THIRD EDITION

Victimology
Theories and Applications

Ann Wolbert Burgess, RN, DNSc, APRN, BC, FAAN

Professor of Psychiatric Nursing
William F. Connell School of Nursing
Boston College

JONES & BARTLETT
LEARNING

World Headquarters
Jones & Bartlett Learning
5 Wall Street
Burlington, MA 01803
978-443-5000
info@jblearning.com
www.jblearning.com

Jones & Bartlett Learning books and products are available through most bookstores and online booksellers. To contact Jones & Bartlett Learning directly, call 800-832-0034, fax 978-443-8000, or visit our website, www.jblearning.com.

Substantial discounts on bulk quantities of Jones & Bartlett Learning publications are available to corporations, professional associations, and other qualified organizations. For details and specific discount information, contact the special sales department at Jones & Bartlett Learning via the above contact information or send an email to specialsales@jblearning.com.

09177-9

Production Credits

VP, Product Management: David D. Cella
Director of Product Management: Matthew Kane
Product Specialist: Audrey Schwinn
Product Assistant: Loren-Marie Durr
Senior Production Editor: Nancy Hitchcock
Marketing Manager: Lindsay White
Production Services Manager: Colleen Lamy
Manufacturing and Inventory Control Supervisor: Amy Bacus

Composition: SourceHOV LLC
Cover Design: Kristin Parker
Interior Design: Theresa Manley
Rights & Media Specialist: Thais Miller
Media Development Editor: Shannon Sheehan
Cover Image: © Peyker/Shutterstock
Printing and Binding: LSC Communications
Cover Printing: LSC Communications

Library of Congress Cataloging-in-Publication Data

Names: Burgess, Ann Wolbert, author.
Title: Victimology : theories and applications / Ann Wolbert Burgess.
Description: Third edition. | Burlington : Jones & Bartlett Learning, 2017. |
    Revised edition of Victimology, c2013.
Identifiers: LCCN 2017045599 | ISBN 9781284130195 (paperback)
Subjects: LCSH: Victims of crimes. | BISAC: LAW / Criminal Procedure.
Classification: LCC HV6250.25 .B87 2017 | DDC 362.88–dc23
LC record available at https://lccn.loc.gov/2017045599

6048

Printed in the United States of America
21 20 19 18 17   10 9 8 7 6 5 4 3 2 1

Brief Contents

© Peyker/Shutterstock.

Contents

CHAPTER 3
Theories of Victimization.............................69

CHAPTER 13
Homicide: Victims, Their Families, and the Community . . .486

CHAPTER 16
Victims of Cybercrime 591

CHAPTER 17
Other Forms of Victimization 636

Preface

In the 19th century and early part of the 20th century, few scholars discussed or wrote about the victim's role in a criminal situation. It was not until the 1940s that interest in the victim developed. Von Hentig's paper titled "Remarks on the Interaction of Perpetrator and His Victim" (1941) and his book *The Criminal and His Victim* (1948); Mendelsohn's paper "New Bio-Psycho-Social Horizons: Victimology" (1947); and Ellenberger's study on the psychological relationship between the criminal and his victim (1954) brought clear scholarly focus to the plight of the victim.

The last quarter of the 20th century brought even more focus to the victim. The First International Symposium on Victimology held in Jerusalem in 1973 gave the discipline of victimology international recognition as a distinct focus separate from the discipline of criminology. The scholarly papers presented at the symposium were divided into five volumes that aimed to provide new data, theoretical inputs, and analyses to encourage the building of ideas and the development of intellectual dialogues in the field of victimology. In particular, the volumes sought to contribute to a discourse within the international community of scholars and to bring together scholars whose paths might not easily cross, despite their common interest.

At the opening ceremony of the symposium, Professor Israel Drapkin, chairman of the Organizing Committee, identified five purposes of the meeting:

1. To reach agreement on the scope of victimology

2. To establish a valid typology of victims as an indispensable tool for future developments

3. To analyze the role of the victim, both in juridical and judicial settings, to improve the current situation

4. To analyze the offender–victim relationship, particularly with regard to the main categories of criminal offense

5. To develop strategies to improve society's reaction toward victims, be it by means of compensation, insurance, prevention, or treatment

Although the science of victimology has expanded over the decades, it is upon this early scholarly and research foundation that this text on victimology has been conceptualized. This text provides an overview of issues related to people who become victims of a wide variety of crimes. At times, these crimes are specific to particular populations, such as children, the elderly, women, or individuals and groups of a specific race or religion. At times, these crimes are more general in who is targeted, such as in the case of Internet crime. We have focused on the incidence of each type of victimization, the impact of the crime on victims, the motivations of the perpetrators, strategies for intervention, laws that define the nature of the crime, and legal attempts to punish offenders and protect victims and society at large.

This third edition of the text includes chapter cases for discussion and expands the traditional academic concepts and theories of victimology to include an applied component for those students who will assess and/or treat victims or offenders. The text emphasizes data from North America regarding the scope of the problem, measurement of victimization, the typologies of victims and offenders, victim impact statements, policies, services, and future research areas. This text is written for students whose work or careers will bring them into contact with victims, offenders, and/or the justice system.

This third edition of the text includes updated information on opening chapter cases on Amanda Knox, Anders Behring Breivik, Kobe Bryant, Casey Anthony, Jaycee Dugard, Brandon McInerney, Rihanna and Chris Brown, Catherine Zeta-Jones, the St. Guillen's family, Mickey Rooney, David Russell Williams, and Brandon Piekarsky and Derrick Donchak. New chapters address social media, cybercrime, forensic victimology, and investigative profiling.

Two important trends have materialized in the five years since the last edition of this text. First, reporting rates on homicides in the United States increased in 2016, and the rate at which murders are cleared through arrest dropped to the lowest level on record. FBI statistics estimate that only 59.4% of homicides were cleared through arrest in 2016. This was the first time the national clearance rate dropped below 60% (Murder Accountability Project, 2017).

Second, mass shootings are increasing. In June 2016, a shooter, Omar Mateen, fired more than 50 rounds into patrons at the Pulse nightclub with an AR-15. He took hostages and shot at police. Forty-nine people died and dozens were wounded. Authorities noted that Mateen had pledged his allegiance to the Islamic State in a 911 call just before the attack. He ultimately died in a gun battle with SWAT team members (Velasquez, 2016). In October 2017, another mass shooting occurred, with the shooter firing from the Mandalay Bay hotel in Las Vegas. It is considered the deadliest U.S. mass shooting committed by one person. The gunman, identified as Stephen Paddock, fired hundreds of rifle rounds into a concert crowd at the Route 91 Harvest Music Festival. Paddock fired from his suite on the 32nd floor of the Mandalay Bay. Fifty-eight victims were killed and hundreds injured. Paddock died from a self-inflicted gunshot wound. His motive remains unclear.

As crime and criminology in our society are ever-changing, the study of victims needs to keep pace and evolve to better serve both victims and the many professionals and practitioners who work with them. Whether a student is considering a career in the criminal justice system, health care, first responder services, social work, or academia, this text will guide the reader toward a deeper understanding of the multifaceted world of victimology and prepare them to better serve this complex population.

■ REFERENCES

Hargrove, T. (2017). Murder Accountability Project. Retrieved from: http://www .murderdata.org

Velasquez, M. (2016, June 12). 2016 Pulse nightclub shooting in Orland, a look back at the worst mass shooting in history. *OCR Daily News*. Retrieved from: http:// www.ocregister.com/2017/06/11/2016-pulse-nightclub-shooting-in-orlando-a -look-back-at-the-worst-mass-shooting-in-us-history/

Acknowledgments

© Peyker/Shutterstock.

The author would like to thank Stefan Treffers for his research additions to all three editions as well as the following for their contributions to the third edition of *Victimology: Theories and Applications*:

Paul Thomas Clements

Dr. Clements is a clinical professor at the College of Nursing and Health Sciences at Drexel University, where one of his online courses for Drexel's forensic health certificate is Victimology for Health Professionals. Dr. Clements has been a psychiatric forensic specialist for more than 20 years, specializing in intrapsychic sequela and behavioral manifestations following exposure to interpersonal violence, crime, and sudden traumatic death.

Grace Cummings

Grace Cummings, Morrissey College of Arts and Science, Boston College, Class of 2020, is one of three student workers who assisted with updates to Chapter 16.

Elizabeth S. Dillon

Elizabeth Dillon, Esq. is a graduate of the University of Pennsylvania and of the Washington University School of Law in St. Louis. She is an associate attorney at Cetrulo, LLP in Boston, Massachusetts. Elizabeth focuses her practice primarily on employment, business, real estate, and probate litigation, as well as employment advice and counseling.

Elizabeth B. Dowdell

Elizabeth Burgess Dowdell is a professor of Pediatric Nursing in the College of Nursing at Villanova University. She is a graduate of Vanderbilt University, Boston College, and the University of Pennsylvania. Her program of research has focused on studying vulnerable populations such as high-risk adolescents, grandmother caregivers, and infants who have been abducted from homes and hospitals. Dr. Dowdell is an expert in the area of forensic pediatric nursing and Internet safety.

Sarah B. Gregorian

Sarah B. Gregorian is a graduate of Northeastern University and the University of Pennsylvania. She has been a research associate at Boston College in the areas of victimology and has coauthored articles on elder abuse and fetal abduction. Her current research is on hate crimes and social justice.

James Hendren

James Hendren, Carroll School of Management, Boston College, Class of 2020, is one of three student workers who assisted with updates to Chapter 16.

Kevin R. Powers, J.D.

Kevin Powers is the founding director for the Master of Science in Cybersecurity Policy and Governance Program at Boston College and an assistant professor of the practice in Boston College's Carroll School of Management's Business Law and Society Department. With a combined 20 years of law enforcement, military, national security, business, higher education, and teaching experience, he has worked as an analyst and an attorney for the U.S. Department of Justice, the U.S. Navy, the U.S. Department of Defense, law firms in Boston and Washington, DC, and as the general counsel for an international software company based in Seattle, Washington. Along with his teaching at Boston College, Kevin has taught courses at the U.S. Naval Justice School and the U.S. Naval Academy, where he was also the deputy general counsel to the superintendent. Kevin regularly provides expert commentary regarding cybersecurity and national security issues for varying local, national, and international media outlets. He is a program lead for the Collegiate Working Group for the U.S. Department of Homeland Security's National Initiative for Cybersecurity Education (NICE), and he also serves as a board member for a regional bank and an international software company. Kevin received his J.D. from Suffolk University Law School and his B.A. in history from Salem State College.

Stefan Treffers

Stefan Treffers is a doctoral candidate in the sociology department at York University. His previous degrees include an M.A. in criminology at the University of Windsor and a B.A. in health sciences at the University of Ottawa. Aside from studies in criminology and victimology, his interests include urban sociology, poverty, race and ethnicity, and urban governance. His current research focuses on austerity and municipal finance in the context of urban decline, including the effects of service withdrawal on residents in the city of Detroit.

Benjamin Twohig

Benjamin Twohig, Carroll School of Management, Boston College, Class of 2019, is one of three student workers who assisted with updates to Chapter 16.

In addition, the author would like to thank the following for their review of this edition and previous editions of *Victimology: Theories and Applications*:

Ashley G. Blackburn, University of Houston–Downtown
Audrelee Dallam-Murphy, Westfield State College
Aric Dutelle, University of Wisconsin–Oshkosh
Kathleen A. Fox, Sam Houston State University
Ray Greenwood, Retired Virginia Beach Police Captain, and Old Dominion University
J. Greg Gullion, Texas Wesleyan University
Susan C. Herrick, West Liberty University
Philip D. Holley, Southwestern Oklahoma State University
Liz Marie Marciniak, University of Pittsburgh at Greensburg
Raisa Martinez, Miami Dade College
Nancy J. Merritt, Front Range Community College, Larimer Campus

Finally, the author and publisher would like to thank Dr. Cheryl Regehr and Dr. Albert R. Roberts for their work and contributions as authors of the previous two editions of this text.

About the Author

Ann Wolbert Burgess, RN, DNSc, APRN, BC, FAAN, is a professor of Psychiatric Mental Health Nursing at Boston College's Connell School of Nursing. She received her bachelors and doctoral degrees from Boston University and her master's degree from the University of Maryland. She teaches five forensic courses: Victimology, Forensic Mental Health, Forensic Science, Forensic Science Lab, and Wounded Warriors in Transition. Together with Lynda Lytle Holmstrom (Boston College), she cofounded one of the first hospital-based crisis intervention programs for rape victims at Boston City Hospital. She is licensed as an advanced practice nurse in Pennsylvania and Massachusetts, where she also maintains prescriptive authority. Dr. Burgess has testified as an expert witness in 31 states and has received grants and published articles on the topics of rape trauma, child sexual abuse, child pornography, serial offenders, crime classification, posttraumatic stress, elder abuse, and wounded warriors.

Dr. Burgess served as chair of the first Advisory Council to the National Center for the Prevention and Control of Rape of the National Institute of Mental Health, was a member of the 1984 U.S. Attorney General's Task Force on Family Violence, served on the planning committee for the 1985 Surgeon General's Symposium on Violence, and served on the National Institute of Health National Advisory Council for the Center for Nursing Research from 1986 to 1988. She was a member of the 1990 Adolescent Health Advisory Panel to the Congress of the United States Office of Technology Assessment and Chair of the National Institutes of Health AIDS and Related Research Study Section (ARRR 6) from 1992 to 1994. She was elected to the National Academy of Sciences Institute of Medicine in October 1994 and chaired the 1996 National Research Council's Task Force on Violence Against Women. She was inducted into the Sigma Theta Tau. Her current research is on patterns of murder-suicide and combat PTSD.

CHAPTER 1

Crime and Victimology

Stefan R. Treffers

OBJECTIVES

- To define victimology and criminology
- To describe victims of crime
- To describe trends in crime and victimization
- To outline the costs and consequences of criminal victimization

KEY TERMS

Cold case

Crime victim

Crime victims' rights

Criminology

Double victimization

National Crime Victimization Survey (NCVS)

Repeat victimization

Victimology

CASE

The November 2, 2007 murder of British exchange student Meredith Kercher in Perugia, Italy, set into motion an investigation that resulted in the arrest, trial, and conviction of her roommate, Amanda Knox, an exchange student from Seattle, Washington. Knox's boyfriend, university student Raffaele Sollecito, and a neighbor of Kercher, Rudy Guede, described as a drifter, were also convicted for the murder. The prosecution's theory was that the victim was forced to participate in a sex game, fueled by drugs, which spiraled out of control. Testimony focused on telephone records, text messages, DNA evidence, bloody fingerprints, and shoe prints. However, 23-year-old Knox, who

FIGURE 1-1 The Amanda Knox Case.
© Antonio Calanni/AP Photos.

served 4 years of a 26-year prison sentence, consistently denied any involvement in the murder (FIGURE 1-1). An appeal of Knox's conviction began in 2010. Independent experts claimed that the collection of evidence fell below international standards and that because of the errors made by police during the original investigation, the evidence against Knox and Sollecito should not be admissible (Vargas & Natanson, 2011).

This case raises three important points with respect to the field of victimology. First, who are the victims? Clearly, Meredith Kercher was a rape-murder victim. But what about the status of Knox and Sollecito, who denied the prosecution's theory and have steadfastly maintained their innocence? Second, forensic evidence, if present, is critical to link a person to a crime. Did the strength of the evidence in this case justify their conviction? Third, this case involved the trial of an American citizen in a foreign jurisdiction. How might differences between international justice procedures and American law procedures have influenced the case? The lack of physical evidence, specifically DNA, to implicate Knox and Sollecito in the murder was not the only problem with this case. Many complained of incompetent police work and

investigators inexperienced in working homicide cases. Knox and Sollecito both asked for attorneys but were denied counsel. The prosecution failed to establish motive or intent for the rape and murder. Knox could barely speak or read Italian. She was interrogated for 41 hours over 4 days, did not even realize that she was a suspect in the case, was pressured into signing a confession that wrongly accused her employer, and held a naive belief in the Italian justice system.

Both she and Sollecito continued to plead their innocence despite serving 4 years in prison. In October of 2011, the Idaho Innocence Project, a nonprofit focused on correcting and preventing wrongful convictions, helped to prove Knox and Sollecito's innocence via DNA testing. The appeal process for both Knox and Sollecito was favorable, and they were acquitted of the murder charges. The defense said the evidence unequivocally pointed to a single attacker, Guede, a drug dealer who fled to Germany after the murder. He was arrested there, brought back to Italy, and tried and convicted of the killing. His conviction was upheld on appeal, and he remains in prison.

After the acquittal, Amanda Knox returned to her home in Seattle, Washington. The case, one of the most-watched trials in Italy, tapped into an intense debate over Italy's justice system (Donadio & Povoledo, 2011).

Once back in Seattle, Knox continued her studies at the University of Washington where she majored in creative writing. Her days as a student did not last long however, as she was soon ordered back to the Italian court for the murder of Kercher. The court of appeal had overturned the previous acquittal and a new trial started in late September of 2013. A piece of evidence was found on a kitchen knife, which was believed to be the murder weapon—one that allegedly contained a minuscule amount of Knox's DNA on the handle. Once again, the court concluded that she was guilty. As a result, she was sentenced to 28.5 years in prison, while Sollecito received 25 years.

In an interesting turn of events, Italy's Supreme Court again overturned the convictions in the spring of 2015. In September 2015, the delegate Supreme Judge, Court adviser made public the reasons for the absolution. First, the evidence did not demonstrate the presence of either Knox or Sollecito at the crime scene. Second, they could not have "materially participated in the homicide"

because there were no "biological traces that could be attributed to them in the room of the murder or on the body of the victim, where in contrast, numerous traces were found attributable to Guede" (Vargas & Natanson, 2011).

Since returning home for a second time, Knox, now 29, has shared much of her journey in her memoir, *Waiting to be Heard: A Memoir*, which has since become a best seller. She is working as a freelance journalist and has attended a number of Innocence Project events—the same organization that helped prove her own innocence (Carter, 2017).

Introduction

The unsettling reality regarding crime in the world today is that it is widespread, often violent in nature, and completely disregards all moral, legal, and geographic boundaries. No home, no community, and no region in North America can consider itself "safe" from the risk of criminal victimization. With recent estimates of the number of crime victims in the United States reaching as high as 22 million, including violent, personal, and property crime, it behooves all of us, both individually and collectively, to support emerging efforts aimed at two distinct but related areas: crime prevention and crime victim assistance. To be sure, averting criminal behavior and victimization through prevention is the more preferable of the two. However, this would likely necessitate substantial investments in crime prevention initiatives that not only aim to deter and alter criminal behavior, but also strive to address fundamental root causes of crime (Hastings, 2008). Although there has been increasing support for situational crime prevention since the 1970s (especially those programs oriented toward victims), rehabilitation of offenders and social investments to mitigate systemic inequalities have largely fallen out of political favor (Garland, 2001), further cementing the notion that crime is an inevitable fact of life. Given the reasonable assumption that not all crimes are preventable under these circumstances, it becomes all the more urgent to be prepared to assist those who are victimized. TABLE 1-1 provides data on the numbers of victims of violent crime for the years 2005 and 2015.

TABLE 1-1 Violent Victimization in the United States (National Crime Victimization Survey), 2005 and 2015

	2005	Rate per 1,000 Persons (12 or older)	Percent of Violent Crime	2015	Rate per 1,000 Persons (12 or older)	Percent of Violent Crime	Percent Change 2005 to 2015
Total population (12 or older)	244,505,300			266,665,160			
Violent crime	6,947,800	28.4	100.00%	5,359,570	18.6	100.00%	−34.6%
Domestic violence	1,242,290	5.1	17.88%	1,109,880	4.1	22.04%	−19.6%
Rape/sexual assault	207,760	0.8	2.99%	284,350	1.6	8.60%	+100.0%
Robbery	769,150	3.1	11.07%	664,210	2.1	11.29%	−32.3%
Aggravated assault	1,281,490	5.2	18.44%	1,092,090	3.0	16.13%	−42.4%

Bureau of Justice Statistics, 2016. *Criminal Victimization, 2015*. Retrieved from https://www.bjs.gov/content/pub/pdf/cv15.pdf.

Despite the general trend of decreasing victimization rates over the past 10 years, a significant number of victims turn to victim assistance programs, mental health centers, domestic violence shelters, and victim compensation programs each year. Research, as well as experience, has shown that these individuals frequently suffer from significant emotional pain and trauma, physical injuries, and/or financial loss as a result of their victimization, while "secondary victims"—relatives and close friends of victims—may also endure both mental anguish and economic hardship. Emergency medical care, mental health counseling, social services, financial aid, victim compensation, and law enforcement protection must be readily available for those injured as a result of either violent or property-related offenses. Despite remarkable advances made in terms of our understanding of the nature of crime victimization and our awareness of the need for victim support, to date most victim assistance policies and programs are limited in their ability to service the diverse needs of all victims. This chapter presents victimology as a discipline as well as provides information on victims of crime, the costs of victimization, and trends in crime and victimization.

Discipline of Victimology

Criminology, defined as the scientific study of nonlegal aspects of crime, arose in the 18th century out of concerns about the use of what was perceived to be cruel and arbitrary means of justice. Through the use of scientific methods, criminologists sought to refocus approaches to crime on prevention of criminal activity and reformation of offenders. Edwin H. Sutherland defined the objectives of criminology as the development of general and verified principles and knowledge regarding the process of law, crime, and treatment (Sutherland & Cressey, 1973, p.3). The etiology of crime and the characteristics of the criminal became the focus of criminological study. Drawing on diverse fields such as sociology, psychology, economics, human geography, and statistics, present-day criminologists use a variety of research and analysis methods to better understand crime and criminal activity (DeFlem, 2006; *Merriam-Webster Dictionary*, 2016).

In contrast, victimology is the study of the victim, including the offender and society. Victimology is a social-structural way of viewing crime, the law, the criminal, and the victim. Victimology, which Fattah (2000) characterized as a young and promising discipline as old as humanity itself, did not emerge as a scientific subject for study until after World War II. In the 1940s and 1950s, based on the research of Benjamin Mendelsohn and Hans Von Hentig, victimology began to emerge as a distinct and viable field of study (Schafer, 1968). Historically, victimology was a branch of criminology, and as such the early criminologists and victimologists focused their analyses and writings on typologies of crime victims, assessing the ways in which a victim may contribute, knowingly or unknowingly, to his or her own victimization. Von Hentig's work (1946) identified categories of individuals who were prone to becoming crime victims. Marvin Wolfgang's doctoral dissertation at the University of Pennsylvania in the 1950s built on Von Hentig's theories and led to Dr. Wolfgang's research conclusions that the majority of criminal homicides in the city of Philadelphia were victim precipitated because the victim either provoked the perpetrator or the victim was motivated by an unconscious desire to commit suicide (Wolfgang, 1958). As one might expect, such findings inevitably resulted in a gross misunderstanding of the plight of crime victims and a categorical dismissal of the validity of their rights and needs.

Because the victim component of crime represented a serious theoretical void, a struggle developed as to the independence of this new discipline in relationship to the established field of criminology. Many, including Fattah, continue to view victimology as an integral part of criminology, whereas others, especially those who work directly with victims, see the field as separate and independent. Fattah (2000) argues that the study of crime victims and of criminal victimization has the potential of reshaping criminology and that it may be the paradigm shift that criminology needs. Recent developments in victimology have undergone a transformation through major achievements in the applied field. This remarkable phase in the evolution of victimology, continues Fattah, was one of consolidation, data gathering, theory formulation, victim legislation, and sustained efforts to improve victims' lot and alleviate their plight.

Advances in the various theoretical victimology models explain the variations in victimization risks, the clustering of victimization in certain areas and certain groups, and the phenomenon of repeat victimization. Many countries have passed victim bill of rights legislation, including the adoption of the U.N. Declaration of Basic Principles of Justice for Victims of Crime and Abuse of Power by the General Assembly of the United Nations (1985). State compensation programs for victims of violent crime have been created, the concept of restitution by offenders has reemerged, and numerous victim–offender mediation programs have been established. Victim therapy has become an acknowledged means of dealing with the traumatic aftereffects of victimization.

Fattah predicts that future developments in victimology will include an emphasis on scientific research, particularly qualitative research, and that the need for advocacy, partisanship, and therapy will decline. In its place will be the rise of the restorative justice paradigm with victimology developing into a scientific discipline with a truly humanistic practice (Fattah, 2000).

Victims of Violent Crime in the Media

People are fascinated by crime. Crimes and the legal proceedings that surround them excite the public's interest for a variety of reasons: some, according to Fletcher (1988), because they involve celebrities, some because they are gruesome, some because they raise important social or legal issues, some because of their racial character, some because of the bizarre behavior of the parties, and some because of the plight of the victim. The growing number of television dramas that depict criminal behavior and victimization, police and forensic work, and the prison system is a testament to crime's prominence in popular culture. However, it has been argued that attributing the fascination with crime media to entertainment and voyeurism alone limits our understanding of its other social functions; namely, that cultural representations of crime reflect (and propagate) social anxieties and fears associated with crime (Sparks, 1990; Young, 2008). Instances of violent crime, especially those that are unpredictable or sporadic in nature and those perpetrated by strangers, often provoke a sense of fear that the mass media is quick to capitalize on. Cases that have received wide media attention for these reasons include murdered children, professionals as victims, victims of revenge, and victims of workplace violence.

Murdered Children

In 1996, almost 2,000 children were murdered in the United States, but none of those murders fascinated the American public and attracted the mass media like that of JonBenét Ramsey, a child beauty pageant contestant. Although the spotlight has dimmed over the years, the case has been reopened, and public bias regarding the parents as suspects, similar to the Caylee Anthony (a two-year-old girl who went missing in Florida in 2008) case, remains.

In the early morning of December 26, 1996, in Boulder, Colorado, Patsy Ramsey reportedly found a ransom note on the family's back staircase demanding $118,000 for her 6-year-old daughter, JonBenét (see FIGURE 1-2). The Ramseys quickly realized that JonBenét was missing from her bedroom and called 911. Later that day, John Ramsey discovered JonBenét's body covered in her special white blanket in the wine cellar. She had been strangled with a garrote made from a piece of cord and the broken handle of a paintbrush; to add to the horror there was evidence of sexual assault. The official cause of death was asphyxiation due to strangulation associated with blunt force head trauma.

FIGURE 1-2 JonBenét Ramsey.

© ZUMA Wire/Alamy Images.

The early investigation focused on the three-page ransom note, and police took hair and blood samples from members of the Ramsey family. The district attorney's office strongly supported a family member theory to the murder, whereas a private investigator, Lou Smit, and Federal Bureau of Investigation (FBI) profiler John Douglas, supported an intruder theory. A Boulder County grand jury was convened on September 16, 1998, and for a year heard testimony, forensic evidence, analysis of handwriting, DNA evidence, and hair and fiber evidence. No indictment was returned by the grand jury because of conflicting testimonies and theories.

In 2002, the Ramseys filed and defended a series of libel lawsuits against media outlets that tried to implicate them in their daughter's murder. In 2003, an Atlanta federal judge dismissed a civil lawsuit against John and Patsy Ramsey, stating there was no evidence showing the parents killed JonBenét and abundant evidence that an intruder killed the child. The judge criticized the police and the FBI for creating a media campaign designed to make the family look guilty. That same year, Mary Keenan, recently elected district attorney, agreed to look at all the evidence in the case, including foreign, male DNA that was found in JonBenét's underwear that had never been tested. In 2006, Patsy Ramsey died of a recurrence of ovarian cancer. Nevertheless, in February 2010, the Boulder Police Department took the case back from the district attorney to reopen the investigation.

Over the years, several theories have been raised regarding the death of JonBenét. One theory suggests that Patsy Ramsey injured her child in a burst of anger over bedwetting, proceeded to kill her either in rage or to cover up the original injury, and then wrote the ransom note. Another speculates that John Ramsey had been sexually assaulting his daughter and murdered her as a cover. Others look to the brother of JonBenét, who they say was jealous of his sister and murdered her. A final theory suggests that an intruder sexually assaulted and murdered the child. To complicate the family murder theory, DNA evidence did not match the mother, father, or brother and failed to find a match in the FBI CODIS database. This **cold case** remains focused on a forensic evidence match to JonBenét Ramsey or the crime scene and/or confession from the offender.

Professionals as Victims

Dr. George Tiller, age 67, was one of the few doctors who performed late-term abortions, raising concerns among citizens in Wichita, Kansas, that Dr. Tiller was contravening state law, public morality, and religious values. For more than 20 years, groups protested outside his offices, people signed petitions, and individuals made death threats against him. On May 31, 2009, Tiller was shot in the head at point-blank range (despite wearing a bulletproof vest) by Scott Roeder, an antiabortion activist. Tiller was killed during a Sunday morning service at the Reformation Lutheran Church in Wichita, where he was serving as an usher. Tiller's killing has been labeled an act of domestic terrorism and an assassination.

Scott Roeder took the stand in his own defense on January 28, 2010. He admitted to killing Dr. Tiller, described his views on abortion, and defended his act as an attempt to save unborn children. On January 29, 2010, the jury returned a verdict of guilty on all three charges (one count of first-degree murder and two counts of aggravated assault) after less than 40 minutes of deliberation. On April 1, 2010, in Wichita, Kansas, Sedgwick County District Judge Warren Wilbert sentenced Roeder to the maximum time allowed in Kansas, known as a "hard 50," meaning he had no possibility of parole for 50 years.

Assassinations have been part of human history from early times. Victims who are killed for political reasons are sometimes aware of their danger, as in the case of Dr. Tiller, or sometimes totally unaware, as in the case of President Abraham Lincoln. In either case, such murders trigger great public outcry for the victims, their families, and their communities.

Victims of Revenge

On Christmas Eve, 2008, Bruce Jeffrey Pardo arrived at the home of Joseph and Alicia Ortega, the parents of his ex-wife, dressed in a Santa Claus suit. He opened fire and killed nine people inside the house, including his ex-wife Sylvia, three of their children, the elder Ortegas, two daughters-in-law, and a teenager working at a computer. Pardo had no criminal record and had no history of violence. Police speculate the motive of the attack was related to marital problems, as Pardo's wife of 1 year had settled for divorce the prior week. Pardo owed his wife $10,000 as part of the divorce settlement, according to court documents, which detailed a bitter split. He also lost a dog he doted on and did not get back a valuable wedding ring. Pardo had also lost his job in July.

Pardo complained in a court declaration that Sylvia Pardo was living with her parents, not paying rent, and had spent lavishly on a luxury car, gambling trips to Las Vegas, meals at fine restaurants, massages, and golf lessons. Some speculated that the divorce may have been caused by Pardo concealing a child from a previous relationship. This child had been severely injured and disabled in a swimming pool accident. It was also revealed that Pardo planned to kill his own mother because she apparently displayed sympathy for Sylvia Pardo during the divorce.

Although there was no history of domestic conflict in the divorce papers, this mass murder might have had some warning signs, such as the rage and anger toward the in-laws and resentment of financial expenditures and revenge toward the distribution of marital property. Clearly, the victims were taken by surprise in a blitz attack and had no time to defend themselves.

Victims of Workplace Violence

"We're now just trying to figure out who's shot, who's not accounted for," said Brett Hollander, the director of marketing at Hartford Distributors (Martinez, 2010). This chilling statement was quoted in one of the initial press reports from the summer of 2010 shooting in a beer distribution company in Manchester, Connecticut. Approximately 60 people were in the warehouse at the 7:00 a.m. shift change when Omar Thornton fatally shot eight fellow employees and then himself. The shooting occurred minutes after Thornton was confronted by management with video evidence that he was stealing beer. He was given the option of quitting the job or being fired. Thornton did not deny the allegations, signed the release papers, and then withdrew a gun from his lunch box. Witnesses on the scene described Thornton as cool and calm as he proceeded to shoot those around him in the head.

During the past decade, newspapers rarely have missed an opportunity to report the latest murder, robbery, physical or sexual assault, or stalking incident occurring in the workplace. Of these incidents, the ones that receive the most attention are, not surprisingly, workplace shootings. In many cases, violent episodes in the workplace can be prevented. With this in mind, some companies have begun to provide employee assistance programs, stress management and anger control workshops, and fitness and exercise facilities. In addition, corporate security and human resource personnel often receive training in crisis intervention, psychological risk assessments, and critical incident debriefing. No office, business, or institution is immune to the threat of violence, and careful planning and program development are crucial to handling threats appropriately and containing and preventing future violent incidents.

Who Is a Victim?

The examples above depict several cases of victimization that have garnered significant media attention over the years. Important questions should be asked about why certain crimes become focal points of news, documentaries, television series, and other productions whereas others are largely ignored. Although the answers to these questions are complex, it is evident that the mass media is drawn to crimes that are especially unpredictable and violent in nature. Because a great deal of peoples' perceptions and knowledge of crime and victimization are informed by sensationalized media accounts, ideas about victims are subject to considerable distortion. As a result, peoples' perceptions of the regularity or frequency of victimization, of who is most likely to become a victim, or what constitutes the most common forms of victimization can become considerably divorced from reality. Media accounts may also lead to an exceedingly narrow conception of what constitutes a victim, silencing accounts of harm that arise in cases that may seem more mundane, such as workplace injuries that result from corporate negligence or acute and chronic illness linked to environmental pollution. As a corrective, victimology can provide a more accurate picture of crime and victimization through data and trends as well as provide a more encompassing conceptualization of the victim that takes into account a wide range of crimes and harms. The following section details a brief definitional history of *victim*, describing the term's historical and contemporary usage.

Defining the "Victim"

The word *victim* is derived from the Latin *victima*, and originally included the concept of sacrifice. The sense of an offering to the temple is implied in the Bible (Leviticus 1.2, 1.14, 2.1, etc.), and though the word *victim* does not appear in the Bible, the notion of persons suffering from acts committed by an aggressor is found throughout. One of the most prominent cases of victimhood found in the holy text is the murder involving Adam and Eve's first- and second-born sons, in which in a fit of jealousy Cain murdered his brother because God had favored Abel's thanksgiving offerings over his (Genesis 4:9–10). The relationship between victim and sacrifice had similar resonance in ancient civilizations where individuals were sacrificed during religious ceremonies to appease the gods. In early Anglo-Saxon society, victims were perceived as persons suffering from injury at the hands of perpetrators, and laws typically enforced restitution and compensation paid to victims or their families by offending parties. While sanctions were initially enforced locally and through informal means, the emergence of a stronger sovereign state transformed the concept of victimhood by implicating the state in processes of justice. No longer was an offense solely viewed as a transgression against the victim, but was considered an offense against God and a breach of the king's peace, and as such, the state increasingly became an instigator of charges against offenders while the victim's role was reduced to that of a witness (Walklate, 2007). As this system of justice evolved, compensation by the offender became increasingly seen as a debt owed to society (often paid in the form of fines), rather than to the individual victim. These arrangements bear some resemblance to the contemporary justice process whereby the prosecution team, as the state's representative, pursues a case against the accused. The role of the victim is limited to that of a witness who may give a testimony on behalf of the prosecution.

Contemporary ideas about what constitutes a victim have largely been shaped and influenced by criminal law. Federal law defines the term *victim* and outlines the rights of crime victims. A **crime victim** in a purely legal sense refers to a person, organization, or business that has been directly harmed (physically, emotionally, or financially) as a result of the commission of an offense. In general, crime victims' rights apply after charges have been filed by a U.S. Attorney's office. Some individuals are viewed to not have the capacity to exercise their own rights. Such individuals include victims of crime who are younger than 18 years of age, incompetent, incapacitated, or deceased. In these cases, the legal guardians of the crime victim or the representatives of the crime victim's estate, family members, or any other persons appointed as suitable by the court may assume the crime victims' rights. A person who is a defendant in the crime being investigated or prosecuted cannot act as a proxy for a victim. In the United States, **crime victims' rights** are the eight rights included in the Justice for All Act (2004), Section 3771 of Title 18 of the U.S. Code, Crimes and Criminal Procedure:

1. The right to be reasonably protected from the accused.

2. The right to reasonable, accurate, and timely notice of any public court proceeding, or any parole proceeding, involving the crime or any release or escape of the accused.

3. The right not to be excluded from any such public court proceeding, unless the court, after receiving clear and convincing evidence, determines that testimony by the victim would be materially altered if the victim heard other testimony at the proceeding.

4. The right to be reasonably heard at any public proceeding in the district court involving release, plea, [or] sentencing, or any parole proceeding.

5. The reasonable right to confer with the attorney for the government in the case.

6. The right to full and timely restitution as provided in law.

7. The right to proceedings free from unreasonable delay.

8. The right to be treated with fairness and with respect for the victim's dignity and privacy.

For purposes of these rights and services, victims are defined in specific ways in the federal law (FBI, 2011).

However, not all contemporary notions of the victim have emerged from within the confines of formal law. The term's first use as a scientific concept originated from the work of Benjamin Mendelsohn. In his scientific study of crime victims, Mendelsohn's (1976) concept of victimhood featured four fundamental criteria:

1. *The nature of the determinant that causes the suffering.* The suffering may be physical, psychological, or both, depending on the type of injurious act.

2. *The social character of the suffering.* This suffering originates in the victim's and others' reaction to the event.

3. *The importance of the social factor.* The social implications of the injurious act can have a greater impact, sometimes even more severe than the physical or psychological impact.

4. *The origin of the inferiority complex.* The term *inferiority complex*, suggested by Mendelsohn, manifests itself as a feeling of submission that may be followed by a feeling of revolt. The victim generally attributes his or her injury to the culpability of another person.

Mendelsohn would later become known for his typology of crime victims that focused on the extent to which victims played a role in their own victimization. However, he also acknowledged that human suffering extended beyond the confines of criminal victimization and proposed that victimology should incorporate causal factors of victimization derived from the self, technology, the social environment, and the natural environment, as well as from criminal offences (Mendelsohn, 1976). As such, the term *victim* has been greatly expanded to imply a wide range of circumstances of human suffering and to include victims of deliberate self-harm, victims of accidents, victims of war and political crises, victims of economic and social problems, victims of natural disasters, and victims of identity theft. The following sections briefly discuss victims of crime as well as victims of "noncriminal" harms.

Victims of Personal and Property Crime

Modern distinctions between what constitutes a crime and what does not are usually drawn from legal definitions inscribed in criminal codes. Additionally, victimization surveys provide us with measures of crime defined in particular ways, the legality of which is largely consistent with criminal law. The **National Crime Victimization Survey (NCVS)** provides definitions of crimes resulting in victimization for the purposes of data collection and reporting.

This information includes the specific type of crime experienced, the location of the incident, whether the incident was reported to police or other officials, the type and value of the property involved, and the identity and personal characteristics of the victim. Personal crime as defined by the NCVS includes rape or sexual assault, robbery, aggravated or simple assault, and personal larceny. A violent crime includes rape or sexual assault, robbery, and aggravated or simple assault characterized by the "use or threat of force." Property crime may involve theft or damage of personal property, but does not usually involve the presence of the victim. **TABLE 1-2** provides a summary of crimes resulting in victimization.

TABLE 1-2 Crimes Resulting in Victimization

Type of Crime	Definition
Burglary	The unlawful or forcible entry or attempted entry of a structure with the intent to commit an offense therein. This crime usually, but not always, involves theft. It is a property crime.
Larceny	The theft or attempted theft of property or cash without using force or illegal entry. An alternate label for this crime is *theft*. It is a property crime.
Personal crime	A criminal act affecting a specific person. Crimes against persons, as defined by NCVS, include rape, sexual assault, robbery, assault, and purse snatching/pocket picking. The victimization is personal either through the direct experience of force or threat of force or by theft directly from one's person.
Personal larceny	Purse snatching and pocket picking. Personal larceny involves the theft or attempted theft of property or cash directly from the victim by stealth, but without force or threat of force. It is both a property crime and a personal crime.
Property crime	The illegal taking or damaging of property, including cash and personal belongings. Examples include burglary, theft, robbery, vandalism, and arson. In many instances, the offender acts furtively, and the victim is often not present when the crime occurs.
Robbery	The taking of property or cash directly from a person by force or threat of force. Robbery is both a property crime and a violent crime.
Vandalism	The willful or malicious destroying, defacing, or damaging of property without the consent of the owner. It is a property crime.
Violent crime	Rape, sexual assault, robbery, and assault, including both attempted and completed crimes. The defining element is the use of force or threat of force. Violent crimes involve contact between the victim and the offender. The NCVS definition of violent crime excludes murder.

Data from National Crime Victimization Survey (NCVS) and the National Incident-Based Reporting System (NIBRS).

Crime victims do not fit a standard profile. Persons of all ages, races, ethnicities, and socioeconomic backgrounds are subject to criminal victimization of one form or another. However, victimization statistics from the U.S. Bureau of Justice Statistics (2016) reveal that not all groups have an equal likelihood or probability of becoming a crime victim. Research indicates that young black males, 16 to 24 years of age and living in high-crime, urban areas, are the most likely to fall victim to serious violent crime due in large part to socioeconomic factors such as poverty and lack of adequate housing, education, and/or employment. In sharp contrast, elderly white females who live in low-crime areas and generally do not venture out at night are the least likely to become victimized. Lifestyle, location, and race appear to be the primary predictors of who is most likely to become a victim of crime. However, one of the best predictors of future victimization is past victimization. As with repeat offenders whose criminal activity constitutes a disproportionate amount of all crime, some individuals are involved in a similarly disproportionate amount of all victimization events (see Tseloni & Pease, 2004). This observation has been supported by a growing field of research on repeat victims of violent crime, including victims of sexual abuse, domestic abuse, bullying, assault, and hate crimes, as well as property crimes such as burglary and vandalism (Arata, 2002; Frank, Brantingham, & Farrell, 2012; Tseloni, Knuttson, & Laycock, 2005). A greater appreciation of patterns in victimization may shed light on which factors make these individuals susceptible to **repeat victimization** and may have further implications for crime prevention policy.

Beyond Criminal Victimization: Victims of "Noncriminal" Harms

In heeding Mendelsohn's suggestion that there are victims outside the domain of crime, our definition of what it means to be a victim expands accordingly. One way in which the term becomes more accommodating is by considering victims who suffer from harmful activities that are not deemed by law to be criminal. It is widely acknowledged among critical criminologists that labeling processes involved in defining what is considered a criminal act cannot be divorced from questions of power and politics. It is not necessarily true that all harmful behaviors are criminalized, nor is it necessarily true that all criminals are pursued with equal intensity by the criminal justice system. Many criminologists and victimologists in the critical and radical traditions have increasingly challenged the stereotypical conception of offenders and victims that narrowly reduce problems of crime to problems associated with traditional "street" crime. For example, in 1939, Sutherland introduced the term *white-collar crime* to bring attention to crimes committed by persons of high respectability and social status that tended to be ignored by law enforcement and society in general (Sutherland, 1949). Other scholars have followed Sutherland's lead, focusing on corporate and occupational crimes that escape criminal definition and tend to be treated with considerable impunity. It has been argued that even when codified in law some forms of corporate and white-collar crimes tend to be unregulated in practice or are prosecuted through administrative and informal channels. It is common in these cases for victims not to receive justice or compensation.

Indeed, some victimologists believe that our understandings of environmental, economic, social, and other forms of victimization cannot and should not be bound by criminal definition, but should rather be seen in terms of "social harms" (see Hillyard and Tombs, 2007). This perspective is especially important for understanding environmental victimization given the various environmentally harmful practices and activities that are regulated (and facilitated) but not prevented by law (White, 2015). Although a more encompassing notion of victimhood can bring a greater emphasis to the experiences of victims adversely affected by pollution, climate change, and other environmental hazards, challenging issues emerge regarding measurement and evidence of environmental harm, determining culpability for environmental harm, and agreeing on appropriate sanctions while providing redress to victims affected. Further complicating matters is the fact that environmental victims may not be aware that they have been victimized, may suffer from repeat exposure to environmental hazards over a long period of time, may not experience symptoms until long after exposure, and may be unsure about who or what is responsible for their victimization (Skinnider, 2011). Despite these challenges, victimologists are increasingly drawn to these matters as they continue to affect a growing number of people across the world.

Similarly, victimology has been concerned with conceptualizing state actions that violate national or international law while in pursuit of economic and political ends, but do not result in criminal sanction. Although this tradition derives from earlier global concerns regarding genocide, Nazi atrocities, and state-sanctioned apartheid, it has also had a more domestic relevance with regard to "victims of police force, the victims of war, the victims of the correctional system, the victims of state violence, the victims of oppression of any sort" (Quinney, 1972, p. 315). Although radical victimology and the study of state crime has yet to develop into a major subfield of criminological research (Kauzlarich, Matthews, & Miller, 2001), the current context of racialized violence and police shootings in the United States, which is not limited to this historical moment, demands a return to thinking about these forms of victimization.

Trends in Crime and Victimization

Among news reporters, historians, and criminologists who review and interpret these findings, there are predictable reactionary stances, including those of the alarmists, the skeptics, and the realists. Frequently, members of the press tend toward alarmism, singling out and sensationalizing specific violent cases of victimization. Such instances include cases like that of Lorena Bobbit, who in 1993, cut off half of her husband's penis while he lay sleeping; or of Lyle and Erik Menendez, who in 1993, murdered their parents; or the 2006 arrest of three Duke lacrosse players for rape. Some historians fall into the skeptic category, where a 5- or 20-year period of cyclical decline in most crime categories is viewed as temporary because history sometimes repeats itself. The realists are many of the academic scholars and criminologists who can examine a 10- or 25-year trend analysis and with reasonable certainty predict that 10, 20, or 25 years of overall declines in crime rates are not necessarily temporary, but coincide with a number of underlying, though complex, factors that remain a subject of debate (see Zimring, 2007). Their goals include understanding why crime rates fluctuate and determining which root causes may explain why people commit crime.

Crime in the United States is a significant criminal justice and public health problem, and the serious nature of homicide, forcible rape, robbery, aggravated assault, domestic violence, burglary, larceny/theft, carjacking, and motor vehicle theft impact millions of victims and their families each year. Repeated depictions of violent crime in the news and television dramas can give the impression that American society is more violent today than ever before and that violence is increasing. The facts are, however, much more complex, and simple generalizations can be misleading (Reiss & Roth, 1993).

Crime data collected by national surveys can help us construct a partial picture of crime and victimization longitudinally, allowing us to make sense of crime trends in a historical context. Generally, data on crime rates show a sharp rise in crime after 1963 until the early 1990s. A snapshot of violent crime trends reported by the FBI's Uniform Crime Reports (UCR) Program for the year 1991, during which violent crime peaked, shows higher rates of violent crime during the summer months and in western states. Aggravated assault accounted for 57% of all reported violent crimes, followed by robberies (36%) and forcible rapes (6%). The number of violent crimes exceeded 1.9 million offenses (Bureau of Justice Statistics, 1992). According to NCVS data, in 1991, violent victimization was highest among males, persons aged 20 to 24 years, persons identified as Black, and persons earning less than $7,500 annually. In addition, those residing in a central city were more likely than those residing in either a suburban or nonmetropolitan area to be victims of violent crime (Bureau of Justice Statistics, 1993).

In the mid-1990s, overall rates of crime began to steadily decline. Rates of violent crime (i.e., crimes involving force or threat of force) are generally consistent with this trend. According to NCVS data, from 1993 to 2015, violent crime dropped from 79.8 to 18.6 violent victimizations per 1,000 persons over the age of 11. Nonfatal firearm violence also declined, falling from 7.3 victimizations per 1,000 persons in 1993 to 1.1 in 2015. Furthermore, the rate of property crime declined from 351.8 to 110.7 per 1,000 persons, with the decline in theft accounting for the majority of the overall fall in property crime (Bureau of Justice Statistics, 2016).

In 2015, the most common type of violent crime recorded by the NCVS was simple assault, accounting for approximately 64% of all violent crimes, followed by aggravated assault (16%), robbery (11%), and rape/sexual assault (9%). In contrast to the previous year, females were more likely than males to be a victim of violent crime. Individuals were more likely to be victimized if they were between the ages of 12 and 17, followed by those aged 18 to 24. Those identifying as Black or Other (e.g., Aboriginal, Asian, and Biracial), as separated or divorced, or as having a household annual income of less than $9,999 showed an elevated risk for violent victimization. When looking only at *serious* violent crime (rape or sexual assault, robbery, and aggravated assault), all the above-mentioned sociodemographic factors remain relevant risk factors, but those between the ages of 18 and 24 are the most at-risk demographic for serious violent victimization (Bureau of Justice Statistics, 2016).

With regard to geography, victims residing in urban areas have been at the highest risk for both violent and property crime, while those living in rural areas have been at the lowest risk. This holds true for years 1996, 2005, and 2015. Regional rates of violent and property crimes have fluctuated over the years, but western states consistently show the highest rates of crime across all three reference years. TABLE 1-3 provides data on violent crime and property crime by household location and region for the years 1996, 2005, and 2015.

The main source for murder rates in the United States is the FBI's UCR. In 2014, the murder rate hit a 51-year low at 4.5 murders per 100,000 inhabitants. In 2015, the murder rate increased slightly to 5 murders per 100,000 inhabitants, levels comparable to 2009. TABLE 1-4 shows the steady decline in rates of murder and nonnegligent manslaughter from 1995 to 2014.

Although the overall murder rate has shown a general decline over the last few decades, the National Center for Victims of Crime (2015) reported that active shooter events, mass murders, and active shooter cases have increased over recent years.

TABLE 1-3 Rate of Violent Victimization by Household Location and Region Based per 1,000 (National Crime Victimization Survey), 1996, 2005, and 2015

Location of Residence	Violent Crime			Property Crime		
	1996	2005	2015	1996	2005	2015
Urban	78.9	37.2	22.7	361.3	202.5	135.4
Suburban	61.1	25.6	17.3	266.3	146.8	98.4
Rural	53.2	22.4	14.0	232.9	126.2	95.7
Region*						
Northeast	52.9	25.9	17.1	234.8	113.3	81.6
Midwest	66.3	34.6	19.6	266.7	165.9	105.0
South	57.9	23.4	16.9	286.8	148.8	107.6
West	85.1	32.0	21.3	371.9	209.3	144.7

*Midwest includes the 12 states of Illinois, Indiana, Iowa, Kansas, Michigan, Minnesota, Missouri, Nebraska, North Dakota, Ohio, South Dakota, and Wisconsin. Northeast includes the nine states of Connecticut, Maine, Massachusetts, New Hampshire, New Jersey, New York, Pennsylvania, Rhode Island, and Vermont. South includes the District of Columbia and the 16 states of Alabama, Arkansas, Delaware, Florida, Georgia, Kentucky, Louisiana, Maryland, Mississippi, North Carolina, Oklahoma, South Carolina, Tennessee, Texas, Virginia, and West Virginia. West includes the 13 states of Alaska, Arizona, California, Colorado, Hawaii, Idaho, Montana, Nevada, New Mexico, Oregon, Utah, Washington, and Wyoming.

Calculated from Bureau of Justice Statistics, Criminal Victimization, by Location of Residence and Region, 1993–2015.

Crime in Canada shows similar historical trends. According to Statistics Canada (2015), violent victimization rates for 2014 (76 per 1,000 persons aged 15 years and older) were 28% lower than those for 2004, with robbery declining by 39% and physical assault by 35%. However, sexual assault victimization rates have remained relatively stable since 1999. In terms of household victimization (which includes break-ins, motor vehicle theft, vandalism, and theft of household property), the 2014 rate of 143 incidents per 1,000 households was 42% lower than the rate in 2004. Key risk factors for violent crime included age, drug use and alcohol consumption, mental health problems, history of homelessness and/or child maltreatment, and residence in a neighborhood with low social cohesion (Statistics Canada, 2015). TABLE 1-5 provides data on violent and property (household) victimization rates per 1,000 persons aged 15 years and older in Canada by type of offence for the years of 1999, 2004, 2009, and 2014.

TABLE 1-4 Murder Rates in the United States (Uniform Crime Reports) from 1995 to 2014

Rate: Number of Crimes per 100,000 Inhabitants						
by Population Group, 2015						
	Violent crime		Murder and nonnegligent manslaughter		Number of agencies	2015 estimated population
Population group	Number of offenses known	Rate	Number of offenses known	Rate		
TOTAL ALL AGENCIES:	**1,154,081**	**385.9**	**14,856**	**5.0**	**15,010**	**299,091,598**
TOTAL CITIES	**922,794**	**454.1**	**11,571**	**5.7**	**10,645**	**203,209,630**
GROUP I (250,000 and over)	436,315	734.2	5,990	10.1	79	59,428,247
1,000,000 and over (Group I subset)	188,291	687.1	2,231	8.1	11	27,404,679
500,000 to 999,999 (Group I subset)	138,863	836.0	2,081	12.5	23	16,609,970
250,000 to 499,999 (Group I subset)	109,161	708.2	1,678	10.9	45	15,413,598
GROUP II (100,000 to 249,999)	147,363	471.0	1,934	6.2	210	31,285,733
GROUP III (50,000 to 99,999)	111,334	337.9	1,231	3.7	474	32,952,951
GROUP IV (25,000 to 49,999)	85,566	293.8	980	3.4	841	29,124,007
GROUP V (10,000 to 24,999)	75,676	269.8	820	2.9	1,752	28,049,861
GROUP VI (under 10,000)	66,540	297.5	616	2.8	7,289	22,368,831
METROPOLITAN COUNTIES	185,490	258.4	2,424	3.4	1,954	71,792,662
NONMETROPOLITAN COUNTIES[1]	45,797	190.1	861	3.6	2,411	24,089,306
SUBURBAN AREA[2]	323,651	249.2	3,822	2.9	8,263	129,863,798

Data from Federal Bureau of Investigation (FBI). 2015. Number of Crimes per 100,000 inhabitants.

[1] Includes state police agencies that report aggregately for the entire state.

[2] Suburban areas include law enforcement agencies in cities with less than 50,000 inhabitants and county law enforcement agencies that are within a Metropolitan Statistical Area. Suburban areas exclude all metropolitan agencies associated with a principal city. The agencies associated with suburban areas also appear in other groups within this table.

TABLE 1-5 Victimization Rates per 1,000 Persons Aged 15 Years and Older in Canada by Type of Offense (General Social Survey), 1999, 2004, 2009, and 2014

	1999	2004	2009	2014
Total violent victimization	111	106	118	76
Sexual assault	21	21	24	22
Robbery	9	11	13	6
Physical assault	80	75	80	48
Total household victimization	218	248	237	143
Break and enter	48	39	47	31
Motor vehicle/parts theft	41	44	34	18
Theft of household property	62	88	83	54
Vandalism	66	77	74	40

Data from Statistics Canada (2015). Table 1: Victimization incidents reported by Canadians, by type of Offense, 1999, 2004, 2009, and 2014.

Costs and Consequences of Crime

Many government agencies and independent organizations have been tasked with measuring crime rates and providing estimates of the costs of crime. While acknowledging that many of these agencies and organizations use distinct crime-costing methods, which inevitably leads to variation in cost estimations, it can be informative to go beyond the simplicity of crime rates by assessing the impact of crime in economic terms. A two-year multidisciplinary research effort, funded by the National Institute of Justice and published in 1996, estimated the costs and consequences of personal crime for Americans (Miller, Cohen, & Wiersema, 1996). The report estimated annual direct tangible costs to crime victims of $105 billion in medical expenses, lost earnings, and public programs related to victim assistance. Pain, suffering, and reduced quality of life increased the cost to $450 billion annually (Miller et al., 1996). Anderson (1999) estimated the total annual cost of criminal behavior in the United States, arguing that past research typically focused on particular costs, regions, or crime categories. Anderson estimated the direct and indirect costs that extend over the expenses of the legal system to consider ancillary costs that had not yet been included into an overall formula for the cost of crime. These costs included victims', criminals', and prisoners' time; the fear of being victimized; and the cost of private deterrence. Anderson estimated the net annual burden of crime to exceed $1 trillion. According to a systematic review of crime costs by Wickramasekera, Wright, Elsey, Murray, and Tubeuf (2015), the total costs of crime in the United States ranged from $450 billion to $3.2 trillion.

Canada has approximately one-tenth the population of the United States (Statistics Canada, 2016) and significantly lower levels of crime and victimization per capita. Zhang (2008) estimated that the total (tangible) social and economic costs of *Criminal Code* offenses in Canada were approximately $31.4 billion annually. This amounted to a per capita cost of $943 per year. However, Zhang pointed out that this was likely to be a conservative estimate due to the unavailability of data in many areas. Despite best efforts to account for all the financial impacts of crime, only a partial picture of the true range of costs is ever available. The costs identified are borne by the criminal justice system, victims of crimes, and third parties in general (Zhang, 2008). For instance, it is estimated that the Canadian criminal justice system cost $15 billion in 2008. This includes policing, courts, prosecution, legal aid, correctional services, and mental health review boards. Individual victims, however, paid an estimated $14.3 billion for crimes committed against them that same year. Their costs included medical attention, hospitalizations, lost wages, missed school days, and stolen/damaged property. Of the total costs, 47.0% represented lost wages and productivity and 42.9% lost or stolen property (Zhang, 2008). Indirect victims also bear costs due to grieving the loss of a loved one or caring for a victim. When all costs were taken into account, Zhang (2008) estimated total costs of crime for a 1-year period in Canada to be $99.6 billion. A more recent study by Easton, Furness, and Brantingham (2014) estimated the overall costs of crime to be $85.2 billion, the majority of which ($47 billion) was borne by victims directly. Victim costs included the value of damaged or stolen property, pain and suffering, loss of income and productivity, and health services. The authors note that although the crime rate in Canada has fallen over the years, the cost of crime has risen due to increased criminal justice system expenditures such as police, courts, and correctional services, which comprise $19.3 billion of the estimated total cost of crime. The remaining costs include those associated with private security, crime prevention services, and productivity and business losses.

A breakdown of the costs of crime can be organized into four main categories: health-related costs, direct financial costs, intangible costs, and criminal justice costs. Each category is detailed below.

Health-Related Costs

Tangible losses consisting of direct costs for damages and injuries as a result of victimization include medical and mental health expenses. Physical means of violence to a victim include a person's body (hands, fists, feet), instruments such as firearms and knives, flammable liquids and explosives, poisons, and animals (such as attack dogs); all of these can produce serious injuries.

Physical injury can range from minor harm, such as bruises and lacerations, to serious harm, such as broken bones and need for hospitalization, to lethal injury and death. Some violent crimes leave no visible sign of physical injury. This is true in some rape cases where there are no general body injuries or pelvic or genital injuries. Wallace and Roberson (2011) list four general classifications of physical injuries to victims.

First, *immediate injuries* include cuts, contusions, and/or broken bones that generally heal fairly quickly and are not viewed as serious by the victim. Immediate injuries can take longer to heal in persons who are elderly, have existing disabilities, are taking certain medications, or have an immune disorder. In a Nevada case, a 23-year-old man was hit over the head and robbed of his wallet by four men in a restaurant parking lot. At the hospital emergency room the physician stitching the victim's head remarked that the patient was lucky—that the last man who was attacked in that parking lot did not survive. The victim filed a civil lawsuit, the case went to trial, and the victim received a jury verdict of $200,000. The restaurant was on notice that its parking lot was not secure, as there was no security surveillance system or security officers patrolling the lot.

Second, *some injuries leave visible scars*, such as facial scaring, loss of teeth or fingers, or loss of mobility. Victims who have been shot will have permanent scars that remind them daily of the crime. Child abuse victims or victims of domestic violence may have lasting scars from physical beatings. In a Florida case, a young woman was exiting her car at her apartment complex when she was forced at gunpoint back into the passenger side of the car and carjacked. After being forced to withdraw money from an ATM, the victim was ordered out of the car and instructed to keep on walking and not to look back. Despite her following instructions she was shot three times in the back. She managed to crawl to a porch and call for help. The three men were found and prosecuted. The victim won a jury award of $1.3 million. Scars from the shootings have continued to remind the victim of her ordeal.

Third, *unknown long-term physical injuries* can cause a change in life activities. Rape victims, for example, may be exposed to a permanent sexually transmitted disease such as herpes virus or HIV/AIDS. In Pennsylvania, a student was working in a convenience store when a man forced her into a back room at gunpoint and raped her orally. Later she developed gonorrhea of the throat and experienced permanent voice changes due to scarring of her vocal cords.

Fourth, *long-term catastrophic injuries* can restrict a victim's mobility. In a Colorado rape case, the perpetrator intentionally broke a victim's neck, resulting in a paraplegic outcome. These severe injuries result in great stress on victims' families, who also need to alter their lifestyle to care for their loved ones. Such injuries may also reduce the victim's life span and alter quality of life.

The use of weapons, namely guns and knives, in incidents of interpersonal violence is considered an insidious public health danger. This violence causes strain to its victims, their families, community members, healthcare practitioners, and law enforcement officials. Gunshot wounds, sometimes called *ballistic trauma*, refer to the physical trauma caused by the discharge of a gun during a conflict. In terms of public health, it is estimated that over 500,000 injuries are sustained annually from the use of firearms. In terms of economic cost, estimates are that the expenditures of shootings and stabbings in the United States are greater than $20 billion each year. In the state of Massachusetts alone, expenditures related to stabbings and shootings are estimated to be greater than $18 million each year and do not account for the emotional impact of these events on victims and their families (Hume, McKenna, & McKeown, 2007).

Although insurance may cover partial or full restitution for such costs, victims can still be required to pay insurance deductibles and face higher premiums when renewing their insurance ("Statistics: Costs of Crime," 2002). Complications from injuries can cause functional, cognitive, and emotional disability as well as the presence of significant comorbid conditions and potential death.

Additionally, where physical manifestations of harm are absent, victims of violent crimes may show signs of significant psychological and emotional trauma endured during and after their victimization. Consequences of violence may be delayed or cumulative, and stress induced by violent acts, especially when repeated within a partner relationship, may culminate in severe emotional trauma or physical illness. Although these psychological consequences are difficult to measure in financial terms, they may manifest in more tangible costs associated with postvictimization counseling and rehabilitation, medication used to cope with resultant psychological trauma, as well as reduced productivity or lost days at work.

Direct Financial Costs

Financial costs for crime victims are staggering. In 2007, for crimes both reported and not reported in the United States, the total economic loss to victims was $2 billion for violent crime and $16 billion for property crime (Bureau of Justice Statistics, 2008). Tangible economic costs include stolen or damaged property; loss of productivity in terms of wages and salary; and days lost from school, work, and other activities. An impaired capacity to work, to continue in school, or to maintain one's quality of life are less often recognized, but consequential, costs of violent victimization. In 2000, 36% of rape and sexual assault victims lost more than 10 days of work after their victimization, and property crimes cost victims more than $11.8 billion (Bureau of Justice Statistics, 2002). State compensation programs paid crime victims and their families $370 million in benefits in the federal fiscal year 2001, which represents an increase of $52 million from 2000 and an increase of $120 million from 1998 (National Association of Crime Victim Compensation Boards [NACVCB], 2002). Vandalism costs totaled $1.7 billion in damages to U.S. households in 2000 (Bureau of Justice Statistics, 2000). Today, victim compensation funds provide nearly $500 million to victims and survivors (NACVCB, 2016). According to the Office for Victims of Crime (2013), the largest sum paid out was to victims of assault ($230 million), followed by homicide ($59 billion), child abuse ($28.4 billion), robbery ($19.6 billion), and sexual assault ($16 billion).

Intangible Costs

Intangible costs usually impact victims in a way that is difficult to measure, at least in a financial sense. However, they are arguably the most significant consequences of crime because they can impede healthy functioning and restrict the ability to carry out the normal functions in one's daily life. These costs include fear of crime, psychological distress, decreased quality of life, suffering, and stigma. In a study on the fear of crime in a sample of college students by Fox, Nobles, and Piquero (2009), it was found that particular types of prior victimization increased fear of crime, especially among females. They also noted that daytime fear was associated with stalking, sexual assault, and theft, whereas nighttime fear was only associated with sexual assault. With regard to psychological distress, victims can exhibit symptoms of a variety of different mental health issues as a result of the trauma experienced during and after their victimization. These may include posttraumatic stress disorder (PTSD), major depressive episode, agoraphobia, obsessive-compulsive disorder (OCD), and other social phobias (Boudreaux, Kilpatrick, Resnick, Best, & Saunders,

1998). Furthermore, young children have been found to be especially vulnerable to mental health problems later in life as a result of victimization (Turner, Finkelhor, & Ormrod, 2006). In terms of overall well-being, Hanson, Sawyer, Begle, and Hubel (2010) found that victimization can indirectly influence life satisfaction by affecting parenting skills, occupational functioning, employment, and intimate relationships. And finally, victimization, particularly events related to child abuse, domestic abuse, and sexual assault, may lead to feelings of shame, self-blame, guilt, and/or self-imposed stigma (Ulman, Townsend, Filipas, & Starzynksi, 2007). These resultant feelings are particularly troubling consequences not only for their substantial psychological impact, but also because they can serve as a barrier for reporting victimization events to police (see Sable, Danis, Mauzy, & Gallagher, 2006).

Criminal Justice Costs

Additional costs to society arise from the discretionary collective response to violent victimization. Law enforcement, adjudication, victim services, and correctional expenditures add thousands of dollars of cost to each criminal event. Although these costs may not be incurred by victims directly, they constitute a significant proportion of expenditures by the state that are financed by the collection of taxes. Additionally, the criminal justice system may impose additional costs on victims beyond those experienced from the criminal incident. The concept of **double victimization** suggests that victims can be revictimized by the criminal justice system in the form of time lost in interviews and completing paperwork, waiting in corridors for hearings and trials, and delays and postponements of the case. This is especially pertinent for victims of sexual assault or abuse who harbor feelings of guilt or shame that may be exacerbated during processes of justice. Several examples include when victims are required to recite the details of their victimization in front of a jury or law enforcement individuals who may doubt their accounts or when victims must come face to face with the accused.

▇ Conclusion

The definition of *victim* dates back to early religious practice and sacrifices. Although victimology emerged as a branch of criminology, the tradition has evolved to become a discipline in its own right. As a corrective to the distortions of victimhood by mass media and culture, victimology vis-à-vis the study of victimization statistics can provide a more accurate picture of the "crime" problem. Most notable is that victimization rates, including violent victimization, property victimization, and murder, have generally been decreasing since the mid-1990s. Despite these declines, the costs of victimization remain significant, including the various costs to victims and their families, as well as costs to society through the criminal justice system. The dynamics of victimization provide important information about the impact to the victim, and victimology is a critical component of investigating violent crime. However, the need exists to understand the experiences of victims who do not fall within the traditional sphere of *criminal* victimization.

Key Terms

Cold case: A criminal investigation that has not been solved for (generally) at least 1 year and, as a result, has been closed from further regular investigations.

Crime victim: A person who has been directly and proximately harmed (physically, emotionally, or financially) as a result of the commission of an offense.

Crime victims' rights: Eight rights included in Section 3771 of Title 18 of the U.S. Code, Crimes and Criminal Procedure.

Criminology: The study of the etiology of crime and the characteristics of the criminal.

Double (or secondary) victimization: The retraumatization of the victim or experience of other adverse consequences as a result of the justice process.

National Crime Victimization Survey (NCVS): A series of surveys, previously called the National Crime Survey, that has collected data on personal and household victimization since 1973.

Repeat victimization: Repeated criminal offences committed against a victim who has experienced prior victimization.

Victimology: The study of the victim from a social-structural way of viewing crime and the law and the criminal and the victim.

Discussion Questions

1. Compare and contrast victimology and criminology.
2. How do you think the JonBenét Ramsey murder will be solved?
3. Are Amanda Knox and Raffaele Sollecito victims of the justice system?
4. How important was DNA evidence in the Meredith Kercher murder case?

5. Why might there be a disconnect between public and media perceptions of victimization and statistics that suggest crime has declined?

6. Can "noncriminal" forms of victimization or harms that are not currently defined by the criminal code be adequately addressed through criminal law?

7. What are the implications of repeat victimization? How can this phenomenon be helpful in understanding vulnerability and the social determinants of victimization?

8. Is thinking about victimization in terms of financial costs to victims and society helpful? Why is there a desire to think of victimization in terms of costs?

Resources

American Statistical Association Committee on Law and Justice Statistics http://ww2.amstat.org/committees/commdetails.cfm?txtComm=CCNARS04

Bureau of Justice Statistics http://www.ojp.usdoj.gov/bjs/

Centers for Disease Control and Prevention Division of Violence Prevention http://www.cdc.gov/ncipc/dvp/dvp.htm

Crimes Against Children Research Center http://www.unh.edu/ccrc/

National Center for Juvenile Justice http://www.ncjj.org

National Institute of Justice's Data Resources Program http://www.nij.gov/funding/data-resources-program/welcome.htm

Office for Victims of Crime http://www.ojp.usdoj.gov/ovc/

Office of Justice Programs: Violence Against Women and Family Violence Program http://www.nij.gov/topics/crime/violence-against-women/welcome.htm

WISQARS™ (Web-based Injury Statistics Query and Reporting System) https://www.cdc.gov/injury/wisqars/index.html

References

Anderson, D. (1999). The aggregate burden of crime. *The Journal of Law and Economics, 42*(2), 611–642.

Arata, C. (2002). Child sexual abuse and sexual revictimization. *Clinical Psychology, 9*(2), 135–164.

Boudreaux, E., Kilpatrick, D., Resnick, H., Best, C., & Saunders, B. (1998). Criminal victimization, posttraumatic stress disorder, and comorbid psychopathology among a community sample of women. *Journal of Traumatic Stress, 11*(4), 665–678.

Bureau of Justice Statistics. (1992). *Crime in the United States, 1991*. Washington, DC: U.S. Department of Justice. Retrieved from https://www.ncjrs.gov/pdffiles1 /Digitization/138839NCJRS.pdf

Bureau of Justice Statistics. (1993). *A National Crime Victimization Survey report: Criminal victimization 1991*. Washington, DC: U.S. Department of Justice. Retrieved from http://www.bjs.gov/content/pub/pdf/cv91.pdf

Bureau of Justice Statistics. (2000). *Crime and the nation's households, 2000*. Washington, DC: U.S. Department of Justice.

Bureau of Justice Statistics. (2002). *National crime victimization survey: Personal and property crimes, 2000*. Washington, DC: U.S. Department of Justice.

Bureau of Justice Statistics. (2008). *Criminal victimization in the United States, 2008*. Retrieved from http://bjs.ojp.usdoj.gov/content/pub/pdf/cv08.pdf

Bureau of Justice Statistics. (2016). *Violent victimization, 1993–2015*. Retrieved from https://www.bjs.gov/index.cfm?ty=dcdetail&iid=245

Carter, B. (2017, July 22). What happened to Amanda Knox—what she's up to now? *The Gazette*. Retrieved from http://gazettereview.com/2017/04/happened-amanda -knox-news-updates/

DeFlem, M. (2006). *Sociological theory and criminological research: Views from Europe and the United States*. New York: Elsevier/JAI Press.

Donadio, R., & Povoledo, E. (2011, October 4). As Amanda Knox heads home, the debate is just getting started. *New York Times*. Retrieved from http://www .nytimes.com/2011/10/05/world/europe/amanda-knox-freed-after-appeal-in -italian-court.html

Easton, S., Furness, H., & Brantingham, P. (2014). *Cost of crime in Canada: 2014 report*. Fraser Institute. Retrieved from https://www.fraserinstitute.org/sites /default/files/cost-of-crime-in-canada.pdf

Fattah, E. (2000). Victimology, past, present, and future. *Criminologie, 33*(1), 17–46.

Federal Bureau of Investigation (FBI). (2011). Victim rights. Retrieved from http:// www.fbi.gov/stats-services/victim_assistance/victim_rights

Federal Bureau of Investigation (FBI). (2015). Number of crimes per 100,000 inhabitants. Retrieved from https://ucr.fbi.gov/crime-in-the-u.s/2015/crime-in-the -u.s.-2015/tables/table-16

Fletcher, G. P. (1990). *A crime of self-defense: Bernhard Goetz and the law on trial*. Chicago: University of Chicago Press.

Fox, K., Nobles, M., & Piquero, A. (2009). Gender, crime victimization and fear of crime. *Security Journal, 22*(1), 24–39.

Frank, R., Brantingham, P., & Farrell, G. (2012). Estimate the true rate of repeat victimization from police recorded crime data: A study of burglary in metro Vancouver. *Canadian Journal of Criminology and Criminal Justice, 54*(4), 481–494.

Garland, D. (2001). *The culture of control: Crime and social order in contemporary society*. Oxford: Oxford University Press.

Hanson, R., Sawyer, G., Begle, A., & Hubel, G. (2010). The impact of crime victimization on quality of life. *Journal of Traumatic Stress, 23*(2), 189–197.

Hastings, R. (2008). *Achieving crime prevention: Reducing crime and increasing security in an inclusive Canada*. Ottawa: Institute for the Prevention of Crime. Retrieved from http://www.publicsafety.gc.ca/lbrr/archives/cnmcs-plcng/cn35297-eng.pdf

Hillyard, P., & Tombs, S. (2007). From "crime" to social harm? *Crime, Law, and Social Change, 48*(1–2), 9–25.

Hume, B., McKenna, M., & McKeown, L. (2007). *Injuries to Massachusetts residents 2004*. Boston: Department of Public Health.

Justice for All Act. (2004). Office of Victims of Crime, Department of Justice, Washington, DC.

Kauzlarich, D., Matthews, R., & Miller, W. (2001). Toward a victimology of state crime. *Critical Criminology, 10*(3), 173–194.

Martinez, E. (2010, August 3). Hartford Distributors shooting: Angry employee allegedly kills multiple people. CBS News. Retrieved from http://www.cbsnews.com/8301-504083_162-20012503-504083.html

Mendelsohn, B. (1976). Pioneers in victimology. *Victimology: An International Journal, 1*(2), 189–228.

Miller, T. R., Cohen, M. A., & Wiersema, B. (1996). *Victim costs and consequences: A new look*. Washington, DC: National Institute of Justice.

Merriam-Webster Dictionary. (2016). Criminology. Retrieved from http://www.merriam-webster.com/concise/criminology

National Association of Crime Victim Compensation Boards (NACVCB). (2002). Compensation at record highs. *Victim Compensation Quarterly*, 3.

National Association of Crime Victim Compensation Boards (NACVCB). (2016). Crime victim compensation: An overview. Retrieved from http://www.nacvcb.org/index.asp?bid=14

National Center for Victims of Crime. (2015). Crime trends. Retrieved from http://victimsofcrime.org/docs/default-source/ncvrw2015/2015ncvrw_stats_crime trends.pdf?sfvrsn=2

Office for Victims of Crime. (2013). *Crime victims fund*. Washington, DC: Office for Victims of Crime, Office of Justice Programs, U.S. Department of Justice.

Quinney, R. (1972). Who is the Victim? *Criminology, 10*(3), 314–323.

Reiss, A. J., & Roth, J. A. (1993). *Understanding and preventing violence*. Washington, DC: National Academy Press.

Sable, M., Danis, F., Mauzy, D., & Gallagher, S. (2010). Barriers to reporting sexual assault for women and men: Perspectives of college students. *Journal of American College Health, 55*(3), 157–162.

Skinnider, E. (2011). *Victims of environmental crime: Mapping the issues*. Vancouver: International Centre for Criminal Law Reform and Criminal Justice Policy.

Sparks, R. (1990). Dramatic power: Television, images of crime and law enforcement. In C. Sumner (Ed.), *Censure, politics, and criminal justice*. Philadelphia: Open University Press, Milton Keynes.

"Statistics: Costs of Crime." (2002). *Encyclopedia of crime and justice*. Retrieved from http://www.encyclopedia.com/doc/1G2-3403000253.html

Statistics Canada. (2015). *Criminal victimization in Canada, 2014*. Statistics Canada. Retrieved from http://www.statcan.gc.ca/pub/85-002-x/2015001/article/14241 -eng.htm

Statistics Canada. (2016). *Population size and growth in Canada: Key results from the 2016 Census*. Statistics Canada. Retrieved from http://www.statcan.gc.ca /daily-quotidien/170208/dq170208a-eng.htm

Sutherland, E. (1949). *White collar crime*. New York: The Dryden Press.

Sutherland, E., & Cressey, D. (1973). *Principles of Criminology 9th Edition*. Philadelphia, J.B. Lippincott.

Tseloni, A., Knutsson, J., & Laycock, G. (2005). Repeat victimization: Introduction. *International Review of Victimology, 12*(1), 47–49.

Tseloni, A., & Pease, K. (2004). Repeat personal victimization. *British Journal of Criminology, 44*(6), 931–945.

Turner, H., Finkelhor, D., & Ormrod, R. (2006). The effect of lifetime victimization on the mental health of children and adolescents. *Social Science & Medicine, 62*(1), 13–27.

Ulman, S., Townsend, S., Filipas, H., & Starzynksi, L. (2007). Structural models of the relations of assault severity, social support, avoidance coping, self-blame, and PTSD among sexual assault survivors. *Psychology of Women Quarterly, 31*(1), 23–37.

United Nations. (1985). *Declaration of basic principles of justice for victims of crime and abuse of power*. G.A. 40/34, annex, 40 U.N. GAOR Supp. (No. 53) at 214, U.N. Doc. A/40/53.

Vargas, E., & Natanson, P. (2011). Amanda Knox "shocked" when Rudy Guede implicates her in murder. *ABC News*. Retrieved from http://abcnews.go.com/International /amanda-knox-shocked-rudy-guede-implicates-murder/story?id=13936041

Von Hentig, H. (1948). *The criminal and his victim: Studies in the sociobiology of crime*. New Haven, CT: Yale University Press.

Walklate, S. (2007). *Handbook of victims and victimology*. Devon: Willan.

Wallace, H., & Roberson, H. (2011). *Victimology: Legal, psychological, and social perspectives*. Upper Saddle River, NJ: Pearson Education.

Wickramasekera, N., Wright, J., Elsey, H., Murray, J., & Tubeuf, S. (2015). Cost of crime: A systematic review. *Journal of Criminal Justice, 43*(3), 218–228.

White, R. (2015). Environmental victimology and ecological justice (pp. 33–52). In D. Wilson & S. Ross (Eds.), *Crime, victims, and policy: International contexts, local experiences*. Basingstoke: Macmillan.

Wolfgang, M. (1958). *Criminal homicide*. New York: Harper & Row.

Young, A. (2008). Culture, critical criminology, and the imagination of crime (pp.18–29). In A. Thalia & C. Cunneen (Eds.), *The critical criminology companion*. Sydney: Hawkins Press.

Zhang, T. (2008). The costs of crime in Canada. Retrieved from http://www.justice .gc.ca/eng/pi/rs/rep-rap/2011/rr10_5/index.html

Zimring, F. (2007). *The Great American Crime Decline*. New York: Oxford University Press.

CHAPTER 2

Measurement of Crime and Victimization

OBJECTIVES

- To present various sources of data regarding crime and victimization
- To identify means of collecting data on crime and victimization
- To discuss strengths and limitations of various data sources

KEY TERMS

Cleared by exceptional means

Dark figure of crime

Hierarchy rule

Incidence

National Crime Victimization
Survey (NCVS)

National Incident-Based
Reporting System (NIBRS)

Prevalence

Uniform Crime Reports (UCR)

CASE

On July 23, 2011, a 32-year-old Norwegian, Anders Behring Breivik, gave himself up to police after admitting to massacring 69 people, mostly teenagers, attending a summer camp of the youth wing of Norway's ruling Labour Party. Breivik was also charged in the crime of bombing Oslo's government district and killing seven people hours earlier. A video posted on YouTube showed several pictures of Breivik, including one of him in a Navy Seal–type scuba diving outfit, pointing an automatic weapon. "Before we can start our crusade we must do our duty by decimating cultural Marxism," said a caption under the video called "Knights Templar 2083," which also provided a link to a 1,500-page electronic manifesto stating Breivik was the author.

Terrified survivors of the shooting rampage said bullets came from at least two sides. "I heard shots, screams, and people begging for their lives. He just blew them away," a Labour Party youth member said. "I was certain I was going to die." "People ran everywhere. They panicked and climbed into trees. People got trampled." "We are all in sorrow. Everybody is scared," said another Norwegian (*The Daily Star*, 2011). Police took almost an hour and half to stop the massacre, the worst by a single gunman in modern times. Witnesses said the gunman, wearing a police uniform, was able to shoot unchallenged for a prolonged period, forcing youngsters to scatter in panic or to jump into the lake to swim for the mainland (Beaumont, 2011). See **FIGURES 2-1A** and **2-1B**.

Following his conviction, Breivik was held in isolation in Norway's Skien prison. He filed a lawsuit in 2016, claiming that his time in solitary confinement was inhumane. Breivik had

FIGURE 2-1B Anders Behring Breivik's victims.
ODD ANDERSEN/AFP/Getty Images.

been limited to a three-room prison cell with space for sleeping, studying, and working out. He was able to run on a treadmill, watch DVDs, play games on a Sony PlayStation, and take distance-learning courses at the university.

According to Breivik's attorneys, the Norwegian government was in violation of two clauses of the European Convention on Human Rights. First, it had failed to uphold Breivik's right to "respect for his private and family life, his home and his correspondence" and another right that prohibits "inhumane or degrading treatment or punishment." Breivik challenged the government over his solitary confinement, whereby he was kept alone in his cell for 22 to 23 hours a day. He was denied contact with other inmates and was only able to communicate with prison staff through a thick glass barrier (BBC News, 2016).

Breivik's attorney questioned the government's use of excessive strip-searches, frequent handcuff usage and, namely, isolation, which were causing Breivik "mental strain." Breivik's goal in going to trial, his attorney said, was to enable Breivik to have contact with other prisoners and lessen restrictions on his communication with the outside world.

FIGURE 2-1A Anders Behring Breivik.
© FEREX/Associated Press.

Attorneys for the Norwegian government stated that 600 letters had been withheld from about 4,000 letters either sent by Breivik or to him in efforts to prevent him from establishing an "extremist network."

Upon entering the temporary hearing room set up in the gymnasium at the prison, Breivik gave a Nazi salute. After listening to testimony, Judge Helen Andenaes Sekulic gave her ruling, stating that the right not to be subjected to inhumane treatment represented "a fundamental value in a democratic society" and also applied to "terrorists and killers." In her view, Breivik's prison regime deviated so markedly from that enforced upon any other prisoner in Norway, regardless of the severity of their crimes, that it had to be considered an extra punishment. Article three of the European Convention on Human Rights (ECHR) requires that prisoners be detained in conditions that do not exceed the unavoidable level of suffering inherent in detention, given the practical requirements of the particular case. Judge Sekulic also noted that the prison authorities had not done enough to counteract the damage he had suffered from being in isolation. According to her ruling, the prison must work to bring in other prisoners and facilitate a community for Breivik. However, the judge ruled that strict controls on Breivik's correspondence were justified and that his right to a private and family life under article eight of the ECHR had not been violated (Bever, 2016).

Introduction

The mass murder of strangers, as illustrated in the opening case, shatters the sense of safety and security for individuals, their families, their communities, and society as a whole. The level of crime victimization in a community, as well as people's perceptions of their safety, impacts directly or indirectly on the quality of people's lives. Those experiencing direct victimization may suffer financially, physically, or emotionally, but fear of crime has widespread impacts, restricting community engagement, reducing levels of trust, and affecting social cohesion (Fattah, 1997). However, public perceptions regarding the incidence of crime and risk of victimization are not necessarily congruent with actual crime rates. Although the public often expresses fear that crime and victimization are increasing, empirical data suggest that the incidence of violent crime is in fact on the decline.

Measuring crime offenses and its victims is critical to identifying the short- and long-term effects of crime, to increasing knowledge regarding victims' needs, to directing funds toward the development and enhancement of victim service programs, and to adding to the scientific base of victimology. The results of continued study and research efforts assist in policy development in areas of the criminal justice system and in outlining emerging issues or trends in the area of crime victimization.

Individuals, communities, and governments gather information about crime and victimization in a number of ways. Statistical data are a key component of information about crime and are critical to decision-making, research, and policy development. In some instances, results from different data sources may provide a different picture of crime in the community, with administrative data indicating a trend in one direction and survey responses indicating the opposite. Different data sources collected via different methods can produce equally valid but quite varied sets of crime victimization rates. While all sampling methods can be criticized, most of these methods advance the measurement of crime beyond anecdotal evidence or media reports alone. The challenge for data users is to understand the bases of these differences in these data sets based on the approach to data collection and measurement and then subsequently identify the statistics and trends that are most relevant for their needs.

The purpose of this chapter is to outline the major crime and victimization data sources and discuss the comparability of various crime measurement instruments and databases. TABLE 2-1 identifies major data sources in crime and victimization.

Uniform Crime Reports

The U.S. Wickersham Commission, convened by President Herbert Hoover in 1929, and named after its chairman and former Attorney General George W. Wickersham, was composed of 11 committees and convened for 2 years (National Commission on Law Observance and Enforcement, 1931). It was established to address the issue of crime in general, but also as a way to resolve the debate over the continuing problem of Prohibition and organized crime. The Commission conducted the first comprehensive national study of crime and law enforcement in U.S. history and published its findings in 14 volumes covering every aspect of the criminal justice system, including the causes of crime, police and prosecutorial procedures, and the importance of probation and parole (National Commission on Law Observance and Enforcement, 1931).

The Commission proposed a comprehensive national criminal justice statistics program under an independent central statistical agency. Although this plan did not come to fruition, it later led to a cooperative system for statistical crime reporting called the Uniform Crime Reporting (UCR) Program, with the goal of meeting the need for reliable, uniform crime statistics for the nation (National Commission on Law Observance and Enforcement, 1931). The UCR Program was conceived and designed in 1929 for the law enforcement community throughout the United States. The task for implementing the directive went

TABLE 2-1 Crime and Victimization Databases

Database	Source of Data	Type of Data	Aims	Country Served
Measurement of Crime				
Uniform Crime Reports (UCR)	Compiled from law enforcement agency data across the country	Crimes reported to police based on standardized definitions	Allows for cross-jurisdictional comparisons	United States and Canada
National Incident-Based Reporting System (NIBRS)	Compiled from law enforcement agency data across the country	Crimes, offender characteristics, and victim characteristics	Expands the UCR data set to accurately reflect crime rates	United States
National Prisoner Statistics Program (NPS)	Census and survey data collected from prisons and correctional facilities	Prison characteristics, staff characteristics, prisoner characteristics	Identifies trends in crime and incarceration, improves planning of prison resources	United States
Adult Criminal Court Survey (ACCS)	Data reported by court systems	Offender characteristics, nature of crime, sentencing and disposition	Identifies trends in crime and sentencing, improves court procedures	Canada
Measurement of Victimization				
National Crime Victimization Survey (NCVS)	General population survey from nationally representative sample of U.S. population	Victims' experiences of crime victimization	Determines the incidence of both reported and unreported crime to aid in understanding the nature and impact of crime	United States
General Social Survey– Victimization (GSS)	General population survey	Self-report data on victimization, perceptions of crime, and attitudes toward the justice system	To better understand how Canadians perceive crime and the justice system and their experiences of victimization	Canada
British Crime Survey (BCS)	General population survey	Criminal victimization and attitudes toward crime, police, and the justice system	To understand the incidence of victimization and public attitudes	England and Wales
International Crime Victims Survey (ICVS)	Survey of households using a standardized questionnaire	Incidence of particular crimes, victim satisfaction with justice and services, attitudes toward crime	To provide international comparative data on crime and longitudinal trends	Over 80 countries
Interpol	World's largest international police organization	Helps police on the ground understand crime trends, analyze information	To aid in arresting as many criminals as possible	190 member countries

Data from Australian Bureau of Statistics. 2004. Information Paper: Measuring Crime Victimisation. Australia: The Impact of Different Collection Methodologies, 2002, cat. no. 4522.0.55.001, ABS, Canberra. Retrieved from http://www.abs.gov.au/ausstats/abs@.nsf/Lookup/5BF3A030F523595BCA2578B00011A06B?opendocument.

to the Federal Bureau of Investigation (FBI). Initially, whether the FBI should be responsible for data collection was questioned because of concerns about the use of information as a basis for appropriation requests or expansion of powers and equipment by the agency. However, it has remained under FBI control as a major database for law enforcement. The FBI issues **Uniform Crime Reports (UCR)** to disseminate the main findings and trends on crime (Kempf, 1990).

UCR Data Collection

The UCR Program collects offense information for murder, nonnegligent manslaughter, forcible rape, robbery, aggravated assault, burglary, larceny-theft, motor vehicle theft, and arson. These reports are compiled monthly by police departments and submitted to the FBI or state-level UCR program. Crimes selected for inclusion in the UCR are those most likely to be reported and those that occur with sufficient frequency to allow for comparisons. Thus, serious but infrequent crimes, such as kidnapping, are not included. Further, the UCR Program does not gather data on offenses in violation of federal law, many white-collar crimes, commerce and industry violations, or drug offenses such as arrests and drug seizures (MacKenzie, Baunach, & Roberg, 1990).

In addition to offense and arrest data, supplemental data are recorded (FBI, 2011a, 2011b). For instance, in the case of robbery, information on property stolen and recovered is obtained. In the case of homicide, the age, sex, and race of the murder victims and offenders and weapons used are recorded. The FBI also collects data on hate crimes and on cases where enforcement officers are killed or assaulted (James & Rishard, 2008).

During the early years of the UCR Program, the database relied largely on the cooperation of local police departments for the collection of information; however, it has become increasingly mandatory. Over 17,000 law enforcement agencies (98% of agencies) submit data to the UCR Program. Forty-six states submit data every month through a state UCR program, and four states submit data directly to the FBI. The FBI requires the following from each state UCR program (James & Rishard, 2008, p. 6):

- The data must conform to national standards, definitions, and information reported.
- The data must be collected and recorded using acceptable quality-control procedures.
- The percentage of the state's population covered must equal that covered by the national UCR Program.
- Adequate field staff must be available for audits and support.

- The FBI must be provided with duplicates of all data collected.

- The organization must be able to supply data in time to meet deadlines.

It is worthwhile to discuss how the UCR treats the clearance of cases. Law enforcement agencies can clear or close offenses in one of two ways: by arrest or by exceptional means (FBI, 2011b). An offense is cleared by arrest or solved for crime-reporting purposes when at least one person has been arrested, charged with the commission of the offense, and turned over to the court for prosecution (whether following arrest, court summons, or police notice). In its clearance calculations, the UCR Program counts the number of offenses cleared, not the number of persons arrested. The arrest of one person may clear several crimes, and the arrest of many persons may clear only one offense. In addition, some clearances that an agency records in a particular calendar year may pertain to offenses that occurred in previous years.

Case clearances can be classified as exceptional in certain situations where elements beyond law enforcement's control prevent the agency from arresting and formally charging the offender. According to the FBI, an offense can be cleared by exceptional means if (1) there is an identified offender; (2) sufficient evidence has been collected to support an arrest, make a charge, and turn over the offender to the court for prosecution; (3) the offender's exact location has been identified so he or she can be taken into custody immediately; and (4) law enforcement agencies have encountered a circumstance outside their control that prohibits arrest and prosecution. Such cases can include situations where the offender has died, the victim refuses to cooperate with the prosecution after the offender is identified, or extradition is denied because the offender committed a crime in another jurisdiction and is being prosecuted for that offense (FBI, 2009a).

The following are some of the advantages and disadvantages of the UCR Program:

- Advantages:
  - Data are compiled annually from jurisdictions all over the United States, which allows comparisons by location and analysis of trends over time.

  - Crime definitions are standardized. For instance, serious crime is divided into two groups: (1) personal offenses, such as murder, forcible rape, robbery, and aggravated assault, and (2) property offenses, including burglary, larceny-theft, motor vehicle theft, and arson.

  - Information gathered provides data for patterns of crime and criminals.

- Disadvantages:
  - Data only include offenses reported to police, masking the "dark figure of crime" and underestimating the incidence and prevalence of crime.
  - Because the UCR is based on the hierarchy rule, the data only include the most serious crime incident in those instances where multiple offenses were committed.
  - Data may be more consistent with the types of offenses that police pursue, rather than with an accurate picture of all crimes committed, and thus the UCR has been said to reflect police behavior more than criminality itself. For instance, a major critique of the UCR has been its neglect of particular types of criminals such as white-collar and female offenders.

In December 2010, the FBI released a new UCR data tool, developed by the Bureau of Justice Statistics (BJS, 2010; FBI, 2011a), as part of ongoing collaboration between the Department of Justice and the FBI to improve accessibility of crime data for researchers and the public. The online UCR data tool facilitates the search for crime data going back to 1960 and enables users to perform queries on custom variables such as year, agency, and type of offense. Until now, making comparisons within the UCR data required searching the annual reports and then manually calculating trends. The new tool aims to make it easier for users—especially law enforcement partners who supply the data—to make use of the raw numbers.

National Incident-Based Reporting System

For many years after its inception, data collection and dissemination through the UCR Program remained virtually unchanged. However, in the 1970s, an increasing number of criticisms were made on the basis of the following limitations:

- Statistics were maintained only on reported crimes and ignored unreported cases.
- Data could be incomplete and manipulated as a way for a city to boost its image.
- Data were lacking regarding victims and offenders.
- Data were only reported on those who were arrested.

Consequently, critics suggested that the UCR underreported the true level of crime. Thus, in the late 1970s, a thorough evaluation of the UCR was undertaken with the objective of recommending an expanded and enhanced data collection program that would better meet the needs of law enforcement, policy makers, and program developers. The multiyear examination of the UCR resulted in a report titled the *Blueprint for the Future of the Uniform Crime Reporting Program* (FBI, 1985). The *Blueprint*, augmented by a process of consultation with law enforcement agencies, became the basis for the development of the **National Incident-Based Reporting System (NIBRS)** (FBI, 2009b).

Similar to the UCR, the NIBRS collects data on crimes known to the police. However, unlike the UCR, the data are not aggregated. Data for each criminal incident are collected on 53 different dimensions, including the specific offenses in the incident, victim and offender characteristics, characteristics of the person(s) arrested, and types of property lost or recovered. Further, the range of offenses on which data are collected was expanded to include two categories of offenses (22 group A offenses and 11 group B offenses) containing a total of 33 different offenses. Each state must be certified to submit data to the FBI (James & Rishard, 2008). **TABLE 2-2** outlines the advantages of NIBRS.

The NIBRS website (https://ucr.fbi.gov/nibrs-overview) states that its databases are available for online data analysis. Users can perform certain statistical procedures on the data, create custom subsets, or browse the codebook on the Web, without downloading the entire collection and importing the data into a statistical package. NIBRS offers the following options:

- Search for variables of interest in a data set.
- Review frequencies or summary statistics of key variables to determine what further analyses are appropriate.
- Review frequencies or summary statistics for missing data.

TABLE 2-2 Advantages of the NIBRS

- Data collection is not restricted to a limited number of offense categories (i.e., group A offenses).
- Offense definitions can meet state, local, and national reporting needs.
- Details on individual crime incidents (offenses, offenders, victims, property, and arrests) can be collected and analyzed.
- Arrests and clearances can be linked to specific incidents and offenses.
- Distinctions can be made between attempted and completed crimes.
- Linkages can be established between variables for examining interrelationships between offenses, offenders, victims, property, and arrestees.
- Detailed crime analyses can be made within and across law enforcement jurisdictions.
- Strategic and tactical crime analyses can be made at the local and regional levels.
- No hierarchy rule because every offense during an incident is reported provided the incidents are separate and distinct.

Data from James, N., & Rishard, L. 2008. *How Crime in the United States Is Measured*. Document RL34309. Washington, DC: Congressional Research Service, p. 17.

- Produce simple summary statistics for reports.
- Create statistical tables from raw data.
- Create a subset of cases or variables from a large collection to save time and storage space downloading to a personal computer.

Despite the advantages of the NIBRS over the UCR, concerns remain about its representativeness and effectiveness as a crime measurement tool. Addington (2008) stated that, unlike the UCR, the NIBRS is voluntary and requires a lengthy certification process for each law enforcement agency. This has resulted in a gradual, but slow conversion from UCR to NIBRS reporting. As of 2015, 33 states were NIBRS certified and 6,648 law enforcement agencies (36.1% of all law enforcement agencies) were contributing NIBRS data to the UCR (FBI, 2015). Further, those jurisdictions reporting NIBRS data had smaller populations, and none were in communities of over 1 million people (Addington, 2008). In 2016, FBI Director James Comey signed a recommendation to have the UCR Program transition to NIBRS-only data by 2021 (FBI, 2016).

UCR Canada

Established in 1962, the Canadian UCR survey was designed to measure the incidence of crime in Canadian society. Substantiated crime data reported by all police departments across the country are collected and collated by the Canadian Centre for Justice Statistics. Data include the number of criminal incidents, the clearance status of those incidents, and persons-charged information. The original survey (referred to as UCR1.0) consisted solely of aggregate summary data for 100 criminal offenses. In 1988, this was modified to include an incident-based survey (referred to as UCR2.0) that records micro-level data on victims, offenders, and offense characteristics for each criminal incident. Subsequent modifications in 1998 and 2004 simplified the data collection and reporting methods. In both surveys police agencies act as respondents, and the response rate and compliance is nearly 100%. These data are used for crime analysis, planning regarding distribution of policing resources, and program development (Statistics Canada, 2011c).

Challenges in the Measurement of Crime

Attempts to uniformly report and measure crime across a wide variety of jurisdictions are fraught with challenges (Akiyama & Nolan, 1999; Caspi et al., 2002; Chilton & Jarvis, 1999). One issue relates to biases inherent in decisions as to which crimes will be included and which will not. For instance, James and Rishard (2008) identified that neither the UCR nor NIBRS collects data on political crime, price-fixing, or illegal environmental pollution and suggest that both sources undercount corporate and occupational crimes. Political pressure to lower crime rates, the extent to which agencies follow FBI definitions of crime, the efficiency of agencies at detecting crime, the willingness of citizens to report crime, and the effectiveness of record-keeping systems may all affect UCR data (James & Rishard, 2008). Specific challenges addressed in this section include definitional challenges, reporting challenges, and challenges related to policing practices.

Definitional Challenges

UCR classification methods have been criticized for being vague, imprecise, and subject to varying interpretation. Definitions may vary subtly from the jurisdictions' legal definitions of crimes, and each offense definition requires factors to provide sufficient basis for classification. In attempting to deal with the definitional challenges in the UCR, a number of rules have been established, including the hierarchy rule, hotel rule, and the separation of time and place rule.

The hierarchy rule in the UCR definitions requires that when multiple offenses occur in a single incident, only the most serious offense is scored. An example of the hierarchy rule is the Petit triple family murders that occurred in Cheshire, Connecticut, in July 2007. Two men, Steven Hayes and Joshua Komisarjevsky, followed Jennifer Hawke-Petit and her 11-year-old daughter Michaela home from a grocery store and targeted the family as wealthy. According to Hayes's confession, the two men planned to rob the house and flee the scene with the family bound and unharmed. However, upon their early morning arrival, they found William Petit sleeping on a couch on the porch. With a bat he had found in the yard, Komisarjevsky bludgeoned Petit and then restrained him in the basement at gunpoint. The children and their mother were each bound and locked in their respective rooms. Hayes says he and Komisarjevsky were not satisfied with the small amount of cash found but that a bankbook revealed an available balance. Hayes thus coerced Jennifer Hawke-Petit to withdraw $15,000 from her line of credit. The bank surveillance cameras captured the transaction showing Hawke-Petit the morning of July 23 informing the teller of her situation. The teller then called 911 and reported the details to police. The Cheshire police response to the bank teller's "urgent bid" began with assessing the situation and setting up a vehicle perimeter that took more than half an hour and provided the time used by the assailants to conclude their modified plan.

Upon returning to the house, Komisarjevsky sexually assaulted the young daughter and photographed her on his cell phone, provoking Hayes to rape and strangle Hawke-Petit. A fire was then ignited, and Hayes and Komisarjevsky fled the scene in the Petit family car. William Petit had been able to free himself, escape, and call to a neighbor for help. The car was pursued by police, and the suspects were apprehended and arrested one block away. The whole invasion lasted 7 hours. Two daughters died of smoke inhalation (Folmer & Friedman, 2010).

The eight crimes included home invasion, kidnapping, assault, hostage taking, burglary, rape, murder, and arson. Using the hierarchy rule, the crime with the highest priority was premeditated murder, based on the fact the two men took time to buy gasoline for the cover-up. None of the other crimes would appear in UCR statistics.

The hotel rule states that when multiple dwelling units under a single manager are burglarized and the offenses are more likely to be reported by the manager rather than individual occupants, the burglaries are recorded as one offense in the statistical record. The separation of time and place rule states that when there is a difference in the time interval and distance between different offenses, each incident must be handled separately (hierarchy and hotel rules cannot apply) (James & Rishard, 2008).

Reporting Challenges

The production of data for the crime databases relies on the participation of victims, witnesses, and police. Thus, a number of factors influence whether a particular crime occurrence will be reported in such databases. First, there must be an awareness that the crime has occurred. Sometimes crimes such as theft or larceny may go undetected for prolonged periods of time. Second, citizens must define the crime as worthy of police intervention. Individual citizens may fail to report crimes to police because they are unaware of the procedures of reporting crime, are doubtful that the police can do anything about the crime, believe the police are incompetent or uninterested, or believe the offense was not important enough to warrant police attention. Business owners may not report crimes to police because if the property is uninsured they may believe there is no personal gain in reporting, or, if they are insured, they may fear rate increases in their insurance policies if they report the incident. Additionally, some victims may be reluctant to report crimes that are sensitive and personal in nature or for fear that reporting could exacerbate emotional trauma, such as in the case of rape. Victims of domestic violence may defer from reporting because they may fear retribution or other repercussions by a spouse, because they do not want anyone to know about the incident, or because they worry about the impact of reporting on a known assailant. Third, police must decide whether a crime has occurred. Police may fail to report crimes by overlooking certain violations (e.g., minor drug violations) or succumb to pressure to reduce crime statistics by downgrading offenses. In dealing with youth, police may defer the incident to responsible adults and avoid making formal reports. Finally, when all the preceding decisions have been made, the information must go to the appropriate authorities for inclusion in the UCR (Kempf, 1990; MacKenzie et al., 1990). Thus, data depend on a series of decisions made by a variety of individuals, and challenges with reporting crime can significantly underestimate actual levels of crime.

Challenges Related to Policing Practices

Jurisdictional variations in police practices can affect reported crime rates. For example, police officers who have more discretion to settle disputes on the streets may prevent crimes from developing. Reporting of rape and sexual assault crimes may vary because of the attitudes of police services toward those who are victimized, the creation of victim–witness assistance programs in police departments, and improved treatment of complainants by the criminal justice system. Other police-related factors are as follows:

- *Response time to a call.* In both the case of the Norway massacre and the Petit triple homicide, the crimes were reported. However, police were criticized in their delay in responding to the calls, resulting in higher numbers of victims. Police departments that have tried to study the issue of response time have encountered a number of challenges in collecting accurate data. In 2008, an Arizona police department attempted to collect data on response time for police incidents dating between 2007 and 2008; however, they had difficulty interpreting the data because there was no standard way for officers to report on scene. For example, while the assigned officer responds to a call a second officer arrives on scene, but the response time clock continues to tick for the incident until the first officer logs on scene (Leung, 2011).

- *Level of professionalism.* Citizens expect police to be knowledgeable and professional in their response to victimization. If they are not, people become increasingly reluctant to report crime. Police agencies that have a reputation for not being adequately responsive to reports of crime, for appearing skeptical about victim testimonies, or for frequently engaging in victim-blaming may foster distrust among residents in the community, which can affect reporting rates.

- *Policing styles (reactive vs. proactive).* The large variation in policing styles can affect officially recorded crime rates. In one Milwaukee study, even though the overall number of incidents dispatched to police officers had declined over the past 6 years, response rates to almost every incident category increased. The police department explained the higher response rates as the result of a focus on proactive policing policy (*Dispatch Magazine*, 2011). The allocation of policing resources to high-priority neighborhoods as part of a problem-oriented approach may also increase the frequency of arrests, and thus increase overall crime statistics reported by local agencies.

- *Arrest practices.* The arrest process can vary among jurisdictions and may also be influenced by a variety of factors, including offense seriousness, the relationship between victim and offender, and situational evidence. Kempf (1990) argued that few offenses are a result of direct police observation, and therefore police rely on the report of the victim in making a decision to arrest a defendant. Police discretion may vary, and not all crimes may be followed by a charge. Warnings may be used to avoid formal arrest, and officers may use their discretion to resolve disputes in informal ways.

National Prisoner Statistics Program

Crime can also be measured by collecting data on prisoners. The National Prisoner Statistics Program (NPS), established in 1926, was one of the first crime databases in the United States. Its aim is to provide national and state-level data on the numbers of prisoners in the state and federal prison systems. These data include prisoner characteristics (e.g., race, gender, and age), type of offense, and time in prison. Information is collected on demographic, social, and criminal characteristics of inmates, movement of inmates within and between facilities, and the prison facilities that house them.

As particular challenges arise, additional data are collected to determine the extent and risk associated. For instance, the Summary of Sentenced Population Movement (West, Sabol, & Greenman, 2010) includes the number of prisoners who are HIV positive. Since 1972, the program has been run under the auspices of the Bureau of Justice Statistics (BJS). In 1983, the NPS and the Uniform Parole Reports were combined into the National Corrections Reporting Program.

MacKenzie and colleagues (1990) identified the following objectives and outcomes of the NPS data collection:

- To determine the physical capacity, staffing, and programming needs of prison facilities through an analysis of characteristics of offenders and the crimes they have committed

- To identify and analyze major issues and trends in corrections related to facilities, such as the influence of sentencing patterns on occupancy rates, trends in population growth, expenditures, staffing patterns, and program availability
- To obtain information on special issues, such as the number of inmate deaths related to HIV infection or the number of inmates that are illegal aliens

NPS Data Collection

Two aspects of the NPS data collection are the census and the survey. The census requires the participation of every prison and correctional facility in the United States. The survey includes a representative sample of facilities and a random sample of inmates drawn from those sample facilities. TABLE 2-3 lists the types of information gathered by the NPS census and survey.

TABLE 2-3 Data Collected in the National Prison Statistics Census and Survey

Facility and inmate characteristics	• Community access: ability of inmates to leave the facility to attend work or study release
	• Security level of the institution: maximum, medium, minimum
	• Programs and resources: for example, medical units, general work release or prerelease programs
	• Inmate capacity
	• Age of facility
	• Health and safety conditions: for instance, whether inmates are on medication, the number of assaults on inmates
	• Operating and capital expenditures
	• Staffing: including race, gender, and work assignments
Inmate characteristics	• Number of inmates
	• Program involvement: the number and sex of inmates enrolled in academic, counseling, and work-release programs on the reference date
	• Work assignments: the number and sex of inmates enrolled in industries, maintenance jobs, and vocational training on the reference date, and the average hourly wage paid to each inmate
	• Special inmate counts: for instance, the number of illegal aliens and persons younger than age 18
Criminal characteristics	• Prior criminal involvement
	• Current offense
	• Victim–offender relationships
Noncriminal characteristics	• Demographic and socioeconomic characteristics
	• Military service
	• History of drug and alcohol abuse

Data from MacKenzie, D. L., Baunach, P. J., & Roberg, R. R. (1990). *Measuring Crime: Large-Scale, Long-Range Efforts.* New York: State University of New York.

Adult Criminal Court Survey

The goal of the Canadian Adult Criminal Court Survey is to develop and maintain a database of statistical information on appearances, charges, and cases in adult criminal courts (Statistics Canada, 2011a). Information is collected on age and gender of the accused, case decision patterns, sentencing information, amount of fine, and case elapsed time. These statistics are collected by the Canadian Centre for Justice Statistics in collaboration with provincial and territorial departments and is a census for provincial and superior criminal courts in Canada.

Information is collected every fiscal year (April 1 to March 31) and includes persons 18 years or older at the time of offense, companies, and youths who have been transferred to adult criminal court. No sampling is required because the census includes all populations who come into contact with criminal courts (Statistics Canada, 2011a).

Challenges in Measuring Crime with Prisoner Data

The use of surveys to collect prisoner and corrections data has several limitations. First, the NPS does not allow for generalizability of findings to all offenders because the survey is limited to those inmates who serve time in facilities. Similarly, the Adult Criminal Court Survey reports data only on those who appear in court. Thus, as discussed in the issues related to measurement of crime above, the data are skewed to reflect those offenders for whom their crime was reported, the police chose to arrest, the prosecutor chose to proceed with charges, and, in the case of the NPS, the jury chose to convict and the judge chose to sentence.

The second limitation is the lack of sufficient data to make conclusions about the causes of crime because only a select sample of offenders is represented in the data. Data collection in census methods relies on the interpretation of questionnaires by administrators who work in jurisdictions with different policies and practices. Further, the definitions of each data item are often not sufficiently clear and may change from year to year because societal mores and political pressures influence what factors are of interest and importance.

Third, there is a lack of a consistent sample. For example, in the case of the NPS, youthful offenders were included in the 1974 consensus and excluded in the 1979 and 1984 censuses (MacKenzie et al., 1990).

Victimization Surveys

Two important factors converged to catapult victim surveys into the criminal justice and victimology arena. First, by the 1960s, 30 years after its creation, the UCR Program was increasingly being called into question by official and journalistic investigations of police offense statistics and by critical social science analyses regarding its ability to provide a full picture of crime and its consequences. Second, the crime victim movement was exerting pressure on criminologists to provide crime statistics that included victims. Some social scientists were already promoting the adaptation of self-report national household surveys to describe the nature of and changes in the crime problem that would be less vulnerable to the limitations of the UCR.

The development of the crime victimization survey was initiated by two commissions appointed in 1965 by President Lyndon B. Johnson and headed by Nicholas Katzenbach, the U.S. Attorney General: the President's Commission on Crime in the District of Columbia and the President's Commission on Law Enforcement and Administration of Justice, precursor of the National Institute of Justice. The surveys intended to capture individuals' experiences with crime and with justice agencies. A goal of both commissions was to reduce the amount of crime that eluded the attention of the police.

The results of the first victimization survey pilot showed that, depending on the type of crime, there were 3 to 10 times as many crimes reported by victims than were recorded by the UCR. Since those early surveys, self-report measures of criminal victimization have become widely used social indicators and research tools in criminology and criminal justice. A great deal has been learned about the strengths and weakness of this methodology. Victim surveys substantially improved the information available on the volume of crime and indicated that household surveys could help estimate the extent of the full picture of crime as well as estimate the number of victimizations at a national level. Victim surveys also provided more detailed information on crime events than did national data systems based on police records. These surveys asked respondents to provide information on themselves, the offenders, the nature of the crime, and the context in which it occurred. Although this type of information may have been available in local police files, it was not assembled nationally by agencies like the FBI in a form that allowed easy access. Moreover, the detail available in police files varied substantially, depending on the willingness of police officers to ask victims systematically for the specifics of crime events (Cantor & Lynch, 2000).

Victimization surveys are composed of interview reports from a random sample of people and begin by asking whether the person has ever been a victim of a crime. Community surveys provide a way of asking people directly

TABLE 2-4 Advantages of Victim Surveys for Measuring Crime

Issue	Advantage
Crime causation	Availability of disaggregate data on crime events not known to police
Theory development	New ways to view crime regarding theories of routine activity, opportunity theory, rational choice theory, etc.
Consequences of crime	Identify the aftermath of crime as it affects the victims, families, and communities
New areas of study	Data on why victims call (or do not call) the police and barriers to reporting crimes to police
Response to victims	Mobilization of resources other than police
Building victimology theory	Occurrence of crime events and risk of criminal victimization
Control sample	Surveys include victim and nonvictim samples to test theories
Offender populations	Composition and profiles of offenders that are not arrested
Repeat victimization	Effect on data collection and crime statistics

about their experiences of crime and are designed specifically for statistical purposes. The primary reason for conducting a survey is that many victims of crime do not report their experiences to police and so are not counted in administrative data. TABLE 2-4 details the advantages of victim surveys for measuring crime.

Different types of information are required to effectively describe people's experiences as victims, and the data generated may subsequently be used to:

- Estimate the overall risk of becoming a victim.
- Monitor trends in crime victimization over time and across different geographic locations.
- Identify risk factors in becoming a victim to assist in establishing priorities for service providers, such as police and victim support groups.
- Contribute to understanding long-term outcomes for victims of crime.

Victim Survey Methods

Surveys collect data about different aspects of crime victimization, and some concepts and data items are common across all surveys. The differences are

TABLE 2-5 Considerations for Victim Survey Design

Sample design	• Selection of a sample is dependent on a number of considerations, including:
	— Aims and content of the survey.
	— Required level of accuracy of the survey estimates.
	— Costs and operational constraints of conducting the survey.
Scope of design	• Scope and coverage for the survey may vary (e.g., rural vs. urban areas).
Questionnaire format	• Study results are dependent on the nature of questions asked, including:
	— Target information to be collected.
	— The manner in which questions are phrased.
Data collection procedure	• Mode of the data collection (e.g., short telephone interview, longer face-to-face interviews).
	• Each method has advantages and disadvantages that can impact on the survey results.
Response rate	• Provides an indication of the influence of nonresponse bias on the data collected in the survey.
	• Will vary across the surveys.
	• The influence of nonresponse bias must be addressed.
Interpretation of data	• The goals to interpreting crime victimization data accurately are:
	— To understand the data source.
	— To make informed decisions about which data source meets the particular data requirements under interpretation.

found in the survey methodology used to collect information. TABLE 2-5 provides considerations for victim survey design. Given the factors described in relation to survey design and operations, each survey data set needs to be considered as a unique, stand-alone data set with unique data items, even when appearing to measure similar concepts. They should not be compared across the different survey data sources (Australian Bureau of Statistics, 2004).

Generations of Victim Surveys

Hindelang (1976) described the development of community surveys as falling into "stages" or "generations." Each stage sought to improve the methodology by identifying problems in an earlier stage.

FIRST-GENERATION VICTIM SURVEYS

The first generation of victim surveys included two stages. Stage 1 was the President's Commission that was convened in the mid-1960s. This survey served as pilot work to test the feasibility of counting crime victims. The report contrasted results of its 10,000-household National Survey of Criminal Victims (conducted by the National Opinion Research Center), as well as city-level victim surveys for Washington, Chicago, and Boston (conducted by the Bureau of Social Science Research and the University of Michigan Survey Research Center), with the FBI's UCR. Concluding that a lack of information on offenses not reported to police made it difficult to develop useful crime policy, the commission recommended the development of a nationwide crime victimization survey (President's Commission on Law Enforcement and Administration of Justice, 1967).

Stage 2 was a survey by the National Opinion Research Center that targeted 10,000 households and asked persons to report on incidents in the past year. The interviewer then focused on the two most recent and more serious crimes. The results of this survey indicated that the UCR underreported crime by about 50%. The National Opinion Research Center reported four times as many rapes and more than three times as many burglaries. Of note was the lone exception of motor vehicle theft. This lack of discrepancy was most likely due to insurance company policy requiring a police report for a reimbursement check. The victimization surveys quickly pointed out the magnitude of unreported crimes (Biderman & Reiss, 1967).

SECOND-GENERATION VICTIM SURVEYS

Second-generation surveys sought to correct the problems identified in first-generation surveys and involved several methods:

- *Record checks*. This method sought to compare information from police records to victimization survey data.

- *Reverse record check*. This was done by locating crime victim names in police files and contacting them and administering a victim survey. The responses were checked against police records. Analysis of these data revealed memory decay increased over time and the best recall was within 3 months. Also, the wording of questions and order of presentation affected responses (Hindelang, 1976).

- *Forward record check*. People in a victim survey were asked whether they had contacted police about the incident. Researchers then checked police records for a written case. Police reports for about one-third of cases could not be found. However, when records were found, the record and victim account showed a great deal of similarity (BJS, 2010; Schneider, Griffith, Sumi, & Burcart, 1978).

THIRD-GENERATION VICTIM SURVEYS

In the early 1970s, the Census Bureau conducted the first National Crime Survey (NCS) with a probability sample of 72,000 households. Each member of the household was interviewed every 6 months for a total of seven interviews over a 3½-year period. Many concerns identified in the first- and second-generation surveys were addressed and corrected in this stage (James & Rishard, 2008).

FOURTH-GENERATION VICTIM SURVEYS

Concerns were again addressed over wording, bounding, memory decay, and telescoping of third-generation surveys, leading to a fourth generation. Redesign efforts were made to address questionnaire development and the data collection procedures. Fourth-generation victim surveys include the widely used National Crime Victimization Survey, which was officially adopted in 1990.

National Crime Victimization Survey

The **National Crime Victimization Survey (NCVS)** was designed with four primary objectives: (1) to develop detailed information about the victims and consequences of crime, (2) to estimate the number and types of crimes not reported to the police, (3) to provide uniform measures of selected types of crimes, and (4) to permit comparisons over time and types of areas. The survey categorizes crimes as "personal" or "property." Personal crimes cover rape and sexual assault, robbery, aggravated and simple assault, and purse snatching/pocket picking (personal theft), whereas property crimes cover burglary, theft, motor vehicle theft, and vandalism. For each incident, the NCVS acquires information on the month, time, and location of the crime; the relationship between the victim and offender; characteristics of the offender; self-protective actions taken by the victim during the incident and results of those actions; consequences of victimization; whether the crime was reported to police and the reason for reporting or not reporting; and offender use of weapons, drugs, or alcohol (James & Rishard, 2008). The survey does not measure homicide, kidnapping, verbal threats over the phone, crimes involving social media, public drunkenness, drug abuse, and blackmail. Data from the NCVS survey are particularly useful for calculating crime rates, both aggregated and disaggregated, and for determining changes in crime rates from year to year. **TABLE 2-6** indicates the major steps taken in the development of the NCVS.

Data Collection for the NCVS

NCVS uses a representative sample of households stratified proportionally to represent the larger population. All members of the household older than

TABLE 2-6 Development of the National Crime Victimization Survey

1967	• President's Commission on Law Enforcement and Administration of Justice
1968	• Establishment of the Law Enforcement Assistance Administration in the U.S. Department of Justice
1970	• Pretesting involving reverse record checks • Small-scale samples
1971	• Questions are added to the Census Bureau's Quarterly Household Survey • Sample of 15,000 households are asked to recall events in past 12 months
1972	• New National Crime Survey (NCS) of 72,000 households

1986–1990	• Redesign and testing
	  — More thorough descriptions
	  — Questions added to stimulate participant recall
	  — Computer-assisted interview introduced
	  — Sexual assault questions added
	  — Intimate partner violence questions improved

1990–1992	• Phase in of new questionnaire and rebranding of the National Crime Survey (NCS) to the National Crime Victimization Survey (NCVS)
Mid-1990s	• Context variables on public housing, college or university housing, and attendance or employment at colleges or universities are added to the screening questions
2001	• Questions on cybercrime are added
2004	• Identity theft questions are added
2006	• The Supplemental Victimization Survey (SVS), focusing on stalking

Data from National Academies of Science. 2008. James, N. & Rishard, L. 2008. *How Crime in the United States Is Measured*. Document RL34309. Washington, DC: Congressional Research Service.

age 12 are interviewed, including persons living in group quarters such as dormitories, rooming houses, and religious dwellings, but excluding correctional quarters such as prisons (James & Rishard, 2008). Interviews are conducted every 6 months for 3 years; the first and fifth interviews are conducted in person, and the others are held by telephone whenever possible. The sample includes 49,000 households comprising about 100,000 persons and obtains an average annual response rate of over 96%.

Crime analysts measure crime rates in several different ways, and the distinction between these various forms of reporting is vital to understanding crime studies. **Prevalence** measures how many people experience a particular crime during their lifetimes. **Incidence** gives a snapshot of how many crimes take place during a particular period of time, often a year. The rate of occurrence is calculated by dividing the actual number of occurrences by the number of possible times the outcome could have occurred. Every year the BJS publishes national crime rates, or the incidence of crime in various jurisdictions per 1000 persons or households:

$$\text{Personal crime rate} = \frac{\text{Number of person crimes}}{(N \text{ persons}/1,000)}$$

$$\text{Household crime rate} = \frac{\text{Number of household crimes}}{(N \text{ households}/1,000)}$$

NCVS Summary Findings for 2015

Available data demonstrate differential rates of various crimes, indicating that not everyone has the same chance of being victimized. Groups of people have differing rates of victimization and crime varies by geography. The BJS reports yearly findings from the NCVS. For example, some of the summary findings from BJS for 2015 are as follows (Truman & Morgan, 2016):

- *Gender.* In 2015, men were less likely than women to be victims of violent crime, but were more likely to be victims of serious violent crime. Of all women aged 12 or older, 1.03% (1.4 million women) experienced one or more violent victimizations.

- *Age.* Persons aged 65 and older had the lowest rate of violent victimization (5.2 per 1,000) compared to all other age groups, despite an increase from 3.1 victimizations per 1,000 persons during the previous year. Persons aged 12 to 17 experienced the highest rate of violent crime, while persons aged 18 to 24 experienced the highest rate of serious violent crime.

- *Race:* In 2015, the rate of violent victimization against Blacks was 22.6 per 1,000 persons aged 12 or older, for Whites 17.4 per 1,000, for Hispanics 16.8 per 1,000, and for persons of other races 25.7 per 1,000.

- *Location.* In 2015, the rate of violent crime was highest in the Nation's Western states and cities at 21.3 victimizations per 1,000 persons aged 12 and older. This was followed by the Midwest (19.6 per 1,000), the Northeast (17.1 per 1,000), and the South (16.9 per 1,000). Similar trends for serious violent crime were recorded with the West experiencing the highest rates at 8.8 serious violent victimizations per 1,000 persons. At a more detailed scale, urban areas experienced the highest rates of violent crime, serious violent crime, and property crime when compared to rural and suburban areas, while rural areas experienced the lowest rates of all three types of crime.

National Family Violence Survey

In 1976, the National Family Violence Survey (NFVS) was conducted; in 1985, it used the Conflict Tactics Scale (CTS) as a means of determining rates of aggression in marital relationships. The CTS is the most widely used measure of spousal violence, focusing on three types of aggression: physical assault, psychological aggression, and negotiation (Straus, 2007). Physical violence by the CTS index is often subdivided into two categories: minor violence and severe violence. Minor violence includes throwing an object, pushing, grabbing, shoving, and slapping. Severe violence includes kicking, biting, hitting, beating up, choking, or using a weapon.

The 1985 NFVS resulted in a rate of violence of 116 per 1,000 couples; that is, almost 12% of husbands in the United States perpetrated violence against their wives that year; in 3% of cases this violence was severe. However, unlike previous studies, it suggested that women perpetrated even more violence toward husbands. The rate of violence by women against their husbands was 124 per 1,000 couples, just over 12%, and in 4% of cases the violence was severe.

Bachman (1998) identified discrepancies between the NFVS and other surveys of crime and violence. For instance, estimates of violence against women using the CTS screening instrument in the NFVS almost doubled the rates of intimate partner violence against women estimated by the NCVS. Further, the NCVS finds that women are much more likely to experience an act of intimate partner violence than are men (9.3 per 1,000 vs. 1.4 per 1,000). Bachman (1998) suggested that this discrepancy is in part because the CTS measures acts of violence in isolation from the circumstances under which the acts were committed, ignoring who initiates the violence, the relative size and strength of the persons involved, and the nature of the participants' relationship. In addition, the NCVS uses a sampling strategy different from the NFVS in that, in addition to heterosexual people in traditional marital relationships, it also includes others, such as single, divorced, and never married women. This is critical, because rates of intimate partner violence are eight times higher among separated women when compared to married women (Bachman & Saltzman, 1995). Other factors

TABLE 2-7 Factors That May Contribute to Different Incidence Rates of Violence Against Women

Methodology	National Family Violence Survey	National Crime Victimization Survey
Sample population	Married or cohabiting heterosexual couples over age 18 may result in higher estimates.	Including all individuals over age 12 in sample may result in lower estimates because of decreased violence against women between 12 and 18 and over 65 years.
Number of times interviewed	Interviewed respondents once, which may produce higher victimization rates.	Interviewed respondents multiple times to eliminate duplicate reports.
Context of the survey	Violence is considered "marital conflict."	Violence is considered a crime; some respondents may not view assaults by intimates a crime.
Number of household members interviewed	Interviewed one member of the married or cohabiting couple.	Interviewed all family members; may prevent some respondents from disclosing incidents of violence.
Context of violence	Does not distinguish acts of self-defense.	Asks questions to distinguish acts of self-defense.

Bachman, R. (1998). Incidence Rates of Violence Against Women: A Comparison of the Redesigned National Crime Victimization Survey and the 1985 National Family Violence Survey. Harrisburg, PA: VAWnet, a project of the National Resource Center on Domestic Violence/Pennsylvania Coalition Against Domestic Violence. Retrieved 12/18/11 from: http://www.vawnet.org.

identified by Bachman (1998) include the nature of questions asked (general questions about crime vs. questions about conflict tactics in the home), which results in different definitions of violence, and the multiple time periods over which the NCVS is conducted, which allows for comparisons. TABLE 2-7 compares factors that may contribute to differences in incidence rates of violence.

Rand and Rennison (2005) discuss the apparent differences between violence against women estimates from NCVS and NVAWS stating that contrary to some literature findings, the NVAWS did not produce statistically significant estimates of violence against women greater than NCVS findings. The researchers suggest incident counting protocols used in NVAWS and the recalibrated NCVS increased the error and decreased the reliability of the estimates (Rand & Rennison, 2005). Challenges in determining rates of victimization from surveys are discussed in more detail below.

Canadian General Social Survey

The General Social Survey (GSS) began collecting information in 1985 on how Canadians perceive their health and social supports. The survey is administered through telephone interviews across all Canadian provinces. A stratified sample of households is selected through random-digit dialing. Until 1998, the sample size for the survey was 10,000 persons. In 1999, it was increased to 25,000 persons and covered social topics such as health, time use, victim-ization, education, work and retirement, family, and social support. Addition of new modules and creation of new surveys allows data to be gathered from different topics related to important policy areas (Dryburgh, 2009). One such module is the GSS-Victimization which explores sensitive subjects of criminal victimization and spousal violence.

According to Statistics Canada (2011b), the purpose of the GSS-Victimization module is to better understand how Canadians perceive crime and the justice system. Each survey contains a standard set of demographic questions. The sur-vey then asks respondents about reported and unreported experiences of crime, violence, physical assaults, emotional abuse, and financial abuse. Each cycle includes new information on victimization, such as Internet victimization and cyberbullying, added in 2009 (Dryburgh, 2009). The goal is to determine the extent of both reported and unreported crimes and to better understand why people may or may not choose to report a crime. The results of the survey inform public policy and the development of services and, to date, represents the only national survey data of self-reported victimization for provinces and territories in Canada. Reports from the GSS-Victimization module are as follows:

- Aboriginal people as victims and offenders
- Crime prevention measures taken by Canadians
- Family violence in Canada
- Hate-motivated crime
- Seniors as victims of crime
- Visible minorities as victims of crime
- Criminal victimization in the workplace
- Sexual orientation and victimization
- Violence against women

British Crime Survey

The British Crime Survey, administered to a national representative sample of citizens, produced its first report in 1982. One of the largest social surveys con-ducted in Britain, it was originally administered every 4 years, and then every 2 years; however, from 2001 onward the survey has been conducted annually.

In 2001, the sample included 40,000 respondents as well as "boost" samples of 3,000 non-White respondents and 1,500 respondents aged 16 to 24 years to increase their representation (Jones, 2006).

The British Crime Survey is a face-to-face survey of people in England and Wales in which respondents are asked if they have been a victim of a crime in the past 12 months. The crimes are divided up into personal offenses (assaults, robberies, thefts from a person, other personal thefts, and sexual offenses) and household offenses (car thefts, bicycle thefts, other thefts, vandalism of household property, and domestic burglary). Until recently, the British Crime Survey did not cover crimes against those younger than age 16 years, but since January 2009, children aged 10 to 15 years have been included for interview. The British Crime Survey also collects data regarding public attitudes toward police, the criminal justice system, crime, and antisocial behavior (Economic and Social Data Service, 2001).

International Crime Victims Survey

In 1980, a group of European criminologists initiated an international victimization study for the purposes of generating international comparative crime and victimization data. The project is now known as the International Crime Victims Survey (Van Dijk, van Kesteren, & Smit, 2008). After the first round in 1989, the surveys were repeated in 1992, 1996, 2000, 2004/2005, and 2010. The United Nations became involved in the project in 1992 to organize the surveys in developing countries; respondents come from industrial countries in Europe, North and South America, Asia, Southern Africa, Australia, and New Zealand (Nieuwbeerta, 2002). Since its inception, more than 300,000 people in over 80 different countries have been interviewed about their experiences of victimization (van Kesteren, van Dijk, & Mayhew, 2014).

In the International Crime Victims Survey, respondents older than 16 years are asked whether they have been victims of a crime in the previous year. The survey covers 10 crimes: theft of a car, theft from a car, theft of a motorcycle or moped, theft of a bicycle, burglary, attempted burglary, theft of personal property, robbery, sexual offences, and assault and threat. In several countries, questions have been added about street-level corruption, consumer fraud (including Internet fraud), drug-related crime, and hate crime (Van Dijk et al., 2008). Respondents are first asked about their crime experiences within the past five years, such as when they occurred, what happened, and whether police were notified (Nieuwbeerta, 2002). Other data collected involve concern and fear about crime, attitudes toward police, and recommendations for fair sentencing.

The average victimization rates among participating countries show that victimization peaked halfway through the 1990s and have declined since. The crimes that showed the most significant drops include vehicle-related crime and burglary (van Kesteren, 2014).

Challenges in Measuring Victimization

The task of describing the national pattern of violence from the various reporting systems is complicated because they differ in terms of (1) the domain of events they attempt to capture, (2) the unit of count on which their statistics are based, (3) the timing of the counting and tabulation, (4) the sources of discretion and error in recording the counting events, and (5) counting neglected victims. Victimization surveys are also subject to problems mainly involving ensuring representative samples, dependence on respondents' memories and recall, willingness of victims to talk about their experiences, and failure to realize an incident is relevant to the survey. This section describes three main types of challenges for measuring victimization through national surveys, including challenges related to sampling, victim responses, and interpretation of data.

Challenges Related to Sampling

Victimization surveys use a sample of the population to represent the experiences and perceptions of the entire population. Thus, the representativeness of the sample is key for population-based estimates and generalizations to be accurate. Survey designers go to great lengths to ensure that samples are stratified in such a way as to reflect the general population on a number of demographic, economic, and cultural variables. Nevertheless, the representativeness of the sample is challenged by a number of factors.

Telephone-based surveys are limited to individuals that own phones and have numbers listed in telephone directories. Thus, people from lower socioeconomic groups who do not own a phone and young people who use cell phones rather than home phones are eliminated from the sample. However, the expenses associated with in-person samples limits their practicality, leaving telephone interviews as the most common and cost-efficient method of administration.

Some individuals refuse to participate in surveys, and it is not always clear whether these people represent a particular subsample of the population. For instance, Schwartz, Steffenmeier, Zhong, and Ackerman (2009) focused on gender biases inherent in crime victimization surveys. They suggested an underestimation of rates of victimization against males due to nonresponse

(Schwartz et al., 2009). Other populations that may not respond are those who are fearful of authorities, such as undocumented immigrants, or those who are more generally fearful, such as elderly or other vulnerable individuals.

Challenges Related to Victim Responses

The accuracy of victimization surveys relies on the sincerity of participants, their goodwill, their ability to recall events, and their ability to understand the questions and provide the required answers. Accuracy can be compromised when participants may not want to reveal incidents where they were a victim or may not provide important details about their victimization. In addition, one may exaggerate the frequency, extent, or seriousness of the incidents, or may, for other reasons, underestimate these details. Specific challenges include recall, telescoping, repeated victimizations, and victim knowledge.

RECALL

Victim surveys tend to use either six-month or one-year reference points, for instance, asking "over the past year have you experienced any of the following?" Generally, respondents are able to recall more accurately an event that occurred within three months of the interview rather than one that occurred within six months; they can recall events over a six-month period more accurately than those over a 12-month period. However, a shorter reference period requires more field interviews per year, increasing the data collection costs significantly. These increased costs would have to be balanced by cost reductions elsewhere, such as sample size. Reducing sample size, however, reduces the precision of estimates of relatively rare crimes.

TELESCOPING

Another concern of researchers using reference periods in retrospective surveys is telescoping. Telescoping refers to a respondent's misspecification of when an incident occurred in relation to the reference period. For example, telescoping occurs if a respondent is asked about victimizations within the past six months and the respondent erroneously includes a victimization that occurred eight months ago. Telescoped events, which actually occurred before the reference period, can be minimized at the time of the first interview by a technique known as bounding.

Bounding compares incidents reported in an interview with incidents reported in a previous interview and deletes duplicate incidents that were reported in the current reference period. In the NCS and NCVS designs, each household visit is used to bind the next one by comparing reports in the current interview to those given 6 months prior. When there is a duplicate report, the respondent is reminded of the earlier report and asked if the new report represents the incident previously mentioned or if it is different. The first interview at a household entering the sample is unbounded, and data collected at these interviews are not included in NCS and NCVS estimates. However, if a household in a sample moves and another household moves into that address, the first interview with the replacement household is unbounded but is included in NCS and NCVS estimates (NCVS, 2011).

REPEATED VICTIMIZATIONS

Individuals who have been repeatedly victimized, particularly by family members, may not remember individual incidents or may remember only the most recent event. Thus, information provided on specific incidents may in fact be blended recollections of several incidents. For instance, a person who experiences repeated assaults at the hands of an intimate partner may not be able to fully differentiate one episode from another. Alternatively, a person in a high-risk profession or neighborhood may have experienced multiple victimizations from different people and cannot recall when each occurred, what happened in one incident versus another, or which one involved the police.

In the NCVS, when a respondent experiences six or more similar but separate victimizations with limited recall, the interviewer is instructed to record these as a series of incidents. When calculating annual victimization rates, series victimizations are not included. Furthermore, the incident report may record only the most recent incident.

VICTIM KNOWLEDGE

Victimization surveys do not provide information of crimes for which the victim is not aware. For example, young children may not understand the nature of sexual acts and may not be aware they have been sexually victimized. A new immigrant woman may not define assault by her husband as a crime because it may not be defined as such in her country of origin. For these above-mentioned reasons, the accuracy of self-report surveys on victimization may be affected.

Challenges Related to Interpretation of Data

Some of the shortcomings and limitations of victim surveys relate to the collecting, coding, and processing of statistical data. Face-to-face and telephone interviews depend on the accuracy and training of the interviewers who classify and code responses. Inaccurate coding or classification may introduce bias. Addington (2008) assessed the extent of nonresponse bias on NIBRS estimates of violent crime and found that the overall response rate was low, as expected. However, the study revealed variation in response rates among the subnational population groups with rural areas, suburban areas, and cities (under 10,000 persons) with the highest response rates.

In addition, artificial fluctuations may occur in the interpretation of data due to the influence of extraneous factors. It may be the case, for example, that upward crime trends reflect more careful reporting of offenses, and downward trends may indicate lower reporting or relaxed enforcement rather than changes in the commission of offenses. Thus, heightened public awareness about a particular type of crime may prompt overreporting or, alternatively, may reduce underreporting. Similarly, increased police presence in a community or community confidence in the police may affect reporting of victimization not only to police (thereby affecting crime statistics) but also to survey administrators (thereby affecting victimization statistics). Many of these factors exist outside the control of statisticians.

Finally, changes in legislation may also affect the reporting of crimes. For example, the legalization of pornography in Denmark and the liberalization of sexual attitudes were followed by a decline in reported adult sexual offenses but an increase in child pornography cases.

◼ Conclusion

The search for methods to provide reliable data on the number of crimes occurring in the country has involved a wide variety of approaches, including data collection by police and courts on crimes committed, data collection on offenders, and, more recently, victimization surveys. Victimization surveys have been described as a means to tap into the **dark figure of crime** (Coleman & Moynihan, 1996), referring to the volume of incidents that are not officially recorded. Such data are believed to provide a more accurate representation of the "true" figure of crime.

No single data source is able to provide all the information required to build a full picture of crime and victimization. Rather, multiple sources of information provide data on different aspects of victimization. At times, the results from different sources vary widely, such as in the case of estimates of family violence between the NCVS and the NFVS. Nevertheless, each reporting system provides critical insights into the rate and nature of crime from a particular lens. It remains the responsibility of those analyzing, reporting, and using the data to determine what these various perspectives do and do not tell us about crime and its victims.

Key Terms

Cleared by exceptional means: Occurs when the police are unable to place formal charges against an alleged offender, for example, because the offender is dead, a victim refuses to cooperate, or extradition is denied.

Dark figure of crime: Describes the amount of unreported or undiscovered crime.

Hierarchy rule: This rule requires counting only the highest offense and ignoring all others; it applies only to the crime reporting process and does not affect the number of charges for which the defendant may be prosecuted in the courts.

Incidence: Crimes that take place during a particular period of time.

National Crime Victimization Survey (NCVS): A series of surveys, previously called the National Crime Survey (NCS), that has been collecting data on personal and household victimization since 1973.

National Incident-Based Reporting System (NIBRS): A more detailed version of the Uniform Crime Reporting Program.

Prevalence: How many people experience a particular crime during their lifetime.

Uniform Crime Reports (UCR): Provides some of the most commonly cited crime statistics in the United States and is concerned with index crimes that include attempted or completed murder and nonnegligent manslaughter, forcible rape, robbery, aggravated assault, burglary, larceny-theft, and motor vehicle theft.

Discussion Questions

1. How would you measure both the victim count and the crime offense count for the Anders Behring Breivik mass murders?

2. Debate the judge's ruling of Breivik's complaints to his confinement.

3. Discuss the hierarchy rule and the Petit triple murder.

4. Compare and contrast measurement of crime and offenders and measurement of victims in terms of sample, methodology, data collection, analysis, interpretation, and outcomes.

5. How would you measure the risk of being a victim?

6. What suggestions do you have for measuring and establishing a useful international database for victimization?

7. What actions and attitudes assist law enforcement in measuring crime victimization?

▉ Resources

American Statistical Association Committee on Law and Justice Statistics http://ww2.amstat.org/committees/commdetails.cfm?txtComm=CCNARS04

Bureau of Justice Statistics http://www.ojp.usdoj.gov/bjs/

Centers for Disease Control and Prevention Division of Violence Prevention http://www.cdc.gov/ncipc/dvp/dvp.htm

Crimes Against Children Research Center http://www.unh.edu/ccrc/

National Center for Juvenile Justice http://www.ncjj.org

National Crime Victimization Survey Resource Guide http://www.icpsr.umich.edu/icpsrweb/NACJD/NCVS/

National Institute of Justice's Data Resource Programhttp://www.nij.gov/funding/data-resources-program/welcome.htm

Office for Victims of Crime http://www.ojp.usdoj.gov/ovc/

Office of Justice Programs: Violence Against Women and Family Violence Program http://www.nij.gov/topics/crime/violence-against-women/welcome.htm

National Archive of Criminal Justice Data lists the following data resource guides at http://www.icpsr.umich.edu/icpsrweb/content/NACJD/learning-data-guides.html:

Capital Punishment in the United States

Chicago Women's Health Risk Study

Expenditure and Employment for the Criminal Justice System

Federal Justice Statistics Program

Geographical Information Systems

Homicide

Homicides in Chicago

Law Enforcement Management and Administrative Statistics

National Corrections Reporting Program

National Crime Victimization Survey

National Incident-Based Reporting System

National Juvenile Corrections Data

Project on Human Development in Chicago Neighborhoods

Survey of Inmates in State and Federal Correctional Facilities

Terrorism and Preparedness Data Resource Center

Uniform Crime Reporting Program

Violence Against Women

References

Addington, L. (2008). Assessing the extent of nonresponse bias on the NIBRS estimates of violent crime. *Journal of Contemporary Criminal Justice, 24*(1), 32–49.

Akiyama, Y., & Nolan, J. (1999). Methods for understanding and analyzing NIBRS data. *Journal of Quantitative Criminology, 15*(2), 225–238.

Australian Bureau of Statistics. (2004). Information paper: Measuring crime victimisation, Australia: The impact of different collection methodologies, 2002. Retrieved from http://www.abs.gov.au/ausstats/abs@.nsf/Lookup/5BF3A030F523595BCA 2578B00011A06B?opendocument

Bachman, R. (1998). Incidence rates of violence against women: A comparison of the redesigned National Crime Victimization Survey and the 1985 National Family Violence Survey. Retrieved from http://www.vawnet.org

Bachman, R., & Saltzman, L.E. (1995). Violence against women: Estimates from the redesigned National Crime Victimization Survey (NCJ-154348). Bureau of Justice Statistics, U.S. Department of Justice.

BBC News. (2016, April 20). Anders Behring Breivik, Norway murderer, wins human rights case. Retrieved from http://www.bbc.com/news/world-europe-36094575

Beaumont, P. (2011, July 23). Anders Behring Breivik: Portrait of a mass murderer. Guardian.co.uk. Retrieved from http://www.guardian.co.uk/world/2011/jul/23 /anders-behring-breivik-norway-attacks

Bever, L. (2016, March 15). Mass killer Anders Behring Breivik gives Nazi salute while complaining about his 3-room cell. *Washington Post*. Retrieved from https://www .washingtonpost.com/news/worldviews/wp/2016/03/15/mass-killer-anders -behring-breivik-gives-nazi-salute-while-complaining-about-3-room-cell/?utm _term=.c031bb8a3f4a

Biderman, A. D., & Reiss, A. J. (1967). On exploring the "dark figure" of crime. *Annals of the American Academy of Political and Social Science, 374* (November), 1–15.

Cantor, D., & Lynch, J. P. (2000). Self-report surveys as a measure of crime and criminal victimization. In D. Duffee (Ed.), *Measurement and analysis of crime and justice* (pp. 85–138). Washington, DC: National Institute of Justice. Retrieved from https://www.ncjrs.gov/criminal_justice2000/vol_4/04c.pdf

Carter, L., & Wilson, M. (2006). Measuring professionalism in police officers. *Police Chief, 73*(8), 42–44.

Caspi, A., McClay, J., Moffitt, T., Mill, J., Martin, J., Craig, I., Taylor, A., & Poulton, R. (2002). Role of genotype in the cycle of violence in maltreated children. *Science, 297*(5582), 851–854.

Chilton, R., & Jarvis, J. (1999). Victims and offenders in two crime statistics programs: A comparison of the National Incident-Based Reporting System (NIBRS) and the National Crime Victimization Survey (NCVS). *Journal of Quantitative Criminology*, *15*(2), 193–205.

Coleman, C., & Moynihan, J. (1996). Haunted by the dark figure: Criminologists as ghostbusters? In M. Maguire (Ed.), *Understanding crime data: Haunted by the dark figure* (pp.1–23). Buckingham, UK: Open University Press.

Dispatch Magazine. (2011). Newspaper studies Milwaukee police response times. Retrieved from http://www.911dispatch.com/page/2/

Dryburgh, H. (2009). Introduction to the General Social Survey. *Canadian Review of Sociology*, *46*(4), 273–285.

Economic and Social Data Service. (2011). British Crime Survey. Retrieved from http://www.esds.ac.uk/government/bcs/datasets/

Fattah, E. A. (1997). *Criminology: Past, present, and future. A critical overview*. Basingstoke, UK: Macmillan.

Federal Bureau of Investigation (FBI). (1985). Blueprint for the future of the Uniform Crime Reporting Program (Blueprint). Retrieved from http://www.ucrdatatool.gov/abouttheucr.cfm

Federal Bureau of Investigation (FBI). (2009a). Percent of crimes cleared by arrest of exceptional means. Retrieved from http://www.fbi.gov/ucr/cius2009/offenses/clearances/index.html

Federal Bureau of Investigation (FBI). (2009b). National Incident-Based Reporting System (NIBRS). Retrieved from http://www.fbi.gov/about-us/cjis/ucr/ucr

Federal Bureau of Investigation (FBI). (2010). Cybercrime statistics. Retrieved from http://scamfraudalert.wordpress.com/2010/03/13/fbi-2009-cybercrime-statistics/

Federal Bureau of Investigation (FBI). (2011a). Crime statistics: New online tool makes research easier. Retrieved from http://www2.fbi.gov/news/stories/2010/november/ucrtool_112910/ucrtool_112910

Federal Bureau of Investigation (FBI). (2011b). Preliminary annual Uniform Crime Report for 2010. Retrieved from http://www.fbi.gov/about-us/cjis/ucr/crime-in-the-u.s/2010/preliminary-annual-ucr-jan-dec-2010/

Federal Bureau of Investigation (FBI). (2015). 2015 NIBRS crime data released. Retrieved from https://www.fbi.gov/news/stories/2015-nibrs-crime-data-released

Federal Bureau of Investigation (FBI). (2016). *UCR Program Quarterly April 2016*. Retrieved from https://ucr.fbi.gov/ucr-program-quarterly/ucr-program-quarterly-april-2016

Folmer, K., & Friedman, E. (2010, October 19). Accused Petit murderer Joshua Komisarjevsky: "I lost control" and "enjoyed it." ABC News. Retrieved from http://abcnews.go.com/US/petit-murder-trial-steven-hayes-diary-joshua-komisarjevsky/story?id=11916557

Hindelang, M. (1976). *Criminal victimization in eight American cities: An analysis of common theft and assault*. Cambridge, MA: Ballinger.

James, N., & Rishard, L. (2008). *How crime in the United States is measured*. Document RL34309. Washington, DC: Congressional Research Service.

Jones, S. (2006). *Criminology* (3rd ed.). New York: Oxford.

Kempf, K. L. (1990). *Measurement issues in criminology*. New York: Springer-Verlag.

Leung, L. (2011). Surprise wants better data on police response times. Retrieved from http://www.azcentral.com/community/westvalley/articles/2008/11/27/20081127gl-nwvresponse1128.html#ixzz1Vy8eYbZ0

MacKenzie, D. L., Baunach, P. J., & Roberg, R. R. (1990). *Measuring crime: Large-scale, long-range efforts*. New York: State University of New York.

National Commission on Law Observance and Enforcement. (1931). Guide to federal records in the National Archives of the United States. Retrieved from http://www.archives.gov/research/guide-fed-records/groups/010.html

National Crime Victim Survey (NCVS). (2011). Methodological issues in the measurement of crime. Retrieved from http://www.icpsr.umich.edu/icpsrweb/NACJD/NCVS/

National Prisoner Statistics Summary of Sentenced Populations. (2009). Retrieved from http://bjs.ojp.usdoj.gov/content/pub/pdf/nps1b_09.pdf

Nieuwbeerta, P. (2002). *Crime victimization in comparative perspective: Results from the International Crime Victims Survey, 1989–2000*. Boom Juridische Uitgevers. The Federation Press, Australia.

President's Commission on Law Enforcement and Administration of Justice. (1967). *Task force report: Crime and its impact—an assessment* (p. v). Washington, DC: U.S. Government Printing Office.

Rand, M. R. (2009). National Crime Victimization Survey, Criminal Victimization, 2008. Bureau of Justice Statistics Bulletin, NCJ 227777, 1–7.

Rand, M. R., & Rennison, M. (2005). Bigger is not necessarily better: An analysis of violence against women estimates from the National Crime Victimization Survey and the National Violence Against Women Survey. *Journal of Quantitative Criminology*, 21(3), 267–291.

Schneider, A. L., Griffith, W. R., Sumi, D. H., & Burcart, J. M. (1978). *Portland forward records check of crime victims*. Washington, DC: National Institute of Law Enforcement and Criminal Justice.

Schwartz, J., Steffenmeier, D., Zhong, H., & Ackerman, J. (2009). Trends in the gender gap in violence: Reevaluating NCVS and other evidence. *Criminology*, 47(2), 401–425.

Statistics Canada. (2011a). Adult Criminal Court Survey (ACCS). Retrieved from http://www.statcan.gc.ca/cgi-bin/imdb/p2SV.pl?Function=getSurvey&SDDS=3312&lang=en&db=imdb&adm=8&dis=2

Statistics Canada. (2011b). General Social Survey-Victimization. Retrieved from http://www.statcan.gc.ca/cgi-bin/imdb/p2SV.pl?Function=getSurvey&SDDS=4504&lang=en&db=imdb&adm=8&dis=2

Statistics Canada. (2011c). Uniform Crime Reporting survey (UCR). Retrieved from http://www.statcan.gc.ca/cgi-bin/imdb/p2SV.pl?Function=getSurvey&SDDS=3302&lang=en&db=imdb&adm=8&dis=2

Straus, M. (2007). Conflict tactics scales. In N. A. Jackson (Ed.), *Encyclopedia of domestic violence* (pp. 190–197). New York: Routledge.

The Daily Star. (2016, July 25). *Gunman acted alone: Wanted 'crusade' against spread of Islam*. *The Daily Star*. Retrieved from http://www.thedailystar.net/news -detail-195671

Truman, J., & Morgan, R. (2016). *Criminal victimization, 2015*. U.S. Department of Justice: Office of Justice Programs. Retrieved from: https://www.bjs.gov/content /pub/pdf/cv15.pdf

Van Dijk, J. J. M., van Kesteren, J. N., & Smit, P. (2008). *Criminal victimisation in international perspective: Key findings from the 2004–2005 ICVS and EU ICS*. The Hague: Boom Legal Publishers.

Van Kesteren, J., van Dijk, J., & Mayhew, P. (2014). The International Crime Victims Surveys: A retrospective. *International Review of Victimology, 20*(1), 49–69.

West, H. C., Sabol, W. J., & Greenman, S. J. (2010). Prisoners, 2009. U.S. Department of Justice, Office of Justice Programs. Bureau of Justice Statistics. Washington, DC: NCJ 231675. Retrieved from http://bjs.ojp.usdoj.gov/content/pub/ascii/p09.txt

CHAPTER 3

© Peyker/Shutterstock.

Theories of Victimization

OBJECTIVES

- To describe the history of victimology theories
- To identify and discuss victim-based theories
- To identify and discuss interactional theories of victimization
- To identify and discuss societal theories of victimization
- To introduce ecological theory
- To apply theories to a case

KEY TERMS

Classical criminology

Critical criminology

Just world theory

Lifestyle routine activities theory

Positivistic

Spiritualistic theories

Stockholm syndrome

CASE

On July 2, 2003, NBA professional basketball star Kobe Bryant was charged with sexual assault of a 19-year-old employee of a Colorado hotel. Prosecutors stated Bryant flirted with the woman, a front-desk employee, and after a tour of the resort, the two ended up in his room and began to kiss. While acknowledging that the kissing was consensual, the victim said that "at some point Bryant's voice became deeper and he became rougher. She asked him to stop, but Bryant allegedly blocked her exit, grabbed her, and forced her over a chair to rape her."

The attorneys argued that "Bryant's hands were around the woman's neck, equating a perceived threat of potential strangulation if she resisted his advances" (Johnston, 2004). Testimony from the victim included that she cried during the act and said no at least twice. The bellman told investigators that as the woman left work that night, she was upset and crying, her clothes and hair were disheveled, and she reported that Bryant had choked her and forced sex on her. Evidence included a T-shirt of Bryant's stained with the victim's blood and a small bruise on her jaw.

During his interview with detectives, Bryant initially denied having sex with the woman, then changed his account after the investigators told him they had physical evidence to support a sexual encounter, saying she initiated consensual sex. He continued to say the woman never cried, and she gave him a kiss goodbye before she left his room. Defense counsel challenged the victim's initial inconsistent statements to detectives, forensic evidence, and her past emotional and mental health stability (Johnston, 2004). District Judge Terry Ruckriegle ruled that "the woman's sex life in the three days surrounding her encounter with Bryant could be admitted as evidence, which may have bolstered the defense's contention that she had sex with someone else after leaving Bryant and before she went to a hospital exam—a potentially key blow to her credibility" (ESPN, 2004).

Although victim names are not to be published in the media, blunders by the court made this victim's name, address, telephone number, and photographs available on the Internet. With her identity revealed, the victim received at least two death threats and relentless media attention. As a result, the victim chose to no longer participate in the trial, and the criminal case was dropped by prosecutors in the midst of jury selection. A civil lawsuit filed against Bryant

FIGURE 3-1 Kobe Bryant.
© Domenic Gareri/ShutterStock, Inc.

was settled with specific terms of the settlement not being disclosed to the public. As part of an agreement with the accuser to dismiss the sexual assault charge, Bryant issued an apology to the victim, her family, his family, and community citizens (ESPN, 2004). See **FIGURE 3-1**.

Gavan Polone, a reporter for *The Hollywood Reporter*, wrote the following in the May 6, 2016 issue:

Like many, I followed the Kobe Bryant adulation tour that led up to his final game April 13. Unlike many, I was focused on why such homage was being paid to this particular man. He also was, in my opinion, and that of many others, guilty of rape.

Ahead of Kobe's last game, I asked three friends if they weren't uncomfortable with how he was being portrayed as a hero, given what happened in 2003. I received a couple of shrugs and a "That was a long time ago." Well, I guess our society thinks that certain transgressions by celebrities can be forgiven. What's perplexing is the contrast between which wrongs are and aren't forgivable. Based on what I've read, I believe Kobe most probably raped a woman and still was paid $26 million in 2015 by Nike, Hublot, Panini Authentic, Turkish Airlines, and others to endorse their products; Ben Roethlisberger was accused of raping two women and still made more than $35 million for one year as an NFL quarterback; Greg Hardy certainly beat the shit out of his ex-girlfriend and was signed to play defensive end for the Dallas Cowboys; Jameis Winston was sued for the rape of a student at FSU and didn't even break stride to the NFL (having watched the victim's recounting of events, I believe her). Both R. Kelly and Michael Jackson were accused of sexual misconduct, yet the former still is performing and the latter practically has been deified.

Most celebrities, especially sports stars, have been treated as special since they were young. So why is it more believable that a woman would try to entrap a celebrity by saying consensual sex wasn't consensual and less believable that a celebrity would use his superior size and strength to inflict himself on a woman? The answer is that it is not more believable. Yet when society makes a judgment about these situations, it finds in favor of the accused. And the only reason this can be true is misogyny: The mind-set that a woman entering a famous man's room, and maybe kissing him, has given license to that man to rape her.

If we really want to reduce the incidents of violence against women, we need to first accept that in the vast majority of accusations of rape, as studies have shown, the accusers aren't lying. And second, if the facts strongly suggest that a celebrity has committed a rape, we cannot simply forget what they did and go to their games and buy their jerseys and the sports drinks they promote. Because if you wanted to encourage a culture of rape, the best way to do so would be to endorse and honor the most visible members of society *who have been accused of rape.*

Introduction

From the beginning of time, people have attempted to understand and explain why some individuals become victims of natural disasters, disease, attack by wild animals, and violence by the hand of other humans. For many, the thought that such events are random is intolerable, and thus explanations help create order and dispel generalized fear and anxiety. Theories regarding victimization are shaped by the scientific knowledge, religious beliefs, and social structures of the time in which they originate. However, theories also shape public attitudes and social policy regarding legal responses and justice approaches. If victimization is caused by God as punishment for evil within the person, the person is to be shunned or killed. If victimization is caused by the offender and the victim is innocent, it is the offender who should be punished. If the victim somehow precipitated the crime, culpability is shared. If societal structures are the causes of crime and victimization, then social change is necessary. This chapter traces the development of theories for understanding victimization to present-day constructions. It also examines the issues involved in the theories proposed on social policy and justice. The Kobe Bryant case reflects society's view of a high-profile rape case in 2003. The Bill Cosby case reflects how one jury viewed another celebrity rape case 13 years later.

Prosecutors say that Cosby drugged and sexually assaulted Andrea Constand, the former director of operations for Temple University's women's basketball team, at his home near Philadelphia in January 2004. Cosby pleaded not guilty to the charges.

Prosecutors called 12 witnesses, including the victim, over a week of testimony but presented almost no forensic evidence. Cosby declined to testify in his own defense, and his attorneys called only one witness. Cosby's attorneys argued that the sexual contact was consensual and worked to highlight inconsistencies in the victim's testimony on cross-examination. Legal experts said the trial fit the "he said, she said" arguments common in sexual offense cases. The high-profile case accusing Bill Cosby of aggravated indecent assault ended in a mistrial in June 2017 after a Pennsylvania jury was unable to come to a unanimous decision. The prosecutor plans to retry the case (Sanchez, Levenson, & Crook, 2017).

History of Victimology and Theory Development

The concept of *victim*, one of the most ancient in the history of humanity, emerges from the attempts of people and the societies in which they live to both explain the reasons for victimization and to determine appropriate redress. In his groundbreaking work *Theoretical Criminology*, published in 1958, Vold provided a framework for categorizing theories that relate to victimology beginning with early spiritual explanations, followed by classical and positivist explanations, and then biological, social, and economic explanations.

Spiritual explanations originated in early religious societies as people attempted to make sense of unexplained events. Natural disasters such as floods, earthquakes, and droughts were explained by attributing them to the interference of the spirit world. Thus, human suffering was viewed as a form of universal justice, taking vengeance for an evil committed by the individual or a member of their family. The gods could be appeased through the use of sacred rites, such as offering animals or humans as sacrifices (Vold & Bernard, 1986).

When suffering was caused by another human being, justice was primarily accomplished through individual acts of revenge, with victims or families of victims taking the law into their own hands and, in effect, donning the role of judge, jury, and executioner. Nevertheless, the gods could intervene. Babylonian law as articulated in the Code of Hammurabi (1786 B.C.), for example, represented a system of restitution based on revenge and cruelty and required a victim's family and community to assume responsibility for aiding the victim if the offender was unable to be brought to justice. The code regulated the organization of Babylonian society and ensured the accountability of those in positions of responsibility and authority, primarily through death. For example, a craftsman whose shoddy workmanship resulted in the collapse of a house and the death of its owner was to be slain; if the owner's son was killed, then the builder's son was slain. Additionally, death was the punishment for providing false testimony in court, trading with a minor or slave, or stealing a pig (Van De Mieroop, 2005). Mosaic Law, as described in the Torah and the Bible, tempered earlier forms of punishment outlined in the Code of Hammurabi and moved to a concept whereby the punishment was determined by the severity of the crime. "An eye for an eye, a tooth for a tooth," for instance, is a familiar biblical reference that highlights views regarding crime and punishment (Mathew 5:38). The first reference to this theme is found in the Old Testament book of Exodus (21:23–25) and reads as follows:

> Thou shalt give life for life,
> Eye for eye, tooth for tooth, hand for hand, foot for foot,
> Burning for burning, wound for wound, stripe for stripe.

During the Middle Ages in England, the view toward crime shifted from viewing crime as an offense against a victim to an offense against God and the king. Henry II produced a common law in which the debt for crime was owed not to the victim, but to society and the state. In this system, the victim's needs became subjugated to the more immediate needs of the state. As such, an informal system of extrajudicial activity flourished, including payment of compensation, retribution, and vigilantism (Kearon & Godfrey, 2007). Similarly, in the early 1700s, aboriginal communities responded collectively to criminal offenses, with tribal law tending to view any transgression against an individual as a transgression against the entire community. The community, in essence, appropriated a victim's concerns, and whether the communal response included a long-standing blood feud, vendetta, or even monetary reparation, the core purpose was not the restoration of any moral order but rather the reestablishment of authority and the securing of optimal conditions for survival of the community as a whole.

Under the Code of Hammurabi, grim retaliatory punishments took no note of excuses or explanations with one striking exception—spiritual intervention. Specifically, an accused person could cast himself into the river Euphrates and if the current safely returned him to shore, he was declared innocent (Van De Mieroop, 2005). Similarly, in the 1200s, trial by ordeal was a method of determining if a woman was a witch. By this method, a woman would be tied up and thrown into blessed water. If she sank she was determined to be innocent, but if she floated her status as a witch was confirmed. Running the gauntlet or walking on fire were other examples or ordeals that if passed could determine innocence. Trial by ordeal was condemned by the pope in 1215. Nevertheless, a more recent example of **spiritualistic theories** in action was the famous witches trials in Salem, Massachusetts in 1692 in which 24 suspected witches were put to death for allegedly causing unexplained illnesses in children (Bernard, Snipes, & Gerould, 2010).

Classical criminology emerged from the philosophy of the Enlightenment and the concept that the rights of man needed to be protected from the oppression and corruption of existing institutions. One of the most oppressive of these institutions was thought to be the justice system, which was characterized by arbitrary and harsh punishments and an absence of due process (Taylor, Walton, & Young, 1973). A key contributor to this new ideology was Cesare Bonesana Marchese di Beccaria, whose essay *On Crimes and Punishments* (1764/1963) was based on the concepts of social contract theory or utilitarianism, as elucidated by such philosophers as Hobbes, Locke, Montesquieu, and Rousseau. Beccaria proposed the following: all men are self-seeking and capable of committing crime; society has an interest to maintain social order and humans accept that antisocial behavior must be controlled; punishment must be used to deter crime but this punishment must be proportional to the crime (Taylor et al., 1973; Vold & Bernard, 1986). Beccaria's ideas were so revolutionary at the time that he published his essay anonymously, and in 1766 it was condemned by the Catholic Church and placed on its List of Prohibited Books. Nevertheless, in 1791, following the French Revolution, his principles formed the basis of the French legal code (Bernard et al., 2010).

The classical criminological theory that arose from Beccaria's work had considerable appeal due to the notion of rational choice. That is, individuals will freely determine whether to engage in crime based on an analysis of the relative costs and benefits. The means of deterring crime are therefore straight-forward, and simply rely on ensuring that the pain or cost of committing crime is higher than the pleasure or benefits accrued from the crime. This notion of deterrence remains a central feature of sentencing decision-making today (Regehr & Kanani, 2010). Rasche (1996) identifies that the popularity of the classical school was the degree to which it placed responsibility for crime on the rational decision-making of the individual criminal. However, the focus on the criminal act as the means for determining punishment ignored individual differences between those who committed crime. The rise of science, medicine, and other social research during the 18th and 19th centuries revealed increasing numbers of ways in which people were not self-determining. This included both external factors, such as the physical, social, and economic environment, and internal factors, such as mental capacity and maturity, mental and physical health, and psychopathology. Thus, **positivistic** explanations for crime grew in popularity. These explanations were premised on the assumption that human behavior was influenced, at least in part, by predetermined biological, psychological, and social factors. These models brought with them the appeal of "objectivity," because they promised to understand crime by using the scientific method (Taylor et al., 1973).

Biological theories focused on hereditary and defectiveness and presumed that criminality could be either inherited genetically or produced by biological or physical defects. Early biological approaches included Phillipe Pinel's *Nosographie philosophique ou methode de l'analyse appliquee a la medecine* (1798) and Henry Maudsley's *The Physiology and Pathology of the Mind* (1867). Both authors now have large forensic mental health facilities named in their honor in Montreal, Canada, and London, England, respectively. While some early biological models were later refuted, such as those that focused on physical attributes, including phrenology (the shape of the skull as an indicator of criminal intents) or the analysis of facial features, others continue to hold promise. For instance, recent research has focused on neurotransmitters, hormones, and both the central nervous system and the autonomic nervous system (Bernard et al., 2010). Vold and Bernard (1986) caution that biological factors must be seen solely as a contributor to criminal activity and not a cause. These factors may increase the likelihood of criminal behavior but only in interaction with psychological and social forces.

Psychological theories focus on the notions of personality or mental disorder, beginning with Sigmund Freud's pioneering work in psychoanalytic theory and the unconscious, whereby behavior is driven by the urges and impulses of the id and moderated or controlled by the superego. More recent models such as those of Albert Bandura (1986) focus on behavioral approaches and the individual's cognitive appraisal of the rewards associated with deviant behavior. Such theories differ widely in their assumptions about how the human mind works, but they have in common an attempt to explain human behavior in terms of psychological functioning. Hans Eysenck (1947), for instance, described extraversion and neurosis as leading to criminal behavior. Later, Robert Hare described psychopathic traits and developed the Psychopathy Checklist (Hare, 1991). However, as noted above with respect to biological factors, psychological factors may create a predisposition to criminal behavior, but are unlikely to act in isolation to social factors.

Social structural theories began with the work of Durkheim (1964), who introduced the science of political economy. In order to maintain a society, all members must give up freedoms and make sacrifices; what is in the interests of society is not consistently in the interests of individual citizens. The law plays the role of maintaining order by repressing deviation and enforcing conformity. However, resources and sacrifices are not equally distributed in society and crime results from the dissatisfaction caused by social inequality. This work gave rise to a large body of theory related to the intersection between crime and poverty. Merton (1938) argued that it is the social structure and culture of American society that gives rise to crime. According to this view, accumulated wealth is associated with higher social value, and that society degrades those who do not possess such resources. This produces strain in all members of society, but particularly in those in the less privileged classes. This strain eventually results in criminal behavior (Vold & Bernard, 1986). Rasche (1996) suggests that the conclusion of social structural theories is that a society creates its own problems with crime and that the solution to crime is the transformation of social structures.

Related to social structural theories are social control theories. Rather than assuming that biological, psychological, or social factors cause people who would normally be law abiding to commit crime, control theories assume that all people would naturally commit crime but are controlled by forces in society to refrain from doing so (Bernard et al., 2010). One theorist in this area, Hirschi (1969), suggested that control is exerted by social bonds such as those with family, peer groups, or within important organizations such as school. Subsequently, Hirschi added the concept of self-control, whereby early social bonds with parents and others lead to the formation of internal mechanisms for control. The policy implications of these theories focus on two aspects: (1) improving parenting to increase the likelihood of instilling values that will result in internal control and (2) providing opportunities for social engagement of older youth such as school- or community-based programs that enhance social bonds (Bernard et al., 2010).

Another form of control is labeling (Becker, 1963). Labeling theory suggests that society attempts to control behavior through social stigma by attaching negative labels to it. This stigma has two possible negative outcomes for society. First, it may create further social disengagement, thereby limiting opportunities and increasing the risk of criminal activity. Second, such labeling behaviors may also become self-fulfilling, as those to whom the labels are attached embrace it as their identity and then behave accordingly—the label paradoxically becomes a badge of honor in certain social groups.

Social structural and social control theories gave rise, in turn, to **critical criminology**. This model arose as a revolt against traditional theories for crime and deviance. These emerging models, which included Marxist, feminist, and conflict models, suggest that deviant action must be examined from the perspective of the deviant actor. That is, how does the actor describe his or her intentions? These models also generally acknowledge the unequal distribution of power and wealth in society that can result in differential legal responses to certain groups in society. Further, these models include a denial of absolutism; that is, definitions of social order are not consensual or monolithic, but may reflect the perspectives and interests of dominant groups (Taylor et al., 1973). A present-day example of this concept is the Occupy Wall Street movement and subsequent political protests that have aimed to challenge increasing social and economic inequality as well as the influence of corporate interests in politics. It is a matter of perception whether individuals in these movements who engage in violent activity are social activists using legitimate means of political expression or are terrorists committing punishable crimes.

Researchers continue to use a wide range of theories to attempt to understand crime and victimization. These theories tend to fall into three broad categories: (1) theories that focus on the role of the victim in his or her own victimization, (2) theories that focus on the interaction between the victim and the offender that result in crime, and (3) theories that focus more broadly on societal influences that lead to victimization.

Victim-Based Theories

By the mid-20th century, in an effort to better understand the phenomenon of victimization, criminologists began to develop methods for categorizing different types of victims, referred to as *victim typologies*. These typologies were based on a variety of factors, including biological, sociological, psychological, demographic, and psychiatric. Benjamin Mendelsohn (1940) coined the term *victimology*, proposing that this be an entirely new field of study, not merely a branch of criminology, but rather a separate and distinct discipline that would be the "reverse of criminology" (Schafer, 1968, p. 42). In 1937, Mendelsohn interviewed victims and, from his analysis, concluded that most victims at least unconsciously participated in their own victimization. Mendelsohn's (1940, 1974) original formulation classified victims according to their relative degree of responsibility and power to control or affect situations. These categories, further described by Zur (1994), also judged the degree of guilt or responsibility, ranging from total innocence/no guilt to 100% responsibility/total guilt (TABLE 3-1).

TABLE 3-1 Mendelsohn's Six Victim Types

Victim who is completely innocent. ● Does not share any responsibility of the offense with the perpetrator.	● The ideal victim. ● Includes children and victims of random or rampage shootings, unexpected natural disasters, and who suffer a crime while they are unconscious.
Victim with minor guilt and responsibility due to his or her own ignorance. ● With some thought, planning, awareness, information, or consciousness, the victim could have expected danger and avoided or minimized the risk of harm.	● Adults who were victimized due to being in the wrong place at the wrong time. ● Includes person attacked walking on a dark street.
Victim who is as guilty as the offender (voluntary victim) and shares equally in responsibility. ● Chose to be part of the interaction. He or she is not caught by surprise, and common sense could have anticipated the damage that occurred.	● People victimized while engaging in risky behavior. ● Includes contracting a sexually transmitted disease from a prostitute; or seeking, challenging, or enticing the perpetrator; or being a willing participant in a chicken game, gun dual, or double suicide.
Victim who is slightly guiltier than the offender (provoker). ● An active participant in an interaction where he or she is likely to get hurt. ● Seeks the damaging contact, while the offender can easily withdraw from the situation.	● Someone who provokes or induces someone to commit a crime. ● Includes an abusive husband who is killed by his battered wife, cult members who chose to enter the cult as adults and then were brainwashed and harmed (e.g., Jonestown, Waco).
Victim who is exclusively responsible for his or her victimization. ● Initiates the contact and commits an act that is likely to lead to injury.	● Someone injured while committing a crime. ● Includes a violent perpetrator who is killed by another person in self-defense or a mentally healthy and competent individual who commits a rationally planned suicide.
The imaginary victim. ● Has suffered nothing at all but accuses another falsely.	● The false accusation may be volitional or involitional. ● Includes false allegations of assault and a delusional individual.

Data from Mendelsohn, B. (1940). *Rape in criminology*. Giustizia Penale; Zur, O. (1994). Rethinking "Don't Blame the Victim": Psychology of Victimhood.

Fattah (1967) similarly sought to classify victims according to their level of participation in the crime. His five major classes parallel those of Mendelsohn: the nonparticipating victim, the latent or predisposed victim, the provocative victim, the precipitating victim, and the false victim.

In 1965, Hermann Mannheim suggested that the distinction between criminal and victim often becomes vague and blurred in individual cases. He continued that the deeper and longer one scrutinized the actions of persons involved in a crime, the more doubtful it became to determine who was to blame for the tragic outcome (Mannheim, 1965a, 1965b). Henri Ellenberger (1954), a prominent psychoanalyst of the same era, concentrated his research on the psychological dynamic between offender and victim. Ellenberger stressed the importance of focusing particular attention on what he refers to as "victimogenesis" rather than "criminogenesis," and he urged criminologists to study dangers to which victims could be vulnerable due specifically to their occupation, social class, or physical condition.

Zur (1994) cautioned that these descriptive categories, in their attempt to differentiate among many situations of victimhood, were controversial, inconclusive, and incomplete, particularly with respect to guilt and responsibility. Cultural, demographic, and personal variables, although not accounted for in the above categories, are nevertheless critical for any assessment of guilt and responsibility. It is also important when evaluating the degree of responsibility in a given situation that the following parameters be assessed: ethnicity (minorities are at greater risk of victimization than those in the majority), gender (women are at greater risk than men are in certain personal crimes, such as rape), socioeconomic status, physical attributes (such as strength and ability), mental status, familial background, and cultural values (cultures that promote violence vs. those that promote harmony) (Zur, 1994).

Hans von Hentig, in his classic book, *The Criminal and His Victim* (1948), offered another victim typology that explored the relationship between the offender and the sufferer. A section of his book, titled "The Victim's Contribution to the Genesis of Crime," concluded that many victims may actually contribute to their victimization by inciting or provoking the offender or by fostering a situation in which they are likely to be victimized. Von Hentig's 13-category typology is based on psychological, social, and biological factors, in contrast to Mendelsohn's categories based on guilt and responsibility (TABLE 3-2). A reading of von Hentig's categories quickly highlights the influence of dominant societal beliefs on the development of theory.

TABLE 3-2 Hans von Hentig's 13-Category Typology

The young	• Viewed by criminals as weak or inexperienced and vulnerable to attack.
	• Not usually victims of crimes for profit.
	• May be kidnapped for profit or used by criminals to commit crimes against property.
The female	• Described by von Hentig as another form of weakness because they have less strength against an attacker.
The old	• Likely to be victims of property crimes because they have accumulated wealth and have wealth-giving power.
	• Can be viewed as weaker due to less physical strength than a younger person.
The mentally defective	• Von Hentig identified the mentally ill, intellectually challenged, and substance abusers as handicapped in any struggle against crime.
Immigrants	• Von Hentig described immigrants as vulnerable while adjusting to a new culture in that they can suffer poverty, emotional difficulties, and rejection by groups in the new country.
	• Criminals often understand the immigrant's disturbed situation and take advantage of it.
Minorities	• The position of minorities is similar to that of immigrants.
	• The lack of equality increases their chances of victimization.
	• Racial prejudices can lead to violent criminal–victim relationships.
Dull normals	• Von Hentig said that "dull normals" are born victims in that the criminal or swindler can exploit their vulnerability.
The depressed	• Von Hentig believed that a depressed person's attitude is apathetic and submissive, and thus the person is unable to have any fighting qualities.
	• The depressed person's mental resistance is reduced, and he or she is open to victimization.
The acquisitive	• Von Hentig described how criminal syndicates, racketeers, gamblers, confident men, and others exploit the victim's need for money.
The wanton	• Von Hentig describes this person as dimmed by the generalization of laws and obscured by social conventions.
The lonesome and heartbroken	• Von Hentig cites mass murders as preying on this type of victim and gives the examples of Henri Desire Landru, Fritz Haarmann, and Jack the Ripper.
	• These murderers took advantage of the loneliness of their victims.
Tormentors	• Von Hentig describes tormentors as being in family tragedies.
	• Examples include an alcoholic or psychotic father who tortured his family over time and who is finally killed by his son.
	• This type of victim is said to strain a situation to such a degree that he becomes a victim of the stressful atmosphere he himself creates.
The blocked	• Von Hentig defines the blocked victim as a person who has been so enmeshed in a losing situation that defensive moves become impossible.
	• He gives the example of someone being blackmailed and then unable to seek the assistance of the police.

Data from: von Hentig, H. 1948. *The criminal and his victim: Studies in the sociobiology of crime.* New Haven, CT: Yale University Press.

Another criminologist scholar, Stephen Schafer, reviewed both Mendelsohn's and von Hentig's work and devised his own concept, which he termed "functional responsibility." Titling his book *The Victim and His Criminal*, in direct opposition to von Hentig's title and work, he asserted that victimization occurs as a result of the functional interplay of causative elements. He believed that a typology of criminal–victim relationships, along with the pattern of social situations in which they appear, might be more useful, and he emphasized that victim–risks evaluation was the most promising (Schafer, 1968) (TABLE 3-3).

The concept of victim precipitation has a long history in the victimology literature. It implies that the victim has something to do with his or her own victimization. This concept needs a context for definition. In a small town it may be quite normal to leave a car or house unlocked. However, in a large urban area this act could be seen as precipitation. The person who left keys in a car did not mean for it to be a temptation–opportunity situation, but it can be. Is the husband who has chronically ridiculed and abused his wife only to be shot by her after an assault partially responsible for his own victimization? Studying victim culpability, according to Galaway and Hudson (1981), involves efforts to measure the extent to which culpability may occur for selected types of victimization.

TABLE 3-3 Schafer's Victim Precipitation Typologies

Unrelated victims	No responsibility; the victim was an unfortunate target of the perpetrator.
Provocative victims	The victim shares responsibility, and the offender is reacting to something in the victim's behavior.
Precipitative victims	Victims who leave themselves open for victimization by placing themselves in dangerous settings.
Biologically weak victims	Age or deficit places these victims at risk for victimization.
Socially weak victims	For example, minorities or immigrants are victimized because they have not adjusted to the culture.
Self-victimizing victims	Persons who are involved in crimes, such as drug use, prostitution, or gambling, whereby the victim and offender act in concert.
Political victims	Persons who oppose those in power and are victimized to be kept under control.

Data from Schafer, S. 1968. *The victim and his criminal: A study in functional responsibility*. New York: Random House.

This concept of victim culpability was introduced by Wolfgang as victim precipitation with regard to homicide cases in which he believed the victim to be suicide oriented. He viewed a victim's will to live to be a mitigating factor in the offender's guilt. As Wolfgang stated, "In many cases, the victim has most of the major characteristics of an offender; in some cases two potential offenders come together in a homicide situation and it is probably only chance that results in one becoming a victim and the other an offender" (Wolfgang, 1958, p. 265). Wolfgang (1958, 1959) viewed the victim and offender as separate, distinct entities that simultaneously act as equal participants in the homicide. He conducted a study focused exclusively on criminal homicides committed in the city of Philadelphia (as recorded by the Philadelphia Homicide Squad) from January 1948 to December 1952, during which time there were 588 homicide victims, with 621 suspects taken into custody. Wolfgang's conceptualization of the victim-precipitated homicide was derived from the cases in which the victim had been found to be the direct and primary precipitator of the crime; that is, the first to use physical force immediately before the homicide. Wolfgang's Philadelphia study concluded that just over one-fourth of the 588 homicides (150 homicides, or 26%) were victim precipitated.

Menachem Amir, a student of Marvin Wolfgang's, analyzed Philadelphia police records on rape incidents between 1958 and 1960. He concluded that 19% of the forcible rape cases were victim precipitated (Amir, 1971). One of the risk factors he identified was that of alcohol use, especially if both victim and perpetrator had been drinking. Amir's book was published at the time the women's movement began to focus on the issue of rape, resulting in considerable criticism by feminist activists and researchers. In particular, Weiss and Borges (1973) faulted his study on the basis of relying on police accounts, methodological and procedural errors, and a faulty theoretical framework. For example, Amir suggested that victims might desire the rape as a rebellious behavior.

More recent homicide typologies can also be useful in facilitating our understanding of the dynamics of homicide and victim involvement. One evidence-based homicide typology was developed based on a longitudinal study of 336 homicide offenders in New Jersey (Roberts, Zgoba, & Shahidullah, 2007). A fourfold typology was developed: (1) homicide precipitated by a general altercation or argument, (2) homicide during the commission of a felony, (3) domestic violence–related homicide, and (4) homicide as a result of an alcohol-related accident. An in-depth analysis revealed that most homicides precipitated by an argument involved a perpetrator who easily went into a rage and/or did not value human life (Roberts et al., 2007).

Galaway and Hudson (1981) argued that the concept of victim culpability raises interesting problems. Although there is evidence that some victims may be partially responsible for their victimization, there is also the danger of fueling a widespread phenomenon of blaming the victim. The Lebanese American artist, poet, writer, philosopher, and theologian Kahlil Gibran expressed the victim culpability concept poetically in his 1920 book, *The Forerunner*, through a poem titled "Critics" (BOX 3-1).

Victim blaming is a phenomenon common to both people hearing of a crime and to victims themselves. Of the many factors that contribute to victim blaming is a belief in a just world. Just world theory is based on the concept that in an effort to retain the belief that the world is predictable and essentially safe, people who become aware that another is victimized will search for an explanation and rationalize that the victim must in some way have deserved his or her plight (Learner, 1980). This is a common theme in rape crisis work, where not only does society often blame victims for their own assault, but the victims themselves internalize the sense

3-1 "CRITICS"

One nightfall, a man traveling on horseback towards the sea reached an inn by the roadside. He dismounted and, confident in man and night like all riders towards the sea, he tied his horse to a tree beside the door and entered into the inn.

At midnight, when all were asleep, a thief came and stole the traveler's horse.

In the morning the man awoke, and discovered that his horse was stolen. And he grieved for his horse, and that a man had found it in his heart to steal.

Then his fellow lodgers came and stood around him and began to talk.

And the first man said, "How foolish of you to tie your horse outside the stable."

And the second said, "Still more foolish, without even hobbling the horse!"

And the third man said, "It is stupid at best to travel to the sea on horseback."

And the fourth said, "Only the indolent and the slow of foot own horses."

Then the traveler was much astonished. At last he cried, "My friends, because my horse was stolen, you have hastened one and all to tell me my faults and my shortcomings. But strange, not one word of reproach have you uttered about the man who stole my horse."

Gibran (1920/1963, pp. 33–34).

of culpability and begin to self-blame (Koss, 2000). In the mid-1970s, the women's movement launched a formidable campaign to address this deep-seated myth that female victims of forcible rape and attempted rape had, in some way, provoked the assault. The goal of this national effort was to exorcise the automatic and generally accepted response of blaming the victim and to raise awareness about where the sole responsibility for such violent crimes truly lay: with the perpetrators themselves. In an effort to assist women in crisis, many grassroots community organizations began to develop women's support groups, counseling centers, and rape crisis centers both locally and at major universities and medical centers across North America. As a result of this nationwide initiative, law enforcement officials, prosecutors, hospital emergency department staff, nurses, and social workers began to implement rape crisis intervention programs, distributing a variety of materials aimed at encouraging women to report rape to police and to seek medical attention and crisis counseling. The work of the women's movement extended to victims of domestic violence, and domestic violence shelters as well as domestic violence services were established to help these women.

The challenge in the victimology field is to continue engaging in both conceptual and empirical work regarding victim culpability but to discover ways to be sure this work is appropriately used and to avoid widespread victim blaming (Galaway & Hudson, 1981). Vulnerability refers to the susceptibility of a person to being victimized through no fault of his or her own based on demographics or other characteristics, as described in von Hentig's typology. For example, does age matter in victimization, such as the very young or the very old? Are women more susceptible than men to certain types of victimization? Is race a factor for some groups? Galaway and Hudson (1981) suggested the analysis of victim vulnerability serves at least two useful functions. First, identification of a population group that may be susceptible to victimization may assist in crime prevention efforts for this group. Second, such an analysis may help to dispel common beliefs or myths and direct a more precise focus on the nature of the crime victimization problem. Galaway and Hudson gave the example of evidence that most crimes are intraracial, which helps dispel the myth that Black offenders predominantly victimize White citizens. With respect to age, victimization surveys indicate that the elderly are victimized less frequently than younger population groups; however, as a group they are more fearful of crime. Thus, victim programs might direct attention toward the elders' fear of crime and recommend strategies to reduce these anxieties.

Interactional Theories

Interactional theories consider the intersection between the victim and the offender and their environment. One of the most commonly cited interactional theories of victimization is the **lifestyle routine activities theory** (Cohen & Felson, 1979; Hindelang, Gottfredson, & Garafalo, 1978). This theory proposes that certain personal characteristics and lifestyle activities increase or decrease an individual's risk of victimization. These can include age, gender, employment status, and marital status. With this in mind, certain groups can be expected to have a higher risk for both property and violent victimization. Due to variations in lifestyle, vulnerable groups, which include individuals who are young, male, unemployed, and unmarried, experience greater risks due to increased exposure. Indeed, research suggests that people with risky lifestyles are more prone to victimization (Schreck & Fisher, 2004). Such risky lifestyle activities include substance abuse, indiscriminate socializing, engaging in criminal activities, types of employment, and prior experience with direct or vicarious victimization (Fisher, Sloan, Cullen, & Lu, 1998; Lasley, 1989; Mustaine, 1997; Mustaine & Tewksbury, 1998).

Lifestyle, however, is not purely a personal choice. Hindelang and colleagues (1978) proposed that an individual is constrained by role expectations and structural characteristics based on factors such as age, race, and socioeconomic status. Their adaptations to these constraints are reflected in routine daily activities, both vocational (e.g., school and work) and leisure activities, that may expose an individual to high-risk victimization situations (Walklate, 1989). For instance, a single mother on welfare may have no option but to live in a high-crime neighborhood. Both she and her children are thus exposed to opportunities for victimization that a child born to a professional couple in the suburbs may not share. Hindelang and colleagues suggested that personal victimization is related to a number of interrelated factors, such as those found in TABLE 3-4.

Lifestyle can also be influenced by other social factors. Indeed, a major assumption of routine activities theory is that social changes affect criminal opportunities. For instance, increased demand for expensive goods increases the risk they will be stolen. Further, increases in safety precautions taken by the public may decrease the availability of victims and displace criminals to another location (Meier & Miethe, 1993). Cohen and Felson (1979) proposed a routine activities theory of crime to explain the rising crime rates in the United States after World War II. They suggested that after World War II,

TABLE 3-4 Eight Propositions Regarding Lifestyle and Victimization

- The probability of suffering a personal victimization is directly related to the amount of time that a person spends in public places (e.g., on the street, in parks, etc.) and particularly in public places at night.
- The probability of being in public places, particularly at night, varies as a function of lifestyle.
- Social contacts and interactions occur disproportionately among individuals who share similar lifestyles.
- An individual's chances of personal victimization are dependent on the extent to which the individual shares demographic characteristics with offenders.
- The proportion of time an individual spends among nonfamily members varies as a function of lifestyle.
- The probability of personal victimization, particularly personal theft, increases as a proportion of time that an individual spends among nonfamily members.
- Variations in lifestyle are associated with variations in the ability of individuals to isolate themselves from persons with offender characteristics.
- Variations in lifestyle are associated with variations in the convenience, the desirability, and the vincibility of a person as a target for personal victimizations.

Data from Walklate, S. 1989. *Victimology: The Victim and the Criminal Justice Process.* London. Unwin Hyman Ltd.

Americans began spending more time outside of their homes, either working or engaging in leisure activities; these changes in lifestyle and behaviors put them at a greater risk for victimization. More suitable targets became available because homes were left unattended for extended periods of time, and individuals often found themselves in unfamiliar places. Fattah (2000), in an attempt to develop a comprehensive system for understanding victimization from an interactive-model approach, grouped relevant factors into 10 categories (**TABLE 3-5**). This model incorporates victim characteristics, victim beliefs and behaviors, offender motivations, interactions between victims and offenders, the environment, and social attitudes.

Fattah (1979) identified fear of crime as a factor that influences victimization. Studies suggest that individual characteristics are related to fear of crime, including an individual's gender, age, race, income, and urban residence. This research has generally found that women, the elderly, non-Whites, the poor, and those who live in urban areas are more fearful of crime than are other groups in the population (Clemente & Kleiman, 1977; Kennedy & Silverman, 1985). Not surprisingly perhaps, these groups were identified in von Hentig's categories of victims in 1940. As such, members of these groups often engage in avoidance behaviors that limit their activities and freedom of movement.

Another defensive behavior is victim resistance. Resistance extends the idea of victim responsibility, a concept proposed by Schafer (1968), to include

TABLE 3-5 Factors Affecting Victimization

Opportunities	• Linked to the characteristics and activities of potential targets
Risk factors	• Sociodemographic (age, gender, area of residence)
	• Lifestyle (alcohol use)
Motivated offenders	• Criteria by which offenders choose victims
Exposure	• Degree to which lifestyle and environment precipitate exposure to offenders
Associations	• Degree of homogeneity with offender populations
	• Contacts through personal, social, or professional life
Dangerous times, dangerous places	• Times with higher risk, including nights and weekends
	• Places with higher risk, including bars and clubs
Dangerous behaviors	• Negligence and carelessness for property crimes (not locking)
	• Behavior where ability to defend oneself is reduced (hitchhiking)
High-risk activities	• Illegal activities in the pursuit of fun
	• Dangerous occupations (such as prostitution)
Defensive/avoidance behaviors	• Fear of crime and prevention are important in reducing victimization
	• Elderly people, for instance, curtail activities
Structural/cultural proneness	• Powerlessness and deprivation are associated with increased victimization
	• Cultural marginalization and stigmatization increase risk for instance of hate crimes

Data from E. Fattah. (2000). Victimology: Past, Present, and Future. *Criminologie, 33*(1), 17–46.

responsibility for thwarting the act. Resistance is defined by Claster and David (1981) as action by a potential victim during a confrontation that is designed to interfere in any way with completion of the criminal act or escape. Resistance may comprise active conduct, such as physical retaliation or calling for help, but it can also include a refusal to meet the demands of an offender, similar to the passive or nonviolent resistance made famous by Mahatma Gandhi and his followers. A crucial factor that impinges on the potential victim, affecting his or her behavior with a criminal adversary, is that of social power, as noted by Schafer (1968). Comparing physical size, occupation, sex, age, or number of participants for both parties may reflect the actual power relationship, for example. The practical question that victim resistance raises is this: How should I act if I perceive myself as a potential victim? The issue of resistance—its presence or absence—remains a current concept in victimology research.

An interactional factor that incorporates earlier formulations of victim responsibility (Mendelsohn, 1940) is mutual violence or role reversals. These concepts describe the movement from victim to offender and/or offender to victim over time. Other terms to describe this concept include the *cycle of violence*, *reciprocal violence*, or the *transgenerational transmission of violence*. An example is intimate partner violence where police officers attending an emergency call determine that both parties have been engaged in the violence and they are unable to assess who started the violence. This has led to a major challenge with respect to mandatory reporting laws and an increase in victims being arrested and charged in domestic violence calls (McDermott & Garofalo, 2004). It has further led to the acceptance of "battered woman syndrome" as a defense for murder (Regehr & Glancy, 1995). The link between childhood victimization and juvenile or adult offending has methodological concerns, not the least of which include the lack of uniformity of behaviors, self-report, and baseline data from control groups. However, there is the public perception that in a culture of violence, victims become offenders and vice versa.

Perhaps the most interesting example of the interaction between the victim and the offender is the **Stockholm syndrome**, a term coined after a Swedish incident in 1973. At 10:15 a.m. on Thursday, August 23, 1973, Jan-Erik Olsson, who was on leave from prison, entered the Sveriges Kreditbank in central Stockholm with a submachine gun. "The party has just begun," he announced, taking four of the bank's employees hostage in a vault measuring 11 × 47 feet until late in the evening of August 28. In answer to his demands, another criminal was brought to the bank and joined Olsson in the siege. Over the almost 6 days of captivity a relationship developed between the hostage takers and their victims. Indeed, the victims later identified that they were more frightened of the police than the captors. Further, after their release the victims asked that mercy be shown toward the offenders.

Stockholm syndrome is the dramatic and unexpected realignment of affections to the positive bond between hostage and captor and to the feelings of distrust and hostility on the part of the victim toward authority. Ochberg and Soskis (1982) contended that positive bonds do not form immediately but are usually established by the third day. They identified four factors that promote the Stockholm syndrome: intensity of the experience, duration, dependence of the hostage on the captor for survival, and distance of the hostage psychologically from authority. Based on their research, Grahm and Rawlings (1991) suggested that bonding with an abuser may be a *universal survival strategy for victims of interpersonal abuse*. Studies of other hostage-like groups suggest this concept can be applied to hostages, concentration camp prisoners, cult members, prisoners of war, civilians in Chinese Communist prisons, procured prostitutes, incest victims, physically and/or emotionally abused children, and battered women. In the most famous U.S. case of the Stockholm syndrome, Patty Hearst, the granddaughter of publishing baron William Randolph Hearst, was kidnapped by the leftist Symbionese Liberation Army in 1974 and robbed a San Francisco bank together with her captors.

Societal-Based Theories of Victimology

Societal-based theories of victimology see the basis of crime and victimization in social structures that precipitate and perpetuate unequal relationships, unrest, anger, and need. In this way, violence is politically, economically, and socially induced. These authors frequently look at the impact of crime on the poorest, most vulnerable, and most marginalized members of society and inter-class conflicts caused by inequalities in wealth, power, and authority (Wolhuter, Olley, & Denham, 2009). Theoretical approaches that fall into the category include critical criminology and feminist criminology.

Within critical criminology it is possible to see distinct but related sub-schools of thought. Conflict theory, first suggested by Sellin (1938) in the early 20th century, essentially sees crime as the product of whoever wins the power struggle over the labeling apparatus. Thus, when one nation conquers another and imposes its law over the conquered land, behaviors that might have been acceptable yesterday may become criminalized today and actions that threaten to undermine the status quo are outlawed. Therefore, it is more important to understand the actions of norm creators, norm interpreters, and norm enforcers than it is to understand norm breakers. The social implications of this approach are somewhat fatalistic: we will always have crime because someone will always be the loser in the power struggles in society, so the only real question is how to minimize it.

By comparison, Marxist theory, a second subschool of critical criminology, takes this line of reasoning much further but ends up with a potential cure for crime in a capitalist society. Based on the work of Karl Marx (1904/1959), Marxist theory asserts that crime is primarily the product of structural arrangements within capitalist political economies, which tend to produce widespread social and economic dislocation (Bonger, 1916) and shape a legal system that is used by the dominant classes to subordinate other less powerful groups in society (Spitzer, 1975). Although there is little hope to eliminate crime while capitalist class relations endure, there is the theoretical possibility of a system-wide cure for crime if capitalism can be overthrown. The cure for crime and the broader problem of social, economic, and political inequality is revolution and the transition to socialism, which promises to liberate the means of production from private ownership and more equally distribute material wealth and political power. It would also potentially mean the end to a ruling economic elite who uses the privilege of legal authority to criminalize subordinate groups, but this does not preclude the use of the criminal label on new groups, nor would it necessarily prevent violent victimization that accompanies the transition to a new type of society. Marxist criminology also aims to bring attention to the often neglected crimes of the powerful, many of which are perceived to be more costly and damaging to society than most "street" crimes in both scale and severity. Although governments are tasked with regulating corporate excesses, some argue that pollution, fraud, tax evasion, and negligence have become necessary by-products of highly competitive market conditions where growth and profits must be maximized.

Another popular subject in critical criminology is the concept of social capital, which can be understood as the features of social organization that can generate beneficial outcomes among cooperative individuals and groups. If characterized by norms of trust and reciprocity, these connections or social networks can result in collective action to solve or mitigate intracommunity problems such as high rates of crime and victimization (Coleman, 1988). Early writings on the roots of social capital can be noted in the founding documents of American government, such as James Madison's contributions to the *Federalist Papers* and the commentary of Alexis de Tocqueville in *Democracy in America*, that encourage pluralist and participatory democracy. The concept of social capital has increased in visibility over the past decade because of its intuitive appeal. For example, if the social ties that bind communities together are strengthened, community members will be healthier, happier, and more likely to cooperate to improve the communities in which they live. By contrast, low levels of social capital may constrain informal social control and weaken the inclination of community members to intervene in or sanction deviant behavior (Laub & Sampson, 1993; Rose & Clear, 1998).

Grootaert (1998) suggested that social capital is the missing link that differentiates healthy and prosperous communities from those torn by poverty, conflict, and concentrated disadvantage. Wacquant (1998) has emphasized that dissolution of social capital has been facilitated by the retraction and disassembly of formal institutions traditionally responsible for providing civic goods and services, including public safety, education, housing, health care, and welfare supports. This more critical take on social capital identifies welfare retrenchment and geographically specific disinvestment as catalysts for increasing levels of crime and victimization.

Feminist criminology arose during the 1980s as a result of concern over the inadequacy of existing criminological theories to explain the relationship between women and crime. Traditional models were not seen to adequately consider issues of power and vulnerability. Feminist researchers consistently pointed to the lack of attention to issues such as rape and sexual assault in academic, legal, and legislative forums (Walklate, 1989). Crime surveys ignored crimes committed largely against women, suggesting they were less important or resulted in lower levels of suffering. Thus, crimes against women, such as intimate partner violence, were not only hidden, but were indeed seen as tacitly sanctioned by the state. Dubinsky (1992), for instance, in reviewing historical legal and societal treatment of rape victims, asserted that whether a raped woman is a "designing woman" or a "virtuous maiden" has always been determined by the morals and social values of the time in which she lived. Further, concerns arose over the dominance of victim-based models for understanding victimization and the tendency of these models to assign blame to the victim for his or her own suffering (Wolhuter et al., 2009). Feminist criminology addresses these issues by placing a gender-based lens on power relationships and legally ascribed rights of women.

Ecological Theory

Although not strictly a theory of victimology, ecological theory is increasingly used as an integrative framework for understanding victimization. Ecological theory seeks to understand human experience and behavior within a "person-in-environment" framework (Bronfenbrenner, 1979; Germain & Gitterman, 1996). Ecological theory sees individuals as influenced by intersecting levels of ecological systems: the individual (or ontogenic), which includes factors internal to the individual, such as personal characteristics and formative history; the microsystem, which considers interactions between the individual and the person's context, such as family, peers, and cultural affiliations; the exosystem, which is the environment in which the person resides, his or her neighborhood and community, including its limitations and resources; and the macrosystem, which includes those factors that are economic, social, and political in nature (Belsky, 1980; Bogo, 2006; Bronfenbrenner, 1979; Germain & Gitterman, 1996). Of significance is that each of these ecological subsystems is viewed to influence the range of choices and options available to victims and

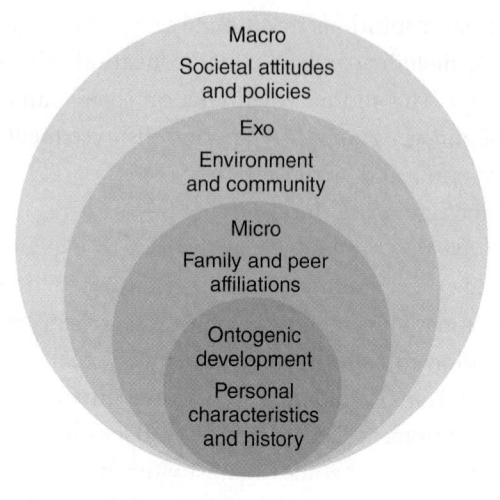

FIGURE 3-2 Four systems of the ecological framework.

Data from: Bronfenbrenner, U. 1979. *The ecology of human development.* Cambridge, MA: Harvard University Press.

ultimately their decisions and behaviors (Bogo, 2006; Bronfenbrenner, 1979). FIGURE 3-2 presents this model.

Alaggia, Regehr, and Jenny (2011) use ecological theory to understand the factors that impede women's disclosure of intimate partner violence. In their analysis of the responses of 118 participants in a mixed-methods study, they identified intrapersonal factors, including levels of posttraumatic stress symptoms, internalized views of love, and the desire to keep their family together and make things work, that interacted in complex ways to inhibit disclosure. At the microsystem level, familial and cultural beliefs about marriage and family and cultural norms regarding the acceptability of abuse impacted women's decisions to disclose. These were often reinforced by mezzosystem, or community, attitudes. For example, fear of losing family support and potential cultural rejection were given as examples of undesirable outcomes of disclosing abuse. Finally, at the macrosystem level, the very policies that were developed and occasionally amended to support women to disclose intimate partner violence have had adverse effects, as reported by the participants. For instance, mandatory charging policies by police that were designed to protect and increase safety for women were actually perceived to take control away from women, further disempowering them.

Case Analysis Using Victimology Theories

In the case of *Commonwealth of Virginia v. Turman* (2007), Myron Turman was convicted of rape and sexual battery. Turman appealed the conviction on the grounds that an America Online Instant Messenger conversation between

Turman and the victim was inadmissible evidence. The court of appeals found that the Commonwealth of Virginia had sufficiently identified Turman as the individual who sent the instant messages. The conviction was upheld.

The victim (we will call her "Ms. S") had known Turman since 1999, and they were considered to be friends. A month before the attack, in September 2002, Turman and Ms. S had consensual sex. On the night of October 5, 2002, she was at a dance club where Turman contacted her to ask when she was planning to leave. When she returned home in the early morning of October 6, Turman was waiting for her in the parking lot of her residence. After allowing Turman into her residence, Ms. S became uncomfortable with his behavior and asked him to leave. Ms. S had lain down on her bed and denied Turman's request to lie down on the bed with her. She then went into another room of her residence and asked Turman to leave. Turman responded by "grabbing [the victim in a bear hug . . . and carrying] her into the bedroom." Turman began performing oral sodomy on the victim and then engaged in sexual intercourse with the victim despite her requests that he stop. Turman then said he wanted to perform anal sodomy and did so despite the victim's denial of the request. After the victim had succeeded in freeing herself of Turman, she insisted that he leave and threatened to call the police. She did not initially call the police because Turman seemed to agree to leave. When the victim restated her intention to call the police, Turman "lunged and took the telephone from her." She then ran to another phone and called the police just before she heard the front door slam. Ms. S was taken to a hospital and examined by a sexual assault nurse examiner; the injuries were consistent with the described sexual assault. She had bruises on her right thigh and left arm and a tear to her anus.

Turman admitted to police officers that he had sex with Ms. S on October 6 but contended that the encounter was consensual. He claimed that he left her residence after she began talking about her boyfriend and that she threatened to call the police and claim that he raped her if he told anyone about the encounter. A key piece of evidence was an America Online Instant Messenger conversation between Turman and the victim several months after the attack. In the conversation, Turman indirectly confessed to the assault, apologizing and claiming he was high on ecstasy. The conversation was presented to the jury during the testimony of the victim; although she did not print or save a copy of the conversation, she recalled the conversation from memory. Turman argued that the instant messages were not admissible because they were hearsay and he could not be definitely identified as the sender of the messages because two of his friends and his estranged wife had access to his account. The court found that the AOL Instant Messenger conversation was admissible in its presentation to the jury in the testimony of the victim. The jury was instructed to consider the flight of Turman from the scene after the victim called the police. While she was on the line with the authorities, she heard the door slam, an indication that Turman had left.

Analysis

This attack was premeditated. Turman had called Ms. S to find out when she would be going home, and when she arrived Turman was waiting for her. Turman made indirect advances that were clearly rejected before he carried Ms. S against her will into the bedroom; he asked if he could lie down on the bed with her, and she said no. He had gained access to the victim's residence because of his friendship with the victim. The attack can be classified as an acquaintance rape, where the perpetrator abuses the trust of the victim. Acquaintance rape provides a perfect example of the tension or conflict between different theoretical formulations. What is the responsibility of the victim relative to the responsibility of the offender and society? This tension is played out in media accounts of date rape trials and in the courtroom.

Victim-based theories of victimology would place Ms. S in von Hentig's victim category of "the female." From this perspective, her physical strength relative to that of the offender was a significant factor leading to the assault. Mendelsohn's classifications consider the concept of victim responsibility. Someone using this classification might argue that either Ms. S has "minor guilt" in that she could have anticipated the danger and minimized the risk. Finally, an analysis using Schafer's victim precipitation typologies may focus on the facts that Ms. S let Turman into her home and had previously had sex with him. Using these facts one could argue that her behavior could be misinterpreted by Turman as an invitation. Looking at the four phases of a sexual assault, the victim had an early awareness of danger before the attack. She rejected his advances from the very beginning and asked him to leave without a major unwanted advance from Turman. The threat of attack in this case was so sudden that the victim had no time to stall, bargain, or to perform any sort of evasive tactic. Turman responded violently to the victim's request that he leave, grabbing her and carrying her to the bedroom. The victim repeatedly expressed verbal resistance throughout the attack. She was also struggling with the realization that she was being raped: "[I was] trying to figure out what in the world was going on, why was this gentleman acting like this." Considering each fact, victim responsibility and victim precipitation were found by the court to be outweighed by offender responsibility.

Interactive theories would consider Ms. S's lifestyle and the manner in which her activities (such as attending bars) put her at higher risk of victimization. Fattah's (2000) factors affecting victimization would consider the danger associated with her relationships with others, the places she frequents, and her behaviors, including engaging in high-risk behaviors and defensive/avoidance behaviors. As with victim-basing theories, application of these theories can lead to victim-blaming and excusing of offender culpability. Further, from a just world perspective, people can focus on the behavior of the victim and not that of the offender to ease fears that they themselves are at risk of harm.

From a feminist criminology perspective, the motive for all sexual violence is clearly the need for power and control. Brownmiller (1975), for instance, suggested that rape was traditionally defined by men rather than women and that men use and benefit from the use of rape as a means of perpetuating male dominance by keeping all women in a state of fear. In this case, Ms. S was initially going to call the police in response to the attack, but she stopped when Turman began to put his clothing on. There is a high frequency of nonreporting among rape victims. Reasons for this include secondary victimization in the courtroom and during police investigations, self-blame, and avoidance of reexperiencing traumatic stimuli.

Ecological theory would integrate each of these perspectives into a comprehensive understanding. From the court's perspective, this was a clear case of acquaintance rape. Her injuries were consistent with her description of the assault. The combination of the injuries and the Instant Messenger conversation gives credence to the victim's story. If Turman's testimony was true—that he became uncomfortable when the victim began to talk about her boyfriend and that she subsequently threatened to falsely accuse him of rape if he told anyone about the sexual encounter—then the victim would have likely never followed through on her threat to call the police after he left. Turman also claimed there was no definitive way to prove he was the individual who sent the message through his Instant Messenger account; however, what was said in the conversation was specific to the case and would most likely not have come from one of the other individuals with access to his account.

Conclusion

Victimology draws on both traditional concepts of the victim–offender relationship, victim resistance, cultural and community factors, prevention and rehabilitation, victim vulnerability, and victim precipitation that have been the foundation of the discipline. Modern theories of victimization can be divided into three main categories: victim-based theories, interactive theories, and societal-based theories. Victim-based theories of victimology consider characteristics of individuals that make them vulnerable to victimization, including biological, sociological, psychological, demographic, and psychiatric. Interactional theories consider the intersection between the victim and the offender and their environment. Societal theories include both critical criminology and feminist criminology. These theories in large part turn the focus away from attempting to explain just criminal behavior and toward understanding social responses to crime. Ecological theory attempts to integrate aspects of all other theories. This theory seeks to understand human experience and behavior within a "person-in-environment" framework. As such, it considers the individual, his or her associations, the community in which he or she resides, and social and political influences on choice.

Key Terms

Classical criminology: A view that people have free will and that appropriate and timely punishment will deter crime.

Critical criminology: Combines an analysis of the state with the lived experience of victims. This model includes radical, Marxist, and feminist approaches.

Just world theory: Tendency of people to attribute blame to victims of crime to retain a sense that the world is safe.

Lifestyle routine activities theory: Certain personal characteristics and lifestyle activities increase or decrease an individual's risk of victimization.

Positivistic: Derives knowledge from the scientific method.

Spiritualistic theories: Attribute victimization to the acts of gods, demons, cosmic forces, and other supernatural forces.

Stockholm syndrome: Dramatic and unexpected realignment of affections to the positive bond between hostage and captor and to the feelings of distrust and hostility on the part of the victim toward authority.

Discussion Questions

1. Provide two examples of victim blame.
2. Debate the Kobe Bryant case and the Bill Cosby case in terms of criminology and victimology theories.
3. How does victim precipitation differ (if at all) from victim vulnerability?
4. What type of prevention program would you recommend for a change in college students' lifestyle routine?

5. Discuss the following case in terms of theories of victimization.

Two suspects arrived in town two days before a shooting. The suspects began dealing drugs out of different units in a housing project and hired residents, including the victim, as drug runners to deliver drugs to prospective buyers. These runners were alleged to have planned to rob the suspects, and at one point all the runners went to the unit where the suspects were staying but were unsuccessful in their robbery attempt. The suspects then stopped dealing and left the area. During the early morning hours the victim and two others were seen talking in the housing project when the suspects pulled up in a car without lights. The suspects got out and ran up to the victim, ordered the others out of the way, and then began to fire point blank eight times into the 21-year-old's body. He was transported unconscious to the hospital, where he died 16 days later. During the autopsy, five .22-caliber bullets were removed from his body. No casings were found at the scene. Victimology noted that the victim lived in a high-drug, low-income, high-unemployment, single-parent area. The victim was described as a drug dealer, user, and enforcer who was known to be combative and argumentative.

References

Alaggia, R., Regehr, C., & Jenny, A. (2011). Risky business: An ecological analysis of intimate partner violence disclosure. *Research on Social Work Practice*. doi:10.1177/1049731511425503

Amir, M. (1971). *Patterns in forcible rape*. Chicago: University of Chicago Press.

Bandura, A. (1986). *Social foundations of thought and action: A social cognitive theory*. Englewood Cliffs, NJ: Prentice-Hall, Inc.

Beccaria, C. (1963). *On crimes and punishments* (H. Paolucci, Trans.). Indianapolis, IN: Bobbs-Merrill (original work published 1764).

Becker, H. (1963). *The outsiders*. New York: New York Free Press.

Belsky, J. (1980). Child maltreatment: An ecological integration. *American Psychologist*, *35*(4), 320–335.

Bernard, T., Snipes, J., & Gerould, A. *Vold's theoretical criminology* (6th ed.). New York: Oxford University Press.

Bogo, M. (2006). *Social work practice: Concepts, processes, and interviewing*. New York: Columbia University Press.

Bonger, W. (1916). *Criminality and economic conditions*. Boston: Little, Brown.

Bronfenbrenner, U. (1979). *The ecology of human development*. Cambridge, MA: Harvard University Press.

Brownmiller, S. (1975). *Against our will: Men, women, and rape.* New York: Simon and Schuster.

Claster, D. S., & David, D. S. (1981). The resisting victim. In B. Galaway & J. Hudson (Eds.), *Perspectives on crime victims* (pp. 183–188). St. Louis, MO: Mosby.

Clemente, F., & Kleiman, M. B. (1977). Fear of crime in the United States: A multivariate analysis. *Social Forces, 56,* 519–531.

Cohen, L. E., & Felson, M. (1979). Social change and crime rates: A routine activity approach. *American Sociological Review, 44,* 588–608.

Coleman, J. S. (1988). Social capital and the creation of human capital. *American Journal of Sociology, 94*(Suppl.), S95–S120.

Commonwealth of Virginia v. Turman. (2007). 39 Va. App. at 337 n. 4.

Dubinsky, K. (1992). Maiden girls or designing women? The crime of seduction in turn-of-the-century Ontario. In F. Iacovetta & M. Valverde (Eds.), *Gender conflicts: New essays in women's history.* Toronto: University of Toronto Press.

Durkheim, E. (1964). *The Division of Labor in Society.* New York: Free Press of Glencoe.

Ellenberger, H. (1954). Psychological relationships between the criminal and his victim. *Revue Internationale de Criminologie et de Police Technique, 2,* 103–121.

ESPN. (2004, September 2). Kobe Bryant's apology. Retrieved from http://sports.espn .go.com/nba/news/story?id=1872928

Eysenck, H. (1947). *Dimensions of personality.* London: Routledge.

Fattah, E. (1967). Towards a criminological classification of victims. *International Criminal Police Review, 209,* 162–169.

Fattah, E. (1979). Recent theoretical developments. *Victimology: An International Journal, 4*(2), 199–213.

Fattah, E. (2000). Victimology, past, present, and future. *Criminologie, 33*(1), 17–46.

Fisher, B. S., Sloan, J. J., Cullen, F. T., & Lu, C. (1998). Crime in the ivory tower: The level and sources of student victimization. *Criminology, 36,* 671–710.

Galaway, B., & Hudson, J. (1981). *Perspectives on crime victims.* St. Louis, MO: Mosby.

Germain, C., & Gitterman, A. (1996). *The life model of social work practice: Advances in theory and practice* (2nd ed.). New York: Columbia University Press.

Gibran, K. (1963). *The forerunner: His parables and poems* (Trans.). London: Heinemann (original work published 1920).

Grahm, D., & Rawlings, E. (1991). Bonding with abusive dating partners: Dynamics of Stockholm syndrome. In B. Levy (Ed.), *Dating violence, women in danger.* Seattle, WA: Seal Press.

Grootaert, C. (1998). Social capital: The missing link? Social Capital Initiative Working Paper No. 3. Washington, DC: World Bank.

Hare, R. (1991). *Manual for the revised psychopathy checklist.* Toronto: Multihealth Systems.

Hindelang, M. J., Gottfredson, M. R., & Garafalo, J. (1978). *Victims of personal crime: An empirical foundation for a theory of personal victimization.* Cambridge, MA: Ballinger.

Hirschi, T. (1969). *Causes of delinquency*. Los Angeles: University of California Press.

Johnston, L. (2004, August 16). *Kobe records released*. CBS News. Retrieved from http://www.cbsnews.com/stories/2004/08/16/national/main636205.shtml

Kearon, T., & Godfrey, B. (2007). Setting the scene: A question of history. In S. Walklate (Ed.), *Handbook of victims and victimology* (pp. 17–36). Portland, OR: Willan Publishing.

Kennedy, L. W., & Silverman, R. A. (1985). Significant others and fear of crime among the elderly. *International Journal of Aging and Human Development*, *20*, 241–256.

Koss, M. P. (2000). Blame, shame, and community: Justice responses to violence against women. *American Psychologist*, *55*(11), 1332–1343.

Lasley, J. R. (1989). Drinking routines/lifestyles and predatory victimization: A causal analysis. *Justice Quarterly*, *6*, 529–542.

Laub, J., & Sampson, R. (1993). Turning points in the life course: Why change matters to the study of crime. *Criminology*, *31*(3), 301–325.

Lerner, M. (1980). *Belief in a just world*. New York: Plenum Press.

Mannheim, H. (1965a). *Ideologie und utopie* (3rd enlarged ed.). Frankfurt: Schulte-Bulmke (original published in 1929).

Mannheim, H. (1965b). *Comparative criminology*. London: Routledge & Paul.

Marx, K. (1959). *Critique of political economy* (Trans.). New York: International Library (original work published 1904).

Maudsley, H. (1867). *The Physiology and Pathology of Mind*. London: Macmillan

McDermott, J. M., & Garofalo, J. (2004). When advocacy for domestic violence victims backfires. *Violence Against Women*, *10*(11), 1245–1266.

Meier, R., & Miethe, T. (1993). Understanding theories of criminal victimization. *Crime and Justice: A Review of Research*, *7*, 459–499.

Mendelsohn, B. (1940). *Rape in criminology*. Giustizia Penale.

Mendelsohn, B. (1974). The origin of the doctrine of victimology. In L. Drapkin & E. Viano (Eds.), *Victimology*. Lexington, VA: Lexington Books.

Merton, R. (1938). Social structure and anomie. *American Sociological Review*, *3*, 672–682.

Mustaine, E. E. (1997). Victimization risks and routine activities: A theoretical examination using a gender-specific and domain-specific model. *American Journal of Criminal Justice*, *22*, 41–70.

Mustaine, E. E., & Tewksbury, R. (1998). Predicting risks of larceny theft victimization: A routine activity analysis using refined lifestyle measures. *Criminology*, *36*, 829–857.

Pinel, P. (1798). *Nosographie philosophique ou methode de l'analyse appliquee a la medecine* (Paris, an VII).

Polone, G. (2016, April 20). Remember when Kobe Bryant was charged with rape? I didn't forget and neither should you. *Hollywood Reporter*. Retrieved from http://www.hollywoodreporter.com/news/kobe-bryants-rape-charge-i-885653

Ochberg, F. M., & Soskis, D. A. (Eds.). (1982). *Victims of terrorism*. Boulder, CO: Westview Press.

Rasche, C.E. (1996). *Theorizing about homicide: A presentation on theories explaining homicide and other crimes—Proceedings of the 1996 meeting of the homicide research working group.* Santa Monica, CA: National Institute of Justice.

Regehr, C., & Glancy, G. (1995). Battered woman syndrome defense in the Canadian courts. *Canadian Journal of Psychiatry, 40*(3), 130–135.

Regehr, C., & Kanani, K. (2010). *Essential law for social work practice in Canada.* Toronto: Oxford University Press.

Roberts, A., Zgoba, K., & Shahidullah, S. (2007). Recidivism among four types of homicide offenders: An exploratory analysis of 336 homicide offenders in New Jersey. *Aggression and Violent Behavior, 12*(5), 493–507.

Rose, D., & Clear, T. (1998). Incarceration, social capital, and crime: Implications for social disorganization theory. *Criminology, 36*(3), 441–480.

Sanchez, R., Levenson, E., & Crook, L. (2017, June 17). Bill Cosby trial: Mistrial declared after jury deadlocks. CNN. Retrieved from http://www.cnn.com/2017/06/17 /us/bill-cosby-verdict-watch/index.html

Schafer, S. (1968). *The victim and his criminal: A study in functional responsibility.* New York: Random House.

Schreck, C. J., & Fisher, B. S. (2004). Specifying the influence of family and peers on violent victimization: Extending routine activities and lifestyle theories. *Journal of Interpersonal Violence, 19,* 1021–1041.

Sellin, T. (1938). *Culture, conflict, and crime* (Bulletin No. 41). New York: Social Science Research Council.

Spitzer, S. (1975). Toward a Marxian theory of deviance. *Social Problems, 22*(5), 638–651.

Taylor, I., Walton, P., & Young, J. (1973). *The new criminology: For a social theory of deviance.* London: Routledge & Kegan Paul.

Van De Mieroop, M. (2005). *King Hammurabi of Babylon: A biography.* Malden, MA: Blackwell.

Vold, G. (1958). *Theoretical criminology.* New York: Oxford Press.

Vold, G., & Bernard, T. (1986). *Theoretical criminology.* New York: Oxford University Press.

von Hentig, H. (1948). *The criminal and his victim: Studies in the sociobiology of crime.* New Haven, CT: Yale University Press.

Wacquant, L. (1998). Negative social capital: State breakdown and social destitution in America's urban core. *Netherlands Journal of Housing and the Built Environment, 13*(1), 25–40.

Walklate, S. (1989). *Victimology: The victim and the criminal justice process.* London: Unwin Hyman.

Weiss, K., & Borges, S. S. (1973). Victimology and rape: The case of the legitimate victim. *Issues in Criminology, 8,* 71–115.

Wolfgang, M. (1958). *Patterns of criminal homicide.* Philadelphia: University of Pennsylvania Press.

Wolfgang, M. E. (1959). Suicide by means of victim precipitated homicide. *Journal of Clinical and Experimental Psychopathology and Quarterly Review of Psychiatry and Neurology, 20,* 335–349.

Wolhuter, L., Olley, N., & Denham, D. (2009). *Victimology: Victimization and victims' rights.* London: Routledge-Cavendish.

Zur, O. (1994). Rethinking "don't blame the victim": Psychology of victimhood. *Journal of Couple Therapy, 4*(3/4), 15–36.

CHAPTER 4

© Peyker/Shutterstock.

Victim Rights and Services

OBJECTIVES

- To describe the basis and rise of the victims' rights movement
- To describe victim compensation and restitution
- To describe the psychological impact of victimization
- To outline assessment and treatment options for crime victims

KEY TERMS

Primary victimization

National Organization for Victim Assistance (NOVA)

Secondary victimization

Tertiary victimization

Victim Information and Notification Everyday (VINE) Program

Victims of Crime Act (VOCA)

CASE

On the morning of September 11, 2001, 19 Al-Qaeda terrorists hijacked four commercial passenger jet airliners and intentionally crashed two of the airliners into the Twin Towers of the World Trade Center in New York City, killing more than 2,000 people (FIGURE 4-1). Both towers collapsed within two hours, destroying nearby buildings and damaging others. A third airliner crashed into the Pentagon (FIGURE 4-2). Hijackers had redirected the

FIGURE 4-1 American Airlines Flight 11 hit the North Tower at 8:46 a.m. and United Flight 175 hit the South Tower at 9:03 a.m.

© Str Old/Thomson Reuters.

FIGURE 4-2 American Airlines Flight 77 crashed into the Pentagon at 9:03 a.m.

© Hyungwon Kang/Thomson Reuters.

FIGURE 4-3 Shanksville crash site of United Airlines Flight 93 at 10:03 a.m.

© Jeff Swensen/Getty Images.

fourth plane toward Washington, DC, targeting either the U.S. Capitol or the White House, but crashed it in a field near Shanksville in Stony Creek Township, Pennsylvania, after passengers attempted to retake control of the airliner (FIGURE 4-3). There were no survivors from any of the flights. Al-Qaeda leader Osama Bin Laden claimed responsibility (CBC News, 2004).

The most expansive Federal Bureau of Investigation (FBI) inquiry in history was launched, given the code name "PENTTBOM." At the peak of the case, more than half of the agents employed by the agency worked with other agencies to identify the hijackers and their sponsors and to head off any possible future attacks. They followed more than half a million investigative leads, including several hundred thousand tips from the public (FBI, 2011).

Among the 2,753 victims who died in the attacks on the World Trade Center were 343 firefighters, 60 police officers, and 8 paramedics. Another 184 people were killed in the attack on the Pentagon. The Shanksville crash killed all 44 people onboard, including the 4 hijackers. In the immediate aftermath of the attack, emergency victim services were established for victims and their families, and psychological first aid services were made available to the thousands of rescue and recovery workers who were sifting through the wreckage to look for survivors and remains of humans for identification and burial. Longer-term counseling services reached out to victims and survivors who were experiencing symptoms of posttraumatic stress and loss. The U.S. government instituted a no-fault compensation program targeted at the 3,000 families who had lost someone in the attacks. Over 97% of those eligible applied for the compensation, with an average award of $2 million for surviving families (Feinberg, 2004).

A national commission was formed shortly after the attack to analyze the events and make recommendations to prevent such an attack from happening on American soil ever again. The strategy recommended by the National Commission on Terrorist Attacks Upon the United States (2004) is elaborate:

> To implement it will require a government better organized than the one that exists today, with its national security institutions designed half a century ago to win the Cold War. Americans should not settle for incremental, ad hoc adjustments to a system created a generation ago for a world that no longer exists.
>
> Our detailed recommendations are designed to fit together. Their purpose is clear: to build unity of effort across the U.S. government. As one official now serving on the front lines overseas put it to us: "One fight, one team."
>
> We call for unity of effort in five areas, beginning with unity of effort on the challenge of counterterrorism itself:
>
> - Unifying strategic intelligence and operational planning against Islamist terrorists across the foreign-domestic divide with a National Counterterrorism Center;
>
> - Unifying the intelligence community with a new National Intelligence Director;
>
> - Unifying the many participants in the counterterrorism effort and their knowledge in a network-based information sharing system that transcends traditional governmental boundaries;
>
> - Unifying and strengthening congressional oversight to improve quality and accountability; and
>
> - Strengthening the FBI and homeland defenders.

Introduction

The unpredictable nature of crime results in a major impact on the victim, on his or her family, and on the community in which he or she lives. Sellin and Wolfgang (1964) identified three levels of victim impact:

- **Primary victimization**, which affects the targeted or personalized victim.

- **Secondary victimization**, which involves impersonal victims, such as commercial establishments, churches, schools, and public transportation. More recently, the definition of secondary victimization has been modified to include those assisting victims such as emergency responders and therapists (Figley, 1995; Stamm, 1995).

- **Tertiary victimization**, which is diffuse and extends to the community at large.

The consequences of crime vary depending on the nature of the crime and the level of victimization. As a result, victim services must comprise a range of legal, psychological, medical, and financial supports and interventions that address the varying needs of those affected.

Four case examples of single victimization are depicted below that elucidate the variable nature of crime and the services available to those victimized:

- *Robbery case.* Sam, a 21-year-old auto parts salesman, was robbed at gunpoint upon returning to his apartment in Yonkers, New York. Sam's most vivid recollection of his encounter was staring into the barrel of a 9mm, semiautomatic gun. The perpetrator got away with $169.00 in cash, several credit cards, and Sam's coat, watch, glasses, and shoes. For a month after the attack Sam was plagued by nightmares several nights a week, and finally he went for counseling at the local mental health center. In addition, the victim advocate at the local victim assistance agency in Westchester County helped Sam complete a victim compensation application so that he could be compensated for his monetary and property losses. He was also eventually reimbursed for 6 weeks of mental health counseling.

- *Rape case.* Julie, a 28-year-old advertising executive, was raped at knifepoint when at midnight she returned from work to her apartment in Brooklyn, New York. She noticed the lock on the front door of her building was broken, which concerned her, but nevertheless she proceeded to the tenant mailboxes. Suddenly, someone grabbed her from behind, put a knife to her throat, and ordered her to remove her clothes suggesting he would stab her in the throat if she refused. In terror, she complied and was raped. The rapist told her she had a great body just like his sister and that he might be back in a week or two. Julie told the female detective in the sex crimes unit she feared the rapist might have AIDS or another sexually transmitted disease and that he would return. She was tested for the HIV virus during her rape examination and returned every 6 months for routine testing.

- *Domestic violence case.* Dani, age 36, was stabbed to death by her ex-husband, Mustapha Sandi, in October 2007. Dani's two sons, ages 9 and 3, witnessed the fatal stabbing of their mother. The first police officer to arrive at the scene indicated that the 9-year-old child said: "My daddy stabbed my mommy, don't let my mommy die. Take care of my mom." There was a history of domestic violence complaints; a temporary restraining order against Mustapha Sandi had recently expired. Mustapha was a recently retired professor from a mathematics and physics department at a community college and the head of a construction-management company. The victim, Dani Sandi, was the director of a licensed practical nurse program in

New Jersey at the time of her murder. Social services placed the children with relatives of the mother and arranged for grief counseling.

- *Felony murder case.* James Stevenson owned a liquor store with his brother-in-law. A man brandishing a gun robbed him on Christmas Eve, and in the ensuing struggle James Stevenson was shot to death. The California State Victim Compensation Board reimbursed Mr. Stevenson's wife for funeral expenses, and she now attends a homicide survivors' support group in Los Angeles.

Pervasive media attention that tends to focus on high-profile crime cases sometimes serves to confuse the general public with respect to who is most likely to be a victim of crime. For example, Ronald Goldman and Nicole Brown Simpson were certainly victims of a violent crime, but their case is in no way typical or representative. They were White, they resided in two of the wealthiest areas in the United States (Beverly Hills and Brentwood, California), and Ms. Brown Simpson was a spouse in an interracial marriage—all conditions that would make her statistically less likely to become a homicide victim (studies have shown that in most cases of domestic homicide where the spouse or former spouse is the perpetrator, interracial marriage was not a factor). On the contrary, although anyone can be a victim of crime, those that are at highest risk of crime are young people living in low-income neighborhoods.

Regardless of their demographic or social situation, victims of crime are physically or emotionally injured by the intentional, premeditated act of a fellow human being. Whether the victim was robbed, raped, assaulted, or murdered, the resulting trauma usually consists of psychological pain and torment, physical injuries, and intense fear of being victimized again.

Victims' Rights Movement

The development of American law with respect to victims' rights is built on a 4,000-year history that includes Babylonian, Roman, Mosaic, and English laws. American law combined common law, written statutes enacted by a legislative body, and constitutionally enshrined rights. From the 16th century until early in the 19th century, victims were largely responsible for pursuing justice themselves. In many cases, the victim arranged for a posse to capture the thief, paid an attorney to prosecute the case, and may have even paid the expenses for a circuit judge to come to that jurisdiction. A major shift from this arrangement was the advent of public prosecutors, first established in 1704 in Connecticut. While other states similarly adopted legislation enshrining public prosecutors' offices, private models continued to be widespread until the late 1800s (Derene, Walker, & Stein, 2007).

This shift to a public prosecution model coincided with two other factors that reduced the centrality of victims in the process of justice. First, the focus of crime turned to the general welfare of the community, emphasizing concepts from traditional English theory that posited that crime was primarily a wrong against the public and only secondarily against the individual. Second, stemming from this focus, restitution was seen as being owed to society, not to the victim. Thus, punishment no longer focused on fines paid to the victims in compensation, rather incarceration had become the primary logic of punishment by the early 19th century. Restitution to the victim became an afterthought that, along with victims' rights, was relegated to the civil court system for almost 125 years (Derene et al., 2007). Not until the mid-20th century did societal views of criminals' and victims' rights begin to change.

The crime victims' movement that began in the 1970s ushered in an array of changes to the social, economic, and political forces that encouraged harsh and neglectful treatment of crime victims, directly confronting damaging notions of victim blaming. This movement also led to landmark federal legislation that resulted in major funding initiatives throughout the nation for prosecutor-based victim/witness assistance programs, state crime victim compensation programs, police victim assistance programs, domestic violence shelters, restitution programs, and sexual abuse treatment and prevention programs (Young & Stein, 2004).

Although the victims' movement in the United States has been thoroughly documented, victims' rights have resonated globally as well. In 1973, a dedicated group of victim advocates and scholars from around the globe assembled in Jerusalem, Israel, for the first International Symposium on Victimology (Drapkin & Viano, 1974). This pivotal event further demonstrated an international awareness of and interest in the victim experience and revitalized advocacy for victims' rights. A broad cross-section of concerned citizens, victim advocates, and feminist leaders began to merge their efforts, forming a number of effective advocacy coalitions. As international pressure grew with respect to concerns about victims and their rights, the United Nations (1985) brought into effect the Declaration of the Basic Principles of Justice for Victims of Crime and Abuse of Power, which identified the need for state action in protecting the rights of victims (TABLE 4-1).

In recognition of the U.N. Declaration, various provincial governments in Canada agreed to the basic principles of justice for victims of crime by enacting victims' rights legislation, beginning with Manitoba's Justice for Victims of Crime Act (1986). The Manitoba legislation included provisions such as crime

TABLE 4-1 United Nations Declaration of the Basic Principles of Justice for Victims of Crime and Abuse of Power

Access to Justice and Fair Treatment
• Victims should be treated with compassion and respect.
• Judicial systems should be established that enable victims to seek redress.
• Victims should be informed.
• Victims' views should be presented and considered.
• Victims should be assisted in the process.
• Privacy and safety should be ensured.
• Informal mechanisms for dispute resolution should be available.

Restitution
• Offenders should be responsible for their behavior and make restitution.
• Governments should consider restitution.
• Where public officials acting in an official capacity violated national laws, victims should receive restitution from the state.

Compensation
• Where compensation is not fully available from the offender, the state should endeavor to provide financial compensation.

Assistance
• Victims should receive material, medical, psychological, and social assistance.
• Police, justice, health, and social service personnel should receive training to sensitize them to the needs of victims.

Data from: United Nations. 1985. *Declaration of Basic Principles of Justice for Victims of Crime and Abuse of Power*. G.A. 40/34, annex, 40 U.N. GAOR Supp.

prevention, mediation, conciliation, and reconciliation procedures as means of assisting victims. By contrast, 10 years later in 1995, Ontario enacted the Victims' Bill of Rights that focused entirely on crime control. Although such differences and others exist, victims' bills of rights throughout Canada generally contain the following rights (Young, 2001):

- To be informed of the final disposition of the case
- To be notified if any court proceeding for which they have received a subpoena will not occur as scheduled
- To receive protection from intimidation

- To be informed of the procedure for receiving witness fees

- To be provided with a secure waiting area (when practical)

- To have personal property in the possession of law enforcement agencies returned as soon as possible

- To be provided with appropriate employer intercessions to minimize loss of pay due to court appearances

Although victims' rights legislation in North America has been viewed by many as a positive step, critics have expressed concern that despite the best intentions, these bills of rights fail to meet the needs of victims for several reasons. For one, there exists no remedy for lack of compliance by law enforcement and the courts with notification requirements. For instance, the Ontario Victims' Bill of Rights (1995) states as follows: "No new cause of action, right of appeal, claim, or other remedy exists in law because of this section or anything done or omitted to be done under this section." This was upheld in an Ontario case in which the judge stated, "I conclude that the legislature did not intend for section 2(1) of the Victims' Bill of Rights to provide rights to the victims of crime . . . they have no claim before the courts because of it" (*Vanscoy and Even v. Her Majesty the Queen in Right of Ontario*, 1999).

Similarly, during the 1980s and 1990s, important legislation was enacted in the United States that expanded victims' rights and allocated critical funding for victim/witness assistance programs, domestic violence shelters, sexual assault treatment and prevention programs, and victim compensation programs. Society's fear of crime, fueled by advances in the women's movement, the report of the President's Task Force on Victims of Crime (1982), the passage of the Federal Victim and Witness Protection Act in 1982, and the **Victims of Crime Act (VOCA)** in 1984, resulted in federal subsidies to state and local victim services, victim compensation, victim/witness assistance, domestic violence programs, and sexual assault prevention programs. The VOCA legislation created a substantial federal fund within the U.S. Treasury accumulated from federal criminal fines, penalties, and asset forfeitures. In 1988, amendments to VOCA required that victim compensation eligibility in all states be extended to include victims of domestic violence and drunk-driving accidents.

During the 1990s, the U.S. federal government and a growing number of states adopted victims' rights legislation. In April 2004, the U.S. Congress enacted the Crime Victims' Rights Act, which identifies the following rights:

- To be reasonably protected from the accused

- To reasonable, accurate, and timely notice of proceedings

- To not be excluded from any such public proceeding
- To be reasonably heard
- To confer with an attorney for the government in the case
- To full and timely restitution as provided by law
- To be free from unreasonable delay

This federal act formed a basis on which many state legislatures moved to expand rights and services for victims of crime with measures that address such things as victim notice, participation, restitution, and compensation. In addition, many states have instituted additional protections for victims of violence. Wisconsin, for instance, prohibits district attorneys and police officers from insisting or suggesting that a victim of sexual violence should submit to a polygraph examination. Colorado allows victims to use pseudonyms and issues orders to protect identity. As of 2007, there were approximately 12,000 victim/witness assistance and service programs, including sexual assault treatment programs, domestic violence shelters, self-help and support groups for families of homicide victims, support groups for abused spouses, and community coalitions and task forces on sexual assault and domestic violence.

While criminal justice and other social service agencies may appear to be responsive to the needs of victims, the lack of *legally enforceable* rights is seen as a major limitation of rights-based victim reform. If agencies fail to adequately meet their service obligations, victims may have little recourse other than lodging complaints, which may only produce further frustrations. Moreover, stringent conditions of eligibility for compensation have meant that only a small proportion of victims end up receiving any compensation (Fattah, 2000). As a consequence of these limitations, some have advocated for a discourse of needs that involves developing more robust systems of victim support. This may include efforts to make victims feel more confident about reporting crimes, to develop stronger systems of victim-centered assistance (e.g., witness care and protection, counseling, etc.), to cater to the needs of those who experience gender- or race-specific victimization, and to foster effective methods of victim healing.

Despite the hurdles faced by victims' rights movements in North America, many laws and policies generated by victim advocacy have made some advancements toward fostering greater inclusion of victims in processes traditionally seen as the exclusive domain of the state and the offender. The following sections describe some of the principles and procedures that have been shaped by this movement.

Restitution

Restitution is the money a judge orders an offender to pay to the victim. It is part of the offender's sentence and is based on the victim's expenses resulting from the crime and the offender's ability to pay. The expenses might include medical/dental expenses, lost wages due to the crime, and stolen or damaged property. Courts in every state have the statutory authority to order restitution, and in more than one-third of all states they are required to do so unless there are compelling or extraordinary circumstances that make this unjust or impossible (Office for Victims of Crimes [OVC], 2002). Nationally, restitution is imposed in about 13% of violent offenses (Ruback & Bergstrom, 2006). Many problems exist with this system however. For instance, research indicates that poor offenders are less likely to be ordered to pay restitution than nonpoor offenders, resulting in an inequity among victims depending on the wealth of their offender. Further, there is ambiguity in many jurisdictions about who is responsible for enforcing restitution orders. Although the U.S. Department of Justice does not oversee the collection of restitution, most Department of Justice compensation programs do have a collections unit that works to recapture claim costs back from offenders and liable third parties. This unit also monitors and collects punitive damage award judgments, which helps fund Department of Justice crime victims programs. To determine the amount of restitution ordered, a copy of the sentencing order includes the time frame in which the defendant is expected to begin making payments.

Victims' Compensation

Although restitution refers to money paid by an offender for the losses and damages incurred by a victim, victims' compensation refers to funds paid by the state to ameliorate the personal costs of crime. Crime victim compensation does not depend on whether the case is charged or if the offender is found guilty. Internationally, the unrelenting advocacy work of Marjory Fry, a Quaker and magistrate, is credited with spearheading the notion of state-funded compensation for victims. Fry succeeded in focusing attention on the inadequacy of court-ordered restitution, where offenders were rarely apprehended or convicted and, when convicted, historically did not have the financial resources available to reasonably compensate a victim (Fry, 1957). This resulted in the first legislation of its kind, the New Zealand Criminal Compensation Act of 1963, followed one year later by similar legislation in England.

In 1965, California led the way for crime victim compensation in the United States by becoming the first state to establish a statewide victim compensation program, with a number of other states quickly following suit with similar legislation: New York in 1966, Hawaii in 1967, and Massachusetts in 1968. The principal objective of these early programs was to establish a system that would enable victims to receive financial compensation for injuries sustained, including ongoing, crime-related medical expenses.

At present, victim compensation in the United States is handled in one of four ways: (1) as a component of victim witness programs, (2) through victim–offender reconciliation programs, (3) in conjunction with parole or probation supervision, or (4) through court-based employment programs (Ruback & Bergstrom, 2006). In most states, victim compensation or restitution programs give victims an opportunity to claim all relevant losses, and usually this is limited to economic losses.

The Crime Victims Fund in the United States was established through the VOCA in 1984. This fund is supported by money collected through criminal fines, forfeited bail bonds, penalties, and special assessments. These funds come entirely from offenders and not from taxpayers. Victims can apply to this fund to cover crime-related medical costs, funeral costs, mental health counseling, or lost wages, which are beyond the costs covered by insurance programs. Maximum awards generally range from $10,000 to $25,000, although some states have different maximums, which may be higher or lower. Generally, victims are required to report the crime within 3 days of the offense and file the claim within 2 years. Despite good intentions, McCormack's study (1989) of the New Jersey Violent Crime Compensation Board revealed that in 1987, as few as 8% of the reported 45,000 violent crime victims had actually filed a compensation claim, leading researchers to conclude there was a need for more claims offices, particularly in high-crime neighborhoods.

In Canada, Alberta developed the first legislation in 1969 that led to the development of a victim compensation program (Young, 2001). However, in 1992, the Canadian federal government discontinued transfer payments for victim compensation, and as a result Newfoundland, the Yukon, and the Northwest Territories abandoned their compensation programs (Roach, 1999). Although in Canada, as in the United States, an award for compensation does not depend on a criminal conviction, in some jurisdictions (Alberta, Ontario, Prince Edward Island [PEI], and Nova Scotia) a claim may be denied or reduced if the victim failed to report the offense within a reasonable time or refused reasonable cooperation with a law enforcement agency. Where eligibility is determined, entitlement is not automatic and falls within the discretionary power of the board. For instance, in determining whether to make an order for compensation, all provinces except Saskatchewan allow the board to consider the behavior of the victim that may have contributed to his or her injury (Regehr & Kanani, 2010). In some circumstances, consideration may also be given to the applicant's character. Awards can include compensation for expenses actually and reasonably incurred, loss due to disability and inability to work, maintenance of a child born due to sexual assault, and pain and suffering (Regehr & Kanani, 2010).

It should be noted that awards made under victim compensation programs are generally perceived to be quite low. However, studies of victims receiving this compensation suggest they view the compensation not as financial assistance or compensation but rather as a public acknowledgment of the harms committed against them (Regehr, Alaggia, Lambert, & Saini, 2008).

The Office for Victims of Crime (OVC) administers funds using a formula from the crime victims fund (CVF) as follows. First, the largest amount of money (approximately $20 million) is allocated to fund child abuse investigation and prosecution. Second, funds are then earmarked to Victim Witness Coordinator positions in U.S. Attorney's Offices ($22 million in 2012). Third, Victim Specialists in the FBI received $16 million in 2012. Fourth, the Victim Notification System received $5 million in 2012. Fifth, for the remaining funds, up to 95 percent is split between state victim compensation grants that reimburse victims and survivors for expenses related to victimization, and victim assistance grants that fund state victim service programs. Finally, the OVC uses the remaining five percent as discretionary grant funds to support training, technical assistance, and demonstration projects (Office of the Inspector General 2013). Federal compensation for victims does not exist except in the event that a U.S. citizen is the victim of terrorism while traveling abroad (National Association of Crime Victim Compensation Boards).

Eligibility for Compensation

The amount of compensation awarded is limited and depends on the category in which the crime falls (e.g., primary, secondary, tertiary). Some have successfully challenged the policy of limiting compensation, as evidenced by the following case reported in *Crime Victim Compensation Quarterly* (2011). In this case, an 11-year-old girl sought compensation as a secondary victim to crime. The girl was on a school bus when a fellow student was stabbed and then collapsed, bleeding, on the claimant's lap. The state compensation program provided funding for up to $1,000 for counseling to people "exposed" to crimes who were not the subject of an attack themselves. However, the girl remained in counseling for 5 years at the expense of $20,000. Her lawyer argued that the girl should be treated as a "primary victim," eligible for the program's full maximum of $35,000.

Discussion surrounding this case focused on whether the girl should be treated as "primary" or "secondary" under state law. A group of advisors approached by the *Crime Victim Compensation Quarterly* stated that the primary consideration should be whether the girl was in a "zone of danger"; that is, in reasonable fear for her own safety because of the proximity of the attack. They argued that the case should consider that the girl was trapped on the bus, had no route of escape, and thus faced possible harm herself. Most victim compensation programs do not have a special category for witnesses, so the choice for the program administrator was to either to deny the claim because the girl was not the direct victim or to find a way to consider her a primary victim. Most of the advisors consulted argued that given these facts she should be considered a primary victim (*Crime Victim Compensation Quarterly*, 2011).

Costs of Victim Compensation

U.S. compensation programs spent a record combined total of $499.9 million in state and federal funds in federal fiscal year 2010. The amount was 16% more than was spent in 2005 and almost 72% more than in 2000, when spending was under $300 million. Over the same period the number of violent crimes went down 12.5%, as measured by the FBI's Uniform Crime Reports (UCR), from 1,425,486 in 2000 to 1,390,745 in 2005, and an estimated preliminary figure of around 1,250,000 violent crimes in 2010 (a remarkable 5% drop from 2009's 1,318,398). Thus, a 12.5% drop in the number of violent crimes corresponded with a 67% increase in compensation claims. This increase reflects larger numbers of compensation claims, inflation in medical costs, and new eligible benefits, including forensic exam payments and domestic violence relocation (*Crime Victim Compensation Quarterly*, 2011). More recent numbers from 2013 to 2014 show that 275,470 victims received compensation payments totaling over $750 million in federal and state funding (Office for Victims of Crime, 2015a).

Innovative Compensation Laws

As society encounters new types of crimes, legislation is written to deal legally with the offender. One such example is dealing with pimps of teenage prostitutes. A bill drafted in December 2008 by Assemblyman John Hambrick of Las Vegas directed proceeds from convicted pimps to fund a shelter for underage prostitutes. Data indicated that every Wednesday morning for 28 months, 385 teenage prostitutes between the ages of 12 and 15 appeared in District

Judge William Voy's court where they received minor sentences. Voy called the teenagers a unique kind of victim in that they did not realize they were victims but rather developed a form of Stockholm syndrome whereby they believed the pimp was their friend. In the Hambrick bill, 60% of funds raised by the forfeitures would go to the district attorney's office to help prosecute pimps and 40% would go toward a secure facility to provide safe housing and psychological services for the teens. This bill was modeled after laws used to confiscate assets of drug dealers (Hambrick, 2011).

9/11 U.S. Compensation Fund

In response to the overwhelming needs of those who lost family members and victims who survived the 9/11 attacks, the September 11th Victim Compensation Fund was created by an Act of Congress, the Air Transportation Safety and System Stabilization Act (49 USC 40101). The act sought to compensate the victims of the attack (or their families) in exchange for their agreement not to sue the airlines involved. Kenneth Feinberg was appointed by Attorney General John Ashcroft to be special master of the fund. He worked for 33 months pro bono and developed the regulations governing the administration of the fund and also administered all aspects of the program. After an application for compensation, an offer was made to each family who lost someone in the 9/11 attacks and each victim based on an estimate of how much each victim would have earned in a full lifetime (on average this was $1.8 million). If a family accepted the offer, it was not possible to appeal. Families unhappy with the offer were able to appeal in a nonadversarial, informal hearing to present their case however they wanted. In the end, 7,300 claims for death and injury were received, representing 98% of families who experienced loss for a total of $7 billion (U.S. Government Benefits Help, 2011).

In addition to the 9/11 fund, the U.S. government has developed a support program for all victims of terrorism. Kathryn Turman, program director of the FBI Office for Victim Assistance, described the program's work (Turman, 2004). The 56 FBI field offices have a total of 122 full-time victim specialist positions, in addition to 20 staff at the main office at FBI headquarters, who oversee all programs and positions and provide support and assistance to them. The FBI Victim Assistance Program has also provided services to victims of bank robberies, kidnappings, aviation accidents, and the shootings at Virginia Tech and at Red Lake reservation in Minnesota. It also assisted in the aftermath of Hurricane Katrina, providing support not only for federal employees but also working side by side with the Red Cross. TABLE 4-2 shows the services provided for federal terrorism cases.

TABLE 4-2 FBI Victim Assistance Programs for Terrorism Cases

Tasks and Issues	Action
Notification of death or injury of U.S. citizens within the first few hours	Victim assistants will reach out to the family, offer condolences, and provide information on what will happen next and why and what help they can expect from the FBI.
Managing deaths that have occurred overseas	Responsible for transporting the victim's remains back to the United States, coordinating the autopsy (which is necessary for the investigation), collecting dental records and DNA from family members, and making arrangements for the final journey home.
Managing personal effects and death certificates	Provide comfort and support. One letter from the 7-year-old son of a terrorism victim: "Thank you for bringing my Daddy home," he wrote. "Thank you for sending Ms. B_____ to give me my Daddy's jewelry. I didn't get to say goodbye to him on the phone but I got to say goodbye at the church."
Survivors need information provided from an official source	The FBI will continue to keep survivors informed no matter how many years an investigation may last.
9/11 terrorist attack had strong assistance from the PENTTBOM team of investigators	Worked with over 10,000 victims and family members of the 9/11 attacks, created a special informational webpage for families as well as a toll-free number and Internet address where they could directly reach the FBI.
Lessons learned	Rights and needs of victims must be built into our response to terrorism from the beginning.
Systems in place	Need to provide ongoing information and answer difficult questions, and help survivors find assistance resources regardless of how many victims there are and where they live.
Terrorism is now a part of our daily reality	Must never forget that the impact on individuals and families lasts long after the crime scenes have been cleared; memorials, erected; and perpetrators, tried and sentenced.

Data from: Roberts, A. R. 1990. *Helping Crime Victims: Research, Policy, and Practice.* Thousand Oaks, CA: Sage Publications.

Restorative Justice

Processes of offender–victim mediation have become an increasingly accepted form of resolution in the aftermath of victimization. Although defined in various ways, the central features of restorative justice include processes of dialogue, mutual understanding, and healing between offenders, victims, and the wider community. For victims, processes of restorative justice provide an avenue for greater participation in the criminal justice process by allowing them to express to the offending party the impacts and consequences of their victimization. They may also wish to gain a greater insight into motivations related to the offense, while giving the opportunity to offenders to express remorse and apologize for harms inflicted. For offenders, restorative justice allows for the making of amends through the expression of remorse and guilt, the acknowledgment of harms caused, the demonstration of accountability for their actions, and the attempt to repair damage done. If successful, the process may provide some form of closure to victims and facilitate reintegration of the offender back into the community (Dignan, 2005). Restorative justice processes can take several forms, including direct and indirect mediation between offenders and victims, family group conferencing, community conferencing, restitution panels, sentencing circles, and reparation orders.

One of the first restorative justice programs was developed in Ontario, Canada, in 1974 and sponsored by the Mennonite Church, though the principles of restorative justice date back to ancient Arab, Greek, and Roman civilizations (Braithwaite, 2002). Many modern principles of these programs reflect the diversity of Aboriginal traditions, including the concept of healing circles, and there have been increasing efforts to integrate restorative justice practices into Aboriginal communities. The efficacy of restorative justice approaches can be measured in several ways. With regard to recidivism, several meta-analyses have shown that offenders exposed to restorative justice programs are less likely to offend compared to controls, but this varies significantly according to the type of crime (Bonta, Jesseman, Rugge, & Cormier, 2006; Bradshaw, Roseborough, & Umbreit, 2006). In addition, restorative justice conferences have been deemed to be a highly cost-effective means of reducing repeat offending (Sherman, Strang, Mayo-Wilson et al., 2015). According to a meta-analysis by Latimer, Dowden, and Muise (2005), these programs are also an effective method of improving victim and offender satisfaction with the criminal justice process and increasing offender compliance with restitution obligations. Restorative justice presents a promising alternative to the traditional methods encompassed in the adversarial system of justice: one that strives less for retribution and attempts to repair relations between offenders, victims, and communities.

Victims' Rights and the Courts

Victim Impact Statements

Courts have traditionally not allowed victims to participate in the sentencing process. In 1982, for instance, in Canada, Justice McLachlin, in denying a victim's request to have input into the sentencing of an offender, concluded that crime victims have no standing under the Criminal Code. Similarly, considerable concern has existed in the United States that victim presence will interfere with the process of justice. Nevertheless, victim impact statements were first introduced in the United States in the mid-1970s, and by the end of the 1990s they were admissible in 49 states. Some states provide additional measures regarding victim impact statements. Illinois requires that any written statement submitted to the state attorney be considered by the courts. Virginia ensures that victim impact statements are heard by the courts after any guilty finding or plea bargain that accepts guilt. Mississippi has enshrined a right that allows victims to make oral and written statements to the presiding judge.

Case law in the United States has similarly underlined the important role of victim impact statements. The case of *R. v. Jacob* (2002) involved a horrific crime of home invasion in the middle of the night, whereby the victim's hands, feet, and face were bound, her hair cut by use of a knife, and multiple physical and sexual assaults were perpetrated. The victim impact statement was read in court. Sentencing judge Stuart Barry in his judgment emphasized four contributions of victim impact statements:

- *Fostering experience of justice.* Victims must be able to participate in the decision-making process of sentencing in a manner that is meaningful to and needed by them. Although it is necessary to leave the ultimate responsibility for the decision with the court and to retain the primacy of the state voice in sentencing, the victim must be afforded a meaningful opportunity to participate if justice, as well as law, is to be served.

- *Making offenders aware.* Offenders are rarely exposed to the tragedies they cause. If offenders can avoid exposure to the pain they cause, they can cling to their rationalizations for crime. Offenders immersed in the gamelike nature of the adversarial system need to confront the human dimensions of their actions.

- *Measuring the severity of crime.* In addressing many of the sentencing principles, the court must be acutely aware of the specific impacts of the crime on victims and on the community. After hearing the legal facts surrounding numerous crimes; after reading numerous presentence reports and psychological assessments, victim impact statements, and various supporting documents; and after listening to countless submissions from counsel, judges may not fully appreciate the uniqueness of each case if the victim's voice is left out.

- *Community awareness.* The community must hear from the victim. Crime, in many ways, isolates a victim from the community. Communities need to hear from the victim to be fully cognizant of what needs to be done in the community to prevent similar acts and to know what is needed to support this survivor and other victims and survivors.

Although victim impact statements have been around for a considerable period of time, their use remains limited. For instance, the government of Canada introduced victim impact statements as part of the revisions to the Criminal Code of Canada in 1988, yet a study published in 1992 determined that in British Columbia victim impact statements were obtained in only 2% to 6% of cases and filed into court in only 1% to 2% of cases. It has been suggested that this, in part, is due to the reluctance of victims to expose their suffering to adversarial challenge (Roberts, 1992). Another study found that between 14% and 18% of victims expressed concerns about participating in preparing impact statements, fearing retribution from the offender and/or his friends (Giliberti, 1991). Similarly, in a U.S. study conducted before the 2004 legislation, it was found that less than 18% of victims or families attended sentencing, only 15% prepared written statements, and only 9% were permitted oral submissions (Finn-DeLuca, 1994).

Victim impact statements are generally prepared statements detailing physical, psychological, financial, and social harms the victim suffered as a result of a crime committed against them. These statements, either in oral or written form, are presented to the sentencing judge after the defendant has been proven guilty in the sentencing phase of the trial (Garkawe, 2007). A family member or other individual may deliver the statement if the victim, such as a child or a homicide victim, is incapable of doing so (Englebrecht, 2011). Impact statements may also be subject to varying degrees of regulation regarding who may testify to the impact of the crime, the content of the impact statement, the number of individuals allowed to speak, the degree of opinionated narratives, and the nature of the discussion in which the statement is shared (Englebrecht, 2011).

Victim support groups have argued that victim impact statements benefit victims by increasing their recognition in the criminal justice system, increasing their satisfaction with the sentencing process, and increasing their cooperation with the system (Garkawe, 2007). In addition, these statements may reveal harms suffered by the victim that were not otherwise apparent to the judge, especially in cases where a guilty plea has been issued, resulting in a limited amount of evidence. According to Trueblood (2011), "victim impact statements provide a way for victims of crime to participate in the criminal justice system process and allow the victims to help focus the court on the human costs of crime" (p. 616).

However, there have been conflicting views on whether victim impact statements should be accepted as evidence and whether they should have any influence on sentencing decisions. According to section 718.1 of the Criminal Code of Canada, "a sentence must be proportionate to the gravity of the offense and the degree of responsibility of the offender" (Criminal Code of Canada, 1985). It is clear that the impact of a crime on the victim is relevant to the seriousness of the crime. However, among many other sentencing factors that are considered during the sentencing process, harms identified in the victim impact statement may play a relatively small role in determining the offender's punishment (Garkawe, 2007). Some empirical research has shown that "in a vast majority of cases the use of VIS [victim impact statement] had no effect on the final result" of sentencing decisions (Garkawe, 2007, p. 107). In their study of impact statements in 500 felony cases, Erez and Tontodonato (1990) concluded that victim impact statements do not have an impact on the length of sentences; nevertheless, they do have some impact on the nature of the sentence. That is, whether an offender is sentenced to incarceration or probation is to some degree influenced by the victim impact statement. However, they conclude that the nature of the crime and the character of the offender continue to be the primary considerations (Erez & Tontodonato, 1990).

A cited reason for using victim impact statements is so victims have the opportunity to have their voices heard. Research conducted by Regehr and colleagues (2008) found that those victims who were able to present their victim impact statement in court felt empowered and positive about the experience. However, those who were not able to read their statement for such reasons as the offender pled guilty or there was a plea bargain felt cheated by the process. Researchers concluded that completing a victim impact statement neither necessarily leads to victim satisfaction nor increases a victim's willingness to cooperate with systems in the future (Young, 2001). Rather, satisfaction depends on whether the statement is considered and acknowledged by the judge and the degree to which the victims continued to be informed of the process.

National Victim Information and Notification Everyday Program

The **Victim Information and Notification Everyday (VINE) Program** is a national initiative that enables victims of domestic violence or other indictable crimes to access reliable information about criminal cases and custody status of offenders 24 hours a day—via phone, Internet, or email. Through VINE, victims can register to be notified immediately in the event of their offender's release, escape, transfer, or court appearance. Currently available in over 2,100 communities across the United States, including most large metropolitan areas, the VINE program has been able to successfully provide a certain degree of comfort and peace of mind to crime victims and their families.

Services for Victims

Victim services have risen exponentially over the past 40 years. For instance, in the United States, the **National Organization for Victim Assistance (NOVA)** was established in 1975 as a national umbrella organization dedicated to expanding current victim services, developing new programs, and supporting passage of victims' rights legislation. In addition to this vital work, NOVA also serves as a conduit of information and technical assistance for local and regional victim assistance programs (NOVA, 1983).

In 1988, through an amendment to the 1984 VOCA, the federal Office for Victims of Crimes (OVC) was formally established. An official agency of the U.S. Department of Justice, the OVC is an important resource for crime victims and the service organizations charged with assisting them. Its mission, according to the OVC website (www.ovc.gov) is "to oversee diverse programs that benefit victims of crime. The OVC provides substantial funding to state victim assistance and compensation programs and supports training designed to educate criminal justice and allied professionals regarding the rights and needs of crime victims" (OVC, 1988). The OVC offers a vast array of tools and resources for service providers, including funding, research, training and technical assistance, maintenance of an extensive list of relevant publications, and coordination of the National Calendar of Crime Victim Assistance–Related Events, a leading resource for locating and promoting events that address crime victims' rights and services, where users can search or submit events for free. In addition to NOVA and OVC, which offer a broad range of services to victims of many types of crime, other services exist that target people who have encountered specific types of victimization such as rape and intimate partner violence.

Women's Movement and Services for Rape Victims

In the early 1970s, when police departments and rape crisis centers first began to address the crime of rape, little was known about rape victims or sex offenders. Feminist groups had just begun to raise the issue of rape, and in 1971, the New York Speak-Out on Rape event was held, drawing widespread attention to sexual violence. Contemporary feminists who raised the issue early were Susan Griffin (1971) in her now classic article on rape as the "all-American" crime, and Germaine Greer (1973) in her essay on "grand rapes" (legalistically defined) and "petty rapes" (everyday sexual rip-offs). Susan Brownmiller (1975) wrote about the history of rape and urged people to deny its future.

The general public was not particularly concerned about rape victims; very few academic publications or special services existed; funding agencies did not see the topic as important; and health policy was almost nonexistent. But by 1972, the anti-rape movement began to attract women from all walks of life and political persuasions. Various strategies began to emerge, particularly the self-help program now widely known as the "rape crisis center." One of the first such centers was founded in Berkeley in early 1972, known as Bay Area Women Against Rape. Within months of the opening of the Berkeley center, similar centers were established in Ann Arbor, Michigan; Washington, DC; and Philadelphia, Pennsylvania. Concurrently, hospital-based rape counseling services began in Boston and in Minneapolis. Soon, centers replicated and services flourished. Although volunteer ranks tended to include a large number of university students and instructors, they also included homemakers and working women. The volunteer makeup usually reflected every age, race, socioeconomic class, sexual preference, and level of political consciousness. Volunteers were, however, exclusively women. Among the women, the most common denominators were a commitment to aiding victims and to bringing about social change (Largen, 1985).

THE "SECOND ASSAULT": EARLY RESPONSE BY THE SYSTEM TO RAPE VICTIMS

The rape crisis centers provided victims with the support and counseling that enabled them to move through the traumatizing experience of rape, both mentally and emotionally. However, rape survivors would often experience victim-blaming treatment from system personnel that would often worsen the victim's physical and mental distress. Additionally, the physical ordeal of the medical exam and subsequent investigation could often be a humiliating and dehumanizing experience for the victim. These post-assault experiences, which became known as the "second assault," consisted of a series of uncomfortable experiences after their victimization. First, rape victims were traditionally seen in the emergency department by male physicians and generalist nurses, who often lacked the time and experience to do a thorough examination of the victim that would assist law enforcement and prosecutors. Rape victims were not a high priority for emergency care, and even when medical needs were satisfied, their emotional needs were not. Before the sexual assault nurse examiner (SANE) programs, medical staffs had an image of the "real" rape victim and much energy went into determining the "legitimacy" of the rape case (i.e., was the victim really raped?). Rape victims often felt depersonalized, lost, and neglected.

Second, the environment of the emergency department and needs of the victim were often at odds. Many victims complained about the long wait, having to wait alone, a lack of privacy, and not being informed of exam results. Rape victims were not a priority with emergency department physicians. Physicians were reluctant to do the rape examination because they lacked experience and training in forensic evidence collection and because they were vulnerable to being subpoenaed and required to testify. Physicians were able to examine the victim's body for bruises and prepare slides to look for sperm and other biological evidence; however, they were often unaware of the procedures for collecting biological evidence. Medical staff often lacked knowledge as to how to preserve evidence on clothing and other biological evidence such as hair samples and fingernail scrapings that may have been left by an assailant. Continuity of care was also lacking. Medical providers did not communicate with each other, so victims returning for follow-up care found it difficult to be asked again by new people why they needed medical attention.

Finally, documentation collected on the victim would often include damning information, such as prior sexual experience, or phrases that included judgmental statements about the victim. Medical records were also found to be illegible. Ultimately, victims were left on their own to cope financially, legally, and emotionally with the aftermath of the crime (Holmstrom & Burgess, 1983).

SANE-SART: PAST AND PRESENT

It was against this backdrop of problems that prompted communities throughout the United States to involve nurses in the care of the sexual assault victim. Nurses, medical professionals, counselors, and advocates working with rape victims agreed that services provided to sexual assault victims in the emergency department were inadequate when compared to the standard of care given to other patients (Ledray, 1999). Thus, SANE programs and sexual assault response teams (SARTs) emerged in the 1970s, with the first SANE program in Tennessee. SANE programs were created whereby specially trained forensic nurses provide 24-hour coverage as first-response care to adult and adolescent sexual assault victims in emergency departments and nonhospital settings (Campbell, Townsend, Long, & Kinnison, 2005).

Nurses have always cared for patients who have been victims of violence. However, it was not until the 20th century that forensic nursing was recognized as an emerging specialty area of contemporary nursing practice. Forensic nursing history has been traced to the 18th century when midwives were called into court to testify on issues pertaining to virginity, pregnancy, and rape. Clinical forensic nursing practice focuses on the collection of evidence from living patients who have been victims of crimes or traumatic injuries. The forensic and clinical training SANEs receive prepare them to care for victims of crime who have needs for crisis intervention and physical and emotional care often within an emergency department. SANE programs have grown in number, and many are still reaching maturity. Ciancone, Wilson, Collette, and Gerson (2000) conducted a survey of SANE programs in the United States. Of the 58 programs that responded, 55% had been in existence for fewer than 5 years and 16% had been in existence for more than 10 years. Campbell and colleagues (2005) surveyed SANE programs and reported on the rapid growth of programs; 58% had emerged within the past 5 years. Trends noted included newer programs created through a joint task force or through collaboration with other community groups, more diverse funding available as opposed to using hospital funds, and significantly larger programs with more staff and serving more patients, which reflected organizational growth.

SANE programs soon became an integral part of a team of primary and secondary responders known as a SART, which included law enforcement, detectives, victim advocates, and healthcare providers. The main goal of a SART is to assist the sexual assault victim through the criminal justice process. The second goal is to increase the odds of successful prosecution by enhancing evidence collection and facilitating communication among all parties in the process. The third goal is to help victims recover and cope from their experience through counseling and support (Girardin, 2005; Wilson & Klein, 2005). Recent assessments of SANE programs are mixed, but some studies have shown that patients perceive these programs to be beneficial and help with processes of healing and empowerment (e.g., see Campbell, Greeson, Bybee, Kennedy, & Patterson, 2011). Other studies suggest that SANE programs may also facilitate sexual assault case progression and may potentially increase prosecution rates via expert testimony and collection of forensic evidence (Campbell et al., 2014).

Domestic Violence and Intimate Partner Violence Services

A distinct victim classification is found among women who are physically and/or emotionally abused by their spouse or intimate partner, abuse that is often long term and sometimes fatal. Estimates indicate that approximately 8.7 million women are battered by their current or former intimate partners each year (Roberts, 2007; Roberts & Roberts, 2005), and an extensive survey conducted in 2005 focused specifically on programs for battered women and their children

(Roberts, Robertiello, & Bender, 2007). According to a survey conducted by the National Coalition Against Domestic Violence (2015), one in five women and one in seven men have been severely physically abused by an intimate partner, with intimate partner violence accounting for 15% of all violent crime. The notion of tailoring victim services specifically for women experiencing intimate partner abuse took hold in the late 1970s, in the wake of wide-ranging legislation. In the beginning, domestic violence shelters served primarily as temporary "safe havens" for women and children in the throes of violent domestic crisis, but by the mid-1990s, a substantial number of shelters had gone beyond simply providing emergency shelter to implementing more comprehensive services, including counseling, legal advocacy, and job placement. With regard to program administration, the intimate partner violence movement has matured from a grassroots movement of paraprofessionals and former abused women to one of trained professional social workers and counselors, many of whom have bachelor's and/or master's degrees (Roche & Sadoski, 1996).

By 1989, 48 states had provisions for the funding of domestic violence intervention programs, 34 states had funding mechanisms in place for general victim service and witness assistance programs at the local level, and 25 states had provided funding for local sexual assault crisis services. Money for such services was garnered through a variety of sources, including alcohol taxes, notoriety-for-profit laws, bail forfeiture, state income tax checkoffs, surcharges on criminal fines, variable penalty assessments levied by judges on convicted felons, and fixed penalty assessments on convicted offenders of criminal offenses and/or traffic offenses.

By the end of the 20th century, the intimate partner violence movement had become well established in terms of funding and staffing, with approximately 1,250 domestic violence shelters in operation throughout the United States and Canada (Roberts, 1990). By the early 21st century, police departments throughout the United States had made major progress in implementing mandatory and pro-arrest intimate partner violence policies and procedures (Roberts & Kurst-Swanger, 2002). With the passage of civil and criminal statutes to protect abused women in all 50 states, police administrators, police officers, and policy makers have become more sensitive and responsive to victims of intimate partner violence. All 50 states and most highly populated cities and counties throughout the United States have implemented mandatory and warrantless arrest laws, in which either some evidence of probable cause or a copy of a temporary or permanent restraining/protective order is all that is needed. In addition, police dispatchers, police officers, and investigators are responding quickly and efficiently to intimate partner violence calls (Roberts & Kurst-Swanger, 2002).

The latest developments within law enforcement agencies are specialized intimate partner violence and crisis intervention units. These include police social worker teams as well as police–crisis worker teams. Such teams can be found in Arizona, California, Florida, Georgia, Illinois, Maryland, Massachusetts, Michigan, Missouri, New Jersey, New York, North Carolina, Ohio, Pennsylvania, South Carolina, Tennessee, Texas, Virginia, Washington, and Wisconsin.

Although the intimate partner violence movement has made, and continues to make, great strides, a number of categories of women remain underserved in many of the states surveyed. The most frequently noted categories included non–English-speaking (and/or undocumented), rurally based, those with mental health issues, gay/lesbian/bisexual/transgender, those with cultural/racial issues, the elderly, children, and the disabled.

Comprehensive Continuum of Services for Crime Victims

Arlene Bower Andrews (1992), building on the victim assistance program guides outlined by the NOVA and the OVC, developed a step-by-step description of victim services. Her continuum focused on the specific role and functions of victim advocates and social workers, including crime prevention, early intervention and risk reduction, crisis intervention, recovery assistance, collaboration, and advocacy. Prevention is proactive and focuses on competence building and empowerment of individuals, including promoting basic life skills such as communication, problem-solving, and stress reduction. Community prevention activities include neighborhood crime watch programs, graffiti and trash removal, and school–police liaison programs. Risk reduction strategies include considerable increase in street lighting, video surveillance cameras, alarms, fences, and/or open building designs in high-crime areas. Recovery assistance includes medical assistance, mental health treatment, and social services ranging from court transportation assistance, case management, home care and emergency food assistance, and services for disabled crime victims with special needs.

CRIMINAL JUSTICE ADVOCACY

Criminal justice assistance for crime victims may well be comprehensive and include police investigation, victim/witness notification of court hearings, witness preparation, help completing and expediting restitution and compensation claims, and so on. Collaboration involves interagency assessment and treatment planning, weekly interagency case analysis, joint staff training, and interagency purchase agreements. Advocacy includes individual case advocacy, group advocacy, community advocacy, and legislative advocacy. More specifically, victim advocates may be involved in advocating for housing rental assistance or emergency food assistance one day and lobbying with legislative aides and legislators the next day for new legislation to provide increased funding and resources to vulnerable victims of violent crimes.

The National Coalition Against Domestic Violence (NCADV), established in 1978 as an alliance of state coalitions and emergency shelters, consists of a representative from each state (Roche & Sadoski, 1996). The NCADV and the 50 statewide domestic violence coalitions lobby and advocate for improved social services and legal rights for battered women and their children. The NCADV (http://www.ncadv.org) is a nationwide organization of intimate partner violence advocates; self-identified formerly battered women; professional social workers, nurses, and attorneys; and service providers and lobbyists. Its mission includes coalition building on the local, state, and national levels; its board of directors represents local and state coalitions as well as diverse groups of women affected by intimate partner violence (Brownell & Roberts, 2002). The coalition not only serves as a national toll-free information and referral center but also has an active public policy office in Washington, DC, that lobbies Congress, monitors state and federal legislative developments, and advises grassroots organizations on legislative developments.

The National Network to End Domestic Violence (NNEDV), established in 1990, is another membership and advocacy organization of state domestic violence coalitions. Similar to its sister organization the NCADV, the NNEDV provides assistance with coalition building and advocacy to strengthen the responsiveness of federal public policies that concern vulnerable battered women and their children. "The NNEDV developed domestic violence policy that was instrumental in the drafting of the VAWA 1994 legislation. The national network has been successful in having the federal funding appropriation for intimate partner violence coalitions and programs raised from $20 million to almost $90 million between 1995 and 2000" (Brownell & Roberts, 2002, pp. 86–87). The network views itself as the voice of domestic violence advocates before Congress, the executive branch, state legislative bodies and committees, and the courts (Brownell & Roberts, 2002).

VICTIM SERVICES AND WITNESS ASSISTANCE

The history of victim services and witness assistance begins in the mid-1970s. By the end of the decade, Viano (1979) counted 265 such programs. Victim/witness assistance programs were usually located either within the local county prosecutor's offices, the county court house, or adjacent to the court building.

These programs were designed to encourage witness cooperation in the filing of criminal charges as well as testifying in court. In general, these programs included a witness notification and case monitoring system in which staff kept witnesses advised of indictment, continuances, and postponements; specific trial and hearing dates; negotiated pleas; and trial outcomes. In addition, many of these programs provided secure and comfortable reception rooms for witnesses waiting to testify, transportation services, and an escort to accompany the witness to court and to remain with that individual to explain and interpret the court proceedings. Typically, these programs also prepared and distributed court-orientation pamphlets about the adjudication process, with titles such as "Crime Victims' Bill of Rights," "Witness Guidelines for Courtroom Testimony," "What You Should Know About Your Criminal Court and the Court Process," and "Information Guide for Crime Victims."

A full array of services was not available even in the 1990s. According to a national organizational survey of victim service and witness assistance programs (Roberts, 1990), slightly under one-third of these programs reported having childcare available for the children of victims and witnesses while parents testified in court. Criminal justice agencies often remained unaware of the impact of victimization on the children of victims and witnesses, in particular a victim/parent's emotional reactions, losses, physical injuries, and disruptions. Victim/witness assistance programs needed to be concerned with the special needs of children not only because many parent witnesses would not be able to testify if they couldn't find adequate child care during a traumatizing court ordeal, but, more important, because it was the humane thing to do. Additionally, some children may have witnessed the crime and could provide additional identifying characteristics of the perpetrator (Roberts, 1990). The deficiencies in services began to be addressed as studies provided evidence-based information.

In 1981, the first national survey of victim service and witness assistance programs was published by Albert Roberts, examining patterns of program development and the state-of-the-art in victim services, based on 184 responding programs. Survey results indicated availability of a broad range of services that have continued into the 21st century and are identified in TABLE 4-3. In addition to these core services, approximately three-fourths of survey respondents were able to provide legal advocacy for clients, two-thirds offered services for the disabled, and one-third had bilingual counselors available. Forms of assistance less likely to be available in the early history of victim services included batterer intervention, crime scene advocacy, and transitional housing, whereas important services such as medical advocacy, employment or financial

TABLE 4-3 Services Offered by Victim Service and Witness Assistance Programs

Crisis intervention	This service is offered in the immediate days or weeks following a victimizing experience. The goal is to reduce the acute trauma symptoms.
24-hour hotline	This service is available to anyone telephoning in to report or require assistance as a victim or the witnessing of a crime.
Assistance with the court process	Trained staff focus on the victim to explain the various aspects of the court process and provide a bridge between the victim and court.
Assistance with completing victim compensation forms	Trained staff explain the various victim compensation forms and can help with filling out of the forms, especially if the victim has any type of disability.
Court advocacy	A member of a victim crisis center acts as an advocate to the victim by explaining the court process and accompanying the victim to court. Child care is provided wherever possible.
Shelter	Crisis centers have lists of shelters where victims of violence and their children may live safely for a short time.
Referral to a mental health agency	Crisis intervention staff have a list of therapists for victims who need more than crisis care. A referral list for offenders is also available.
Transportation to court	Advocacy staff will transport victims to court.
Public education	An important part of crisis services is to educate the public on crime and victimization. The education is conducted in schools, community groups, and to healthcare and law enforcement groups.

Data from Roberts, A. R. 1990. *Helping Crime Victims: Research, Policy, and Practice*. Thousand Oaks, CA: Sage Publications.

aid, elder abuse assistance, and youth education and mentoring were, proportionately speaking at that time, almost nonexistent.

Programs for victims have proliferated but still cannot meet the need for such services. In 2014, Family Violence Prevention & Services Programs (FVPSP) grantees reported 196,467 unmet requests for shelter—a 13% increase over those reported in 2010. This represents a count of the number of unmet requests for shelter due to programs being at capacity (Family Violence Prevention & Services Program, Family & Youth Services Bureau, 2015).

Evaluating Victim Assistance Programs

Between 2010 and 2012, the Office of Victims of Crime (OVC) funded Vision 21 projects whose objectives were to examine the existing framework of the victim assistance field nationwide and explore new and existing challenges facing the field. Data for the report included a review of the research literature and a series of five stakeholder forums. These projects were able to engage a broad spectrum of stakeholders that included service providers, advocates, criminal justice professionals, allied practitioners, and policy makers with the goal to discover crime victim issues through a lens broader than their everyday work (OVC, 2015b).

The Vision 21: Transforming Victim Services was the first major evaluation in 15 years, with the goal of transforming the treatment of crime victims in the United States. It recognized that practitioners in the victims of crime field, which began as a transformative movement, would not be content with maintaining the status quo or a less than bold exploration of the issues. To that end, Vision 21: Transforming Victim Services Final Report discusses the following (OVC, 2015b):

- Challenges in integrating research into victim services.
- Availability of legal assistance for crime victims to help them address the wide range of legal issues that can arise following victimization.
- Impacts of advances in technology, globalization, and changing demographics on the victim assistance field.
- The capacity for serving victims and infrastructure issues that must be overcome to reach that capacity.

In addition, the report outlined recommendations for bringing about this transformation, which are summarized in four broad categories (OVC, 2015b):

1. Conducting continuous rather than episodic strategic planning in the victim assistance field to effect real change in research, policy, programming, and capacity building.

2. Supporting research to build a body of evidence-based knowledge and generate, collect, and analyze quantitative and qualitative data on victimization, emerging victimization trends, services and behaviors, and victims' rights enforcement efforts.

3. Ensuring the statutory, policy, and programmatic flexibility to address enduring and emerging crime victim issues.

4. Building and institutionalizing capacity through an infusion of technology, training, and innovation to ensure that the field is equipped to meet the demands of the 21st century.

Code of Ethics for Victim Services

Concerns have been raised at times about the oversight of victim services and the degree to which they adhere to a common set of ethical principles and professional standards. As a result the Canadian Department of Justice undertook a project to identify what jurisdictions had codes of ethics for their victim services providers and to identify and compare the common elements present in these codes, as well as in the development of these codes (McGibbon, 2011). The study identified great variations in practice across Western nations but nevertheless identified some common themes and issues across jurisdictions:

- *Striking a balance between respecting the voice of victims and protecting clients.* Clients have the right to choose services that meet their needs and to refuse service, even if such refusal may increase the risk of danger. For instance, a victim of intimate partner violence may refuse to enter a shelter and may instead decide to return home.

- *Providing information to clients.* This includes not only information about the rights of victims and services available, but also information about the limits of confidentiality, such as when might their statements be subpoenaed into court.

- *Providing safe space.* Including both physically and psychologically safe space, and as well as safeguarding their identity from the public and media, as necessary.

- *Ensuring the safety of children.* Despite concerns for confidentiality, service providers must report child abuse and neglect to appropriate authorities.

- *Maintaining professional boundaries.* Service providers must ensure they do not establish personal or sexual relationships with clients.

- *Providing advocacy.* Victim service providers see their responsibility not only to the individual victim, but also to provide advocacy to improve the services for all victims.

Psychological Response to Victimization

The traumatic memories that haunt people after experiencing overwhelming terror has been a theme in literature from Homer to Shakespeare's *Macbeth* Act V, iii. By the late 1850s, Briquet suggested a link between the symptoms of hysteria and childhood histories of trauma (Mai & Merksey, 1980). During this time, a small Anglo-Saxon literature emerged documenting responses to accidents (e.g., "railway spine" after train accidents) and war trauma ("soldier's heart").

The relationship between trauma and psychiatric illness, however, began to be explored only in the last two decades of the 19th century when neurologist Charcot lectured on the functional effects of trauma on behavior (see a review by van der Kolk, 1994). Charcot's student, Pierre Janet, undertook one of the first systematic studies of the relationship between trauma and psychiatric symptoms and delivered a major paper at the Harvard Medical School in 1906 (van der Kolk, Brown, & van der Hart, 1989). Janet realized that different temperaments predisposed people to deal with trauma with different coping styles. He coined the term *subconscious* to describe the collection of memories that form the mental schemes that include the person's interaction with the environment. He suggested it was the interplay of memory systems and temperament that made each person unique and complex (van der Kolk et al., 1989).

Similarly, Freud, in one of his earliest published works, *Studies in Hysteria*, suggested the concept of "anxiety neurosis" or "hysteria" in which a horrific psychological event leads to physical consequences (Breuer & Freud, 1895). He later shifted from a trauma-related paradigm of neurosis to a paradigm that centered on intrapsychic fantasy. In a later work, *Beyond the Pleasure Principle*, he once again addressed the issue of traumatic neurosis and looked at trauma as disequilibrium (Freud, 1961).

Posttraumatic Stress Disorder

The history of the development of trauma theory was intensified around war and combat stress during both the First and Second World Wars. However, despite such recognition systematic inquiry into the phenomenon of posttraumatic stress was remarkably late in coming. Indeed, it was not until the mid-1970s that the concept of posttraumatic stress disorder (PTSD) emerged due to two social factors: the return of soldiers from the Vietnam War and the emergence of "rape trauma syndrome" (Burgess & Holmstrom, 1974). In 1980, PTSD was determined to be a separate and distinct diagnostic category by the American Psychiatric Association (APA). Clinicians use the *Diagnostic and Statistical Manual of Mental Disorders* (DSM) to understand the clusters of symptoms that qualify a person as suffering from posttraumatic stress disorder.

Prior to the 5th edition of the DSM, PTSD was considered a type of anxiety disorder. The 5th edition placed it into a new category: "Trauma and Stress-Related Disorders." This change is intended to help destigmatize PTSD by treating it as a disorder connected to an external event rather than an anxiety-related mental illness (Staggs, 2013).

Diagnostic criteria for PTSD in the 5th edition include a history of exposure to a traumatic event and symptoms from each of four symptom clusters: intrusion, avoidance, negative alterations in cognitions and mood, and alterations in arousal and reactivity. Criterion also concern duration of symptoms and functioning; and, the eighth criterion clarifies symptoms as not attributable to a substance or co-occurring medical condition. Additionally, two categories include delayed expression and a dissociative subtype of PTSD, the latter of which is new to DSM-5. In both specifications, the full diagnostic criteria for PTSD is required first (DSM, 2013).

CRITERION A: STRESSOR

The person was exposed to: death, threatened death, actual or threatened serious injury, or actual or threatened sexual violence, as follows: (one required)

1. Direct exposure.

2. Witnessing, in person.

3. Indirectly, by learning that a close relative or close friend was exposed to trauma. If the event involved actual or threatened death, it must have been violent or accidental.

4. Repeated or extreme indirect exposure to aversive details of the event(s), usually in the course of professional duties (e.g., first responders, collecting body parts; professionals repeatedly exposed to details of child abuse). This does not include indirect non-professional exposure through electronic media, television, movies, or pictures.

CRITERION B: INTRUSION SYMPTOMS

The traumatic event is persistently re-experienced in the following way(s): (one required)

1. Recurrent, involuntary, and intrusive memories. Note: Children older than six may express this symptom in repetitive play.

2. Traumatic nightmares. Note: Children may have frightening dreams without content related to the trauma(s).

3. Dissociative reactions (e.g., flashbacks), which may occur on a continuum from brief episodes to complete loss of consciousness. Note: Children may reenact the event in play.

4. Intense or prolonged distress after exposure to traumatic reminders.

5. Marked physiologic reactivity after exposure to trauma-related stimuli.

CRITERION C: AVOIDANCE

Persistent effortful avoidance of distressing trauma-related stimuli after the event: (one required)

1. Trauma-related thoughts or feelings.

2. Trauma-related external reminders (e.g., people, places, conversations, activities, objects, or situations).

CRITERION D: NEGATIVE ALTERATIONS IN COGNITIONS AND MOOD

Negative alterations in cognitions and mood that began or worsened after the traumatic event: (two required)

1. Inability to recall key features of the traumatic event (usually dissociative amnesia; not due to head injury, alcohol, or drugs).

2. Persistent (and often distorted) negative beliefs and expectations about oneself or the world (e.g., "I am bad," "The world is completely dangerous").

3. Persistent distorted blame of self or others for causing the traumatic event or for resulting consequences.

4. Persistent negative trauma-related emotions (e.g., fear, horror, anger, guilt, or shame).

5. Markedly diminished interest in (pre-traumatic) significant activities.

6. Feeling alienated from others (e.g., detachment or estrangement).

7. Constricted affect: persistent inability to experience positive emotions.

CRITERION E: ALTERATIONS IN AROUSAL AND REACTIVITY

Trauma-related alterations in arousal and reactivity that began or worsened after the traumatic event: (two required)

1. Irritable or aggressive behavior.

2. Self-destructive or reckless behavior.

3. Hypervigilance.

4. Exaggerated startle response.

5. Problems in concentration.

6. Sleep disturbance.

CRITERION F: DURATION

Persistence of symptoms (in Criteria B, C, D, and E) for more than one month.

CRITERION G: FUNCTIONAL SIGNIFICANCE

Significant symptom-related distress or functional impairment (e.g., social, occupational).

CRITERION H: EXCLUSION

Disturbance is not due to medication, substance use, or other illness.

SPECIFY IF: WITH DISSOCIATIVE SYMPTOMS

In addition to meeting criteria for diagnosis, an individual experiences high levels of either of the following in reaction to trauma-related stimuli:

1. Depersonalization: experience of being an outside observer of or detached from oneself (e.g., feeling as if "this is not happening to me" or one were in a dream).

2. Derealization: experience of unreality, distance, or distortion (e.g., "things are not real").

SPECIFY IF: WITH DELAYED EXPRESSION

Full diagnosis is not met until at least six months after the trauma(s), although onset of symptoms may occur immediately.

TRAUMA AND THE LIMBIC SYSTEM

One way to explain the long-term effects of trauma is to understand the neurobiology of trauma and its effect on the limbic system. The limbic system is the alarm system for the body that protects the individual in the face of danger. It is the place where all sensory information enters the human system and is encoded. When trauma is experienced the neurohormonal system releases and is regulated by epinephrine, which helps mobilize resources during dangerous states. However, when individuals are trapped and cannot remove themselves either through fleeing or fighting, a particular type of learning, termed *trauma learning*, occurs that does not allow a reduction of stress through adaptive means of the fight-or-flight response. Due to excesses and depletion of hormones in the brain structures responsible for interpreting and storing incoming stimuli, alterations occur in memory systems. The individual becomes immobilized, and as the level of autonomic arousal increases, there is a move into a numbing state through the release of opiates in the brain. This numbing state accounts for disconnection of the processing and encoding of information. In a sense, when the trauma is over the alarm system remains somewhat stuck between the accelerated fight-or-flight response and the numbing state, resulting in an alteration in an adaptive capacity. This alteration is a cellular change that becomes fixed in its patterning and is difficult to change or extinguish. Of particular importance are various theories of modulating effects in the brain. There is now a greater understanding of how trauma can have a lasting effect on basic processes of adaptation and growth.

Because these neurosystems of arousal and numbing are intricately related to information processing and memory, a distinctive type of memory is formed in which experiences are recalled as if they were happening (i.e., a *flashback*). Thus, when external events trigger an association to the abuse itself, the person is thrown into this panic memory and feels subjected to a hostile exploited environment even though nothing like that is going on. Internal events can also trigger trauma-specific reactions, such as night terrors. These experiences are not like typical dreams. Rather, they are vivid, visceral responses as if the trauma is occurring.

ASSESSMENT MEASURES AND PROTOCOLS FOR PTSD

Clinicians have the responsibility of assessing trauma in a victim, making a diagnosis, and devising a treatment plan. Many assessment tools are available to screen for PTSD. The National Center for PTSD, part of the U.S. Department of Veterans Affairs, has a list of assessment tools written by their staff that can be downloaded, and they list measures available from other organizations/clinicians as well. A few of the tools are briefly described in TABLE 4-4.

TABLE 4-4 Assessment Measures for PTSD and Other Symptomatology

Tool	Description
Clinician Administered PTSD Scale-1 (CAPS-1)	Structured interview designed to make a categorical PTSD diagnosis, as well as to provide a measure of PTSD symptom severity.
The Brief Trauma Questionnaire (BTQ)	A 10-item self-report trauma exposure screen that asks for a "yes" or "no" answer to the question. The BTQ screens for different types of experiences including combat trauma, car accidents, natural disasters, exposure to violent death, and physical or sexual abuse.
Impact of Event Scale (IES)	A 22-item self-report measure constructed to assess intrusion, avoidance, and hyperarousal symptoms of PTSD experienced over the past week.
Beck Depression Inventory-2	A 21-item scale contains four statements reflecting current manifestations of depression in increasing intensity, from neutral to severe.
Trauma Symptom Inventory (TSI)	Assesses acute and chronic posttraumatic symptomatology, including the effects of rape, spouse abuse, physical assault, combat experiences, major accidents, and natural disasters, as well as the lasting sequelae of childhood abuse and other early traumatic events.
Symptom Checklist-90-R (SCL-90-R)	A 90-item self-rating scale of general symptoms, scored on nine subscales.

Source: Measures authored by National Center for PTSD staff are available as direct downloads or by request. Measures developed outside of the National Center can be requested via contact information available on the information page for the specific measure (see National Center for PTSD).

Data from: Acierno at the National Violence Against Women Prevention Research Center at the Medical College of South Carolina.

Treatment Interventions

Roberts's Crisis Intervention Model

In terms of crisis resolution, Roberts's seven-stage crisis intervention model (Yaeger & Roberts, 2015) provides a structured and targeted framework that can lay the foundation for more comprehensive, long-term service plans. TABLE 4-5 shows the stages of crisis intervention.

The goal of Roberts's crisis intervention model is to ensure a victim's immediate safety and stabilization, followed by problem-solving and the exploration of alternative options that will culminate in a meaningful action plan. The use of standardized test measurements is highly recommended in making a comprehensive assessment, and several are available that can enable crisis workers to retrieve specific and relevant information: the Expanded Conflict Tactics Scales of Aggression—both verbal and physical (Straus, Hamby, Boney-McCoy, & Sugarman, 1996); the Beck Depression Inventory (Beck & Steer, 1984); the Derogatis Symptom Checklist-90-Revised (Derogatis, 1992); and the Trauma Symptom

TABLE 4-5 Roberts's Seven-Stage Crisis Intervention Model

Stage 1: Assessing Safety	Evaluate (1) the severity of the crisis, (2) the client's current emotional state, (3) immediate psychosocial and safety needs, and (4) level of client's current coping skills and resources.
Stage 2: Establishing Rapport and Communication	Goals are assessment and identification of critical areas of intervention, recognition of the duration and severity of violence, and acknowledgment of what has happened.
Stage 3: Identifying the Major Problems	Prioritize the problems or impacts by identifying them in terms of how they affect the survivor's current status.
Stage 4: Dealing with Feelings and Providing Support	Demonstrate empathy and an anchored understanding of the survivor's experience so symptoms and reactions are normalized and can be viewed as functional strategies for survival.
Stage 5: Exploring Possible Alternatives	Explore alternatives of (1) situational supports or social agencies to help resolve crisis-related problems; (2) coping skills and strategies to help the client reach a precrisis level of functioning; and (3) positive and rational thinking patterns, to lessen the client's levels of anxiety, stress, and crisis.
Stage 6: Formulating an Action Plan	Help the client achieve a level of functioning and maintain coping skills and resources and have a manageable treatment plan, allowing the client to follow through and be successful.
Stage 7: Follow-Up Measures	Crisis resolution addressed: (1) physical safety and survival, (2) ventilation and expression of feelings, (3) cognitive mastery, and (4) interpersonal adjustments and adapting to a new environment.

Data from: Roberts, A. R. 2005. Bridging the past and present to the future of crisis intervention and crisis management. In A. R. Roberts (Ed.), *Crisis Intervention Handbook: Assessment, treatment, and research* (3rd ed., pp. 3–33). New York: Oxford University Press.

Checklist-40 (Briere & Runtz, 1989). These are intended to elicit responses that can provide clinicians with a multifaceted snapshot of a victim's trauma history and current psychological state, including varying degrees of depression, anxiety, sexual problems, dissociation, sleep disturbances, and post–sexual abuse trauma. Although the seven-stage model can be viewed as a stand-alone protocol for initial crisis intervention, it is imperative that it be functionally viewed as the first step on a continuum of established strategies and supports designed to facilitate long-term treatment, cognitive reorientation and empowerment of the victim, and freedom from the abusive environment.

Treatment Models

Once preliminary assessment and stabilization have been accomplished, the more chronic difficulties must be addressed to progress toward significant and lasting emotional, behavioral, and environmental change. **TABLE 4-6** outlines some of the treatment models.

COGNITIVE-BEHAVIORAL THERAPY

A number of reviews of the effectiveness of cognitive-behavioral approaches for PTSD have been conducted and conclude that cognitive-behavioral therapy is effective in reducing the severity of posttraumatic stress symptoms in individuals who have experienced a wide range of traumatic events and in individuals who suffer from both acute and chronic symptoms (Regehr & Glancy, 2010). The basis of cognitive therapeutic methods is that behavior is a learned rather than an innate process. Operant conditioning, described by B. F. Skinner in his 1938 book, *The Behavior of Organisms: An Experimental Analysis*, postulates that a response that is reinforcing (rewarded) will reoccur, whereas the

TABLE 4-6 Treatment Models

Cognitive Behavioral Therapy (CBT)	Psychotherapy based on modifying everyday thoughts and behaviors, with the aim of positively influencing emotions.
Problem Identification and Problem-Solving	Redirection of the client's emotions and skills *away from* fear, powerlessness, and subjugation, and *toward* self-confidence, self-reliance, and competent decision making.
Psychotherapy	A range of techniques based on experiential relationship building, dialogue, communication, and behavior change.
Eye Movement Desensitization and Reprocessing (EMDR)	Client attends to past and present experiences in brief sequential doses while simultaneously focusing on an external stimulus.

premise of social learning theory proposed by Bandura in 1977 is that learning takes place by modeling (observing and imitating others), as well as through self-reinforcement and self-evaluations. Treatment strategies include systematic desensitization, aversion therapy, shaping behaviors by rewarding successive approximations of the desired result, positive and negative reinforcement, and role modeling of adaptive behaviors. Cognitive restructuring, identifying dysfunctional core beliefs, role-plays and rehearsals, relaxation and stress management training, self-monitored homework assignments, and problem-solving are used to reinforce the goals of positive learning and change.

The general approach for cognitive-behavioral therapy, a widely accepted, evidence-based, cost-effective psychotherapy for many disorders, developed out of behavior modification and cognitive therapy. The particular therapeutic techniques commonly include relaxation and distraction techniques; keeping a diary of significant events and associated feelings, thoughts, and behaviors; questioning and testing assumptions or habits of thoughts that might be unhelpful and unrealistic; gradually facing activities that may have been avoided; and trying out new ways of behaving and reacting.

ADDITIONAL TREATMENT INTERVENTIONS

Psychotherapy is an interpersonal, relational intervention used by trained psychotherapists to aid victims in problems of living. This usually includes increasing individual sense of well-being and reducing subjective discomforting experience. These include psychodynamic, cognitive-behavioral, interpersonal, experiential, and body-centered therapies. Eye movement desensitization and reprocessing (EMDR) integrates elements of many effective psychotherapies in structured protocols that are designed to maximize treatment effects. EMDR is an information-processing therapy and uses an eight-phase approach.

TERMINATION, REFERRALS, AND EVALUATION

Primary treatment effectively ends when a client has stabilized enough to pursue his or her own goals of independent living with appropriate supports and resources. Referrals for legal, financial, and educational assistance should be made, and regular follow-up contact should be part of any treatment plan. Clinicians must also stress the importance of seeking help immediately for any crisis situation or safety concerns, ensuring the client of the availability of prompt intervention and assistance.

Ideally, evaluation of strategies and interventions conducted will be an ongoing practice at each stage along the recovery continuum, not just with regard to a specific client but also to the future implementation of intervention and therapeutic models vis-à-vis broader program policies and procedures.

Conclusion

As individuals and communities worldwide have risen up in an effort to be more compassionate to the suffering of their fellow citizens, so, too, has society as a whole evolved from barbarianism to humanitarianism vis-à-vis vast and complex criminal justice systems. Governments and citizens have made tremendous strides with regard to their understanding and treatment of crime victims. Advocacy, legislation, and education have provided the cornerstones for advancing the belief that crime victims deserve compassion and assistance rather than blame. Society remains, however, on the precipice of a successful, fully realized legacy of programs and services for victims of crime and are therefore charged with vigorously continuing the work.

Key Terms

National Organization for Victim Assistance (NOVA): Established in 1975 as a national umbrella organization and is dedicated to expanding current victim services, developing new programs, and supporting passage of victims' rights legislation.

Primary victimization: Affects the targeted or personalized victim.

Secondary victimization: Affects impersonal victims, such as commercial establishments, churches, schools, and public transportation.

Tertiary victimization: Diffuse and extends to the community at large.

Victim Information and Notification Everyday (VINE) Program: Enables victims of intimate partner violence to access court information.

Victims of Crime Act (VOCA): The VOCA established the Crime Victim's Fund that is supported by fines collected from persons who have been convicted of criminal offenses.

Discussion Questions

1. Consider the rights of the victim delineated by the United Nations. Select one that requires greater focus and attention in our country and discuss means for improvement.

2. Considering different models of victim compensation, what do you believe victims should be compensated for? Who do you think should be responsible for paying victims?

3. Should victim witness statements be admissible in court? Why or why not?

4. How have rights movements contributed to the development of services for victims? What has been neglected by this advocacy approach to legislative change?

5. Read and research how many of the recommendations from the National Commission on Terrorist Attacks Upon the United States (2004) have been implemented by the Bush, Obama, and Trump administrations.

Resources

American Probation and Parole Association http://www.appa-net.org

Canadian Resource Centre for Victims of Crime http://www.crcvc.ca/en /compensation.php

Criminal Injuries Compensation Board http://www.cicb.gov.on.ca/en/index .htm

National Institute on Mental Health, Post-traumatic Stress Disorder http:// www.nimh.nih.gov/health/publications/post-traumatic-stress-disorder-easy -to-read/index.shtml

National Commission on Terrorist Attacks Upon the United States http:// govinfo.library.unt.edu/911/report/911Report_Exec.htm

Office for Victims of Crime http://www.ojp.usdoj.gov/ovc/about/index.html

References

Andrews, A. B. (1992). *Victimization and survivor services*. New York: Springer.

American Psychiatric Association (APA). (2013). *Diagnostic and Statistical Manual of Mental Disorders* (5th edition). Washington, DC: Author.

Bandura, A. (1977). *Social learning theory*. New York: General Learning Press.

Beck, A. T., & Steer, R. A. (1984). Internal consistencies of the original and revised Beck Depression Inventory. *Journal of Clinical Psychology, 40*(6), 1365–1367.

Bonta, J., Jesseman, R., Rugge, T., & Cormier, R. (2006). Restorative justice and recidivism: promises made, promises kept. In D. Sullivan & L. Tifft (Eds.), *Handbook of restorative justice: A global perspective* (pp. 108–120). London: Routledge.

Bradshaw, W., Roseborough, D., & Umbreit, M. (2006). The effect of victim offender mediation on juvenile offender recidivism: A meta-analysis. *Conflict Resolution Quarterly, 24*, 87–98.

Braithwaite, J. (2002). *Restorative justice and responsive regulation*. Oxford: Oxford University Press.

Breuer, J., & Freud, S. (1895). *Studies in hysteria*. Boston: Beacon Press.

Briere, J., & Runtz, M. (1989). The Trauma Symptom Checklist (TSC-33): Early data on a new scale. *Journal of Interpersonal Violence, 4,* 151–163.

Brownell, P., & Roberts, A. R. (2002). National organizational survey of domestic violence coalitions. In A. R. Roberts (Ed.), *Handbook of domestic violence intervention strategies* (pp. 80–98). New York: Oxford University Press.

Brownmiller, S. (1975). *Against our will: Men, women, and rape.* New York: Simon & Schuster.

Burgess, A. W., & Holmstrom, L. L. (1974). Rape trauma syndrome. *American Journal of Psychiatry, 131*(9), 981–986.

Campbell, R., Bybee, D., Townsend, S., Shaw, J., Karim, N., & Markowitz, J. (2014). The impact of sexual assault nurse examiner programs on criminal justice case outcomes: A multisite replication study. *Violence Against Women, 20*(5), 607–625.

Campbell, R., Greeson, M., Bybee, D., Kennedy, A., & Patterson, D. (2011). *Adolescent sexual assault victim's experiences with SANE-SARTs and the criminal justice system.* Washington, DC: National Institute of Justice.

Campbell, R., Townsend, S. M., Long, S. M., & Kinnison, K. E. (2005). Organizational characteristics of sexual assault nurse examiner programs: Results from the national survey project. *Journal of Forensic Nursing, 1*(2), 57–64.

CBC News. (2004, October 29). Bin Laden claims responsibility for the 2001 attacks against the United States. Retrieved from http://www.cbc.ca/world/story/2004/10/29/binladen_message041029.html

Ciancone, A. C., Wilson, C., Collette, R., & Gerson, L. W. (2000). Sexual assault nurse examiner programs in the United States. *Annals of Emergency Medicine, 35*(4), 353–357.

Criminal Code of Canada. RSC, 1985, c C-46.

Crime Victim Compensation Quarterly. (2011). 2012 VOCA cap may remain level as budget issues grow. Retrieved from http://www.nacvcb.org/NACVCB/files/ccLibraryFiles/Filename/000000000114/newsletter.2011-2final.pdf

Derene, S., Walker, S., & Stein, J. (2007). History of the crime victim's movement in the United States. *Senator Tommy Burks Victim Assistance Academy Participant Manual.* Nashville, TN: The Tennessee Coalition Against Domestic Violence and Sexual Assault.

Derogatis, L. R. (1992). *SCL-90-R: Administration, scoring, and procedures manual. II.* Baltimore, MD: Clinical Psychometric Research.

Dignan, J. (2005). *Understanding victims and restorative justice.* Maidenhead: Open University Press.

Drapkin, I., & Viano, E., eds. (1974). *Victimology: A new focus.* Lexington, MA: Lexington Books. From International Symposium on Victimology, 1st, Jerusalem, 1973. 5 volumes.

Englebrecht, C. (2011). The struggle for "ownership of conflict": An exploration of victim participation and voice in the criminal justice system. *Criminal Justice Review, 36*(2), 129–151.

Erez, E., & Tontodonato, P. (1990). The effect of victim participation in sentencing on sentence outcome. *Criminology, 28*, 451–474.

Family Violence Prevention & Services Program, Family & Youth Services Bureau. (2015). Domestic Violence Services Provided by State and Tribal Grantees. Washington, DC.

Fattah, E. (2000). Victimology: Past, present, and future. *Criminologie, 33*, 17–46.

Federal Bureau of Investigation (FBI). (2011). 9/11 Investigation. Famous cases. Retrieved from http://www.fbi.gov/about-us/history/famous-cases/9-11-investigation/9-11 -investigation

Feinberg, K. (2004). What have we learned about compensating victims of terrorism? Retrieved from http://www.rand.org/publications/randreview/issues/summer 2004/33.html

Figley, C. (1995). *Compassion fatigue: Coping with secondary traumatic stress disorder in those who treat the traumatized*. New York: Brunner/Mazel.

Finn-DeLuca, V. (1994). Victim participation at sentencing. *Criminal Law Bulletin, 30*, 403–428.

Freud, S. (1961). *Beyond the pleasure principle (The Standard Edition)*. Trans. James Strachey. New York: Liveright Publishing Corporation.

Fry, M. (1957, July 7). Justice for victims. *Observer* (London, England), p. 8.

Garkawe, S. (2007). Victim impact statements and sentencing. *Monash University Law Review, 33*, 90–114.

Giliberti, C. (1991). Evaluation of victim impact statement projects in Canada: A summary of findings. In G. Kaiser, H. Kury, & J. Albrecht (Eds.), *Victims and criminal justice*. Freiburg, Germany: Max-Planch Institute.

Girardin, B. (2005). The sexual assault nurse examiner: A win-win solution. *Topics in Emergency Medicine, 27*(2), 124–131.

Greer, G. (1973, January). Seduction is a four-letter word. *Playboy*, 80–82, 164, 178, 224–228.

Griffin, S. (1971). Rape: The all-American crime. *Ramparts, 10*(3), 26–35.

Hambrick, B. (2011). Sex trafficking bill passes Senate. Retrieved from http://hambrick 4assembly.com/2011/05/17/press-release-sex-trafficking-bill-passes-senate-to-be -signed-by-governor/

Holmstrom, L. L., & Burgess, A. W. (1983). *The victim of rape: Institutional reactions*. New Brunswick, NJ: Transactions.

Largen, M. A. (1985). The anti-rape movement: Past and present. In A. W. Burgess (Ed.), *Rape and sexual assault* (pp. 1–13). New York: Garland Press.

Latimer, J., Dowden, C., & Muise, D. (2005). The effectiveness of restorative justice practices: A meta-analysis. *The Prison Journal, 85*(2), 127–144.

Ledray, L. (1999). *Sexual assault nurse examiner (SANE) development and operation guide*. Washington: U.S. Department of Justice, Office of Victims of Crime.

Mai, F. M., & Merskey, H. (1980). Briquet's treatise on hysteria. A synopsis and commentary. *Archives of General Psychiatry, 37*, 1401–1405.

Manitoba Victims' Bill of Rights. (1986). Retrieved from http://www.canlii.org/mb
/laws/sta/v-55/20050110/whole.html

McCormack, R. J. (1989, April). A perspective on United States crime victim compensation. Paper presented at the annual meetings of the Academy of Criminal Justice
Sciences, Washington, DC.

McGibbon, A. (2011). Codes of ethics for victim services. Retrieved from http://www
.justice.gc.ca/eng/pi/rs/rep-rap/rd-rr/rr07_vic4/p2.html

National Center for PTSD. (2017). U.S. Department of Veterans Affairs. White River Junction, VT. Retrieved from https://www.ptsd.va.gov/professional/assessment
/all_measures.asp

National Coalition Against Domestic Violence. (2015). Domestic violence: Fact sheet.
Retrieved from http://ncadv.org/images/Domestic%20Violence.pdf

National Commission on Terrorist Attacks Upon the United States (2004). The 9/11
Commission report. Retrieved from http://govinfo.library.unt.edu/911/report
/911Report_Exec.htm

National Organization for Victim Assistance (NOVA). (1983). *The victim service
system: A guide to action.* Washington, DC: Author.

Office of the Inspector General. (2013). Audit of the Federal Bureau of Investigation's
accounting and reporting of funds distributed from the Crime Victims Fund.
Washington, DC: U.S. Department of Justice.

Office for Victims of Crime (OVC). (1988). Restitution: Making it work. Retrieved
from http://www.aardvarc.org/victim/restitution.shtml

Office for Victims of Crime (OVC). (2002). Restitution—making it work. Department
of Justice, Office of Justice Programs. Retrieved from http://www.ovc.gov/archive
/index.html

Office for Victims of Crime (OVC). (2015a). VOCA compensation and assistance statistics. Department of Justice, Office of Justice Programs. Retrieved from https://
www.ovc.gov/pubs/reporttonation2015/VOCA-compensation-and-assistance
-statistics.html

Office for Victims of Crime (OVC). (2015). OVC Report to the Nation: Fiscal Years
2013–2014 Building capacity through research, innovation, technology, and
training. Retrieved from https://www.ovc.gov/about/initiatives.html

Ontario Victims' Bill of Rights, 1995, S.O. 1995, c. 6 http://www.e-laws.gov.on.ca
/DBLaws/Source/Statutes/English/2000/S00032_e.htm

President's Task Force on Victims of Crime. (1982). *Final report.* Washington, DC: U.S.
Government Printing Office.

R. v. Jacob. (2002). YKTC 15.

Regehr, C., Alaggia, R., Lambert, L., & Saini, M. (2008). Victims of sexual violence in
the Canadian criminal courts. *Victims and Offenders, 3*(1), 1–15.

Regehr, C., & Glancy, G. (2010). *Mental health social work in Canada.* Toronto:
Oxford University Press.

Regehr, C., & Kanani, K. (2010). *Essential law for social work practice in Canada.*
Toronto: Oxford University Press.

Roach, K. (1999). *Due process and victim's rights: The new law and politics of criminal justice.* Toronto: University of Toronto Press.

Roberts, A. R. (1981). *Sheltering battered women: A national study and service guide.* New York: Springer.

Roberts, A. R. (1990). *Helping crime victims: Research, policy, and practice.* Thousand Oaks, CA: Sage.

Roberts, A. R. (2007). Overview and new directions for intervening on behalf of battered women. In A. R. Roberts (Ed.), *Battered women and their families: Intervention strategies and treatment programs* (3rd ed., pp. 3–32). New York: Springer.

Roberts, A. R., & Kurst-Swanger, K. (2002). Police responses to battered women: Past, present, and future. In A. R. Roberts (Ed.), *Handbook of domestic violence intervention strategies* (pp. 101–126). New York: Oxford University Press.

Roberts, A. R., Robertiello, G., & Bender, K. (2007). National survey of 107 shelters for battered women and their children. In A. R. Roberts (Ed.), *Battered women and their families: Intervention strategies and treatment programs* (3rd ed., pp. 109–132). New York: Springer.

Roberts, A. R., & Roberts, B. S. (2005). *Ending intimate abuse: Practical guidance and survival strategies.* New York: Oxford University Press.

Roberts, T. (1992). *Assessment of the Victim Impact Statement Program in British Columbia.* Canada: Department of Justice, Research and Development Directorate [and] Corporate Policy and Programs Sector.

Roche, S. E., & Sadoski, P.J. (1996). Social action for battered women. In A. R. Roberts (Ed.), *Helping battered women: New perspectives and remedies* (pp. 13–30). New York: Oxford University Press.

Ruback, R., & Bergstrom, M. (2006). Economic sanctions in criminal justice: Purposes, effects, and implications. *Criminal Justice and Behavior, 33*(2), 242–273.

Sellin, T., & Wolfgang, M.E. (1964). *The measurement of delinquency.* New York: Wiley.

Sherman, L., Strang, H., Mayo-Wilson, E., Woods, D., & Ariel, B. (2015). Are restorative justice conferences effective in reducing repeat offending? Findings from a Campbell systematic review. *Journal of Quantitative Criminology, 31,* 1–24.

Skinner, B. F. (1938). *The behavior of organisms: An experimental analysis.* New York: Appleton-Century.

Stagg, S. (2013). Symptoms and diagnosis of PTSD. Psych Central. Retrieved from https://psychcentral.com/lib/symptoms-and-diagnosis-of-ptsd/

Stamm, B. (1995). *Secondary traumatic stress: Self-care issues for clinicians, researchers, and educators.* Lutherville, MD: The Sidran Press.

Straus, M. A., Hamby, S. L., Boney-McCoy, S., & Sugarman, D. B. (1996). The revised Conflict Tactics Scales (CTS2): Development and preliminary psychometric data. *Journal of Family Issues, 17*(3), 283–316.

Trueblood, C. (2011). Victim impact statements: A balance between victim and defendant rights. *Phoenix Law Review, 3*(2), 605–640.

Turman, K. (2004, March 26). Helping terrorism victims and their families. Retrieved from http://www2.fbi.gov/page2/march04/turman032604.htm

United Nations. (1985). *Declaration of basic principles of justice for victims of crime and abuse of power*. G.A. 40/34, annex, 40 U.N. GAOR Supp. (No. 53) at 214, U.N. Doc. A/40/53.

U.S. Government Benefits Help. (2011). Victims compensation fund. Retrieved from http://www.usgovernmentbenefits.org/hd/index.php?t=victims+compensation+fund

Van der Kolk, B. A. (1994). The body keeps score: Memory and the evolving psychobiology of post-traumatic stress. *Harvard Review of Psychology, 1*(5), 253–265.

Van der Kolk, B. A., Brown, P., & van der Hart, O. (1989). Pierre Janet on post-traumatic stress. *Journal of Traumatic Stress, 2*, 365–378.

Vanscoy and Even v. Her Majesty the Queen in Right of Ontario. (1999). O.J. No. 1661 (Ont. Sup. Ct. Jus.).

Viano, E. (1979). *Victim/witness services: a review of the literature*. Washington, DC: U.S. Department of Justice.

Wilson, D., & Klein, A. (2005). *An evaluation of the Rhode Island sexual assault response team (SART)*. National Criminal Justice Research Service. Washington: U.S. Department of Justice.

Yaeger, K. & Roberts, A. R. (2015). Bridging the past and present to the future of crisis intervention and crisis management. In A. R. Roberts (Ed.), *Crisis intervention handbook: Assessment, treatment, and research* (4th ed). New York: Oxford University Press.

Young, A. (2001). *The role of the victim in the criminal justice process: A literature review 1989–1999*. Ottawa, Ontario, Canada: Policy Centre for Victims' Issues, Department of Justice, Research and Statistics Division.

Young, M., & Stein, J. (2004). *The History of the Crime Victims Movement in the United States*. Office of the Victims of Crime. Retrieved from https://www.ncjrs.gov/ovc_archives/ncvrw/2005/pg4c.html#d

CHAPTER 5

Justice Systems

OBJECTIVES

- To outline the history of the evolution of laws
- To describe the victim process in the criminal justice system
- To describe the civil court system
- To describe the juvenile justice system
- To describe the death penalty

KEY TERMS

Adjudication

Civil justice system

Criminal charges

Criminal law

Defendant

English common law

Grand jury

Juvenile justice system

Law

Pretrial

Third-party liability

Victim impact statement

CASE

The Anthony case riveted the public for three years. Two-year-old Caylee Marie Anthony went missing on Monday, June 9, 2008, in Orlando, Florida. Five weeks later her mother reported her missing, and a nationwide search ensued for the missing child. Over time, evidence accumulated that Casey Anthony, Caylee's mother, had lied to police, and questions were raised about her inappropriate behavior for a mother of a supposed missing child. The strong odor of decomposition was also discovered in her car trunk, Anthony was charged with child neglect, jailed, and believed guilty by public vote.

Meanwhile, Casey Anthony's parents made an appeal to the media to help in the search for their missing grandchild. In December 2008, a meter reader reported a grisly finding: a bag with bones and duct tape hanging from a child's skull in swampy woods near the Anthony home. DNA identified the skeletal remains of Caylee. Her mother, Casey Anthony (FIGURE 5-1), was charged with first-degree murder, a capital death penalty case. In June 2011, however, she was acquitted of three murder charges and convicted of four counts of lying to the police. She was released on July 13, 2011, for time served but was required to complete one-year probation on check fraud charges she admitted to in 2010.

In 2017, after her acquittal of her daughter's murder, Casey Anthony lives with and works for Patrick McKenna, a private investigator who worked as the lead investigator for the defense teams of both Casey and O.J. Simpson.

FIGURE 5-1 Casey Anthony.
© Joe Burbank/Orlando Sentinel/MCT via Getty Images.

She tried to start a photography business in 2015, filing papers to open Case Photography in West Palm Beach, Florida. News of the launch hit the media the following month, and incensed online readers bombarded the company's Facebook page with negative messages, prompting it to be taken down (McPadden, 2017). She has given only one media interview (to the Associated Press) and is rarely seen in public.

Introduction

Victims of crime may come into contact with one of two aspects of the justice system: the criminal justice system or the civil justice system. If the crime is reported to the police, the victim enters the criminal justice system. A police investigation may involve interviewing the witness and gathering evidence, arresting and charging a suspect, prosecuting and sentencing the accused, and perhaps ultimately incarcerating of the offender. In the criminal justice system, a crime has been committed against the state, and the victim is a witness in the service of justice. The prosecuting attorney represents the interests of the state against the accused offender; he or she does not represent the interests of the victim. Further, the decision to pursue **criminal charges** and proceed to court rests with the prosecution, not the victim. Although programs that assist victims in the criminal justice system may be available, the criminal justice process is designed to judge the guilt or innocence of accused offenders and, if found guilty, to punish and/or rehabilitate them for the greater good of society.

The civil justice system, by contrast, is designed to ensure the rights of individual citizens who have suffered the direct impact of the crime. Regardless of whether there was a prosecution, victims can bring their claims before the court and ask to have the responsible parties held accountable. Control over initiating a legal process rests with the citizen, not the state.

This chapter focuses on the importance of the development of laws over time and the victim process and role in the criminal and civil justice systems. Cases, including that of Casey Anthony, who was charged with the murder of her child; Jaycee Dugard, a victim of kidnapping; and the Petit triple murders, are used to illustrate various components of the justice systems. The chapter also provides information on crime in North America, noting that the justice systems of the United States and Canada are governed by local, state, or federal laws.

In addition to the civil and criminal justice systems, victims may encounter two other justice systems not covered here. First, the family law system considers issues related to family disputes and obligations. These include legal relationships surrounding divorce, child custody, and child support. From the perspective of victims of crime, family law may be relevant in cases of spousal violence, child abuse, and child abduction (*West's Encyclopedia of American Law*, 1998a). Second, the juvenile justice system is responsible for handling cases involving young offenders. The first juvenile court in the United States was established in 1899 with the goal of controlling serious juvenile offending. Similarly, Canada created an Act Respecting the Arrest, Trial, and Imprisonment of Youthful Offenders in 1894 followed by the Juvenile Delinquents Act in 1908. These acts saw offenses of youth as conditions of delinquency and offenders in need of guidance and supervision (Regehr & Kanani, 2010). In 1974, the U.S. Juvenile Justice and Delinquency Prevention Act created the Office of Juvenile Justice and Delinquency Prevention. The establishment of this office was an acknowledgment that young people in crisis, whether they are serious, violent, and chronic offenders or victims of abuse and neglect, pose a challenge to the nation (Office of Juvenile Justice and Delinquency Prevention, 2011). Individuals who are victims of youthful offenders may access information from the Office of Juvenile Justice and Delinquency Prevention to better understand the process they will encounter in the justice system.

Evolution of Laws

English writer and historian Colin Wilson (1984) referred to the "warrior tradition" that once typified much of everyday life millennia ago, stating that it is not known exactly when piracy and banditry became common in Europe, but that it was probably toward the end of the third millennium B.C. Wilson notes that the Greek historian Thucydides, writing in the 5th century B.C., stated that in times ancient to him, the world was commanded by leaders of powerful bands of raiders who plundered towns and villages with such intensity that all Greeks were required to carry weapons in defense of their homes and persons. The "warrior mentality" was both myth and a very current dangerous reality to the people of those times. These ancient civilizations attempted to deal with their reality by developing criminal justice systems (Wilson, 1984).

A crime is an act prohibited by criminal law that involves a victim and a perpetrator. The justice system is based on law; that is, a set of rules usually enforced through a legal institution. The purpose of law is to provide an objective set of rules for governing conduct and maintaining order in a society. This justice system can be confusing and frustrating to the victims who must navigate it. However, a review of the history of laws helps to explain the various aspects and steps involved in the criminal and civil justice systems.

Historical Perspective

Greek Mythology

The ancient Greek myths include stories of gods and goddesses that were used to describe and enforce moral standards and to explain natural phenomenon and the events that befell people. For example, thunder and lightning were believed to be caused by Zeus hurling his thunderbolt. The list of writers through whom the myths have been told is not lengthy. Homer heads the list with his two famous poems, *The Iliad* and *The Odyssey*, which were written sometime around 1000 B.C. Homer's Zeus is a person living in a world where civilization has made an entry and where he has established a standard of right and wrong. Zeus punishes men who lie and break their oaths; he is angered by the ill treatment of the dead; he pities and helps others; and he intervenes in disputes, beseeching others to show mercy. In *The Odyssey*, Homer describes a concept familiar to many today, writing that those who fail to help the needy and strangers are in fact sinning against the god Zeus (Hamilton, 1942).

The Greek poet Hesiod also wrote about the Greek myths. Writing in approximately 750 B.C., Hesiod addressed the concept of evil and suggested that a man who inflicts evil on vulnerable people invokes the wrath of Zeus. As a peasant who lived among the poor, Hesiod believed the poor must have a just god. He wrote, "Fishes and beasts and fowls of the air devour one another. But to man, Zeus has given justice. Besides Zeus on his throne Justice has her seat" (Hamilton, 1942, p. 20). Hesiod's work introduced the victim concept and showed that the great and bitter needs of the helpless were reaching up to heaven and changing the god of the strong into a protector of the weak (Hamilton, 1942).

Urukagina

The concept of law is as old as civilization itself. Urukagina was a ruler of the city-state Lagash in Mesopotamia from 2380 to 2360 B.C. The reforms he enacted to fight corruption have been cited as a key example of an early legal code. Urukagina exempted widows and orphans from taxes, compelled the city to pay funeral expenses (including the ritual food and drink for the journey of the dead into the lower world), and decreed that the rich must use silver when purchasing from the poor. He also said that powerful rich men could not force poor people to sell if they did not wish to.

Code of Ur-Nammu

The Code of Ur-Nammu (ca. 2112–2095 B.C.) is the oldest known surviving tablet containing a law code, dating 300 years older than the Code of Hammurabi. The tablet was written during the Sumerian dynasty in Mesopotamia. In contrast to the *lex talionis* principle of Babylonian law of an "eye for an eye," this code is viewed as advanced because it set monetary fines for crimes. However, the capital crimes of murder, rape, robbery, and adultery were punishable by death.

Code of Hammurabi

The Code of Hammurabi was established around 1786 B.C. in ancient Mesopotamia with Hammurabi's founding of Babylon, the world's first metropolis. As the first ruler of the Babylonian empire, Hammurabi holds the claim of restoring order and justice to Mesopotamia. Although Hammurabi did conquer other city-states to expand his empire, he let the rulers of the cities-states live and justly rule the people with fair laws. He wrote 282 laws governing family, criminal punishment, civil law, ethics, business, prices, trade, and other aspects of ancient life that came to be known as the "Code of Hammurabi." His stated purpose was "to promote the welfare of the people and cause justice to prevail in the land by destroying the wicked and the evil, that the strong might not oppress the weak" (Stearns, Adas, Schwartz, & Gilbert, 2003). These laws were carved on an 8-foot-high stone monument in public view so that all people could read and know what was required of them. Putting the laws into writing was important in itself because it suggested the laws were immutable and above the power of any earthly king to change.

In the prologue to his code, Hammurabi declared his desire to "establish justice," and at the end he declared that through his enactments the strong would not injure the weak and that there would be justice for widows and orphans. Although Hammurabi had the right motives for producing these laws, which he believed Marduk, the chief god of Babylon, had given him the commission to write, many of the laws seem strict, harsh, and cruel by today's standards. For example, the code called for cutting off the hand of a son who would strike his father and putting to death someone who had stolen the minor son of another man (Stearns et al., 2003). Punishments varied depending on the class of offenders and victims, with those from the upper classes, who were expected to be more responsible, receiving harsher punishments. Nevertheless, the code is one of the earliest examples of the idea of presumption of innocence, suggesting that the accused and accuser had the opportunity to provide evidence in a dispute or conflict.

Mosaic Law

Moses (between 1300 and 1150 B.C. in Egypt) is one of the most important figures in Judaism. According to the Old Testament, through Moses, God gave the Israelites the Ten Commandments on stone tablets. The Mosaic Law begins with these commandments and also includes a variety of rules with regard to religious observance. In Judaism, the first five books of the Bible are called the Torah, or "the Law." The 10 Commandments have become the basis of Judeo-Christian morality and underpin many of the criminal laws in our modern society (e.g., the prohibition against murder, theft, and perjury).

Roman Law

The development of Roman law ranges over more than 1,000 years, from the Law of the Twelve Tables (ca. 451 B.C.) to the Corpus Juris Civilis (Corps of Civil Law) of Emperor Justinian I (ca. 530). A critical feature of Roman law was the Law of the Twelve Tables, the earliest Roman code of law, that was written by a special commission of 10 men in approximately 451 B.C. The tables were supposedly written to address plebeians' protests that the patrician judges were able to discriminate against them with impunity because the principles governing legal disputes were known only orally. No complete text of the code survives; it is known only from quotations and references. The Law of the Twelve Tables served as the foundation of Roman law and encompassed all spheres of law—private, criminal, public, and sacred. The laws set forth were never abolished, but later enactments made them obsolete. The Law of Twelve Tables made the law more concrete, and a product of the Roman citizenry itself. It was a publicly stated and accessible guide for the average citizen's course of conduct.

Code of Justinian

Justinian I is one of the most famous of the Byzantine, or Eastern Roman, emperors. One reason for this is his role in creating the Code of Justinian. Born a barbarian, Justinian became a powerful ruler and reformer. After solidifying his rule, Justinian found the laws of the empire to be in great confusion. Many laws were out-of-date; some contradicted others; and nowhere did a complete collection of the laws exist. Justinian appointed a commission to study the problem. The work of the commissioners resulted in the publication of the *Code of Justinian*, a three-book collection that encompassed the decrees of emperors, the opinions of the lawyers and judges who had interpreted these decrees, and a description of the legal principles in simple terms. A fourth book, *Novella Constitutions*, included the ordinances of Justinian after the codification. These four books together constitute the *Code of Justinian*, or Civil Law (*Corpus Juris Civilis*), and mark the beginning of recording case law.

Feudalism

Feudalism emerged in 8th-century France. Initially, feudalism was a manner of law that established fiefs, or the granting of labor and law, as a reward for contributing to military service. In England in 1066, William the Conqueror established feudalism after the defeat of the Anglo-Saxons as a reward to those who were loyal to him. By the Middle Ages, feudalism had become a system of duties and rights that bound nobility or an upper class in loyalty and responsibility to a king or lord. This loyalty to the king was in exchange for land (fiefs) that was worked by lower-class labor (serfs). In return for their servitude, the serfs received the protection of the landowner. This type of system clearly benefited the monarchy and the upper class. The king or monarchy held public power privately, and the nobles were bound to the monarch in both military and civil capacities.

In colonial America, the principles of feudalism continued as an extension of the English nobility system. Feudal domains were established by the early colonists to secure property and wealth. Colonies were established by the Puritans and the Protestants in New England; proprietary colonies were established by the Anglicans in Maryland, the Carolinas, and Delaware; and similar systems were established by the Dutch in New Amsterdam (later New York) and New Jersey.

English Common Law

English common law has its foundations in the traditional unwritten law of England, based on custom and usage. Centuries before the Norman Conquest, decisions regarding legal issues were made by councils of the king and passed down to village meetings. Each community then developed its own set of customs and expectations. It was not until the 9th century that King Alfred moved to unify the various kingdoms into a single kingdom of England and similarly attempted to create a more unified approach to legal decision-making. His wife, Queen Martia, is credited with writing down the pre-Saxon compendiums of the common law, known as Alfred's Code. With his invasion of England in 1066, William the Conqueror combined the Anglo-Saxon law with Norman law to form what we now know as English common law. This particular form of law is based on custom and precedent rather than statutory laws, in that the recorded legal decisions of one court shape future decisions (Baker, 2002).

The common law of the United States is based on Sir William Blackstone's *Commentaries on the Laws of England*, completed in 1769 and based on a course of study he undertook at Oxford University (the commentaries can be found online at http://www.lonang.com/exlibris/blackstone/). Over time, English common-law precedents were enacted into the legislation of various states, with the exception of Louisiana, which is still influenced by the Napoleonic Code due to its initial colonization by the French. Similarly, in Canada all provinces use common law, with the exception of Quebec, which also follows a system based on Napoleonic Code.

Contemporary Codes and Laws

Early English common law forms the basis for much of our contemporary legal system. The Magna Carta of England and the U.S. Constitution both stand as great documents and great moments in the history of Western law. The Magna Carta grants basic liberties for all British citizens. The U.S. Constitution, adopted in 1787, established certain individual rights, defined the powers of the federal government, and limited punishment for violation of laws.

Constitutional law is a form of American criminal law. It does not define crimes, but rather sets limits on laws as they apply to individuals (Wallace & Roberson, 2010). Similarly, the Constitution Act, part of the Canada Act of 1982, established the Constitution of Canada to be the supreme law of Canada. The Canadian Constitution sets out the basic principles of democratic government and defines the three branches of government: (1) the executive, which includes the prime minister and other ministers, which is responsible for administering and enforcing laws and which answers to the legislature; (2) the legislature, which has the power to make, alter, and appeal laws; and (3) the judiciary, which interprets and applies the law (Regehr & Kanani, 2010).

Concepts Related to Justice and Alternative Forms of Justice

The concept of justice is one of the key features of a society. Justice, according to Rawls (1971), is the concept of moral rightness based on ethics, rationality, law, natural law, fairness, and equity. Theories of justice vary greatly, but Rawls (1971) argued that there is evidence that everyday views of justice can be reconciled with patterned moral preferences. Justice concerns the proper ordering of things and persons within a society. As a concept it has been subject to philosophical, legal, and religious reflection and debate throughout history. According to most theories of justice, it is overwhelmingly important. Rawls, for instance, claimed that "[j]ustice is the first virtue of social institutions, as truth is of systems of thought" (Rawls, 1971, p. 3).

Several types of justice have been delineated. However, those that concern the issue of crime victims and the offenders are retributive justice, utilitarian justice, distributive justice, and restorative justice (TABLE 5-1).

Retributive Justice

Retributive justice is based on the principles that the guilt of an accused must be proven, and once established, the offender's punishment must be proportional to the crime committed. As is noted in ancient codes of law,

TABLE 5-1 Types of Justice

Type	Definition
Retributive justice	A theory of justice that dictates a proportionate response to crime proven by lawful evidence so that punishment is justly imposed and considered as morally correct and fully deserved. For retributionists, punishment is backward-looking and strictly for punishing crimes according to their severity.
Utilitarian justice	For utilitarians, punishment is forward-looking, justified by a purported ability to achieve future social benefits, such as crime reduction.
Distributive justice	This concept of justice is directed at the proper allocation of things—wealth, power, reward, respect—between different people. A number of important questions surrounding justice have been fiercely debated over the course of Western history. What is justice? What does it demand of individuals and societies? What is the proper distribution of wealth and resources in society: equal, meritocratic, according to status or some other arrangement?
Restorative justice	The focus is on the needs of victims and offenders in contrast to a focus on punishing the offender. Victims are active participants in the process, whereas offenders are encouraged to take responsibility for their actions.

such as the Code of Hammurabi, the law has a role in maintaining social order, and retributive justice models work to restore equilibrium by enforcing action against the offender. Retributive justice is often associated with harsh punishment and societal vengeance. One example of retributive justice is the practice of imposing differential prison sentences on first-time offenders and repeated offenders. For example, in the 19th century, New York State introduced the Persistent Felony Offender Act that established longer sentences for repeat offenders. Despite the legislation, however, judges had considerable discretion regarding the term of incarceration imposed, allowing them to take into consideration other factors in addition to number of previous offenses (Zimring, Hawkins, & Kamin, 2001). Several states enacted habitual offender laws in the 1990s that impose mandatory prison sentences for criminals convicted on three or more occasions (known as "three strikes" laws).

Utilitarian Justice

Utilitarianism, a term proposed by John Stewart Mill in 1863, is a principle of justice based on the greatest good for the greatest number. The moral worth of an action is judged by its overall utility. Thus, punishment for crime is not retribution against the offender but rather an attempt to prevent future harms. Future harm may be prevented by keeping a dangerous person safely incarcerated; however, punishment of offenders can also serve as a deterrent to others. This concept is differentiated from *deontology*, which is based on a form of absolutism or irrefutable moral laws. Certain acts are wrong and others are right, independent of the goodness or badness of their outcomes (Craig, 1998).

Distributive Justice

Distributive justice is concerned with the fair allocation of resources among diverse members of a community. Different distributions advance various social goals. For example, John Rawls (1971) noted that one's place of birth, social status, and family influences are matters of luck and that a goal of distributive justice is to limit the influence of luck so that goods might be distributed more fairly and to everyone's advantage. Robert Nozick (1977), in contrast, believes that a goal of distributive justice is setting down rules that individuals should follow in acquiring and transferring resources and benefits to ensure a fair process of exchange. Others believe distributive justice must be a matter of both process and outcome (Maiese, 2003).

Restorative Justice

The term *restorative justice* refers to informal and nonadjudicative forms of dispute resolution, such as losses suffered by a victim (Cheon & Regehr, 2006). This concept also includes offender mediation, family conferences, neighborhood accountability boards, and peacemaking circles that promote joint decision-making power (Bazemore & Schiff, 2001; Roach, 2000). A central concept of restorative justice is that it can repair the harms of crime and restore what has been lost (Zehr, 1995). This notion of justice posits that victims and offenders, when put together in the right circumstances, can negotiate a mutually agreeable plan for easing the burden on the victim both psychologically and materially (Umbreit, 1995). Restorative justice is not about determining guilt or innocence; it is rather a means for negotiating ways to mediate the effects of crime. It attempts to move from punishment to repairing the harms caused by the crime by balancing the needs of the victims, citizens, and offenders (Cheon & Regehr, 2006).

Restorative justice models have a number of elements. First, restorative justice generally involves not only the victim and the offender, but also the members of the community, because the community is viewed to have a stake in the outcome. Community members are expected to have an ongoing role in supporting victims in the healing process, enforcing agreements, and influencing the offender's behavior to prevent further offending (Dodd, 2002; Presser & Gaarder, 2000). The involvement of community members has another purpose, however: to bring the crime out of the closet and into the open light. This exposure has been described as shaming by people important to the offender, including family and community members (Braithwaite, 2000). This shaming is then followed by gestures of reintegration and support, which are seen to deter antisocial behavior and enable more prosocial behavior in the future.

A second key element is the role of the victim. The model generally involves a meeting or series of meetings attended by community members, the offender, and the victim. The victim describes the impact of the offense and what might be needed to assist him or her in healing. During the process of restoration, victims of crime are provided with opportunities to discuss how the crime affected them, get information about the offender's motivation, and have input into sanctions and restitution (Bazemore, 2001). This is a significant departure from the retributive model, in which the needs of the victim are considered secondary to the needs of police, judges, and prosecutors, and in which resources to assist victims are scarce. In the end, victims are expected to benefit from reparative words such as an apology by the offender or statements of support by others and actions offered by the offender and/or community. This can be augmented by the provision of financial compensation by the offender or material assistance by the community.

Finally, the role of the offender is key to the success of the model. The offender is expected to accept responsibility for his or her harmful actions and to make amends (Dodd, 2002). As stated above, an important part of this process often includes apologies to the victim and some type of restoration. For instance, if the offender is a juvenile who has committed a property crime against a member of the community, the juvenile might be expected to pay for the repair of the damage or offer his or her physical labor to restore the damage. The goal is to return offenders to a law-abiding life and reintegrate them into the community (Presser & Van Voorhis, 2002).

Criminal Law

Criminal law is concerned with actions that are dangerous or harmful to society as a whole, in which prosecution is pursued not by an individual but rather by the state. The purpose of criminal law is to define what constitutes a crime and to prescribe punishments for committing such a crime. Criminal law must include both factors. Criminal justice is concerned with the enforcement of criminal law.

The U.S. and Canadian court systems are based on the principles of federalism. Federalism is a system of government in which a constitution separates out the power and authority between a central governing authority and units called states or provinces. Federalism is a system in which sovereignty is shared between the national and state or provincial governments. Proponents of this federation system are often called *federalists*.

The U.S. Constitution established the rules under which the federal government could operate. *The Federalist Papers*, one of the most important documents in American political history, is a compilation of 85 essays. They were written for the people of the state of New York to support and vote for ratification of the new constitution. The essays, written by Alexander Hamilton, James Madison, and John Jay, analyzed the deficiencies of the Articles of Confederation and the benefits of the new, proposed Constitution and argued the political theory and function behind the various articles of the proposed Constitution.

In Canada, a common federal Criminal Code applies in all jurisdictions. The Canadian Constitution defines the powers of government; the Canadian Charter of Rights and Freedoms protects the fundamental rights of Canadians; the legislatures make, alter, and repeal laws; and the judiciary and administrative bodies interpret and apply the law.

The first U.S. Congress established the federal court system and permitted individual states to continue their own judicial structure, maintaining a dual system of state and federal courts. Thus, a victim may be a witness in a state or federal (or both) court (Wallace & Roberson, 2010). The 1991 Rodney King case, where an African American taxi driver was stopped, beaten, and arrested by four Los Angeles policemen, offers an example of this dual system. The four officers charged with beating King were tried in a state court for using excessive force but were acquitted. News of the acquittal triggered the Los Angeles riots of 1992. By the time the police, the U.S. Army, the Marines, and the National Guard restored order, the casualties included 55 deaths, 2,383 injuries, more than 7,000 fires, damage to 3,100 businesses, and nearly $1 billion in financial losses. On May 1, 1992, the third day of the L.A. riots, King appeared in public before television news cameras to appeal for calm. After the riots, the U.S. Department of Justice reinstated the investigation and obtained an indictment of violations of federal civil rights against the four officers. The federal trial focused more on the evidence as to the training of officers instead of just relying on the videotape of the incident. The jury found two officers guilty, who were subsequently sentenced to 30 months of prison, and two officers were acquitted of all charges.

A second characteristic of the U.S. court system is the lack of oversight or supervision it has as it carries out its duties. However, the U.S. Supreme Court and the various state supreme courts do review appellate cases from lower courts; in that sense there is supervision of the district, or first level, of the court system. A third feature of the U.S. court system is one of specialization that occurs primarily at the state and local levels. For example, special courts are designated to hear juvenile cases or family law cases. At the federal level, certain courts hear specific types of cases, such as for bankruptcy (Wallace & Roberson, 2010).

Levels of the U.S. Court System

In the early days of the federation, each of the original 13 states had its own court system. The framers of the U.S. Constitution wanted the state governments to have general jurisdiction while granting the federal government only limited power. Thus, the framers of the Constitution limited the kinds of cases federal courts can decide. The result is that most laws that affect daily life are passed by state governments, and state courts handle disputes involving those laws. The federal courts, however, serve an important role in that they defend many of our most basic rights, such as freedom of speech and equal protection under the law (Judicial Learning Center, n.d.).

Over time, several reform movements have assisted in streamlining and modernizing the state systems. These reforms have resulted in many states adopting a three-tier judicial system of trial courts, appellate courts, and state supreme courts. Victims of violence appear at the trial court level, because this level is where criminal cases start and finish.

The flowchart in FIGURE 5-2 shows the steps in the criminal justice system; this chart updates the original chart prepared by the President's Commission on Law Enforcement and the Administration of Justice in 1967. The chart summarizes the most common events in the criminal and juvenile justice systems, including entry into the criminal justice system, prosecution and pretrial services, adjudication, sentencing and sanctions, and corrections. A discussion of the events in the criminal justice system follows.

DISTRICT COURT LEVEL

Courts of general jurisdiction are granted the authority to hear and decide issues brought before them. These courts generally hear all major civil or criminal cases. They may be known by various names, including *superior courts*, *circuit courts*, or *district courts*. A case may have its verdict appealed by either the prosecution or the defense. The intermediate level is called the *courts of appeals*. These

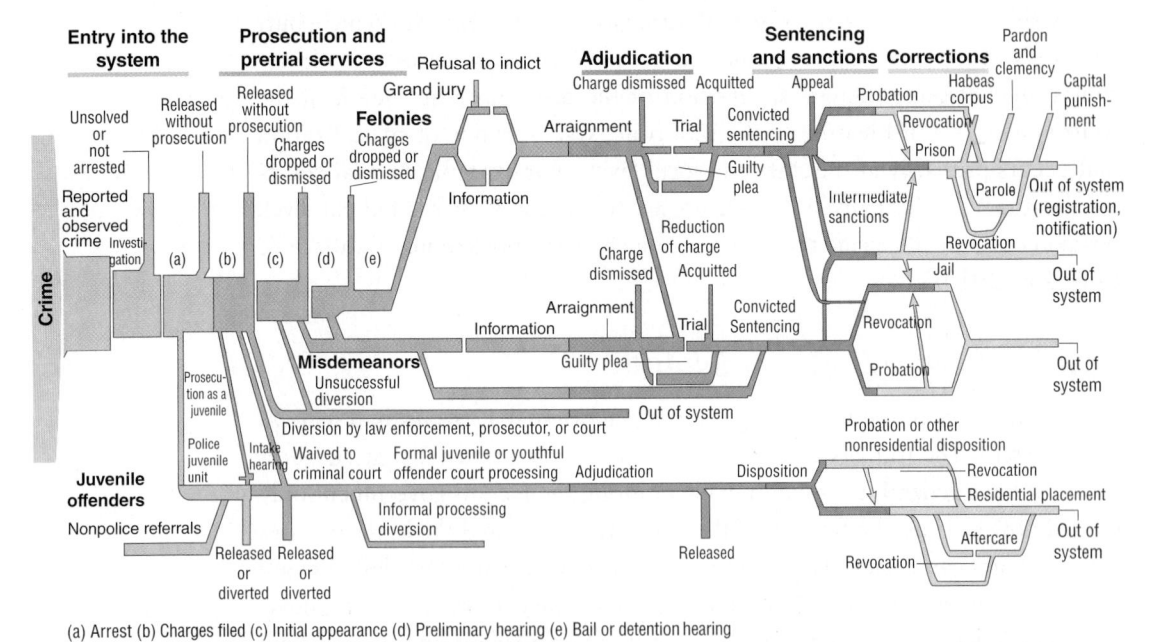

(a) Arrest (b) Charges filed (c) Initial appearance (d) Preliminary hearing (e) Bail or detention hearing

Note: This chart gives a simplified view of caseflow through the criminal justice system. Procedures vary among jurisdictions. The weights of the lines are not intended to show actual size of caseloads.

FIGURE 5-2 Steps in the criminal justice system.

Reproduced from: Bureau of Justice Statistics.

courts hear and decide issues of law. A jury is not used to decide factual disputes. The *appellate level* has the authority to uphold the decision or to reverse the decision of the lower courts and to send the case back with instructions. Again, in either situation the party who loses the appeal at this level may file an appeal to the next higher appellate court (Wallace & Roberson, 2010).

The final appellate courts are the highest level of appeal in a state and are known as the *supreme courts*, or courts of last resort. Multiple justices may sit on this court depending on the state. Supreme courts rule on state constitutional or statutory issues. Once a state supreme court has decided an issue, the only appeal left is to file in the federal court system.

FEDERAL COURT SYSTEM

In contrast to state courts, whose origins are traced to historical accident and custom, the federal courts were created by the U.S. Constitution. From this point Congress enacted various legislation that resulted in the contemporary federal court system. The Judiciary Act of 1789 created the U.S. Supreme Court and established district courts and the circuit of appeals. The federal system has three levels: federal district courts, federal circuit courts, and the U.S. Supreme Court (Wallace & Roberson, 2010). The federal district courts are the first level of the federal court system. These courts have jurisdiction over all cases having a violation of federal statutes. Examples of cases heard in federal district court are infant and child abductions, domestic violence or rape cases where the victim has been taken across state lines, certain homicide cases, and child pornography cases. The federal circuit courts are the intermediate level of appeal within the federal system. The federal system is divided into 11 circuits. An appeal is heard by three appellate court judges.

The U.S. Supreme Court is the highest court in the United States. It can provide judicial review for all lower state and federal court decisions. The court meets on the first Monday in October and usually remains in session until June. It hears very few cases. The justices' caseload has increased steadily to a current total of over 10,000 per term. Plenary review, with oral arguments by attorneys, is granted in about 100 cases per term. Formal written opinions are given in 80 to 90 cases. About 50 to 60 additional cases are disposed of without granting plenary review.

Canadian Court System

The Canadian court system has four levels (Department of Justice, 2003; Regehr & Kanani, 2010):

- *Provincial courts.* These courts handle criminal offenses, family law matters (except divorce), and young offender cases. In addition, some provinces and territories have established provincial courts dedicated to particular offenses or offenders, such as small claims courts, drug treatment courts, youth courts, and domestic violence courts.

- *Provincial/territorial superior courts.* These courts deal with the most serious criminal and civil cases. In addition, most superior courts have family law divisions to deal with particularly difficult divorce and property claims.

- *Provincial and federal courts of appeal.* These courts deal with appeals from the lower courts and with constitutional questions.

- *Supreme Court of Canada.* This is the highest court of appeal. This court also decides questions on the Constitution and other controversial questions.

Generally, a decision made in a lower court can be appealed to the next level of court until the case reaches the Supreme Court of Canada. Lower courts must follow precedents set by higher courts, and thus decisions made by the Supreme Court of Canada direct decisions at all other levels. When new legislation is passed, however, the courts must include these directives in the decision-making process. Furthermore, as stated earlier, the Canadian Charter of Rights and Freedoms must ultimately govern judiciary decisions in that the courts must ensure legislation does not violate individual rights and freedoms (Regehr & Kanani, 2010).

Entering the Criminal Justice System

The act of reporting a crime starts a complicated process. A number of institutions immediately swing into motion. Victims find themselves caught up in protocols that are routine to authorities but new and not completely understood by them. At the very least, victims will be questioned by authorities and their statements recorded in official files. These things may not be done against a victim's will, but more may be done than he or she bargained for. It thus becomes especially important that victims understand the process, which is one reason that victim services have been established.

Reporting the Crime: Interactions with the Police

The police are generally the first official a victim encounters. The questions police ask tend to focus on what happened, who is involved, where it happened, and why it happened. The style of questioning used in the interview of a victim by law enforcement depends on the officers, their training, and the nature of the crime. The opening statement made by an officer is crucial in setting the tone of the interview. Officers who want to put a victim at ease will give a brief explanation by saying, "I will need some information about what happened. And I have to ask some questions." Other officers are blunt and simply begin by asking questions without any introductory comments, such as "Tell me what happened."

In most interviews the officers will ask about the incident, the relationship (if any) of the victim to the assailant, and the victim's background. The tone and demeanor of the officers make a difference in the reaction of the victim to the interview. Officers who are empathetic will end an interview with a supportive question, such as "Is there anything else you can tell me that would help me?" Officers who are less sympathetic may ask more confrontational questions, perhaps about a victim's past behavior, that sound abrasive. This style of officer may also end the interview with a statement about the possible consequences for the assailant, such as "It can be a life sentence for this." This officer may seem intent on testing the strength of a victim's motivation to follow through in the court process.

Once the crime is reported, the next step is making a decision about pressing charges. Victims quickly learn that the state has an interest in what happens in a case. Legally, the crime is committed against the state and the victim is a witness. One rape victim, laughing at the irony, said, "What kills me is that the Commonwealth got raped and I'm only a witness" (Holmstrom & Burgess, 1983, p. 55).

Police officers differ in the degree of enthusiasm they express for pursuing some cases. Crimes committed by strangers are responded to more enthusiastically than are interpersonal violence cases. For example, police officers do not see all claims of rape as being equal. Instead, they have in their minds an image of what constitutes an ideal victim case. Such cases are often described as being "strong" or "weak." Holmstrom and Burgess (1983) identified four types of criteria police officers use in making this distinction in rape cases.

First, police look at the quality and consistency of the information they received. To be strong, the case cannot rest on the victim's statement alone but must have corroborating evidence. Police like to have forensic findings, injuries, and/or a witness. Conversely, in describing a weak case, officers are skeptical of a victim who changes his or her story. Police prefer a consistent and unchanging statement.

Second, police officers look to characteristics of the victim, especially his or her behavior and moral character. A case is strong if the victim was forced to accompany the offender and weak if he or she accompanied the offender willingly. Characteristics of a strong case include the victim not exposing him- or herself to risk, being sober, being upset, and being emotionally stable.

Characteristics of weak cases include being drunk or on drugs, having a psychiatric history, having a history of attempted suicide, taking chances, or being unconcerned (in demeanor) about the incident.

Third, police look at the relationship between victim and offender. It is a strong case if the offender is a stranger, if the victim is a teenager, or if the offender is in his or her 20s or 30s. Police are less enthusiastic about cases where both parties are teenagers with only a year or so difference in ages or are known to each other.

Fourth, police look at the characteristics of the offender. They are very enthusiastic if they find the offender has other charges against him or her or a prison record. In one case, the offender had both a prior rape charge and a charge of armed robbery on a male victim who was severely injured during the crime. In the incident, a knife penetrated the victim's back, breaking two ribs and puncturing a lung. The victim was taken to the hospital where a team of surgeons worked on him. Complications occurred, and he was a month in the hospital. The robbery victim and the rape victim both made a positive identification of the assailant. The police were anxious to see the assailant "off the streets" and kept saying, "He's a goner" (Holmstrom & Burgess, 1983, p. 43).

Fifth, the police officer has the serious task of writing the police report. Although there are various training methods for report writing, the first rule of thumb in police report writing is to describe what happened in chronological order. The first line is almost always the same: "On [date] while working with [name of officer] we received a call from 911 dispatcher [name] to 123 Anywhere St. for a Man with a Gun." Police officers are questioned in court as to whom they were working with, who gave them the call, the time of the call, and/or what the call was about. The remaining report describes the action taken by the officer. The report is viewed as highly credible, and thus accuracy is essential and the report is necessary for the prosecution of a case.

POLICE AND THE VICTIM

Considerable publicity is given to the emotional difficulties victims face in dealing with police. But the difficulties police face in dealing with crime victims has received less attention. Holmstrom and Burgess (1983) identified several reasons police take crime victims seriously. They are often the first professional group to arrive on the scene, occasionally even arriving while the crime is in progress. They observe victims who are distraught, screaming, bleeding, injured, and crying. Furthermore, police stay with the victims as they go through the criminal justice system. Other professionals, such as physicians, nurses, forensic examiners, and prosecutors, are with the victims for a relatively short time period. However, the same teams of police officers usually follow victims through the system. They take victims to the hospital, talk to them during the investigation, sit with them during waiting time at the hospital or courthouse, and attend court sessions. Thus, they come to know certain individual victims better than other groups do and also observe firsthand much of the aftermath of the crime (Holmstrom & Burgess, 1983).

Police officers, like health professionals and court officials, are asked to engage in work that can be emotionally disturbing. They see victims who have been robbed, injured, beaten, raped, and murdered. They must deal with the violence of rape, arson, and death. They see the suffering of victims. They need access to information about injury to bodies. They must ask for information about the private lives of victims. They need this information for investigative purposes and also to prepare for court. Their work is in the realm of uncertainty. What really happened and who is telling the truth?

Thus, one would expect to find institutionalized roles and social control mechanisms in place for police to carry out their work. Professional protocol is one example of this control mechanism. For example, police are never present during the physical examination of a victim. They wait in a designated area for a staff member to provide information. It is appropriate for police officers to develop what might be called "professional armor" to protect themselves against the emotional aspects of their work to remain "affectively neutral" (Parsons, 1951). Media reports have portrayed both positive and negative police treatment of crime victims. Positive reactions focus on victims feeling they were treated well and that the police officer made them feel better. Negative reactions include victims feeling as though people stared at them, that they had no privacy when talking, or that they felt pressured into pressing charges.

Pressing Charges

The criminal justice system does put pressure on victims to participate in the court process. Once victims talk with police, the police must decide whether to press charges. In large part this depends on whether the victim is willing to participate in the justice system. Victims may get entangled in the legal process before they can get their own thoughts straight. Victims may be ambivalent about involving the full weight of the justice system, especially in cases where they know the perpetrator or the perpetrator is a family member, as in domestic violence. Victims may not want to participate in the judicial system to avoid the ordeal of court; because they are afraid of the perpetrator taking revenge; to avoid sending a person to jail; because they feel sorry for the perpetrator; because they just want to forget the whole thing; or because they are afraid of identifying the wrong person (Holmstrom & Burgess, 1983).

The government brings criminal cases to court through the criminal justice system. The American and Canadian systems of justice have evolved from English common law into a complex series of procedures and decisions. Founded on the concept that crimes against an individual are crimes against the state, the justice system prosecutes individuals as though they have victimized all of society. However, crime victims are involved throughout the process, and many justice agencies have programs that focus on helping victims.

Once a law enforcement agency has established that a crime has been committed, a suspect must be identified and apprehended for the case to proceed through the system. Sometimes, a suspect is apprehended at the scene; however, identification of a suspect sometimes requires an extensive investigation. Often, no one is identified or apprehended. In such situations, the case remains open. Statutes exist in every jurisdiction for how long a case may remain open. Currently, murder cases are not subject to statutory time limits. In such cases, the file is classified in the cold case division of a police department.

In some instances, a suspect is arrested and later the police determine that no crime was committed, charges are dropped, and the suspect is released. In other instances, the assailant, his or her social network, and the defense counsel may pressure the victim to drop charges. Holmstrom and Burgess (1983) found that 24 of 115 rape victims were so pressured. In addition, seven victims reported "mysterious happenings," such as unexplained phone calls, that they interpreted as efforts at intimidation. Assailants and their networks used three main approaches: threats (14 cases), sympathy appeals (5 cases), and bribes (2 cases). In addition, harassment from the defense counsel before the court occurred in 11 cases.

Pretrial

After an arrest, law enforcement agencies present information about the case and about the accused to the prosecutor, who will decide if formal charges will be filed with the court. Victims usually have knowledge of the police officer's role but are less certain of the role of the prosecutor or district attorney. Victims need to understand that the prosecutor represents the state's interests, is supposed to be on their side, and that they do not need their own lawyer. The prosecutor will interview the victim. Some prosecutors try to put the victim at ease with introductory phrases and an explanation as to why they need to know the answers to certain questions.

Prosecutors, like police and hospital staff, have an image of what constitutes an ideal case. Police talk of strong and weak cases. Hospital staff talk of whether a rape case is "legitimate," and prosecutors talk about whether or not the victim will make a "good witness." Prosecutors want witnesses to be explicit and consistent in their testimony. It is important that victims work with the prosecutor and his or her team on the preparation of the case. The victim's appearance and demeanor are important, too. Court is a stressful and controlling environment. Victims need to be able to hold up under the pressure of cross-examination. In one case a victim became so upset she walked out in the middle of her testimony. Most prosecutors' offices have victim witness staff that assist in working with witnesses to prepare them for their testimony.

If no charges are filed, the accused must be released. The prosecutor can also drop charges after making efforts to prosecute (*nolle prosequi*). A suspect charged with a crime must be taken before a judge or magistrate without unnecessary delay. At the initial appearance, the judge or magistrate informs the accused of the charges and decides whether there is probable cause to detain the accused person. If the offense is not very serious, the determination of guilt and assessment of a penalty may also occur at this stage.

The defense attorney represents the rights and interests of the suspect. Often, the defense counsel is assigned at the initial appearance. All suspects prosecuted for serious crimes have a right to be represented by an attorney. If the court determines the suspect is indigent and cannot afford such representation, the court will assign counsel at the public's expense. The four types of defense attorneys are public defenders, contract defense services, assigned defense counsel, and private defense counsel.

PRETRIAL RELEASE

A pretrial-release decision may be made at the initial appearance. This decision may also be made at other hearings or at another time during the process. Pretrial release and bail were traditionally intended to ensure appearance at trial. However, many jurisdictions permit pretrial detention of **defendants** accused of serious offenses and deemed to be dangerous to prevent them from committing crimes before trial. The court often bases its **pretrial** decision on information about the defendant's drug use, as well as residence, employment, and family ties. The court may decide to release the accused on his or her own recognizance or into the custody of a third party after the posting of a financial bond or on the promise of satisfying certain conditions such as taking periodic drug tests to ensure drug abstinence.

Preliminary Hearing

In many jurisdictions a preliminary hearing may follow the initial appearance. The main function of this hearing is to discover if there is probable cause to believe the accused committed a known crime within the jurisdiction of the court. If the judge does not find probable cause, the case is dismissed; however, if the judge or magistrate finds probable cause for such a belief or the accused waives his or her right to a preliminary hearing, the case may be bound over to a grand jury.

Grand Jury

A **grand jury** hears evidence against the accused presented by the prosecutor and decides if there is sufficient evidence to cause the accused to be brought to trial. If the grand jury finds sufficient evidence, it submits to the court an indictment, which is a written statement of the essential facts of the offense charged against the accused. In some jurisdictions, defendants, often those without prior criminal records, may be eligible for diversion from prosecution subject to the completion of specific conditions such as drug treatment. Successful completion of the conditions may result in the dropping of charges or the expunging of the criminal record where the defendant is required to plead guilty before the diversion.

Given the time and effort put into an investigation and arrest of a suspect, the police and prosecutors sometimes pressure victims to persevere in the court process. They may be firm ("Be at court") or try to appeal to the victim's sympathies ("You can't back out on me after all the work I did to arrest him"), or they may appeal to the victim's sense of civic duty or a duty to protect other potential victims. The pressure to testify may also be placed on other witnesses that know of the crime or the victim or the defendant.

Plea Bargain

A plea bargain is an agreement in which a defendant pleads guilty to a lesser charge and the prosecutor in return drops more serious charges. The plea bargain is then presented to the judge who may or may not accept it. For example, Joanne Thompson faced five counts of felony embezzlement after she and another employee, Mike Nemeyer, were arrested in separate cases in June 2010. Both were accused of stealing money from her former employer, New York City–based billionaire Edgar Bronfman, and his property, Georgetown Farms. Bronfman's family once owned the Seagram's liquor empire, and Bronfman has an estimated net worth of $2.6 billion. Nemeyer was found not guilty on all counts after a three-day jury trial in October. Thompson testified against Nemeyer in his trial in hopes of lightening her own sentence. Defense attorney Scott Goodman and Commonwealth's Attorney Elliott J. Casey reached an agreement that would have spared Thompson any jail time. The prosecutor argued that it would be unfair for Thompson to endure any incarceration whatsoever while the other walked free. His conclusion was based on Thompson's willingness to cooperate during the Nemeyer trial. However, Judge Cheryl Higgins did not accept the agreement, stating she was uncomfortable agreeing to this particular sentence, adding that the proposed punishment was a deviation from guidelines (Koon, 2011).

Suppression Hearings and Change of Plea Hearings

A victim is generally entitled to be present at a suppression hearing or a change of plea hearing, which both occur in open court. At a suppression hearing the defense challenges the prosecution's evidence and whether law enforcement complied with legal rules in collecting evidence. A victim, along with a victim advocate, may be present in court during the hearing, which ordinarily involves testimony of witnesses, including police officers. If the motion to suppress is granted, evidence may be excluded from the county prosecutor's case, which may impact whether the case can be proven at trial. If the motion is overruled, the evidence may be presented at trial to assist in proving the case. In the Anthony case in March 2011, there were several days of testimony in a suppression hearing to determine if statements made by Casey Anthony to detectives after being placed in custody, in jail, through video visitations with family, and letters to another inmate should be suppressed.

A change of plea hearing is when the accused, upon consulting with his or her criminal defense attorney, decides to change the plea from not guilty to a plea of guilty as part of an agreed sentence recommendation to resolve the case short of trial. The accused agrees to waive his or her constitutional rights, including the right to a jury trial in adult cases, which results in a criminal conviction. The court is required to inform the accused of the rights being waived and ensure that the change of plea is voluntary. In the Garrido case, at the last minute Phillip Garrido decided against pleading guilty—as expected—to Jaycee Dugard's kidnapping, with his lawyer citing problems with the grand jury. However, they subsequently made a surprise change of plea after prosecutors agreed to drop some charges against Nancy Garrido, Phillip's wife, if Phillip pleaded guilty to almost the full indictment. Their change in pleas meant Jaycee Dugard and her children would not have to testify at a trial. Nancy Garrido was sentenced to 36 years to life in prison for her role in the abduction and rape and husband Phillip was sentenced to 431 years to life in prison after pleading guilty to kidnapping and multiple counts of sexual assault (Glynn, 2011).

Many cases of conviction result from *guilty pleas* rather than *guilty verdicts* in trials. Victims may believe they have no say in plea bargaining; this can have a negative effect on victims, who may believe the criminal justice system has let them down. To avoid this situation a victim should be present in court for this hearing, along with a victim advocate. The court may ask whether the victim has been consulted about the change of plea and the sentence recommendation agreed upon between the parties to the case. A presentence investigative report may be ordered, which provides the court with background information about the accused and the crime committed for purposes of the court considering the appropriate sentence to be ordered in the case. A sentencing hearing may take place at a change of plea hearing if prison is jointly recommended between the parties in the case. Therefore, it is important that a victim be present to speak to the court if a sentencing takes place immediately after the defendant's change of plea.

Criminal Justice Trials

The criminal justice system features two types of trials: bench trials, which are conducted before a judge, and jury trials, which are conducted before a group of citizens. It is the jury trial that is written into every document significant to the notion of American independence and justice. It finds voice in the Magna Carta, Declaration of Independence, all the state constitutions enacted between 1776 and 1786, and in the body of the U.S. Constitution and three of the Bill of Rights. Even before the enactment of the U.S. Constitution, the jury trial had become an important protection from false accusations of crime for colonial Americans (Antkowiak, 2006).

Consistent with the overall philosophy of the criminal justice system, the government faces the hurdle of having to prove the guilt of an accused to a nongovernmental body (a jury) to the highest standard known to the law: proof beyond a reasonable doubt. That is, the government must prove each element of the offense to convince a jury of the guilt of a defendant. To prove its case, the government needs evidence. Besides the testimony of witnesses, the government seeks to offer a wide variety of physical evidence it has obtained during its investigation. Evidence includes the collection of such items as body fluids, fingerprints, and fibers that then can be subjected for forensic testing for a match to the crime scene, to the defendant, and to the victim.

Victims are often confronted with repeated postponements or continuances in court proceedings. Postponements may be due to the request of the defense because the defendant has defaulted or changed lawyers or the lawyer has not had time to prepare the case. Sometimes a trial is postponed due to the prosecution because a witness is not available or the victim does not appear. The amount of time passing between the date of the crime and the final verdict may easily be over a year.

Each time the case is scheduled at the district court level or the superior court level, witnesses, including the victim, are to appear. For victims, witnesses, and the defendant, this involves a lot of waiting. Victim services were implemented in prosecutor offices as a way to ease the pain of waiting and to reduce the cost, both financial and emotional, on victims and their families.

IN THE COURTROOM

The victim enters the courtroom, which has a formal, authoritative, solemn atmosphere. The placement of furniture indicates who has the authority. The judge's bench is on a raised platform, and behind the judge's chair are the seal of the jurisdiction and the flags of the appropriate federal and state governments, symbolizing the power and authority of the state. Court personnel wear special uniforms. The judge usually wears a black robe and enters the courtroom through a special door.

Adjacent to the judge's bench are the witness stand and the desks where the court clerk and the court reporter sit. The courtroom is divided into two parts by a barrier known as the bar. On one side is the judge's bench, the tables for the plaintiff, the defendant and his or her respective counsel, and a separate group of seats known as the jury box where the jury sits. Apart from the parties to the case and any witnesses, only the lawyers can literally pass the bar (court personnel and jury members usually enter through separate doors), which is how the term "the bar" has come to refer to the legal profession as a whole. The bailiff stands against one wall and keeps order in the courtroom.

The ideology of both the American and Canadian legal systems is the adversarial system of law. Both systems feature the presumption of innocence of the defendant, the defendant's right to counsel, the right of the defendant not to testify, placing the burden of proof on the state, and the standard of proof of beyond a reasonable doubt. Three rules that can create difficulties for victims include the defendant's right to a public trial, to see his or her accuser, and to cross-examine the state's witnesses.

Although many people in a courtroom have specific reasons for being present, spectators are able to sit in the courtroom during a trial. These spectators may be family and friends of either the prosecution or the defense. Spectators may also include lawyers waiting for their turn in court, members of the general public, and court watchers who regularly pass the time of day watching cases. Victims are questioned in front of these strangers. They may be asked identifying information, such as where they live and work, as well as minute details on the crime itself. In rape cases, detailing the sexual aspects of the incident can be embarrassing and difficult.

The right of the defendant to see his or her accuser means that both the victim and the defendant are present in the courtroom. Thus, the victim comes face to face again with the person who has injured him or her and must testify in that person's presence. The prosecution and defense have the right to question each other's witnesses. The cross-examination recapitulates, on a psychological and verbal level, the original crime.

JURY TRIAL

Once the legislative body has defined the crime, the final determination of whether the crime was committed is turned over not to a body of governmental officials but to a committee of the governed: the jury. The jury trial became an important protection from false accusations of crime for colonial Americans. A great deal of faith was placed in the common law jury as providing this important protection of liberty (Antkowiak, 2006). The right to trial by jury can be found in every document relevant to the notion of American independence and justice. As stated above, reference to a trial by jury can be found in the Magna Carta; the Declaration of Independence; all state constitutions enacted between 1776 and 1786; the body of the U.S. Constitution, where it is found in Article III; and three of the Bill of Rights (Antkowiak, 2006).

Members of a jury are drawn from a group of citizens who sit in judgment of the defendant. The number of jury members varies by jurisdiction and depends on the state constitution. The jury listens to the evidence and testimony presented. Both the prosecution and the defense give opening and closing statements. After closing arguments, the judge provides instructions to the jury as to the meaning of the law. The jury deliberates and tells the bailiff when they have reached a verdict. The verdict is then taken into court and presented to the judge. The judge then asks the foreperson of the jury to read the verdict.

VICTIM'S RIGHT TO HEAR TESTIMONY

Victims have the right to be present at a trial and likely will be called as a witness in the state's presentation of evidence. A separation of witnesses order, however, may prevent a victim from being in the courtroom during testimony heard before the victim testifies. This separation order prevents a possible claim that the victim tailored his or her testimony by hearing the testimony of other witnesses first. Once a victim has testified, a victim ordinarily can be present in court to hear the testimony of other witnesses and closing arguments, as long as the victim does not disrupt the proceedings in some way.

A judicial release hearing is when a defendant who has been convicted of a felony and sentenced to prison requests that the court release him or her from prison on a term of community control. If the court is considering granting early release, a hearing in open court must be held, and the victim is entitled to be present and provide input to the court on whether the court should grant early release from prison on community control. The decision to grant or deny judicial release is made by the court, upon reviewing legal guidelines and evaluating factors present in a specific case, including any agreed upon sentence recommendation (Seneca County Prosecutor's Office, 2009).

Civil Commitments for Sex Offenders

Some states have used civil commitment proceedings to remove habitual sex offenders from society for extended periods of time. The U.S. Supreme Court ruled in *Kansas v. Hendricks* (1997) that such laws do not violate the Constitution's double jeopardy or *ex post facto* clauses. The commitment is intended to reduce the risk of future dangerous sexual behavior. It is not meant to serve as punishment for past crimes. Civilly committed sex offenders may be held for an indeterminate amount of time. In other words, they may be held as long as warranted to successfully treat them and to satisfy public safety concerns (Denner & Pellegrino, 2011).

Other Postconviction Hearings

Postconviction hearings include a direct appeal of a conviction, a judicial release hearing, and other possible hearings, including community control violation hearings. If a convicted criminal files a direct appeal upon being found guilty at trial, a victim has a right to be notified and present at the oral arguments on the appeal and to be informed of the outcome of the appeal. An appeal that results in a judgment of conviction being affirmed upholds the trial court's proceedings and its sentencing order. An appeal that results in a reversal of the conviction means there was a significant error in the lower court proceedings, which may allow for a retrial.

Sometimes cases have occurred in which the victim should have been told of a postconviction hearing or of a parole hearing and is not aware that an offender has been released. Even with the Victims' Bill of Rights, the correctional system sometimes fails in its accountability that the victim be notified when the offender is released. In such cases, the victim advocacy office or attorney general's office should be notified to address this.

Other postconviction hearings may involve notice to a victim of an upcoming parole hearing. Communication to the parole board is given through the county prosecutor's office or victim assistance program for serious felony offenses. A community control violation may involve victim notification, particularly if the nature of the alleged violation relates to the victim. A victim may receive a subpoena to testify at a revocation hearing.

Casey Anthony's Trial and Acquittal

Both the prosecutor and defense attorney make opening and closing statements about the evidence in the case. In the opening statements, the attorneys on both sides state what they plan to present, such as "you will hear X and Y," contrasted with the closing argument when the prosecutor can state that "X and Y" together prove guilt because of their conclusion. The defense attorney, in contrast, usually argues that the case has ample reasonable doubt.

The Casey Anthony case was an example of "reasonable doubt" and citizen reaction to the justice system. On July 5, 2011, people outside the courthouse in Orange County, Florida, and across the nation were outraged by the acquittal verdict in the trial for the murder of her toddler daughter, Caylee. The verdict surprised many legal analysts and commentators and spared the 25-year-old from a possible death penalty, which prosecutors planned to seek if Anthony had been found guilty as charged of first-degree murder. The prosecution's case argued that Casey Anthony used chloroform on her daughter before leaving her in the trunk of a car and duct taping her mouth and nose. The prosecutor's rationale was that Casey Anthony was a party girl who wanted to enjoy her personal life and free herself from parental responsibility. The defense's theory was that the death was accidental, and attorney Baez contended that there were holes in the prosecution's forensic evidence, saying it was based on a "fantasy."

A *not guilty verdict* generally implies that a jury did not have adequate evidence and testimony to connect a defendant to the crime. In the Casey Anthony case, the following key points suggest some of the issues with the testimony the jury considered that resulted in the failure of the State of Florida's case:

THE CAR

Casey Anthony's car became the first piece of evidence. The maternal grandmother, Cindy Anthony, called 911 on July 15, 2008, told the emergency dispatcher she had not seen the child for 31 days, and that Casey's car smelled as though there had been a dead body inside it. Prosecutors immediately took Casey into custody, interrogated her, and began to analyze the contents of the car in an attempt to prove that she was responsible for Caylee's body being in the trunk of her car based on the following:

- *Trunk odor.* Testimony was given on two odors found in the car trunk: the smell of human decomposition and chloroform. The trunk odor of decomposition (i.e., dead body, dead fish, maggots) was discussed by Cindy, George, and Casey Anthony as well as two yard employees and a dog handler. Testimony was given on unusual levels of chloroform found in the trunk, the chemical believed to be used to kill Caylee. Tests conducted on the air in the trunk by the Federal Bureau of Investigation (FBI) laboratory and by Dr. Vass's odor-analysis technique long after Caylee's disappearance indicated high levels of chloroform. At trial, the defense argued that chloroform was a volatile liquid that would dissipate quickly into the surrounding air, that Dr. Vass's odor-analysis technique was unreliable and untested for proving decomposition of a body, and blamed the stench on garbage found in the trunk.

- *Hairs.* Investigators testified that the hairs found in the trunk contained no roots or tissues and that the only test that could be used would be for mitochondrial DNA, which is passed down through female ancestors. This meant that the hairs could belong to as many as five people: Casey, her mother, grandmother, brother, and Caylee. Two experts examining the same hair could have two opinions: that the darkening was caused by either decomposition or air pockets. Identifying human hairs is not an exact science.

- *Insects.* Insects are common in murder cases where a body is found outside, but without a body in the trunk forensic entomology experts could not prove it was a human body in the trunk.

CAYLEE ANTHONY'S BODY

The child's body was not found until Roy Kronk, a meter reader, again called law enforcement on December 11, 2008. Four months before, in August 2008, Kronk had called law enforcement three times when he saw a partially submerged bag in the same area where the remains were found in December 2008. Deputy sheriffs claimed to have searched the area without success. By December 2008, six months after the child was last seen, her body had decomposed in a wooded area 20 feet off the road and less than a mile from her grandparents' home. Investigators found 350 pieces of evidence at the crime scene, including a handful of bones, a blanket that matched the bedding at her grandparents' home, laundry bags, and a relatively rare brand of duct tape:

- *Plastic bag.* Lorie Gottesman, a 20-year forensic specialist at the FBI, testified that she found no match between the black plastic bags containing a portion of Caylee's skeletal remains and similar black plastic bags collected from the Anthony home.

- *Skull.* Some crime scene photos showed the skull with a piece of duct tape around the lower facial region. In others it appeared to be lying alongside the skull. Kronk claims in December that he placed a stick in the right eye socket of the skull and "pivoted" it back and forth, thus indicating interference.

- *Duct tape.* Prosecutors contended that Anthony placed the duct tape over Caylee's nose and mouth. To support that theory, they used a video demonstration of an image of Caylee's decomposing duct-taped skull superimposed over a photograph of the toddler cheek-to-cheek with her mother as they both smiled.

CAUSE OF DEATH

Juries usually need to hear how the victim died and by what means. Medical examiners were unable to pinpoint the cause of Caylee's death or the manner of death, although a medical examiner, Dr. Jan Garavaglia, testified that she determined Caylee's manner of death to be homicide but listed it as "death by undetermined means." Forensic pathologist Dr. Werner Spitz said he could not determine Caylee Anthony's manner of death but said there was no indication to him that she was murdered. Additionally, Spitz testified that he believed the duct tape found on Caylee's skull was placed there after the body decomposed, opining that if tape was placed on the skin there should have been DNA left on it, and suggested that someone may have staged some of the crime scene photos.

THE COMPUTER

Computer-based evidence is believed to be reliable. To try to prove their assertion that Anthony searched the Internet for homemade chloroform recipes, prosecutors called on digital forensics experts who recovered searches from Anthony's laptop, even after they had been erased. However, investigators could not place a person at the computer. Prosecutors emphasized that the Internet searches occurred on Anthony's computer, whereas defense lawyers stressed that many people other than Anthony had access to the computer.

A jury generally needs three issues answered for a guilty verdict: motive, opportunity, and intent. Despite the claim by the state that Casey wanted to live the life of a party girl, there was no evidence Casey wanted Caylee dead for any reason. The fact that Casey had neither car nor child at various times on the 16th and 17th means that there is much doubt as to whether Casey had the opportunity to kill Caylee. In light of Lee's testimony, the only way Casey could get Caylee back was to stay quiet and *not* talk to the police. There was no evidence of intent to harm Caylee (Murphy, 2011).

Wendy J. Murphy, a former child abuse prosecutor, was not surprised at the verdict and called for full disclosure of the sealed evidence of photographs. It is true, writes Murphy, that Casey Anthony's failure to report Caylee missing for more than a month is powerful evidence of her consciousness of guilt. The question is guilt about what? It's just as possible Casey did not kill her child, that she was afraid to call the police, and that her fear was related to some unknown evidence such as those sealed photographs of Caylee. As Casey's brother Lee testified at trial, Casey was told Caylee was taken from her to "teach her a lesson." If Casey knew the people who had Caylee and stayed quiet in the hope they would give her child back, her failure to report Caylee missing makes sense (Murphy, 2011).

Sentencing

If a defendant is acquitted, the judge thanks the jury for their work and releases the defendant. If the defendant is found guilty, the trial moves into the sentencing phase. The court considers principles of sentencing in its deliberations, including punishment of the offender, denunciation of the crime, general (the public) and specific (the offender) deterrence from committing crimes of this nature, and protection of the public. In arriving at an appropriate sentence, a sentencing hearing may be held at which evidence of aggravating or mitigating circumstances is considered. In assessing the circumstances surrounding a convicted person's criminal behavior, courts often rely on presentence investigations by probation agencies or other designated authorities. Although sentencing is proportional to the crime, not the harms caused by it, courts may also consider victim impact statements.

A restitution order ordinarily is included in the sentencing order. All documented economic losses, such as loss of income due to lost time at work because of any injury caused to the victim, and any property losses, medical costs, or funeral expenses incurred as a result of the commission of the offense may be submitted to the court to determine restitution.

VICTIM IMPACT STATEMENT

The 1991, case of *Payne v. Tennessee* (501 U.S. 808) is believed to be the first case to recognize the rights of crime victims to make a **victim impact statement** in the sentencing phase of a criminal trial. On June 27, 1987, Pervis Tyrone Payne took cocaine and drank malt liquor and, after viewing pornography, attempted to rape and then murdered an acquaintance of his, Charisse Christopher, and her 2-year-old daughter. Police were called by neighbors who witnessed a bloody Payne exiting the apartment building.

Forensic evidence noted 42 stab wounds to Charisse's body. Payne had also made multiple stab wounds to Charisse's 3-year-old son, who was rushed to the hospital. The evidence of fingerprints, the victim's blood-soaked clothes, and Payne's property left at the scene was sufficient to cause a jury to convict Payne of two counts of first-degree murder, two counts of attempted murder, and a related charge. During sentencing the prosecutor introduced victim impact statements to show the effect of the murders on the victims' friends, family, and neighbors.

Payne appealed the sentence, claiming it was an unconstitutional violation of his Eighth Amendment right against cruel and unusual punishment and argued that the victim impact statements emotionally influenced the jury to recommend the death penalty. Payne pointed to the U.S. Supreme Court decisions that held that victim impact statements were *not* admissible during the sentencing phases of capital murder trials.

The case was appealed, and the Tennessee Supreme Court upheld the sentence. Payne appealed again, and the Tennessee Supreme Court found that the victim impact statements did not create a constitutionally unacceptable risk of an arbitrary imposition of the death penalty. The U.S. Supreme Court upheld the sentence finding that the introduction of victim impact statements was not an unconstitutional violation of the Eighth Amendment, overruling two prior cases, *Booth v. Maryland* (1987) and *South Carolina v. Gathers* (1989). That ruling left it up to the states to allow or disallow victim impact statements (*Payne v. Tennessee*, 90-5721, 501 U.S. 808 [1991]).

Correctional System

After a conviction, the sentence is imposed. In most cases the judge decides on the sentence, but in some jurisdictions the jury, particularly for capital offenses, determines the sentence. Offenders sentenced to incarceration usually serve time in a local jail or a prison. The difference between jail and prison is the length of stay for inmates. Jails are usually run by local law enforcement and/or local government agencies, and are designed to hold inmates awaiting trial or serving a short sentence. Thus, offenders sentenced to less than 1 year generally go to jail (2 years in Canada); those sentenced for longer periods of time go to prison. Persons admitted to the prison system may be held in prisons with varying levels of custody or in a community correctional facility. A prisoner may become eligible for parole after serving a specific part of his or her sentence. **Parole** is the conditional release of a prisoner before the prisoner's full sentence has been served. The decision to grant parole is made by an authority such as a parole board, which has power to grant or revoke parole or to discharge a parolee altogether. The way parole decisions are made varies widely among jurisdictions (Bureau of Justice Statistics, n.d.).

Offenders may also be required to serve out their full sentences before release (expiration of term). Those sentenced under determinate sentencing laws can be released only after they have served their full sentence (mandatory release) less any "good time" received while in prison. Inmates get good time credits against their sentences automatically or by earning them through participation in programs. If released by a parole board decision or by mandatory release, the release will be under the supervision of a parole officer in the community for the balance of his or her unexpired sentence. This supervision is governed by specific conditions of release, and the release may be returned to prison for violations of such conditions (Bureau of Justice Statistics, n.d.).

Impact of Trials on Juries

Some cases can have a tremendous emotional impact on a jury. Such was the case in the trial of the two defendants of the Petit family murders of the mother and two daughters (*New York Times*, 2010). To address the secondary trauma of that case, the Connecticut state judicial branch, for the first time in state history, offered posttraumatic stress assistance to jurors who served in the Petit family triple-murder trial. Because the jurors were required to look at disturbing images and hear grisly testimony during the two-month trial, their service necessitated these actions. A spokesperson confirmed that such posttraumatic assistance has never been done before by the state's judicial branch. The trial of Casey Anthony is another example of a case that took a toll on the jurors. Because of public outrage and death threats, the judge refused initially to release the names of the jurors in the Anthony trial, and most did not respond to requests for media interviews.

Restitution

Courts in 17th-century England are believed to have been the first courts to have used restitution as a contractual remedy. This concept of giving back to an injured party migrated to courts in the United States, and has since become an integral part of the U.S. criminal justice system. The basic principle is to achieve fairness and prevent unjust enrichment of a party.

The criminal is generally perceived as the appropriate source of benefits for the victim of crime. Yet those remedies that involve the criminal—self-help, civil actions, and restitution ordered by a criminal court—are inadequate for most victims of crime because in theory, victims of crimes have, for centuries, had the option of bringing tort (civil) actions against individuals who have wronged them. All too often, however, offenders remain unidentified, rendering it impossible to file any sort of claim. Further, even when the perpetrator is known, victims frequently cannot afford to bring suit, or if a successful suit is accomplished, offenders are often poor, making actual financial compensation highly unlikely. Civil actions are also commonly subject to delays of several months or even years, which can discourage such actions at the outset and certainly diminish a victim's hope for any tangible satisfaction.

Restitution may take the classic form of return or repair of stolen or damaged property. It most often involves monetary payments, either lump sum or periodic, for property loss or damage. It may also involve payments for personal injuries. The increased use of restitution in contemporary times started at the Minnesota Restitution Center in the 1970s. It has since spread throughout the United States, with restitution experiments at various stages in the criminal justice process funded by the Law Enforcement Assistance Administration (LEAA/OJP Retrospective, 1996).

The sentencing court can order the defendant to pay restitution to the victim, known as a *direct order of restitution*, or restitution fines. With regard to the federal courts, the U.S. Parole Commission can establish the repayment of this restitution as a condition of parole or supervised release. Inmates may even begin payment of fines and restitution during their incarceration (U.S. Department of Justice, 2015a).

A second, less formal method of achieving restitution in the mid-1970s, the neighborhood justice center, was the forerunner of the current restorative justice concept. Many communities in the United States established programs, with the cooperation of police departments and prosecutors, in which victims of minor crimes were brought together with offenders to resolve original or resulting disputes. The supposed advantage to the victim of mediation or arbitration is restitution rather than merely the satisfaction that the offender has been prosecuted.

Parole Hearings

The purpose of a parole hearing is to determine whether an inmate should be released from prison to parole supervision in the community for the remainder of the inmate's sentence. A Hearing Examiner of the United States Parole Commission reviews the inmate's record and conducts the hearing. A Commissioner of the Parole Commission makes the parole decision (U.S. Department of Justice, 2015b).

Specific criteria must be met in order to hold a parole hearing. Usually a minimum term of incarceration must be met (determined by the sentencing court) prior to an inmate's parole eligibility. Inmates cannot be released to parole prior to their eligibility date. Also, the scheduling of a parole hearing does not guarantee release. Inmates may have several parole hearings before being released, and some parole-eligible inmates are never released for parole supervision. Federal law may also require a parole hearing every two years (U.S. Department of Justice, 2015b).

ATTENDANCE AT HEARINGS

The parole hearing is not an open hearing. Aside from the parole board and the offender, the parole hearing is generally limited to the victim and the victim's next-of-kin or immediate family members. A support person may accompany the victim or family member to the hearing but this person cannot participate in the hearing. Victims and their families also have the opportunity to assign a representative to speak on their behalf at the hearing (U.S. Department of Justice, 2015b).

NOTIFICATION OF HEARINGS

Victims of crime who wish to be notified of parole hearings can register for the Federal Victim Notification System (VNS) by contacting the Commission's Victim Support Program Victims can obtain automated status information by calling the VNS Call Center at 1-866-365-4968 (1-866-DOJ-4YOU) or by accessing the VNS Internet site at www.notify.usdoj.gov. A Victim ID# and PIN# are required to access the VNS Call Center or VNS Internet site. The website is https://www.justice.gov/criminal-vns/automated-victim-notification-system.

VICTIM APPEARANCE

The victim can participate in a parole hearing in a number of ways. The victim may be present at the hearing, make a video statement from a United States Attorney's Office, submit a written or recorded statement to the Commission prior to the hearing or request to present an oral statement to a Hearing Examiner at the Commission's office in Washington, DC, who will prepare a statement for the inmate's case record (U.S. Department of Justice, 2015b).

The Victim Support Program can assist in helping crime victims participate in the parole hearing by any of the methods identified above. Victims may call the toll-free telephone number 1-888-585-9103 or send an email to USPC. VictimAdv@usdoj.gov or mail a request to 90 K Street NE, 3rd Floor, Washington, DC, 20530-0001 (U.S. Department of Justice, 2015b).

For additional information on the Commission's procedures for the attendance of a victim at a parole hearing, persons are directed to the Commission's Rules and Procedures Manual (see section 2.13(b) and 2.13–11 regarding federal offenders and section 2.72(e) regarding District of Columbia Code offenders).

RESULTS OF THE PAROLE HEARING

The outcome of the parole hearing will be given to victims and witnesses upon request. The outcome requires completion of a victim/witness notification request form. This form is usually sent to witnesses along with the subpoena (U.S. Department of Justice, 2015b).

O.J. Simpson's Parole Hearing

In 2008, O.J. Simpson and an associate were convicted of kidnapping, armed robbery, and assault with a deadly weapon for attempting to steal pieces of Simpson sports memorabilia at gunpoint. At the time of the incident, Simpson said that he had gone to the room in the Palace Station Hotel & Casino in Las Vegas to reclaim family heirlooms and other personal items that had been taken from him. In addition, he claimed not to know his associates were armed. Simpson stated that he was not there to hurt anyone but only sought the return of personal possessions. Simpson was convicted and sentenced to 9 to 33 years. He served his time in the medium-security Lovelock Correctional Center. At his parole hearing 9 years later, in 2017, he further said it was "stupid" of him and that he was sorry.

At his televised 2017 parole hearing, Simpson spoke clearly as to why he should be granted parole. He identified several mitigating factors that made him a good candidate for release. He had been discipline-free in prison, he had stable release plans, he had family and community support—and he had no prior criminal convictions. Simpson also apologized, saying that he had spent the past nine years making no excuses about anything. He was *sorry* things turned out the way they did. Simpson emphasized that he told inmates all the time not to complain about their grind and to just do their time. He said he believed in the jury system and would honor the parole board decision. He said he had done his time and wanted to get back to his friends, and stressed that he did have friends (Boren, 2017).

Four members of the board of the Carson City, Nevada, Probation and Parole Division office heard Simpson's case. In addition to his lawyer, Malcolm LaVergne, his elder daughter, Arnelle, attended the hearing, along with his sister, Shirley Baker, and his friend Tom Scotto. Bruce Fromong, who described himself as a friend of 27 years, was one of the victims of the crime and read a statement on Simpson's behalf, "time for him to go home for his family and friends" (Boren, 2017). All four board members voted for Simpson's release, and board member Tony Corda said he was graded a "low risk to reoffend."

Capital Punishment and Death Penalty Cases

Early Roots of Capital Punishment

Early laws that encouraged individuals to seek retribution by killing their offenders began the tradition of defining and listing the crimes that would deserve a death penalty and set a precedent for Western legal codes. For example, the Babylonian Code of Hammurabi, written around 1786 B.C., arbitrarily made the selling of beer and revealing the location of sacred burial places crimes punishable by death (Henderson, 2000). In the 7th century, government leaders concluded that crime harmed society's collective interests, and thus the government became more involved in controlling and punishing crimes. To protect society, leaders passed laws and devised lists of punishments to fit specific crimes. Laws were focused more on keeping the peace in society than on serving justice, with the Justinian Code of A.D. 529 standing as an example.

In ancient Greece and Rome, the prime reason for execution was to punish those who had attacked the state. The use of capital punishment for two specific offenses were Socrates's execution for heresy, ca. 399 B.C., and the crucifixion of Jesus Christ, ca. A.D. 33, whose formal charge was sedition against the state (Henderson, 2000). In the ancient world, punishment was violent and often a means of inflicting torture, as well as death.

During the Middle Ages, a number of methods were used to determine the guilt of an offender, including physical fights between the offender and the victim (or victim's family member), the torture of the accused to see if he or she would survive, and testimony as to the truthfulness of the accused. This latter method of determining innocence or guilt was reserved for the members of the higher classes of society (Banks, 2005). These three methods slowly lost popularity as governments realized they were ineffective. Trial by jury became the accepted and effective way of establishing guilt and was widely used by the mid-13th century. As civil and criminal law developed, torture was slowly phased out. Common methods of torture including chopping off the hands and feet, impaling the body on a large stake, stripping off the skin, boiling a person alive in oil, drawing and quartering, burning at the stake, and crucifying. The period between 1400 and 1800 was marked by enough executions that the laws on capital punishment were later dubbed the "Bloody Code" (Levinson, 2002).

The 18th-century European Enlightenment focused on ideas that emphasized the value of humankind and individual potential. Reformists began thinking about how the government could serve the common good, and the use of incarceration and taking away liberty as punishment grew in favor (Banks, 2005).

Capital Punishment in America

The American system of capital punishment, based on British law, grew out of the Western basis for capital punishment: personal retribution. As the colonies began to define American legal codes, patterns of punishment surfaced. The Bill of Rights, ratified in 1791, controlled the use of capital punishment by prohibiting "cruel and unusual punishment" in the Eighth Amendment. In the first half of the 19th century, prisons began to provide tailored punishment to convicts, offering probation and other rehabilitative programs. Hanging was criticized as too brutal, the product of a more barbaric society, and a growing faith in science as the means of ameliorating aspects of the human condition led to the advent of the electric chair. The first chair was built in New York in 1888, and used in 1890 to execute William Kemmler. On the morning of March 29, 1889, William Kemmler, 30, was drinking beer when John Debella, one of his employees, arrived to take him to work. Kemmler became angry when his common-law wife, Tillie Ziegler, talked to Debella. He accused her of deceiving him, stealing money from him, and planning to leave him. Tillie admitted that it was all true. Kemmler became quiet, left the house, returned with a hatchet, and struck Tillie in the head more than 20 times. When he was finished he went to a neighbor's house and said, "I killed her. I had to do it. I meant to. I'll take the rope for it." Kemmler was tried, convicted, and executed August 6, 1890 (MacLead, 2011).

Capital punishment was on the decline around the turn of the 20th century. Crime continued to be seen as the result of a criminal's environment, and science was suggesting it was also the result of inborn genetic traits. As the criminal was viewed as a victim of outside forces, the death penalty became less and less just. The shift away from capital punishment changed when America entered World War I. Because of the fear generated by the Russian Revolution and class conflicts, many states that had abolished the death penalty reinstated it, and no states abolished capital punishment until the 1950s. In fact, support for and use of capital punishment grew from 1920 to 1935. Ten American states abolished the death penalty between 1897 and 1917, but by the end of the 1930s, eight of these states had reinstated capital punishment (Galliher, Ray, & Cook, 1992).

In the mid-1950s, the death penalty debate resurfaced. Caryl Chessman, 27, convicted of kidnapping, robbery, sexual mistreatment, and attempted rape, was sentenced to death because kidnapping carried a mandatory death sentence in California, based on the passage of the 1933 Lindbergh federal law. Chessman appealed his sentence 42 times and remained on death row for 12 years before being executed in 1960 (*West's Encyclopedia of American Law*, 2011). Chessman wrote several books while in prison, one of which was an autobiography, titled *Cell 2455, Death Row*. Chessman's case brought the death penalty question back to the forefront of issues facing society.

Simultaneously, support for capital punishment was waning as many nations around the world abolished the death penalty (Death Penalty

Information Center, 2009). The main points of the worldwide debate currently surrounding the death penalty are not new but seem to accumulate and converge as societies progress.

Death Penalty Case

Legal experts have dubbed the Petit triple-family murders in Cheshire, Connecticut, as a "poster child" for the debate on capital punishment (*New York Times*, 2010). Defendant Hayes's own defense attorney alluded to the difficulty of producing a jury who would not be so outraged as to incline toward the death penalty. He acknowledged that even someone opposed to the death penalty in general would have difficulty not recommending it in this case. The notoriety of this crime extends well beyond Cheshire and even the state; indeed, it has national implications and genuine human interest.

In early 2009, the Connecticut General Assembly sent legislation to abolish the state's death penalty to Governor Rell, ostensibly to be signed into law. However, on June 5, 2009, Rell vetoed the bill instead, and cited the Cheshire murders as an exemplary reason for doing so (Governor Rell Vetoes HB 6578, 2009). On November 8, 2010, Governor Rell issued the following statement regarding the jury's recommendation of a sentence of death for Hayes (Rell, 2009):

> The crimes that were committed on that brutal July night were so far out of the range of normal understanding that now, more than three years later, we still find it difficult to accept that they happened in one of our communities. I have long believed that there are certain crimes so heinous, so depraved, that society is best served by imposing the ultimate sanction on the criminal. Steven Hayes stands convicted of such crimes—and today the jury has recommended that he should be subjected to the death penalty. I agree.

However, by 2016, the Connecticut Supreme Court had voted a second time to abolish the death penalty and reclassified 11 death row inmates, including Hayes. Dr. Pettit was dismayed:

> Now people have decided to change the game. . . . You end up not having much faith in the criminal justice system because it's really not a justice system. It's a legal system moved by the winds of different opinions and who has been appointed. I think it's a sad day for jurisprudence in the state of Connecticut.
>
> (Griffin & Kauffman, 2016)

Critical Issues in the Criminal Justice System

The following issues on pretrial detention, reintegration after incarceration, and probation have been debated in criminal justice circles in the last decade.

Period from Arrest to Pretrial Detention

Since the 1980s, there has been a significant, nationwide move away from courts allowing nonfinancial forms of pretrial release (such as release on own recognizance) to money bail, although this varies substantially depending on jurisdiction. Almost all defendants will have the opportunity to be released pretrial if they meet certain conditions, and only a very small number of defendants will be denied a bail bond, mainly because a court finds that individual to be dangerous or a flight risk. The national data on pretrial detention comes from the Bureau of Justice Statistics' Felony Defendants in Large Urban Counties series. Nationally, in 2009, 34% of defendants were detained pretrial for the inability to post money bail (Joyce, 2016).

Reintegration of the Incarcerated into Society

In his review of criminal justice policy in the United States, sociologist Bruce Western (2003) examined the societal reintegration of the formerly incarcerated and suggested that the challenge was to draw people back into communities rather than exclude them. He emphasized addressing incarceration itself as well as reentry policies. One of the unexpected findings from Western's study was the prevalence of a history of victimization among those who would later serve time in prison, regardless of demographic variables. He noted that there was little distinction between victims and offenders, noting that many of the formerly incarcerated had long histories of trauma and victimization. Western raised the ethical question about the role of punishment in the criminal justice system, stating that incarceration is fundamentally disruptive and that society needs to readjust how it views life after incarceration (Western, 2013).

Probation

Since the beginning of the statistics almost 40 years ago, the probation population has grown much more quickly than either the number of people on parole or the number of people in federal, state, and local prisons and jails. Whereas about 2.3 million U.S. residents were behind bars in 2012, almost 4 million were under probation (Wagner, 2015).

Civil Justice System

Civil laws are rules and regulations that govern transactions and grievances between individual citizens. The civil justice system is really a system of private justice. In the legal system of continental Europe, the civil justice system is referred to as *private law*. This is in contrast to *public law*, such as in criminal law where the government or the public is always a party (Cafardi, 2006). In the civil justice system parties are private individuals or corporations or companies who are either suing or being sued. The parties involved are the plaintiff and the defendant, and it is the plaintiff's burden to prove the elements of a civil claim against a defendant. If the elements of the claim are proven, the defendant will have to pay the plaintiff. Criminal justice deals with alleged crimes and can lead to fines or prison. A civil justice case deals with civil claims and can lead to money damages and injunctions (Cafardi, 2006). Crime victims seek civil justice by filing lawsuits against criminal perpetrators or other responsible parties to be compensated for the damages incurred as a result of the criminal act.

In 2015, U.S. residents age 12 or older experienced an estimated 5.0 million violent victimizations, according to the Bureau of Justice Statistics' (BJS) National Crime Victimization Survey (NCVS). The consequences of crime frequently extend far beyond the criminal act. All too often victims are left with expenses for medical procedures, physical rehabilitation, counseling, and lost wages. It is estimated that crime costs victims $345 billion annually. Although many crime victims and their families have some knowledge about the legal system, they are often unaware that two systems of justice are available in which to hold the offender accountable: the criminal justice system and the civil justice system.

The criminal courts can provide crime victims with a sense of justice and can sometimes provide victims compensation through restitution orders. Unfortunately, even when restitution is ordered, it is rarely enforced. This lack of enforcement combined with statutory restrictions on the type of damages that may be included in a restitution order often result in restitution falling far short of meeting victims' needs. Compensation may also be available from the state's crime victims' compensation board; however, these programs are often subject to restrictions and limitations that may prevent crime victims from being fully compensated.

Civil Procedures

The civil justice system, unlike the criminal justice process, does not attempt to determine the innocence or guilt of an offender and does not seek to incarcerate the offender. Rather, the civil courts attempt to ascertain whether an offender or a third party is civilly liable for the injuries sustained as a result of the crime. In civil cases, the "crime" is referred to as a *tort*. For most criminal offenses there is a corresponding tort for which a crime victim may bring a civil suit. TABLE 5-2 provides examples of causes of civil action.

Most often, a civil court's finding of liability means the defendant must pay the victim and/or the victim's family monetary damages. In this respect, the civil justice system can provide victims with more of the monetary resources needed to help rebuild their lives. Furthermore, the civil justice system often provides victims and their families with a sense of justice the criminal courts cannot. Rather than holding a defendant accountable for his or her "crime against the state," the civil justice system holds a defendant who is found liable directly accountable to the victim for the harms he or she has suffered.

TABLE 5-2 Causes of Civil Action

Cause	Definition
Assault	Putting the victim in fear of being injured while the perpetrator has the present and immediate capacity to inflict that injury.
Battery	Any intentional physical contact that offends the victim. Battery includes, but is not limited to, the crimes of sexual battery, rape, molestation, fondling, forcible sodomy, malicious wounding, and attempted murder.
Wrongful death	A death caused by another person that occurs without justification or excuse, including murder, manslaughter, and vehicular homicide.
False imprisonment	Holding a victim against his or her will for any amount of time, no matter how brief. This often occurs in rape and kidnapping situations.
Intentional or reckless infliction of emotional distress	Causing a victim emotional distress or anxiety through extreme, outrageous, and offensive conduct. Emotional distress is usually claimed in conjunction with another tort rather than standing alone. Emotional distress is frequently seen in stalking cases.
Fraud	An intentional misrepresentation of facts made to deceive the victim, resulting in damages. This is often seen in white collar or economic crimes such as criminal fraud, telemarketing schemes, racketeering, etc.
Conversion	The theft or destruction of personal property, other belongings, or money. This includes larceny, concealment, embezzlement, etc.

Process for a Civil Claim

The first step in the civil process is to file the claim or complaint. The victim and the victim's attorney have control over the causes of action against the third party or offender, in contrast to the criminal justice process whereby the prosecutor controls the filing of charges. The claim or complaint is a written document usually called a *pleading*. There are three components to a claim: (1) it establishes the subject-matter jurisdiction, (2) it sets for the facts constituting the cause of action, and (3) it asks for certain types of relief (Wallace & Roberson, 2010). The causes of action, or legal theories, need to be proven for the victim, called the *plaintiff*, to receive compensation for injuries.

Two types of monetary awards are available. *Compensatory damages* in the form of monetary amounts are awarded to plaintiffs for the injuries they suffered. *Punitive damages* are monetary amounts awarded to the plaintiff to punish the defendant and to send a message to other similarly situated persons, usually third parties such as a corporation for failing to provide adequate security. The complaint lists the issues and parties involved in the lawsuit. The complaint also asks for relief. This relief is known as the *prayer* and generally cites a specific amount of money or, if unknown at the time, states "damages according to proof."

Once the complaint is filed in the proper jurisdiction, the defendant(s) is served with a copy. A response is generally required in 30 days or a default judgment may be entered for the plaintiff.

PRETRIAL ACTIVITIES

A number of pretrial activities may occur before either mediation or a trial. These legal maneuvers often account for the delays in the process. The most important motion that can be filed by the defense is a *summary judgment*. This motion is used to dismiss the entire case or to strike portions of the complaint. *Discovery* allows each side to learn the facts and theories each side is claiming. The tools of discovery include depositions, interrogatories, and requests for production of documents. The chart in FIGURE 5-3 flows from top to bottom unless indicated otherwise by arrows and is a useful schematic for both U.S. and Canadian civil justice processes.

BURDEN OF PROOF

In the civil justice system, liability must be proven by a preponderance of the evidence, which simply means that one side's evidence is more persuasive than the other's. This standard is far less than the proof beyond a reasonable doubt required for a conviction in the criminal justice system. Therefore,

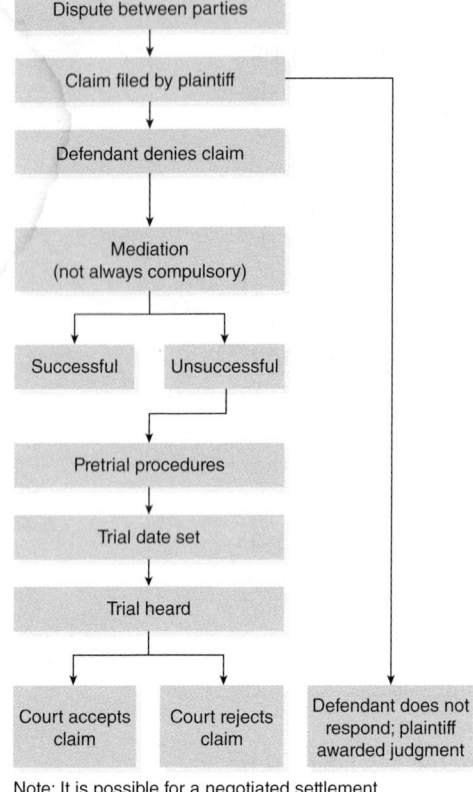

Dispute between parties

↓

Claim filed by plaintiff

↓

Defendant denies claim

↓

Mediation
(not always compulsory)

↓

Successful | Unsuccessful

↓

Pretrial procedures

↓

Trial date set

↓

Trial heard

↓

Court accepts claim | Court rejects claim | Defendant does not respond; plaintiff awarded judgment

Note: It is possible for a negotiated settlement to occur at any stage in the process.

FIGURE 5-3 Civil justice process flowchart.

Data from: Alberta Justice. 2008. Justice Process. (Civil Claims).

FIGURE 5-4 In 1995, O.J. Simpson was found not guilty of the murder of Nicole Brown and Ron Goldman but was later found liable in a civil case.

© Pool/Getty Images.

it is sometimes possible to find the defendant liable in a civil case even though a verdict of "not guilty" was rendered in the criminal case—or even if the offender was never prosecuted. A good example of this principle is the O.J. Simpson case (**FIGURE 5.4**). Simpson, a former professional football player and well-known sports commentator, was prosecuted for the murder of his former wife, Nicole Brown, and her friend, Ron Goldman. In 1995, the jury found Simpson not guilty of the murders. Despite Simpson's acquittal in the criminal justice system, the families of Nicole Brown and Ron Goldman filed a wrongful death lawsuit against Simpson. A civil trial was held in 1997, and Simpson was found liable for the deaths of Brown and Goldman. The jury in the civil case awarded the victims' families $33.5 million in damages. Although a criminal conviction may increase the chances of a perpetrator being held civilly liable, it is by no means a requirement for bringing a civil action.

Third-Party Liability

Civil courts have been used successfully to obtain reparations for the victim from third parties instead of the offender. The courts view that those who could have prevented the commission of a crime through the exercise of due care are civilly liable to the victim for his or her injuries. Such **third-party liability** extends to those having a duty to have interfered with the offender on behalf of the victim. Third-party defendants are not the persons who actually commit the acts but instead are those parties who may have contributed to or facilitated them. The following are a few examples of possible third-party defendants in a victim's case:

- Hotel, motel, and apartment owners who do not have adequate security measures, such as locks on doors and windows, and proper lighting to provide for the safety of their guests.

- Colleges and universities that fail to provide adequate security for students or fail to notify students of campus assaults, leaving students vulnerable to victimizations.

- Shopping malls that do not employ security patrols or other necessary measures despite a likelihood or a history of criminal attacks on customers.

- A person who allows a child access to a firearm or other dangerous instrument and the child, in turn, uses the weapon to injure another person.

- Child-care centers, schools, and churches that do not properly check the backgrounds of their employees or simply transfer employees to other locations following allegations of abuse.

- A tavern owner or social host who continues to serve alcohol to an inebriated person who subsequently injures someone in a drunk driving crash.

It should also be noted that successful civil lawsuits could have a significant deterrent effect. Actions against negligent third parties can promote enhanced safety practices and encourage the exercise of greater caution, thereby reducing the likelihood that others will become victims of crime. For example, in a 1998 case, *Fough v. Texas Health Enterprises, Inc.*, Texas's largest nursing home operator agreed to pay $4.65 million to the estate of a partially paralyzed woman who was sexually abused repeatedly by a male nurse's aide. Trial evidence established that the defendant nursing home was negligent in hiring the nurse's aide by (1) failing to check job references, (2) ignoring a two-year gap in his employment history, (3) failing to verify his nurse's aide certification status with the State of Texas and the State of Kansas, and (4) failing to submit the criminal history checks required under law. It was undisputed that the nurse's aide had previously served time in the penitentiary for felony crimes, which made him ineligible for employment in a nursing home.

Jaycee Dugard was abducted at the age of 11 in 1991 by convicted sex offender Philip Craig Garrido. It was not until 18 years later that she was discovered and freed by law enforcement officials. In July 2010, the State of California approved a $20 million settlement with Jaycee Dugard to compensate her for lapses in supervision of Garrido by the Corrections Department that prolonged Dugard's continued captivity, ongoing sexual assault, and mental abuses (La Ganga & Goldmacher, 2010). The settlement, part of AB1714, was approved by the California State Assembly by a 70 to 2 vote and by the California State Senate by a 30 to 1 vote. San Francisco County Superior Court Judge Daniel Weinstein, who mediated the settlement, stated that the settlement was reached to avoid a lawsuit that would be an added invasion of privacy and publicity for California (La Ganga & Goldmacher, 2010).

Considerations for Pursuing Civil Justice

A significant difference between the criminal and civil court systems is that in a civil case the victim, usually through the advocacy of a privately retained attorney, controls essential decisions shaping the case. It is the victim who ultimately decides, usually on the advice of his or her attorney, whether to sue, accept a settlement offer, or go to trial.

Through civil litigation more and more victims are obtaining payment for medical expenses, psychological counseling, lost wages, earning ability, and property loss. In addition, they are more frequently recovering damages for "pain and suffering," a remedy traditionally unavailable through restitution ordered by criminal courts. However, a victim contemplating a civil lawsuit should bear in mind that obtaining a civil judgment is only half the battle. In many cases in which the victim wins a judgment, it may be difficult to collect the money awarded by the court. Victims, their lawyers, and advocates recognize that justice demands that such judgments be satisfied. Unfortunately, many defendants do not pay these judgments, and the victim and his or her attorney before filing a civil lawsuit should consider this possibility seriously. Nevertheless, there are numerous sources of assets with which perpetrators can satisfy civil judgments. Many of those sources fall into three broad categories:

- *Current and expected assets.* These include cash, securities, wages, and both real and personal property as well as expected assets such as inheritances, interests in estates, pensions, and annuities.

- *Insurance.* Many perpetrators will have some kind of insurance coverage: homeowners, automobile, professional, general liability, etc. Although most insurance policies exclude intentional acts from coverage, in some circumstances perpetrators are able to use insurance coverage to satisfy civil judgments.

- *Windfalls.* Perpetrators sometimes come into sums of money that no one could have anticipated such as unexpected inheritances or proceeds from lawsuits. Some prisoners have even won lotteries.

Statutes of Limitations

Laws have been passed that have established time limits for filing civil suits. These statutes of limitation vary from state to state but usually are from one to three years. Any suit filed after the expiration of the statute of limitations is time barred and cannot proceed. However, in certain circumstances, such as those involving child victims and victims with repressed memories, the time in which victims can file suit has been extended. Although there is a limited time in which to file a suit, once a judgment is obtained, it is valid for a minimum of 20 years and can often be extended. In other words, even if a perpetrator has no assets today, filing suit and securing a judgment may allow the victim to seize assets the perpetrator may obtain many years in the future.

The Juvenile Justice System

Juvenile courts usually have jurisdiction over matters concerning children, including delinquency, neglect, and adoption. They also handle *status offenses*, such as truancy and running away, that are not applicable to adults. State statutes define which persons are under the original jurisdiction of the juvenile court. The upper age of juvenile court jurisdiction in delinquency matters is 17 in most states.

The processing of juvenile offenders is not entirely dissimilar to adult criminal processing, but there are crucial differences. Many juveniles are referred to juvenile courts by law enforcement officers, but many others are referred by school officials, social services agencies, neighbors, and even parents, for behavior or conditions that are determined to require intervention by the formal system for social control.

At arrest, a decision is made either to send the matter further into the justice system or to divert the case out of the system, often to alternative programs. Examples of alternative programs include drug treatment, individual or group counseling, or referral to educational and recreational programs.

When juveniles are referred to the juvenile courts, the court's intake department or the prosecuting attorney determines whether sufficient grounds exist to warrant filing a petition that requests an adjudicatory hearing or a request to transfer jurisdiction to criminal court. At this point, many juveniles are released or diverted to alternative programs.

All states allow juveniles to be tried as adults in criminal court under certain circumstances. In many states, the legislature statutorily excludes certain (usually serious) offenses from the jurisdiction of the juvenile court regardless of the age of the accused.

Juveniles are afforded many of the due process safeguards associated with adult criminal trials. For example, most states do not make provisions for juries in juvenile courts.

In disposing of cases, juvenile courts usually have far more discretion than adult courts. In addition to such options as probation, commitment to a residential facility, restitution, or fines, state laws grant juvenile courts the power to order removal of children from their homes to foster homes or treatment facilities. Juvenile courts also may order participation in special programs aimed at shoplifting prevention, drug counseling, or driver education.

Once a juvenile is under juvenile court disposition, the court may retain jurisdiction until the juvenile legally becomes an adult (at age 21 in most states). In some jurisdictions, juvenile offenders may be classified as youthful offenders, which can lead to extended sentences.

Following release from an institution, juveniles are often ordered to a period of aftercare that is similar to parole supervision for adult offenders. Juvenile offenders who violate the conditions of aftercare may have their aftercare revoked and may be subject to adult sanctions.

▪ Conclusion

Throughout the Middle Ages, laws were often created or abolished according to the ruling nobility, and law could be established by philosophers or religion. In contemporary societies, laws are typically created and enforced by governments. These laws may coexist with or contradict other forms of social control, such as religious proscriptions, professional rules and ethics, or the cultural mores and customs of a society.

Under the U.S. form of government, each state and the federal government has its own criminal justice system. In Canada, a federal criminal code covers all jurisdictions. All systems must respect the rights of individuals set forth in court interpretation of the constitutional rights of individuals and defined in case law.

Although money awarded in civil lawsuits can never fully compensate a victim for the trauma of his or her victimization or the loss of a loved one, it can provide valuable resources for crime victims to help rebuild their lives. Furthermore, the exposure to civil liability is a powerful incentive for landlords, businessmen, and other proprietors to enact the security measures necessary to prevent future victimizations.

◾ Key Terms

Adjudication: Includes all formal and informal steps within the criminal process.

Civil justice system: A network of courts and legal processes that enforce, restore, or protect private and personal rights.

Criminal charges: A formal accusation of having committed a criminal offense.

Criminal law: Concerned with actions that are harmful to society in which prosecution is pursued by the state, not the individual.

Defendant: A person or institution against whom an action is brought in a court of law; the person being sued or accused.

English common law: The traditional, unwritten law of England that forms the basis of modern statutes.

Grand jury: A jury convened to inquire into accusations of crime and to evaluate the grounds for indictments.

Juvenile justice system: Has jurisdiction over cases involving persons age 17 and younger.

Laws: Define the criminal justice system within each jurisdiction and delegate the authority and responsibility for criminal justice to various jurisdictions, officials, and institutions.

Parole: Release of a prisoner who agrees to certain conditions before the completion of the maximum sentence period.

Pretrial: A conference held before the trial begins to bring the parties together to outline discovery proceedings and to define the issues.

Third-party liability: Responsibility held by a person or organization that did not commit the offense but may have contributed to or facilitated the offense.

Victim impact statement: A statement given by the victim(s) that details how the crime has affected him or her.

Discussion Questions

1. How did Greek mythology contribute to the development of laws?

2. Give examples of the contributions of primitive laws under various rulers.

3. Identify the key documents that contributed to the development of American and Canadian law.

4. Why do you think that criminal justice professionals failed to recognize until late 1980s that victims deserved to have their legal and constitutional rights protected?

5. How is the victimization experience different or similar for a crime victim versus a victim of a social or public health problem?

Questions for debate:

1. Does the death penalty protect society by ridding it of evil and actually deterring people from committing crimes?

2. Does the death penalty exact retribution from criminals appropriately, in fair proportion to the crime committed?

3. Is the death penalty used fairly in terms of the race and class of its victims?

4. Is capital punishment barbaric, or does it have a place in civilized society?

5. Is the death penalty justified in the vast monies saved by not having to support such criminals with incarceration for their lifetimes, or is its cost to society's humanity even dearer?

6. During her interview with the Associated Press, Casey Anthony said that she had become fascinated with the 1994 O.J. Simpson murder trial, stating that there were a lot of parallels to her own case, adding, "I can empathize with his situation." Is she correct?

Resources

National Center for Victims of Crime https://victimsofcrime.org

Office of Juvenile Justice and Prevention Programs http://www.ojjdp.gov

References

Antkowiak, B. A. (2006). Criminal law and procedure. In C. H. Wecht & J. T. Rago (Eds.), *Forensic science and the law*. Boca Raton, FL: Taylor & Francis, pp. 67–99.

Baker, J. (2002). *An introduction to English legal history.* London: Butterworths.

Banks, C. (2005). *Punishment in America.* Contemporary World Issues series. Santa Barbara, CA: ABC-CLIO.

Bazemore, G. (2001). Young people, trouble, and crime: Restorative justice as a normative theory of informal social control and social support. *Youth & Society, 33*(2), 199–226.

Bazemore, G., & Schiff, M. (2001). *Restorative justice: Repairing harm and transforming communities.* Cincinnati, OH: Anderson Press.

Boren, C. (2017, July 20). An apologetic OJ Simpson is given parole. *Washington Post.* Retrieved from https://www.washingtonpost.com/news/early-lead/wp/2017/07/20/what-to-expect-from-the-o-j-simpson-parole-hearing/?utm_term=.dce7ebd22e1d

Braithwaite, J. (2000). Shame and criminal justice. *Canadian Journal of Criminology, 42*(3), 281–298.

Bureau of Justice Statistics. (n.d.). The justice system. Retrieved from https://www.bjs.gov/content/justsys.cfm#contents

Bureau of Justice Statistics. (2015). National Crime Victimization Survey (NCVS), 1993–2015. Retrieved from https://www.bjs.gov/index.cfm?ty=dcdetail&iid=245

Cafardi, N. P. (2006). The civil justice system. In C. H. Wecht & J. T. Rago (Eds.), *Forensic science and the law.* Boca Raton, FL: Taylor and Francis, pp. 139-148.

Cheon, A., & Regehr, C. (2006). Restorative justice in cases of intimate partner violence: Reviewing the evidence. *Victims and Offenders, 1*(4), 369–394.

Craig, E. (1998). *Encyclopedia of philosophy.* London and New York: Routledge.

Death Penalty Information Center. (2009). Introduction to the death penalty. Retrieved from http://www.deathpenaltyinfo.org/part-i-history-death-penalty

Denner, J., & Pellegrino, R. (2011). Civil commitment. Retrieved from http://criminal.findlaw.com/crimes/more-criminal-topics/sex-offenders/civil-commitment.html

Department of Justice. (2003). Canada's court system. Retrieved from http://www.justice.gc.ca/en/dept/pub/trib/page1.html

Dodd, J. D. (2002). Justice Options for Women Project. Dialogue on restorative justice and women who are victims of violence: A discussion paper in preparation for the Restorative Justice and Violence Against Women workshop. Retrieved from www.isn.net/~tha/justiceoptions/4pagediscussionpaper.pdf

Galliher, J. F., Ray, G., & Cook, B. (1992). Abolition and reinstatement of capital punishment during the Progressive Era and early 20th century. *Journal of Crime & Criminology, 83*(3), 538.

Glynn, C. (2011). Phillip and Nancy Garrido sentenced for Jaycee Dugard kidnapping. CBS New. Retrieved from https://www.cbsnews.com/news/nancy-and-philip-garrido-sentenced-for-jaycee-lee-dugard-kidnapping/

Griffin, A., & Kauffman, M. (2016, May 26). CT Supreme Court upholds abolishment of death penalty, including for death-row inmates. *Hartford Courant.* Retrieved from http://www.courant.com/news/connecticut/hc-connecticut-supreme-court-death-penalty-ruling-upheld-20160526-story.html

Hamilton, E. (1942). *Mythology*. New York: Mentor Books.

Henderson, H. (2000). *Capital punishment* (rev. ed.). New York: Facts on File.

Holmstrom, L. L., & Burgess, A. W. (1983). *The victim of rape*. New Brunswick, NJ: Transaction Books.

Joyce, E. (2016). Detaining the poor: How money bail perpetuates an endless cycle of poverty and jail time. Prison Policy Initiative. Retrieved from https://www .prisonpolicy.org/graphs/arrest_pretrialdetention.html

Judicial Learning Center. (n.d.). State courts vs. federal courts. Retrieved from http:// judiciallearningcenter.org/state-courts-vs-federal-courts/

Koon, S. (2011, December 6). Judge rejects plea bargain from woman accused of stealing from Brofman. Retrieved from http://www2.dailyprogress.com/news/2011 /dec/06/judge-rejects-plea-bargain-woman-accused-stealing--ar-1525299/

La Ganga, M. L., & Goldmacher, S. (2010, July 2). Jaycee Lee Dugard's family will receive $20 million from California. *Los Angeles Times*. Retrieved from http:// articles.latimes.com/2010/jul/02/local/la-me-0702-dugard-settlement–20100702

LEAA/OJP Retrospective. (1996). 30 years of federal support to state and local criminal justice. Washington, DC: U.S. Department of Justice. Retrieved from https://www .ncjrs.gov/pdffiles1/nij/164509.pdf

Levinson, D. (2002). Capital crimes. In *Encyclopedia of crime and punishment* (Vol. 4). Thousand Oaks, CA: Sage.

MacLead, M. (2011). The electric chair. Retrieved from http://www.trutv.com/library /crime/notorious_murders/not_guilty/chair/5.html

Maiese, M. (2003). Distributive justice. Retrieved from http://www.beyondintractability .org/bi-essay/distributive_justice/

McPadden, M. (2017). What's been up with Casey Anthony since she got off: 4 crucial updates. Crime Feed. Retricved from http://crimefeed.com/2017/04/casey-anthony -since-she-got-off-5-crucial-updates/

Mill, J. S. (1863). *Utilitarianism*. London: Parker, Son, and Bourn.

Murphy, W. J. (2011). Not guilty verdict was the right result but we're not done yet. Retrieved from http://www.patriotledger.com/opinions/x1498054785/WENDY-MURPHY-Anthony-verdict-was-right-but-we-re-not-done

New York Times. (2010, November 8). Petit family killings. Retrieved from http:// topics.nytimes.com/top/reference/timestopics/people/p/petit_family/index.html

Nozick, R. (1977). *Anarchy, state, and utopia*. New York: Basic Books.

Office of Juvenile Justice and Delinquency Prevention. (2011). About OJJDP. Retrieved from http://www.ojjdp.gov/about/about.html

Parsons, T. (1951). *The social system*. Glencoe, IL: Free Press.

Payne v. Tennessee (90-5721), 501 U.S. 808 (1991).

President's Commission on Law Enforcement and Administration of Justice. (1967). *The Challenge of Crime in a Free Society*. Washington, DC: U.S. Government Printing Office.

Presser, L., & Gaarder, E. (2000). Can restorative justice reduce battering? Some preliminary considerations. *Social Justice*, *27*(1), 175–195.

Presser, L., & Van Voorhis, P. (2002). Values and evaluation: Assessing processes and
outcomes. *Crime and Delinquency*, *48*(1), 162–188.

Rawls, J. (1971). *A theory of justice*. Harvard, MA: Harvard University Press.

Regehr, C., & Kanani, K. (2010). *Essential law for social work practice in Canada*.
Toronto: Oxford University Press.

Rell, M. J. (2009). *An Act Concerning the Penalty for a Capital Felony*, HB 6578.
Hartford, CT. Executive Chambers. Retrieved from http://www.ct.gov/governorrell
/cwp/view.asp?A=3675&Q=441204

Roach, K. (2000). Changing punishment at the turn of the century: Restorative justice
on the rise. *Canadian Journal of Criminology*, *42*(3), 249–280.

Seneca County Prosecutor's Office. (2009). Seneca County victim rights. Retrieved from
http://www.senecapros.org/victims_rights.html

Stearns, P., Adas, M., Schwartz, S., & Gilbert, M. (2003). *World civilizations: The
global experience* (AP edition). New York: Pearson Education.

Umbreit, M. (1995). The development and impact of victim–offender mediation in the
United States. *Mediation Quarterly*, *12*(3), 263–276.

U.S. Department of Justice. (2015a). Restitution. Retrieved from https://www.justice
.gov/uspc/restitution

U.S. Department of Justice. (2015b). Parole hearing guidelines. Retrieved from https://
www.justice.gov/uspc/parole-hearings

Wagner, P. (2015). Bureau of Justice Statistics' *Annual Probation Survey* and *Annual Parole Survey* data series and Prison Policy Initiative *in Tracking State Prison
Growth in 50 States*. Washington, DC.

Wallace, H., & Roberson, C. (2010). *Victimology: Legal, psychological, and social
perspectives* (3rd ed.). Boston: Allyn and Bacon.

Western, B. (2013). Leaving prison as a poverty transition: Preliminary results . . .
Boston Reentry Study. Retrieved from https://www.youtube.com/watch?v=e7y
H39B563k

West's Encyclopedia of American Law. (1998a). Family law. Retrieved from http://
www.answers.com/topic/family-law#ixzz1fy4yedCi

West's Encyclopedia of American Law. (1998b). Feudalism. Retrieved from http://
www.answers.com/topic/feudalism

West's Encyclopedia of American Law. (2011). Caryl Chessman. Retrieved from http://
www.answers.com/topic/caryl-chessman#ixzz1WQjXf896

Wilson, C. (1984). *A criminal history of mankind*. New York: G.P. Putnam's Sons.

Zehr, H. (1995). Justice paradigm shift? Values and visions in the reform process.
Mediation Quarterly, *12*(3), 207–216.

Zimring, F. E., Hawkins, G., & Kamin, S. (2001). *Punishment and democracy: Three
strikes and you're out in California*. New York: Oxford University Press.

CHAPTER 6

Child Abuse and Neglect

OBJECTIVES

- To define and describe the various forms of child maltreatment and their dynamics
- To outline the short- and long-term consequences of child maltreatment
- To describe resources for intervening in child maltreatment

KEY TERMS

Child maltreatment

Complex child trauma

Developmental disability

Developmental traumatology

Disclosure

Eye movement desensitization and reprocessing (EMDR)

Fetal homicide

Fetal rights

Incest

Statutory rape

Trauma-focused cognitive-behavioral therapy (TF-CBT)

CASE

Scott Brown, a junior senator from Massachusetts, stunned the public by disclosing that he had endured both physical and sexual abuse as a child in his book, *Against All Odds* (2011). He revealed that his stepfather repeatedly beat both him and his mother and that he was sexually abused by a counselor at a summer camp when he was 10 years old. Senator Brown kept this secret for over 40 years due to shame, embarrassment, the threat that he would be hurt badly if he ever told, and the belief that boys don't tell (FIGURE 6-1). Brown wrote that the incident showed him there were no safe havens and no one he could truly trust. He continued to disclose that, as a teen,

FIGURE 6-1 Senator Scott Brown, victim of child abuse.

© Win McNamee/Getty Images.

FIGURE 6-2 Oprah Winfrey discloses child abuse.

© Helga Esteb/ShutterStock, Inc.

he engaged in numerous incidents of shoplifting, including stealing a three-piece suit from a department store and steaks and hamburger from the supermarket. When he was caught shoplifting albums by Black Sabbath and other rock artists, he was admonished by a judge to straighten up. He did. He went to college, attended law school, ran for political office as a Republican in an overwhelmingly Democratic state, and was elected in 2009 to fill the U.S. Senate seat vacated by Senator Edward Kennedy, a Democrat, who had died. On June 8, 2017, the Senate easily confirmed the former senator to be President Trump's ambassador to New Zealand and the independent state of Samoa. The senators voted 94 to 4 in favor of their former colleague, who was considered a lock for the position. Only four senators voted against the nomination.

Brown is not the only public figure whose sexual abuse has become public knowledge. When she was nine years old and living in Milwaukee, Oprah Winfrey and her siblings were left alone with their 19-year old cousin. It was this cousin who sexually abused Oprah for the first time: she was raped and then taken out for ice cream and told to keep it a secret—which she did. She was again abused by a family friend and an uncle years later, ongoing abuse about which she kept silent. Without receiving much direction from her

mother and unable to discuss her sexual abuse, Oprah resorted to acting out: skipping school, dating, stealing money from her mother, and running away. She was sent back to live with her father in Nashville. At age 14, Oprah discovered she was pregnant, although she hid this news from her parents until she was in her seventh month. The day she told her father the news of her pregnancy she went into early labor and delivered her baby that day, a boy, who died within two weeks of his birth (Fry, 2011; Oprah.com, 2006).

Oprah Winfrey is one of the richest people in the world, according to *Forbes* magazine, but there is no doubt her legacy extends beyond her massive wealth (**FIGURE 6-2**). Throughout her career, Oprah has used her celebrity status to promote issues she is passionate about, most notably racism and sexual abuse. She also broke barriers and forged a bigger space for African American women in media, TV, and business. She engages in generous philanthropic efforts and charitable giving. Oprah regularly gives generous portions of her wealth to educational causes.

The message from these public figures is that childhood victimization occurs across gender, race, and socioeconomic factors, that nondisclosure is not uncommon, that resiliency is possible, and that the abuse is never forgotten.

Introduction

Childhood is supposed to be a happy, conflict-free time of life; however, negative life events can converge on a child to create victimization and trauma. As the case examples illustrate, many children remain silent about their abuse for years, may have episodes of acting out, or may become pregnant; when there is disclosure, they risk the public reaction from their family, the abuser, and the community.

The U.S. Department of Health and Human Services Administration on Children, Youth, and Families, Children's Bureau (2016) reported an estimated 702,000 children were confirmed by child protective services as being victims of abuse and neglect in 2014. At least one in four children have experienced child neglect or abuse (including physical, emotional, and sexual) at some point in their lives, and one in seven children have experienced abuse or neglect in the last year (Finkelhor, Turner, Shattuck, & Hamby, 2015). *Child neglect* includes failure to provide, physical neglect, emotional neglect, medical/dental neglect, educational neglect, failure to supervise, or exposure to a violent environment.

Child abuse and maltreatment have been linked to a variety of short- and long-term health consequences, including poor physical and mental health, changes to brain architecture and development, altered biological factors, reduced cognitive ability and educational achievement, and impaired psychosocial functioning (Merrick & Latzman, 2014).

Child abuse has been persistent across history, and has even been traced to the prehistoric period. Children have been maltreated and exploited throughout history, given that they were long considered family property. Fathers in ancient times could sell, mutilate, or kill their children. Many religions used child sacrifice to please and appease gods. Infanticide was common. Children born with infirmities, intellectual or physical disabilities, or deformities were killed to maintain and strengthen society. In most cultures severe punishment and harsh treatment were deemed necessary for rearing and educating children (Volpe, 2011).

In the past several decades, childhood victimization has been formally categorized as a pervasive public health problem and at pandemic levels globally. This formal recognition has resulted from media campaigns, increased reporting, enhanced comprehensive and sensitive assessment of childhood victims, and giving children a "voice" and recognizing their human rights (American Public Health Association, 1975, 1986; deMause, 1998; National Association of Counsel for Children, n.d.a; World Health Organization, 2004, 2006).

deMause (1998) described the history of childhood as a nightmare that society has only recently begun to address. He suggested the further back in history one goes, the lower the level of child care and the more likely children were to have been killed, abandoned, beaten, terrorized, and abused. Congruent with these thoughts, Hopper (2007) offered a similar yet contemporary statement. Hopper (2007) agreed that children have been abused throughout human history, but emphasized that society's acknowledgment that it is a root cause of many people's suffering and personal problems is recent. Some believe that only now is society beginning to face the true prevalence and significance of child abuse, whereas others worry that many people have become obsessed with child abuse and deny any personal responsibility for their problems, instead "blaming" them on abuse and bad parenting.

On any given day people can pick up a newspaper or turn on a television and hear yet another report of a missing, abused or neglected, or, even worse, murdered child (Mugavin, 2005). On June 25, 2015, a dog walker found the partially decomposed body of a small girl on the shore of Deer Island, a peninsula in Boston Harbor opposite Logan Airport. The girl was found with a fleece blanket and wrapped in a trash bag. It took months to identify her as Bella Bond, but in 2016, the mother and her boyfriend were arrested and charged with the two-year-old's murder. At the 2017 trial, the boyfriend, who was obsessed with the occult, said the girl was a demon and that it was her time to die (Levenson, 2017).

The seemingly significant increase in the frequency of child abuse is not necessarily a reflection of elevated occurrence or prevalence but rather that society, over time, has come to terms with the reality of the large numbers of children who experience or witness violence, abuse, or neglect; consequently, we have become more aware and understanding of the importance of reporting to child protective agencies, forensic nurses, and law enforcement (National Association of Counsel for Children, n.d.b; Pleck, 2003). Further expanding and enhancing such reporting, all 50 states, as well as all major healthcare-related associations and professional licensing and credentialing bodies, have passed some form of a mandatory child abuse and neglect reporting law to provide assessment, protection, and intervention for all children with suspected or documented abuse or neglect (National District Attorneys Association, n.d.).

One of the greatest challenges for child survivors of abuse, their families, and their healthcare providers is grappling with the perception of the abused child as "damaged goods." Sgroi (1982) considered the "damaged goods syndrome" as one of the "impact issues," wherein the physical damage caused to the child causes the child to believe that he or she has been damaged.

By expanding awareness and understanding of the risk and plight of children relative to abuse, while simultaneously enhancing assessment, therapeutic intervention, and the medicolegal interface with law enforcement and the judicial system, actions can promote adaptive mental health and on-time emotional growth and development of survivors of abuse, neglect, and other forms of interpersonal violence (Clements & DeRanieri, 2006; LaSala & Lynch, 2006; World Health Organization, 2006).

Scope of the Problem

The National Child Abuse and Neglect Data System, a reporting system for all cases that come to the attention of child protective services (CPS), provides a primary approach for obtaining statistics related to child abuse and neglect. Four other approaches are used to examine the occurrences of maltreatment (Levanthal, 2005):

1. Collection of prospective data in selected communities to identify cases of child maltreatment even if not reported to CPS. This approach has been used in four national studies. In each study, the number of identified victims of child maltreatment has been substantially higher than the number of cases substantiated by CPS over the comparable time period (Levanthal, 2005).

2. Asking adults about the details of how they have treated their children over a specific period, such as the previous month or a year (Straus, Hamby, Finkelhor, Moore, & Runyon, 1998).

3. Asking children about their experiences of violence, including their experiences of maltreatment (Finkelhor & Dziuba-Leatherman, 1994).

4. Asking adults how they were treated during childhood (Finkelhor & Dziuba-Leatherman, 1994).

This last approach has helped in gaining an understanding of how many adults have experienced different types of maltreatment during childhood. For example, many studies have asked adult men and women about their experiences of sexual abuse in childhood and adolescence. A review of studies of community samples in the United States and Canada found the prevalence of sexual abuse reported by women ranged from 2% to 62% and by men, 3% to 16% (Finkelhor & Jones, 2006). Finkelhor and Dziuba-Leatherman (1994) suggested that a reasonable summary statistic for women would be 20% and for men, 5% to 10%.

National Child Abuse and Neglect Data System

The National Child Abuse and Neglect Data System (NCANDS) is a voluntary reporting system in the United States developed by the Children's Bureau of the U.S. Department of Health and Human Services to collect and analyze annual statistics on child maltreatment from state child protection agencies. The data are then used to create reports on child maltreatment based on data submitted to NCANDS by all 50 states, the District of Columbia, and Puerto Rico. The data include all children with an allegation of maltreatment who are involved in investigations or assessed and reach disposition during the year. TABLE 6-1 summarizes the findings of this report for 2015.

TABLE 6-1 U.S. Child Protective Services Report, 2015

Incident	Findings
Reporters of child maltreatment More than three-fifths (63.4%) of all reports of alleged child abuse or neglect were made by professionals.	18.4% education personnel 18.2% legal and law enforcement personnel 10.9% social services staff 9.1% medical personnel 18.2% nonprofessionals, including friends, neighbors, sports coaches, and relatives 18.3% anonymous and unknown reporters
Confirmed child victims to CPS An estimated 683,000 children were victims of abuse and neglect nationwide, which is a rate of 9.2 victims per1,000 children in the population. African American children had the highest rates of victimization at 14.5 per 1,000 children in the population of the same race or ethnicity, and American Indian or Alaska Native children had the second highest rate at 13.8 per 1,000 children.	Birth to 1 year had the highest rate of victimization at 24.2 per 1,000 children of the same age group 50.9% of victims were girls and 48.6% were boys. Gender unknown for 0.5% 21.4% were African American 23.6% were Hispanic 43.2% were White
Types of child maltreatment	75.3% of victims suffered neglect 17.2% of victims suffered physical abuse 8.4% of victims suffered sexual abuse 6.2% suffered psychological maltreatment 2.2% suffered medical neglect 6.9% experienced "other" maltreatment, such as parents' substance abuse

(continues)

TABLE 6-1 U.S. Child Protective Services Report, 2015 (*Continued*)

Incident	Findings
Child fatalities NCANDS defines "child fatality" as the death of a child caused by an injury resulting from abuse or neglect or where abuse or neglect was a contributing factor.	An estimated 1,670 children died due to abuse or neglect. The overall rate of child fatalities was 2.25 deaths per 100,000 children. Close to three-quarters (74.8%) of the children who died due to child abuse or neglect were younger than 3 years of age. Nearly three-quarters (72.9%) of child fatalities were attributed to neglect only or a combination of neglect and another maltreatment type, and 43.9% of the children died exclusively from physical abuse or from physical abuse in combination with another maltreatment type. Boys had a slightly higher child fatality rate than girls, at 2.42 boys per 100,000 boys in the population compared with 2.09 girls per 100,000 girls in the population.
Perpetrators of child maltreatment More than three-fifths (61.5%) of perpetrators maltreated one victim, more than one-fifth (21.5%) maltreated two victims, and the remaining 10.3% maltreated three or more victims. Seven percent of perpetrators were involved in more than one report.	The great majority of perpetrators were parents—one or both parents maltreated 91.6% of victims. Women comprised 54.1% of perpetrators; 45.0% of perpetrators were men, and 0.9% were of unknown sex. Approximately 13.3% of victims were maltreated by a perpetrator who was not the child's parent and who sometimes acted alone and sometimes with other perpetrators. The largest categories in the nonparent group were male relatives, male partner of parent, and "other," but the category also included other options, such as daycare providers, foster parents, and unknown.
Who received services for the child and family	61.9% of victims and 29.7% of nonvictims received postresponse services. 20.8% of victims were removed from their homes. More than one-fifth (22.9%) of victims who received services and 2.1% of nonvictims who received services were removed from their homes and received foster care services. The remaining victims and nonvictims who received services received in-home services only.

Source: *Child Maltreatment 2015*, a report based on data submissions by State child protective services (CPS) agencies for Federal fiscal year (FFY) 2015.
Child Welfare Information Gateway. (2017.) *Child maltreatment 2015: Summary of key findings*. Washington, DC: U.S. Department of Health and Human Services, Children's Bureau.

National Incidence Study

The National Incidence Study (NIS) is a congressionally mandated, periodic effort of the U.S. Department of Health and Human Services. In 1974, Public Law 93-247 mandated the first NIS (NIS-1), which collected data in 1979 and 1980. Three additional cycles of data were collected in 1986–87 (NIS-2), 1993–94 (NIS-3), and 2005–06 (NIS-4). The NIS serves as the nation's needs assessment on child abuse and neglect. It offers a unique perspective on the scope of the problem beyond the children that CPS agencies investigate. Although the NIS includes children investigated by CPS agencies, it also obtains data on other children who were not reported to CPS or who were screened out by CPS without investigation. These additional children were recognized as maltreated by community professionals. Thus, the NIS estimates include both abused and neglected children who are in the official CPS statistics and those who are not.

The NIS follows a nationally representative design, so the estimates reflect the numbers of abused and neglected children in the United States who come to the attention of community professionals. Because the three previous cycles used comparable methods and definitions, one can compare NIS-4 estimates with those earlier studies to identify changes over time in the incidence and distribution of abused and neglected children.

The NIS-4 identified some major changes in the incidence of child maltreatment since the time of the NIS-3. First, the NIS-4 documented declines in rates of all categories across definitional standards. These declines in physical and sexual abuse are consistent with trends in CPS data. The increase in rate of emotional neglect since 1993 could reflect a real increase or be due to some change in policy and focus. The NIS-4, for the first time, found race differences in maltreatment rates, with African American children experiencing maltreatment at higher rates than White children in several categories, including low socioeconomic circumstances and family structure of a single parent with a partner in the household (Sedlak et al., 2010).

Canadian Incidence Child Abuse Statistics

The Canadian Incidence Study of Reported Child Abuse and Neglect (CIS) is a national initiative to collect data on children who come to the attention of a child welfare authority due to alleged or suspected abuse and/or neglect in the year the study is conducted. The objectives of the CIS are to provide reliable estimates of the incidence of reported child abuse and neglect and to compare findings over time as data collection for the CIS is usually completed in 5-year cycles; however, the Public Health Agency of Canada decided not to collect data in 2013 (Potter, Nasserie & Tonmyr, 2015).

The third cycle of the study, CIS-2008, tracked 15,980 child maltreatment investigations conducted in a representative sample of 112 child welfare service organizations in all provinces and territories in Canada (Trocme, Fallon, MacLaurin, Sinha, & Black, 2008). In this study, the largest proportion of substantiated cases was for neglect (34%) or for exposure to domestic violence

TABLE 6-2 Canadian Child Abuse: Major Findings

- One-third of Canadians aged 15 and older (33%) experienced some form of child maltreatment before age 15. Child maltreatment includes physical and/or sexual abuse by someone aged 18 or older, and/or witnessing violence by a parent or guardian against another adult. Childhood physical abuse was reported by 26% of Canadians, while 8% reported sexual abuse.
- For 6 in 10 (61%) victims of childhood physical violence, a parent or step-parent was identified as the abuser in the most serious incident of abuse.
- One in 10 Canadians (10%) stated that, before age 15, they had witnessed violence by a parent or guardian against another adult in the home. The majority of child witnesses—7 in 10 (70%)—also reported having been the victim of childhood physical and/or sexual assault. Those who witnessed parental violence were more likely to have suffered the most severe forms of physical abuse.
- More than 9 in 10 (93%) victims of childhood physical and/or sexual abuse did not report the abuse to either police or child protection services before they turned 15. In fact, the majority of victims (67%) did not speak to anyone, including friends or family.
- Almost half of people aged 15 and older who identified as gay, lesbian, or bisexual reported having experienced childhood physical and/or sexual abuse (48%). This compared to 30% of heterosexual people.

Data from Statistics Canada. 2015 Family violence in Canada, A Statistical Profile. Burczycka, M. and Conroy, S. (2017 Retrieved from http://dsp-psd.pwgsc.gc.ca/Collection/Statcan /85-224-X/85-224-XIE.html.

(34%), whereas 20% of children were physically abused, 9% were emotionally abused, and 3% were sexually abused (Trocme et al., 2008). In addition, Statistics Canada collects population-based data, the findings of which can be found in **TABLE 6-2**.

Tonmyr, Quimet, and Ugnat (2014) analyzed 37 peer-reviewed articles derived from three cycles of the CIS published between 2001 and October 2011. These articles revealed an increased likelihood of substantiation or placement if investigations (1) uncovered the presence of emotional or physical harm in a child, (2) involved older children, (3) identified the presence of risk indicators in caregivers, or (4) documented unstable or unsafe housing. The researchers found that several issues were understudied, such as neglect and emotional maltreatment, especially using multivariate approaches.

Legislative Framework

The protection of children is a primary responsibility of any society, and, as such, child protection (or child welfare) legislation has a long history in North America and Europe. According to UNICEF (2011), *child protection* is the response to violence, exploitation, and abuse of children by both governments and citizens. This protection is inclusive of the commercial sexual exploitation, trafficking, child labor, and harmful traditional practice. In 1989, the United Nations brought leaders together to establish the first internationally binding legislation to protect children. The U.N. Convention on the Rights of the Child spells out basic human rights for children: the right to survival; to develop to the fullest; to protection from harmful influences, abuse, and exploitation; and to participate fully in family, cultural, and social life (United Nations, 2009). The Convention protects children's rights by setting standards in health care; education; and legal, civil, and social services. Each nation that signed the agreement is responsible for establishing legislation that ensures the protection of children.

In both Canada and the United States, children who were not cared for by their parents often were taken into mandated servitude. In Ontario, for instance, the Orphan's Act of 1799 empowered town wardens to bind orphaned children to apprentices. This legislation and similar legislation throughout North America viewed children as small adults and perpetrated the belief that hard work was the solution to social ills (Regehr & Kanani, 2010). By the 1800s, charitable and religious organizations began to establish children's homes to care for orphans and abandoned and neglected children. However, concerns were raised about the treatment of children in these homes, and in 1909, the first White House Conference on the Care of Dependent Children was convened with the aim of preventing the removal of children from homes. State laws followed that for the first time addressed the protection of children. However, it was not until some time later that the state took responsibility for the care of children.

The 1935 Social Security Act authorized the first federal grants for child welfare services in the United States. The first Children's Aid Society in America opened in New York City in 1953. In 1954, in Canada, the first legislation, the Child Welfare Act, was enacted that placed accountability for child protection on the state. In 1974, the U.S. Congress enacted the Child Abuse Prevention and Treatment Act that required each state to establish policies and procedures for the reporting and investigation of child abuse and neglect. Today, the U.S. government is a major funder of child protection services that are provided by state and local authorities and by nonprofit social service organizations.

Mandated Reporting

In general, child welfare legislation throughout North America mandates the reporting of suspected child abuse to child welfare authorities. The types of professionals mandated to report child maltreatment has expanded over the years to include almost anyone who comes in contact with children, such as physicians, dentists, nurses, teachers, mental health professionals, social workers, police, and clergy. Mandated reporters are expected to report both by telephone to a central hotline and in writing. Most state laws indicate that mandated reporters must report if there is a reasonable suspicion of abuse or neglect; they do not have to be 100% certain. State statutes protect the reporter for reporting in good faith. The failure to report a suspected case can place the child at risk of a more serious episode of maltreatment, and this inaction can result in prosecution by the state.

Role of Child Protective Services

Child protective services have advanced in major ways. They investigate cases of suspected child maltreatment and place children in foster care. In some localities they have expanded into helping families receive additional services, such as with home visits by nurse practitioners and substance abuse referral for parents. Major changes have occurred in how child maltreatment cases are investigated. Investigations can include CPS and the police, and many states have passed legislation for the development of regional multidisciplinary investigative teams. Increasing attention has been paid to research on children as reporters of their experiences, in particular children reporting suspected sexual abuse. Research has assisted in studying the short- and long-term memories of children, how they describe events, and factors that affect reporting. Guidelines have been published, and forensic interviewers have been specially trained in asking children nonleading questions about their experiences.

Child Fatality Review Boards

Some states have established fatality review panels or boards. The rationale for such panels is based on the fact that child deaths are often regarded as an indicator of the health of a community. The ultimate purpose of review boards is to reduce the incidence of preventable child deaths, with the following goals:

- To promote cooperation, collaboration, and communication between all groups that serve families and children

- To maintain a database of all child deaths to develop an understanding of the causes and incidence of those deaths

- To recommend and develop plans for implementing local service and program changes, and to advise the department of health of aggregate data, trends, and patterns found in child deaths

Typology of Child Maltreatment

The term *child abuse* has been broadened into an all-encompassing term of child maltreatment. Maltreatment of children includes neglect, physical abuse, sexual abuse, and emotional maltreatment. Physical abuse against children was first recognized in the 1960s with the advent of both the women's movement and its concern for vulnerable members of society and with the advent of improvements in medical technology (such as the x-ray). This was then followed by recognition of child sexual abuse in the 1970s and 1980s. Recognition of the emotional aspects of child maltreatment has been particularly important for understanding both short- and long-term outcomes of child abuse. It has become increasingly clear that children reported for one type of maltreatment have often suffered from other types as well.

Neglect

Child neglect is generally characterized by omissions in care resulting in significant harm or risk of significant harm. Neglect is frequently defined in terms of a failure to provide for the child's basic needs, such as of adequate food, clothing, shelter, supervision, or medical care. It may include abandonment of the child and failure to see that the child receives adequate education and nutrition. Although neglect can be a one-time incident, such as leaving a child unsupervised in an unsafe setting, it is usually a pattern of unsafe care caused by a serious mental health problem or substance abuse on the part of the parent or caregiver (TABLE 6-3).

Physical Abuse

Joel Steinberg, a former New York criminal defense attorney, was convicted of manslaughter in the November 2, 1987 death of a six-year-old girl, Lisa, whom he had "adopted." Court records indicated Steinberg ate dinner and freebased

TABLE 6-3 Possible Signs of Child Neglect

Consider the possibility of neglect when the *child:*
- Is frequently absent from school.
- Begs for or steals food or money.
- Lacks needed medical or dental care, immunizations, or glasses.
- Is consistently dirty and has severe body odor.
- Lacks sufficient clothing for the weather/is dressed inappropriately.
- Abuses alcohol or other drugs.
- States that there is no one at home to provide care.

Consider the possibility of neglect when the *parent or other adult caregiver:*
- Appears to be indifferent to the child.
- Seems apathetic or depressed.
- Behaves irrationally or in a bizarre manner.
- Is abusing alcohol or other drugs.

Data from Recognize Child Abuse.

cocaine as Lisa lay unconscious for hours in the bathroom of a Greenwich Village apartment after being felled by a "staggering blow" to her head. When Lisa died in a hospital, she weighed 43 pounds and her little body was covered in bruises. Hedda Nussbaum, Steinberg's partner, was found to have suffered extensive and permanent injuries at Steinberg's hands and became a figure of pity and revulsion as the history of her dysfunctional relationship with Steinberg was revealed.

Child physical abuse is the intentional act of injury to a child. Such acts may cause harm to the child or they may intend to harm. Examples include punishing a child severely, such as when a parent loses control and shakes a crying infant. Injuries for abuse or neglect must be distinguished from accidental or unintentional injuries.

The two most common instruments used in child abuse, other than the hand, are belts and electrical cords. Cases of child abuse due to intentional burns are important to identify. These injuries account for approximately 6% to 20% of all abuse cases (Peck and Priola-Kapel, 2002) and severe burns are reported in an estimated 10% of all children suffering physical abuse (Maguire, Moynihan, Mann, Potokar, & Kemp, 2008). Most deliberate burns are from very hot tap water. Contact burns are usually of the branding type and will mirror the object used to cause the injury. The most common type of instrument used to inflict contact burns in child abuse cases is a cigarette. Clinicians are taught to distinguish intentional signs of injury from accidental. For example, in deliberate immersion burns, the depth of the burn is uniform. The wound borders are very distinct, sharply defined "water lines," with little tapering of depth at edges. The evidence will not reflect that the child thrashed about during the immersion, indicating the child was held in place. On occasion there may be bruising of soft tissue to indicate that the child was held down.

The term *shaken baby syndrome* was developed to explain instances in which severe intracranial trauma has occurred in the absence of signs of external head trauma. The mechanism of injury in shaken baby syndrome results from a combination of physical factors, including the proportionately large cranial size of infants, the laxity of their neck muscles, and the vulnerability of their intracranial bridging veins, due to the subarachnoid space (the space between the arachnoid membrane and the pia matter, which are the inner two of the three membranes that cover the brain) being somewhat larger in infants. However, the primary factor is the proportionately large size of the adult relative to the child. Shaking by admitted perpetrators has produced remarkably similar injury patterns.

Munchausen's syndrome by proxy is a form of child abuse in which the abuser fabricates an illness in a child for the purposes of obtaining attention by medical professionals. The child is taken for medical care with fabricated symptoms or feigned illness knowing this will most likely result in hospitalization of the child victim for tests or observation. As a consequence, the parent obtains attention and sympathy. The syndrome was first identified in 1977 by Professor Roy Meadow, a pediatrician at the University of Leeds, England. He described two initial cases, the first in which a mother poisoned her toddler with excessive salt and second in which the mother put her own blood in the baby's urine.

A number of terms have been suggested for Munchausen's syndrome by proxy. Roesler and Jenny (2009), for example, suggested retiring the name Munchausen and replacing it with a more fitting name to appreciate that children can be abused by their parents in the medical environment. The term *pediatric condition falsification* has been offered as an alternative (Ayoub & Alexander, 1998). This term clearly labels the problem as the caretaker, who provides a false history to the medical community.

In DSM-5 (American Psychiatric Association, 2013), this disorder is listed under *301.51 Factitious disorder*. This, in turn, encompasses two types (APA, 2013, 324-326):

- *Factitious disorder imposed on self* (formerly Munchausen syndrome).

- *Factitious disorder imposed on another* (formerly Munchausen syndrome by proxy); diagnosis assigned to the perpetrator; the victim may be assigned an abuse diagnosis (e.g., child abuse).

Caution must be taken regarding different cultural norms. Some cultural practices are generally not defined as physical abuse but may result in physically hurting children. For example, "coining," or *cao gio*, is a practice used to treat illness by rubbing the body forcefully with a coin or other hard object; similarly, *moxabustion* is an Asian folkloric remedy that burns the skin. The rule of thumb for practitioners is that such minor forms of injury due to cultural practices are generally respected. However, if the injury or harm is significant, professionals typically work with parents to discourage harmful behavior and suggest preferable alternatives.

Child Sexual Abuse

Infants, preadolescent children, and teenage boys and girls can all be targets of sexual abuse. In adult relationships, sexual encounters occur in three ways: through negotiation and consent, through pressure and exploitation, or through force and assault. The first method is regarded as a healthy and mature manner of relating sexually to another person. In the second method, one adult takes sexual advantage of another, usually through a position of dominance, and the subordinate person agrees to the sexual activity to achieve some nonsexual goal. Depending on the nature of the power imbalance in the relationship, this can result in criminal prosecution and/or civil liability. The third method, legally termed rape, involves the threat of harm or injury and/or actual physical assault to establish sexual contact and is a criminal activity.

Only through negotiation and consent can sexual relations properly be achieved. However, negotiation and consent are precluded between an adult and a preadolescent or underage person because such a person has not developed sufficient knowledge or wisdom to be able to negotiate such an encounter on an equal basis with an adult. Although the youngster may be sexually mature, she or he is not psychologically equipped to deal with sexual situations on an equal basis with an adult, and can therefore be easily manipulated. By definition, children are immature; thus, adults can capitalize in self-serving ways on this immaturity and can exploit the child in a variety of ways: physically, socially, psychologically, and emotionally (Groth, 1979).

Sexual abuse includes physical contact, including the touching or exposing of sexual or other intimate parts of a person for the purpose of arousing or gratifying sexual desire in either the perpetrator or the subject child.

Statutory rape is defined as the crime of engaging in sexual activity with a person who has not yet reached the age of consent. Even if the activities are consensual, the adult can still be charged with statutory rape if the other party is younger than the age of consent. Minors and physically and mentally incapacitated persons are deemed incapable of consenting to sex under rape statutes in the United States and Canada (*West's Encyclopedia of American Law*, 1998). An age of consent statute is believed to have first appeared in 1275 in England as part of the rape law. The statute was considered a misdemeanor to "ravish" a "maiden within age." The phrase "within age" was interpreted by jurist Sir Edward Coke as meaning the age of marriage, which at the time was 12 years of age (Robertson, n.d.).

Child pornography, another form of child sexual abuse, can be behaviorally defined as the sexually explicit reproduction of a child's image, including sexually explicit photographs, negatives, slides, magazines, movies, videotapes, and computer disks. In essence, it is the permanent record of sexual abuse or exploitation of a child. To legally be child pornography, it must be a visual depiction (not the written word) of a minor (as defined by statute) that is sexually explicit (not necessarily obscene, unless required by state law). Child pornography by itself represents an act of sexual abuse or exploitation of a child and by itself does harm to the child.

The case of John Edward Sullivan, 73, illustrates the use of an affidavit for purposes of law enforcement finding child pornography in order to bring charges against a suspect they believed was sexually abusing teenaged boys. On the basis of evidence presented in the affidavit, a search warrant was issued March 26, 2014. Sullivan was present when the warrant was executed, and due to the findings, was arrested on charges of possession of child pornography and online solicitation of a minor. Seized in the search were several photos of naked young boys, VHS and 8mm tapes, a computer and a laptop, miscellaneous written notes, financial statements, passport copies, CDs, and a brown paper sack containing condoms (Reinhardt, 2014).

Psychological Maltreatment

Psychological maltreatment—also known as *emotional abuse* and *neglect*—refers to a repeated pattern of caregiver behavior or extreme incident(s) that conveys to children that they are worthless, flawed, unloved, unwanted, endangered, or only of value in meeting another's needs. Psychological maltreatment is the most difficult form of child maltreatment to identify. In part, the difficulty in detection occurs because the effects of psychological maltreatment, such as lags in development, learning problems, and speech disorders, are often evident in both children who *have* and those who *have not* experienced maltreatment. Additionally, the effects of psychological maltreatment may become evident only in later developmental stages of the child's life (Hart & Brassard, 1987) (TABLE 6-4).

TABLE 6-4 Forms of Psychological Maltreatment

Form of Maltreatment	Definition
Terrorizing	Threatening violence against a child, placing a child in a recognizably dangerous situation, terrorizing a significant other of the child
Spurning	Belittling, hostile rejecting, ridiculing
Isolating	Confining the child, placing unreasonable limitations on the child's freedom of movement, restricting the child from social interactions
Exploiting or corrupting	Modeling antisocial behavior such as criminal activities, encouraging prostitution, permitting substance abuse
Denying emotional responsiveness	Ignoring the child's attempts to interact, failing to express affection
Mental health, medical, and educational neglect	Refusing to allow or failing to provide treatment for serious mental health or medical problems, ignoring the need for services for serious educational needs

Data from Hart, S. N. & Brassard, M. R. 1987. A major threat to children's mental health: psychological maltreatment. *American Psychologist, 42*, 161–165.

Fetal Death

In 1969, Teresa Keeler, eight months pregnant, was beaten unconscious by her jealous ex-husband, Robert Keeler, who told her during the attack he was going to "stomp it out of her." Later, at the hospital, Keeler delivered a stillborn baby girl who had suffered a fractured skull. Prosecutors attempted to charge Robert Keeler with the beating of his wife and the murder of the fetus, but the California Supreme Court dismissed the charges, stating that only someone born alive could be killed and that the fetus was not a human being (Montaldo, 2011).

Fetal death refers to the spontaneous intrauterine death of a fetus at any time during pregnancy. Fetal deaths later in pregnancy (such as 20 to 28 weeks or more, for example) are also sometimes referred to as *stillbirths*. In the United States, state laws require the reporting of fetal deaths, and federal law mandates national collection and publication of fetal death data. Most states report fetal deaths of 20 weeks of gestation or more and/or 350 grams birth weight. However, a few states report fetal deaths for all periods of gestation. Fetal death data are published annually by the National Center for Health Statistics in reports and as individual-record data files. Historically, under both English common law and U.S. law, the fetus has not been recognized as a person with full rights. Instead, legal rights have centered on the mother, with the fetus treated as a part of her. Nevertheless, U.S. law has in certain instances granted the fetus limited rights, particularly as medical science has made it increasingly possible to directly view, monitor, diagnose, and treat the fetus as a patient.

Due to public pressure, the debate over **fetal rights** intensified and legislation began to define the fetus as a person under fetal homicide, or "feticide," laws. Such legislation has been debated under names such as the Fetal Protection Act, the Preborn Victims of Violence Act, and the Unborn Victim of Violence Act. On April 1, 2004, President Bush signed into federal law the Unborn Victims of Violence Act, also known as "Laci and Conner's Law." This law states that any "child in utero" is considered to be a legal victim if injured or killed during the commission of a federal crime of violence. The bill defined "child in utero" as "a member of the species homo sapiens, at any stage of development, who is carried in the womb" (p. 1).

The **fetal homicide** law was used to prosecute Scott Peterson with two counts of murder of Laci Peterson, his wife, and their seven-month unborn son, Conner. Peterson, 36, was sentenced to death by lethal injection in March 2005 after being convicted of both homicides and disposing of his pregnant wife in the San Francisco Bay on Christmas Eve day of 2002. His case is currently on appeal ("Scott Peterson," 2005). Further, former pro football player for the Carolina Panthers, Rae Carruth, was convicted of conspiracy to commit the murder of Cherica Adams, who was seven months pregnant with their child. He was also found guilty of shooting into an occupied vehicle and of using an instrument to kill a fetus. Adams died as a result of the gunshot wounds, but her son was born 10 weeks premature in an emergency department before she died. Carruth received close to the maximum sentence of 19 to 24 years in prison. Codefendant Michael Kennedy, 35, testified against Carruth and spent 14 years and 9 months behind bars for second-degree murder at the Central Prison in Raleigh. He was released July 2011. Carruth is set to be released in October 2018, and the shooter, codefendant Van Brett Watkins, is expected to be released in March 2048 (*Charlotte Observer*, 2011).

A case out of Massachusetts connected child neglect and fetal death to a 31-year-old mother (Fisher, 2017). Investigators searched the home after a 10-year-old boy living there told a neighbor that two severely neglected children, a three-year-old girl and a five-month-old baby, were being kept in bedrooms of the home. A 13-year-old also lived there. The neighbor was alerted to the situation in August 2014.

The house was infested with flies, various other bugs, dead animals, mice, and decomposed remains of infants. The four living children were immediately removed from the dwelling and placed into temporary foster care.

On December 29, 2014, a grand jury sitting in Worcester, Massachusetts indicted Erika Murray on two counts of murder, one count of fetal death concealment related to the remains of the three infants, and two counts of assault and battery in connection with the neglected and abused children. According to prosecutor, two of the dead infants had lived from one week to a month.

In speaking to reporters, the prosecutor said that the defendant had admitted to investigators that even though she knew her boyfriend did not want any more children after the first two, they continued to have unprotected sex. She gave birth to all of the infants in the home's only bathroom, and birthed the children herself. She hid their tiny corpses among the trash in the squalid dwelling.

The younger children, the two born in secret, had spent their lives inside that house. The three-year-old had poor muscle tone and couldn't walk. The baby showed signs of having lived entirely in the dark and had maggots in its ears (Fisher, 2017).

Theories of Child Maltreatment

Theories of child maltreatment drive an understanding of how abuse and neglect occur and underscore the need for an understanding of etiology to focus intervention efforts where they will be most effective. Theoretical frameworks that explain the complex causes of child maltreatment are helpful to the measurement, study, and treatment of the child victim. Several frameworks have been proposed over the years, such as the intergenerational transmission of violence, social learning theory, ecological theory, and psychopathology.

Intergenerational Transmission of Violence

Punitive child-rearing practices were the focus of early longitudinal studies on the etiology of antisocial and criminal behavior (Glueck & Glueck, 1950; Robins, 1966). Paternal discipline (corporal punishment, authoritarian attitudes, strict discipline), maternal supervision (laxness), parental affection toward the child (rejection), family disruption (divorce), and deviant parental characteristics (substance abuse, mental problems, criminality) were core elements in the Glueck model of criminality prediction. Later studies included factors such as lack of interaction between parents and the child, parental conflicts and disagreement on child-rearing methods, socioeconomic difficulties, parental criminality, alcoholism, and mental health problems (Eron, Huesmann, & Zelli, 1991).

The longitudinal findings that show both child abuse and child neglect may lead to antisocial and criminal behavior and/or abuse of one's own children have been called the *intergenerational transmission of violence*, the *cycle of violence*, the *abused to abuser theory*, and the *victim to offender approach*. Even before Kempe, Silverman, Steele, Droegemuller, and Silver (1962) reported prevalence of parental violence directed at their children and described the "battered child syndrome," psychiatric case studies suggested that cruel punishment, severe discipline, and other kinds of physical abuse could produce later violent behavior (Satten, Menninger, Rosen, & Mayman, 1960; Silver, Dublin, & Lourie, 1969).

One important issue concerns "abuse-resistant" or resilient children who were maltreated but who managed to survive without later antisocial or aggressive behaviors. Most reviews of the cycle of violence hypothesis suggest that the severity, frequency, and perpetrator of abuse; the absence or presence of compensatory or protective factors; and the intrinsic vulnerabilities or strengths of the child may play an important role in determining the consequences (Haapasalo & Pokela, 1999).

Social Learning Theory

Social learning theory argues that abusive parents provide aggressive models for their children (Huesmann & Eron, 1986). McCord (1988) proposed that parental aggressiveness may be transmitted to children in the cycle of aggression by two processes: (1) teaching them that expressive behavior, including injurious actions, is normal and justified and (2) teaching that egocentrism is both normal and desired and that aggression is permissible in getting others to do what one wishes.

Ecological Theory

Initially, the focus was on parental psychopathology; however, a more useful approach has focused on the abnormalities in the parent–child relationship (Bavolek, 2000) in the context of an ecological model of parenting (Belsky, 1985). Bavolek (2000) noted the following four abnormalities in the parent–child relationship that can lead to abuse or neglect:

- Inappropriate parental expectations of the child.
- Lack of empathy toward the child's needs.
- Parent's belief in physical punishment.
- Parental role reversal.

According to Belsky (1985), these parental thoughts, feelings, and behaviors need to be considered in an ecological model in which the parent–child relationship is viewed as existing in layers of systems, including the family, the extended family, the social setting, and the cultural context. How parents feel about and behave toward their child is influenced by characteristics of the child (e.g., unwanted), parent (abused during childhood), family (domestic violence), social setting (poor housing), and cultural contact (violence in the neighborhood). This more complex approach to understanding parenting behaviors in general also can be used in targeting interventions to support the parent–child relationship, such as helping families by linking them to services for depressed parents, housing, treatment facilities, and so on.

Part of the ecological theory includes environmental circumstances that can elicit stressful behaviors. Gil (1979) termed the social setting in which life experiences aggravate the "triggering context" for abusive parents. Several stressors include family structure such as the single parent, lack of family support, and extreme levels of economic deprivation.

Psychopathology

One of the early theories of child maltreatment was that psychopathology would be found in persons such as parents or caregivers who seriously mistreated children under their care. Some cases had diagnoses of mental disorders but no consistent profile of parental psychopathology was sustained in the research literature, rather, the mistreaters were classified as anxious or troubled persons but not with extreme psychopathology (National Research Council, 1993, p. 111).

Attention to Prevention

A primary focus has been on the prevention of child maltreatment. A major strategy has been the use of regular and frequent home visits for socially high-risk, first-time mothers, beginning during pregnancy or shortly after the child's birth and through the first several years of life. The home visitors, who are often nurses, focus on the following:

- Providing advice about and modeling effective parenting
- Helping mothers develop parenting skills and good relationships with their infants
- Helping mothers make good decisions about returning to school, choice of day care, and their relationship with the baby's father
- Recognizing early problems related to family violence and maltreatment in the home
- Ensuring the child receives appropriate medical care
- Helping families link to community-based services, such as mental health services for the mother or developmental services for the child

Dynamics of Disclosure in Child Abuse

Disclosure, or telling someone of the abuse, varies by type of child maltreatment. Usually, visible signs of physical abuse, such as cuts, bruises, burns, or broken bones, are present. In neglect, there will be poor hygiene, weight loss, or withdrawn behavior. Sexual abuse symptoms include stomachaches, headaches, and development of fears, anxiety, or sexualized behaviors. However, in sexual abuse, typically children do not immediately or directly tell someone they have been abused. Disclosures are more likely to arise after an extended period of time when the perpetrator is no longer in the environment or after some type of emotional upheaval.

Several factors influence a child's ability and willingness to disclose sensitive information, especially around the identity of an abuser. One influence is the response of the caregiver, professional, or police officer to the child's disclosure of abuse. If the person reacts with shock or negativity or disbelieves the child, the child may not provide further information or even deny or recant what he or she has said. The dynamics of child sexual abuse are pressure, sex, and secrecy in cases in which there is a known relationship between the victim and abuser. First, the abuser must pressure the child by developing a relationship and then groom the child for the sexual relationship. This grooming can take weeks and months before a sexual intent is started. Second, the abuser then engages the child in sexual activities that can range from fondling to penetration. Third, for an abuser to be successful with a child victim, he or she must try to conceal the deviant behavior from others. More likely than not, he or she will try to pledge the child to secrecy in several ways. The dynamics are the setting for the various causes of delayed disclosure. The psychological factors that can lead a victim to disclose after a delay usually depend on who is a trusted person in the victim's support network. Delay can be days, weeks, months, or years. Victims may give a subtle message to see a person's reaction, may become symptomatic and an alert adult picks up the cues and helps the victim disclose, or victims learn more about sexual abuse and are able to report themselves (TABLE 6-5).

TABLE 6-5 Causes of Delayed Disclosure of Abuse

Cause	Explanation
Relationship of victim and offender	When the relationship involves family, it is less likely a victim will disclose due to the issue of family loyalty.
Age difference	The younger the victim, the more likely it is the victim will not disclose.
Pressure by the offender	The offender may use various strategies to ensure secrecy or merely direct the victim not to tell; for example, "this is our special secret."
Threats	The offender may threaten the victim with some consequence or harm if he or she tells. The victim may fear punishment if he or she tells.
Repercussions	The victim may believe he or she will not be taken seriously or that there will be negative repercussions from telling.
Communication	The victim may not know what or how to tell about the sexual abuse. He or she may not know the words to use.
Fears	The victim may fear abandonment or rejection if he or she tells.
Emotions	The victim may have a wide range of emotions such as fear, guilt, shame, and embarrassment. If the abuser has authority over the victim, it will be difficult for the victim to disclose, as he or she may fear betrayal of the relationship.

Effects of Traumatic Events on Children

Research in the field of child maltreatment has had an impact on practice, experts' understanding of the scope of the problem, and knowledge of the short- and long-term consequences of child maltreatment. Numerous studies have made clear that child maltreatment is just not a childhood problem but can leave lasting problems. Research has also contributed to describing the phenomenon of child maltreatment and the range of clinical presentations and findings (National Research Council, 1993).

A traumatic event may be a sudden and unexpected occurrence that causes intense fear and may involve a threat of physical harm or actual physical harm. Or, a traumatic event may occur over time and include multiple types of abuses. A traumatic experience, whether sudden or chronic in nature, can have a profound effect on the child's physical health, mental health, and development.

Children exhibit a wide range of symptoms depending on the type of maltreatment. Common general symptoms include withdrawn behavior, depression, sleeping and eating changes, development of fears and phobias, and psychosomatic symptoms (stomachaches, headaches). School problems may begin, such as absences or drops in grades. Children can begin to ignore health habits and develop poor hygiene or, in contrast, excessive bathing. Children may become highly anxious or feel guilty. Children can feel stigmatized and develop symptoms such as feelings of guilt/responsibility for the abuse. Children can develop feelings around betrayal that include lack of trust, especially of those who were supposed to be protective and nurturing. Children also feel powerlessness.

Children who are victims of sexual abuse may develop aversive feelings about sex, overvaluing sex, sexual identity problems, and hypersexual or sexual avoidance. No standard or typical symptoms can be used to identify an individual as having survived incest. Individual reactions and symptoms depend on age at time of abuse, age at time of disclosure, support (or lack of support) from other caregivers, length of abuse, sex of the victim, and perpetrator.

Developmental Traumatology

Developmental traumatology is key to understanding child trauma. Developmental traumatology describes how children process trauma based on their age and level of development. By understanding how children experience traumatic events and how they express their lingering distress over the experience, parents, clinicians, and school personnel can better respond and help them through this challenging time.

In general, for children a traumatic experience may cause ongoing feelings of concern for their own safety and the safety of others. These children may become preoccupied with thoughts about their actions during the event, oftentimes experiencing guilt or shame over what they did or did not do at the time. They might engage in constant retelling of the traumatic event or may describe being overwhelmed by their feelings of fear or sadness.

Preschool children may lose recently acquired developmental milestones and may increase behaviors such as bedwetting and thumb sucking, and regress to simpler speech. They may become clingy to their parents and worry about their parent's safety and return. These young children may also become more irritable with more temper tantrums and more difficulty calming down. A few children may show the reverse behavior and become very withdrawn, subdued, or even mute after a traumatic event. These children may have difficulties falling or staying asleep or have nightmares about the event or other bad dreams. Typically, these children will process the event through posttraumatic play. For example, one child bitten by a dog would, months later, go under a dinner table and bite the legs of people. This is an example of repetition of the traumatic event and will continue until the child's anxiety is reduced.

Children exposed to a traumatic event feel self-conscious about their emotional responses to the event. They often experience feelings of shame and guilt about the traumatic event and may express fantasies about revenge and retribution. A traumatic event for adolescents may foster a radical shift in the way these students think about the world. Some of these adolescents may begin to engage in self-destructive or accident-prone and reckless behaviors. There may be a shift in their interpersonal relationships with family members, teachers, and classmates. These adolescents may show a change in their school performance, attendance, and behavior.

Children with Developmental Disabilities

Children with a **developmental disability** or other physical challenges are exposed to abuse at a significantly high rate (National Child Traumatic Stress Network, 2004). These situations continue to be fraught with issues relative to lack of reporting and accurate assessment, often due to impaired communication or the perception by others that these cases cannot be successfully prosecuted or treated.

Although violence is widespread in the United States, the rate of this problem related to those with a developmental disability is misunderstood, and, at times, the survivors are virtually "invisible." Of interest to the interdisciplinary team including family, psychiatric nurses, and other community health practitioners are the mental health consequences for those persons with developmental disabilities. In the flurry of activity after traumatic events, the loss and related bereavement process, along with long-term effects, may be misinterpreted and overlooked in "translation" as the team endeavors to assess and understand the impact. What may be different in comparison with other survivors are the ways they think about themselves as victims, react to the violent event, and express their fears and ongoing concerns (Focht-New, Clements, Barol, Service, & Faulkner, 2008).

Violence and abuse against children with developmental disability often results in intense and confusing feelings and can activate fears and concerns regarding their own vulnerability (including the awareness they may be unable to protect themselves). They may also become fearful of the potential for future violence. Children with a developmental disability, however, can have responses that are uniquely difficult because they are not always adequately prepared to decipher and manage what they are feeling. Numerous feelings may arise simultaneously and be difficult for the individual to articulate and the caregiver to understand. They may experience multidirectional anger at the offender, those they perceive did not protect them, or toward themselves for feeling they could have done something to prevent the violence. Feelings of abandonment by their caregivers may surface or great physical and emotional pain and sorrow that may have accompanied the violence. The child may express their anger, pain, and trauma by becoming withdrawn or depressed or developing physical symptoms (Burgess, Hartman, & Clements, 1995; Sunderland, 1995).

Epidemiological Approaches to the Study of Child Maltreatment

Major efforts have been made to understand the consequences of maltreatment. The following three epidemiological approaches have been used to investigate this problem:

- Use of longitudinal cohorts to follow maltreated children over time to examine developmental problems, juvenile or adult violence, mental health problems, and substance abuse.

- Use of case-control design in which cases are adults with a specific problem, such as depression, and controls are adults who do not have the problem. The subjects are then asked about childhood experiences with maltreatment.

- A sample of adults from a specific population or geographic area is asked about physical and sexual abuse. Rates of the outcomes are then compared to groups with and without certain past experiences.

In addition to epidemiologic studies concerning the consequences of child maltreatment, there is new interest in how early experiences affect the development of the brain and the neuroendocrine system.

Complex Child Trauma

Complex child trauma appears most frequently after extreme exposures to traumatic stress in early life. The areas of impairment include (1) attachment and affective disorders in infancy and childhood; (2) aggression, social anxiety, and eating disorders; (3) dissociative and physical problems; (4) sexual disorders in adolescence and adulthood; and (5) the risk of revictimization (Dube et al., 2001).

Causes of Complex Trauma

Developmental traumatology is a growing field and is providing insights as to how the mechanisms of abuse and neglect can influence behavior. Early sustained abuse can produce physiological changes in the developing brain resulting in difficulty modulating emotional responses (including anger and depression), difficulty interpreting social situations, and difficulty in thinking that contributes to impulsivity, antisocial behavior, and sexual misconduct (Schwartz, Prentky, Pimental, & Cavanaugh, 2006).

The National Child Traumatic Stress Network describes complex child trauma on their website. The website emphasizes the serious effects of trauma on a child's development. In addition, complex trauma can create a wide range of problems in adulthood such as substance abuse, depression and anxiety, self-harming behaviors, and other psychiatric disorders.

There is great importance tied to bonding (establishing early life attachments). Research has shown that bonding establishes a blueprint of how the child will interpret situations outside of family relationships. Primary emphasis is on warmth, affection, caring, protective behaviors, and establishment of accountability, which in turn leads to a foundational establishment of basic trust. These remain at the core of building a social human being (Hazelwood & Burgess, 2016).

Children who lack protection by their caretaker can experience serious stress and anxiety, be overwhelmed, and dissociate themselves from the trauma. This dissociation limits their sense of feeling connected to their environment. As a result, children become isolated from others.

Case of Complex Trauma

A powerful force that impacts children's development is their caregiver history. Homes in which a parent abuses drugs or alcohol, is sexually indiscriminate, has long prison confinement, is absent from the home, or has serious psychiatric history affects a child negatively. The lack of consistent caregiving that occurs when a child is born into an abusive or neglectful family and/or has inconsistent care or institutional placement can lead to deficits in social and interpersonal skills. Positive childhood caregiving facilitates neurological development so that impulses arising from the brain are integrated with the reasoning capacities in the cognitive levels of the brain. However, inconsistent caregiving may disrupt normal development in a variety of ways.

Reactive attachment disorder is one condition that may develop because the child's basic needs for comfort, affection, and nurturing are ignored and positive, caring attachments with others are never established. This may permanently change the child's growing brain, hurting the ability to establish future relationships (Mayo Clinic staff, 2011).

This reactive attachment disorder may take many paths depending on the child's abusive upbringing. Children who are subjected to changes in caregivers never learn to develop secure attachments of any sort and often develop highly ambivalent attachment styles. These children have problems empathizing with others and may act out in aggressive and sexually inappropriate ways. The following case is one example.

Jane was a low-birth-weight infant (2 pounds); her mother was addicted to and took drugs during pregnancy. The house also had high amounts of lead. Jane developed a learning problem, thought to be caused by the high lead levels in the home, that required her to be placed in special schools and learning programs.

Jane was one of eight children, all from different fathers. Two brothers (one died at birth) and a sister were deceased. Her father, now deceased, was absent from her life. Jane received inconsistent caregiving. She lived with an aunt and uncle when her mother could not care for her children; she was returned to the mother when she was six years old. Her mother served a significant amount of time in prison for theft, burglary, and drug use. The uncle, although not a blood relative, also lived with the family for over 40 years. A man named Ralph also lived at the house around the mid-1990s; the mother had planned to marry him but he started using drugs. The mother stated she stopped using drugs. A female friend of her mother's also lived at the house on occasion, as she and the mother were romantically involved. Jane reported sibling incest when she was six or seven with her brother, who was four years older. He offered her to some of his friends for sex. Jane began taking money for sex as a young adolescent.

Jane was already having major conflicts with family, school, and peers in her early teens. She had run away from home, was using drugs, and was homeless. She was hospitalized for fighting her brothers. They teased her and called her a whore; she argued with them and stated she felt like punching them in the face. She claimed her mother cursed at her, hit her with a stick, and threatened to kick her out of the house before a suicide attempt. She also had a case pending for retail theft.

Diagnostic Considerations

Childhood exposure to various types of victimization is not uncommon and can contribute to serious short- and long-term psychological distress and functional impairment (D'Andrea, Ford, Stolbach, Spinazzola & van der Kolk, 2012). Children who experience interpersonal victimization often meet criteria for psychiatric disorders other than posttraumatic stress disorder (PTSD). Such diagnoses can include attention deficit hyperactivity disorder, depression, oppositional defiant disorder, conduct disorder, anxiety, and separation anxiety disorder, to name a few.

Suicidal Impulses and Violence Against Others

Childhood physical and sexual abuse are related to numerous problems for victims later in life, including attempted suicide (Joiner et al., 2007) and repeated suicidal behavior (Ystgaard, Hestetun, Loeb, & Mehlum, 2004). A powerful graded relationship exists between adverse childhood experiences and risk of attempted suicide throughout the life span (Dube et al., 2001). Childhood physical and sexual abuse, abuse-related injuries, and traumatic brain injuries were found to be prevalent in populations of female prison inmates who had engaged in high rates of suicidal behaviors (Brewer-Smyth, Burgess, & Shults, 2004). Sexual abuse by a family member has been related to a decreased diurnal variation of the stress hormone cortisol and increased homicidal behavior in females (Brewer-Smyth & Burgess, 2008). Yet little is understood about risk factors for violent, homicidal, and suicidal behaviors of females. In particular, relationships between these behaviors and physiological associations with previous abuse-related injuries and neurological impairment need to be defined.

Suicide attempts, also described as *parasuicidal behavior* or *nonfatal suicide-related behavior*, are failed attempts to kill oneself (Hauenstein, 2001). Self-directed violence is a significant cause of morbidity and mortality in the United States. Trend analysis data from 9th through 12th grades in public and private schools is showing an increased rate of adolescents who seriously considered attempting suicide (Youth Risk Behavior Surveillance, 2013).

Risk factors for attempted suicide by youth include depression, physical or sexual abuse, and disruptive behavior (Petronis, Samuels, Moscicki, & Anthony, 1990; U.S. Public Health Service, 2001).

Violence that is related to abuse is not only directed toward the self. In a study of school shootings in 37 communities across the United States, Vossekuil, Fein, Reddy, Borum, and Modzeleski (2002) found that in 78% of cases perpetrators exhibited some form of suicidal behavior or ideation before or during the attack. Even among teenagers who engage in less brutal forms of violence, studies suggest they also are more likely to struggle with suicidal thoughts and behaviors than their nonviolent peers (Borowsky, Hogan, & Ireland, 1997; Coker et al., 2000; Swahn, Lubell, & Simon, 2004). Lubell and Vetter (2006) suggested that it should not be terribly surprising that suicidality and interpersonal violence are correlated.

However, despite this expanding research, efforts to develop and implement effective suicide and violence prevention strategies continue to occur in relative isolation from one another. Lubell and Vetter (2006) argued that this bifurcation between researchers and practitioners does not take advantage of opportunities to integrate knowledge and maximize the impact of prevention programs.

Not only are suicide and interpersonal violence leading health problems in the United States, but these two problems have also been linked in the psychiatric literature for over a century. Early psychological formulations by Freud (1963) and Menninger (1933) suggested that hostile and aggressive impulses underlying suicidal and violent behavior develop from similar frustrations within the individual (Lubell & Vetter, 2006). Expanding on these theories, Plutchik and colleagues developed a two-stage model of the relationship between "outward and inward directed aggressiveness" (Plutchik, 1995; Plutchik, van Praag, & Conte, 1989).

Case of Matricide

A 16-year-old youth was convicted of stabbing and beating his 48-year-old mother after a dispute over a letter from the school regarding his nonattendance. The argument continued into the following day; the juvenile threw bleach at this mother and picked up a kitchen knife. She followed him into the bathroom; he stabbed her numerous times and then struck her over the head with a baseball bat. He ransacked the bureaus and threw his blood-stained clothes and bat into a nearby marsh. The juvenile later returned to the house with a friend and found the body. After intensive investigation, the son confessed. The crime is cause-specific, family violence. There was information that the mother had physically and sexually abused the youth as a small child.

Treatment for Child Victims

The immediate and long-term consequences of child abuse and neglect point to the fact that many child victims will need treatment intervention. Such intervention can occur on a crisis basis or may address more longstanding issues.

Crisis Intervention

The immediate concern in crisis situations involving children is safety and security. Child protection services focus on assessing immediate risk and ensuring the child is safe from further harm in the immediate future. Once safety is established, crisis intervention focuses on helping the child and whatever supportive adults may be in his or her life. This is a highly supportive intervention that builds on client strengths, helps identify short-term goals, and helps clients identify how they will go about attaining them.

Crisis workers provide stability to families and guide them to appropriate organizations and services and they give the name of a specific person rather than simply a telephone number. During the initial crisis, crisis workers may even need to accompany the clients to appointments. As a support system, the crisis worker should always be available. Advocacy for clients, in helping them access and use resources, dramatically enhances the therapeutic relationship.

As identified by the U.S. Department of Health and Human Services (1994), abusive families' diverse needs require services from many different organizations. Presently, services are fragmented into various aspects, including investigation, crisis intervention, concrete services, and long-term treatment, and health, social, legal, housing, education, employment, mental health, spiritual, and financial all fall under the mandates of different governmental and community organizations. So-called wraparound services provide whatever the family thinks it needs to stabilize. This requires strong, collaborative efforts among community resources (U.S. Department of Health and Human Services, 1994).

Individual Treatment for Children

Two types of treatment, eye movement desensitization and reprocessing (EMDR) and trauma-focused cognitive-behavioral therapy (CBT), are widely used in the treatment of posttraumatic stress disorder (PTSD). Seidler and Wagner (2006) conducted a study on the efficacy of the two treatment methods for PTSD and found both therapy methods to be equally efficacious.

EYE MOVEMENT DESENSITIZATION AND REPROCESSING (EMDR)

Eye movement desensitization and reprocessing (EMDR) was developed and introduced by Francine Shapiro in 1987 (Shapiro, 2001) and has mainly been used in the treatment of PTSD. With EMDR the client is instructed to focus both on a disturbing image or memory and on the emotions and cognitive elements connected with it. Once the client has established contact with the disturbing material, the therapist induces a bilateral stimulation. The simplest method involves moving the fingers back and forth in front of the client's face after instructing the client to follow the movement with his or her eyes. Bilateral stimulation can also be induced through auditory or tactile stimuli (Seidler & Wagner, 2006).

TRAUMA-FOCUSED COGNITIVE-BEHAVIORAL THERAPY

Evidence is growing that **trauma-focused cognitive-behavioral therapy (TF-CBT)** is an effective treatment for sexually abused children, including those who have experienced multiple other traumatic events. Most studies that have evaluated TF-CBT have been well designed (Cohen, Deblinger, Mannarino, & Steer, 2004; Cohen, Mannarino, & Knudsen, 2005). This treatment model represents a synthesis of trauma-sensitive interventions and well-established CBT principles (Beck, 1993).

TF-CBT takes a child and parent psychotherapy approach for children and adolescents who are experiencing major emotional and behavioral difficulties related to traumatic life events. It is a components-based treatment model that incorporates trauma-sensitive interventions with cognitive behavioral, family, and humanistic principles and techniques (Cohen, Mannarino, & Deblinger, 2006).

The therapy was developed to resolve PTSD and depressive and anxiety symptoms, as well as to address underlying distortions about self-blame, safety, the trustworthiness of others, and the world (Cohen, Mannarino, & Deblinger, 2006). The treatment also fits traumatic experiences into a broader context of children's lives so their primary identity is not that of a victim.

Core components of TF-CBT are psychoeducation about child trauma and PTSD, affective modulation skills, individualized stress-management skills, an introduction to the cognitive triad (relationships between thoughts, feeling, and behaviors), creating a trauma narrative, cognitive processing, safety skills, and a parental treatment component. Parents are seen separately from their children for most of the treatment and receive interventions that parallel those provided to the child, along with parenting skills. Several joint parent–child sessions are also included to enhance family communication. Most TF-CBT treatment studies have consisted of 12 treatment sessions (Cohen, Mannarino, & Deblinger, 2006).

ATTACHMENT TRAUMA THERAPY

Traditional therapy techniques are usually ineffective with attachment-impaired children, because they rely on the child's ability to form trusting relationships, which an attachment-impaired child is unable to do. Attachment therapy is a multidimensional intervention with the primary goal of creating or restoring a secure bond of trust between a parent and child, not between the therapist and child. Attachment therapy involves the parents and the child working together rather than the therapist working with the child alone. Attachment therapy is directive, experiential, and confrontational, in that it deals with the drama, trauma, and truth of the child's life.

Consequently, one needs to examine the nature of their framework for not only assessing the individual child but for assessing the social and family contexts of a child. Those children whose sense of other and self has been compromised by abuse and who have withdrawn from the world of people and personal achievement and satisfaction often display an array of avoidant behaviors. Sometimes the pressure of unhappiness and unchanging family patterns often find these children and youth pressed to a singular alternative; that is, to eliminate the people who are abusing them, resulting in the tragic outcome of isolated youths killing a parent or parents or people who have been subjecting them to continuous harmful situations. At times, in the context of running away from home, these same youths can find themselves in a peer relationship following someone who commits aggressive acts toward strangers.

Conclusion

The challenges to providing intervention and treatment to victimized children and their families are clear. Early recognition of child maltreatment provides an opportunity to reduce the pain of the child and help families to change their behaviors to assist their children. Neutralizing the impact of trauma on the development of the child may prevent victim to offender role reversal and also decrease any suicidal thoughts. It would be beneficial if intervention programs for children were a part of every mental health center.

Key Terms

Child maltreatment: Describes the four types of child mistreatment: physical abuse, sexual abuse, emotional abuse, and neglect. In many cases, children are the victims of more than one type of abuse. The abusers can be parents or other family members, caretakers such as teachers and babysitters, acquaintances (including other children), and (in rare instances) strangers.

Complex child trauma: Describes both children's exposure to multiple traumatic events, often of an invasive, interpersonal nature, and the wide-ranging, long-term impact of this exposure. These events are severe and pervasive, such as abuse or profound neglect.

Developmental disability: A cognitive, emotional, or physical impairment, especially one related to abnormal sensory or motor development, that appears in infancy or childhood and involves a failure or delay in progressing through the normal developmental stages of childhood.

Developmental traumatology: The systemic investigation of the psychiatric and psychobiological impact of overwhelming and chronic interpersonal violence on the developing child. This relatively new area of study synthesizes knowledge from an array of scientific fields, including developmental psychopathology, developmental neuroscience, and stress and trauma research.

Disclosure: A child telling that someone has abused or hurt him or her. This can be very difficult, and how the professional/investigator responds can be critical for all facets of subsequent intrapsychic and interpersonal recovery.

Eye movement desensitization and reprocessing (EMDR): A psychotherapy treatment designed to alleviate the distress associated with traumatic memories.

Fetal homicide: Also called feticide, it is an act that causes the death of a fetus.

Fetal rights: The rights of any unborn human fetus, which is generally a developing human from roughly eight weeks after conception to birth.

Incest: Sexual intercourse with a descendent by blood or adoption.

Statutory rape: Sexual intercourse with a person under the age of consent and by an adult age 18 years or older.

Trauma-focused cognitive-behavioral therapy (TF-CBT): A psychotherapy approach for children and adolescents who are experiencing significant emotional and behavioral difficulties related to traumatic life events.

▎ Discussion Questions

1. Do you believe there were more instances of child abuse 100 years ago? Why or why not?

2. Why might the rates of reported child abuse be decreasing in recent surveys?

3. Is it actually possible for a 10-year-old to be at risk for suicide? Explain.

4. Should fetal death be included as child abuse?

5. Why is the age of the child when the violence occurred an important part of assessment and planning?

6. How do you explain Ericka Murray's abuse of her children?

7. What type of treatments would you recommend for abused children of different ages?

Resources

American Bar Association. Invisible Victims: Violence Against Persons with Developmental Disabilities http://www.abanet.org/irr/hr/winter00human rights/petersilia.htm

Centers for Disease Control and Prevention: Violence Prevention http://www.cdc.gov/ncipc/dvp/dvp.htm

Disability, Abuse & Personal Rights Project http://www.disability-abuse.com

Kid-Safe Network http://www.kidsafenetwork.com

National Center for Missing and Exploited Children (NCMEC)—CYBERTIPLINE: Reporting categories http://www.missingkids.com/missing kids/servlet/PageServlet?LanguageCountry=en_US&PageId=2447

References

American Psychiatric Association. (2002). *Diagnostic and statistical manual of mental disorders* (4th ed.). Washington, DC: American Psychiatric Association.

American Public Health Association. (1975). Policy statement database. Child abuse. Policy Date: 1/1/1975. Policy Number: 7512. Retrieved from http://www.apha.org/advocacy/policy/policysearch/default.htm?id=790

American Public Health Association. (1986). Policy statement database. Prevention of child abuse. Policy Date: 1/1/1986. Policy Number: 8614(PP). Retrieved from http://www.apha.org/advocacy/policy/policysearch/default.htm?id=1129

Ayoub, C., & Alexander, R. (1998). Definitional issues in Munchausen by proxy. *American Professional Society on the Abuse of Children Advisor*, 11(1), 7–10.

Bavolek, S. J. (2000). *The nurturing parenting programs*. Washington, DC: Office of Juvenile Justice and Delinquency Prevention, U.S. Department of Justice.

Beck, A. (1993). *Cognitive therapy and the emotional disorders*. New York: Penguin.

Belsky, J. (1985). The determinants of parenting: A process model. *Child Development*, 55(1), 83–96.

Borowsky, I. W., Hogan, M., & Ireland, M. (1997). Adolescent sexual aggression: Risk and protective factors. *Pediatrics*, 100(6), E7.

Brewer-Smyth, K., & Burgess, A. W. (2008). Childhood sexual abuse by a family member, salivary cortisol, and homicidal behavior of female prison inmates. *Nursing Research*, 57(3), 166–174.

Brewer-Smyth, K., Burgess, A. W., & Shults, J. (2004). Physical and sexual abuse, salivary cortisol, and neurological correlates of violent criminal behavior in female prison inmates. *Biological Psychiatry*, 55(1), 30–40.

Brown, S. (2011). *Against all odds*. New York: Harper.

Burczycka, M., & Conroy, S. (2017). Family violence in Canada: A statistical profile, 2015. Canadian Centre for Justice Statistics. Retrieved July 24, 2017 from http://www.statcan.gc.ca/pub/85-002-x/2017001/article/14698-eng.pdf

Burgess, A. W., Hartman, C. R., & Clements, P. T. (1995). The biology of memory in childhood trauma. *Journal of Psychosocial Nursing*, 33(3), 16–26.

Centers for Disease Control and Prevention. (2004). Web-based Injury Statistics Query and Reporting System (WISQARS). Retrieved from www.cdc.gov/ncipc/wisqars

Charlotte Observer. (2011). Driver in Carruth murder case released from prison. Retrieved from http://www.charlotteobserver.com/2011/07/20/2469034/driver-in-carruth-murder-case.html#ixzz1T2bwfqT2

Child Welfare Information Gateway. (2017). *Child maltreatment 2015: Summary of key findings*. Washington, DC: U.S. Department of Health and Human Services, Children's Bureau.

Clements, P. T., & DeRanieri, J. T. (2006). Youth exposure to violence, terrorism, and sudden traumatic death. In R. M. Hammer, B. Moynihan, & E. M. Pagliaro (Eds.), *Forensic nursing: A handbook for practice* (pp. 305–320). Sudbury, MA: Jones & Bartlett.

Cohen, J. A., Deblinger, E., Mannarino, A. P., & Steer, R. A. (2004). A multisite, randomized controlled trial for children with sexual abuse-related PTSD symptoms. *Journal of the American Academy of Child and Adolescent Psychiatry*, 43, 393–403.

Cohen, J. A., Mannarino, A. P., & Deblinger, E. (2006). *Treating trauma and traumatic grief in children and adolescents*. New York: The Guilford Press.

Cohen, J. A., Mannarino, A. P., & Knudsen, K. (2005). Treating sexually abused children: 1 year follow-up of a randomized controlled trial. *Child Abuse & Neglect*, 29, 135–145.

Coker, A. L., McKeown, R. E., Sanderson, M., Davis, K. E., Valois, R. F., & Huebner, E. S. (2000). Severe dating violence and quality of life among South Carolina high school students. *American Journal of Preventive Medicine*, 19(4), 220–227.

D'Andrea, W., Ford, J., Stolbah, B., Spinazzola, J. & vander Kolk, B. (2012). Understanding interpersonal trauma in children: Why we need a developmentally appropriate trauma diagnosis. *American Journal of Orthopsychiatry*, 82(2), 187–200.

deMause, L. (1998). The history of child abuse. *Journal of Psychohistory*, 25(3), 216–236.

Dube, S. R., Anda, R. F., Felitti, V. J., Chapman, D. P., Williamson, D. F., & Giles, W. H. (2001). Childhood abuse, household dysfunction, and the risk of attempted suicide throughout the life span: Findings from the Adverse Childhood Experiences Study. *Journal of the American Medical Association, 286*(24), 3089–3096.

Eron, L. D., Huesmann, L. R., & Zelli, A. (1991). The role of parental variables in the learning of aggression. In D. J. Pepler & K. H. Rubin (Eds.), *The development and treatment of childhood aggression* (pp. 169–188). Hillsdale, NJ: Erlbaum.

Finkelhor, D., & Dziuba-Leatherman, J. (1994). Children as victims of violence: A national survey. *Pediatrics, 94,* 413–420.

Finkelhor, D., & Jones, L. (2006). Why have child maltreatment and child victimization declined? *Journal of Social Issues, 62,* 685–716.

Finkelhor D., Turner, H. A., Shattuck, A., & Hamby, S. L. (2015). Prevalence of childhood exposure to violence, crime, and abuse: Results from the National Survey of Children's Exposure to Violence. *JAMA Pediatrics, 169*(8), 746–754.

Fisher, J. (2017, March 20). Erika Murray's squalid house of horrors. True Crime Blog. Retrieved from http://jimfishertruecrime.blogspot.com/2014/09/erika-murrays-squalid-house-of-horrors.html

Focht-New, G., Clements, P. T., Barol, E., Service, K., & Faulkner, M. (2008). Persons with developmental disabilities exposed to interpersonal violence and crime: The impact of intrapsychic trauma. *Perspectives in Psychiatric Care: The Journal for Advanced Practice Psychiatric Nurses, 44*(1), 3–13.

Freud, S. (1963). In J. Strachey (Ed.), *The standard edition of the complete psychological works of Sigmund Freud* (Vol. 14). London: Hogarth Press.

Fry, E. (2011). A childhood biography of Oprah Winfrey. Retrieved from http://oprah.about.com/od/oprahbiography/p/oprahchildhood.htm

Gil, D. G. (1979). *Child abuse and violence.* New York: AMS Press.

Glueck, S., & Glueck, E. T. (1950). *Unraveling juvenile delinquency.* Cambridge, MA: Harvard University Press.

Groth, A. N. (1979). *Men who rape.* New York: Plenum.

Haapasalo, J., & Pokela, E. (1999). Child-rearing and criminality. *Aggression and Violent Behavior, 4*(1), 107–128.

Hart, S. N., & Brassard, M. R. (1987). A major threat to children's mental health: Psychological maltreatment. *American Psychologist, 42,* 161–165.

Hauenstein, E. J. (2001). Case finding and care in suicide: Children, adolescents, and adults. In M.A. Boyd (Ed.), *Psychiatric nursing: Contemporary practice.* Philadelphia: Lippincott Williams & Wilkins.

Hopper, J. (2007). Unavoidable controversies & biases, in historical contexts. Retrieved from http://www.jimhopper.com/abstats/#s-intro

Huesmann, L. R., & Eron, L. D. (1986). *Television and the aggressive child: A cross-national comparison.* Lawrence Erlbaum.

Joiner, T. E., Sachs-Ericsson, N. J., Wingate, L. R., Brown, J. S., Anestis, M. D., & Selby, E. A. (2007). Childhood physical and sexual abuse and lifetime number of suicide attempts: A persistent and theoretically important relationship. *Behaviour Research and Therapy, 45*(3), 539–547.

Kempe, C. H., Silverman, F. N., Steele, B. F., Droegemuller, W., & Silver, H. K. (1962). The battered-child syndrome. *Journal of the American Medical Association, 181,* 17–24.

Laci and Conner's Law. (2004). Unborn Victims of Violence Act. Legislative Report of 2004, Washington, DC.

LaSala, K. B., & Lynch, V. A. (2006). Child abuse and neglect. In V. A. Lynch & J. B. Duval (Eds.), *Forensic nursing* (pp. 249–259). St. Louis, MO: Mosby.

Leeb, R. T., Paulozzi, L., Melanson, C., Simon, T., & Arias, I. (2008). Child maltreatment surveillance: Uniform definitions for public health and recommended data elements, Version 1.0. Retrieved from http://www.cdc.gov/ViolencePrevention /pub/CMP-Surveillance.html

Levenson, E. (2017, May 30). "She was a demon": Trial for murder of two-year-old Bella Bond begins. CNN. Retrieved from http://www.cnn.com/2017/05/30/us/bella -bond-murder-trial/index.html

Leventhal, J. M. (2005). Overview of child maltreatment. In A.P. Giardino & R. Alexander (Eds.), *Child maltreatment.* St. Louis, MO: G. W. Medical Publishing.

Levanthal, J. M., Martin, K. D., & Gaither, J. R. (2012). Using US data to estimate the incidence of serious physical abuse in children. *Pediatrics, 129*(3) 458–464.

Lubell, K. M., & Vetter, J. B. (2006). Suicide and youth violence presentation: The promise of an integrated approach. *Aggression and Violent Behavior, 11*(2), 167–175.

Maguire, S., Moynihan, S., Mann, M., Potokar, T., & Kemp, A. M. (2008). A systematic review of the features that indicate intentional scalds in children. *Burns.* Dec; 34(8):1072–81.

Mayo Clinic Staff. (2011). Reactive attachment disorder. Retrieved from http://www .mayoclinic.com/health/reactive-attachment-disorder/DS00988

McCord, J. (1988). Parental behavior in the cycle of aggression. *Psychiatry, 51*(1), 14–23.

Menninger, K. A. (1933). Psychoanalytic aspects of suicide. *International Journal of Psychoanalysis, 14,* 376–390.

Merrick, M., & Latzman, N. (2014, January 31). Child maltreatment: A public health overview and prevention considerations. *OJIN: The Online Journal of Issues in Nursing, 19*(1), Manuscript 2.

Montaldo, C. (2011). Retrieved from http://www.CharlesMontaldo.About.com

Moscicki, E. K. (2001). Epidemiology of completed and attempted suicide: Toward a framework for prevention. *Clinical Neuroscience Research, 1,* 310–323.

Mugavin, M. E. (2005). A meta-synthesis of filicide classification systems: Psychosocial and psychodynamic issues in women who kill their children. *Journal of Forensic Nursing, 1*(2), 65–72.

National Association of Counsel for Children. (n.d.a). Child maltreatment. Retrieved from http://www.naccchildlaw.org/childrenlaw/childmaltreatment.html

National Association of Counsel for Children. (n.d.b). Children and the law: Reporting child abuse. Retrieved from http://www.naccchildlaw.org/childrenlaw/reporting childabuse.html

National Child Traumatic Stress Network. (2004). Facts on traumatic stress and children with developmental disabilities. Retrieved from http://www.nctsnet.org /nctsn_assets/pdfs/reports/traumatic_stress_developmental_disabilities_final.pdf

National District Attorneys Association. (n.d.). Mandatory reporting of child abuse and neglect: State statutes and professional ethics. Retrieved from http://ndaa.org/pdf /mandatory_reporting_state_statutes.pdf

National Research Council. (1993). Etiology of child Maltreatment. In *Understanding child abuse and neglect* (pp. 106–160). Washington, DC: National Academies of Sciences, Engineering, and Medicine.

Oprah.com. (2006). Why 15-year-old Jessica Coleman killed her baby. Retrieved from http://www.oprah.com/oprahshow/All-American-Tragedy

Peck, M. D., & Priolo-Kapel, D. (2002). Child abuse by burning: a review of the literature and an algorithm for medical investigations. *Journal of Trauma and Acute Care Surgery.* Jul; *53*(5):1013–22.

Petronis, K. R., Samuels, J. F., Moscicki, E. K., & Anthony, J. C. (1990). An epidemiologic investigation of potential risk factors for suicide attempts. *Social Psychiatry and Psychiatric Epidemiology, 25*(4), 193–199.

Pleck, E. (2003). Criminal approaches to family violence: 1640–1980. In M. Silberman (Ed.), *Violence and society: A reader* (pp. 161–173). Upper Saddle River, NJ: Prentice Hall.

Plutchik, R. (1995). Outward and inward directed aggressiveness: The interaction between violence and suicidality. *Pharmacopsychiatric, 28*(Suppl 2), 47–57.

Plutchik, R., van Praag, H. M., & Conte, H. R. (1989). Correlates of suicide and violence risk III: A two-stage model of countervailing forces. *Psychiatric Research, 28*(2), 215–225.

Potter, D., Nasserie, T. & Tonmyr, L. (2015). A review of recent analyses of the Canadian Incidence Study of Reported Child Abuse and Neglect (CIS). *Health Promotion and Chronic Disease Prevention in Canada: Research Policy and Practice, 35*(8/9), p. 120.

Regehr, C., & Kanani, K. (2010). *Essential law for social work practice in Canada* (2nd ed.). Toronto: Oxford University Press.

Reinhardt, C. (2014). Affidavits detail how Sullivan preyed upon young boys. *San Angelo News.* Retrieved from http://sanangelolive.com/news/crime/2014-06-06 /affidavits-detail-how-sullivan-preyed-upon-young-boys

Robertson, S. (n.d.). Age of consent laws, in children and youth in history, item #230. Retrieved from http://chnm.gmu.edu/cyh/teaching-modules/230

Robins, L. (1966). *Deviant children grown up.* Baltimore, MD: Williams & Wilkins.

Roesler, T., & Jenny, C. (2009). *Medical child abuse: Beyond Munchausen syndrome by proxy.* Washington, DC: American Academy of Pediatrics.

Satten, J., Menninger, K., Rosen, I., & Mayman, M. (1960). Murder without apparent motive: A study in personality disorganization. *American Journal of Psychiatry, 117*, 48–53.

Schwartz, D., Prentky, R. A., Pimental, A., & Cavanaugh, D. (2006). Descriptive study of precursors to sex offending among 813 boys and girls: Antecedent life experiences. *Victims & Offenders, 1*(4), 61–77.

"Scott Peterson sent to San Quentin." (2005). MSNBC. Retrieved from http://www.msnbc.msn.com/id/7217582/

Sedlak, A. J., Mettenburg, J., Basena, M., Petta, I., McPherson, K., Greene, A., & Li, S. (2010). *Fourth National Incidence Study of Child Abuse and Neglect (NIS-4): Report to Congress, Executive Summary.* Washington, DC: U.S. Department of Health and Human Services, Administration for Children and Families.

Seidler, G. H., & Wagner, F. E. (2006). Comparing the efficacy of EMDR and trauma-focused cognitive-behavioral therapy in the treatment of PTSD: A meta-analytic study. *Psychological Medicine, 36,* 1515–1522.

Sgroi, S. (1982). *Handbook of clinical intervention in child sexual abuse.* Toronto: Lexington Books.

Shapiro F. (2001). Eye movement desensitization and reprocessing (EMDR): basic principles, protocols, and procedures. 2nd ed. New York, NY: The Guilford Press.

Silver, L. B., Dublin, C. C., & Lourie, R. S. (1969). Does violence breed violence? Contributions from a study of the child abuse syndrome. *American Journal of Psychiatry, 126,* 404–407.

Straus, M. A., Hamby, S. L., Finkelhor, D., Moore, D. W., & Runyon, D. (1998). Identification of child maltreatment with the Parent-Child Conflict Tactics Scales: Development and psychometric data for a national sample of American parents. *Child Abuse & Neglect, 22,* 249–270.

Sunderland, R. (1995). *Helping children cope with grief: A teacher's guide. Picking up the pieces* (2nd ed.). Fort Collins, CO: Services Corporation International.

Swahn, M., Lubell, K., & Simon, T. (2004). Suicide attempts and physical fighting among high school students—United States, 2001. *Journal of the American Medical Association, 292,* 428–429.

Tonmyr, L., Quimet, C., & Ugnat, A. M. (2012). A review of findings from the Canadian Incidence Study of Reported Child Abuse and Neglect (CIS). *Canadian Journal of Public Health, 103*(2), 103–112.

Trocme, N., Fallon, B., MacLaurin, B., Sinha, V., & Black, T. (2008). *Canadian Incidence Study on child abuse and neglect.* Ottawa: Public Health Agency Canada.

UNICEF. (2011). Child protection from violence, exploitation, and abuse. Retrieved from http://www.unicef.org/protection/index_3717.html

United Nations. (2009). The Convention on the Rights of the Child. Retrieved from http://www2.ohchr.org/english/law/crc.htm

U.S. Department of Health and Human Services. Administration on Children, Youth, and Families, Children's Bureau. (2016). Child maltreatment 2014 [online]. Retrieved from http://www.acf.hhs.gov/sites/default/files/cb/cm2014.pdf

U.S. Department of Health and Human Services. (1994). Crisis intervention in child abuse and neglect user manual series. *Child Welfare Information Gateway.* Retrieved from http://www.childwelfare.gov/pubs/usermanuals/crisis/crisisj.cfm

U.S. Public Health Service. (2001). Suicide in the U.S.: Statistics and prevention. Retrieved from http://www.nimh.nih.gov/health/publications/suicide-in-the-us-statistics-and-prevention/index.shtml

Volpe, R. (2011). The Canadian encyclopedia. Retrieved from http://thecanadianencyclopedia.com/index.cfm?PgNm=TCE&Params=A1ARTA0001576

Vossekuil, B., Fein, R. A., Reddy, M., Borum, R., & Modzeleski, W. (2002). *The final report and findings of the safe school initiative: Implications for the prevention of school attacks in the United States.* Washington, DC: U.S. Secret Service and the U.S. Department of Education.

West's Encyclopedia of American Law. (1998). Statutory rape. Farmington Hills, MI: The Gale Group.

World Health Organization. (2004). Guidelines for medico-legal care for victims of sexual violence. Retrieved from http://whqlibdoc.who.int/publications/2004/924154628X.pdf

World Health Organization. (2006). Prevention of child maltreatment—WHO scales up child maltreatment prevention activities. Retrieved from http://www.who.int/violence_injury_prevention/violence/activities/child_maltreatment/en/index.html

Youth Risk Behavior Surveillance. *Morbidity and Mortality Weekly Report (MMWR).* (2013). Retrieved from http://www.cdc.gov/mmwr/pdf/ss/ss6304.pdf

Ystgaard, M., Hestetun, I., Loeb, M., & Mehlum, L. (2004). Is there a specific relationship between childhood sexual and physical abuse and repeated suicidal behaviour? *Child Abuse and Neglect, 28,* 863–875.

CHAPTER 7

Child Abduction and Exploitation

OBJECTIVES

- To define the types of missing children
- To identify groups of children who are vulnerable for abuse
- To describe laws that address child labor and child trafficking
- To describe fetal, infant, and child abduction
- To identify grooming techniques used by child molesters

KEY TERMS

Alien

Child pornography

Child prostitution

Child trafficking

Fetal abduction

Grooming

Infant abduction

Missing children

Thrownaways

CASE

Child Prostitution

Three major forms of commercial sexual exploitation of children are prostitution, child pornography, and sex trafficking. Although the actual statistics on the number of child victims is not known, British Columbia and Canada estimate between 10 to 12% of youth involved in prostitution are less than 18 years old. Disproportionately represented in the sex trade in Canada are aboriginal children (Hay, 2004).

Where there is prostitution, writes Zurita (2012), you can expect to find sex trafficking. Simply stated, when the supply of prostitutes fails to meet the demand for prostitutes, at-risk or vulnerable persons are forced into sex work. The vulnerable persons include children because more money can be made by the traffickers/pimps if they can supply younger children believing they are disease-free. If johns stopped buying sex, argues Zurita (2012), pimps and sex traffickers would have no business. However, Mitchell, Finkelhor, and Wolak (2010) found in their study that 31% of cases had no pimp, 57% of cases did have a pimp, and 12% of the cases involved child abuse with payment. The researchers suggest that the children with no pimp were most likely runaways that needed money for a drug habit or for survival for food and shelter (Mitchell et al., 2010).

In Canada, one of the areas for child prostitution is the Downtown Eastside, known as "Low Track." This location, known because of the high incidence of drug abuse, drug-related crime, and prostitution, is a notorious neighborhood in Vancouver, British Columbia, a beautiful city bordered by the Pacific Ocean and the Rocky Mountains. Well known as Canada's poorest postal code, the area has been described as "a world of misery crammed into 10 blocks" (Matas & Peritz, 2008, p. 1). Drugs of choice are heroin and crack cocaine, supplied by motorcycle gangs or Asian cartels that stake out choice blocks and use brute force in defending their territory. In 1998, the area averaged one death per day from drug overdoses, the highest rate in Canadian history (Newton, n.d.).

Most of Eastside's female addicts support their habits via prostitution, trolling the streets night and day, feeding on crack cocaine. Safe sex is an illusion in this neighborhood, which includes the highest HIV infection rate in North America (Newton, n.d.).

Although statistics on prostitution are difficult to determine, in 2012 there were almost 14,000 child and youth victims of sexual offenses in Canada, a rate of 205 victims for every 100,000 child and youth. Unfortunately, only one in five (21%) of cases of sexual offenses with a child or youth victim are reported to the police (Statistics Canada, 2012).

The prevalence of fentanyl and carfentanil place child and youth prostitutes and drug users in the Downtown Eastside at risk of overdose and death. Although much of Canada has felt the effects of the fentanyl-driven overdose crisis, British Columbia has been hardest hit, experiencing more fatal overdoses in 2017 than in three decades of record-keeping. The death toll is expected to climb to more than 800. Eight overdose deaths have been recorded in the Downtown Eastside in a single day. In the troubled neighborhood, more than 6,300 people draw social assistance and more than half the 18,000 residents are thought to be drug users (Woo et al., 2017).

The United Nations Office on Drugs and Crime (UNODC) published statistics in 2012 that stated that the number of child victims had increased from 20% to 27% over a three-year period, with two out of three child victims being girls. Profiling by gender and age, UNODC reported that globally, 17% of victims were girls and 10% were boys, compared to 59% women and 14% men.

When internal trafficking victims are added to the estimates of 600,000 to 800,000 persons trafficked globally, the number of victims annually is in the range of 2 to 4 million. And of these numbers, 50% of those victims are estimated to be children. The Internet is believed to be the blame for more than 75% of sex transactions with underage girls (Ark of Hope, 2017).

Child Kidnapping

On June 10, 1991, 11-year-old Jaycee Dugard was kidnapped on her way to the school bus stop. She was abducted by a couple in a gray sedan as her stepfather watched from his driveway two blocks away. Eighteen years later she was discovered at the age of 29. Jaycee Dugard had been kept in a small concealed area behind the home of Phillip and Nancy Garrido in Antioch, California, for 18 years. On August 26, 2009, she was discovered by serendipity in the course of another investigation. The day earlier, convicted sex offender Phillip Craig Garrido had visited the campus of UC Berkeley accompanied by two young girls. Their unusual behavior sparked a police investigation. It was later revealed the girls were the children of the long-missing Jaycee Dugard.

Phillip and Nancy Garrido were charged with abduction, rape, and forcible confinement. At the trial, Jaycee testified that she was forced to have sex with Garrido and was threatened with a stun gun if she did not comply. It was further revealed that Nancy Garrido was fully involved with the kidnapping and confinement of Jaycee. Jaycee's testimony stated that she and Nancy would watch television and have dinner together and that Nancy would at times offer to have sex with Garrido to spare Jaycee. During her time in captivity, Jaycee Dugard bore two daughters, ages 11 and 15, at the time of her reappearance in 2009. She testified that she never tried to escape because she feared what would happen to her. On June 2, 2011, Phillip Garrido was sentenced to 431 years; his wife received 36 years to life in prison.

Victims have the opportunity to read or to have read a victim impact statement at the time of a criminal trial against their victimizer. The following is the victim impact statement made by Jaycee Dugard at the April 28, 2011, sentencing hearing, where Phillip and Nancy Garrido pled guilty to kidnapping and rape. Dugard, who did not attend the sentencing, sent a written statement that was read in court (Dugard, 2011):

> I chose not to be here today because I refuse to waste another second of my life in your presence. I've chosen to have my mom read this for me. Phillip Garrido, you are wrong. I could never say that to you before, but I have the freedom now and I am saying you are a liar and all of your so-called theories are wrong. Everything you have ever done to me has been wrong and someday I hope you can see that. What you and Nancy did was reprehensible. You always justified everything to suit yourself but the reality is and always has been that to make someone else suffer for your inability to control yourself and for you, Nancy, to facilitate his behavior and trick young girls for his pleasure is evil. There is no God in the universe that would condone your actions. To you, Phillip, I say that I have always been a thing for your own amusement. I hated every second of every day of 18 years because of you and the sexual perversion you forced on me. To you, Nancy, I have nothing to say. Both of you can save your apologies and empty

words. For all the crimes you have both committed I hope you have as many sleepless nights as I did. Yes, as I think of all of those years I am angry because you stole my life and that of my family. Thankfully I am doing well now and no longer live in a nightmare. I have wonderful friends and family around me. Something you can never take from me again. You do not matter anymore.

Due to Garrido's failed parole supervision, Jaycee and her daughters were awarded $20 million by the State of California. Since their rescue, Jaycee and her daughters have lived a secluded life in Southern California with Jaycee's mother and stepsister.

Introduction

Children suffer abuse and neglect at the hands of their parents, guardians, and other family members. Such forms of abuse are by far the most common forms of victimization children experience at the hands of adults in North America. However, public awareness and fear are often focused on other forms of victimization of children, most commonly that perpetrated by a stranger. These include the abduction of children and the exploitation of children, particularly sexual exploitation. Indeed, for certain groups of children, such forms of victimization are all too common. UNICEF summarized these concerns as follows: "All children have the right to be protected from violence, exploitation, and abuse. Yet, millions of children worldwide from all socio-economic backgrounds, across all ages, religions, and cultures suffer violence, exploitation, and abuse every day. Millions more are at risk" (UNICEF, 2010, p. 1).

Scope of the Problem

The 2002 World Health Organization study on violence against children provided a wealth of international data on the abduction and exploitation of children. This study estimated that 150 million girls and 73 million boys under the age of 18 experience forced sexual intercourse or other forms of physical sexual violence (World Health Organization, 2002). This abuse comes in many forms, one of which is children forced to work in the sex trade. UNICEF, in its publication *State of the World's Children* (2010), concluded that in the United States alone at least 100,000 children are involved in commercial sexual exploitation. Similarly, the U.S. Department of Labor publication "Forced Labor: The Prostitution of Children" (1999) reported that there were approximately 100,000 child prostitutes working in the United States. An estimated 14,500 to 17,500 foreign nationals are trafficked into the United States each year, and the number of U.S. citizens trafficked within the country is even higher, with an estimated 200,000 American children at risk for trafficking into the sex industry. UNICEF estimates that 1.2 million children are trafficked worldwide (UNICEF, 2010).

One of the outcomes of the 2002 study by WHO was "INSPIRE," a plan of seven strategies to reduce violence against children that was launched in July 2017 (WHO, 2017). The seven strategies of INSPIRE include the following:

- Implementation and enforcement of laws by limiting young people's access to firearms and other weapons and criminalizing parents for violently punishing their children.
- Changing beliefs and behaviors around gender roles.
- Ensuring safe environments by improving home environments.
- Providing parent and caregiver support.
- Increasing incomes.
- Providing support and treatment programs for juvenile offenders.
- Providing education and life skills to improve children's life and social skills.

The Federal Bureau of Investigation (FBI) reports that the average age of a child targeted for prostitution is between 12 to 14 for girls and 11 to 13 for boys. These youth are dependent on their pimps for everything and should they try to escape they are often subject to brutal beatings or even killed (2003).

The FBI, in conjunction with the nearly 400 law enforcement agencies at all levels, the U.S. Department of Justice, and the National Center for Missing and Exploited Children (NCMEC), launched the Innocence Lost National Initiative to address the growing problem of children recruited for prostitution (FBI, 2003). In a May 29, 2014 audio broadcast of *FBI This Week*, FBI spokesperson Mollie Halpern reported the importance of the initiative in combatting the growing crime of domestic minor sex trafficking. Additionally, Supervisory Special Agent Jake Hardie reported that 69 FBI-led Child Exploitation Task Forces located across the country are also addressing minor sex trafficking. Since its inception, the Innocence Lost initiative has led to the recovery of more than 3,400 children—some as young as 9 years old. Hardie emphasized that the FBI has a very victim-centered approach, removing children from the lifestyle and ensuring they go somewhere where they will be safe. The initiative has also led to the convictions of more than 1,450 pimps, madams, and their associates, many resulting in lengthy sentences (including 13 life sentences) and the seizure of property, vehicles, and other monetary assets. (Halpern, 2014).

Child abduction and exploitation occur not only in faraway countries characterized by political corruption, tyranny, and severe poverty, but also in North America. In the United States, statistics on child abduction and exploitation are collected by the National Incidence Studies of Missing, Abducted, Runaway, and Thrownaway Children (NISMART). Studies and data collection by NISMART have been undertaken in response to the Missing Children Act of 1982 and the subsequent Missing Children Assistance Act of 1984, which requires the Office of Juvenile Justice and Delinquency Prevention to conduct periodic studies to determine the number of U.S. children reported missing and the number of children recovered during a given year.

Stereotypical kidnappings are defined as abductions in which a slight acquaintance or stranger moves a child at least 20 feet or holds the child at least 1 hour, or in which the child is detained overnight, transported at least 50 miles, held for ransom, abducted with the intent to keep permanently, or killed (Wolak, Finkelhor, and Sedlak, 2016).

NISMART-3 compared the characteristics of stereotypical kidnappings of children in 2011 with the findings from 1997 and identified the following key results (Wolak et al., 2016):

- The estimates of child victims of stereotypical kidnappings in 2011 matched the estimates of 1997. The use of force or threats were involved in most kidnappings, and about 60%—or three in five victims—were sexually assaulted, abused, or exploited.

- The average age of child victims were ages 12 to 17, girls, White, and not living with biological or adoptive parents. Fifty percent of the 2011 stereotypical kidnappings were classified as sexually motivated crimes.

- The perpetrators of these stereotypical kidnappings were usually males ages 18 to 35, and were White or Black in equal proportions. About 70% were unemployed, and about 50% had substance abuse problems.

- Fewer stereotypical kidnappings ended in homicide in 2011 than in 1997 (8% vs. 40%). The kidnappers lured almost 70% of victims through tricking the child or nonthreatening pretexts rather than being violent. Almost all kidnappings (92%) involving child victims in 2011 resulted in recovering the child alive, compared with 57% of victims in 1997.

- Estimates of detaining child victims overnight were three times the 1997 estimates (80% vs. 26%).

- Cell phones and the Internet assisted law enforcement to solve crimes involving two-thirds of the child victims.

Of particular interest was the way in which electronic devices aided in finding the missing child. Wolak et al. (2016) noted that in cases involving two-thirds of victims (67%), law enforcement respondents stated that electronic devices such as cell phones and computers provided evidence, leads, or other information that was key to recovering the child or identifying the perpetrator. Investigators were able to trace calls made on cell phones to identify suspects. Through global positioning systems (GPS) they located children who used their cell phone to call or text for help. Surveillance cameras, in several cases, recorded kidnappings. A woman was recorded by camera picking up and walking away with a toddler from a playground; a man was recorded exiting a building late at night with a child wrapped in a blanket; and a stranger on the street was recorded approaching a boy who was later reported missing. Social networking sites were used by some victims to seek help. In one case, a girl taken and sold for sex escaped from her room to the motel lobby where she then used a computer to contact her family via Facebook. Electronic databases were used to help investigators quickly access critical information, such as ownership of a car. In another case, a woman received an AMBER Alert on her cell phone and notified law enforcement. She was able to provide information on an electronic credit card transaction that enabled law enforcement to identify the perpetrator (Wolak et al., 2016).

The Canadian missing children program website is a partnership between the Royal Canadian Mounted Police (RCMP), the Canada Border Services Agency, the Department of Foreign Affairs and International Trade, and the Department of Justice. The RCMP operates the Our Missing Children program as a national initiative under the umbrella of the National Missing Children Services and the National Child Exploitation Coordination Centre in Ottawa. As part of the Our Missing Children program, the RCMP assists all law enforcement agencies in their efforts to find and return missing children. This program also coordinates investigations on missing children nationally and internationally. As well, when an AMBER alert is activated, Our Missing Children is responsible for disseminating an emergency alert to the various North American partners. The Our Missing Children program is managed by a member of the Federal Investigation Section (RCMP, 2011).

The National Missing Children Services (NMCS) reported that from December 1988 to December 31, 2009, 11,144 cases were opened and 8,410 cases closed. As of 2009, 2,734 cases were still active. Canadian statistics indicate a significant decrease in children missing since 2005 (RCMP, 2011).

The first Canadian statistics on missing children were released in 1987, with 57,233 children reported missing that year. In 2016, the RCMP reported

45,609 reports of missing children in Canada, using numbers provided by the Canadian Police Information Centre (CPIC). Of these:

- 58% were female.

- 75% were runaways.

- 59% were removed because the child was found within 24 hours, while 92% were found within a week.

Legal Framework

The 1948 Universal Declaration of Human Rights was the first international statement addressing issues of slavery, justice, and the status of refugees and minority groups. This declaration clearly articulated that children are entitled to the rights and procedures in international law. This was further enshrined in 1959 by the Declaration of the Rights of the Child and in 1989 by the Convention on the Rights of the Child.

The Global Missing Children's Network was instituted in 1998 as a joint program of the NCMEC and International Centre for Missing and Exploited Children. This Network includes a multilingual database that contains photos of and information about missing children from around the world.

One of the most effective tools in the search for missing children is photographs of the child. The rapid distribution of a child's photo can make the difference between a rapid recovery of the child rather than a prolonged search.

The Global Missing Children's Network contains a number of websites that transfer into a central multilingual database. Members of the international network are trained and given access to a website interface that allows them a number of opportunities to find a missing child such as the following:

- Customize their country's website to contain specific information and individual needs.

- Link their website to the global network and access the database to display information and photos of missing children in their country.

- Create posters rapidly and easily using the customized information entered.

The information for the posters is entered on the Global Missing Children's Network website pages and is managed by the organization that is responsible for managing a particular country's website. In other words, NCMEC does not determine any content on website pages hosted by the Global Missing Children's Network. Twenty-five countries now use the network (http://www.missingkids.com/GMCN).

Child Abduction and Murder

Child abduction and murder that is not associated with child abuse and neglect is a relatively rare occurrence in our society, and consequently legislation has largely been reactive to high-profile cases that capture the public attention, beginning in 1932 with the Lindbergh kidnapping. Charles Augustus Lindbergh, Jr., 20-month-old son of the famous aviator and Anne Morrow Lindbergh, was kidnapped at about 9:00 p.m. on March 1, 1932, from the nursery on the second floor of the Lindbergh home near Hopewell, New Jersey. A ransom note demanding $50,000 was found on the nursery windowsill. After the Hopewell police were notified, the report was telephoned to the New Jersey State Police, who assumed charge of the investigation, with the Federal Bureau of Investigation soon to join. The toddler's body was found on May 12, 1932, in a wooded area; the cause of death was determined to be a severe blow to the skull. Bruno Hauptmann was eventually charged, found guilty, and executed, although he continued to proclaim his innocence. The crime inspired the Lindbergh Law, which made kidnapping a federal offense.

Adam John Walsh was abducted from a Sears store in Hollywood, Florida, on July 27, 1981, and later found murdered. This crime prompted Adam's father to become an advocate for victim's rights and to assist in the formation of the NCMEC. John Walsh continued his work in the victim's area by hosting the television series *America's Most Wanted*. The Code Adam program, named for Adam Walsh, established a protocol to find missing children in department stores.

On October 22, 1989, Jacob E. Wetterling, age 11, was riding his bicycle with his brother and a friend when a masked gunman ordered the boys to stop. The man asked the boys their ages and then grabbed Jacob. He has never been found. The Jacob Wetterling Crimes Against Children and Sexually Violent Offender Registration Act was passed as part of the Federal Violent Crime Control and Law Enforcement Act of 1994. This law requires states to implement registries for those convicted of sex offenses and crimes against children.

Megan Kanka, age 7, was abducted, raped, and murdered by Jesse Timmendequas, who lived across the street. Timmendequas was a repeat child sexual offender. He was found guilty and is serving life without parole in a New Jersey prison. Megan's parents, Richard and Maureen Kanka, began the Megan Nicole Kanka Foundation with the belief that parents should have the right to know if a dangerous sexual predator moves into their neighborhood. The Kankas circulated a petition demanding immediate legislative action. The petition garnered over 400,000 signatures, and the law was passed in an unprecedented 89 days. Megan's home state of New Jersey passed the first so-called Megan's Law in 1994.

Child Trafficking and Child Prostitution

The UN Convention Against Transnational Organized Crime came into force in 2003 and was supplemented with a protocol titled "The Protocol to Prevent, Suppress, and Punish Trafficking in Persons, Especially Women and Children." Under this protocol, all signatory countries must criminalize trafficking in persons and undertake other initiatives to combat trafficking, including education campaigns and social and economic programs. An additional protocol under the Convention on the Rights of the Child addresses the sale of children, **child prostitution**, and **child pornography**. It specifically requires states to criminalize such acts as transferring a child's organs for profit or engaging in forced child labor (United Nations, 2002a). This protocol requires the following:

- Recognize the vulnerability of child victims and adapt procedures to meet their needs.
- Inform child victims of their rights.
- Provide supports for child victims.
- Protect the privacy and identity of child victims.
- Ensure child victims and their families are free from intimidation and retaliation.
- Avoid unnecessary court delays or delays in granting of compensation.

The trafficking of women and children has a long history in the United States. In response to concerns about national trafficking rings, the Mann Act (or the White Slave Traffic Act) was passed into law in 1910, making interstate transportation of women for the purposes of prostitution, debauchery, or "immoral purposes" a felony offense (PBS, 2005). The law, however, differentiated between foreign-born (i.e., **alien**) and American-born children and women. Immigration officials were to maintain information on foreign-born women and children and brothel owners. Specifically, the law designated the Commissioner-General of Immigration to keep records concerning the "procuration of alien women and girls with a view to their debauchery, and to provide supervision over them" (PBS, 2005). The law continues that persons who control or harbor females for the work of prostitution within three years after her entry to the United States and party to the suppression of White slave traffic need to file with the Commissioner-General of Immigration information as to the alien girl's or woman's name, age, nationality, parentage, address, facts as to the date and port of entry to the United States, and her "procuration to come to this country within the knowledge of such person" (PBS, 2005).

Over the years, multiple changes have been made to the Mann Act, and additional legislation has addressed many of the concerns of the original act. These concerns include making the act gender neutral, increasing the focus on juveniles, limiting the focus to prostitution, adding the issues of child pornography, and addressing international trafficking. In 2000, the Trafficking Victims Protection Act (TVPA; 22 U.S.C. §7101 et seq.) was enacted to prosecute traffickers as a better way to protect victims in the United States. The TVPA was reauthorized in 2003, 2005, and 2008, each time enhancing and strengthening the law. The Justice for Victims of Trafficking Act (JVTA, S. 178/P.L. 114-22), an omnibus bill that primarily includes anti-human-trafficking provisions, was signed into law on May 29, 2015. The JVTA amends the TVPA as the federal law that deals with human trafficking, as well as several additional federal statutes. The JVTA addresses and expands the federal response to trafficking into four important areas: (1) victims' benefits and services, (2) criminal justice, (3) sex trafficking of children within the United States, and (4) interagency coordination and training. The United States has implemented its anti-trafficking efforts of victim assistance by providing services and helping victims recover from the victimization. A major objective of the JVTA is to improve victim services. JVTA directs the Department of Justice to provide a database for trafficking victim stakeholders on victim support resources, especially counseling.

In addition, the JVTA strengthens the federal response to crimes perpetrated by traffickers through financial penalty assessments for traffickers. These monies collected are deposited into a Domestic Trafficking Victims' Fund. Monies may be used to fund grants authorized by the TVPA or to develop programs for child pornography victims served under the Victims of Child Abuse Act.

The JVTA has updated its policies on domestic sex trafficking of children to include missing and exploited children, runaway youth, the child welfare system, and juvenile justice. Law enforcement agencies are required to report additional information to a federal data system on missing children. JVTA now has a trafficking deterrence program to assist child victims of both sex and labor trafficking in addition to supporting investigations and prosecutions of trafficking offenses.

The JVTA reviews other agencies for any duplication of efforts or lack of coordination specific to anti-trafficking activities. It directs the President's Interagency Task Force to Monitor and Combat Trafficking on prevention efforts of child trafficking within the United States. The Government Accountability Office by federal law requires a report to Congress on federal and state law enforcement agencies' efforts to combat human trafficking.

As in the United States, mid-1800s prostitution laws in Canada did not differentiate between children and adults. Children were seen as little adults who were responsible for their own behavior and were not afforded the protection of the state. By the late-1800s, however, the law began to recognize the emergence of "White slavery" and the trafficking of women and children. Thus, in 1892, the Canadian government made a number of amendments to the Criminal Code of Canada aimed at protecting children and young women from sexual predators. Additional legislation in the early 1900s focused on rehabilitation approaches for young prostitutes but largely ignored the actions of male customers and conditions that led to prostitution. Beginning in the 1970s, there was renewed interest in protecting children from sexual exploitation, and the government convened at the Committee on Sexual Offences Against Children and Youth, which resulted in a report in 1984 (known as the Badgley Report). The Committee found that (1) most young prostitutes were girls, (2) 27.6% of girls and 13.1% of boys in prostitution were under the age of 16, and (3) many of the youth in prostitution had run away from intolerable home situations, often including child sexual abuse (Committee on Sexual Offences Against Children and Youth, 1984). One recommendation of this report was the suggestion that criminalization of youth prostitution would aid in protecting these young people. This recommendation was highly criticized for ignoring structural issues and blaming victims who became child prostitutes and was not enacted.

In 1988, the Canadian government introduced a bill to protect child victims of sexual abuse that increased the severity of sentences, improved conditions for child witnesses, and criminalized the sexual procurement of youth. This made it easier for police to target pimps and customers of child prostitutes. Nevertheless, in the early days this law was rarely enforced, in large part due to the attitudes of police and others toward child prostitutes. For instance, in the first six years of the new law, only six charges were laid in Vancouver despite awareness of a severe problem in that city. By the mid-1990s, however, the belief grew that youth in the sex trade are victims, and the focus shifted to services and policies to help those who wanted to leave prostitution to do so (Justice Canada, 2011).

In addition, Canada has provisions in the Criminal Code regarding trafficking; however, 2002 amendments to the Immigrant and Refugee Protection Act provide that "persons shall knowingly organize the coming into Canada of one or more persons by means of abduction, fraud, deception, or use or threat of force or coercion" (Raaflaub, 2006, p. 1). The maximum penalty for this offense is a fine of $1 million life imprisonment, or both (Parliament of Canada, 2011).

The Department of Justice Canada (2016a) has made the following advances with regard to combatting human trafficking and supporting victims:

- Public Safety Canada joined with the Canadian Women's Foundation to sponsor the 2016 National Forum on Human Trafficking in Toronto. Stakeholders came together at this forum to discuss new issues, develop cooperation, and strengthen anti-exploitation efforts.

- In August 2016, the government funded the National Inquiry into Missing and Murdered Indigenous Women and Girls and, during consultations, the causes and consequences of sexual exploitation and trafficking of Indigenous women and girls were considered.

- Also, in August 2016, the government provided $16.17 million in funding over four years to develop Family Information Liaison Units in each province and territory, to increase funding for Victims Services, and to provide culturally sensitive services for families of missing and murdered Indigenous women and girls and for survivors of violence.

- The fifth edition of Operation Northern Spotlight was launched in October 2016 by the RCMP. This coordinated Canadian law enforcement program seeks to proactively identify and assist those who are being exploited or at risk of human trafficking. A total of 53 law enforcement partners, across nine Canadian provinces were involved in the project. They held 334 interviews and removed 16 individuals from exploitative situations. This initiative involves multiple Canadian police forces and a partnership with U.S. law enforcement counterparts (Department of Justice, Canada, 2016b).

Infant Abduction

The taking of a fetus or infant under 6 months of age by nonfamily members is not a crime of epidemic proportion; however, such cases result in anguish for those involved. Cases of fetal and infant abduction have been documented by the NCMEC, the International Association for Healthcare Security & Safety, and the FBI's National Center for the Analysis of Violent Crime. Infant abductions usually involve the kidnapping of newborns/infants (birth to 6 months) from healthcare facilities, homes, and other places. A nonfamily member is defined as someone who is not a parent or legal guardian. According to the NCMEC, a total of 317 infants were abducted from 1965 to August 2017. Of those, 15 are still missing. Seventy-two (22.71%) of the cases involved violence; the mother died in 36 (11.36%) of the cases. In nine cases (2.84%), the infant died (NCMEC, 2017).

Fetal Abduction

A **fetal abduction** is the kidnapping of a fetus by the criminal removal of the fetus from the uterus of the pregnant mother. Yutzy, Wolfson, and Resnick (1993) reported the first case of fetal abduction by cesarean section in the literature. In 1987, Darci Pierce, age 19 and married, approached a pregnant woman as she left a prenatal clinic at Kirtland Air Force Base in Albuquerque, New Mexico. Using a gun (replica), the abductor forced the mother into her car and initially drove to her own home, where she had surgical instruments and medical books. When Pierce discovered her husband was at home, she drove to an isolated desert area, strangled the mother to unconsciousness, and then, using a set of car keys, performed a cesarean section and delivered a live baby girl. She then hid the body of the mother under some bushes. Needing a birth certificate, Pierce drove to a local car dealership where she told a friend she had just delivered a baby. She was taken to the local hospital where the on-call physician performed a gynecological examination that revealed she had not recently given birth to a baby. The authorities were notified and Pierce was taken into custody (Yutzy et al., 1993). She was found guilty but mentally ill and received a 30-year prison sentence.

A 2002 study by Burgess, Baker, Nahirny, and Rabun concluded that cesarean section murder is a new category of personal cause homicide. The researchers found that in most instances it was evident that considerable planning had occurred before the crime was committed. In many cases, the abductor first befriends the pregnant victim to gain access to the eventual goal of extracting the baby by cesarean section. The motivations for such a gruesome crime include the desire to solidify a relationship with a romantic partner and to fulfill a fantasy of bearing a child (Burgess et al., 2002).

Infant Abduction

An **infant abduction** is a kidnapping where the infant has been born, is less than 6 months of age, and is then abducted from a hospital, clinic, home, or other location. The abduction of infants by nonfamily members is a subject of concern to healthcare staff in all specialty fields because a primary agency standard is patient safety. Some hospitals use video surveillance to monitor the movements of infants. Other hospitals now use an electronic security system for infants by which a security tag is placed around the infant's wrist or ankle. The security system is alerted when the child is removed from a specified area. However, the RCMP report that these security tags have been removed by infant abductors and are not a fail-safe method (RCMP, 2011).

More than 38 hospitals have infant footprinting programs. As with fingerprints, footprints are unique to individuals and can be used to identify a person throughout their lifetime. Footprinting programs involve obtaining the infant's digital footprint. The digital footprint can be used to identify an infant in cases of abduction, lost child, natural disaster, or other emergency. In cases of multiple births, the technology can resolve mix-ups in the home, helping to identify Baby A from Baby B, C, or D. The new technology, based on years of experience in the maternity setting and with the guidance from the NCMEC, is now considered the gold standard for identifying infants and has been included as a recommendation for hospitals in the NCMEC's "Infant Security Guidelines" (Makin, 2017).

This technology would have been helpful during Hurricane Sandy's devastation when New Jersey hospitals needed to evacuate newborns, and babies were separated from their mothers and their ID bracelets could slip off. In addition, years from now such systems could even help locate adults with dementia or amnesia if they had been digitally footprinted as newborns (Makin, 2017).

In July 2007, Shameka Pittman, dressed in purple hospital scrubs and posing as a nurse, took an infant from his mother in the maternity ward. Hospital staff sounded an alarm, causing the elevators to shut down and doors to lock. The infant was found in a diaper bag hidden behind a couch. In court, the prosecutor noted that in the 13 months preceding the kidnapping, Pittman had repeatedly gone to doctors, claiming to be pregnant but testing negative. In June 2007, Pittman went to an emergency department claiming she was 38 weeks pregnant and her water had broken. The doctor asked Pittman's visitors to leave the room and then told her she was not pregnant. Pittman replied, "OK. I'm glad you didn't say it in front of my visitors." The prosecutor argued that had the hospital's alert system failed to work, Pittman's family would never have known she had not given birth to the child herself. The defense attorney argued that Pittman's repeated doctor visits showed mental health issues that were compounded by her drug and alcohol abuse, stating that "What she needs is an order for mental health treatment." The judge sentenced Pittman to 5 years in prison, far longer than the probationary term suggested by her sentencing guidelines. In addition to the prison sentence, the judge ordered Pittman never to visit a maternity ward unless admitted there as a patient. She was also required to seek mental health and substance abuse counseling.

Regardless of security and identification measures used by hospitals, hospital-based staff in maternity centers, neonatal centers, and pediatric units need to know the red flags for infant abduction. Also, staff in emergency centers, home nursing, and community-based facilities need to be alert to this type of criminal behavior in females seeking to kidnap infants.

In a study conducted by Burgess, Carr, Nahirny, and Rabun (2008) based on data from 248 NCMEC cases from 1983 through 2007, significant differences were noted in abduction patterns from earlier to later time periods. Specifically, the abductions of Hispanic infants went from 17% to 32%, with a corresponding decrease in the proportion of White children abducted, whereas African American infants remained more or less constant at 40% and 43%. Similarly, the proportion of Hispanic abductors nearly doubled from 14% to 25%, whereas the proportion of White abductors decreased from 46% to 32%. The percentage of unmarried suspects increased from 32% to 52%. The total number of parental injuries went from 11 (9%) in the earlier period to 21 (17%) in the later period. The number of lethal injuries doubled, from 7 (6%) to 15 (12%). The proportion of abductions involving the use of a weapon nearly doubled, from 11% in the earlier period to 20% in the later one. The number of suspects arrested increased from 90 (88%) to 101 (94%); the number indicted increased from 82 (87%) to 99 (93%). TABLE 7-1 shows the profile of infant abductors according to this study.

Family responses in cases where the infant is returned unharmed and no violence was used against the victim include severe stress and anxiety during the period when the infant is missing. Despite relief when the baby is returned, however, parental distress does not end. The family members have to rebond with the infant and testify in a criminal case. In cases with violence, family members experience feelings of fear, terror, distress, and anger. Some report having little appetite, difficulty sleeping, and feelings of irritability and numbness (Burgess et al, 2008).

In cases of child abduction where the mother of the infant or fetus had been killed, joy of the infant's return is mixed with grief. In the study by Burgess and colleagues (2008), a maternal grandmother described how difficult it was to have to produce her daughter's dental records (because a fire had been set to hide her murder). The grandmother's distress led to psychiatric hospitalization as she reported repeatedly hearing auditory memories of her daughter's voice crying out to her. Time, sometimes thought to assist in healing wounds, did not help in many of the infant and fetal abduction cases involving violence.

TABLE 7-1 Profile of Infant Abductors

- A woman between the ages of 12 and 50 years who is often overweight.
- Is compulsive and often uses manipulation and deceit to gain access.
- Often indicates she has either lost or cannot have a baby.
- Lives in, or is familiar with, the community where the abduction occurs.
- Can provide good care for the baby once the abduction occurs.
- Is often married or living with a man.
- Visits nursery and maternity units before the abduction and asks detailed questions about procedures and unit layout; the abductor may also try to abduct from the home setting.
- Usually plans the abduction but does not necessarily target a specific infant; often seizes any opportunity that presents.
- Frequently impersonates a nurse or other healthcare personnel.
  - The typical abductor who doesn't target a healthcare setting has these characteristics:
    - Significantly more likely to be single while claiming to have a partner.
    - Often targets a mother, whom she may find by visiting hospitals, and tries to meet the target family.
    - Often both plans the abduction and brings a weapon, although the weapon might not be used.
    - Often impersonates a healthcare or social services professional when visiting the home.

Data from Burgess, A. W., Carr, K. E., Nahirny, C., & Rabun, J. B. Non-Family Infant Abductors: 1983-2006, 2008. *American Journal of Nursing. 108*(9), 32–38.

A maternal grandmother who had been shot at the time of the incident in which her daughter was killed said, "Although it had been 14 years, the situation still hits me." She vividly remembered her daughter's last words to the perpetrator, "Don't kill my mother!" This woman was particularly dismayed five years later when the perpetrator blamed her for the violence inflicted on her daughter (Burgess et al., 2008).

Missing Children

The term missing children refers to children whose whereabouts are unknown to their parent, guardian, or legal custodian. This includes two categories of children: those who are taken in either familial or nonfamilial abductions and those who are runaways, thrownaways, or otherwise missing. In the United States, resources are provided for missing children, their families, and the professionals who serve them through clearinghouses.

The United States Department of Justice's Office of Juvenile Justice and Delinquency Prevention (OJJDP) has a strong commitment to missing children and their families. The office has funded three research projects called NISMART, or the National Incidence Studies of Missing, Abducted, Runaway, and Throwaway Children, to comply with the mandate of the 1984 Missing Children's Assistance Act (Pub.L. 98-473). NISMART-1 in 1988 developed categories from missing children reports and estimated the number of missing and recovered children in each (Finkelhor, Hotling, & Sedlak, 1990). NISMART-2 in 1999 then compared categories and interviewed youth directly (Sedlak, Finkelhor, Hammer, and Schultz, 2002). The 2013 NISMART-3 surveyed parents and caretakers about missing child episodes in the previous year (Sedlak, A. J., Finkelhor, D., & Brick, J. M., 2017).

In addition to the research projects, the NCMEC works closely with all missing-child clearinghouses and ensures they know of the resources available through NCMEC. NCMEC provides training, technical assistance, and information to help them handle missing-child cases. Missing-child clearinghouses focus on networking, information dissemination, training, data collection, and technical assistance in cases of missing and sexually exploited children (Missing child websites, n.d.).

Family Abductions

Although the abduction of children by strangers is the greatest fear of all parents, in fact the abduction of children by a member of the family is the most common occurrence. Family abductions typically involve the violation of a custody agreement or decree, such as the failure to return a child at the end of a legal or agreed on visit. For such a violation to be considered an abduction, the child must be away at least overnight and attempts made to conceal the child's location and prevent contact with the child. Further, the abductor must have the intent to keep the child indefinitely or to permanently alter the custody arrangements. The exact number of parental abductions is unknown, but estimates suggest several hundred such abductions per year occur in Canada and the United States (Kiedrowski & Dalley, 2008). In a review of the existing literature in the area, Kiedrowski and Dalley (2008) developed a profile of parental abductions of children, as shown in TABLE 7-2.

The after effects of such abductions are seen in both children and parents. The parenting relationship is obviously severely affected, permeated by distrust and fear. Funds available to support and raise the child are redirected to extensive legal costs, travel, accommodation, and search and recover fees, which are compounded by income loss. Emotional harm to the child is another outcome. For instance, children are forced to hide their identity (and, in some cases, to cross-dress to hide their identity), may be told the other parent died or does not love them anymore, may lose all contact

TABLE 7-2 Profile of Parental Abductions of Children

- Either parent may abduct his or her own child; male and female children are equally likely to be abducted.
- Mothers are more likely to abduct after a court order, whereas fathers are more likely to abduct before a court order.
- Fathers who abduct are more likely to be employed, whereas mothers who abduct are more likely to be unemployed.
- Most children taken are between 3 and 7 years of age.
- Communication usually occurs between the abducting parent and the searching parent.
- Accomplices are used in half the cases, usually family members or current partners.
- Most cases are resolved within 1 week.

Data from Kiedrowski, J & Dalley, M. 2008. Parental Abduction of Children: An Overview and Profile of the Abductor. Royal Canadian Mounted Police.

with family and friends, and are forced to live like fugitives. Less frequently, the child may be subject to physical or sexual abuse. After returning home children experience nightmares, sleeplessness, and emotional distance from others (Dalley, 2007).

The Missing Children Society of Canada (n.d.) offers a fact sheet to assist parents in these circumstances, with the following suggestions:

- File a missing person's report with police and provide identifying data, such as birth certificates, fingerprints, pictures, and so on.
- Flag the child's birth certificate, school records, and medical records, in case requests for information or transfer of records are made.
- Inquire about change of address of the abductor in records pertaining to employment, professional licensing bodies, motor vehicle registration, pension, tax records, and so on.
- Keep a notebook and record any forms of contact.

Nonfamily Abduction

According to U.S. law, *nonfamily abductions* are defined as the coerced and unauthorized taking of a child into a building, a vehicle, or a distance of more than 20 feet and/or the detention of a child for a period of more than 1 hour. Attempted abductions include luring of a child for the purposes of committing another crime. This definition includes abductions conducted by friends and acquaintances as well as strangers, and most of these abductions occur within a quarter mile of the child's home. The findings from NISMART-1 indicated more than 65% of children abducted by nonfamily members are girls; of these 46% are sexually abused and 31% are physically abused. In 75% of cases the perpetrator is a male, 67% of them are below 29 years of age, and most target children within their own ethnic group (Sedlak, Finkelhor, Hammer, & Schultz, 2002).

The FBI has delineated four categories of nonfamilial child abductors (Wilson, 2010):

- *Pedophiles* are the largest single category of nonfamilial child abductors. These individuals are able to connect easily with children and obtain their confidence, which then makes the child vulnerable to abduction. The child often initially has confidence in the person and then becomes aware the person is exploitative.

- *Serial killers* are methodical and ritual in their approaches, using power, dominance, and control as tactics. Such abductors are more likely to use a blitz attack method in which the offender suddenly approaches and over-whelms the child.

- *Profiteers* abduct children for the purpose of criminal exploitation, for instance, in prostitution, pornography, or illegal adoption rings.

- *Childless psychotics* tend to abduct children in a delusional state, attempting to correct the reality that they are unable to have children or have lost their own children, for instance, to child protection services.

Thrownaways/Runaways

Runaways make up the majority of missing children. They are often described by family and others in their social network as delinquents or troublemakers; in actual fact, however, they are often not running to something but rather away from something. **Thrownaways** is a term used by NISMART to describe children who have experienced any of the following situations: the child was told to leave the household, the child was away from home and the parent/guardian refused to allow the child back, the child ran away but the parent/guardian made no effort to recover the child or did not care whether or not the child returned, or the child was abandoned or deserted. Thus, the distinction between runaways and thrownaways is not entirely clear. NISMART-2 (2003) estimated in 1999 that 1,682,900 children in the United States had a runaway/thrownaway episode. Only 21% of these situations were reported to the police for the purposes of relocating them. Youths aged 15 to 17 made up two-thirds of children in this category (Sedlak et al., 2002).

Children and youth in the thrownaway category are at highest risk of exploitation by child traffickers. The child is usually homeless and in need of food and shelter. The trafficker plays the role of parent or romantic friend, offering care, understanding, and attention. Offering free drugs is often a part of this package. In the end, the child is manipulated into survival sex, frequently in exchange for drugs. A series of FBI sting operations in 2009 resulted in 2,300 arrests and the recovery of 170 children in this circumstance (McLaughlin, 2009).

Lost, Injured, or Otherwise Missing Children

This category includes children missing for varying periods of time that do not fit into any other category. Nearly half of the children in this category are younger than 5 years of age. Often, they suffer from some sort of disability or challenge that puts them at risk for becoming lost or injured. It is important to note that this group of children suffers the most physical harm compared to every other category, except those children abducted by strangers.

AMBER Alert

AMBER, America's Missing: Broadcast Emergency Response, was created in 1996 in Texas after the abduction of 9-year-old Amber Hagerman. The purpose of AMBER was to develop an early warning system, with collaboration between law enforcement agencies, broadcasters, and transportation agencies to activate an urgent bulletin in the most serious child abduction cases. Since its inception, the program has gained national attention, and now all 50 states have implemented the system. As of June 2017, 881 successful recoveries have been reported as a result of these alerts (NCMEC, 2017).

When a child goes missing, law enforcement is contacted. An AMBER alert is issued after certain criteria have been met. Although there are no national guidelines, most states have similar stipulations for issuing an alert. First, the abduction must be confirmed: the child cannot just be a runaway. Second, the child must be at risk of injury or death. Third, law enforcement needs information about the child and the captor and his or her vehicle. Finally, the child must be younger than 17 years of age. It is recommended that all missing child data be entered into the National Crime Information Center (NCIC) run by the FBI (FBI, 2008). The success of AMBER alert is due in large part to the efforts of the media, law enforcement, and observant citizens.

Child Labor

Forms of child labor, including indentured servitude and child slavery, have existed throughout history. Children's role in the family was often to help earn money for the family's survival. Even today, in the 21st century, in parts of Peru many working children are active in the country's informal economy, which accounts for nearly 50% of the country's economic output (U.S. Department of Labor, n.d.). Child labor is prevalent in the brick-making sector of Huachipa, where the children as young as 3 years old help their parents to meet daily brick-making quotas. The children carry heavy loads of brick or sand throughout the day, and, as a result, many suffer from spinal and bone deformities (U.S. Department of Labor, 1999).

In Canada, children were considered cheap farm labor until the end of the 19th century. As an economic asset they were counted and treated as such along with cows, chickens, and horses. The residue of this history remains in current Canadian attitudes toward the use of corporal punishment and in the legal sanction of physical punishment by parents provided by current provisions of the Criminal Code of Canada (Volpe, 2011).

In the United States, as industrialization moved workers from farms and home workshops into urban areas and factory work, children were often viewed as being better able to conform to work requirements. They were also cheaper to employ than adults and less likely to strike. Child labor began to decline as the labor and reform movements grew and labor standards in general began improving, increasing the political power of working people and other social reformers to demand legislation regulating child labor. Women-led organizations, such as state Consumers' Leagues and Working Women's Societies, prompted the formation of the National Consumers' League in 1899 and the National Child Labor Committee in 1904, which shared goals of challenging child labor. Efforts were successful to provide free, compulsory education for all children and culminated in the passage of the Fair Labor Standards Act in 1938, which set federal standards for child labor (Child Labor Education Project, 2004).

Child Trafficking

In 2000, the United Nations General Assembly adopted the Protocol to Prevent, Suppress, and Punish Trafficking in Persons, Especially Women and Children. This act marked a significant milestone in international efforts to stop the trade in people. As the guardian of the protocol, the United

Nations Office of Drugs and Crime (UNODC) addresses human-trafficking issues through its Global Programme against Trafficking in Persons (GPAT). While more than 147 states have signed and ratified the protocol, translating the protocol into reality has been problematic. Very few criminals have been convicted, and most victims are probably never identified or assisted (UNODC, 2006).

The United Nations (2002b) defines trafficking as follows:

> [T]he recruitment, transportation, transfer, harbouring, or receipt of persons, by means of threat or use of force or other forms of coercion, of abduction, of fraud, of deception, of the abuse of power or of a position of vulnerability or of the giving or receiving of payments and benefits to achieve the consent of a person having control over another person for the purposes of exploitation. Exploitation shall include, at a minimum, the exploitation or the prostitution of others or other forms of sexual exploitation, forced labour or services, slavery or practices similar to slavery, servitude or the removal of organs.
>
> (p. 1)

Although the transport of slaves on British ships was abolished in 1807 and slavery is illegal today in virtually every country, human trafficking, the modern-day equivalent to slavery, remains rampant throughout the world. In 1865, the Thirteenth Amendment to the Constitution was ratified abolishing slavery in the United States. The U.S. Department of State initiated monitoring human trafficking in 1994, when the issue began to be covered in the department's annual country reports on human rights practices. Originally, coverage focused on trafficking of women and girls for sexual purposes. Coverage of the issue in the annual country reports has broadened over the years, and U.S. embassies worldwide now routinely monitor and report on cases of trafficking in men, women, and children for all forms of forced labor, including agriculture, domestic service, construction work, and sweatshops, as well as trafficking for commercial sexual exploitation (U.S. Department of State, 2008).

Trafficking is a transnational criminal enterprise that recognizes neither boundaries nor borders. Profits from trafficking feed the coffers of organized crime. It is estimated that human trafficking is a $32-billion-a-year industry, that it is on the rise, and it is in all 50 states in America. It has surpassed sales of the illegal sale of arms and will soon surpass the illegal sale of drugs (Arc of Hope, 2016).

Trafficking is linked to other criminal activities, such as document fraud, money laundering, and migrant smuggling. Moreover, as a matter of policy, the U.S. government opposes prostitution and any related activities as contributing to the phenomenon of trafficking in persons. These activities are inherently harmful and dehumanizing (Ashcroft, 2).

In describing the types of human trafficking in the Mekong subregion, which includes Laos, Thailand, Vietnam, and Cambodia, the United Nations Inter-Agency Project (UNIAP) notes it takes many forms. For instance, children are taken from Cambodia to beg or sell flowers on the streets of Thailand, Chinese boys are stolen and sold to those who want a son, Cambodian babies are stolen and then adopted by well-meaning parents in the United States, young Vietnamese brides go to meet their new husbands in Taiwan only to discover that he is a pimp, and adults are taken and then held to work in factories, brothels, houses, or fishing boats (UNIAP, 2001–2005).

World Vision's Child Sex Tourism Prevention Project aims to deter potential child sex tourists before they harm children and provides assistance to U.S. and other law enforcement agencies in their work to identify and prosecute offenders (World Vision International, 2008). An estimated 2 million children are enslaved in the global sex trade market. Children in countries such as Cambodia, Thailand, Costa Rica, Mexico, and Brazil are coerced, abducted, or sold by their parents to work in brothels catering to wealthy Western customers (World Vision International, 2008). These children not surprisingly suffer from physical, emotional, and social harms, including HIV infection, rejection by families and society, shame, fear, and despair. As another example, in Eastern Europe, Romanian women are deceived and taken to Germany and other parts of the world, including North America, to work as exotic dancers or prostitutes, unable to free themselves due to torture, extortion, and their illegal status in the country in which they now reside (UNODC, 2006). In **child trafficking**, children are recruited and trafficked to earn money by begging or selling goods. Child beggars are sometimes maimed by their captors to generate sympathy and generosity from potential buyers.

Over the past 15 years, "trafficking in persons" and "human trafficking" have been used as umbrella terms to describe activities in which one person obtains or holds another person in compelled service. The TVPA, mentioned earlier, describes this compelled service using a number of different terms: *involuntary servitude*, *slavery*, *debt bondage*, and *forced labor*. The 11th Trafficking in Persons report ranks 184 countries as to their level of accomplishment in combating human trafficking (UNODC, 2006) (TABLE 7-3).

TABLE 7-3 Types of Child Trafficking

Type of Child Trafficking	Example	Reference
Infant adoption	Guatemalan infants are trafficked for adoption by couples in North America and Europe.	UNICEF (2010) estimates that 1,000 to 1,500 Guatemalan infants are trafficked each year.
Mail-order brides as young as age 13	Mainly from Asia and Eastern Europe.	UNICEF (2010) states these girls and women are powerless, isolated, and at great risk of violence.
Domestic work and sexual exploitation	Large numbers of children are trafficked in West and Central Africa.	UNICEF (2010) estimates 90% of the domestic workers are girls.
Child sex workers	Mekong subregion of Southeast Asia.	Surveys indicate that 30% to 35% of all sex workers are between 12 and 17 years of age. The global market of child trafficking is over $12 billion a year, with over 1.2 million child victims (UNODC, 2006).
Child prostitution and child pornography	Lithuania Mexico reports tourist destinations have the highest number.	20% to 50% of prostitutes are believed to be minors. More than 16,000 children are reported to be engaged in prostitution (Patt, 2011).
Forced child labor	Child performs work that financially benefits someone outside the child's family and does not offer the child the option of leaving.	Forced child labor has been reported in cocoa production in Ghana, the cotton industry in Uzbekistan, and the production of soccer balls in India (U.S. Department of Labor, 2012a).
Child soldiers	Involves the unlawful recruitment or use of children—through force, fraud, or coercion—as combatants or for labor or sexual exploitation by armed forces.	The use of child soldiers is an issue in Burundi, the Congo, and Rwanda (U.S. Department of Labor, 2012b).

Child Prostitution

Child and juvenile pornography and prostitution are difficult topics to study for several reasons. First, it is hard to determine the numbers of children being exploited due to the clandestine nature of the activity. Second, law enforcement is often handicapped in investigating cases because of the child's attachment to the caregiver. Third, estimates of the number of child prostitutes and children who are trapped into pornography, both nationally and internationally, are exceptionally variable and impressionistic. Child pornography has increasingly moved to the Internet, and is thus covered in reviews on cybercrime as well.

Children involved in prostitution are victims who are vulnerable targets for trafficking. The children are coerced and manipulated by pimps and traffickers who physically, emotionally, and psychologically abuse them and keep them controlled through drugs. Child victims are often beaten, raped, or tortured (Ark of Hope, 2017).

The commercial sexual exploitation of children has been facilitated by the Internet, which provides worldwide marketing. Websites are used to advertise, schedule, and purchase sex with minors. Technology enables pimps and traffickers to reach more children which, in turn, exposes victims to greater risks and dangers.

Child victims can be exposed to physical and mental health injuries, including sexually transmitted diseases, tuberculosis, infections, drug addiction, malnutrition, as well as injuries resulting from the abuse inflicted upon them. Short-term and long-term psychological effects include depression, low self-esteem, and feelings of hopelessness (U.S. Department of Justice, n.d.).

Although there are barriers to our understanding the origins of child prostitution, law enforcement recognizes it is a problem of considerable magnitude. Most of our knowledge of child prostitution comes from children and juveniles who have run away from home and are existing on the street or who are institutionalized. These runaways, often around the ages of 14 and 15, have told their histories of prostituting to police and mental health staff. Although these estimates are, at best, crude and vary widely, they appear to reflect a problem of considerable magnitude. For the most part, these young runaway prostitutes are escaping from chaotic and abusive home environments and are subsisting on the streets by prostituting themselves. Children who have been initiated into a life of prostitution, often at a very young age, constitute a population that remains largely invisible. Their invisibility stems, in part, because they are living with families in the community and are often being prostituted by caregivers, relatives, and acquaintances. Unless they come to the attention of the child welfare system, they do not become "known" until after they run away, get into trouble, and eventually fall into the category of teenage prostitutes struggling to survive on the street. It is at that point that law enforcement becomes aware of them because of committing delinquent acts. Three parties are usually involved in prostitution: the pimp (who receives the goods or money), the prostitute (who provides the sex), and the john (or client). The principle-defining characteristic of prostitution is a barter of sexual services in exchange for goods or money. Typically, the exchange goes from the adult clients, or "johns," to the adults who are sexually exploiting the children. The exploitative adults typically receive drugs and/or money from the clients as payment for sex with the children. When the child receives something in exchange for sex, it is invariably "goods" (e.g., clothing, video games, records, toys, and books). Prostituting a child is an extreme form of sexual abuse.

Making of Teenage Prostitutes

Several entrances into youth prostitution have been identified (TABLE 7-4). The first comprises children who run away from abusive, dysfunctional families and are prostituted by professional pimps who run stables of sexually exploited children. The second comprises children who are reared in environments in which sexual exploitation and sexual barter are simply one feature of the over-all pattern of abuse to which they are exposed. Frequently, their caretakers were either prostitutes themselves or were involved with other sexually abusive adults.

The typical pattern of sexual exploitation involves initial abuse of the child by either a pedophile or incestuous caretaker. The sexual abuse evolves into sexual exploitation when the caretakers discover a market for the sexual

TABLE 7-4 Avenues into Child Prostitution

Avenue	Definition
Parent as role model	Some children are exposed to the world of prostitution from birth by their parents, for example, a mother as a professional prostitute brings her daughter with her from motel to motel as she engages in her illicit activities or a child whose father was her mother's pimp.
Parental incest	Some children are initiated into sexual activity through parental sexual abuse. The parent begins the incest, then videotapes and photographs the child, and then brings adults in for sex.
Chaotic and abusive, sexualized home environments	Some children live in multiple abusive and sexualized homes. The child learns that it is both acceptable and appropriate to trade sexual favors for shelter, love, and money.
Child sex rings	Child sex rings include adults who sexually exploit multiple children.
Sibling incest	Older siblings can sexually exploit younger siblings and use threats to provide sexual services promised to peers.
Incest and prostitution normalized	Some children grow up in a home in which there is physical, psychological, and sexual abuse; gross neglect; and extensive drug use. The eventual exchange of sex for drugs outside the home is a logical and inevitable outgrowth of such upbringing.
Unclear origin	Not all cases of child prostitution can be traced to early life events. In general, however, child prostitutes are clearly a product of a highly sexualized home environment.

services their children could provide. These "caretaker pimps" begin by bringing in known like-minded friends and acquaintances, who provide money and drugs in exchange for sex with the children. Eventually, the "business" might branch out to include strangers. To ensure some degree of compliance, the children are given material goods but rarely money. Eventually, these children can strike out on their own unless the social welfare system or law enforcement becomes aware of their plight and intervenes.

Typologies of Sex Offenders of Children

An overriding feature of the descriptions of the many victimizations of children described in this chapter is sexual exploitation. This section thus focuses on sexual offenders who victimize children in an attempt to explain the underlying factors that fuel many of these crimes. In most cases, offenders gain sexual access to the child in one of two ways: (1) by pressuring the child into sexual activity through enticement, encouragement, or instruction or (2) by forcing the child into the sexual activity through threat, intimidation, or physical duress.

The concept of **grooming** has evolved and spread into more common usage by law enforcement, other professionals, and the media and laypersons. Lanning (2018) was one of the first to use the term early in his lectures to law enforcement on child molesters. Lanning defines grooming as the use of nonviolent techniques by one person to gain sexual access to and control over child victims. The grooming (sometimes called *seduction*) process has several stages including identifying child targets; learning about child interests and vulnerabilities; and gaining access to the child through games, sports, religion, food, alcohol, and online computer. The molester seeks to fill emotional and physical needs of the child, lower the child's inhibitions, and gain and maintain control of the child through bonding, competition, challenges, peer pressure, and sympathy (Lanning, 2010). Grooming techniques take time and skills in relating to children and, most important, for the offender to be perceived as a nice guy. Offenders often use similar grooming techniques with parents, guardians, caretakers, and youth-serving organizations to gain and maintain access to the child.

The type of grooming or seduction process that is used by the molester is dependent on the age, developmental stage, needs, and vulnerabilities of the preferred child victim and his or her relationship with the offender (Lanning & Dietz, 2014). To varying degrees, all children are vulnerable to this process and not just those who are somehow naïve, poor, or from troubled families.

However, when the techniques work and the child victim is compliant, it is often improperly interpreted by some as consent and a lack of true victimization (Lanning, 2005).

Coerced Versus Forced

In the *coerced* situation, the offender initially establishes a nonsexual relationship with the child so that the child comes to trust and feel comfortable with the offender. Then, the offender influences the child to engage in sexual activity through the offer of some type of reward (such as candy or money), by misrepresenting moral standards (such as telling the child that all boys and girls do this), or through trickery and deception (e.g., "This is going to be a game, and we're going to wrestle"). The most commonly used technique of luring the child into this coerced sexual activity is by capitalizing on the child's need for attention, approval, and human contact. In such situations, the offender spends considerable time with the child, gives the child a lot of attention, and makes the child out to be special or a favorite. Children respond to attention and are taught to be obedient, so the intended victim cooperates and goes along with the sexual demands of the offender. The child does this to secure the promised reward because of confusion and lack of understanding or to get approval and recognition. As one offender said:

> I can look at kids in a schoolyard and tell you who is an easy mark. It will be the child alone and off by himself, the one who appears lonely and has no friends. The quiet kid—the one no one is paying any attention to—that's the one who will respond to some attention.
>
> (Groth, 1979, p. 142)

In coerced sex encounters, the offender does appear to have a high emotional investment in his or her victim and uses the child to gratify the unmet needs for approval, recognition, and affiliation in his or her own life. The child makes the offender feel good. This type of offender does not find satisfaction in his or her adult relationships but in his or her encounters with children; the sexual activity serves to validate his or her worth as a person. When this is the dominant motive, the offense is characterized by a relative lack of physical force in the commission of the offense. Such offenders describe their victims in positive terms, such as innocent, clean, loving, open, warm, affectionate, attractive, and undemanding. They feel safe and secure with children. They are usually dissuaded if the child resists or refuses them. They do not resort to force but instead seek out another, more cooperative or accommodating victim.

In the *forced* situation, the offender gains access to the child through intimidation in the form of verbal threats (e.g., "Do what I say and you won't get hurt") or physical actions, such as grabbing hold of the child or using a weapon. Or the offender resorts to physical force to overcome the child's resistance and, in some cases, derives pleasure from hurting and sexually abusing the child.

These situations are comparable to rape. In these assaults, sexuality becomes an expression of power and anger. Such offenders describe the victim as small, weak, helpless, unable to resist, easily controlled, and vulnerable. They feel stronger and more dominant in regard to a child. Any resistance on the part of the child may result in increased aggression on the part of the offender. The offender does not take no for an answer and will enforce his or her sexual demands. In most of these cases, whatever force is used is directed toward having control over the child (Burgess, Groth, Holmstrom, & Sgroi, 1978).

Multiple factors impact the selection of a child as the target of a sexual assault. An adult is physically superior to a child, and the offender may feel stronger and more powerful in regard to a child victim compared to an adult victim. The child does not pose as much of a physical or psychological threat. The child is sexually immature and inexperienced, and the offender may believe there is less risk his or her sexual performance will be compared to others'. The offender may not feel as sexually inadequate with a child as he or she would with an adult. The child may represent everything negative the offender believes about him- or herself, and the abuse, in part, serves as a punishment for the offender's self-hatred. Or the child may be a means by which the offender attempts to control or retaliate against another adult. These represent some of the dynamics suggested by clinicians who have worked with child molesters (Groth, 1979). In addition, two types of child molesters are described by whether the sexual abuse is a situational event or whether it is a preferential choice.

Situational Predators Versus Preferential Predators

In the situational offense, there is evidence of impulsive, opportunistic, predatory behavior, such as the victim being present or a spur-of-the-moment decision to offend. Situational child molesters do not have a true sexual preference for children but engage in sex with children for varied and sometimes complex reasons, ranging from child availability to offender inadequacy (e.g., raping a child because she is available and vulnerable). For such a child molester, sex with children may range from a one-time episode to a long-term pattern of behavior. The more long term the pattern, the harder it is to distinguish it from preferential molesting. The situational child molester usually has fewer numbers of different child victims. Vulnerable individuals such as the elderly, sick, or disabled may also be at risk of sexual victimization. For example, the situational child molester who sexually abuses children in a daycare center might leave the job and begin to abuse elderly people in a nursing home.

Preferentially motivated sexual offenses usually involve strong patterns of behavior or sexual rituals that are difficult for the offender to change. Sexual ritual involves repeatedly engaging in an act or series of acts in a certain manner because of a sexual need. In other words, for a person to become sexually aroused and/or gratified, he or she must engage in the act in a certain way. This sexual ritualism can include such things as the physical characteristics, age, or gender of the victim; the particular sequence of acts; the bringing or taking of specific objects; or the use of certain words or phrases.

Sexual ritual is more than the concept of method of operation or *modus operandi* (MO). The MO is something done by an offender because it works. Sexual ritual is something done by an offender because of a psychological need. Therefore, it is much harder for an offender to change, vary, or adjust the ritual than his or her MO. Both preferential and situational sex offenders may have an MO, but the preferential offender is more likely to have a sexual ritual.

The preferential offense often has clear evidence that the offender thought, planned, and went searching for a particular victim. Preferential child molesters have a definite sexual preference for children. Their sexual fantasies and erotic imagery focus on children. Preferential child molesters almost always have access to children, molest multiple victims, and collect child pornography or child erotica.

A preferential child molester (pedophile) might have other psychosexual disorders, personality disorders, or psychosis, or may be involved in other types of criminal activity. A pedophile's sexual interest in children might be combined with other sexual deviations (paraphilias), which include indecent exposure (exhibitionism), obscene phone calls (scatophilia), exploitation of animals (zoophilia), urination (urophilia), defecation (coprophilia), binding (bondage), baby role-playing (infantilism), infliction of pain (sadism, masochism), real or simulated death (necrophilia), and others. The preferential child molester must have (1) high amount of victim contact and (2) high level of fixation or pedophilic interest (Prentky & Burgess, 2000).

High Contact Versus Low Contact Offenders

A preemptory distinction is made between those offenders who have spent a substantial amount of their time in close proximity to victims (high contact) and those offenders who have spent little or no time with victims outside of rape and sexual assaults (low contact). Amount of contact is a behavioral measure of the time spent with victims. It includes both sexual and nonsexual situations but excludes the contact that results from parental responsibilities. The contact distinction must be distinguished from the fixation decision, which attempts to assess the strength of an individual's pedophilic interest.

Evidence for high contact includes structured and nonstructured involvement with a victim through an occupation or through recreation (e.g., schoolteacher, bus driver, carnival worker, riding stable attendant, newspaper delivery person, scout leader, sports coach, youth group volunteer, babysitter). These occupational criteria are only intended to help identify the level of contact for those already determined to be child molesters. Other evidence for high contact may include regular visits by the victim to the offender's home or the offender acting as an adopted father or big brother. In addition, we assume that repeated sexual (nonincestuous) encounters with a victim imply the development of a relationship that goes beyond sexual involvement. For that reason, when there are three or more sexual encounters with the same victim, the offender is coded as having high contact (Prentky & Burgess, 2000).

Case of a Preferential Child Molester/Spree Crime and Multiple Victims

The following case provides examples of the multiple factors and complex dynamics that can occur in crimes of abuse committed against children. These examples provide insight into the multilevel and multidimensional facets of assessment that will enhance comprehensive assessment and intervention with child victims.

1. On August 28, around 10:00 p.m., Elizabeth, age 15, was walking with her girlfriend, Kate. A man on a bicycle kept riding by them, asking if they wanted to buy any weed. They said no. He then asked if they wanted a joint and asked their names. Elizabeth said she did not have a name. The girls walked faster; however, the man rode by and grabbed Elizabeth's backside. The girls were stunned and then ran and called 911.

2. Two days later, on August 30, around 6:40 p.m., Kathleen, age 13, was rollerblading at a school with friends and noticed someone following them.

A man asked Kathleen if she liked Bones, Thugs, and Harmony (a music group). She said no. Then he asked her if she wanted to "get it on." She again said nothing but felt nervous and scared. Then he put his bike in front of her and grabbed her backside and sped away on his bike. Kathleen told people at the apartment who called 911 and the police came.

3. On August 30, around 7:00 p.m., Amanda, age 9, was riding her bicycle and a man came up to her, put his hand on the brake handle and his other hand around her, and asked if she wanted to go bike riding with him. He asked her name and address. She said nothing. He tried to grab her backside, but she pushed his hand away. He left and she told her mother, who then called the police.

4. On August 30, around 8:20 p.m., Morris, age 76, had bought food at Wendy's, and as he approached his car a large figure said hello and then said, "Let me help you, Pop." Morris was trying to open the door with keys. The man began struggling; the door flung open. The man asked for his keys and wallet, threatening he was going to kill him with a gun. He tried to get in the car, but Morris fought him. Suddenly the man left, and Morris reported the incident to the police.

5. On August 30, around 9:20 p.m., Robert, age 15, was approached by a man on a bicycle and asked if he and his friend had any money. They said no. The man threatened to kill them if they reported him. The boys told their parents and the police were called.

6. On August 30, around 9:35 p.m., Chris, age 17, was with his friend Robert playing "Manhunt." The boys saw a man biking in and out of people's driveways checking to see if anybody was home. The man then "cut the boys off" with his bike and asked if they had any money. Then he said they should be sure to forget they saw his face.

7. On August 30, around 10:00 p.m., Mrs. Peck and her husband were watching TV when they heard a noise in their back room and thought it was the cat. The wife walked back and noticed the screen had been pushed in. She checked outside and noticed a lawn chair had been moved from the pool, pulled up underneath the window, and the toys for her two daughters, ages 4 and 9, were strewn around. She called the police.

8. On August 30, around 10:15 p.m., Mrs. Fried heard a noise downstairs and asked her husband to check the back door. He found it open with the handle forced. Mrs. Fried discovered her purse was missing (from the dining room table), which held her money and credit cards. She later found her

6-year-old daughter's black glove to her Nerf football missing from the outside sandbox.

9. On August 30, about 10:55 p.m., Laura, age 8, was lying in her bed on the second floor listening to music. She saw someone walk into the room. First she thought it was her dad, and then thought it was the exterminator "that kills bugs," but then realized it was a stranger. She asked, "Who are you and what are you doing?" He said to "be quiet" and "be calm." He said he had a knife. He picked her up, put his hands around her neck and over her mouth, and told her not to scream. He dragged her down the stairs when her dog, Rocky, a Rhodesian ridgeback, suddenly came down the stairs from the third floor and leapt at the man. He loosened his hand and Laura was able to scream. The man dropped her on the stairs. The dog bit the man on the wrist and he ran out of the house. Laura's mother came out of her room and called the police. The backyard had a trampoline, a rope, a shed with toys, and a garage with basketballs and bikes and scooters.

10. An investigating officer was dispatched to the scene and observed a blue mountain bike, a woman's handbag containing a CD player and headphones, and numerous items bearing the name "Lisa." The officer saw the defendant at the softball field park, tackled him, and took him into custody. Upon searching him, the officer found a set of GM car keys, a GE keypad, as well as a rabies tag in his right front pants pocket. The officer also found a CD for Bones, Thugs, and Harmony and solar sunglasses. The defendant had blood on his shirt (which was turned inside out) and puncture marks on his wrist. He admitted to the burglaries. In reference to the girl, he said he just knocked her down the steps, did not take her, and was using her as a shield against the dog. No weapon was found. He claimed he was just burglarizing the house and that he needed a car to "get out of town."

CASE ANALYSIS

This was a spree crime, that is, one continuous event that started on August 28 and continued through August 30 with multiple locations and no cooling-off period. The offender was consistently looking for victims. He was mission oriented, and the crimes accelerated with the buildup of emotion. He first talked to the children, then touched them, and then attempted to abduct one. He targeted homes that had children's toys present outside.

Burton was a preferential child molester with a sexual preference for children. He had a long history of indecent exposure to children, for example, calling them over to his car to ask directions, staring at them, using obscene language, and exposing himself. In many ways he fit the old stereotype of the man hanging around playgrounds with a bag of candy. He liked to watch children or engage in brief sexual encounters; however, he lacked interpersonal skills for grooming the child. This type of offender is more likely to abduct because he or she cannot seduce the child because of poor social skills.

There were phases of buildup to the abduction. He had a fantasy about sex with a child that led to a need to carry out the plan. His mission was to obtain a child, but he needed money and mobility or a vehicle for escape. He selected a child who was a stranger so as not to be caught. Fantasy driven, he took increased risks to get a child. Part of the pleasure was the complete control over the child. He usually rehearsed before the abduction.

In summary, Burton had a crime spree pattern with a classic escalation of intent. He targeted vulnerable victims (children, older man with hands occupied, people in bed sleeping). His nonsexual crimes had sexual and aggressive language. He sought out homes with toys in yards and probably had them under surveillance. The child victims in this case were referred to victim counseling programs through the prosecutor's office. The child most traumatized due to the offender's direct contact with her was Laura. Her therapy required individual as well as family work. Laura was unable to sleep in her own room for months, sleeping instead with her parents. Her parents redecorated and rearranged furniture before her return to her room.

Conclusion

Children are at risk of multiple forms of exploitation and abduction. Although not crimes of large numbers, the theft of fetuses through cesarean section and infant abductions are a problem. However, older children who are missing due to abduction, running away, or being "thrown away" is a far greater issue. The Jaycee Dugard case revealed problems with California's system for monitoring convicted sex offenders after it was determined that parole agents had missed numerous clues and chances (more than 18 years) to find her. At the federal level, the 10th anniversary reauthorization TVPA law was groundbreaking legislation because it was the first comprehensive federal law that addressed child trafficking in the modern era. One of its most important contributions was the formulation of a victim-centered paradigm for addressing the crime and a three-pronged approach for prevention of trafficking, protection of victims, and prosecution of perpetrators. Issues of impact for child victims and their families who survive exploitation illustrate the resiliency as well as long-term memories. Jaycee Dugard tells us she had no choice but to endure and that the sounds of her imprisonment continue to haunt her.

Key Terms

Alien: Term used in the Mann Act to denote foreign-born persons.

Child pornography: Obscene photographing, filming, or depiction of children for commercial purposes or for arousal of self, subject child, or viewing audience.

Child prostitution: Inducing or encouraging a child to engage in sex for financial or other gain.

Child trafficking: Abduction and sale of children.

Fetal abduction: Kidnapping before a fetus is born by the criminal removal of the fetus from the uterus of the pregnant mother.

Grooming: Use of nonviolent techniques by one person to gain sexual access to and control over a child victim.

Infant abduction: Kidnapping after the infant is born and is less than 6 months old, usually from a hospital, clinic, home, or other location.

Missing children: Children whose whereabouts are unknown to their parent, guardian, or legal custodian.

Thrownaways: Children who have been told to leave the household, are refused reentry into their home after running away, are not sought by parents or others when they run away, or are abandoned or deserted.

Discussion Questions

1. What is the role of international law and law enforcement in child trafficking?

2. What challenges are presented to law enforcement and service providers with respect to child prostitution?

3. If you were to design an educational campaign with respect to child abduction, what would be the focus?

4. What services would you request for a 14-year-old found by police on "Low Track" in Vancouver, British Columbia?

5. Debate the pros and cons of treating youth prostitution as a victimless crime.

6. Discuss the failed attempts at grooming in the Burton spree case.

Resources

Canadian Missing Children Program: a partnership between the Royal Canadian Mounted Police (RCMP), Canada Border Services Agency, Department of Foreign Affairs and International Trade, and the Department of Justice http://www.rcmp-grc.gc.ca

Child Labor Public Education Project http://www.continuetolearn.uiowa.edu /laborctr/child_labor/

Citizen's Guide to U.S. Federal Law on the Prostitution of Children https:// www.justice.gov/criminal-ceos/citizens-guide-us-federal-law-prostitution -children

Missing Children Society of Canada http://www.mcsc.ca

National Center for Missing and Exploited Children http://www.missingkids .com/missingkids/servlet/PublicHomeServlet?LanguageCountry=en_US

National Incidence Studies of Missing, Abducted, Runaway, and Thrownaway Children (NISMART) https://www.ncjrs.gov/html/ojjdp/nismart/04/

References

Ark of Hope. (2017). Child trafficking statistics. Retrieved from http://arkofhopeforchildren .org/child-trafficking/child-trafficking-statistics

Ashcroft, J. (2004). *U.S. Department of Justice Report to Congress from Attorney General John Ashcroft on U.S. Government Efforts to Combat Trafficking in Persons.* Washington, DC: U.S. Printing Office.

Burgess, A., Baker, T., Nahirny, C., & Rabun, J. (2002). Newborn kidnappings by Cesarean section. *Journal of Forensic Science, 47*(4), 827–830.

Burgess, A. W., Carr, K. E., Nahirny, C., & Rabun, J. B. (2008). Non-family infant abductors: 1983–2006. *American Journal of Nursing, 108*(9), 32–38.

Burgess, A. W., Groth, A. N., Holmstrom, L. L., & Sgroi, S. (1978). *Sexual assault of children and adolescents.* Lexington, MA: Lexington Books.

Canadian Broadcasting Corporation. (2001). Child prostitution widespread: Experts. Retrieved from http://www.cbc.ca/news/canada/story/2001/02/27/hooker_folo010227 .html

Child Labor Education Project. (2004). University of Iowa Labor Center. Retrieved from http://www.continuetolearn.uiowa.edu/laborctr/child_labor/about/us_history.html

Committee on Sexual Offences Against Children and Youth. (1984). *Sexual offences against children.* Ottawa: Department of Supply and Services.

Dalley, M. (2007). The left-behind parents' view of the parental abduction experience. National Missing Children Services. National Police Services Publ. Ottawa: Royal Canadian Mounted Police.

Department of Justice Canada. (2016). Combatting human trafficking and supporting victims. Retrieved from https://www.canada.ca/en/department-justice /news/2017/02/combatting_humantraffickingandsupportingvictims.html ?=undefined&wbdisable=true

Department of Justice Canada. (2016). National Forum on Human Trafficking Report 2016. Retrieved from https://www.publicsafety.gc.ca/cnt/rsrcs/pblctns/2016-ntnl -frm-hmn-trffckng-smmry/2016-ntnl-frm-hmn-trffckng-smmry-en.pdf

Dugard, J. (2011). Victim impact statement. *ABC News*. Retrieved from http://abcnews .go.com/GMA/jaycee-dugards-victim-impact-statement/story?id=13745897

Federal Bureau of Investigation. (2003). Innocence Lost National Initiative. Retrieved from http://www.missingkids.com/missingkids/servlet/PageServlet?LanguageCountry =en_US&PageId=4166

Federal Bureau of Investigation. (2008). National Crime Information Center (NCIC). Retrieved from http://www.fas.org/irp/agency/doj/fbi/is/ncic.htm

Finkelhor, D., Hotaling, G., and Sedlak, A. (1990). Missing, Abducted, Runaway, and Thrownaway Children in America. First Report: Numbers and Characteristics, National Incidence Studies. Washington, DC: U.S. Department of Justice, Office of Justice Programs, Office of Juvenile Justice and Delinquency Prevention. Available online: www.ncjrs.gov/pdffiles1/ojjdp/nismart90.pdf.

Groth, A. N. (1979). *Men who rape*. New York: Plenum.

Halpern, M. (2014, May 29). Innocence Lost National Initiative. Transcript of *FBI This Week*. Retrieved from https://www.fbi.gov/audio-repository/news -podcasts-thisweek-innocence-lost-national-initiative.mp3/view

Justice Canada. (2011). Youth involvement in prostitution: A literature review and annotated bibliography. Retrieved from http://canada.justice.gc.ca/eng/pi/rs/rep -rap/2001/rr01_13/a12.html

Kiedrowski, J., & Dalley, M. (2008). Parental abduction of children: An overview and profile of the abductor. Retrieved from http://www.rcmp-grc.gc.ca/pubs/omc-ned /parent-eng.htm

Lanning, K. V. (2005). Compliant child victim: Confronting an uncomfortable reality. In E. Quayle and M. Taylor (Eds.), *Viewing child pornography on the Internet* (pp. 49–60). Dorset, United Kingdom: Russell House Publishing.

Lanning, K. V. (2010). *Child molesters: A behavioral analysis* (5th ed.). Alexandria, VA: National Center for Missing & Exploited Children.

Lanning, K. V. (2018). On grooming. *Journal of Interpersonal Violence*, Vol. 33 (2).

Lanning, K. V. & Dietz, P. E. (2014). Acquaintance child molesters and youth-serving organizations. *Journal of Interpersonal Violence*, 29(15), 1–24.

Makin, C. (2017) Footprints keep babies safe for lifetime. My Central Jersey. Retrieved http://www.mycentraljersey.com/story/news/local/outreach/2017/07/11 /footprints-keep-babies-safe-lifetime/468223001/

Matas, R., & Peritz, I. (2008). Canada's poorest postal code in for an Olympic clean-up? Retrieved http://www.theglobeandmail.com/news/national/canadas-poorest-postal -code-in-for-an-olympic-clean-up/article704374/page2/

McLaughlin, E. (2009). Expert: Child trafficker target runaways, "throwaways." Retrieved from http://edition.cnn.com/2009/CRIME/11/18/domestic.child.trafficking/index .html?eref=edition

Missing child websites, n.d. Retrieved from http://bannerb.missingkids.com/missingkids /servlet/ServiceServlet?LanguageCountry=en_US&PageId=1421

Missing Children Society of Canada. (n.d.). What do I do? Parental abductions. Retrieved from http://www.mcsc.ca/my-child-is-missing

Mitchell, K, Finkelhor, D., & Wolak, J. (2010). Conceptualizing juvenile prostitution as child maltreatment: Findings from the National Juvenile Prostitution Study," *Child Maltreatment, 15*(1).

National Center for Missing and Exploited Children (NCMEC). (2012). AMBER alert program. Retrieved from http://www.ncmec.org/missingkids/servlet/PageServlet ?LanguageCountry=en_US&PageId=4319

National Center for Missing and Exploited Children (NCMEC). (2017). Missing kids. Retrieved from www.missingkids.org/InfantAbduction

Newton, M. (n.d.). Robert Pickton: The missing Vancouver women. Ch. 2, Tru/Crime Library. Retrieved from http://www.missingpeople.net/robert_pickton.htm

Parliament of Canada. (2011). Human trafficking. Retrieved from http://www.parl .gc.ca/Content/LOP/ResearchPublications/prb0425-e.htm#intllaw

Patt, M. (2011). Child prostitution—Lithuania. Retrieved from http://gvnet.com /childprostitution/Lithuania.htm

PBS. (2005). The Mann Act—Full text. Retrieved from http://www.pbs.org /unforgivableblackness/knockout/mannact_text.html

Prentky, R. A., & Burgess, A. W. (2000). *Forensic management of the sex offender*. New York: Plenum.

Raaflaub, T. (2006). Human trafficking in Canada. Retrieved from http://www.parl .gc.ca/Content/LOP/ResearchPublications/prb0425-e.htm

Royal Canadian Mounted Police (RCMP). (2011). Assistance to Federal Agencies and Joint Project: Our missing children. Retrieved from http://www.rcmp-grc.gc.ca /pubs/index-eng.htm#r6.5

Sedlak, A. J., & Finkelhor, D. (2011) National Incidence Studies of Missing, Abducted, Runaway, and Thrownaway Children (NISMART), 2011.

Sedlak, A. J., Finkelhor, D., & Brick, J. M. (2017). National Estimates of Missing Children: Updated findings from a survey of parents and other primary caretakers. OJJDP Juvenile Justice Bulletin. Washington, DC: Office of Juvenile Justice and Delinquency.

Sedlak, A. J., Finkelhor, D., Hammer, H., & Schultz, D. J. 2002. *National Estimates of Missing Children: An Overview*. Washington, DC: U.S. Department of Justice, Office of Justice Programs, Office of Juvenile Justice and Delinquency Prevention. Available online: www.ncjrs.gov/ pdffiles1/ojjdp/196465.pdf

Sedlak, A. J., Finkelhor, D., Hammer, H., & Schultz, D. J. (2002). National estimates of missing children: An overview. In *National incidence studies of missing, abducted, runaway, and thrownaway children*. Washington, DC: Office of

Juvenile Justice and Delinquency Prevention, Office of Justice Programs, U.S. Department of Justice.

Statistics Canada. (2012). Canadian Centre for Justice Statistics, Incident-based Uniform Crime Reporting Survey Trend Database.

Thorn (2017). Child sex trafficking statistics. https://www.wearethorn.org/child-trafficking -statistics/

UNICEF. (2010). UNICEF releases startling report on child protection from http:// www.fouryearsgo.org/2010/08/19/world-news/child-protection-from-violence -exploitation-and-abuse/violence, exploitation and abuse

United Nations Inter-Agency Project (UNIAP). (2001–2005). Human trafficking in the Greater Mekong subregion. Academy for Educational Development. Retrieved from http://www.humantrafficking.org/organizations/36

United Nations Office on Drugs and Crime (UNODC). (2006). Trafficking in persons report. Retrieved from http://css.unodc.org/pdf/brazil/Trafficking%20in%20Persons %20Report%202006_US%20gov.pdf

United Nations. (2002a). Rights of the Child. Retrieved from http://www.amnesty.ca /themes/children_un_convention.php

United Nations. (2002b). Trafficking in Women and Girls. Retrieved from http://www .un.org/womenwatch/daw/egm/trafficking2002/reports/WP-DAW.PDF

U.S. Department of Justice. (n.d.) Prostitution of children. Retrieved from https://www .justice.gov/criminal-ceos/prostitution-children

U.S. Department of Labor. (1999). Child Labor Report press conference. Retrieved from https:///www.dol.gov/oasam/programs/history/herman/speeches/990325ah.htm

U.S. Department of Labor. (2012a). Office of Child Labor, Forced Labor, and Human Trafficking. Retrieved from http://www.dol.gov/ilab/programs/ocft/

U.S. Department of Labor. (2012b). Fact sheet: Child soldiers. Retrieved from http:// www.dol.gov/ilab/programs/iclp/childsoldiers/factsheet.htm

U.S. Department of State. (1999). Human rights report, Section 6d. Retrieved from http://www.state.gov/www/global/uman_rights/1999_hrp_report

U.S. Department of State. (2008). 2007 Country Report. Released by Bureau of Democracy, Human Rights, and Labor. Retrieved from http://www.state.gov/j/drl /rls/hrrpt/2007/

USA Trafficking Victims Protection Act (TVPA). (2008). 50 key provisions. Retrieved from http://www.wunrn.com/news/2008/12_08/12_15_08/121508_usa2.htm

Volpe, R. (2011). The Canadian encyclopedia, historica-dominion. Retrieved from http:// thecanadianencyclopedia.com/index.cfm?PgNm=TCE&Params=A1ARTA0001576

Wilson, S. (2010). Child abduction, abductors, and warning signs. Kidproof. Retrieved from http://kidproofblog.com/2010/05/01/child-abduction-abductors-and-warning-signs/

Wolak, J., Finkelhor, D., & Sedlak, A. J. (2016). Child victims of stereotypical kid-nappings known to law enforcement in 2011. OJJDP Juvenile Justice Bulletin. Retrieved from https://www.ojjdp.gov/pubs/249249.pdf

Woo, A., Dhillon, D., Stueck, W., Hager, M., Hume, M., Bailey, I., & Lope, L. (2017, December 30). On cheque day in Downtown Eastside. *The Globe and Mail*. Retrieved

from https://www.theglobeandmail.com/news/british-columbia/on-cheque-day-a
-toxic-mix-of-money-and-drugs-in-vancouvers-downtowneastside/article33462579/

World Health Organization. (2002). *World Health Report. Reducing risks: Promoting
health life*. Retrieved from http://www.who.int/whr/2002/en/

World Health Organization. (2017). New strategies to end violence against children.
Retrieved from http://www.who.int/mediacentre/news/notes/2016/new-strategies
-violence-children/en/

World Vision International. (2008). Child sex tourism prevention project partners. Retrieved
from http://www.worldvision.org/content.nsf/learn/globalissues-stp-partners

Yutzy, S., Wolfson, J., & Resnick, P. (1993). Child stealing by cesarean section. *Journal
of Forensic Science, 38*(1), 192–196.

CHAPTER 8

School Violence

OBJECTIVES

- To describe the nature and prevalence of corporal punishment
- To discuss bullying in schools
- To discuss cyberbullying
- To discuss gangs as an element of school violence
- To identify issues related to school shootings
- To outline the effect of school-based violence on victims

KEY TERMS

Bullying

Conditional threat

Corporal punishment

Direct threat

Indirect threat

Personality

Physical bullying

School dynamics

Social bullying

Threat

Veiled threat

Verbal bullying

Youth gang

CASE

Lawrence (Larry) King was different from most kids who attended E.O. Green Junior High School in Oxnard, California. After being taken from the home of his adoptive parents, he lived in a youth center called Casa Pacifica that provided foster care for children. He wore mascara, jewelry, lipstick, and stiletto shoes to school. He interacted primarily with girls and openly spoke about his attraction to boys. At one point he asked his teachers to call him Leticia and indicated that he wanted a sex change. It was for these reasons that his eighth-grade classmate Marissa Moreno said others taunted him and called him gay. In response to the taunting, Larry would suggest that the other boys were sexually interested in him and would flirt with them. Larry became a central focus of discussion in the school, mainly surrounding whether he should be allowed to dress differently or should conform to school dress code policies. Memos were circulated to teachers about tolerating difference. As a preventive measure, Larry was removed from gym class due to issues in the changing room.

Larry then took a particular interest in a fellow student, 14-year-old Brandon McInerney. Brandon was also a troubled boy; both his parents were drug addicts with criminal records, and he seemed to have an unusual interest in World War II Nazism. One day in February, Larry initiated a game with the girls, asking who they wished would be their special love on Valentine's Day. Larry then walked up to Brandon, who was playing basketball nearby with friends. Interrupting the game, he asked Brandon to be his valentine. Friends responded with taunts that the two were going to make gay babies. Rumors flew through the school that Brandon would seek revenge. The next day, February 2, 2008, Brandon followed through on his threats. While students sat together in the school's computer lab, Brandon pulled out a concealed handgun and shot Larry

in front of his stunned classmates. Two days later, Larry died in the hospital (Cathcart, 2008; Setoodeh, 2008).

A timeline for the criminal process revealed that a decision was made on July 24, 2008, that McInerney would stand trial as an adult; on August 7, 2008, McInerney pleaded not guilty to premeditated murder and a hate crime. In December, he was found competent to stand trial. In March 2009, Brandon's father was found dead from an accidental head injury, and Brandon received permission to leave the juvenile detention facility and attend his father's funeral.

In September 2009, a lying-in-wait allegation was added to the list of charges, which automatically meant that the case would be heard in an adult court. In May 2011, an appeals court ruled that the juvenile records of the victim, Lawrence King, would remain sealed. In September 2011, a mistrial was declared after the jury reported that they were deadlocked after four votes with the last vote was split between seven votes for voluntary manslaughter and five jurors voting for either first-degree or second-degree murder.

In September 2011, the district attorney's office announced that they intended to retry McInerney and drop the hate crime charge. A hearing was scheduled for October 2011. In November 2011, McInerney pleaded guilty to second-degree murder, voluntary manslaughter, and use of a firearm. He will serve 21 years behind bars, with no credit given for time served prior to the trial and no credit will be given for good behavior. He will initially serve his sentence in a juvenile facility and then be transferred to prison upon turning 18.

Introduction

In the past, physical punishment within schools was tolerated or condoned, and the physical discipline of children within schools continues in some parts of the United States. More than a million cases of **corporal punishment** in U.S. schools are reported annually, with states located in the Southeast and Southwest accounting for the vast majority of instances. Today, corporal punishment is prohibited in 28 states and Washington, DC. Seven states do not prohibit corporal punishment, and 15 states expressly permit corporal punishment (Dupper & Dingus, 2008).

Education Week, using data from the Department of Education Civil Rights division, reported that in the 2013–2014 school year about 110,000 students were physically punished nationwide (Education Week, 2016). Most of these instances occurred in states such as Mississippi, Alabama, Arkansas, and Texas, where tens of thousands of students are paddled every year. Child advocates are working toward zero paddling in North Carolina by asking state legislators to outlaw the practice in schools (Sparks & Harwin, 2016).

North Carolina state law describes corporal punishment, as "The intentional infliction of physical pain upon the body of a student as a disciplinary measure." Robbinsville High School in North Carolina permits corporal punishment in the form of paddling, which administrators have described as a "few licks on the backside" delivered with a long wooden paddle. School policy allows students to request a paddling in place of in-school suspension. In 2016, 22 students chose paddling over suspension (Clark, 2017).

Many organizations are working to prohibit corporal punishment. Organizations include the American Academy of Child and Adolescent Psychiatry, the American Academy of Family Physicians, the Canadian Academy of Child and Adolescent Psychiatry, and the American Psychological Association, to name a few. As early as 1992, the Society for Adolescent Medicine took a strong position condemning corporal punishment:

> The Society for Adolescent Medicine concludes that corporal punishment in schools is an ineffective, dangerous, and unacceptable method of discipline. The use of corporal punishment in the school reinforces the notion that physical aggression is an acceptable and effective means of eliminating unwanted behavior in our society. We join many other national organizations recommending that it be banned and urge that nonviolent methods of classroom control be utilized in our school systems. We must abandon such a technique that overtly promotes more violence on our children.
>
> (p. 245)

Similarly, bullying among peers used to be viewed as a normal part of the maturation process and generally not a cause for adult intervention. Thus, schools have not traditionally been seen as places where children and adolescents can be safe from violence. Now, however, there is widespread concern about physical abuse that students may suffer at the hands of adults or other children. In light of high-profile cases of violence in schools, considerable concern also exists regarding gang violence and school shootings.

Scope of the Problem

School violence is violence that occurs on school property, on the way to or from school or school-sponsored events, or during a school-sponsored event. A young person can be a victim, a perpetrator, or a witness of school violence. School violence may also involve or impact adults. Youth violence includes various behaviors. Some violent acts—such as bullying, pushing, and shoving—can cause more emotional harm than physical harm. Other forms of violence, such as gang violence and assault (with or without weapons), can lead to serious injury or even death.

In the United States, statistics on the incidence of school violence are compiled by the National Center for Education Statistics using data from the U.S. Department of Education, the Centers for Disease Control and Prevention (CDC), the Bureau of Justice Statistics, and the National Crime Victimization Survey. Annual reports produced by the National Center for Education Statistics present a comprehensive picture on the incidence of school violence in the United States (Musu-Gillette, Zhang, Wang, Zhang, & Oudekerk, 2017). TABLE 8-1 provides summary statistics on school violence. In the most recently reported school year (2013–2014), 48 violent deaths of students, teachers, staff, or parents occurred on school property, including 26 homicides and 20 suicides (Musu-Gillette et al., 2017).

However, these figures are only a small percentage of homicides and suicides of youth aged 5 to 18 years. It is sobering to note that approximately 50 times more homicides and 150 times more suicides occurred in this population off school property during the same time period. Nonfatal crimes show a different picture, however. Young people were more likely to experience both theft and violent crimes at school (841,100 reports) than away from school (545,100 reports). This pattern differs according to age, with younger adolescents (aged 12 to 14) more likely to be victimized at school and older students (aged 15 to 18) more likely to be victimized away from school. Of all types of school violence, bullying is most prevalent in middle schools, with 25% of middle schools in the United States reporting that the problem occurs at least once a week. In 2010, it was

TABLE 8-1 School Violence in the United States

- 6% of students in grades 9–12 reported being threatened or injured with a weapon on school property.
- 23% of students in grades 9–12 reported they had been in a physical fight at least one time during the previous 12 months anywhere.
- 8% of students in grades 9–12 said they had been in a fight on school property during the previous 12 months.
- Students ages 12–18 were victims of about 841,000 nonfatal crimes (theft plus violent crime) at school (2015).
- 65% of public schools recorded that one or more incidents of crime had taken place at school, amounting to an estimated 757,000 crimes.
- Of the 48 student, staff, and nonstudent violent deaths on school property occurring during the 2008–2009 school year, 26 were homicides and 20 were suicides.
- In 2007, approximately 3% of students aged 12 to 18 reported they were afraid of attack or harm at school. 7.8% reported being in a physical fight on school property in the 12 months before the survey.

Data from Musu-Gillette, L., Zhang, A., Wang, K., Zhang, J., & Oudekerk, B. (2017). *Indicators of School Crime and Safety*: 2016 NCJ250650. National Center for Education Statistics, U.S. Department of Education, and Bureau of Justice Statistics, Office of Justice Programs, U.S. Department of Justice. Washington, DC.

reported that gang violence was the most prevalent form of violence in high schools; indeed, 43% of high schools in the United States have reported gangs as a problem (Robers, Kemp, and Truman, 2010). Recent data demonstrate that student reports of gang presence have declined quite considerably since 2010. Furthermore, though total victimization rates for students aged 12 to 18 have declined since 1992 (Musu-Gillette et al., 2017), its prevalence still poses a significant problem for parents, administrators, and the students themselves.

Teachers are also victims of crime at school. Survey results from 2007–2008 reported by Robers and colleagues (2010) indicate that 7% of teachers had been threatened and 4% had been physically attacked on the job. This rate was higher for teachers in inner-city schools, 10% of whom reported being threatened and 7% of whom reported being attacked. Rates of crime victimization were also comparatively higher for high school teachers than for middle school teachers, and for male teachers than for female teachers. More recent statistics show that 10% of elementary and 9% of secondary school teachers reported being threatened by a student from their school between 2011 and 2012 (Musu-Gillette et al., 2017).

Legislation Addressing School Violence

Addressing school violence through legislation is complex given the diverse nature of this issue. At the federal level, in the United States the Gun-Free Schools Act was introduced in 1994 as an amendment to the 1964 Elementary and Secondary Schools Education Act. It requires that "each State receiving

Federal funds under this Act shall have in effect a State law requiring local educational agencies to expel from school for a period of not less than one year a student who is determined to have brought a weapon to a school" (Section 14601(b)1). Individual states were required to enact legislation in compliance with this act by October 1995. Florida, for instance, enacted the following legislation (Section 790.115):

> A person who exhibits a sword, sword cane, firearm, electric weapon or device, destructive device, or other weapon, including a razor blade, box cutter, or knife . . . at any school-sponsored event or on the grounds of facilities of any school, school bus, or school bus stop, or within 1,000 feet of the real property that comprises a public or private elementary school, middle school, or secondary school, during school hours or during the time of a sanctioned school activity, commits a felony of the third degree.

Under the Gun-Free Schools Act, education agencies must also have a policy that refers any student with a weapon to the criminal or juvenile justice system.

Individual states have attempted to address school violence beyond weapons use. For instance, the New York legislature passed the Safe Schools Against Violence in Education (SAVE) legislation in 1990. This legislation is broad based and has requirements for violence prevention training for teachers, school safety plans, building emergency response plans, codes of conduct, reporting requirements, and procedures for dealing with violent students. Penalties for assaults on teachers were increased in the SAVE legislation, changing them from misdemeanors to felony offenses. Colorado introduced the Safe Schools Bullying Policy that defines bullying and requires each school district to develop policies and committees that address bullying.

In the aftermath of a highly publicized school shooting at Sandy Hook Elementary School in Newtown, Connecticut, several gun laws were proposed at both the state and federal levels. At the federal level, the Obama administration announced the formation of a task force premised on reducing gun violence by implementing a number of policies that, among other things, aimed to address loopholes in background checks for firearm acquisition, to ban assault firearms and high capacity magazines, to increase access to mental health services, and to improve data sharing and coordination between agencies. Gun laws and rights associated with gun ownership continue to be some of the most highly contentious issues in American society today. While there are fierce advocates on both sides of the debate surrounding gun control, the laws are frequently subject to change and reflect a long political battle between

Second Amendment rights and the potential for gun-related violence. Recently, the Trump administration signed a bill to reverse a ban on the purchase of firearms by those deemed mentally ill, fulfilling a campaign promise that had been strongly supported by many gun advocates. And though critics have condemned recent reforms to reverse firearm regulations, others have long been critical of legislative responses in the aftermath of school shootings, claiming that they are largely routine, ineffective, and serve as "feel good" legislation (see Schildkraut & Hernandez, 2014, for further discussion). In any case, it is evident that much more research is required to identify the complex etiology of school shootings and gun violence that includes but likely goes beyond the issue of access to guns.

Gang violence is also a serious problem in North American schools, and yet law enforcement has been largely unable to effectively address the issue. Some have argued that this ineffectiveness is in large part due to difficulties in obtaining convictions through criminal justice processes. In the United States, some states have attempted to address the problem through civil means. At present, most states have legislation addressing various aspects of gang activity, such as prohibiting gang participation or wearing gang-related clothing. For instance, the California Education Code does not allow the wearing of gang clothing in schools. Arizona law allows for extended sentences if a felony is committed in a school safety zone. Illinois law makes it a felony to recruit for a gang on school property. Nevada directs boards of trustees of school districts to adopt antigang policies.

Many police departments across the United States have developed specialized gang units. It has been estimated that 365 gang units employed 4,300 officers in the United States in 2007 (Langton, 2010).

In 2009, Canada introduced specific legislation to address gang violence (Bill C-14, 2009). Changes to the Criminal Code of Canada included the following:

- Murders connected to organized crime activity are automatically classified as first-degree and are subject to a mandatory sentence of life imprisonment without eligibility for parole for 25 years.

- A new offense for drive-by and other reckless shootings was added. The minimum sentence for this offense is longer if the offense was committed for a criminal organization or with a prohibited or restricted firearm.

- Two new offenses of aggravated assault against a peace or public officer and assault with a weapon on a peace or public officer were added with maximum penalties of 14 and 10 years, respectively.

Bullying

Bullying is an insidious problem, with the potential for devastating emotional and physical effects. Unfortunately, it has likely existed since the beginning of time. According to the stopbullying.gov website, "Bullying is unwanted, aggressive behavior among school-aged children that involves a real or perceived power imbalance. The behavior is repeated, or has the potential to be repeated, over time" (U.S. Department of Health and Human Services, n.d.). In a large U.S. survey, more than 15,000 students reported on their bullying experiences. Thirty percent reported moderate to frequent involvement with bullying, 13% indicated they were bullies, 10.6% indicated they were victims, and 6.3% indicated they were both (Nansel et al., 2001). In 2015, the National Center for Education Statistics reported that 21% of students aged 12 to 18 identified they were bullied in the past year. Of those who were bullied, 12% were ridiculed, 18% were the subject of rumors, 5% were physically bullied, and 4% were threatened (Musu-Gillette et al., 2017).

Types of Bullying

Bullying can occur in many forms; the broad categories are physical, emotional, and social bullying. Bullying can occur through direct contact or indirectly through rumors and social exclusion. Increasingly, bullying is occurring via electronic means, called *cyberbullying*.

Physical bullying can include pushing, hitting, tripping, spitting at, or, more rarely, physical beating. This type of bullying peaks during grades 6 through 8 and is reported about twice as often by boys than by girls. Verbal bullying includes taunts, threats, name calling, and derogatory comments. Approximately twice as many students indicate they are victims of verbal bullying than those who admit to perpetrating it. Social bullying involves rumors and behaviors aimed at deliberate social exclusion. This is more commonly reported by girls than by boys.

Factors Contributing to Bullying

Inevitably, when researchers attempt to determine factors that contribute to bullying they reach the conclusion that it is caused by multiple aspects. These aspects can include individual factors of both the victim and the bully, family of origin factors, the peer group, and the school setting.

A study of 185 ninth-grade students in Sweden revealed that students were most likely to attribute the causes of bullying to individual characteristics of the bully (69%) and secondarily to characteristics of the victim (42%) (Thornberg & Knutsen, 2011). In this study, students were most likely to believe that others were bullies because of personal flaws, such as low self-esteem, psychological problems, issues with hostility, or coming from a problematic family with poor parenting. Students also believed that the bullying behavior was motivated by a desire for social positioning and attempting to protect oneself from social exclusion. The most common victim characteristic thought by students to result in bullying was that the victim was deviant, irritating, or weak. Only 13% of this sample thought bullying was caused by peer group pressure. A mere 7% attributed it to school factors, such as boredom or poor anti-bullying policies, and, similarly, 7% thought it was due to societal or human nature factors (Thornberg & Knutsen, 2011).

Many studies have confirmed that students who are victims of bullying do have distinguishing characteristics. They are more likely to report being physically hurt by a family member (23.2% of bullied students compared to 6.2% of nonbullied students), and 22.8% report witnessing violence in their families (compared to 6.6% of nonbullied students) (CDC, 2011). The rate of family violence among bullied students is also higher than among students who admit to being bullies (CDC, 2011). Other studies have demonstrated that it is the interaction between these individual variables and other variables that lead to bullying behavior. For instance, Lee (2011) demonstrated that although individual factors of both the victim and the bully were important, these were mediated by parenting factors (including authoritarian parenting and domestic violence), teacher interventions, and peer group interactions. Another study demonstrated that students with high self-esteem were *less* likely to bully in a positive school environment where students did not believe violence was normal. However, high self-esteem students were *more* likely to bully in negative school environments where violence was the norm (Gendron, Williams, & Guerra, 2011).

A particularly confusing aspect of bullying, however, is that bullying is often perpetrated by someone the victim believes to be a friend. Mishna, Wiener, and Pepler (2008) conducted qualitative interviews with a subsample of children who identified being bullied in a citywide survey. Of those interviewed, 89% indicated they had been bullied by a friend. In this study, parents and teachers were also interviewed, and, interestingly, for the most part they had not identified the child as being bullied by friends. Thus, this type of bullying is more insidious and less recognizable. Parents may unwittingly place the child in difficult situations by encouraging interactions with the bullies and questioning the child when they do not wish to participate in activities. For children, this type of bullying resulted in high levels of distress, and due to the sense of betrayal and isolation, these children experienced self-blame for the bullying and difficulty in disclosing the bullying to others for fear of losing the friendship and expectations that adults will not intervene (Mishna & Alaggia, 2005).

Cyberbullying

Another form of bullying that has caught the attention of researchers, the public, and the media is cyberbullying, which is typically defined as "aggression that is intentionally and repeatedly carried out in an electronic context (e.g., email, blogs, instant messages, text messages) against a person who cannot easily defend him or herself" (Kowalski, Guimetti, Schroeder, & Lattanner, 2014, p. 1073). Highly publicized media accounts of cases in which cyberbullying victims tragically committed suicide have galvanized public support for tougher legislation against this type of behavior, such as Canada's Bill C-13, which promises to combat online harassment and nonconsensual distribution of intimate images, as well as individual state laws in the United States that prohibit cyberbullying. Without a doubt the growth of technology, the spread of the Internet, and the proliferation of social media platforms have provided new avenues for aggressive behavior. Indeed, some suggest that certain features of online communications may increase the likelihood of such behavior, including the ability for perpetrators to remain anonymous, the absence of emotional reactivity, victim perception of uncontrollability, and the ability to reproduce messages, images, and other forms of media that can be easily shared with others (Kowalski et al., 2014). It is less clear whether the psychological effects of cyberbullying markedly contrast from those of more traditional face-to-face forms of bullying, though some suggest that the public nature of some cyberbullying acts may involve larger audiences, and thus greater feelings of shame and embarrassment for the victim (Slonje & Smith, 2008). Nevertheless, both traditional and cyber forms of bullying appear to share many common adverse effects that can significantly influence physical and mental health.

Effects of Bullying

Outcomes for both bullies and those who are bullied are serious. Those who bully have been shown to experience academic problems, poor psychological adjustment, and later, delinquency (Nansel et al., 2001). Bullies often have higher rates of alcohol and drug abuse, are more likely to engage in early sexual activity, are more likely to have criminal convictions later in life, and are more likely to be perpetrators of intimate partner violence. Those who are bullied experience psychological distress and adjustment problems, heightened anxiety, and low self-esteem. Bullied students can exhibit avoidant and withdrawal behaviors, such as refusing to attend school, or self-protective behaviors, such as carrying a weapon or joining a gang (Wynne & Joo, 2011). From a mental health perspective, bullying has been associated with depression, anxiety, eating disorders, and a wide range of somatic symptoms (CDC, 2011; Ttofi & Farrington, 2008). Musu-Gillette and colleagues (2017) found that bullying at school had negative effects on how victims felt about themselves, on their relationships with friends and family, on their performance in school, and on their physical health. In 2015, approximately 5% of students aged 12 to 18 reported that they avoided at least one activity, one class, or one location on school grounds because they feared being attacked or harmed. Moreover, those who have been bullied are considerably more likely to have seriously considered suicide (24.9%) than students who have not been bullied (4.5%) and have much higher rates of intentional self-injury (40.9% vs. 8.4%) (CDC, 2011).

On January 2, 2002, J. Daniel Scruggs, a 12-year-old boy, was found dead, hanging by a tie in his closet. The fact that such a young child would commit suicide baffled many. As it turns out, Scruggs was the victim of relentless bullying at the middle school he attended. Daniel was a small boy, weighing only 63 pounds, and, although he had a high IQ, suffered from a learning disability. As a result, he was a lonely outcast who was severely tormented by the peers at his school. His classmates would push him around and call him names because he wore mismatched clothes, acted strangely, and smelled like he rarely bathed. He was hit, kicked, spit on, laughed at, thrown down a flight of stairs, and sometimes made to eat his lunch off the cafeteria floor. Classmates reported that Daniel was bullied every day he was in school and teachers rarely did anything to stop the behaviors or hold the bullies accountable. His gym teacher stated that he had witnessed Daniel being physically picked up by a peer and spun in the air. The incident had been reported to school administrators, but no disciplinary action had been taken (Stowe, 2003). By the seventh grade Daniel often refused to bathe and even soiled himself so he would not have to go to school. He had been moved to a trailer behind the school designated for children who had trouble fitting in with other students. School officials had also recommended to Daniel's mother that she seek counseling for him. As a result of Daniel's chronic truancy, the Department of Children and Families became involved. The appointed caseworker suggested that Daniel change schools but nevertheless failed to see how serious the case really was. In fact, the case was closed six days before Daniel's death despite the fact that he had missed 74 of the 78 preceding schools days (Santora, 2003).

Daniel's mother was a single mother who worked two jobs and raised Daniel and his sister all on her own. Their father had physically abused his wife and abandoned his family when Daniel was only 3 months old. Daniel's mother worked at Daniel's school as a teacher's aide and said that she complained to school officials about the bullying but stated she had no idea how severe the abuse really was until it was too late. After Daniel's death, his mother had planned to sue the school for ignoring how badly he had been mistreated and not intervening or providing the help he needed. However, the mother was arrested and charged with three counts of risk of injury to a minor and one count of cruelty to persons. The police alleged that Ms. Scruggs had raised Daniel in an unhealthy home environment and failed to provide him with the proper medical and psychological care he needed. Their home was filled with piles of debris, clothing, dirty dishes, garbage, and other clutter (Santora, 2003).

Ms. Scruggs went on trial and was found guilty on one count of risk of injury to a minor for an unhealthy home environment. Jurors report the decision was based on the fact that every night Daniel slept surrounded by steak knives out of fear. The judge spared Ms. Scruggs from having to serve a prison sentence and instead placed her on probation for 5 years with 100 hours of community service. The judge also ordered her to undergo mandatory counseling. This was the first case in Connecticut in which a parent was held criminally accountable for a child's suicide (Salzman, 2004). After pronouncing the sentence, the judge affirmed that "the law requires parents and caregivers to protect their children, to keep them safe, and to make sure they're not subjected to risks to their health" (Salzman, 2004, p. 4). He further admonished Ms. Scruggs for the lack of remorse she displayed regarding her son's death and the horrible circumstances in which he was forced to live (Salzman, 2004).

An investigation conducted by the state's child advocate and chief state's attorney found that school officials, the state's child protection system, and Ms. Scruggs had all failed Daniel in one way or another. Not one of these parties acted in a way to ensure Daniel received the care he so desperately needed. Instead, his frantic cries for help were ignored and left unanswered. Daniel's experience of relentless bullying and subsequent suicide led to a new law in Connecticut that now requires schools to report bullying to the authorities (Santora, 2003).

Managing and Preventing Bullying

Given the nature of bullying, approaches to managing and preventing it are necessarily broad based. Successful programs to address bullying use a whole-school approach that involves strong teacher leadership; clear expectations of behaviors and adherence to norms; adult awareness, supervision, and monitoring; student involvement in program development and delivery; and age- and gender-appropriate social skills training (Public Safety Canada, 2008). In 1994, the Cherry School District in Colorado developed a program titled Bully-Proofing Your School that has served as a model to other communities. In this program, members of the school community work together to identify and alter the factors that allow bullying to occur. The program focuses on "the caring majority" of students and involves teaching students strategies for developing and maintaining a caring environment. Similarly, the Olweus Bullying Prevention Program (also from Colorado) has now been implemented in over a dozen countries and involves individual-, classroom-, and school-level interventions. Farrington and Ttofi (2009) conducted a systematic review of 30 studies examining the efficacy of school-based intervention programs in reducing bullying. They concluded that such programs reduce bullying by 20% to 23%. In their meta-analysis, the most important factors associated with decreased bullying were consistent disciplinary methods, parent meetings, playground supervision, and cooperative peer group work.

In response to the troubling results of a national survey on bullying published in 2001 (Nansel et al., 2001), the U.S. Department of Health and Human Services launched the Stop Bullying Now! campaign. This national media campaign focused on youth aged 9 to 13 and the adults in their lives. It sought to raise awareness about bullying, to shape attitudes and behaviors, and to identify strategies for intervention. Today, the U.S. Department of Health and Human Services provides an interactive website (www.stopbullying.gov) that features tools to help kids, teens, and teachers recognize and stop bullying. It also identifies that parents have a role to play in preventing and/or stopping bullying and recommends that parents watch for the signs identified in TABLE 8-2. Although the information in Table 8-2 can be helpful, relying on signs of bullying does have risks. One study found that parents and teachers frequently did not identify a child who was being bullied or questioned the veracity of a child's disclosure of bullying because the child did not "fit" expectations about how a victimized child presents (i.e., grades had not dropped, child appeared to have friends, child remained calm and focused) (Mishna, Pepler, & Weiner, 2006). It is thus important for parents and teachers to not only watch for warning signs but also to be open to disclosures from children and youth who do not fit the model.

Low-level violent behavior, particularly school bullying, remains a critical public health issue that has been associated with negative mental and physical health outcomes. School-based prevention programs, while a valuable line of defense for staving off bullying, have shown inconsistent results in terms of decreasing bullying.

TABLE 8-2 Signs of Bullying

Signs a Child May Be a Victim of Bullying
• Comes home with damaged clothing or belongings.
• Frequently loses books and/or personal belongings.
• Has unexplained injuries.
• Attempts to avoid school because of headaches, stomachaches, feeling sick.
• Does not want to visit with friends or has fewer friends.
• Changes in eating habits.
• Feels helpless, bad about themselves, moody, anxious, or angry.
• Afraid of going to school, doing activities with friends.
Signs a Child May Be a Bully
• Becomes violent or gets into fights with others.
• Gets sent to the principal's office or has frequent detentions.
• Has extra money or belongings.
• Blames others.
• Has friends who are bullies.

Data from www.stopbullying.gov.

A study by Blosnich and Bossarte (2011) explored whether school safety measures (e.g., security guards, cameras, ID badges) were associated with student reports of different forms of peer victimization related to bullying. Analyzing data from the 2007 School Crime Supplement of the National Crime Victimization Survey produced several results. Of the school safety measures examined, the only one that resulted in a significant reduction in odds of being physically bullied, having property vandalized, or having rumors spread was having adults in hallways. Having adults and/or staff supervising hallways was associated with an approximate 26% decrease in students experiencing an additional form of peer victimization (Blosnich & Bossarte, 2011).

With regards to cyberbullying, Slonje, Smith, and Frisén (2013) have suggested that many school-based programs suited for traditional forms of bullying can be extended and modified to incorporate cyberbullying as well. These may include schoolwide anti-bullying policies and awareness training programs that highlight the negative consequences of bullying on victims as well as the potential legal consequences for perpetrators.

School Bullying Climate

Educational research emphasizes the complexity of bullying behavior and finds that the school climate plays a central role in its development, or elimination of bullying behavior among students. Wang, Berry & Swearer (2013) highlight the importance of school climate in bullying prevention and made the following findings from their study on school culture. First, positive relationships among students and teachers, and negative attitudes toward harmful behavior such as bullying are critical elements of a healthy school climate. Second, to create a positive school climate, school personnel need to promote and demonstrate attitudes and behaviors, such as caring, empathy, and respectful interactions between students and teachers. Third, teachers and staff need to take reports of any bullying incident seriously, according to school rules, and not ignore or minimize bullying behavior. Fourth, adults should refrain from bullying students and other adults at school. Fifth, teachers can build school climate interventions into the curriculum and openly discuss topics related to bullying, such as popularity, power, and social ostracism. Sixth, bullying is not only a behavior problem, but also a mental health problem and consultation needs to be sought for both the victim and the bully.

Gang Violence in Schools

Modern-day gangs began in the United States in the 1820s in New York in the context of large-scale immigration. These early gangs were populated by White Europeans who faced extreme economic and social conditions (Howell, Egley, Tita, & Griffiths, 2011). The next documented wave of gang activity occurred in the 1920s, when 1,313 gangs were reported to be active in Chicago. Sociologist Frederick Thrasher (1927) described the manner in which European-born and first-generation youth joined gangs in response to societal conditions in which they found themselves. These youth, he observed, were struggling with the clash between cultural customs from the homeland and the expectations of their new country. Their lives lacked the organizing and stabilizing structures experienced by peers with longer family histories in America, and thus they were prey to the organization offered by gangs (Thrasher, 1927). Gang problems in many cities began to emerge again in the 1970s and expanded throughout the 1980s and 1990s. At that time most gang members were African American or Latino youth. Conditions believed to contribute to this rise were the losses of hundreds of thousands of factory jobs, leading to poverty, economic marginalization, and social disorganization in some U.S. cities. An informal economy involving illegal activity grew and flourished. By 2000, however, the membership of gangs had again shifted in response to large-scale immigration from Latin America and Asia (Moore & Hagedorn, 2001).

A **youth gang** is a self-formed association of peers who have the following characteristics: three or more members, generally aged 12 to 24 years; a name and some sense of identity, generally indicated by such symbols as style of clothing, graffiti, and hand signs; some degree of permanence and organization; and an elevated level of involvement in delinquent or criminal activity (National Youth Gang Center, 2008). They control their territories through violence and intimidation. They increase their size through recruiting members, often from single-parent, low-income households. As of September 2005, Los Angeles County had over 1,400 gangs, with a total membership exceeding 160,000. Estimates based on law enforcement reports in 2009 suggested there were 28,100 gangs and 731,000 gang members in the United States (Egley & Howell, 2011). Recent estimates show that gang membership is much higher, with approximately 33,000 street gangs and 1.4 million members, though there is uncertainty to what extent these numbers are affected by more accurate reporting and more active gang surveillance by law enforcement (Federal Bureau of Investigation, 2010).

Youth Gang Participation

Gangs frequently are formed in response to an awareness that other gangs are forming. Members are drawn together because of a perceived need for protection from various forms of victimization. Rivalries exist over neighborhood dominance, drug turf, and symbolic ascendance or power. In general, these gangs are not well organized and have weak control over their members. The response to perceived threat from others outside the gang is violence. One attraction to gangs is the loyalty that members have to one another. Gangs provide a family system that is often very alluring to youth. According to the National Youth Gang Center (2011), several factors contribute to the development of youth gangs:

- Conventional socializing agents, such as families and schools, are largely ineffective and alienating and adult supervision is absent.

- Adolescents have a great deal of free time that is not consumed by other prosocial roles.

- Members have limited access to appealing careers or jobs.

- Young people have a place to congregate—usually a well-defined neighborhood.

TABLE 8-3 Theories for Understanding Gang Participation

Theory	Characteristics
Strain theory	Multiple strains, including poverty and social disintegration, challenge youth. Unable to achieve success in socially defined manner. Look to achieve success through gang activities.
Social learning theory	Family disorganization. Family structures do not model healthy development. Gang provides normative model for behavior.
Systems theory	Family disorganization and inability to meet need. Other systems (school, church) do not fill the gap. Gang provides a protective, structured environment.
Social control theory	Lack of clear community expectations of behavior. Gang provides clear rules and expectations.
Self-control theory	Inability to control own impulses. Fits with gang activities.

Data from Sharkey, J., Shekhtmeyster, Z., Chavez-Lopez, L., Norris, E. & Sass, L. 2011. The protective influence of gangs: Can schools compensate? *Aggression and Violent Behavior. 16,* 45–54.

Sharkey, Shekhtmeyster, Chavez-Lopez, Norris, and Sass (2011) have provided a summary of theories to explain youth attraction to gangs (TABLE 8-3).

Nevertheless, gangs are very rarely a safe haven for members. As a result of the weak organizational structure and lack of control over members, violence is used as a threat if members are not compliant (Decker & Curry, 2002). When joining a gang, an initiate must prove his or her worthiness. In some gangs initiation involves committing a crime, or new members might have to be "beaten in," where members punch and kick them for a period of several minutes while they cannot fight back (Carlie, 2002). Female gang members are either "beaten in" or "sexed in," which includes sex with numerous members and may result in violent sexual assault (Walker, 2008). Without question, initiations are generally very brutal; however, before this initial step is complete the promise of love, belonging, and protection can be quite alluring.

Some evidence suggests that gang presence at schools is declining, or at least that their presence is less noted by other students. Musu-Gillette and colleagues (2017) found that between 2001 and 2015 the percentage of students who reported gang presence at their schools decreased from 20% to 11%. Reports of gang presence were more prevalent in urban areas and in public schools.

Gang Violence

Gang members account for a disproportionate amount of violence in our society. In large part this is because gangs play an important role in facilitating drug sales and defending territory, resulting in a concomitant need for self-protection. As more guns were drawn into the urban drug markets in the early 1990s, they eventually became diffused throughout the youth population and contributed to a sudden spike in homicides in the United States between 1990 and 1994. Between 1998 and 2003 gang members were believed to have committed 6% of violent crime in the United States (Harrell, 2005). Trends in youth gang activity show that the frequency of gang problems reported by law enforcement agencies in the United States increased from the 1970s until the mid-1990s, decreased for several years, and then increased again from 2002 to 2008 (Howell, 2010). Not surprisingly perhaps, gang violence is most likely to occur in large cities and least likely to occur in rural areas, as reflected by the data in FIGURE 8-1 (National Youth Gang Center, 2011). Individuals between the ages of 12 and 19 were 4 times more likely to be victims of gang violence than those aged 20 to 49 and 10 times more likely than those over the age of 50. Young males were at highest risk (Harrell, 2005). Of those young people who are victims of gang crime, it is gang members themselves who are at highest risk (Delisi, Barnes, Beaver, & Gibson, 2009).

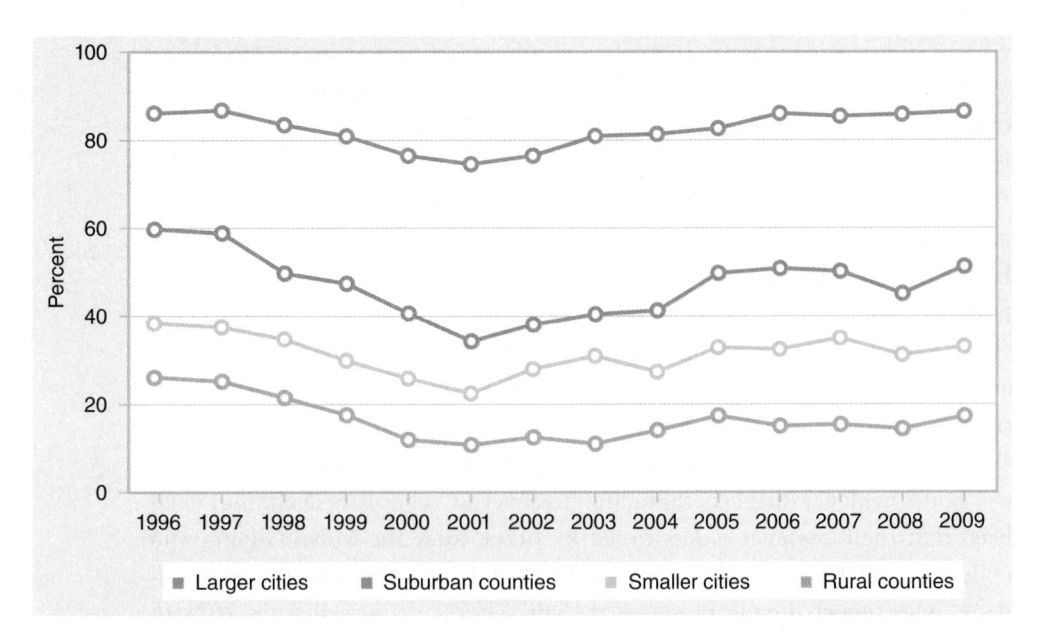

FIGURE 8-1 Prevalence of gang violence by area type.

Data from National Youth Gang Center. 2011.

In Chicago, gang-motivated homicides represented approximately one-fourth of all homicides between 1993 and 1995, and 45% of homicides in Los Angeles between 1994 and 1995 were gang related (Decker & Curry, 2002). Gang homicides are more likely to occur between members of the same ethnic group and involve younger offenders and victims than nongang homicides. The peak risk ages to be killed in a gang homicide are between 15 and 19 years. The homicides are more likely to have multiple participants, occur in the street, and involve the use of automobiles. They are significantly more likely to involve firearms (Decker & Curry, 2002). The issue of perceived threat from a rival gang is key to understanding gang homicide. Further, many of the killings are retaliatory in nature. Gang violence escalates rapidly as one event triggers another.

Victims of Gang Violence

A special report from the Office for Victims of Crime (Seymour & Ray, 1996) identified several characteristics unique to victims of gang violence. First, victims and witnesses generally live among the perpetrators of their crimes. They frequently face the entire gang, as opposed to a sole perpetrator, even at the funeral of their murdered friend or family member. Victims and witnesses are often intimidated into not cooperating with the criminal justice system and are fearful of retaliation if they do. Second, victims and survivors are often seen as contributing in some way to the crime. This is particularly true for surviving family members of murdered children, some of whom were members of gangs. Third, victims are frequently afraid or unable to exercise victims' rights. As a result of intimidation, fear of retaliation, or due to cultural norms, many victims of gang violence do not exercise their rights, which often include the right to be notified of, attend, and be heard at court proceedings; to be informed when the defendant is released or escapes; and to receive restitution. Safety and protection issues for victims are a serious concern. See TABLE 8-4 for characteristics of victims of gang violence that were compiled and published by the Office of Victims of Crime as one of the first educational reports on gangs in America.

Addressing Gang Violence in Schools

Gangs have proven to be a significant problem in schools and have put increasing burdens on teachers and school administrators. With respect to prevalence, a U.S. national survey released in 2017 revealed that 11% of students between the ages of 12 and 18 reported the presence of gangs at their schools (Musu-Gillette et al., 2017), though this number was considerably higher in 2010, with 45% of high school students and 35% of middle school

TABLE 8-4 Characteristics of Victims of Gang Violence

- Victims and witnesses generally live with and/or among the perpetrators of their crimes, similar to domestic violence victims.
- Victims and survivors are often seen as contributors to the crime.
- Victims are frequently afraid or unable to exercise victims' rights.
- Victims may be fearful of seeking or receiving restitution for fear of intimidation or retaliation.
- Despite legislation that allows for relocation, prosecutors lack funding for relocating victims and witnesses of gang violence.
- Lack of English language skills often prohibits engagement in the judicial process.
- Victims may be affected by cultural norms and mores that include a general distrust of government, and hence they may not access, or even be aware of, available services or participate in any way within the criminal justice system.

Data from: Office for Victims of Crime. 1996.

students claiming there were gangs or gang members in their schools (Arciaga, Sakamoto, & Jones, 2010). Further, an earlier study revealed that 7.6% of secondary school boys and 3.8% of girls reported belonging to a gang (Gottfredson & Gottfredson, 2001). Although earlier views considered girls in gangs to be largely "possessions," it is increasingly clear they are intricately involved in criminal activity and violence (Moore & Hagedorn, 2001). It is interesting to note that only 5% of principals surveyed indicated gang activity in their schools (Arciaga et al., 2010), suggesting that school authorities are much less aware of the presence of gangs compared to students.

Gangs can be identified in schools through gang attire (clothing, jewelry, belt buckles, customized T-shirts), hand signs, behaviors, gang insignia, and graffiti, some of which are purposefully displayed by members. These identifying characteristics serve several purposes: scaring off enemies, getting victims to comply, discouraging bystanders from interfering, and discouraging witnesses from coming forward. Although there is partial evidence that the presence of gangs in schools has decreased over the last several years, potentially attributable to focused prevention programs, proactive policies are still needed that have been proven to mitigate the formation of youth gangs. Considering the factors that attract youth to gangs discussed in Table 8-3, school-based interventions are vital and should include the following:

- Programs to strengthen families and parenting skills
- Programs that promote and strengthen social and academic competencies
- Programs that enhance a sense of community among students, teachers, and academic leaders

- Engagement of community groups and community leaders
- Provision of social and instrumental supports for youth at risk

Teachers as Victims of School Violence

Violence against teachers is an area that has received surprisingly little attention considering the rates at which teachers are victims of aggression and assault. During the 2007–2008 school year, 8% of U.S. secondary school teachers and 7% of elementary school teachers reported being threatened with injury by a student; 6% of elementary school teachers and 2% of high school teachers reported being assaulted (Robers et al., 2010). In another study of 731 teachers, analyses showed that 80% of respondents (n = 585) had experienced some type of violence during their teaching careers. Actual, attempted, or threatened physical violence was reported to be 27.6% (Wilson, Douglas & Lyon, 2011).

Reports from other countries indicate shocking rates of violence against teachers. For instance, 49% of teachers in Slovakia reported experiencing violence in the past 30 days (Dzuka & Dalbert, 2007). Other studies have focused on student reports of violence toward teachers. A study conducted in Taiwan, for instance, found that over 30% of students in grades 4 through 12 reported being involved in at least one aggressive behavior toward teachers in the past 12 months (Chen & Astor, 2008). Students reported mocking, cursing, insulting, teasing, or playing harmful tricks on teachers. A much smaller number (2.4%) reported actual acts of physical violence. Reported reasons for violence, in order of frequency, were what were perceived to be unreasonable requirements (55.7%), unfair treatment (48.6%), disagreements (41.6%), in response to punishment (23.2%), being upset (16.1%), and perceived provocation (11.5%) (Chen & Astor, 2008). A small number of students indicated that teachers were simply easy targets (5.9%) (Chen & Astor, 2008).

A national survey of students in Israel revealed lower yet still significant rates of violence (Khoury-Kassabri, Astor, & Benbenishty, 2009). In this survey 14% of students reported verbal aggression against a teacher, almost 7% reported destroying personal belongings of a teacher, and slightly less than 4% of students reported physical violence against a teacher. Factors associated with higher reported rates of violence and aggression included male gender, lower family income, and lower educational attainment of parents. Further, violence against teachers was higher in areas with greater amounts of community violence.

School Shootings

School shootings are a sad and disturbing part of crime culture. Although rare, when they do occur school shootings shock the conscience of society and generate expedient demands for such actions as tighter gun controls, stronger mental health intervention, and faster, more efficient law enforcement responses. The issues facing educators, law enforcement agencies, and the mental health community are how to identify students at risk of lethal violence, how to assess the degree of threat, and, tragically, how to manage the aftermath of these horrifying events.

Columbine

The name "Columbine" has become synonymous with school shootings. The Columbine High School massacre occurred on Tuesday, April 29, 1999, when two students, Eric Harris and Dylan Klebold, shot and killed 12 students and a teacher, as well as wounding 24 others, before committing suicide. It remains the third-deadliest school shooting in U.S. history, after the 1966 University of Texas mass shooting and the 2007 Virginia Tech shootings.

The massacre began with Eric and Dylan hauling two bombs hidden in duffle bags into the school cafeteria, each consisting of a propane tank, a gasoline tank, a detonator, and a timer. The bombs, set to explode at 11:17 a.m., were placed within close range of the table occupied by the "jocks," who were among the 480 students eating lunch. Dylan and Eric left the cafeteria and strategically positioned themselves outside the building, ready to shoot students as they fled the bombs. Their weapons, a semi-automatic handgun and a 12-gauge, sawed-off shotgun, were hidden under black trench coats. They carried duffle bags with backup weapons, including explosive devices, ammunition, and knives. Their cars were fixed with bombs timed to explode while emergency response personnel were on scene. The plan was to kill 500 people. Mercifully however, the bombs did not explode and the young men therefore changed plans, ran into the school, and began their shooting spree (Larkin, 2007).

Time Magazine (Gibbs & Roche, 1999) described the content of videos taped by Dylan and Eric prior the attacks. In the tapes they itemize their hatred towards all "niggers, spics, Jews, gays, f____ing whites," students who abused them and others who did not defend them. They brag with anticipation that "It's going to be like F___ing Doom." Eric and Dylan prepared extensively for the massacre, trying on their coats with weapons concealed, carrying weapons in their duffle bags, and concealing equipment in their bedrooms. It has been determined, in hindsight, that there were clues that these students were dangerous (Achenbach & Russakoff, 1999). In a composition for class, as a young child Eric created a story in which he and his brother were Rambo-like heroes armed with M-16s and fighting off an army. In the year before the Columbine shooting, he kept a journal in which he detailed year-long plans for killing others that he hoped would result in 500 dead and he and Dylan hijacking a plane and crashing into New York City. In creative writing class in high school, neither young man attempted to conceal their dark interests, consistently turning in violent stories that they shared with the class. In the fall, they made a video for a government and economics class in which they pretended to be hit men who could be hired to bring justice to jocks who picked on other students, ending it with a violent scene in which they bludgeoned the head of a dummy covered in fake blood (Achenback & Russakoff, 1999). Added to this were violent blogs and a violent website that hosted the first-person shooting game DOOM. Further videos documented their shooting practice, and a final one contained a goodbye and apology to friends and family. Despite all of this and an arrest in January 1998 for stealing a computer, the true danger was tragically never noted.

Although school homicides are considered rare, the following TABLE 8-5 details some of those taking place between 2010 and 2017.

A Note on Frequency

Despite common perception, there is little evidence that the frequency of school shootings has increased dramatically over last several years or that there has been a national epidemic. In fact, Schildkraut, Elsass, Stafford, 2015 found that there are on average approximately 10 events per year; a rate that has been relatively consistent over time, though other estimates seem to vary widely given the absence of an agreed upon definition of a school shooting incident. This definitional ambiguity, along with extensive media coverage, can lead some to believe that they are at a higher likelihood of becoming victims, which may provoke increased levels of fear and anxiety among students and staff, has the potential to divert budgets to excessive security measures in schools, and can encourage zero-tolerance disciplinary policies that do more harm than good (Schildkraut, Elsass, Stafford, 2015). Instead, it has been suggested that a more comprehensive understanding of the relative risk of victimization and thorough threat assessment to evaluate troubling student behavior and resolve conflicts before they lead to more violent behavior are essential (Elsass, Schildkraut, & Stafford, 2016).

TABLE 8-5 School Shootings, 2010–2017

Date	City, State	Victim	Offender	Outcome
April 10, 2017	San Bernardino, California	Jonathan Martinez, 8, and his teacher, Karen Smith, shot.	Smith's estranged husband walked into her special needs classroom and opened fire with a large-caliber revolver.	Two other students were wounded. Cedric Anderson killed himself.
September 28, 2016	Greenville, South Carolina	Father killed; 14-year-old drove truck into elementary school fence and shot three people, killing a 6-year old	14-year-old teen overheard saying, "I hate my life" before shooting three people. Security guard tackled him on playground.	Pending trial and decision whether to be tried as an adult.
June 14, 2014	Troutdale, Oregon	14-year-old Emilio Hoffman shot in the school gym.	Jared Padgett took own life following shooting.	
October 24, 2014	Marysville, Washington	Four victims shot in school cafeteria.	Freshman Jaylen Fryberg died from self-inflicted gunshot.	Five dead, including gunman.
December 13, 2013	Centennial, Colorado	17-year-old Claire Davis died on December 21, 8 days after being shot.	Karl Pierson, 18, opened fire inside school, injuring one student and then taking his own life.	
October 21, 2013	Sparks, Nevada	Three people shot, killing teacher Mike Landsberry.	12-year-old Jose Reyes used parent's handgun to shoot three people and then took his own life.	
December 14, 2012	Newtown, Connecticut	Deaths of 20 children ages 6 and 7 and 6 adults (school staff/faculty) from gunshot wounds.	Adam Lanza killed mother before coming to Sandy Hook elementary.	Turns gun on himself; final count dead is 28.
February 27, 2012	Chardon, Ohio	Daniel Parmertor, 16, is killed and four others wounded. On February 28, Demetrius Hewlin, 16, dies from his wounds and Russell King Jr., 17, is declared brain dead.	T.J. Lane, 17, opened fire in the school.	Lane was sentenced to life in prison on March 2013. On September 11, 2014, Lane escaped from prison. He was captured early the next morning.
January 5, 2011	Omaha, Nebraska	Vice Principal Vicki Kasper died later at hospital.	17-year-old Robert Butler, Jr. opened fire on Principal Curtis Case and Vice Principal Kasper.	Butler killed himself a mile from the school.
February 5, 2010	Madison, Alabama	14-year-old Todd Brown died after being shot in a school hallway.	Fellow ninth-grader Hammad Memon pleads guilty to murder.	Sentenced to 30 years in prison; eligible for parole in 15 years.

Indications and Threats of Violence

After a violent incident has taken place, retracing an offender's past and identifying clues that in retrospect could have been signs of danger can yield significant, useful information. However, even clues that appear to help interpret past events cannot be taken as predictors of similar events in the future. At this time no research has identified traits and characteristics that can reliably distinguish school shooters from other students, including those who may threaten but never carry out their threats. Many students appear to have traits and characteristics similar to those observed in students who were involved in school shootings. They dress a similar way, they have similar tastes in music, they are loners, many even have felt bullied, yet the vast majority of these students have never acted out in a violent way. Simply put, there is no "profile" of a school shooter. However, lessons can be learned from every school shooting incident and every school shooter. In 1999, following the mass shooting at Columbine High School, the U.S. Federal Bureau of Investigation's (FBI) National Center for the Analysis of Violent Crime hosted the first of its kind conference on school shootings. Based on the data generated from this conference on types of threats, combined with the FBI's extensive experience in the area of threat assessment, in 2000 the FBI published a monograph titled, "The School Shooter: A Threat Assessment Perspective" (O'Toole, 1999). The following is based on those conclusions.

A **threat** is defined by *Webster's* dictionary as an expression of intention to inflict evil, injury, or damage. A threat can be spoken, written, or symbolic; for example, motioning with one's hands as though shooting at another person. Threats also carry varying levels of intensity, and, fortunately, most people who threaten are unlikely to carry out their threat. However, as in the case example at the beginning of this chapter, a relatively common threat of one student toward another can at times result in tragic consequences. Thus, all threats must be taken seriously and evaluated. A comprehensive threat assessment program should include not only procedures to assess a threat but also to assess a student's behavior and other communications that could indicate future violence. Threats can be classified into four types: direct, indirect, veiled, and conditional (TABLE 8-6).

Threat assessment requires specialized training and generally consists of four elements: (1) personality dynamics of the individual issuing the threat, (2) family dynamics, (3) school dynamics, and (4) social dynamics. Hong, Cho, Allen-Meares, and Espelage (2011) developed an ecological assessment of the Columbine tragedy using this multiple element analysis. *Personality dynamics* included means of managing stress and conflicts, expression of anger,

TABLE 8-6 Types of Threats

Type of Threat	Definition
Direct threat	Identifies a specific act against a specific target. Delivered in a straightforward, clear, and explicit manner: "I am going to place a bomb in the school's gym."
Indirect threat	Tends to be vague, unclear, and ambiguous. Plan, intended victim, motivation, and other aspects of the threat are masked or equivocal. Suggests that a violent act *could* occur, not that it *will* occur: "If I wanted to, I could kill everyone at this school!"
Veiled threat	Strongly implies but does not explicitly threaten violence. Clearly hints at a possible violent act but leaves it to the potential victim to interpret the message: "We would all be better off without you around anymore."
Conditional threat	Often seen in extortion cases. Warns that a violent act will happen unless certain demands or terms are met: "If you don't pay me 1 million dollars, I will place a bomb in the school."

Data from: O'Toole, M.E. 1999. *The School Shooter: A Threat Assessment Perspective*. FBI Critical Incident Response Group, National Center for the Analysis of Violent Crime, Quantico, VA.

resiliency, response to authority, need for control, and ability to empathize with others. From this perspective both Eric and Dylan had undergone counseling for depression, impulsivity, and antisocial behavior. Eric had paranoid traits and unconstrained aggression, and Dylan was described as overly sensitive to shame and humiliation. Thus, consistent with literature on risk factors, the perpetrators were primarily male, had histories of mental and emotional distress, and also had histories of aggression and antisocial behavior (Hong, Cho, & Lee, 2010). *Family dynamics* encompasses both role-modeling in the family and the ability of the family to provide a supportive environment. Questions have been raised about the family environments of Dylan and Eric and the fact that parents did not see the evidence reported in the youth's journals, the accumulation of weapons, and the concerns reported by friends and neighbors (Hong et al., 2011). Strong parent–child relationships and positive parental modeling are protective factors against violence. School dynamics include the culture, rules, and roles of people within the school. Dylan and Eric did not fit into the school culture and were frequently taunted by kids. Peer victimization and poor peer relationships are common themes in postmortem examinations of school shootings (Hong et al., 2010). Finally, *social dynamics* involve issues related to larger society. Dylan and Eric were obsessed by violent video games and attended gun shows, both of which are common features of American society. Lack of access to mental health services

TABLE 8-7 Levels of Threat Risk

Level of Risk	Characteristics
Low level: Poses a minimal risk to the victim and public safety.	Vague and indirect. Information is inconsistent, implausible, or lacks detail. Lacks realism. Content suggests person is unlikely to carry it out.
Medium level: Could be carried out, although it may not appear to be entirely realistic.	More direct and concrete. Wording suggests some thought as to how the act will be carried out. May be a general indication of a possible place and time that still falls well short of a detailed plan. No strong indication of preparatory steps, although there may be some veiled reference or ambiguous or inconclusive evidence pointing to that possibility. May contain an allusion to a book or movie that shows the planning of a violent act or a vague, general statement about the availability of weapons. May be a specific statement seeking to convey that the threat is not empty: "I'm serious!" or "I really mean this!"
High level: Appears to pose an imminent and serious danger to the safety of others.	Direct, specific, and plausible. Suggests concrete steps have been taken toward carrying it out, for example, has acquired or practiced with a weapon or has had the victim under surveillance. Example: "At 8 o'clock tomorrow morning, I intend to shoot the principal. That's when he is in the office by himself. I have a 9mm. Believe me, I know what I am doing. I am sick and tired of the way he runs this school." Direct, specific as to the victim, motivation, weapon, place, and time, and indicates the threatener knows his or her target's schedule and has made preparations to act on the threat.

Data from O'Toole, M.E. 1999. *The School Shooter: A Threat Assessment Perspective*. FBI Critical Incident Response Group, National Center for the Analysis of Violent Crime, Quantico, VA.

and availability of weapons are risk factors for violence of all types (Hong et al., 2010). For most individuals this does not result in violence, but when **personality** and other factors interact, it can support unhealthy beliefs and provide access to means of violence. The FBI divides risk into the categories listed in **TABLE 8-7**.

Effects of School Shooting

The tragic events of Virginia Tech, Northern Illinois University, and Columbine have had a wide range of impacts on campuses. One impact is the increase of security systems, including emergency communication systems through text, email, and phone alerts; increased security staff; and allowing security staff and others to carry concealed weapons on campus (Kaminsky, Koons-Witt,

Thompson, & Weiss, 2010). A second impact is on students who were present at schools where shootings occur. Such exposure not surprisingly can result in symptoms of posttraumatic stress. Factors that are protective and are associated with fewer posttraumatic stress symptoms include having a strong social support network, family support, and a sense of self-worth (Grills-Taquechel, Littleton, & Axsom, 2011). Interestingly, student exposure to media attention of the event has not been found to be associated with higher posttraumatic stress among those at the school, but being interviewed by the media was associated with higher levels of posttraumatic stress when compared to those who refused to be interviewed or those who were not approached by reporters (Haravuori, Suomalainen, Berg, Kiviruusu, & Marttunen, 2011). Another impact is generalized fear. In one of the few studies examining fear in college students on other campuses after the Virginia Tech and Northern Illinois University shootings, researchers found that students had significantly higher fears of being attacked with a weapon or murdered on campus. The authors concluded that this is largely due to media coverage of mass shootings that highlight and magnify this relatively rare yet devastating form of school violence (Kaminsky et al., 2010).

◼ Conclusion

Violence is a tragic yet all too common aspect of children's and youths' experience in North American schools. The most common form of violence involves bullying, where one child or young person experiences physical, verbal, or social violence caused by peers. Society has become increasingly aware that students as well as teachers can be victims of such behaviors. Although some may argue this has always been a reality of school life, the consequences can be devastating, leading to mental health problems and further violence directed at one's self (in the form of suicide) or others. Gang activity is the second most common form of violence on school property, preying on vulnerable youth both as gang members and victims. Violence in this case is often paradoxically caused by perceived threats from rival groups. School shootings are rare occurrences, but the dramatic nature and the simultaneous loss of multiple lives results in large-scale media attention, fueling fears and reinforcing the offenders' need for attention. Solutions to school violence are complex and require system-wide interventions that provide mental health and social services to young people in distress, provide support for families who are struggling, address violence attitudes within the culture of the school, and consider societal influences that condone violent actions.

Key Terms

Bullying: A form of habitual aggressive behavior that is hurtful and deliberate.

Conditional threat: Warns that a violent act will happen unless certain demands or terms are met.

Corporal punishment: punishment intended to cause pain.

Direct threat: Identifies a specific act against a specific target.

Indirect threat: Tends to be vague, unclear, and ambiguous.

Personality: Pattern of collective character, behavioral, temperamental, emotional, and mental traits of an individual.

Physical bullying: Pushing, hitting, tripping, spitting at, and physical beating.

School dynamics: Patterns of behavior, thinking, beliefs, customs, traditions, roles, and values that exist in a school's culture.

Social bullying: Rumors and behaviors aimed at deliberate social exclusion.

Threat: Expression of intent to do harm or to act out violently against someone or something.

Veiled threat: Strongly implies but does not explicitly threaten violence.

Verbal bullying: Taunts, threats, name calling, and derogatory comments.

Youth gang: A self-formed association of peers who have in common some sense of identity, some degree of permanence and organization, and an elevated level of involvement in delinquent or criminal activity.

Discussion Questions

1. Given the multiple factors that contribute to bullying, what advice would you give a parent who is concerned his or her child might be bullied?

2. What types of legislation and/or school-based policies may more effectively address issues of gang violence in schools?

3. How might teacher training programs more effectively educate teachers to deal with violence in schools?

4. How might the media influence the phenomenon of school shootings? How can such influence be mitigated?

5. Discuss the factors that might influence fluctuations in school violence.

Resources

Bullying Canadahttp://www.bullyingcanada.ca

CDC Division of Violence Prevention www.cdc.gov/violenceprevention/

CDC Division of Adolescent and School Health www.cdc.gov/healthyyouth/

National Gang Intelligence Center (FBI) http://www.fbi.gov/about-us/investigate /vc_majorthefts/gangs/ngic

National Youth Gang Center (U.S. Bureau of Justice Assistance) http://www .nationalgangcenter.gov

RCMP Gang Awareness Quick Facts http://bc.rcmp.ca/ViewPage.action?site NodeId=453&languageId=1&contentId=3871

StopBullying.gov http://www.stopbullying.gov

STRYVE www.cdc.gov/violenceprevention/stryve/

Surgeon General's Report on Youth Violence http://www.ncbi.nlm.nih.gov /books/NBK44294/

References

Achenbach, J., & Russakoff, D. (1999, April 29). Teen shooter's life paints and anti-social portrait. *Washington Post*, p. A1.

Arciaga, M., Sakamoto, W., & Jones, E. (2010). *Responding to gangs in school settings*. National Gang Center Bulletin. Washington, DC: U.S. Department of Justice.

Blosnich, J., & Bossarte, R. (2011). Low-level violence in schools: Is there an association between school safety measures and peer victimization? *Journal of School Health*, 81(2), 107–113.

Bill C-14. (2009). An act to amend the Criminal Code (organized crime and protection of justice system participants) LS-633E. Retrieved from http://www.parl.gc.ca/About/ Parliament/LegislativeSummaries/Bills_ls.asp?lang=E&ls=c14&Parl=40&Ses =2&source=library_prb

Carlie, M. K. (2002). Into the abyss: A personal journey into the world of street gangs (Part 11: How to join a gang). Available from http://faculty.missouristate.edu/M /MichaelCarlie/what_I_learned_about/gangs/join_a_gang.htm

Casteel, C., Peek-Asa, C., & Limbos, M. (2007). Predictors of non-fatal assault injury to public school teachers in Los Angeles City. *American Journal of Industrial Medicine*, 50, 932–939.

Cathcart, R. (2008, February 23). Boy's killing labeled a hate crime, stuns a town. Retrieved from http://www.nytimes.com/2008/02/23/us/23oxnard.html

Centers for Disease Control and Prevention (CDC). (2011). Bullying among middle school and high school students—Massachusetts, 2009. *Morbidity and Mortality Weekly Report, 60*, 465–471.

Chen, J., & Astor, R. (2008). Students' reports of violence against teachers in Taiwanese schools. *Journal of School Violence, 8*(1), 2–17.

Clark, J. (2017). Where corporal punishment is still used in schools: Its roots run deep. North Carolina Public Radio: Hear on all things considered. April 12, 2017.

Decker, S., & Curry, D. (2002). Gangs, gang homicides, and gang loyalty: Organized crimes or disorganized criminals? *Journal of Criminal Justice, 30*, 343–352.

Delisi, M., Barnes, J., Beaver, K., & Gibson, C. (2009). Delinquent gangs and adolescent victimization revisited. *Criminal Justice and Behavior, 36*(8), 808–823.

Dupper, D. R., & Dingus, A. E. M. (2008). Corporal punishment in U.S. public schools: A continuing challenge for school social workers. *Children & Schools, 30*(4), 243–250.

Dzuka, J., & Dalbert, C. (2007). Student violence against teachers. *European Psychologist, 12*(4), 253–260.

Education Week (2016). Department of Education Civil Rights division, 2013–2014.

Egley, A., & Howell, J. (2011). *Highlights of the 2009 National Youth Gang Survey.* Juvenile Justice Fact Sheet. Washington, DC: U.S. Department of Justice.

Elsass, H. J., Schildkraut, J., & Stafford, M. (2016). Studying school shootings: Challenges and considerations for research. *American Journal of Criminal Justice, 41*(3), 444–464.

Farrington, D., & Ttofi, M. (2009). How to reduce school bullying. *Victims & Offenders, 4*(4), 321–326.

Federal Bureau of Investigation (FBI). (2010). *2011 National gang threat assessment: Emerging trends.* Retrieved from https://www.fbi.gov/stats-services/publications/2011-national-gang-threat-assessment

Gendron, B., Williams, K., & Guerra, N. (2011). An analysis of bullying among students within schools: Estimating the effects of individual normative beliefs, self-esteem, and school climate. *Journal of School Violence, 10*(2), 150–164.

Gibbs, N., & Roche, T. (1999, December 20). The Columbine tapes. *Time.* Retrieved from http://www.time.com/time/magazine/article/0,9171,992873,00.html

Gottfredson, G., & Gottfredson, D. (2001). Gang problems and gang programs in a national sample of schools. Retrieved from www.gottfredson.com/Gang_Problems_%20Programs/report.pdf

Grills-Taquechel, A., Littleton, H., & Axsom, D. (2011). Social support, world assumptions, and exposure as predictors of anxiety and quality of life following mass trauma. *Journal of Anxiety Disorders, 25*, 498–506.

Haravuori, H., Suomalainen, L., Berg, N., Kiviruusu, O., & Marttunen, M. (2011). Effects of media exposure on adolescents traumatized in a school shooting. *Journal of Traumatic Stress, 24*(1), 70–77.

Harrell, E. (2005). *Violence by gang members, 1993–2003*. Washington, DC: Bureau of Justice Statistics.

Hong, J., Cho, H., Allen-Meares, P., & Espelage, D. (2011). The social ecology of the Columbine High School shootings. *Children and Youth Services Review, 33*, 861–868.

Hong, J., Cho, H., & Lee, A. (2010). Revisiting Virginia Tech shootings: An ecological systems analysis. *Journal of Loss and Trauma, 15*, 561–575.

Howell, J. (2010). *Gang prevention: An overview of resources and programs*. Juvenile Justice Bulletin. Washington, DC: Department of Justice, Office of Juvenile Justice and Delinquency Prevention.

Howell, J., Egley, A., Tita, G., & Griffiths, E. (2011). *US gang problem trends and seriousness, 1996–2009*. National Gang Center Bulletin, no. 6. Washington, DC: U.S. Department of Justice.

Kaminsky, R., Koons-Witt, B., Thompson, N., & Weiss, D. (2010). The impacts of the Virginia Tech and Northern Illinois University shootings on fear of crime on campus. *Journal of Criminal Justice, 38*, 88–98.

Khoury-Kassabri, M., Astor, R., & Benbenishty, R. (2009). Middle Eastern adolescents' perpetration of school violence against peers and teachers. *Journal of Interpersonal Violence, 24*(1), 159–182.

Kowalski, R., Guimetti, G., Schroeder, A., & Lattanner, M. (2014). Bullying in the digital age: A critical review and meta-analysis of cyberbullying research among youth. *Psychological Bulletin, 140*(4), 1073–1137.

Langton, L. (2010). *Gang units in large local law enforcement agencies, 2007*. Bureau of Justice Statistics Special Report. Washington, DC: U.S. Department of Justice.

Larkin, R. (2007). *Comprehending Columbine*. Philadelphia: Temple University Press.

Lee, C. (2011). An ecological systems approach to bullying behaviors among middle school students in the United States. *Journal of Interpersonal Violence, 26*(8), 1664–1693.

Mishna, F., & Alaggia, R. (2005). Weighing the risks: A child's decision to disclose peer victimization. *Children & Schools, 27*(4), 217–226.

Mishna, F., Pepler, D., & Weiner, J. (2006). Factors associated with perceptions and responses to bullying situations by children, parents, teachers and principals. *Victims and Offenders, 1*, 255–288.

Mishna, F., Wiener, J., & Pepler, D. (2008). Some of my best friends—Experiences of bullying within friendships. *School Psychology International, 29*(5), 549–573.

Moore, J., & Hagedorn, J. (2001). *Female gangs: A focus on research*. Juvenile Justice Bulletin. Washington, DC: U.S. Department of Justice.

Musu-Gillette, L., Zhang, A., Wang, K., Zhang, J., & Oudekerk, B. (2017). *Indicators of School Crime and Safety*: 2016. NCJ250650. National Center for Education Statistics, U.S. Department of Education, and Bureau of Justice Statistics, Office of Justice Programs, U.S. Department of Justice. Washington, DC.

Nansel, T., Overpeck, M., Pilla, R., Ruan, W., Simons-Morton, B., & Scheidt, P. (2001). Bullying behaviors among US youth: Prevalence and association with psychological adjustment. *Journal of the American Medical Association, 285*, 2094–2100.

National Youth Gang Center. (2011). Frequently asked questions. Retrieved from http://www.nationalgangcenter.gov

O'Toole, M. E. (1999). *The school shooter: A threat assessment perspective.* Quantico, VA: FBI Critical Incident Response Group, National Center for the Analysis of Violent Crime.

Public Safety Canada. (2008). *Bullying prevention: Nature and extent of bullying in Canada.* Ottawa: National Crime Prevention Centre.

Robers, S., Kemp, J., & Truman, J. (2010). Indicators of School Crime and Safety: 2010 https://nces.ed.gov/pubs2011/2011002.pdf. National Center for Education Statistics, U.S. Department of Education, and Bureau of Justice Statistics, Office of Justice Programs, U.S. Department of Justice. Washington, DC. Retrieved at https://nces.ed.gov/pubs2011/2011002.pdf

Salzman, A. (2004, May 15). Mother of boy in suicide is spared prison term. *New York Times*, B(6), p. 4.

Santora, M. (2003, September 27). Case tries to link a mother to her boy's suicide. *New York Times*, B(2), p. 1.

Schildkraut, J., Elsass, J., & Stafford, M. (2015). Could it happen here? Moral panic, school shootings, and fear of crime among college students. *Crime, Law and Social Change, 63*(1–2), 91–110.

Schildkraut, J., & Hernandez, T. (2014). Laws that bit the bullet: A review of legislative responses to school shootings. *American Journal of Criminal Justice, 39*(2), 358–374.

Setoodeh, R. (2008, July 19). Young, gay and murdered. Retrieved from http://www.newsweek.com/2008/07/18/young-gay-and-murdered.html

Seymour, A., & Ray, D. (1996). *Victims of gang violence: A new frontier in victim services*, special report. Washington, DC: U.S. Department of Justice, Office for Victims of Crime.

Slonje, R., & Smith, P. (2008). Cyberbullying: Another main type of bullying? *Scandinavian Journal of Psychology, 49*(2), 147–154.

Slonje, R., Smith, P., & Frisén, A. (2013). The nature of cyberbullying, and strategies for prevention. *Computers in Human Behavior, 29*(1), 26–32.

Sharkey, J., Shekhtmeyster, Z., Chavez-Lopez, L., Norris, E., & Sass, L. (2011). The protective influence of gangs: Can schools compensate? *Aggression and Violent Behavior, 16*, 45–54.

Society for Adolescent Medicine. (1992). Position paper: Corporal punishment in the schools. *Journal of Adolescent Health, 13*, 240–246.

Sparks, S.D., & Harwin, A. (2016) Corporal punishment: Inside Education Week analysis. Inside School Research. Retrieved from http://blogs.edweek.org/edweek/inside-school-research/2016/08/corporal_punishment_frequently_asked_questions.html

Stowe, S. (2003, October 7). Boy who sought help was seen as target. *New York Times*, B(1), p. 5.

Thornberg, R., & Knutsen, S. (2011). Teenager's explanations of bullying. *Child and Youth Care Forum, 40*, 177–192.

Thrasher, F. (1927). *The gang: A study of 1,313 gangs in Chicago.* Chicago: University of Chicago Press.

Ttofi, M., & Farrington, D. (2008). Bullying: Short-term and long-term effects, and the importance of defiance theory in explanation and prevention. *Victims and Offenders, 3,* 289–312.

U.S. Department of Health and Human Services. (n.d.). What is bullying? Retrieved from http://www.stopbullying.gov/what-is-bullying/definition/index.html

Walker, R. (2008). Gangs or us: Gangsta girls. Retrieved from http://www.gangsorus .com

Wang, C., Berry, B., & Swearer, I. S. (2013). The Critical Role of School Climate in Effective Bullying Prevention, *Theory into Practice,* Vol. 52, (4) pp. 296–302.

Wilson, C. M., Douglas, K.S., & Lyon, D. R. (2011). Violence against teachers: Prevalence and consequences. *Journal of Interpersonal Violence, 26*(12).

Wynne, S., & Joo, H. (2011). Predictors of school victimization: Individual, familial and school factors. *Crime and Delinquency, 57*(3), 458–488.

CHAPTER 9

Intimate Partner Violence

OBJECTIVES

- To identify the scope of intimate partner violence
- To identify legal responses to intimate partner violence
- To discuss dating violence
- To identify impacts of intimate partner violence on victims and on children who witness the violence
- To discuss typologies of offenders
- To discuss homicide in the context of intimate partner violence
- To review intervention programs that address intimate partner violence

KEY TERMS

Battered woman syndrome

Battered woman syndrome defense

Complex posttraumatic stress disorder

Domestic violence

Intimate partner violence (IPV)

Learned helplessness

Posttraumatic stress disorder (PTSD)

Protection orders

Wife battering

CASE

By all accounts R&B singers Rihanna, then aged 20, and Chris Brown, then aged 19, had it all (**FIGURE 9-1**.) They were frequently pictured together in the press and were referred to as having a fairy-tale romance. Rihanna, a Barbados-born star, had sold nearly 10 million tracks in 2008, the highest number of any singer that year. Brown had made his debut at the age of 16 with a self-titled album that sold over 2 million copies and featured a hit single that topped the Billboard 100 list. He continued to roll out albums, and by 2009 his eighth top 20 hit was on the charts. But in February 2009, the night both he and Rihanna were scheduled to appear on the Grammys, Chris Brown surrendered himself to the Los Angeles Police Department and was booked on felony assault of an unidentified female (Cruz, 2009; *LA Times*,

FIGURE 9-1 Rihanna: A victim of intimate partner violence.

© Featureflash Photo Agency/Shutterstock, Inc.

2009). Ten days later a photograph showing Rihanna's bruised and bloodied face, reported to be part of the police investigation, was leaked online (Swash, 2009). Gossip reports suggested that in interviews with the police Rihanna had indicated that this was not the first time Brown had been abusive toward her, and that his abuse was becoming more frequent and more violent. That same year Chris Brown pled guilty for the assault and was sentenced to five years of probation and six months of community service. He was also issued a five-year restraining order that required him to stay at least 10 yards away at events. In July 2009 Brown released a YouTube video in which he apologized for his behavior, explaining he would have made an apology earlier but was advised not to by his attorneys (CNN, 2009).

Rihanna has since dated Drake, Travis Scott, and Matt Kemp, and was even linked with actor Leo DiCaprio in the years since her breakup with Chris Brown, but the two have not publicly been seen together in years.

As for Chris Brown, he reportedly is not giving up his obsession with Rihanna. The rapper, whose relationship with Rihanna ended when he assaulted her back in 2009, reportedly believes that the two will reunite in the future. According to *Hollywood Life*, the musician claims that there is still a chance for a reunion with his ex. "[At] the end of the day, Chris knows he's still on Ri's mind," an insider source claims. "And he still loves her dearly. Chris doesn't believe for a second that romance and intimate relationship with Rihanna is over for good. It's just a matter of time" (Skwiot, 2016).

Introduction

Intimate partner violence (IPV) is any behavior within an intimate relationship that causes physical, psychological, or sexual harm to those in the relationship. It includes acts of physical aggression (slapping, hitting, kicking, or beating), psychological abuse (intimidation, constant belittling), forced sexual intercourse, or any other controlling behavior (isolating a person from family and friends, monitoring a person's movements, or restricting access to information or assistance). This definition includes current and former spouses and dating partners and people in both heterosexual and lesbian, gay, bisexual and transgender (LGBT) or same-sex relationships. This is differentiated from the previously used terms **wife battering** and **domestic violence**, which focused on violence between spouses and tended to be used synonymously with the abuse of women. These terms reflect the history of study, policy, and interventions in the area of IPV that began with the recognition of assaultive behavior toward women that was perpetrated by their husbands.

Wife battering was an issue for concern in North America from the time the Puritans arrived from England. Family violence was seen to threaten an individual's and the community's standing before God. It threatened the social and political stability of the Puritans' Godly settlement. The wife-beating husband shamed Christianity, dishonored God, and dishonored himself. The Puritan communities dealt with family violence with the combined forces of the church, the state, and the community. Meddling was considered to be a virtue, and consequently neighbors watched, church courts extracted confessions, and civil courts upheld laws and punished wrongdoers. The consequence for wrongdoing was often shame and disgrace before the entire congregation (Pleck, 1987).

However, the goal of this vigor was to restore family order, not to protect individual rights (Pleck, 1987). Abused members were never removed from the home, and despite the reported vigor in exposing and punishing family violence, Pleck (1987), an American historian, could locate only four cases in the Plymouth courts from 1663 to 1682. Yet, although the Puritan laws against family violence were rarely enacted, they did serve as a guide for community moral principles. As the religious community gave way to pluralism, the state relinquished its commitment to enforce morality.

During the 1800s women were viewed as guardians of the domestic fireside. Women had the power to reform the morals of their husbands and sons, but this power was to remain in the home. The temperance movement challenged this, highlighting the plight of abused women and placing women's rights ahead of preservation of the family. Although they originally did not advocate policies to aid victims of wife assault directly, they considered violence to be an evil consequence of alcohol. Therefore, if alcohol was prohibited, violence would end. In the 1840s American women's rights activists joined the temperance movement and called for divorce for drunkards' wives and the right for women to have their own earnings. Nevertheless, divorce was advocated only in the most extreme circumstances (Pleck, 1987).

In 1641, following the British precedent, the Massachusetts Body of Liberties provided that "Everie marryed woeman shall be free from bodile correction or stripes by her husband, unless it be in his own defense upon her assault" (as cited in Pleck, 1987). However, divorce on the grounds of severe cruelty was not permitted until 1870. Also in the 1870s, legislation was enacted in America for public flogging at whipping posts for abusive husbands. In three states these laws were not abolished until 1948 to 1952. Although this punishment was infrequently used, many believed the threat to be an effective deterrent.

In 1885 the Chicago Protective Agency for Women and Children was established for the purposes of providing legal aid, court advocacy, and personal assistance to battered women and their children. This is the first recorded women's shelter in North America, and women and their children could stay for up to 4 weeks. Between 1915 and 1920 another 25 cities established protective agencies for women, although most were closed by the 1940s. The next period of interest and assistance for women who were battered did not occur until the 1970s, during which time the feminist rights movement successfully pushed for the opening of assistance programs and shelters in the United States, Canada, and the United Kingdom (Roberts, 2002).

By 1977 there were 89 shelters in the United States for women who were abused, and by 1990 this number had risen to 850. As of 2017, 1,500 emergency battered women shelters exist in the United States with the goal of enabling each woman to be independent in order to care for herself and her family (Tracy, 2017). In Canada in 1980 Linda MacLeod made the first attempt to estimate the incidence of wife assault in Canada and suggested that 1 in 10 Canadian women were victims of intimate violence (MacLeod, 1980). As public awareness and outrage over the issue grew, commitment to services for women, public education, and legislative reform increased. By 1987 MacLeod documented significant gains, applauding the progress in bringing the problem of woman abuse from the private sphere into the public domain (MacLeod, 1987).

The number of shelters across Canada increased from 78 to 400 between 1978 and 1989 (Denham & Gillespie, 1998). By April 16, 2014, 627 shelters for abused women were operating across Canada (Statistics Canada, 2015). Funding for woman abuse programs in North America continued to build until the passage of the Violence Against Women Act of 1994 by the U.S. federal government. This legislation included a $1.2 billion appropriation for 1995 to 2000 to improve criminal justice responses, expand community services, improve safety measures, and provide support for education and health-based services.

Although the attention to woman abuse has been critical to improving the lives of women who are affected by violence, more recently views of IPV have expanded to include others who are affected by violence. One focus has been the impact on children as witnesses of parental violence. Another focus has been on men as victims either in heterosexual relationships or in same-sex relationships. A final focus has been on women who are victimized in lesbian relationships. The important focus on women traditionally has left these other victims in the shadows, and their suffering has gone unacknowledged.

Scope of the Problem

In the United States, IPV accounted for 22% of violent crimes against women and 4% of violent crimes against men between 2001 and 2005. Both academic research studies and national agencies have continued publishing their findings and their methodologies provide an opportunity to understand trends of both increase and decrease in a victimization such as intimate partner violence. In 2007, 24% of female homicide victims were killed by a spouse or ex-spouse, 21% were killed by a boyfriend or girlfriend, and 19% were killed by another family member. In 2008, 99% of the IPV against women was committed by male offenders, and 83% of IPV against men was committed by female partners. Black females were twice as likely as White females to be killed by a spouse and four times more likely to be killed by a boyfriend or girlfriend. Of male homicide victims, 2% were killed by a spouse or ex-spouse and 3% were killed by a girlfriend or boyfriend (Catalano, Smith, Snyder, & Rand, 2009). From 2001 to 2005 women who lived in households with lower annual incomes experienced the highest average annual rates of nonfatal intimate partner victimization; however, women remained at greater risk than men within each income level. On average, between 2001 and 2005, children were residents of households in 38% of cases where women were victims of IPV and 21% of the incidents involving men as victims. The presence of alcohol or drugs was reported in 42% of all cases of nonfatal IPV (Catalano, 2007). The National Crime Victimization Survey estimated that more than 50% of homes with calls to law enforcement for severe domestic violence contained children younger than 12 years of age (Catalano, 2007).

Efforts have been made to determine global figures on IPV. Since the 1993 World Conference on Human Rights and the Declaration on the Elimination of Violence Against Women, the international community has acknowledged that violence against women is an important public health, social policy, and human rights concern. However, documenting the magnitude of violence against women and producing reliable comparative data to guide policy and monitor progress has been difficult (Devries et al., 2013).

Based on U.S. national and state data analyzed by NISVS (Smith et al., 2017), physical violence by an intimate partner was experienced by almost a third of women (32.4%) and more than a quarter of men (28.3%) in their lifetime. State estimates ranged from 25.4% to 42.1% (all states) for women and 17.8% to 36.1% (all states) for men. Data on severe physical violence reported nationally was experienced by 23.2% of U.S. women and 13.9% of U.S. men during their lifetime (NISVS, 2017).

According to Statistics Canada, in 2015 almost 92,000 people in Canada were victims of IPV, representing just over a quarter (28%) of all victims of police-reported violent crime. Four out of five victims of police-reported intimate partner violence were women (79%), representing about 72,000 female victims. Victimization by an intimate partner was the most common form of police-reported violent crime committed against females (42% of female victims, compared to 12% of male victims). In contrast, more males relative to females were victimized by a friend or an acquaintance (40% vs. 28%) or by a stranger (36% vs. 15%). Violence within dating relationships was more common than violence within spousal relationships, according to police-reported data. A current or former dating partner was the perpetrator against 54% of IPV victims, compared to a current or former legally married or common-law spouse (44% of victims). These proportions were similar among male and female victims (Allen, 2016).

Similar to previous years, close to 7 out of 10 Canadian victims of family violence reported to police in 2015 were young girls or women (67%). One-third (33%) of all female victims of police-reported violent crime had been victimized by a family member, a proportion almost double that of male victims (18%). Meanwhile, males were proportionally more likely than females to have been victimized by someone outside the family (82% vs. 67%) (Burczycka, 2016).

In 2015, police reported a total of 163 family-related homicides in Canada, translating into a rate of 4.5 victims per 1 million population. The rate of family-related homicide has decreased by 49% since 1985, in line with the overall decrease in the Canadian homicide rate over the same time period (−44%) (Mulligan, 2016).

On November 24, 2005, the first-ever World Health Organization (WHO) study on domestic violence revealed that IPV is the most common form of violence in women's lives, much more so than assault or rape by strangers or acquaintances. The study reported on the enormous toll that physical and sexual violence by husbands and partners has on the health and well-being of women around the world and the extent to which IPV is still largely hidden. The study was based on interviews with over 24,000 women residing in urban and rural areas in 10 countries, including Brazil, Ethiopia, Japan, Peru, Samoa, Serbia, and Thailand, and the findings indicated that women are at much greater risk from violence in their own homes than on the street (WHO, 2005). One-fourth to one-half of the study's female victims of physical assault by their husbands or partners stated they had sustained physical injuries as a result of the battering, and more than 20% of the women who reported physical violence said they had never told anyone about the abuse before the interview. Despite serious medical consequences, only a very small percentage of victims ever sought help from healthcare providers or the police; instead, those who sought help tended to reach out to neighbors and extended family members. Also significant was the finding that in most countries studied 4% to 12% of pregnant women interviewed reported they had been beaten by the unborn child's father during pregnancy, with a disturbing 50% indicating they had been punched or kicked in the abdomen (WHO, 2005). This landmark WHO study concluded that domestic violence by husbands and other intimate partners is still a largely hidden phenomenon around the world. It highlighted the urgent need for policymakers and public health officials to address the health and human costs and for countries to develop policies and programs aimed at preventing and eliminating violence against women and children (WHO, 2005).

A summary of U.S. IPV statistics can be found in TABLE 9-1.

TABLE 9-1 Intimate Partner Violence: U.S. Statistics

- On a typical day, domestic violence hotlines nationwide receive approximately 20,800 calls.
- The presence of a gun in a domestic violence situation increases the risk of homicide by 500%.
- Domestic violence accounts for 15% of all violent crime
- Domestic violence is most common among women between the ages of 18 and 24.
- 19% of domestic violence involves a weapon.
- Domestic victimization is correlated with a higher rate of depression and suicidal behavior.
- Only 34% of people who are injured by intimate partners receive medical care for their injuries

Data from: Catalano, S. 2007. Intimate partner violence in the United States. Retrieved May 2, 2009 from http://www.ojp.usdoj.gov/bjs/intimate/ipv.htm; Catalano, S., Smith, E., Snyder, H. & Rand, M. 2009. Female victims of violence. Bureau of Justice Statistics. NCJ 228356. Washington: US Department of Justice; World Health Organization. 2005. Landmark study on domestic violence.

Dating Violence

Violence does not occur only in marital or common-law relationships, it also occurs in relationships in the context of dating. *Dating violence* is defined as physical, sexual, psychological, or emotional violence within a dating relationship, including stalking. It can occur in person or electronically and might occur between a current or former dating partner. Different terms have been used to describe teen dating violence, including *relationship abuse, intimate partner violence, relationship violence, dating abuse, domestic abuse,* and *domestic violence.*

Dating violence is widespread with serious long-term and short-term effects. Many teens do not report it because they are afraid to tell friends and family. A 2011 nationwide survey by the Centers for Disease Control and Prevention (CDC) found that 23% of females and 14% of males who ever experienced rape, physical violence, or stalking by an intimate partner first experienced some form of partner violence between 11 and 17 years of age. The 2013 National Youth Risk Behavior Survey found that approximately 10% of high school students reported physical victimization and 10% reported sexual victimization from a dating partner in the 12 months before they were surveyed (Vagi et al., 2015).

Violence is related to certain risk factors. Risks of having unhealthy relationships increase for teens who (CDC, 2017):

- Believe that dating violence is acceptable.
- Are depressed, anxious, or have other symptoms of trauma.
- Display aggression towards peers or display other aggressive behaviors.
- Use drugs or illegal substances.
- Engage in early sexual activity and have multiple sexual partners.
- Have a friend involved in dating violence.
- Have conflicts with a partner.
- Witness or experience violence in the home.

A tragic case of teen dating violence happened in Wayland, Massachusetts, in July 2011. The body of Lauren Astley, 18, was found in a marshy area by a bicyclist. Her throat had been cut and a bungee cord had been wrapped around her neck. Her ex-boyfriend, 18-year-old Nate Fujita, a high school football player, was charged with first-degree murder. Police found blood in his garage and other locations to tie him to the murder. At trial, the prosecutor described the case as teen dating violence. Lauren had broken off the relationship. Fujita did not have a prior criminal record, and there was no indication that he had abused Astley while they were dating. But Astley's friends told police he kept trying to reestablish the relationship in the months following the breakup. He would call her on her cell phone at the mall where she worked and text her constantly; she kept telling him to stop and to leave her alone. In the month after graduation Fujita became angrier at the breakup, isolated himself, and dropped out of the social scene. An analysis of his texts shows Fujita becoming angrier and angrier, sending profanity-laced comments to friends. Phone records indicated three calls between Fujita and Astley the night she was murdered. Lauren agreed to meet him at his house, and that was the last text she sent (Smith, 2013).

The three-week trial ended with a guilty verdict and Nate Fujita was sentenced to life in prison without the possibility of parole.

Teenagers should be made aware of the following warning signs of an abusive dating relationship: the partner checks the person's cell phone or email without permission, constantly puts the other person down, shows extreme jealousy or insecurity, has an explosive temper, isolates the person from his or her family or friends, makes false accusations, has mood swings, physically injures the person, and is possessive and controlling.

Legal Responses to IPV

Despite the history previously described, from a legislative perspective, IPV has been considered a crime in violation of community standards and requiring state intervention for only about 30 years in most parts of the United States and Canada. For example, the right of women to be free of sexual assault committed by their husbands was not acknowledged in the Criminal Code of Canada until the offense of marital rape was formally recognized as a crime in 1983 (MacKinnon, 1987). In the past three decades police and prosecutors have enhanced investigative techniques and the pursuit of charges and convictions. Courts have responded with more severe sentences and mandated interventions for perpetrators (Jaffe, Crooks, & Wolfe, 2003).

A variety of approaches have been attempted over the years to address the issue of IPV from a legal perspective. One approach was the mandatory arrest and charging of perpetrators of IPV that arose because of voiced concerns of victim advocacy groups that due to police discretion and policies of individual police departments male batterers were rarely arrested, prosecuted, or sentenced. Such concerns were substantiated by research on police and prosecutor practices (Fagan, 1996). Most famous among the research studies was the Minneapolis Domestic Violence Experiment, funded by the National Institute of Justice and the first scientifically controlled test of the effects of arrest for any crime (Sherman & Berk, 1984). In the experiment suspects of domestic violence were randomly assigned to three outcomes: (1) arrest, (2) sent away from the scene for eight hours, or (3) given advice and/or mediation. To be included in the study the police officer needed to have probable cause to believe a misdemeanor domestic assault had occurred within the past four hours and both the victim and the offender had to be present. The experiment ran from March 1981 to August 1982 to collect 314 cases.

Outcomes in terms of repeated violence were assessed at six months (Sherman & Berk, 1984). The results were presented in three ways: police reports of repeated violence, victim reports of repeated violence, and victim reports of repeated violence when the victim believed the officer had listened to her or his concerns. The results shown in TABLE 9-2 are impressive and led to the conclusion of the authors that arrest is the most effective method for reducing domestic violence (Sherman & Berk, 1984).

These impressive results raised hopes that this was a relatively simple solution to a complex problem. However, the legislative changes in many places moved more quickly than the training of police officers who were intended to implement the policies. Later attempts to replicate the findings in five different jurisdictions failed to produce the same results. Methodological problems in the replication studies, which were in large part caused by the attempt to conduct experimental research in naturalized settings, do not allow us to draw the conclusion that mandatory arrests do or do not work (Fagan, 1996). However, they do confirm that mandatory arrest is not the magic bullet for ending IPV. A further set of issues was the unintended side effects of such a policy, such as contempt of court charges against victim witnesses who refused to testify in court and perjury charges against those who changed their stories (Jaffe et al., 2003). This resulted in a revictimization of those individuals the policy was intended to protect.

TABLE 9-2 Results of the Minneapolis Domestic Violence Experiment

	Arrest	Advice	Sent Suspect Away
Police report	10%	19%	24%
Victim report	19%	37%	33%
Victim report if "police listened"	9%	26%	35%

Data from Sherman, L. & Berk, R. 1984. *The Minneapolis Domestic Violence Experiment. Police Foundation Reports.* April 1984. Washington: Police Foundation.

Another justice approach to IPV has been the reliance on **protection orders** or restraining orders to increase the safety of IPV victims. A study of 227,941 restraining orders issued in California revealed that in 72.2% of the cases the order was for a woman to be protected from a male abuser and in 19.3% of the cases the protection was from someone of the same sex (Sorenson & Shen, 2005). As originally envisioned, these orders were viewed as potentially more effective than criminal prosecutions because they could enhance the safety of the victim and could reduce the chances of retaliation from an offender who was angered at criminal charges. Further, protection orders were viewed as possible deterrents because offenders would seek to avoid criminal prosecution. Nevertheless, research suggests that 23% to 50% of victims experience revictimization within a two- to four-month follow-up period. Where comparison groups have been used, this has resulted in no differences in victimization rates between victims who did use protection orders and those who did not (Mears, Carlson, Holden, & Harris, 2001). Revictimization rates are higher in those who share biological children, are of lower socioeconomic groups, are of minority status, and when the perpetrator has a history of arrest.

An example of both revictimization and failure of protection orders is that of Jared Remy, the son of a popular Red Sox newscaster and former player. The 27-year-old victim, Jennifer Martel, had been in a six-year relationship with Remy and they had a 4-year-old daughter together. Remy had a history of domestic violence against Martel. Two days before the 2013 murder, Remy had spent the night in jail and was issued a restraining order after slamming the victim's face into a mirror. The night of the murder, two neighbors heard loud banging noises and Jennifer Martel screaming. One neighbor came over to the apartment and tried unsuccessfully to pull Remy off of Martel. Remy had straddled Jennifer, choked and punched her in the face, and knocked her out. Then with both hands he plunged a knife into her several times in the neck and shoulders. Remy said, "Jennifer had a knife in her hand and threatened me with my daughter. So I killed her. I don't think it's right when a woman uses their kids against their fathers." Jennifer had been planning an escape from Remy prior to the fatal stabbing and had changed her Facebook page to "complicated." His criminal record indicated he had stalked harassed, terrorized and assaulted five prior girlfriends. His post-assault behavior indicated remorse and he did plead guilty to the crime despite a possible defense of anxiety, depression, and steroid or prescription drug use. He was one of the only people in Massachusetts to plead guilty to first-degree murder and violation of a protection order. He received a mandatory sentence of life without parole (Moskowitz, 2014).

In January 1991 the California State Assembly passed a bill in which it became a public offense for persons subject to domestic violence restraining orders to purchase a firearm. The law also required law enforcement agencies to report domestic violence restraining orders to a central database (Domestic Violence Restraining Order System) to effectively prohibit these individuals from acquiring firearms (Sorenson & Shen, 2005). In 1996 Congress passed the Domestic Violence Misdemeanor Gun Ban, which prohibits anyone convicted of a misdemeanor crime of domestic violence or child abuse from purchasing or possessing a gun. This is an important legislative step because, according to U.S. Federal Bureau of Investigation (FBI) statistics, in homicides during 1995 in which the weapon was known 50% of domestic violence homicide victims were killed with a firearm (FBI, 1995). Of those female firearm homicides, 75% were killed with a handgun. Canadian statistics reveal that in 1996, 34% of all spousal homicide victims were killed by firearms (Royal Canadian Mounted Police [RCMP], 2012).

Legislative changes in Canada and the United States resulted in the recognition that the exposure of children to violence between their parents constitutes a form of child abuse. As a result, child protection agencies in Canada experienced a dramatic rise in reports of emotional abuse, the largest proportion of which were children exposed to IPV (Black, Trocmé, Fallon, & MacLaurin, 2008). In 1999 in Minnesota the expanded definition of child abuse to include exposure to IPV resulted in such a substantial increase in reports that child protective services agencies were overwhelmed, and a need for $30 million in additional services was identified. The next year the state repealed the law (Taylor & Sorenson, 2007).

In response to legislative changes and in an attempt to better protect children, child welfare services agencies have developed policies and practices to assess and intervene in cases of child exposure to IPV (Shlonsky & Friend, 2007). However, if child exposure to IPV is equated with child abuse, the abused parent is placed in the position of culpability for failure to protect. That is, an abused parent who chooses not to, or cannot, leave the abusive relationship may be held responsible for exposing the child to violence. Ultimately, this may result in the removal of the child, a double jeopardy for the abused parent. If the abused parent discloses abuse to a healthcare or social service professional in an effort to obtain assistance, he or she may be penalized with the loss of the child. In a study conducted by Alaggia, Jenney, Mazzuca, and Redmond (2007), this was particularly true for women who were marginalized due to race, sexual orientation, or immigration status. These women found that the risks associated with seeking help were simply too high.

This policy was tested by a group of mothers who were victims of domestic violence and had their children removed in a class action lawsuit against New York City's Administration of Children's Services (ACS) (*Nicholson v. Williams*, 2004). The district court concluded that ACS violated the federal constitutional rights of battered mothers and their children. The court concluded that ACS unnecessarily prosecuted mothers for neglect and removed their children when the mothers had been the victims of significant domestic violence and when the mothers themselves had done nothing wrong. The district court issued a preliminary injunction ordering ACS to discontinue its practices and ordered the city and the state to pay assigned counsel for battered women in dependency proceedings. ACS appealed the finding, and in October 2004 the New York Court of Appeals ruled that it was unacceptable to presume a child who witnesses domestic violence is neglected or a child who is exposed to domestic violence should be removed from the family home on this basis alone. Furthermore, the court held that any decision to remove a child must be weighed against the psychological harm to the child that could be created by the removal itself (*Nicholson v. Williams*, 2004).

Effects of IPV on Victims

Lenore Walker first proposed the term **battered woman syndrome** in 1979 as a means of describing the effects of IPV on the victims. According to Walker (1979), any woman may find herself in an abusive situation once. However, if violence occurs a second time and the woman remains in that situation, she is described as a battered woman. In her extensive studies with battered women, Walker found that battering relationships have a clearly discernible cycle, and she concluded that battered women respond to events in this cycle in a predictable pattern. The battering cycle, according to Walker, has three phases. The first phase is tension reduction, during which a batterer, in an attempt to reduce his own anxiety and tension, begins to inflict his mate with verbal or minor physical abuse. The woman responds with anger reduction techniques, aimed at placating the batterer to avoid a severely abusive episode. As the tension grows the phase is followed by an acute battering episode. At this time the victim is subject to severe physical and verbal abuse, which may include significant injury and threats of death. At the end of the incident there is a sharp, predictable reduction in the tension. The final phase of the cycle is loving attrition, during which the batterer becomes remorseful, apologetic, and loving. At this time he also assures the victim the battering incident will not be repeated. This loving attrition reinforces the woman's commitment to the relationship by making her feel loved and protective of her partner's evident vulnerability. This phase may last for an extended period of time, but invariably it fades as the tension mounts and the cycle begins again. To qualify for battered woman syndrome, according to Walker's criteria, a woman must have gone through this cycle at least twice.

In addition to the battering cycle, a victim of IPV experiences other forms of totalitarian control, often on a daily basis. Psychological abuse can involve the constant undermining of the victim's sense of self, including that she is an inadequate parent, inadequate lover, unable to think clearly, and an unworthy human being. In a study by Regehr and Glancy (1995), one woman who had just been released from the hospital with a colostomy was told she was smelly and disgusting and was forced to wash the floor with a toothbrush. Another woman, a former beauty queen, was convinced by her spouse that she had become ugly, and as a consequence she totally abandoned her self-care in defeat. These constant negative depictions of the victim are unable to be disputed by positive interactions with others outside the relationship because of enforced social isolation. Victims in the Regehr and Glancy study stated their telephones were monitored or disconnected, and they were no longer allowed to interact with friends or family. This isolation was at times overtly enforced or subtly engineered by insulting, demeaning, or sexually harassing the victim's social supports. Financial abuse was also common, where the abuser takes away the victim's paycheck, monitors all grocery and other receipts to ensure no money is saved, and places all jointly owned assets in the abuser's name, denying the victim the right to access them. Finally, physical abuse took many forms, including breaking favorite objects, smashing walls and furniture, threatening harm to children or other family members, sexual assault, kicking, punching, hair pulling, and so on.

Finkelhor and Yllo (1982) were among the first to describe the phenomenon of forced sex in marriage as a form of physical abuse. They include in this definition sexual aggression (including rape) and coercion to engage in forms of sexual activity that the woman did not wish or enjoy (such as oral or anal sex). Women in their study who were victims of forced sex in marriage reported feeling humiliated, angry, and depressed.

The pattern of control and abuse can lead to a state of **learned helplessness**. That is, the victim has learned to accept abuse as a way of life and does not believe she or he has any influence on its occurrence. Thus, with repeated battering and repeated threats of future violence, a victim becomes passive. Furthermore, the victim's cognitive ability to perceive success is altered. The victim does not believe any response will result in a positive outcome. Finally, the victim's sense of emotional well-being becomes precarious, rendering the victim vulnerable to depression and anxiety (Walker, 1979).

Victims of IPV may also experience **posttraumatic stress disorder (PTSD)** (Randle & Graham, 2011). However, in some situations PTSD is inadequate to explain the significant impacts of repeated abuse over long periods of time. Judith Lewis Herman (1992) proposed a new diagnosis to explain the cluster of symptoms experienced by someone who has endured a situation of abuse and totalitarian control over a prolonged period of time. Herman argued that survivors of prolonged abuse develop characteristic personality changes that affect both their sense of identity and their ability to form and sustain interpersonal relationships. Elements of this disorder include alterations in self-perception, including shame, guilt, self-blame, and a sense of being completely different from others; alterations in perceptions of the perpetrator, such as ascribing unrealistic power to the perpetrator, idealizing the perpetrator, or rationalizing the abusive behavior; alterations in relations with others, including isolation and withdrawal, distrust or overtrusting behavior, and disruption in relationships; and alterations in systems of meaning, such as loss of faith, hopelessness, and despair (Herman, 1992).

Barriers to Disclosing and Ending Abuse

A number of theoretical frameworks have emerged to explain strategies used by women in abusive relationships and their help-seeking actions, obstacles that confront those who attempt to escape partner violence, and decision models for help seeking. Alaggia, Regehr, and Jenny (2011) use ecological theory to describe the multiple factors that influence a victim's decision to disclose abuse and take action to end the abusive relationship. These factors are summarized in **TABLE 9-3**.

At the intrapersonal or individual level, current mental health and emotional status are important factors to consider. Women in abusive relationships have been found to suffer from high levels of posttraumatic stress as described above and often find themselves in a perpetual state of fear (Alaggia et al., 2011). This fear is justified as research confirms that leaving an abusive relationship increases the safety risk; in particular, women who leave are more likely to be killed by their abusive husbands than those who stay. In addition, however, somewhat surprisingly perhaps to others, women in abusive relationships describe feelings of love and commitment to their abusive partners. At an individual level, the dynamic of staying in an abusive relationship is important

TABLE 9-3 Why Battered Women Stay

Individual factors	Posttraumatic stress Fear Love and commitment Resilience and ability to self-protect
Family and cultural factors	Bring shame on the family Religious and cultural beliefs about the family Concern for children Beliefs that abuse is normal
Community services	Inadequate social housing Limited education, retraining, or employment opportunities Insufficient counseling or shelter resources
Social policies	Immigration policies that do not allow sponsored individuals to leave their sponsors Social welfare and housing policies that disadvantage single mothers Mandatory reporting to child welfare of children witnessing abuse

Data from Alaggia, R., Regehr, C. & Jenny, A. (2011) Risky Business: An Ecological Analysis of Intimate Partner Violence Disclosure. *Research on Social Work Practice.*

to determine. One of the most common questions people ask about victims of domestic violence is, "Why don't they just leave?" According to the National Coalition Against Domestic Violence (NCADV, n.d.), people stay in abusive relationships for a variety of reasons, including:

- The victim fears the abuser's violent behavior will escalate if he or she tries to leave.

- The abuser has threatened to kill the victim, the victim's family, friends, pets, children, and/or himself/herself.

- The victim loves the abuser and believes that he or she will change.

- The victim believes abuse is a normal part of a relationship.

- The victim is financially dependent on the abuser.

- The abuser has threatened to take the victim's children away if he or she leaves.

- The victim wants his or her children to have two parents.

- The victim's religious and/or cultural beliefs preclude him or her from leaving.

- The victim has low self-esteem and believes he or she is to blame for the abuse.
- The victim is embarrassed to let others know he or she has been abused.
- The victim has nowhere to go if he or she leaves.
- The victim fears retribution from the abuser's friends and/or family.

The push and pull between service providers can increase the conflict for the victim. The tendency of service providers to push women to leave the relationships is at odds with the goals of some victims and makes them reluctant to seek services. At the intrapersonal level is the resilience of victims and their ability to self-protect that makes staying in the relationship tolerable.

At a microsystem level, participants identified family and cultural factors that impacted disclosure and ending the relationship (Alaggia et al., 2011). For instance, victims from some cultural groups were concerned about the way in which their situation and behavior may bring shame on their family. Cultural and religious practices made it impossible for these women to consider divorce or separation. This was particularly true if women perceived their children would be negatively affected by having separated parents. Further, immigrant women in this study identified they came from countries where abuse was considered normal. One woman was quoted as saying, "Being beaten is normal. There are lots of abuses in my country. In my country you call and they never come. They only come if your eye is falling out of its socket, or if you are almost dying, then they come, then they notice. They always come if the woman is dead" (Alaggia et al., 2011, p. 306).

Exosystems refer to the supports and challenges presented by community services. Ptacek (1999) proposed a *social entrapment* perspective in which women attempting to escape their abusive relationships are often frustrated by inadequate institutional responses. These can include inadequate social housing options, services that do not support the goal of family reunification, inadequate shelters and counseling services, and inability to access education, retraining, or employment. Grauwiler (2008) concluded in her study of women in New York City that women experienced services as being unresponsive to their needs and goals. Of particular concern was the expectation of these services for women to leave their communities and isolate themselves to maintain their safety.

Finally, at the macrosystem level, policies and laws limit the choices available to victims. In their study of immigrant women, Alaggia, Regehr, and Rishchynsky (2009) found that immigration laws seriously hampered disclosure, especially when the abusive partners were their sponsors. That is, immigrant women were frequently sponsored by their partners and faced deportation if they were to leave the relationship. Further, as noted earlier, mandatory reporting to child welfare services when children are witnesses to violence can be highly problematic. Finally, social welfare, housing, and education policies can all serve to trap victims. These structural responses can cause women to retreat within themselves and internalize blame, leading them to stay with their abusive partners.

IPV in LGBT Relationships

IPV between lesbian, gay, bisexual, or transgendered partners has been a relatively unexplored area in both the professional and research literature. Yet studies examining incidence reveal that violence occurs in 21% to 50% of male same-sex couples (Stanley, Bartholomew, Taylor, Oram, & Landolt, 2006) and 25% to 50% of female same-sex couples (Hardesty, Oswald, Khaw, & Fonseca, 2011). Women in lesbian relationships are also more likely to come from heterosexual relationships where violence was an issue (Pattavina, Hirshel, Buzawa, Faggiani, & Bentley, 2007). In one study 50% of participants indicated that the violence in their same-sex relationship was bidirectional; that is, both partners were physically violent at some point (Stanley et al., 2006).

In many ways violence in LGBT relationships is similar to that in heterosexual relationships. For example, there is often a cycle of violence that involves a building of tension, followed by actual violence, followed by a period of reconciliation and remorse. In addition, the level of violence tends to build over time. Social isolation, minimizing of the abuse, victim blame, and a belief the offender will change are also common features. In addition, the offender typologies are very similar (Brown, 2008). In other ways issues are intensified for people in LGBT relationships who are battered, particularly with regard to a fear of exposure and possible rejection from family and friends upon reporting based on the victim's sexual orientation. In lesbian relationships victims also confront a political agenda that has identified violence as a male issue (Stanley et al., 2006).

Specific forms of abuse that may occur in relationships where one partner is transgendered are published on the NCADV website and include the following (Domestic Violence and Lesbian, Gay, Bisexual and Transgender Relationships, n.d.):

- Telling the transgendered partner that he or she is not a real man or woman
- Ridiculing the transgendered partner's identity as "bisexual," "trans," "femme," "butch," "gender," "queer," etc.

- Using offensive pronouns such as "it" to refer to the transgendered partner

- Ridiculing the transgender partner's body or appearance

- Denying the transgendered partner's access to medical treatment or hormones or coercing him or her to not pursue medical treatment

Legal issues can also form an additional barrier for same-sex couples because advances in laws that protect victims from violence in intimate relationships have been primarily directed at heterosexual relationships. Six states (Delaware, Louisiana, Montana, New York, South Carolina, and Virginia) specifically exclude same-sex partners from legal interventions (Hardesty et al., 2011), and only six states specifically provide protection in same-sex couples. Other states use vague terms, such as "partners" and "cohabitants," that leave discretion to individual judges with respect to who qualifies. In addition, three states maintain anti-sodomy laws, forcing victims to admit to illegal behaviors before they can be protected. Finally, several studies have provided evidence that police are less likely to intervene, fail to arrest, and ignore standard domestic violence procedures in the case of same-sex IPV (Pattavina, Hirshel, Buzawa, Faggiani, & Bentley, 2007).

Child Witnesses of IPV

Significant overlap exists between IPV and child abuse. The 2003 Canadian Incidence Study of Reported Child Abuse and Neglect revealed that 34% of all substantiated cases of child abuse in Canada involved some form of children witnessing IPV (Black et al., 2008). Other research has demonstrated that in families reported to child protection where the woman is a victim of IPV, there is a co-occurrence rate of child abuse in 30% to 60% of the cases, with a median rate of 40%. Usually, this abuse is in the form of physical abuse. In community-based studies the co-occurrence rate between IPV and child abuse is 5.6% to 11%. Thus, most studies suggest that the occurrence of IPV in a family increases the risk of physical violence against the child, neglect of the child, sexual abuse of the child, and psychological violence directed at the child (Zolotor, Theodore, Coyne-Beasley, & Runyan, 2007).

Even when children in homes where IPV is present are not victims of direct abuse themselves, considerable evidence indicates that these children suffer the aftereffects of violence. Mothers who experience more severe forms of physical abuse are more likely to report that their children are forced to watch the abuse, suggesting this is part of the abusers' strategy for control and intimidation (Mbilinyi, Edleson, Hagemeister, & Beeman, 2007). When compared to children who have not witnessed abuse, children who are exposed to IPV demonstrate increased internalizing behaviors, including depression, anxiety, and social withdrawal; increased externalizing behaviors, including hyperactivity and aggression; more social integration problems; lower self-esteem; and lower school performance (Alaggia et al., 2007; Wolfe, Crooks, Lee, McIntyre-Smith, & Jaffe, 2003). Indeed, in 63% of cases outcomes for children who witness interparental violence are equivalent to children who are physically abused themselves (Kitzmann, Gaylord, Holt, & Kenny, 2003). In large part these childhood effects are the result of severe stress experienced by the abused parent and the affect this stress has on their ability to parent (Huth-Bocks & Hughes, 2008).

A smaller subset of children exposed to interparental violence will develop PTSD. Community-based studies suggest that approximately 13% of these children will develop PTSD and about 50% will have at least one symptom of PTSD, such as intrusive thoughts of the event. Among children who are abused themselves, studies have found that 26% in a clinical sample and 42% in foster care have PTSD. This is considerably higher than those who witness abuse alone (Margolin & Vickerman, 2007). Despite these alarming findings about the impact that witnessing violence has on children, it is important not to conclude that all children who are exposed to IPV will have negative effects. A meta-analysis of 118 studies of children who were exposed to interparental violence demonstrated that 37% showed outcomes that were similar to or better than nonwitnesses (Kitzmann et al., 2003). Thus, as in all cases of victimization, individual resilience can overcome extremely adverse conditions.

Another outcome of child abuse and children witnessing abuse is the possibility of becoming an abuser later in life. In U.S. national surveys 39% of abusive men reported being abused as children, compared to 11% of nonabusive men (Straus & Gelles, 1980). Nevertheless, exposure to domestic violence is a stronger predictor than physical child abuse that a person will become a perpetrator of IPV (Adams, 2009). Straus and Gelles (1980) found that men who were exposed to domestic violence as children were three times more likely to grow up to become perpetrators of IPV. Men who witnessed severe abuse of their mothers by their fathers had rates of IPV that were 100 times greater than men who had not been exposed to spousal abuse. When these two factors—child abuse and witnessing abuse—are combined, the contributions to IPV are intensified (Adams, 2009).

Holt, Buckle, and Whelan (2008) examined the impact of exposure to domestic violence on the health and developmental well-being of children and young people across four separate yet interrelated domains: domestic violence exposure and child abuse, impact on parental capacity, impact on child and adolescent development, and exposure to additional adversities. They found that children and adolescents living with domestic violence are at increased risk of experiencing emotional, physical, and sexual abuse; of developing emotional and behavioral problems; and of increased exposure to other adversities. However, they noted that a range of protective factors can mitigate against this impact, in particular a strong relationship with and attachment to a caring adult, usually the mother.

These findings advocate for a holistic and child-centered approach to service delivery, derived from an informed assessment, designed to capture a picture of the individual child's experience, and responsive to their individual needs (Truman & Morgan, 2014).

Continuum of Intimate Violence

Roberts and Roberts (2005) conducted in-depth interviews with 501 battered women in a variety of settings, deriving an empirically based continuum of IPV based on the common metrics among their responses. Around these metrics the variables clustered into five levels on the IPV continuum that progress by duration and severity of abuse: (1) short term, (2) intermediate, (3) intermittent long term, (4) chronic/predictable, and (5) homicidal. Two variables in the Roberts (2007) study were empirically related to the duration of the battering relationship: (1) a victim's highest level of education completed and (2) relationship status. That is, victims with higher levels of education and lower levels of commitment to the relationship were more likely to leave.

Socioeconomic status appeared to follow an inverse trend in relationship to the duration and intensity of abuse. Thus, victims on the low-risk end of the continuum (short-term battering relationships) were characterized as having high levels of education (88.3% were college students or graduates), being involved in a dating relationship with their abusive partner (94.7%), and being middle- or upper-middle class (81.5%). In contrast, the vast majority of victims at the high-risk end of the continuum (chronically abusive relationship) were lower or middle class, had low levels of education (88.7% were high school dropouts or graduates), and were either currently or formerly married (70%) or were cohabiting long term (30%) with their abusive partners (Roberts, 2007).

Roberts (2002) developed a conceptual model from his work with battered women based on a continuum of intimate partner violence. This continuum model is presented in TABLE 9-4.

TABLE 9-4 Continuum of Intimate Partner Violence

Level 1 Short term	Level 2 Intermediate	Level 3 Intermittent/ Long term	Level 4 Chronic and predictable	Level 5 Homicidal
Less than 1 year duration; usually college or high school students	Several months to 2 years; cohabiting	Long-term committed relationship; maybe has children	Long-term relationship; maybe a religious or cultural element to commitment	Variable but often long term
1–3 incidents	3–15 incidents	4–30 incidents	Several hundred incidents	Numerous violent incidents
Pushing, shoving, sometimes hitting with object	Moderate to severe injuries	Severe and intense episode with no warning; long periods between episodes	Frequent, predictable pattern of abuse, often involving substances	Violence escalates to homicide and life-threatening injuries
Victim leaves after first, second, or third incident Caring support system	Victim leaves due to bruises or injury Caring support system, parents, friends, new partner	Stays until children grow up Stays for status or prestige No other support system	Abuse continues until abuser is arrested, dies, is hospitalized Few financial resources	Victim has limited education or resources Victim suffers from PTSD or complex PTSD

Data from Roberts, A. R. 2002. Duration and severity of woman battering: A conceptual model/continuum. In A. Roberts (Ed.), *Handbook of domestic violence intervention strategies* (pp. 64–79). New York: Oxford University Press.

Batterer Typologies

Typologies of batterers emanate from two different perspectives: (1) clinically and theoretically derived typologies or (2) empirically derived typologies. In general, clinically and theoretically based models were the first to be proposed, and later empirical testing either confirmed the clinical models or suggested other forms of grouping. Elbow (1977) described four patterns of behavior in batterers, based on clinical reflections emanating from practice: (1) the controller, who sees his partner as an object to be controlled; (2) the defender, who expects his wife to love and forgive him no matter how much he abuses her; (3) the approval seeker, who is so insecure he cannot tolerate the rejection implicit in his wife's leaving and often threatens her with death; and (4) the incorporator, who sees his wife as an extension of himself and often threatens violence because her leaving is such a threat to his ego.

As one of the first empirically derived classifications, Gondolf (1988) developed a typology of batterers based on a cluster analysis of batterer abuse and variables drawn from intake interviews with 6,000 battered women. The goal was to identify treatment approaches that reflect different motivations. The typology included three types of batterers: sociopathic, antisocial, and typical. According to Gondolf (1988) the sociopathic batterer engages in high levels of physical abuse and emotional abuse, is likely to be violent outside the home, and is likely to have been arrested for violent and nonviolent crimes. The antisocial batterer is less likely to have been arrested than the sociopathic batterer because this batterer is generally violent and verbally and physically abusive within the intimate relationship. The typical batterer commits less severe verbal and physical abuse than either of the preceding types, is less likely to use a weapon, and is generally less violent outside the home.

Holtzworth-Munroe and Stuart (1994) conducted a comprehensive review of 15 batterer typologies, including both clinically derived (deductive approaches) and empirically derived models (inductive approaches). An analysis of the data across these studies revealed that those who engage in IPV are a heterogeneous group that varies along theoretically important dimensions (TABLE 9-5). Holtzworth-Munroe and Stuart (1994) proposed that batterer

TABLE 9-5 Typologies of Batterers

Typology	Characteristics
Family only	Least marital violence Lowest levels of psychological and sexual abuse Least violence outside the home Little or no psychopathology Violence resulting from a combination of stress and risk factors (childhood witnessing of IPV, lack of relationship skills) Lack of generalized hostility to women Remorse leading to lower risk of escalating violence
Dysphoric–borderline	Moderate to severe wife abuse Not much violence outside the home Most psychologically distressed Background of parental abuse and rejection Most likely to show borderline characteristics (emotional liability, intense unstable personal relationships, fear of rejection, jealousy)
Generally violent–antisocial	Moderate to severe levels of marital violence Highest levels of extrafamilial violence Most likely to have antisocial personality disorder (criminal behavior, arrests, substance abuse) High levels of family of origin violence Associates with deviant peers Marital violence is part of general use of aggression

Data from Holtzworth-Munroe, A., & Meehan, J. C. 2004. Typologies of men who are maritally violent: Scientific and clinical implications. *Journal of Interpersonal Violence, 19*(12), 1369–1389.

subtypes can be classified along three descriptive dimensions: severity and frequency of marital violence, generality of the violence (i.e., family only or extrafamilial violence), and the batterer's psychopathology or personality disorders. They suggested that using these descriptive dimensions produces three major subtypes: family only, dysphoric–borderline, and generally violent–antisocial. These typologies are useful to predict risk of future violence and to predict treatment success; that is, future violence is most likely to occur with the dysphoric–borderline and generally violent–antisocial abusers. Further, family only abusers are most likely to benefit from traditional batterer treatment programs. Dysphoric–borderline abusers may be amenable to long-term treatment approaches that focus not only on battering but also on significant difficulties with interpersonal functioning. Finally, generally violent–antisocial abusers are least likely to benefit from any treatment approach.

Intersections Between Batterer Typologies and the Continuum of Violence

Bender and Roberts (2007) proposed the batterer typologies intersect with the continuum of violence (TABLE 9-6). That is, Holtzworth-Munroe and Stuart's category of family-only abuser and Gondolf's category of typical batterer will most commonly result in level 1, or short-term, violence. These individuals may also present with moderate severity, or level 2, violence, depending on the characteristics of the victim and the victim's ability to exit the situation. Dysphoric–borderline abusers in Holtzworth-Munroe and Stuart's typology are likely to be found in level 2 (intermediate violence) or level 3 (intermittent long-term violence), again depending on the victim's characteristics and resources. Finally, the most severe abusers, the generally violent, antisocial, and sociopathic types, are most likely to be found in the highest-risk category of the continuum of abuse, which is chronic and predictable and often leads to significant injury or death. Victims in this category frequently have come to expect battering as a part of life, have histories of violence in their families of origin, and have few person resources or social supports to draw upon. Level 5 violence, homicide, may occur in the context of chronic abuse that continues to escalate, as with the antisocial–sociopathic abuser, or it may occur in the course of an emotional rage, such as in the case of a dysphoric–borderline abuser.

Spousal homicide is an all-too-common occurrence in the context of IPV. As noted earlier, in 2007 intimate partners committed 14% of all homicides in the United States; 70% of those people killed by an intimate partner were women (Catalano et al., 2009). Also, 24% of women who were

TABLE 9-6 Intersections Between Batterer Typologies and the Continuum of Violence

Batterer Typologies		Violence Continuum	
Typology	**Description**	**Typology**	**Description**
Low risk			
Family only (Holtzworth-Munroe & Stuart, 1994) Typical batterer (Gondolf, 1988)	Low level of severity Low frequency of violence Little or no psychopathology Usually no criminal history	Level 1 Short term (Roberts & Roberts, 2005)	Mild to moderate intensity of abuse 1–3 incidents Less than 1 year dating relationship Presence of caring, responsive support system
Moderate risk			
Family only (Holtzworth-Munroe & Stuart, 1994) Typical batterer (Gondolf, 1988) OR Dysphoric–borderline (Holtzworth-Munroe & Stuart, 1994)	Moderate severity of violence Moderate frequency of violence Moderate to high psychopathology	Level 2 Intermediate (Roberts & Roberts, 2005) Level 3 Intermittent long term (Roberts & Roberts, 2005)	Moderate to severe abuse 3–15 incidents Cohabitating or recently married Presence of caring, responsive support system Severe and intense violent episodes without warning; long periods without violence between violent episodes 4–30 incidents No alternative support system
High risk			
Generally violent–antisocial (Holtzworth-Munroe & Stuart, 1994) Antisocial type and sociopathic type (Gondolf, 1988) OR Dysphoric–borderline (Holtzworth-Munroe & Stuart, 1994)	High severity of violence High frequency of violence High levels of psychopathology Usually has a criminal record	Level 4 Chronic and predictable (Roberts & Roberts, 2005) Level 5 Homicidal (Roberts & Roberts, 2005)	Severe repeated incidents, frequent, predictable pattern Violence often precipitated by substance abuse Several hundred violent acts Violence escalates to homicide and life-threatening injuries

Data from Bender, K. & Roberts, A. 2007. Battered women versus male batterer typologies: Same or different based on evidence-based studies? *Aggression and Violent Behavior. 12*(5) 519–530.

murdered were killed by a spouse or ex-spouse, 21% were killed by a girlfriend or boyfriend; 2% of male homicide victims were killed by a spouse or ex-spouse and 3% were killed by a girlfriend or boyfriend. Most intimate partner homicides (67% to 80%) occur in the context of ongoing IPV (Catalano et al., 2009).

Data reported by NVDRS from 18 states during 2003–2014 included a total of 10,018 female homicides; among these, 1,835 (18.3%) were part of a homicide-suicide incident (i.e., suspect died by suicide after perpetrating homicide). Homicide victims ranged in age from 18 to 100 years. Approximately 15% of women of reproductive age (18–44 years) were pregnant or ≤6 weeks postpartum. Information available for all 4,442 IPV-related homicides noted that 79.2% deaths were perpetrated by a current or former intimate partner and one in 10 victims experienced some form of violence in the month preceding their death (Petrosky, Blair, Betz et al., 2017).

Research in Canada suggests that spousal homicide is a significant contributor to the overall number of homicides; 17% of Canadians who were accused of murder in 2006 were accused of murdering their current or former spouse. Seventy-two percent of Canadians who were murdered by their spouses in 2006 were female; during the 11 previous years, 82% of spousal homicide victims were women. The youngest person killed by his or her spouse in Ontario between 2003 and 2005 was aged 15 years; the eldest was aged 89 years. The youngest perpetrator was aged 21 years and the eldest, 89 years. Forty-one percent of spousal homicides involved stabbing, 29% were firearms deaths, 9% were due to beating, 6% were due to strangulation, and 3% each were due to poisoning and burns (Selley, 2008). Updated statistics on spousal homicides indicate police services reported 960 domestic homicides in Canada between 2003 and 2013 (Statistics Canda, 2015).

What differentiates battering spouses who kill from those who do not? Campbell and colleagues (2003) reviewed 220 intimate partner murders in 11 cities and identified both preincident and incident risk factors when compared to a control group of abused women. The strongest demographic risk factor was the abuser's lack of employment, followed by an education level of high school or lower. Individual risk factors included the abuser's access to a firearm and the abuser's use of illicit drugs. Substance abuse by the victim was not a risk factor. The risk was lower for victims who had never lived with the abuser and highest for victims who had separated from the abuser. This increased ninefold if the victim was separated from a highly controlling abuser. Stalking, however, was not a risk factor. A previous arrest for spousal assault reduced the risk of murder. Having a child in the home who was not the biological child of the abuser more than doubled the risk of homicide. TABLE 9-7 summarizes risk factors associated with homicide in IPV.

Dixon, Hamilton-Giachristis, and Browne (2008) reviewed the cases of 90 perpetrators of intimate partner homicide and attempted to classify them

TABLE 9-7 Risk Factors Associated with Homicide in Intimate Partner Violence

- Abuser has a lower level of education
- Abuser has access to a firearm
- Use of illicit drugs by abuser
- Abuser separated from victim
- Highly controlling abuser
- No previous abuser arrests for intimate partner violence
- A stepchild lives in the home
- Abuser previously threatened victim with a weapon

Data from Campbell, J., Webster, D., Koziol-McLain, J., Block, C., Campbell, D., et al. 2003. Risk factors for femicide in abusive relationships: Results from a multisite case control study. *American Journal of Public Health, 93*(7), 1089–1097.

on the dimensions of psychopathology and criminality. Most intimate partner murderers fell into the category of high criminality and low to moderate psychopathology (49%) or moderate to high criminality and high pathology (36.1%). These offenders had characteristics that corresponded with Holtzworth-Munroe's classifications of general violence–antisocial batterers and dysphoric–borderline batterers. Compared to community sample rates, which indicated the incidence of both these two types of batterers to be 25%, these two groups are represented at a considerably higher rate in IPV offenders who murder their partners. Low criminality and low pathology cases (akin to family only batterers) represented only 15.3% of the sample, despite the fact that they are the most common type of batterer found in community samples.

Others proposed more dynamic approaches to understanding batterers who kill. Adams (2009), in describing men who murdered their intimate partners, identified five overlapping typologies: jealous, substance abusing, materially motivated, suicidal, and career criminal. Most of the jealous types of killers in Adams's work appeared to have been perpetually vigilant toward their intimate partners, which escalated over the course of their relationships. Adams hypothesized that this distrust had its roots in the offender's family of origin. That is, in many cases adverse childhood events, such as child abuse and exposure to interparental violence, contributed to the development of insecurity and anxiety about intimacy, which led to difficulty establishing meaningful interpersonal relationships. Further, elements of possessive control had their roots in direct paternal modeling of spouse abuse, which was then socially reinforced through peer and cultural supports of male dominance within male–female relationships.

Partner Homicides

Murder charges brought in partner homicides may result in differing judicial rulings especially in high-profile cases. One example is South African blade runner Oscar Pistorius's murder of his girlfriend, model and law graduate Reeva Steenkamp, on Valentine's Day 2013. Pistorius's affidavit states he heard a noise in the middle of the night and retrieved his 9 mm gun that he kept under the bed. He went to the bathroom and saw that the bathroom window was open and that the toilet door was locked. He yelled out to the unknown person he heard making noise, but didn't get an answer. He then claimed that he yelled to Steenkamp to call police and then fired four shots through the bathroom door.

Reeva Steenkamp died of multiple gunshot wounds to the body and head. The fact that the bullet holes were so low to the ground suggested Pistorius was on his stumps, not his prosthetics, when he shot at the door. The door was also damaged by blows from a cricket bat, which suggested an attempt to break down the bathroom door.

Texts from Reeva to Pistorius were introduced into evidence at the trial that painted a profile of him as being hot-tempered, self-centered, insecure, and abusive, particularly to women. Reeva wrote that he would snap at her, told her that her accent and voice were annoying, and that he did not like her touching his neck in a loving manner. She wrote that she was scared of him sometimes and how he snapped at her. She noted how his moods changed quickly, how he sometimes acted cold, distant, and offish, and his telling her of dating another "chick." Testimony at trial revealed a serious argument the day before the murder.

In the trial outcome and sentencing, the judge originally found that Pistorius acted negligently, but not intentionally, when he shot Steenkamp, and sentenced him to five years in prison. He served one year of that sentence and was released to house arrest. The Supreme Court of Appeals overturned that verdict and found him guilty of murder and sentenced to him to six years (out of the minimum 15) in prison with mitigating circumstances such as remorse and good candidacy for rehabilitation due to his disability and emotional state. He is awaiting a decision on his parole.

Honor Killings

Honor killings, previously believed to be a phenomenon found only in other places in the world, have recently become an increasing issue in North America. A Canadian report (Papp, 2010) noted that there were 13 honor-based murders of women in Canada between 2002 and 2010, examples of which can be found

TABLE 9-8 Examples of Honor Killings

Incident	Details of the Case
2003, British Columbia Amandeep Atwal, age 17	Atwal's father was convicted of stabbing her to death because he did not approve of her boyfriend, who was from another ethnic group.
2006, Ottawa, Ontario Khatera Sadiqi, age 20	Sadiqi and her fiancé were shot to death in a shopping mall parking lot by her brother because he believed his sister was being disrespectful of their father.
2007, Mississauga, Ontario Aqsa Parvez, age 16	Parvez was strangled to death by her father and brother. Friends said they were upset she would not wear a hijab.
2011, Vancouver, BC Ravinder Bhangu, age 24	Bhangu was killed when her estranged husband entered her workplace, a Punjabi-English newspaper, and repeatedly struck her with an axe.
2011, Toronto Shaher Shahdady	Shahdady was strangled to death by her husband. Friends reported that her husband was upset she wanted to go to school and get a job. A member of the Canadian Muslim Congress referred to the murder as an honor killing of the worst sort.
2009, Kingston, Ontario Zainab, Sahar, and Geeti Shafia (sisters age 19,17, and 13) and Rona Amir Mohammad (father's first wife age 52)	The women were drowned when their vehicle was submerged in a canal. The sisters' mother, father, and brother were found guilty of murder in 2012. The court heard that the parents refused to let the older daughter attend school because she was dating "unapproved" males. Ms. Amir was seen as supporting the girls' rebellion against their family.

Data from Hopper, T. 2011. Murders spark fears of honor killings. *National Post.* August 3, 2011, p.1; Hildebrandt, A. 2009. Honour killings: domestic abuse by another name. CBC News. July 24, 2009.

in TABLE 9-8. This report sparked considerable attention in the media and government. As a result, Rona Ambrose, the Canadian Minister of Public Works and Government Services, called upon cultural communities, stating,

> honour crimes and to the subjugation, oppression and repression of women and girls wherever it happens. Repression, oppression and violence to maintain a family's honour may even happen because a girl wants to wear westernized clothing, date a boy who may not be from her own religion or culture or simply wanting to wear make-up.
>
> (Wilkes, 2010)

Honor killings originated as a patriarchal tribal custom in Muslim, Sikh, and Hindu cultures. These killings involve the murder of a wife or daughter, usually by her father or brother, to restore a family's or community's reputation. Although originally linked to adultery or premarital sex, increasingly they are associated with a woman's push for independence (Hildebrandt, 2009). The idea that honor is a cause for murder stems from the belief that a person's honor or a family's honor depends on the behavior of others. Status and acceptance in some traditional cultures rests on the family honor, which stems from the behavior of family members, including the purity of female family members. Killing of a wayward woman can be seen as an act of purification for the family to restore the respect of the community (Baker, Gregware, & Cassidy, 1999).

Honor killings have distinct characteristics that differentiate them from other forms of IPV. Honor killings are generally planned in advance and often occur after multiple threats have been made. The honor killings frequently involve the complicity of multiple family members. Those who perpetrate honor killings do not necessarily face stigma in their communities (Hopper, 2011).

Battered Woman Syndrome Defense

An alternative area of study and law related to homicide in intimate relationships pertains to women who kill their abusive husbands. Battered woman syndrome testimony began emerging in the United States during the late 1970s and early 1980s to support defense strategies in criminal cases. In 1990, as a result of a decision by the Supreme Court of Canada, **battered woman syndrome defense** became accepted as a legitimate extension of self-defense in Canadian courts (Regehr & Glancy, 1995). Similar developments are noted in the United Kingdom, Australia, and New Zealand. This defense arose out of concerns that the real-life experiences of battered women had not been reflected in the laws of self-defense. Traditional self-defense law is intended to explain the behavior of an individual who responds to a threat of death or bodily harm with lethal force or force that causes bodily harm. The standard example of this was the barroom brawl and an interpretation of how the average man would have behaved if he had been in a similar situation. The law of self-defense carries an assumption that the force used in self-defense would be applied in the course of mutual combat, but many women who kill their abusive husbands do not do so while they are being assaulted. Faced with memories of previous abuses, fears for the safety of their children who may also be present, and the reality of marked physical strength advantage, those women recoil during the assault. It is only later that these traumatized women protect themselves in the only way they can conceive, by killing their husbands as they lie drunk or asleep (Regehr & Glancy, 1995).

A common question asked of battered women is why they did not just leave the threatening situation. In most American jurisdictions, one is not required to retreat from an imminent threat of death or serious bodily injury, even if such retreat can be accomplished with complete safety. This doctrine, called the "true man rule," states, "There is a strong policy against the unnecessary taking of human life but there is also a strong policy against making one act in a cowardly and humiliating role" (Ewing, 1990, p. 81). Nevertheless, whereas a man's right to stand his ground and defend himself, his family, and his property was generally recognized, a woman who did so in the context of IPV had to demonstrate why she did not flee. The battered woman syndrome defense was an attempt to modify gender-biased self-defense laws to allow for the experiences of battered women. Elements of the battered woman syndrome defense include the following: (1) the existence of **complex posttraumatic stress disorder**; (2) the existence of battered woman syndrome; (3) the uniqueness of events leading to the ultimate offense; (4) elements of the woman's psychological functioning that led to an apprehension that her death was imminent, and she consequently used lethal force; and (5) a description of why the woman remained trapped in the relationship and was unable to leave (Regehr & Glancy, 1995).

The precedent-setting case in the Supreme Court of Canada was *R v. Lavallee*. Ms. Lavallee was a 22-year-old woman who had been living with the victim, Kevin Rust, for three to four years. After a boisterous party the couple had an argument. Ms. Lavallee had hidden in the closet upstairs and was dragged out by Mr. Rust. He gave her a gun and stated, "Either you kill me or I will kill you," and then "he kind of smiled and turned around." Although she claims to have been aiming over his head, Ms. Lavallee killed Mr. Rust with a single shot to the back of the head with a .303 caliber rifle. A psychiatrist with extensive experience working with battered women testified at the trial that Ms. Lavallee had been terrorized by her husband to the point of feeling worthless, trapped, vulnerable, and unable to escape the relationship despite the violence. In his opinion the shooting was a final desperate act of a woman who sincerely believed she would be killed that night. Ms. Lavallee was acquitted at the original trial but was convicted by the Supreme Court of Manitoba. The defense appealed to the Supreme Court of Canada, who restored the acquittal. The written judgment made it clear that battered woman syndrome defense was now an acceptable extension of self-defense. It was stated that although the Criminal Code of Canada does not stipulate imminence, it is an assumed element of self-defense; however, in the case of battered women, the perception of lethality goes beyond the immediate assaultive situation. "The issue is not what an outsider would have reasonably perceived, but what the accused reasonably perceived given her situation and experience. The question the jury must ask itself is whether, given the history, circumstances and perception of the accused, her belief that she could not preserve herself from being killed by the deceased that night except by killing him first, was reasonable" (*R v. Lavallee*, 1990, S. 51).

Although battered woman syndrome defense in both Canada and the United States was heralded by some as a great victory in light of the historical treatment of women in the courts, others suggest that it has disadvantaged women as a group. That is, the defense is thought to reinforce negative stereotypes of women as passive and helpless (Ferraro, 2003). Others suggest that those women who received acquittals on this basis are forced to embrace their victimhood as the sole defining characteristic. Further, it is suggested that this defense, which is based on stereotypes, does not necessarily fit all women. For example, research has shown that stereotypes of women of color do not allow for the overlay of another stereotype of being weak, helpless, and passive (Tang, 2003).

The use of the defense has been extended beyond its original intent to include men who killed their spouses and victims of IPV who committed other crimes, such as fraud. This trend has led some to use the term "abuse excuse," whereby guilty people use previous abuse to justify crime. Cited examples of the abuse excuse as a defense include the Menendez brothers, who killed their parents; Lorena Bobbitt, who is accused of hiding behind "the murky battered woman's defense"; and terrorists (Dowd, 1999; Dershowitz, 2006).

Intervention Programs in IPV

Intervention programs related to IPV fall into three broad categories: programs for child witnesses of violence, which are aimed at preventing future harm; programs for victims of violence, which are aimed at providing emergency assistance and increasing available choices; and programs for batterers, which are aimed at stopping violent behavior. The passage of the Violence Against Women Act (1994) by the U.S. federal government signaled a commitment to improve criminal justice responses, expand community services, improve safety measures, and provide support for education- and health-based services. Similar investments in programs have been made in other Western countries.

Interventions for Victims of IPV

The first line of intervention for victims of IPV is ensuring their safety. Shelters for victims of violence (which in the vast majority of cases are aimed at abused women and their children) provide shelter and offer anonymity. Shelters have security measures that often involve secret locations, electronic security, and arrangements with local police forces. Other safety programs involve hotlines or provide counselors who work with victims to develop a safety plan that may include removing weapons from the home, confiding in friends or family who could help in an emergency, obtaining a protection order, or relocating.

In extreme cases services that are focused on safety can assist victims to relocate to another city and change their identity.

The next level of intervention is programs that provide ongoing treatment and assistance to victims. Many treatment programs, both for victims of IPV and for batterers, use a group work model, which frequently is based on feminist ideology. Even when couples choose to remain together, current clinical wisdom suggests that both victim and offender fare better in gender-specific programs aimed at enhancing self-esteem, recognizing violence, and changing attitudes and behaviors. Groups reduce isolation, normalize the woman's experience, allow for an environment where victims can challenge one another for self-blaming statements or for beliefs that minimize the abuse, and allow victims to support one another in the difficult transition to change. Research evidence for the usefulness of women's support groups demonstrates statistically significant pretest–posttest improvements in areas such as self-esteem, anger, and depression (Tutty, Ogden, & Wyllie, 2006).

Treatment programs for victims of same-sex violence are often far more limited. Traditional feminist-based programs may not provide ideal services for this group of victims because of the basic assumptions about male violence and power that underlie many of the approaches. This may be at odds not only with assumptions about who is the victim and who is the perpetrator but also with issues of mutual violence or alternating violence. Shelters that address personal safety, which is a paramount concern to all victims of IPV, may not be welcoming or available to those who are openly lesbian. Gay men are excluded from these shelters, and the only option is shelters for indigent or substance-abusing men. Yet formal programs that address same-sex violence are available only in large cities that have visible gay and lesbian communities (Gillis & Diamond, 2006). In the end, this population of victims has fewer options and may feel more trapped in relationships than heterosexual victims.

Interventions for Child Witnesses

Interventions for children similarly need to be stratified to address varying needs at different times. Crisis intervention may be necessary at times of acute distress, such as when children enter a shelter. The focus of this intervention is to make the children feel safe, normalize the children's feelings, and develop a plan for when the children feel that either they or their parent are at risk. At the next stage, group therapy can provide support, education, problem-solving skills, and coping skills (Lehmann & Rabenstein, 2002). Many children benefit from the positive, fun atmosphere where they feel validated and appreciated. However, group treatment may be contraindicated for children with particularly poor social skills who are at risk of further rejection (Vickerman & Margolin, 2007). Group treatments are designed to be specific to different developmental stages. Interventions for younger children often incorporate play. Interventions for adolescents draw on adult-oriented treatment models but attend to the unique challenges of adolescents, including peer group pressures and risk taking.

Parents' and children's groups are a newer model of intervention that teaches improved parenting skills and emphasizes discipline techniques that do not involve violence or psychological abuse. The goal is to increase positive and supportive parenting techniques and reduce coercive interactions (Vickerman & Margolin, 2007). These groups also work to improve the relationship between the parent and child. Essentially, the abused parent is encouraged to move beyond his or her own distress to be available to and support the child.

Interventions for Offenders

Glancy and Saini (2005) conducted a meta-analysis of psychological treatments for anger and aggression. Their review concluded that a number of treatment approaches are effective in reducing anger and aggressive behavior in a variety of populations, including both male and female perpetrators of IPV. Programs that used a cognitive-behavioral therapeutic approach were most frequently studied, and all these programs showed at least moderate gains in reducing problematic behavior, often in as few as six to eight sessions. When a follow-up was conducted of male batterers, 85% were still refraining from physical violence one year later. Psychoeducational approaches were also effective in reducing aggressive acts of violence in intimate relationships. Although fewer studies exist on psychotherapeutic approaches, comparative studies with cognitive-behavioral therapy demonstrate equal effectiveness, and the effects were sustained at 12- and 24-month follow-ups.

Despite these successes, anger management groups have been criticized for ignoring the context of IPV and merely concentrating on skills. Conceptualizing IPV as simply a problem with anger ignores the basic belief systems that contributed to the abusive treatment of an intimate partner. From a feminist perspective, problematic beliefs include attitudes that view women as chattels of men and as people who can and should be controlled. The concern that arises from this is that although physical aggression may cease, emotional abuse may remain or increase. That is, a controlling abuser may simply learn more sophisticated means of control, such as emotional blackmail, from the group process. As a result, outcome measures to assess group effectiveness must go beyond physical violence alone and also address attitudes and other controlling behaviors (Tutty et al., 2006).

Conclusion

IPV has a long history. It continues to pervade our society at an alarming rate, causing profound effects on victims and their children. Early work in the area of IPV focused on abuse of women and addressed issues such as unequal treatment and protection under the law and patriarchal structures that condoned the abuse of women. More recent attention has been paid to male victims of interpersonal violence in both heterosexual and same-sex relationships and to women in same-sex relationships.

The continuum of violence spans from single-incident violence, which often occurs within dating relationships, to chronic ongoing abuse with serious bodily injury and ultimately to homicide. Typologies of abusers similarly span people who commit violence only within the confines of their family as a result of a variety of risk factors, to those with significant personality pathology, to those for whom violence is a way of life and a means for achieving their goals. Treatment approaches for both victims and abusers must consider these varying levels and types of abuse and be tailored to address both immediate needs and to maximize the possibilities of success.

Key Terms

Battered woman syndrome: The effects of intimate partner violence on victims.

Battered woman syndrome defense: An extension of self-defense laws that appreciates battered women's perceptions of risk and the possibility of escape.

Complex posttraumatic stress disorder: Reactions experienced by survivors of prolonged abuse, which includes symptoms of posttraumatic stress disorder and personality changes.

Domestic violence: Incidents of interspousal physical or emotional abuse perpetrated by one of the spouses upon the other spouse.

Intimate partner violence (IPV): Any behavior within an intimate relationship that causes physical, psychological, or sexual harm to those in the relationship.

Learned helplessness: A cognitive state in which a victim no longer believes that any action can change an aversive situation.

Posttraumatic stress disorder (PTSD): An anxiety disorder that develops in some individuals who have had major traumatic experiences. It is characterized by intrusive thoughts and images and heightened arousal.

Protection orders: An order made when the court makes a final decision and is satisfied that domestic and family violence has occurred and is likely to occur again.

Wife battering: Assault against a woman by her husband.

■ Discussion Questions

1. Select a legal response to intimate partner violence. What are the pros and cons of the particular approach?

2. What are the long-term effects of intimate partner violence on children who witness abuse?

3. Identify characteristics of various typologies of batterers. What policies and interventions may best address their violence?

4. What intervention strategies can be used for victims at various points along the continuum of violence?

5. In your opinion, is battered woman syndrome defense justifiable homicide? Explain.

6. Compare Jared Remy and Oscar Pistorius in terms of their victims, the murders, and the legal outcomes.

7. What do you predict for the Rihanna–Brown relationship?

■ Resources

Centre for Children and Families in the Justice System, Domestic Violence http://www.lfcc.on.ca

Health Canada, Violence Against Women https://www.canada.ca/en/status -women/news/2017/06/it_s_time_canadasstrategytopreventandaddress gender-basedviolence.html

National Clearing House on Family Violence http://www.phac-aspc.gc.ca/ncfv -cnivf/index-eng.php

U.S. Department of Justice, Office for Victims of Crime http://www.ojp.usdoj .gov/ovc/

Violence Policy Center http://www.vpc.org

■ References

Adams, D. (2009). Predisposing childhood factors for men who kill their intimate partners. *Victims and Offenders, 4*(3), 215–229.

Alaggia, R., Jenney, A., Mazzuca, J., & Redmond, M. (2007). In whose best interest? A Canadian case study of the impact of child welfare policies in cases of domestic violence. *Brief Treatment and Crisis Intervention*, 7(4), 275–290.

Alaggia, R., Regehr, C., & Jenny, A. (2011). Risky business: An ecological analysis of intimate partner violence disclosure. *Research on Social Work Practice*. doi:10.1177/1049731511425503

Alaggia, R., Regehr, C., & Rishchynsky, G. (2009). Intimate partner violence and immigration laws in Canada: How far have we come? *International Journal of Law and Psychiatry*, 32(6), 335–341.

Allen, M. (2016). Police-reported crime statistics in Canada, 2015. *Juristat*. Statistics Canada Catalogue no. 85-002-X.

Baker, N., Gregware, P., & Cassidy, M. (1999). Family killing field: Honor rationales in the murder of women. *Violence Against Women*, 5(2), 164–184.

Bender, K., & Roberts, A. (2007). Battered women versus male batterer typologies: Same or different based on evidence-based studies? *Aggression and Violent Behavior*, 12(5), 519–530.

Black, M. C., Basile, K. C., Breiding, M. J., Smith, S. G., Walters, M. L., Merrick, M. T., Chen, J., & Stevens, M. (2011). *The national intimate partner and sexual violence survey: 2010 summary report*. Atlanta, GA: National Center for Injury Prevention and Control of the Centers for Disease Control and Prevention.

Black, M. C., Basile, K. C., Breiding, M. J., Smith, S. G., Walters, M. L., Merrick, M. T., Chen, J., & Stevens, M. R. (2011). The National Intimate Partner and Sexual Violence Survey (NISVS): 2010 Summary Report. Atlanta, GA: National Center for Injury Prevention and Control, Centers for Disease Control and Prevention.

Black, T., Trocmé, N., Fallon, B., & MacLaurin, B. (2008). The Canadian child welfare system response to exposure to domestic violence investigations. *Child Abuse and Neglect*, 32, 393–404.

Breiding, M. J., Smith, S., Basile, K. C., Walters, M. L., Chen, J. & Merrick, M. (2014). *The national intimate partner and sexual violence survey: 2010 summary report*. Atlanta, GA: National Center for Injury Prevention and Control of the Centers for Disease Control and Prevention. Retrieved from https://www.cdc.gov/mmwr/preview/mmwrhtml/ss6308a1.htm?s_cid=ss6308a1_e

Brown, C. (2008). Gender-role implications on same-sex intimate partner abuse. *Journal of Family Violence*, 23, 457–462.

Burczycka, M. (2016). Trends in self-reported spousal violence, 2014. In *Family violence in Canada: A statistical profile, 2014*. *Juristat*. Statistics Canada. Catalogue no. 85-002-X.

Campbell, J., Webster, D., Koziol-McLain, J., Block, C., Campbell, D., Curry M., . . . Laughon, K. (2003). Risk factors for femicide in abusive relationships: Results from a multisite case control study. *American Journal of Public Health*, 93(7), 1089–1097.

Catalano, S. (2007). Intimate partner violence in the United States. Retrieved from http://www.ojp.usdoj.gov/bjs/intimate/ipv.htm

Catalano, S., Smith, E., Snyder, H., & Rand, M. (2009). Female victims of violence. Bureau of Justice Statistics. NCJ 228356. Washington, DC: U.S. Department of Justice.

Centers for Disease Control and Prevention. (2006). Dating violence fact sheet. Retrieved from http://www.cdc.gov/ncipc/dvp/dating_violence.htm

Centers for Disease Control and Prevention. (2017). Teen dating violence. Retrieved from https://www.cdc.gov/violenceprevention/intimatepartnerviolence/teen_dating _violence.html

CNN. (2009). Chris Brown apology video. Retrieved from http://www.cnn.com /video/?/video/showbiz/2009/07/20/dcl.brown.apology.cnn

Cruz, A. (2009, February 9). Chris Brown and Rihanna: A fairy-tale romance gone awry. Retrieved from http://www.people.com/people/article/0,,20257828,00.html

Denham, D., & Gillespie, J. (1998). *Two steps forward . . . one step back: An overview of Canadian initiatives and resources to end wife abuse 1989–1997.* Ottawa, Ontario, Canada: Family Violence Prevention Unit, Health Canada.

Dershowitz, A. (2006, April 20). The abuse excuse. Zacarias Moussaoui's lawyers float the "Impoverished French Muslim Syndrome." Retrieved from http://www.slate .com/id/2140262/

Devries, K. M., Mak, J. Y. T., García-Moreno, C., Petzold, M., Child, J. C., . . . Watts, C. H. (2013). The global prevalence of intimate partner violence against women. *Science, 340*(6140), 1527–1528.

Dixon, L., Hamilton-Giachristis, C., & Browne, K. (2008). Classifying partner femicide. *Journal of Interpersonal Violence, 23*(1), 74–93.

Dowd, M. (1999). Women and the abuse excuse. Retrieved from http://library.findlaw .com/1999/Nov/1/129404.html

Elbow, M. (1977). Theoretical considerations of violent marriages. *Social Casework, 58*(9), 515–526.

Ewing, P. (1990). Psychological self-defense: A proposed justification for battered women who kill. *Law and Human Behavior, 14*(6), 579–594.

Fagan, J. (1996). *The criminalization of domestic violence: Promises and limits.* National Institute of Justice Research Report. Washington, DC: U.S. Department of Justice.

Federal Bureau of Investigation (FBI). (1995). The structure of family violence An analysis of selected incidents. Retrieved from http://www.fbi.gov/about-us/cjis/ucr /nibrs/nibrs_famvio95.pdf

Ferraro, K. (2003). The words change, but the melody lingers: The persistence of battered woman syndrome in criminal cases involving battered women. *Violence Against Women, 9*(1), 110–129.

Finkelhor, D., & Yllo, K. (1982). Forced sex in marriage: A preliminary research report. *Crime and Delinquency, 28*(3), 459–478.

Gillis, R., & Diamond, S. (2006). Same-sex partner abuse: Challenges to the existing paradigms of intimate violence theory. In R. Alaggia & C. Viner (Eds.), *Cruel but not unusual: Violence in Canadian families* (pp. 127–146). Waterloo, Ontario: Wilfrid Laurier University Press.

Glancy, G., & Saini, M. (2005). An evidence-based review of psychological treatments for anger and aggression. *Brief Treatment and Crisis Intervention, 5*(2), 229–248.

Gondolf, E. F. (1988). Who are those guys? Toward a behavioral typology of batterers. *Violence and Victims, 3*, 187–203.

Grauwiler, P. (2008). Voices of women: Perspectives on decision-making and the management of partner violence. *Children and Youth Services Review, 30*, 311–322.

Hardesty, J., Oswald, R., Khaw, L., & Fonseca, C. (2011). Lesbian/bisexual mothers and intimate partner violence: Help seeking in the context of social and legal vulnerability. *Violence Against Women, 17*(1), 28–46.

Herman, J. L. (1992). *Trauma and recovery*. New York: Basic Books.

Hildebrandt, A. (2009, July 24). Honour killings: Domestic abuse by another name. Retrieved from http://www.cbc.ca/news/canada/story/2009/07/24/f-honour-killings .html

Holt, S., Buckley, H., & Whelan, S. (2008). The impact of exposure to domestic violence on children and young people: a review of the literature. *Child Abuse & Neglect, 32*(8):797–810.

Holtzworth-Munroe, A., & Stuart, G. L. (1994). Typologies of male batterers: Three subtypes and the differences among them. *Psychological Bulletin, 116*(3), 476–497.

Hopper, T. (2011, August 3). Murders spark fears of honor killings. *National Post*, p. 1.

Huth-Bocks, A., & Hughes, H. (2008). Parenting stress, parenting behaviour and children's adjustment in families experiencing intimate partner violence. *Journal of Family Violence, 23*, 243–251.

Jaffe, P., Crooks, C., & Wolfe, D. (2003). Legal and policy responses to children exposed to domestic violence: The need to evaluate intended and unintended consequences. *Clinical Child and Family Psychology Review, 6*(3), 205–213.

Kitzmann, K., Gaylord, N., Holt, A., & Kenny, E. (2003). Child witnesses to domestic violence: A meta-analytic review. *Journal of Counselling and Clinical Psychology, 71*(2), 339–353.

LA Times. (2009, February 8). Singer Chris Brown under investigation for alleged assault. Retrieved from http://latimesblogs.latimes.com/lanow/2009/02/chris-brown -boo.html

Lehmann, P., & Rabenstein, S. (2002). Children exposed to domestic violence. In A. Roberts (Ed.), *Handbook of domestic violence intervention strategies* (pp. 343–364). New York: Oxford University Press.

MacKinnon, C. (1987). *Feminism unmodified: Discourses on life and law*. Cambridge, MA: Harvard University Press.

MacLeod, L. (1980). *Wife battering in Canada: The vicious cycle*. Ottawa: Canadian Advisory Council of the Status of Women.

Margolin, G., & Vickerman, K. (2007). Posttraumatic stress in children and adolescents exposed to family violence: Overview and issues. *Professional Psychology: Research and Practice, 38*(6), 613–619.

Mbilinyi, L., Edleson, J., Hagemeister, A., & Beeman, S. (2007). What happens to children when their mothers are battered? Results from a four city anonymous telephone survey. *Journal of Family Violence, 22,* 309–317.

Mears, D. P., Carlson, M. J., Holden, G. W., & Harris, S. D. (2001). Reducing domestic violence revictimization: The effects of individual and contextual factors. *Journal of Interpersonal Violence, 16,* 1260–1283.

Moskowitz, E. (2014, May 27). Jared Remy pleads guilty to murder of Jennifer Martel. *The Boston Globe.* Retrieved from https://www.bostonglobe.com /metro/2014/05/27/jared-remy-due-woburn-courtroom-today-latest-hearing -jennifer-martel-murder-case/QRd1y01jtYjZFPtZccI9VN/story.html

Mulligan, L. (2016). Homicide in Canada, 2015. *Juristat.* Statistics Canada. Catalogue no. 85-002-X. Retrieved from http://www.statcan.gc.ca/pub/85-002-x/2016001 /article/14668-eng.htm

National Coalition Against Domestic Violence (NCADV) (n.d.). Learn More. Retrieved from https://ncadv.org/learn-more

National Coalition Against Domestic Violence (NCADV) (n.d.) (Domestic Violence Against Lesbian, Gay, Bisexual And Transgender Relationships, n.d.). New York. Retrieved from http://www.mmgconnect.com/projects/userfiles/file/dce-stop_now /ncadv_lgbt_fact_sheet.pdf

Nicholson v. Williams. (2004). U.S. Court of Appeals, 2nd Cir., No. 2, 171 (amicus).

Papp, A. (2010). Culturally driven violence against women: A growing problem in Canada's immigrant communities. Frontier Centre for Public Policy. Retrieved from http://www.fcpp.org/publication.php/3351

Pattavina, A., Hirshel, D., Buzawa, E., Faggiani, D., & Bentley, H. (2007). A comparison of the police response to heterosexual versus same-sex intimate partner violence. *Violence Against Women, 13*(4), 374–394.

Petrosky, E., Blair, J. M., Betz, C. J. et al. (2017). Racial and ethnic differences in homicides of adult women and the role of intimate partner violence. *Morbidity and Mortality Weekly Report (MMWR),* 2017;66(28);741–746.

Pleck, E. (1987). *Domestic tyranny: The making of social policy against family violence from colonial times to present.* New York: Oxford University Press.

Ptacek, J. (1999). *Battered women in the courtroom: The power of judicial certainty.* Boston: Northeastern University Press.

R v. Lavallee. (1990). 55, CCC 3d 97.

Randle, A., & Graham, C. (2011). A review of the evidence of the effects of intimate partner violence on men. *Psychology of Men and Masculinity, 12*(2), 97–111.

Regehr, C., & Glancy, G. (1995). Battered woman syndrome defense in the Canadian courts. *Canadian Journal of Psychiatry, 40*(3), 130–135.

Roberts, A. R. (2002). Duration and severity of woman battering: A conceptual model/ continuum. In A. Roberts (Ed.), *Handbook of domestic violence intervention strategies* (pp. 64–79). New York: Oxford University Press.

Roberts, A. R. (2007). Domestic violence continuum, forensic assessment, and crisis intervention. *Families in Society: Journal of Contemporary Social Services, 88*(1), 30–43.

Roberts, A. R., & Roberts, B. (2005). *Ending intimate abuse: Practical guidance and survival strategies*. New York: Oxford University Press.

Royal Canadian Mounted Police (RCMP). (2012). Research summary: Domestic violence involving firearms. Retrieved from http://www.rcmp-grc.gc.ca/cfp-pcaf /res-rec/violence-eng.htm

Selley, C. (2008, April 11). Spousal homicide: Just the facts. Retrieved from http://www .macleans.ca/article.jsp?content=20080411_141047_4888

Sherman, L., & Berk, R. (1984). *The Minneapolis Domestic Violence Experiment. Police Foundation Reports*. Washington, DC: Police Foundation.

Shlonsky, A., & Friend, C. (2007). Double jeopardy: Risk assessment in the context of child maltreatment and domestic violence. *Brief Treatment and Crisis Intervention, 7*(4), 253–274.

Skwiot, S. (2016, October 9). Report: Chris Brown believes he will end of with Rihanna. *Life & Style*. Retrieved from http://www.lifeandstylemag.com/posts/chris-brown -believes-he-ll-end-up-with-rihanna-115746

Smith, S. G., Chen, J., Basile, K.C., Gilbert, L. K., Merrick, M. T., Patel, N., Walling, M., & Jain, A. (2017). The National Intimate Partner and Sexual Violence Survey (NISVS): 2010–2012 State Report. Atlanta, GA: National Center for Injury Prevention and Control, Centers for Disease Control and Prevention.

Smith, T. (2013, October 28). Lauren Astley murder draws attention to teen breakup violence. *48 Hours*. Retrieved from https://www.cbsnews.com/news/lauren-astley -murder-draws-attention-to-teen-breakup-violence/

Sorenson, S., & Shen, H. (2005). Restraining orders in California. *Violence Against Women, 11*(7), 912–933.

Stanley, J., Bartholomew, K., Taylor, T., Oram, D., & Landolt, M. (2006). Intimate violence in male same-sex relationships. *Journal of Family Violence, 21*(1), 31–41.

Statistics Canada. (2005, July 14). Family violence in Canada: A statistical profile. Retrieved from http://www.statcan.ca/Daily/English/050714/d050714a.htm

Statistics Canada. (2015). Family violence in Canada: A statistical profile, 2013. Juristat, Statistics Canada Catalogue no. 85-002-X.

Statistics Canada. (2015). Shelters for abused women in Canada, 2014. Retrieved from http://www.statcan.gc.ca/pub/85-002-x/2015001/article/14207-eng.htm

Straus, M., & Gelles, R. (1980). *Behind closed doors: Violence in the American family*. Garden City, NJ: Anchor/Doubleday.

Swash, R. (2009, February 20). Rihanna assault photo leaked. Retrieved from http:// www.guardian.co.uk/music/2009/feb/20/rihanna-alleged-assault-photo-leaked

Tang, K. (2003). Battered woman syndrome testimony in Canada: Its development and lingering issues. *International Journal of Offender Therapy and Comparative Criminology, 47*(6), 618–629.

Taylor, C., & Sorenson, S. (2007). Intervention on behalf of children exposed to intimate partner violence: Assessment of support in a diverse community-based sample. *Child Abuse and Neglect, 31*, 1155–1168.

Tracy, N. (2017) Battered women shelters: What are they and how to find one. HealthyPlace.com. Retrieved from https://www.healthyplace.com/abuse/domestic-violence/what-is-domestic-violence-domestic-abuse/

Truman, J. L., & Morgan, R. E. (2014). Nonfatal domestic violence, 2003–2012. Retrieved from http://www.bjs.gov/content/pub/pdf/ndv0312.pdf

Tutty, L., Ogden, C., & Wyllie, K. (2006). An evaluation of the Peer Support Services peer model. Final report to Peer Support Services for Abused Women. Calgary: RESOLVE Alberta.

Vagi, K. J., Olsen, E. O., Basile, K. C., & Vivolo-Kantor, A. M. (2015). Teen dating violence (physical and sexual) among US high school students: Findings from the 2013 National Youth Risk Behavior Survey. *JAMA Pediatrics*, *169*, 474–482.

Vickerman, K., & Margolin, G. (2007). Posttraumatic stress in children and adolescents exposed to family violence: Treatment. *Professional Psychology: Research and Practice*, *38*(6), 620–628.

Walker, L. A. (1979). *Battered women syndrome*. New York: Springer.

Wilkes, J. (2010, July 13). Ottawa condemns honour killings. Retrieved from http://www.thestar.com/news/canada/article/835153--ottawa-condemns-honour-killings

Wolfe, D., Crooks, C., Lee, V., McIntyre-Smith, A., & Jaffe, P. (2003). The effects of children's exposure to domestic violence: A meta-analysis and critique. *Clinical Child and Family Psychology Review*, *6*(3), 177–187.

World Health Organization. (2005). *Landmark study on domestic violence*. Retrieved from http://www.who.int/mediacentre/news/releases/2005/pr62/en/index.html

Zolotor, A., Theodore, A., Coyne-Beasley, T., & Runyan, D. (2007). Intimate partner violence and child maltreatment: Overlapping risk. *Brief Treatment and Crisis Intervention*, *7*(4), 305–321.

© Peyker/Shutterstock.

CHAPTER 10

Stalking Victims

OBJECTIVES

- To discuss the nature of stalking behaviors
- To identify legal responses to stalking
- To identify a typology of stalkers
- To discuss effects of stalking on victims
- To discuss threat assessment
- To discuss risk assessment of offenders
- To discuss treatment for offenders

KEY TERMS

Celebrity stalking	Peace bond
Credible threat	Protection order
Cyberstalking	Psychiatric gating
de Clérambault's syndrome	Restraining order
Erotomania	Sexually violent predator
Obsessional harassment	Stalking

CASE

Catherine Zeta-Jones and Michael Douglas live a life of luxury and have ample resources to ensure their privacy in their several residences around the world. But in March 2004, while staying at a luxury hotel Douglas co-owns in Bermuda, they received a message from a female caller indicating she was going to kill Zeta-Jones. The call was followed by a series

FIGURE 10-1 (a) Dawnette Knight, celebrity stalker of (b) Michael Douglas and Catherine Zeta-Jones.

(a) © Nick Ut/AP Photos; (b) © Alastair Grant/AP Photos.

of letters sent to others, including Zeta-Jones's father-in-law, Kirk Douglas, in which 32-year-old Dawnette Knight (**FIGURE 10-1**) threatened to slice Zeta-Jones up and feed her to the dogs, chop her into pieces, or shoot her in the head.

In July 2004, Knight issued an apology for her threats toward Zeta-Jones, indicating she was a confused young woman who was infatuated with Michael Douglas. However, later on the witness stand she intimated that she and Douglas had had a love affair and that Douglas paid her off to go away. Douglas denied meeting Knight, although he had received a note from her offering to show him a good time. Knight's fiancé in her defense described her as a fun-loving girl who wanted to pursue a career as a child psychologist. Legal proceedings were suspended after Knight took an overdose while in jail awaiting trial; however, a subsequent fitness hearing found her competent to stand trial for 24 felony counts of threatening and stalking. Zeta-Jones testified at trial that she was terrified for the safety of herself and her family. One year after her initial apology, Knight pled no contest to stalking charges and

was sentenced to three years imprisonment and ordered to pay $200 in restitution (Rathi, 2005; Taylor, 2004; *Telegraph*, 2004).

Catherine Zeta-Jones has faced a number of personal and health challenges since 2004, when her stalker was sentenced. In 2010, her husband Michael Douglas was diagnosed with cancer, and shortly after that Zeta-Jones was admitted to a clinic where doctors concluded she was suffering from bipolar II disorder, a form of manic depression that involves periods of excessive energy and extreme depression. She spoke publicly about her illness and sought treatment by checking herself into a hospital in 2011 and again in 2013. Owing to the stress of both their illnesses, the couple decided to live separately in 2013, though without taking legal action toward separation or divorce. They reconciled in 2014. Zeta-Jones has been the recipient of numerous acting awards, and in 2010 she was appointed Commander of the Order of the British Empire (CBE) for her film and humanitarian endeavors. She supports various charities and causes, and is a prominent celebrity endorser of brands.

Introduction

Stalking is defined as a pattern of conduct in which one person inflicts on another repeated, unwanted intrusions and communications to the extent the victim fears for his or her own safety (Pathé & Mullen, 1997). A national survey in 2010 reported 1 in 7 women and 1 in 18 men have been stalked. Stalking causes the target to fear that he or she or someone close to him or her will be harmed or killed (Black et al., 2011).

Stalking behaviors experienced by the victim can seem benign to the outside observer. A person leaves repeated phone messages, sends gifts, or shows up in places where the victim habitually goes, all of which in isolation do not appear to be threatening (Purcell, Pathé, & Mullen, 2004). Yet, the context of the relationship sets the stage for what the victim experiences as intimidation. That is, the stalker pursues a relationship the victim does not desire, often because the victim is a former partner, a famous person who has no relationship with the stalker, or a professional who has no interest in a personal relationship with the victim. What differentiates these behaviors from normal interpersonal interactions and characterizes them as stalking is that they are (1) intentional, (2) repeated, and (3) result in fear (Spitzberg & Cupach, 2007).

Stalking behaviors can cover a wide range of activities. Generally, stalking includes harassing or threatening an individual during his or her repeated activities, such as following the person, appearing at the person's home or place of business, making harassing phone calls, leaving objects or written messages, or vandalizing property. Stalking may or may not involve threatened or actual violence. **TABLE 10-1** provides a list of common stalking behaviors.

TABLE 10-1 Common Stalking Behaviors

- Repeated telephone calls, letters, or emails
- Sending unwanted gifts (flowers, candy, etc.)
- Showing up uninvited at work or home
- Intercepting mail or email
- Following, watching, or tracking
- Collecting photos or videos of the person
- Contacting the victim's employer, colleagues, or family
- Threatening harm to the victim
- Threatening the victim's family, friends, or pets
- Vandalizing the victim's car or property
- Assault (physical, sexual, or emotional)
- Kidnapping or holding hostage

Stalking behaviors have expanded and now include cybermethods of harassment. **Cyberstalking** provides an additional means to harass victims in a manner that is more anonymous and has less chance of detection than other methods of stalking. The advent of virtual social networks, such as Facebook, allows stalkers easy access to information about victims. Pictures posted on multiple sites often reveal friends, common activities, and favorite places to frequent. Messages can be transmitted to the victim, which can be received anytime or anywhere through email and text messaging. A study conducted by Moriarty and Freiberger (2008) revealed that cyberstalking behaviors were most likely to involve, in order of frequency, (1) threatening, harassing, or obscene emails; (2) live chat harassment or online verbal abuse; (3) threatening or obscene calls to a cell phone; (4) improper messages on message boards; and (5) text and instant messaging. Infrequent but highly threatening activities included tracking a person's whereabouts on a GPS system without the person's consent and electronic identity theft. Interestingly, the nature of the stalking differed with cyberstalking when compared to other methods of stalking. In general, stalking is most commonly associated with domestic violence; however, Moriarty and Freiberger (2008) found a full one-third of cyberstalkers were considered to be nuisance stalkers.

An emerging trend in the context of domestic violence is the use of technology to facilitate stalking and other forms of abuse. Woodlock's survey with 152 domestic violence advocates and 46 victims revealed that technology—including phones, tablets, computers, and social networking websites—is commonly used in intimate partner stalking. Technology was used to create a sense of the perpetrator's omnipresence and to isolate, punish, and humiliate domestic violence victims. Perpetrators also threatened to share sexualized content online to humiliate victims. Technology-facilitated stalking is a serious offense and effective practice, policy, and legal responses need to be developed (Woodlock, 2017). See TABLE 10-2 for the various technologies used in stalking.

One of the troublesome issues in stalking is the degree to which stalking behaviors are an exaggeration of normal courtship behaviors. When someone is infatuated with another person, he or she thinks of them constantly throughout the day. Early in an amorous relationship people call each other frequently and want to spend a great deal of time together, and they might send notes and/or purchase small gifts for each other. Initially, therefore, it can be difficult to differentiate between the behaviors associated with love and those associated with **obsessional harassment**. Similarly, with a famous person, fans are encouraged to be adoring. Fan mail is rewarded with signed pictures and personalized letters. In fact, the existence of people waiting in areas where the famous

TABLE 10-2 Use of Technology in Stalking

Technology	Method	Purpose
Telephone	Caller identification	Reveals telephone number, name, and location of caller
	Fax	Reveals name, fax number, and location of sender
	TTY and TTD (text-telephones used by hearing impaired)	Can be used to impersonate others
	Calling card/spoof card	Provides anonymity for stalkers Disguises stalker phone number or allows impersonation Cannot be traced
	Cordless telephones	Conversations can be intercepted by other devices Calls can be made by similar phones on same line
	Cellular and wireless telephones	Analog cell and digital telephones may be intercepted by radio scanners and special hardware Smartphones can be hacked New cellular telephone directory makes numbers available on an opt-in basis Can be used as listening devices Can be used to impersonate or harass through calls and text messages (e.g., SpoofApp) Call history can be monitored Can threaten and harass by flooding victim with texts, messages, and phone calls
GPS and Location Services	GPS (Global Positioning System)	Location may be detected through GPS in cellular telephones or other GPS devices Laptops and tablets can also show location
Computer and Internet	Desktop, laptop, and tablets can be hacked	All data on the computer becomes available to the hacker and can be used to harm victim
	Public websites, social networking sites, and blogs	Can be used to threaten the victim Can be used to encourage others to contact the victim Can be used to publicly post the victim's personal information Can be used to impersonate the victim or others to gain information about or access to the victim Can be used to spread rumors about the victim

(continues)

TABLE 10-2 Use of Technology in Stalking (*Continued*)

Technology	Method	Purpose
	Email, instant messages, and personal social websites (e.g., Facebook) can be hacked	Others or victim can be impersonated Can be used as another method of harassment through spamming or flooding the computer with unwanted email or messages Can be used to send electronic viruses or phishing scams Can subscribe the victim to multiple listservs
	Website browser history	Records Internet activity, allows "cookies"
	Spyware software	Monitors Internet use
	Keystroke logging software	Records keys typed, including passwords, PIN numbers, email, and websites and sends to hacker
	Hidden cameras and built-in camera	Web cameras connected to a remote computer
	Online databases and information brokers	Personal information sold to and published by corporations, court, and government agencies
	Identity theft or other financial harm	Identity theft Purchasing items or services in victim's name
	Malware	Viruses, worms, ransomware

Data from: TK Logan, 2010. *Research on Partner Stalking: Putting the Pieces Together*. Lexington, KY: University of Kentucky, Department of Behavioral Science & Center on Drug and Alcohol Research.

person is expected to arrive in the hopes of getting a picture or autograph is a sign of success and celebrity. When does fan behavior become stalking?

A further problem associated with stalking is the victim's lack of authority to end the behavior. Although laws that address stalking have emerged, beginning with California in 1990, a continuing problem is that many strategies used by stalkers, such as calling a victim or being in the same place as the victim, are basic rights and freedoms guaranteed under law. Thus, victims try to use a number of strategies that are generally unsuccessful. First, the victim often tries to ignore or normalize the behavior, trying to assess whether or not it should be regarded as threatening. Next, the victim may try to negotiate, request, or plead with the offender to stop the behavior. When these attempts fail, the victim may move to threats, such as calling the police, notifying a superior (such as an employer), or other forms of harm to the stalker. Such strategies, however, can serve to escalate the situation because the threats are often unsuccessful (e.g., the police have limited jurisdiction to intervene), and the victim has now demonstrated the impact of the stalker on his or her life. The victim therefore may begin to alter his or her customary patterns and limit his or her activities to avoid contact with the stalker. He or she may change telephone numbers, move to a different residence, restrict excursions, or refrain from going anywhere unless accompanied. Finally, the victim may seek assistance from a shelter or other service or seek legal options. The experience consumes the victim's time and emotional energy and is highly distressing and seemingly without end.

Scope of the Problem

A large number of studies have attempted to determine the nature and incidence of stalking. Spitzberg and Cupach (2007) conducted a meta-analysis of 175 studies using unique samples ranging from large-scale population studies to studies of forensic populations, which in total represented 122,207 individuals. From their analysis, they determined that population-based studies indicate a lifetime prevalence of stalking ranging from 2% to 13% for males and 8% to 32% for females. Across the studies examined, 60% to 80% of the victims were female. Stalking was most likely to emerge from a preexisting relationship; 79% of victims knew their pursuer, and half of all stalking emerged from romantic relationships. Physical violence was reported in 32% of cases, and sexual violence was reported in 12% of cases.

The U.S. National Crime Victimization Survey (U.S. Department of Justice, 1997) found a lifetime prevalence of 8.1% for women and 2.2% for men, which, by extrapolation, translates to 2.04 million women and 820,000 men in the United States who at some time in their lives have been victims of stalking behavior (Douglas & Dutton, 2001). The 2006 Supplemental Victimization Survey estimated that over a 12-month period in the United States, 3.4 million people over age 18 were victims of stalking (Baum, Catalano, Rand, & Rose, 2009). Nearly three-fourths of those reporting stalking knew their attacker. The National Violence Against Women Survey revealed that 87% of stalking victims were women and 87% of stalkers were men. Of all groups in the survey, Native American women were significantly more likely to report being stalked than members of other ethnic and racial groups (Tjaden & Thoennes, 1998).

Ongoing surveys such as the National Intimate Partner and Sexual Violence Survey (NISVS) collect current national- and state-level data on intimate partner violence, sexual violence, and stalking victimization in the United States. The CDC developed the survey to collect data on important public health problems to address violence prevention efforts. The NISVS examined stalking and intimate partner violence victimization using data collected between January and December 2011 by the CDC. The CDC used a conservative definition of stalking for the 2011-2012 survey. First, respondents were classified as a stalking victim if they experienced multiple stalking tactics or a single tactic by the same offender multiple times and second, if the respondents felt very fearful or believed someone would be harmed as a result of the offender's stalking behavior. The specific findings of this survey reported by Breiding and colleagues (2014) include:

- In one year in the United States, 7.5 million people were stalked.
- 61% of female victims and 44% of male victims were stalked by a former or current intimate partner.
- During one's lifetime, an estimated 15% of women and 6% of men have been a victim of stalking.

The General Social Survey in Canada found that 11% of women aged 15 and older (or 1.4 million women) stated they had been stalked in a way that caused them to fear for their safety or the safety of someone close to them (Statistics Canada, 2006). Clearly, stalking is a much more common experience than most of us would expect.

Stalking Laws

California passed the first stalking law in the Western world in 1990 as a result of five stalking-related murders that occurred in Orange County over a 1-year period, the most famous of which was the murder of actress Rebecca Schaeffer (California Penal Code, 1990). In 1996, the National Institute of Justice brought a Model Anti-Stalking Code to Congress. This code defines stalking as "repeatedly maintaining visual or physical proximity to a person, repeatedly conveying verbal or written threats or threats implied by conduct" (p. 43). The code was seen as necessary because generally, legal remedies for victims were covered under laws addressing harassment, trespassing, or vandalism, which addressed very specific aspects of stalking behavior; were frequently misdemeanors that were not given serious attention; and could not be enacted until the stalker had inflicted physical assault or property damage on the victim (Dennison & Thomson, 2005; Purcell et al., 2004). This was exemplified by Sandra Pollard, the mother of a stalking victim, who testified before the 1992 U.S. Senate Judiciary Committee hearings on anti-stalking legislation:

> Despite threats he has made against our lives, despite repeated violations of restraining orders, despite the professional assessment of him as dangerous, both the District Attorney and our own attorney

have said that nothing can be done until he has "done something." What is the "something" they must wait for him to do? Kidnap [my daughter]? Rape her? Kill her?

(Purcell et al., 2004, p. 159)

As a result, public pressure and concern resulted in legislative reform with the goal to better address the needs of stalking victims. Current legislation varies by state but generally covers repeatedly following or harassing an individual where the behavior of the pursuer contains a **credible threat** of harm. Some states specify which acts are included in the term "conduct," whereas others focus on the criminal outcome of the conduct. All states require the prosecution to demonstrate the stalking was intentional (Tjaden, 2009). Some states classify stalking as a misdemeanor, and others define it as a felony, resulting in wide variation in sanctions. Even where stalking is a felony offense, sentences vary from a maximum of 12 months in West Virginia to 7 years for an equivalent offense in Illinois. Further, some states require prior incidents of stalking or the violation of existing protection orders, and others do not (Dennison & Thomson, 2005).

Stalking (defined as criminal harassment) was introduced into the Criminal Code of Canada in April 1993. The Section 264 of the Code stipulates that:

No person shall, without lawful authority and knowing that another person is harassed or recklessly as to whether the other person is harassed, engage in conduct referred to in subsection (2) that causes that other person reasonably, in all the circumstances, to fear for their safety or the safety of anyone known to them.

Prohibited conduct outlined in the Code includes the following (Criminal Code of Canada, 1993, Section 264):

(a) repeatedly following from place to place the other person or anyone known to them;

(b) repeatedly communicating with, either directly or indirectly, the other person or anyone known to them;

(c) besetting or watching the dwelling-house, or place where the other person, or anyone known to them, resides, works, carries on business or happens to be; or

(d) engaging in threatening conduct directed at the other person or any member of their family.

Criminal conviction of stalking behavior carries a penalty of up to five years imprisonment. In England, Wales, and Scotland, the legislation similarly takes the form of protection from harassment in which harassment is defined as conduct that causes distress.

Although these stalking laws are, without question, an improvement over the previous laws that addressed this issue, critics indicate that these laws continue to have limitations (Abrams & Robinson, 1998). For example, in some jurisdictions definitions can be problematic, such as when stalking is viewed as limited to situations where the victim and the offender have a previous relationship (Gilligan, 1992; Lingg, 1993). In many states there is a requirement that a "credible threat" of violence is established, which is defined as a threat causing a reasonable person to fear for his or her physical safety (Perez, 1993). This is potentially problematic in all situations but in particular in cases of intimate partner violence where the threat is perceived differently by the victim because of previous experiences of violence with this offender. Thus, the victim's view may not be equivalent to the "reasonable person" defined by law. Indeed, less than half of the stalking victims in a national survey were directly threatened by their stalker, thereby making them ineligible for assistance under statutes that include the requirement of credible threat (Tjaden & Thoennes, 1998).

A separate set of laws related to stalking emanate out of concerns related to stalking among **sexually violent predators**. This is the least common form of stalking; nevertheless, the serial rapist or serial murderer who stalks and then attacks his or her victim is one of the most primal fears in our society. Sexually violent predator laws provide a means to incarcerate sex offenders judged to be mentally disordered and dangerous to others at the end of their court-imposed sentences for crimes already committed. These laws were developed throughout the United States to address public concerns for safety and provide a mechanism for keeping individuals who are dangerous away from the public (Prentky, Janus, Barbaree, Schwartz, & Kafka, 2006). In essence, these laws attempt to curtail future stalking in an individual who has been tried and convicted of this offense in the past.

Canadian legislation and practice uses four procedures for dealing with sexual predators. In 1997, a federal task force, with input from the Canadian Psychiatric Association and the Canadian Academy of Psychiatry and Law, amended sexual predator legislation to create an indeterminate sentence for dangerous offenders and include the new category of long-term offender. Long-term offenders are those sexual offenders who appear to have a reasonable prospect of successful treatment. Further, a new section that amounts to a preventive peace bond has been enacted for situations where there is a reasonable fear of a sexual offense. Finally, an informal mechanism of **psychiatric gating** exists, where a person is certified under provincial mental health legislation and sent to any hospital (Glancy, Regehr, & Bradford, 2001). Use of this dangerous offender legislation is increasing in most Canadian jurisdictions.

In summary, legislation enacted since 1990 throughout North America and much of Western Europe has led to considerable improvement in legal options that are available to manage stalking behavior. Nevertheless, these laws do not provide perfect protection, and victims of stalking, to a large extent, are still left to their own devices to ensure their safety.

Typology of Stalking

The term *stalking* is used to describe a pattern of behavior that is intrusive, repeated, and fear provoking. However, the motivations behind this behavior are highly variable. In an example discussed below under "Celebrity Stalkers," Robert Bardo, a fan, sought to develop a relationship with Rebecca Schaeffer, a celebrity, based on his idealized fantasies about who she was and how she might change his life. In another example, an abusive husband was rejected by his wife, who sought to secure her safety and improve her life. His motivation was likely a mixture of desire to reconcile and anger at the fact that his wife had left him. These are but two examples of a wide range of motivations for stalking behavior.

Several authors have attempted to develop typologies of stalking based on a number of dimensions, including the psychological characteristics of the stalker and the relationship between the stalker and the victim. Zona, Sharma, and Lane (1993) identified three types of stalkers:

1. The classic erotomania stalker, who is often a woman with a delusional belief that a powerful man is in love with her (e.g., her doctor)

2. The love-obsessed stalker, who is delusionally focused on a famous person (e.g., an actor or politician)

3. The simple obsessional stalker, who stalks a former partner with intense resentment as a result of perceived rejection

Mullen, Pathé, Purcell, and Stuart (1999) identified five types of stalkers:

1. The rejected stalker, who is motivated by a mixture of revenge and desire for reconciliation after a relationship ends

2. The intimacy-seeking stalker, who often has erotomanic delusions

3. The incompetent stalker, who may be intellectually or socially limited

4. The resentful stalker, who seeks to frighten and distress the victim

5. The predatory stalker, who is preparing for a sexual attack

Dziegielewski and Roberts (1995), in an attempt to better understand and treat victims of stalking, suggested three categories:

1. Domestic violence stalking
2. Erotomania or delusional stalking
3. Nuisance stalking

Meloy (1998b) focused on relational typologies: intimates, strangers, and acquaintances. Melton (2000) differentiated between delusional and nondelusional stalkers and known and not-known victims. More recently, authors have focused on cyberstalking, although there is no clear consensus whether this represents another typology of stalker or whether this is simply a method of stalking.

Ben and Fremouw (2002) examined data from a sample of 108 female college students who had experienced stalking behaviors and had responded to questions regarding their perceptions of those behaviors. The victims' perceptions were factor analyzed, and a cluster-analysis grouped those factors to produce a four-cluster typology of stalkers. Cluster 1 (Harmless) appeared to reflect a more casual, less jealous pattern of behavior. Cluster 2 (Low Threat) appeared the least likely to become physically violent or threatening or to engage in illegal behaviors. Cluster 3 (Violent Criminal) appeared to be the most likely to engage in physically threatening and illegal behaviors. Cluster 4 (High Threat) was characterized by a more serious type of relationship where the victim felt restricted by the partner even in early meetings. Glancy (2008) recommended a multiaxial approach that addresses motivation, mental state, method, and victim relationship (TABLE 10-3).

TABLE 10-3 Classification Criteria for Stalkers

Motivation	Mental Status	Method	Relationship
Rejected	Psychotic	Harassment	Known
Intimacy seeking	Nonpsychotic	Threats	Ex-intimate
Incompetent		Assaults	Potential suitor
Resentful			Professional
Predatory			
			Unknown
			Professional
			Potential suitor
			Celebrity
			Head-of-state

Data from: Glancy, G., & Saini, M. 2005. An evidence-based review of psychological treatments for anger and aggression. *Brief Treatment and Crisis Intervention*, 5(2), 229–248.

Although all these typologies are useful, for the purposes of this chapter four main categories of stalking are discussed: (1) **celebrity stalking**, (2) erotomanic stalking, (3) stalking as an extension of intimate partner, and (4) the sexually sadistic stalker.

Celebrity Stalkers

In 1989, 21-year-old actress Rebecca Schaeffer was a star on the rise. She had just completed a three-year run on a CBS situation comedy, was the celebrity spokesperson for a charity for high-risk adolescents, and was preparing for an audition for the movie *The Godfather: Part III.* Although her fan mail was increasing, she continued to try to respond to each letter she received. One of these letters was from 19-year-old Robert John Bardo, a young man who, unknown to Rebecca, had become obsessed with her. He filled his room with photographs and video clips of her, and in 1987, he went twice to the studio where she worked but was turned away. Then, via computer databases, he discovered whom she called, what car she drove, and where she shopped; subsequently, he hired a detective to obtain her address from the California Department of Motor Vehicles. Bardo's love turned to rage, however, when he saw a movie scene in which Rebecca was in bed with a man. Bardo then determined to kill her for this perceived relationship breach and documented on a drawing of her body where he intended to shoot her. On July 18, Bardo went to Rebecca's apartment. Expecting a script delivery she opened the door and, surprised to see a fan, quickly sent him away. A few minutes later he returned and shot her to death. Rebecca's fatality sparked legislation prohibiting the release of addresses through the Department of Motor Vehicles, legislation directed at curtailing stalking, and the creation of the first Threat Management Unit through the Los Angeles Police Department.

The very nature of the activities in which celebrities engage to enhance their fame and fortunes make them ideal targets for stalkers. Celebrities appear on talk shows and tell their innermost secrets, they appear in music videos and sing songs of love and lust while looking directly into the viewers' eyes, and they have a staff that sends signed photos with intimate messages to eager fans. Given the ever-present availability of TV programming—including music video stations and entertainment news shows—tabloids that track every relationship and every excursion, and Internet video footage posted by anyone with a cell phone, information about celebrities is easily accessible to everyone (Philips, 2008).

Although there are several types of celebrity stalkers, one type has been described as "love obsessed," where the adoration of a fan becomes exaggerated and the stalker believes he or she is in love. At times, the belief systems of celebrity stalkers may be related to a psychotic illness and results in delusional beliefs that they have a special relationship with the famous person. These celebrity stalkers closely resemble erotomanic stalkers (discussed below).

A more contemporary case is actress Sandra Bullock, who has been in many award-winning films and serves as a public figure. To ensure her protection she resides deep in the Hollywood Hills in an estate with an elaborate fence armed with a security system and cameras.

In June 2014, a man later identified as Joshua James Corbett stood outside Bullocks's driveway gates for days writing in his journal about Bullock. On the morning of June 9, Corbett rang the doorbell 10 to 12 times before breaking in through a sunroom door. When Bullock went to close her door, she saw Corbett wearing dark-colored clothing. She instantly closed her "safe door" and locked herself in her closet, from where she called the police. On her phone she directed them through her security gate and up to the attic where she saw Corbett going.

When Corbett was arrested (on site) he was holding a notebook with a two-page letter to Bullock professing his love for her as her "husband." As the officers took him away, he shouted, "Sandy, I'm sorry. Please don't press charges." Corbett was held on a $2.185 million bail. He eventually pled guilty and was sentenced to 5 years of probation and 10 years of a protective order not to be within 200 feet of Ms. Bullock. He was also ordered to receive inpatient psychiatric treatment. A search of Corbett's house after his arrest revealed 24 firearms, including machine guns, assault rifles, and explosive devices. Police also found a letter detailing his intent to sexually assault Sandra Bullock after breaking into her home.

Dietz and associates (1991a, 1991b) reviewed thousands of letters, identified as concerning, that had been sent to celebrities and members of Congress. Their study revealed that even though the subjects had no personal relationship with the people to whom they wrote, many believed they did have a relationship, and often an important one. The most common roles individuals believed they had with celebrities were friend or advisor (41%), spouse or would-be spouse (30%), and lover or would-be lover (25%). Twenty-two percent of the letter writers saw themselves as special fans, and only 17% appropriately identified themselves simply as fans or strangers. For those with delusional beliefs, publicity tactics such as encouraging individuals to email the star or offering a phone call from the star only served to intensify their beliefs. When this type of celebrity stalker believes he or she has been rejected, behaviors can be intensified, and the person begins to seek reconciliation and/or revenge. If, as a result of intensified attempts to contact the celebrity, the stalker feels humiliated or mistreated, the motivation for the stalking may change from love to distress or anger. In such a case, for example, that of Rebecca Schaeffer, the outcome may be tragic.

Other celebrity stalkers may engage in stalking behavior out of rage due to a perceived injustice. Robert Philips (2008), in his work as a consulting psychiatrist to the Protective Intelligence Division of the U.S. Secret Service, reviewed various motivations of presidential stalkers. One motivation, retribution, occurs when an individual holds a political figure or the government in general responsible for his or her own personal failures. Such was the case of Samuel Byck, who sent many threatening letters to President Nixon and others and eventually moved to execute a plan to hijack a commercial airliner and fly it into the White House. Byck killed himself with his own gun but not before killing a police officer, the pilot, and the copilot of the plane he was attempting to hijack (Philips, 2008). Other motivations for stalking a political figure include erotomania, such as in the case of Jane Doe and President Clinton, or delusional obsessions, such as in the case of John Hinckley, Jr., and President Reagan.

Erotomanic Stalkers

Erotomania, also known as **de Clérambault's syndrome**, is delusional loving. The symptoms of this syndrome were first delineated by French psychiatrist de Clérambault (1942) in his work *Les Psychoses Passionelles*. However, Jordan and Howe (1980) traced the origins of the disorder back to Hippocrates and later to Pardoux's book, *Disease of the Mind*, published in the late 1500s. One who suffers from this syndrome believes a person of higher social stature or professional standing is passionately in love with him or her but that this person is restricted from expressing this love because of external constraints. For instance, if the object of affection is a professional, the stalker may believe it is regulations that forbid relationships between patients and doctors or students and professors that are standing in the way of their happiness together. Alternately, the stalker may attribute blame to the victim's family, believing, for instance, that if the pregnant wife were out of the way the stalker and victim could be together. Thus, the stalker may confront or harass family members, attempting to convince them or scare them into freeing the loved one to be with the stalker. The delusions of love are fixed and constant, and despite repeated confrontations with reality, the person is unable to let go of the belief (Jordan & Howe, 1980). When the love and hope are not realized, however, they may disintegrate to resentment and anger (de Clérambault, 1942). At that time the stalker may become threatening or assaultive.

Of all categories of stalkers, women who stalk are most likely to fall into this category of erotomanic stalkers (Purcell, Pathé, & Mullen, 2001). Erotomanic stalkers are likely to have a diagnosis of personality disorder, paranoid disorder, or psychotic disorder such as schizophrenia. They are more likely than other types of stalkers to have never been married, to misuse substances, to have a history of assault and self-harming, and to have more repeated hospitalizations.

The most common victims of erotomanic stalkers are professionals who have had contact with the stalker and with whom the stalker desires to establish a close and loving relationship. Mental health professionals are at particularly high risk, and a variety of surveys suggest that 8% to 11% of mental health professionals have been stalked at one point in their career by a patient. Men are the more common victims in this category. Psychiatrists and psychologists are at highest risk, with reported stalking as high as 20% to 33% in these professions (McIvor & Petch, 2006).

The high rate of stalking among mental health professionals is not particularly surprising. Mental health professionals frequently work with individuals who have significant difficulties in forming interpersonal relationships and often have histories of abuse or neglect. The warm, supportive, and accepting relationship that a professional forms with a patient as part of the treatment process can easily be misinterpreted as an indication of love or desire in someone who has not experienced such relationships in the past and can become incorporated into a delusional system (Regehr & Glancy, 2011). Further, mental health professionals are more likely to tolerate harassing and other behaviors that are not tolerated in other circumstances as a standard part of the management of behaviors of psychiatric patients (McIvor & Petch, 2006). As with celebrity stalkers, the behaviors at first are not overtly threatening and begin more as a nuisance and then escalate. Whereas others may stop contact at an earlier stage, the mental health professional may persist in the relationship, reinforcing false beliefs about love, until the situation is more difficult to control.

This group of stalkers is least likely to result in threats of violence or actual violent activity (Rosenfeld, 2000). However, the cost of the harassing behavior to the victim in both emotional and professional terms is often very disturbing. Stalkers in this group have been known to send letters to the spouses and children of victims declaring the imaginary relationship and indicating that the victim has been unfaithful to loved ones. Flowers, gifts, and letters are left at professional offices or on personal property. Items such as photographs or signs with the person's name may be stolen and kept as tokens of imagined love. Declarations of the relationship can be made to other colleagues, raising suspicions of sexual impropriety. Finally, complaints of impropriety may be made to professional licensing bodies, resulting in lengthy and embarrassing investigations (Regehr & Glancy, 2011).

Stalking as an Extension of Domestic Violence

At the time that National Institute of Justice (NIJ) and the National Center for Injury Prevention and Control (NCIPC) formed a partnership to study violence against women, no national data on stalking and its impact existed. Their first-ever national survey made a major contribution and has served as the foundation for additional studies to be added to the history of stalking in America, especially as an extension of domestic violence (Tjaden & Thoennes, 1998). Although legal definitions of stalking can vary widely from state to state, most states define stalking as the willful, malicious, and repeated following and harassing of another person. Women are twice as likely as men to be stalked by their intimate partner. This is not surprising when considering the incidence of intimate partner violence against men and women. When stalking does occur in intimate relationships, it is likely to coexist with other forms of violence. Eighty-one percent of women in the National Violence Against Women Survey who reported being stalked by an intimate partner also reported other forms of physical abuse, and 31% had been sexually assaulted (Tjaden & Thoennes, 1998).

- In examining statistics about stalking, it is important to report, when possible, differences between abusive partners who stalk and abusive partners who do not stalk. The differences will identify characteristics and the dangerousness of the partner stalking. In analyzing the findings from several studies, Logan (2012) reported the following findings: Several studies found that between 50 and 60% of partner violence victims reported being stalked by their partner.

- The majority of partner violence victims (about 90%) who reported being stalked by a violent partner reported being stalked the year prior to obtaining a protective order.

- Thirty percent of domestic violence offenders in offender treatment reported stalking behaviors toward their victim.

Stalking as a form of domestic violence is the most common form of stalking, encompassing an estimated 75% to 80% of all cases (Roberts & Dziegielewski, 2006). Considerable evidence suggests that victims of spousal violence who attempt to separate from their abusive partner may be at higher risk after the separation than before. According to Statistics Canada (2006), in most cases (63%) where intimate partner violence was reported in a general population survey, violence ended at separation; however, 39% of women and 32% of men who had been in violent relationships indicated they were assaulted after the relationship ended. Of these, 24% indicated the violence became worse, and 39% indicated the violence began only after separation. Further, marital separation is a factor that elevates the rate of spousal homicide for women. Ex-marital partners are responsible for 38% of all homicides against women in Canada and 2% of all homicides against men (Hotton, 2002).

Burgess and colleagues (1997) studied 120 people charged with domestic violence who were attending a treatment program, and 30% admitted to stalking their partners. Those that did stalk a former partner had more serious histories of domestic violence. Similarly, Schwartz-Watts and Morgan (1998), using a clinical sample, reported that 80% of violent stalkers had previous relationships with the victims, compared to 55% of nonviolent stalkers. Palarea, Zona, Lane, and Langhinrichsen-Rohlings (1999), in an analysis of stalking cases from the Los Angeles Threat Management Unit, found that stalkers with previous intimate relationships were significantly more likely to threaten, damage property, and physically harm the victim.

Amrita and Sulay were married shortly after being introduced by family members, and they moved into the home of Sulay and his family. Although initially this went well, family problems in Sulay's home resulted in increased distress for all members. During this time, Amrita and Sulay also began to have fights, and on more than one occasion Sulay's mother asked Amrita to leave their home to end the argument. Fights between Amrita and Sulay intensified, at times including physical assaults against Amrita. After nine months of marriage, Amrita elected to leave the marriage and return to the home of her own parents. Sulay began contacting Amrita with increasing intensity, hanging around outside her university classes, parking in front of her home for hours on end, calling her incessantly, and sending cards, flowers, and gifts. In each encounter, he insisted that she was mistaken in breaking up with him and was not telling him the truth about the reason for the breakup, which he believed to be another man. Sulay became increasingly tearful, sleepless, angry, and withdrawn. After a few months of harassment, Amrita's father attempted to intervene by contacting Sulay's family. Shortly thereafter, Sulay physically assaulted Amrita as she was leaving a university class, resulting in severe bruising. He was arrested and charged with assault. After he was released from jail, Sulay continued to contact and follow Amrita. One month later, he approached her at the hospital at which she had a part-time job and stabbed her. Fortunately, Amrita survived the attack.

Stalking behavior in this category is frequently seen to be motivated by the desire for power and control. In this conceptualization, the ending of a relationship is a threat to the power and control that an abuser exercised over his or her partner. Stalking then includes a series of behaviors aimed at regaining control and reestablishing the relationship (Burgess et al., 1997; Dziegielewski & Roberts, 1995). One set of strategies can involve limiting social activities of the victim by contacting family and friends, going to places or events the victim is likely to attend, and driving or walking by the victim's residence to limit who might visit (Brewster, 2003). Other strategies involve influencing children, attempting financial control, and physical violence (Brewster, 2003). The intimidation can be extended beyond the victim and include other vulnerable members of the victim's family, such as children, a sibling, or an elderly parent. Domestic violence stalking is often open in nature, in part because the stalker believes the behavior is justified and a right. When it leads to violence, the stalker believes the violence was provoked by the victim. However, to an outsider the actual behavior of the victim that may result in an attack is not predictable; rather, the nature of the provocation resides in the fantasy world of the stalker (Burgess et al., 1997).

The need for power and control in domestic violence stalkers is generally fueled by rage at abandonment (Douglas & Dutton, 2001). Mullen and colleagues (1999) thus referred to this group of stalkers as "rejected stalkers." In their study of 145 stalkers, people in this category described a complex mixture of desire for reconciliation and revenge. They experienced a sense of loss, alternately combined with frustration, anger, jealousy, vindictiveness, and sadness. The majority of this group carried a diagnosis of personality disorder, although a smaller percentage of them had delusional disorders. Burgess and colleagues (1997) described a process that occurs in these types of stalking situations based on their research of domestic violence cases in Michigan. First, the stalker is open in his or her attempts to contact the ex-partner. When this fails the stalker begins to contact others and discredit the partner. Next, the positive emotion of love becomes converted to hatred, and the stalker goes underground and clandestine, using tactics such as phoning and hanging up or entering the premises without permission. After this comes a phase of ambivalence, where the stalker may send gifts and flowers. When this attempt at reconciliation is unsuccessful, the stalker may become explosive and violent.

Sexually Sadistic Stalkers

Although sexually violent predators are perhaps the most distressing type of stalker from a public perspective, this type of stalking remains relatively rare. Purcell and colleagues (2001) suggested that 7% of male stalkers in their studies (and 0% of female stalkers) fall into the designation of sexually motivated predatory stalkers. Nevertheless, this has been a focus of legislative activity in Canada and the United States in recent years. In this situation, stalking occurs when a violent and dangerous offender seeks a victim to satisfy his desires. A particular victim is selected because she represents a particular type of person to whom the offender is attracted. This type of stalker may identify a potential victim over a period of time, establish her patterns, and in the end sexually assault or murder her.

Alicia Ross, age 25, was killed by her next door neighbor, Daniel Sylvester, a social recluse who fantasized about raping and killing women and spied on women in his neighborhood. In the seven years he lived next door to Ross they had never spoken. Then one evening after her boyfriend left, Sylvester approached Alicia on the driveway. When she rejected his advances, he hit her over the head to subdue her, dragged her away, and raped her, killed her, and then hid the body. The court heard that Sylvester had been treated by mental health professionals beginning at the age of 9 years, and from an early age had fantasies about jumping out of the bushes and raping women (Mitchell, 2007). In these situations, the victim is often unaware that she is being stalked and can do little to protect herself.

Effects of Stalking on Victims

Victims of stalking believe they are under siege. Unwanted phone calls and messages were the most common type of stalking behavior experienced, according to a national study (Catalano, 2012). Victims report receiving repeated unwanted phone calls where the stalker hangs up immediately, remains silent, declares love, shouts obscenities, or threatens. Calls are usually received at inconvenient times, such as in the early morning or at work, and the victim's voice mail is often filled with the stalker's messages. Letters are frequently sent, or written messages are dropped off. Gifts arrive with some frequency. In the current days of electronic communication, email is a common form of communication. The stalker may come to the victim's home or office and refuse to leave. Surveillance is commonly reported by victims in which they are followed or watched. In a study by Pathé and Mullen (1997), 36% of a sample of 100 victims reported property damage. Cars were covered with graffiti, the paint was scratched, and the tires were slashed. Homes were attacked via broken windows and smashed fences. In addition, in more than half the cases, stalkers made threats directly to harm the victims or their families and friends, or they threatened to discredit the victim by spreading malicious gossip. In one-third of cases the victim was assaulted.

In light of these repeated attacks on the privacy, property, and life of the victim, it is not surprising that stalking victims experience a wide range of social and psychological sequelae. Victims who are in a constant state of threat experience feelings of fear, anxiety, and apprehension that sometimes may border on paranoia. Symptoms of depression, anger, and helplessness are also reported, occasionally leading to suicidal ideation (McEwan, Mullen, & Purcell, 2007). The arousal, intrusion, and avoidance symptoms associated with posttraumatic stress disorder (PTSD) are also common (Pathé & Mullen, 1997). Victims are in a constant state of heightened anxiety, are easily startled by any noise (such as the telephone ringing for the 50th time that day), and remain hypervigilant, carefully watching for any sign of the stalker. They check their rearview mirror and drive home by different routes. Thoughts of the stalker begin to intrude throughout the day, and at night they invade the victim's dreams. The victim begins to avoid any possibility of contact, restricting activities such as going outside and answering the telephone, thereby becoming more isolated.

Pathé and Mullen (1997) reported that over half of the victims in their study decreased or ceased work or school attendance. These symptoms are likely to be more pronounced when the stalking involves a former history of violence, because the number of stalking behaviors increases, or when the duration of the stalking is prolonged (Kamphuis & Emmelkamp, 2001; Kamphuis, Emmelkamp, & Bartak, 2003; Pathé & Mullen, 1997). As stalking continues, victims report sleep disturbances, nausea or stomach upset, fatigue, headaches, and exacerbation of preexisting medical conditions, such as asthma. Consequently, according to the National Violence Against Women Survey, 30% of female victims and 20% of male victims seek psychological counseling as a result of their victimization (Tjaden & Thoennes, 1998).

On a social level, the victim's occupational and educational status is affected if he or she reduces his or her attendance or has frequent interruptions at work. Friends and family are called on to accompany the victim to various places or stay at the victim's home. Family members become distraught and angry, as there seems to be no end in sight, and may alternately express anger toward the justice system for failing to protect the victim or anger at the victim for bringing this into their lives. Social supports can diminish with prolonged stalking as friends seek to have their own lives return to normal (Regehr & Glancy, 2011).

Safety Strategies for Victims

Given the highly distressing nature of stalking, victims frequently seek assistance from others, including mental health professionals. It is important to reinforce the victim's perception of being stalked and that he or she is not simply being paranoid or overreacting. Added to this is the provision of education on safety measures. Victims must be made aware that they are primarily responsible for their own safety (Meloy, 1998a). That is, despite even their best efforts, police and others in the justice system will be unable to ensure that no harm comes to the victim.

The victim should first be vigilant about safety risks. Any unusual occurrences or uncomfortable feelings about situations should be addressed. Victims can enlist the assistance of others in this regard by telling neighbors or coworkers about the situation and enlisting their assistance in being alert to dangers. One forensic psychiatrist who was under threat from a previous inmate circulated pictures of the stalker to selected neighbors (in particular, a police officer who lived across the street) and to others in his office building. Security firms can be enlisted to evaluate the safety of the victim's home and install often-inexpensive measures to increase security. The victim should ensure that doors and windows are locked and that outside lights are illuminated. The door should not be answered without verifying the identity of the visitor. Cars should be parked in well-lit areas. Habitual travel patterns should be modified regularly (Dietz, 1989).

Victims should create and maintain documentary evidence of the stalking to assist with apprehension and successful prosecution of the offender. Voice mail messages, although they are upsetting and often abhorrent, should be recorded and stored. All letters, emails, notes, and gifts should be retained. Photos should be taken of damage or messages left on property, such as writing on windows. Contemporaneous recording of incidents is an excellent way of demonstrating a pattern of repetition, for example, that the phone rang on 20 separate occasions in one evening, and when the phone was answered by the victim the caller did not respond. Although any single occurrence seems innocuous, pages of notes that record repeated small events leads to a more compelling argument of threat.

The victim should avoid contact with the stalker and never initiate contact. Although at first glance this suggestion may seem obvious, it is not uncommon for victims to attempt to confront the stalker, plead for him or her to stop, or try to negotiate limited contact. These actual contacts can be reinforcing for the stalker, demonstrating that repeated attempts do result in intermittent rewards (Meloy, 1998b). Alternately, these contacts can serve to incite anger and violence if the stalker feels slighted or rebuked.

Victims who are in need of legal protection can obtain a **restraining order** made under civil law, usually in the context of family court. Such orders forbid a person from molesting, annoying, harassing, or communicating with another person except as set out in the order. A **protection order** may give temporary custody of children and the home to the victim and order the abusive person out of the home. It can include conditions such as not allowing any contact (Department of Justice Canada, 2004). To obtain a protection order, a person must make an application to the court, often done with the assistance of a lawyer. A protection order is not dependent on fear of personal safety.

Although in the United States protection orders are made at the state level, the Interstate Stalking Punishment and Prevention Act of 1996 made the orders enforceable across state lines and the violation of such an order a federal crime. In Canada, the police do not enforce civil orders such as a restraining order, and breach of the civil order does not result in criminal charges. If the designated person ignores the order, a civil contempt proceeding must be initiated. At the contempt hearing the judge can order the named person to be fined or to jail until such time as he or she obeys the court order. Another option for victims in Canada therefore is a **peace bond**, which can be initiated by victims, often through the prosecutor's office or the police, who fear they or their family will be harmed by the offender. The standard of proof for the victim's fears is the balance of probabilities; that is, it is more likely to be true than not. If the conditions of a peace bond are broken, the named person can be charged with a criminal offense (Regehr & Kanani, 2010).

In a review of protection orders, Benitez, McNiel, and Binder (2010) concluded there is clear evidence that orders will be violated and the risk of violation is greatest soon after the order is implemented. Further, the risk of violence tends to increase after a protection order violation. Indeed, the National Violence Against Women Survey revealed that 69% of female stalking victims and 81% of male stalking victims who had obtained restraining orders indicated their stalkers had violated the order (Tjaden & Thoennes, 1998).

Storey and Hart (2011) conducted a case analysis of strategies used by victims immediately before the desistance of a stalker. Effective strategies inevitably involved legal interventions. In 90% of these cases legal intervention occurred, including police monitoring, a peace bond, or conviction. Second, in 23% of the cases the police collaborated with mental health professionals to obtain psychiatric intervention, and in 16% of cases they collaborated with other policing jurisdictions. Interestingly, in 13% of cases the lead detective developed a relationship with the stalker or a member of the stalker's family, which allowed for monitoring of the stalker. On the other hand, in 25% of cases victim attempts to stop the behavior through direct interactions with the stalker in fact worsened the stalking.

If all else fails, victims may have to consider relocation to another home, by staying with a family member or friend, or by staying in a shelter. In Storey and Hart's analysis, this was the final strategy that ended stalking in 13% of cases. Domestic violence shelters are a good option for domestic violence stalking victims, in particular, because they offer immediate assistance and security through established mechanisms. However, this is perhaps the most disruptive option for victims because it feels as though their lives have been placed on hold. TABLE 10-4 provides a summary of safety strategies for victims of stalking.

TABLE 10-4 Safety Strategies for Victims

- Accept responsibility for own safety.
- Develop surveillance strategies.
- Enlist the assistance of others.
- Increase security for home, work, and travel.
- Document incidents and retain evidence.
- Avoid contact and never initiate contact.
- Obtain legal orders (peace bonds, restraining orders, protection orders).
- Relocate or stay in a shelter.

Court Appeals of Stalking Convictions

A not-guilty verdict in a trial normally ends a stalking case because a prosecutor cannot appeal an acquittal. However, with a guilty verdict, there are several options for an appeal: the appellate court may grant a new trial, or send the case back to the trial court for a hearing, or dismiss the case. The appellate court reviews testimony and exhibits presented at trial to see if there was a legal error. The appellate court does not rule on the facts of the case as the judge or the jury in a trial does. (Massachusetts court system, 2017).

Appealed cases of stalking are often listed on the Internet as follows: Appeals court reverses conviction in stalking case; Convicted stalker who sued his victim pushes his case all the way to the Michigan Supreme Court; Court finds double jeopardy in stalking case; Court rejects appeals in three stalking cases; Court upholds attempted stalking case; Tennessee Supreme Court reinstates aggravated stalking conviction; Appeals judges order re-sentencing in stalking case; and Judge recuses herself in stalking case (Stalking cases appealed [n.d.]).

Abstracts of cases that were appealed on the basis of constitutional protection provide an example of an abstract of the court's opinion. An appeal to the United States District Court (Maine) on the basis of First Amendment protection was *U.S. v. Sayer*, 2012 U.S. Dist. LEXIS 67684.

Under a federal statute the defendants were charged with interstate stalking. The defendants argued that the federal stalking law was overbroad and that their conduct was protected by the First Amendment. Both motions were denied by the court. The charge against defendant Sayer was based on the allegations that he posted on the Internet the victim's address and sexually explicit videos of her. The result was that several men showed up at the victim's home asking for sex causing her to fear being sexually assaulted. On the other hand, defendant Thomas sent threatening and harassing letters through the mail to another state. The First Amendment does not protect any of these activities. The court stated that websites and emails involve speech communication, and extortion, bribery, conspiracy, fraud, identity theft, and threats also all involve speech communication and, therefore, are crimes not protected by the First Amendment. The Supreme Court has long recognized that when writing or speech is used as an integral part of conduct that is in violation of a valid criminal statute, it is not protected.

In another case, an appeal to the United States District Court (Washington) on the basis of the Sixth Amendment of doctrine of forfeiture of confrontation rights by wrongdoing was *State v. Dobbs*, 167 Wn. App. 905 (2012).

The defendant in this case was convicted of various charges that included felony harassment and stalking. His argument in his appeal was that the trial court erred when they applied the doctrine of forfeiture of confrontation rights by wrongdoing (Sixth Amendment). He also argued that the state failed to present any evidence that the victim was unavailable due to the defendant's behavior and that the court should have only considered the defendant's actions after the state initiated criminal proceedings. There was no rule, reported the court, that the trial court could only consider acts occurring after the defendant is charged in deciding whether the forfeiture doctrine applies. Specifically, acts of domestic violence may be intended to discourage the victim from getting help and prevent communication with the police or cooperation in a prosecution. When an abusive relationship ends in murder, the evidence may indicate that the crime was intended to stop the victim from reporting abuse to the police or cooperating with a criminal prosecution and thereby rendering her prior statements admissible under the forfeiture doctrine. Prior abuse, or threats that intended to dissuade the victim from seeking outside help would be relevant to this inquiry, as would evidence that the victim would have been expected to testify in a criminal proceeding. The court stated that the evidence in this case showed that the defendant had engaged in persistent acts of violence against the victim and his violence escalated over time. One of his actions included threatening the victim if she reported to or cooperated with the police. Thus, in this case, the doctrine of forfeiture by wrongdoing was correctly applied.

In another case, an appeal to the United States District Court (New Jersey) on the basis of technology was *A.T. v. R.T.*, 2012 N.J. Super. Unpub. LEXIS 189.

The defendant in this case appealed the final restraining order (FRO) entered against him under the Prevention of Domestic Violence Act. The plaintiff's complaint was that the defendant used a GPS tracking device on her car to track her movements. Under N.J.S.A 2C:12-10(a)(1), a course of conduct necessary to constitute stalking includes any behavior, whether directly or indirectly, or any action, device, or method that indicates observing, following, or monitoring a person. The GPS device that was placed in the plaintiff's car was clearly directed at her. After reviewing the relationship history between the defendant and plaintiff, the appeal court found that all of the allegations, including the GPS stalking, were adequate to grant an FRO.

Threat Assessment of Stalkers

As discussed earlier, the threat of violence usually implicit in stalking is highly distressing. Nevertheless, it is important to have a framework for evaluating the likelihood that the stalker will indeed physically harm the victim.

Threat assessments of violence date back the 19th century work of criminologist Caesar Lombroso (Wolfgang, 1961). A major concept in threat assessment is warning behaviors. Warning behaviors, according to Meloy, Hoffmann, Guldimann, and James (2011) are acts that constitute evidence of increasing or accelerating risk. These acts are acute, dynamic, and particularly toxic changes in patterns of behavior that may direct a professional's judgment that a person of concern now poses a threat, whether the actual target has been identified or not.

A framework for threat assessment in action involves three functions: identify, assess, and manage (Miller, 2014). Authorities *identify* threats. To do that, people need to know when, how, and where to report concerns. For example, in New Bedford, Massachusetts, a high school student told a favorite teacher about hearing of a group of students planning a bomb. A serious school incident was averted. The second step is to *assess* and evaluate information that has been identified. The third step is to *manage* the identified and assessed information (Miller, 2014).

Prediction of dangerousness based solely on clinical assessments for offenders of any kind has proven to be remarkably inaccurate and results in very low rates of interrater reliability among professional assessors (Hilton & Simmons, 2001). Consequently, considerable effort in the past decade has focused on the development of actuarial tools with the aim of improving accuracy in predicting dangerousness. Although developers of the tools have reported favorable results in terms of predictive validity, considerable controversy exists about the role of actuarial testing in the assessment of offenders (Sreenivasan, Kirkish, Garrick, Wineberger, & Phenix, 2000; Zonana, 1999, 2000). Also, most of these tools predict the recidivism of physical or sexual violence and are not useful for understanding the risk in someone who has not offended. Further complicating this is that although stalking carries an implicit threat, there may not be overt indications of aggression or violence. Finally, when predicting recidivism, the assessor generally has access to the offender and can conduct a full clinical interview and make use of a large number of biological, psychological, and actuarial tests to aid in the prediction (Glancy & Regehr, 2002).

Research on correlates of violence in stalkers does, however, lead to some indications that stalkers are at higher risk of committing violent acts against the victim (TABLE 10-5). Research suggests that those who threaten are indeed more violent. For example, in one study, 81% of those who did not make threats were, in fact, not violent (Harmon, Rosner, & Owens, 1998). Other factors associated with violence in stalkers are that violent stalkers tend to be young (younger than age 30 years), have lower levels of education, have made prior threats, and had previous intimate relationships with the victims (Rosenfeld & Harmon, 2002). Violent stalkers have been found to be more likely to have a history of violence and abusing substances (Burgess et al., 1997). Schwartz-Watts and Morgan (1998), using a clinical sample, reported that 80% of violent stalkers had previous relationships with the victims, compared to 55% of nonviolent stalkers; Palarea and colleagues (1999) found similar results.

Burgess, Harner, Baker, Hartman, and Lole (2001) have offered useful guidelines for assessing dangerousness in stalkers:

- *Reason for contacts*. There is greater concern when a stalker is seeking contact as a result of a need for retaliation or control than when the stalker is trying to reestablish the relationship or deal with practical details. It is important to note, however, that the motivation for contact can shift as the stalker's attempts to establish or reestablish a relationship are repeatedly met with frustration.

TABLE 10-5 Factors Associated with Increased Risk of Violence Among Stalkers

- History of making threats
- Young age
- Lower level of education
- Previous intimate relationship with the victim
- History of ignoring legal orders to stay away from the victim
- History of violence
- Substance abuse

Data from: Burgess, et al. 1997. Schwartz-Watts and Morgan. 1998. Rosenfeld & Harmon. 2002.

- *Emotional response.* Is the stalker expressing anger or frustration, or is there a sense of acceptance or hope?

- *Thought content.* In terms of thought content, it is important to understand what fantasies the stalker may have about the victim's behavior and attitudes. Are the beliefs simply denial of the reality or are they embedded in a delusional system? What are the stalker's fantasies about what he or she would like to do to or with the victim?

- *Contact pattern and predatory behaviors.* The assessor needs to determine the intrusiveness of the contact pattern and the degree to which the stalker is violating laws, such as trespassing, destruction of property, and making threats. Such violations can suggest an escalating pattern of violence.

- *Preoccupation.* Preoccupation can be determined in part by the frequency of contacts and the ability of the stalker to maintain other roles, such as continuing to work or attend school. When the stalker spends every free moment on attempts to be near to, to monitor, or to make contact with the victim, risk increases.

Treatment of Stalkers

The treatment of stalkers is highly challenging, and generally there is considerable pessimism about the likelihood of success, although there is a lack of studies in the literature to support this contention. Stalkers, by the very nature of their problem, are not motivated for treatment because they rarely see themselves as having a disorder or problem. Nevertheless, treatment approaches to stalking depend on the nature of the stalking behavior.

Delusional stalkers with erotomania are best treated with psychotropic medications aimed at addressing the psychotic symptoms. Involuntary commitment and treatment may be an option when there is a defined mental illness and a probable risk of harm. Each jurisdiction has different legal language related to the nature of illness and the severity and imminence of danger required for involuntary admission to hospital. Further, the lengths of involuntary stays and the ability to enforce treatment are highly variable, depending on legislation in that jurisdiction. This group of stalkers is largely impervious to judicial sanctions, at times regarding court appearances or jail terms as the price of true love (Mullen et al., 1999).

Domestic violence stalkers who are reacting to rejection can at times be persuaded to desist through fines and incarceration. However, this is by no means universal, and recidivism rates of up to 44% have been reported 6 months after sentencing (Koss, 2000); other studies found that for a subgroup of male batterers, arrests tend to actually increase violence (Coker, 2002). Thus, arrest of domestic violence stalkers in no way guarantees the cessation of the behavior or the reduced risk of violence.

The field of batterer intervention has been grappling for over two decades with how to address the seemingly intractable problem of men's violence against their female partners. After a comprehensive review of the literature on psychological treatment for anger and aggression, Glancy and Saini (2005) concluded that there is no consensus among therapists and researchers about the best way to treat and reduce anger and aggression and that little empirical evidence exists to support intervention strategies and guide therapists. Nevertheless, a review of the research on treatment effectiveness reveals two main findings that have important implications for considering the appropriateness of restorative processes. First, it appears that court coercion does not significantly affect whether or not a man will attend treatment. The second major finding is that confrontational treatment approaches that focus on getting men to take responsibility for their abusive behavior have not been very effective. They have failed to promote lasting change in most cases (Babcock & Steiner, 1999; Feder & Dugan, 2002).

Predatory or sexually sadistic stalkers, because of the nature of their planned offense, are generally dealt with only through the justice and correctional systems. When they are incarcerated, the risk of future threat is determined by careful risk assessment, which generally determines long-term disposition. Sexual predator laws in Canada and the United States provide a number of provisions for those at high risk of offending, including indeterminate sentences, mandatory monitoring, and preventive peace bonds (Glancy et al., 2001).

In conclusion, approaches to managing stalking behavior, both from a criminal justice and a mental health treatment perspective, have been met with limited success at best. Clearly, there is little comfort for victims with respect to hope that interventions will stop the behavior.

◼ Conclusion

Stalking is an insidious crime in which victims feel terrorized, isolated, and helpless. Stalking involves a constellation of behaviors that involve repeated and unwanted attempts to contact another person. This behavior can include physical presence at places the victim frequents, telephone calls, email messages, letters and packages, notes and gifts, and, less frequently, identity theft, threats of violence, or actual physical violence. The nature of stalking makes it very difficult for law enforcement personnel to intervene because in many jurisdictions there is a requirement for what is referred to as a "credible threat." Yet the behavior of many stalkers does not include an overt threat; rather, threat is implied through access to the victim and knowledge of the victim's activities.

Victims frequently find it difficult to convey the accumulation of what constitutes a harassing and fear-inducing situation when it appears to others to be relatively harmless behaviors. Although some legal safeguards exist, such as peace bonds and restraining orders, they are difficult to enforce. Even when the offender is charged and/or is brought into treatment, the nature of the underlying pathology limits the success of available treatment approaches. In the end, stalking is a powerful yet largely invisible crime that impacts victims profoundly. Victims are aware of escalating behaviors and fears, yet they are frequently unable to obtain assistance until after a violent incident has occurred.

◾ Key Terms

Celebrity stalking: Harassment of a well-known figure who generally does not know the stalker.

Credible threat: A legal term that indicates a clear threat that, to an outside observer, is a cause for concern for the safety of the victim.

Cyberstalking: Use of the Internet to stalk another person.

de Clérambault's syndrome: A syndrome of delusional loving first described by de Clérambault in 1942.

Erotomania: A syndrome of delusional loving.

Obsessional harassment: Harassment causing fear that originates from the obsession of one individual with another individual who is uninterested in the relationship.

Peace bond: An order from a criminal court that restrains one person from bothering or threatening another.

Protection order: A civil court order that is issued under family violence legislation. It provides various emergency and long-term orders to protect victims of family violence.

Psychiatric gating: Where a sexually violent person is certified under provincial mental health legislation and sent to any hospital.

Restraining order: An order issued after the aggrieved party appears before a judge that tells one person to stop harassing or harming another person.

Sexually violent predator: Any person who has been convicted of or charged with a crime of sexual violence and who suffers from a mental abnormality or personality disorder that makes the person likely to engage in predatory acts of sexual violence if not confined in a secure facility.

Stalking: Any form of harassment that causes the person being harassed to have a reasonable fear for his or her safety.

Discussion Questions

1. To outsiders, the behavior of a stalker can appear to be relatively benign. Explain why this is the case.

2. How useful are stalking laws in protecting victims of stalking?

3. What challenges exist in the treatment of offenders?

4. What advice should be given to victims of stalking to protect themselves?

Resources

Department of Justice Canada, Criminal Harassment: A Handbook for Police and Crown Prosecutors http://www.justice.gc.ca/eng/rp-pr/cj-jp/fv-vf/har/toc-tdm.html

National Institute of Justice, Stalking in America http://www.nij.gov/pubs-sum/169592.htm

RCMP, Criminal Harassment: Stalking—It's NOT Love http://www.justice.gov.yk.ca/pdf/crimhar-eng.pdf

Stalking Resource Center, National Center for Victims of Crime http://victimsofcrime.org/our-programs/stalking-resource-center

Statistics Canada, Stalking—Criminal Harassment http://www.statcan.gc.ca/bsolc/olc-cel/olc-cel?lang=eng&catno=85-224-X20050008645

U.S. Department of Justice, Stalking http://www.ovw.usdoj.gov/aboutstalking.htm

References

Abrams, K., & Robinson, G. (1998). Stalking part II: Victims' problems with the legal system and therapeutic considerations. *Canadian Journal of Psychiatry, 43,* 477–481.

Babcock, J. C., & Steiner, R. (1999). The relationship between treatment, incarceration, and recidivism of battering: A program evaluation of Seattle's coordinated community response to domestic violence. *Journal of Family Psychology, 13*(1), 46–59.

Baum, K., Catalano, S., Rand, M., & Rose, K. (2009). *Stalking victimization in the United States.* NCJ 224527. Washington, DC: Bureau of Justice Statistics.

Ben, K. D. & Fremouw, W. J. (2002). Stalking: Developing an empirical typology to classify stalkers. *Journal of Forensic Sciences, 47*(1):152–8.

Benitez, C., McNiel, D., & Binder, R. (2010). Do protection orders protect? *Journal of the American Academy of Psychiatry and the Law, 38,* 376–385.

Black, M.C., Basile, K. C., Breiding, M. J., Smith, S. G., Walters, M. L., Merrick, M. T., Chen, J., & Stevens, M. R. (2011). The National Intimate Partner and Sexual Violence Survey (NISVS): 2010 Summary Report. Atlanta, GA: National Center for Injury Prevention and Control, Centers for Disease Control and Prevention.

Breiding, M. J., Smith, S., Basile, K. C., Walters, M. L., Chen, J. & Merrick, M. (2014). *The national intimate partner and sexual violence survey: 2010 summary report.* Atlanta, GA: National Center for Injury Prevention and Control of the Centers for Disease Control and Prevention. Retrieved from https://www.cdc.gov/mmwr/preview/mmwrhtml/ss6308a1.htm?s_cid=ss6308a1_e

Brewster, M. (2003). Power and control dynamics in prestalking and stalking situations. *Journal of Family Violence, 18,* 207–217.

Burgess, A., Baker, T., Greening, D., Hartman, C., Burgess, A., Douglas, J., & Halloran, R. (1997). Stalking behaviors within domestic violence. *Journal of Family Violence, 12,* 389–403.

Burgess, A., Harner, J., Baker, T., Hartman, C., & Lole, C. (2001). Batterers stalking patterns. *Journal of Family Violence, 16,* 301–321.

California Penal Code, s. 646.9. (1990).

Catalano, S. (2012). Stalking victims in the United States—Revised. Washington, DC: U.S. Department of Justice, Office of Justice Programs, Bureau of Justice Statistics. Retrieved from https://www.bjs.gov/content/pub/pdf/svus_rev.pdf

Coker, D. (2002). Transformative justice: Anti-subordination processes in cases of domestic violence. In H. Strang & J. Braithwaite (Eds.), *Restorative justice and family violence* (pp. 128–152). New York: Cambridge University Press.

Criminal Code of Canada. (1993). R.S., c. C-34, s. 264. Retrieved from http://www.canlii.org/ca/sta/c-46/whole.html

de Clérambault, C. (1942). Les psychoses passionelles. In *Oeuvres psychiatriques* (pp. 315–322). Paris, France: Nationale Universitaires de France.

Dennison, S., & Thomson, D. (2005). Criticisms or plaudits for stalking laws? What psycholegal research tells us about proscribing stalking. *Psychology, Public Policy, and Law, 3*, 384–406.

Department of Justice Canada. (2004). Criminal harassment. Retrieved from http://www.justice.gc.ca/eng/pi/fv-vf/pub/har/index.htmlhttp://canada.justice.gc.ca/en/ps/fm/harassment.html#rest

Dietz, P. (1989). Defense against dangerous people when arrest and commitment fail. In R. Simon (Ed.), *American Psychiatric Press review of clinical psychiatry and the law* (pp. 205–219). Washington, DC: American Psychiatric Press.

Dietz, P., Matthews, D., Martell, D., Stewart, T., Hrouda, D., & Warren, J. (1991a). Threatening and otherwise inappropriate letters to Hollywood celebrities. *Journal of Forensic Sciences, 36*, 181–209.

Dietz, P., Matthews, D., Martell, D., Stewart, T., Hrouda, D., & Warren, J. (1991b). Threatening and otherwise inappropriate letters to members of the United States Congress. *Journal of Forensic Sciences, 36*, 1445–1468.

Douglas, K., & Dutton, D. (2001). Assessing the link between stalking and domestic violence. *Aggression and Violent Behavior, 6*, 529–546.

Dziegielewski, S., & Roberts, A. (1995). Stalking victims and survivors: Identification, legal remedies, and crisis treatment. In A. Roberts (Ed.), *Crisis intervention and time-limited cognitive treatment* (pp. 73–90). Thousand Oaks, CA: Sage.

Feder, L., & Dugan, L. (2002). A test of the efficacy of court-mandated counseling for domestic violence offenders: The Broward experiment. *Justice Quarterly, 19*(2), 343–375.

Gilligan, M. (1992). Stalking the stalker: Developing new laws to thwart those who terrorize others. *Georgia Law Review, 27*, 285–342.

Glancy, G. (2008). Commentary on attacks on the British Royal Family: The more we know the more we can classify. *Journal of the American Academy of Psychiatry and the Law, 36*, 68–73.

Glancy, G., & Regehr, C. (2002). A step-by-step guide to assessing sexual predators. In A. Roberts & G. Greene (Eds.), *Social work desk reference* (pp. 702–708). New York: Oxford University Press.

Glancy, G., Regehr, C., & Bradford, J. (2001). Sexual predator laws in Canada. *Journal of the American Academy of Psychiatry and the Law, 29*(2), 232–237.

Glancy, G., & Saini, M. (2005). An evidence-based review of psychological treatments for anger and aggression. *Brief Treatments and Crisis Intervention, 5*, 229–248.

Harmon, R., Rosner, R., & Owens, H. (1998). Sex and violence in a forensic population of obsessional harassers. *Psychology, Public Policy, and Law, 4*, 236–249.

Hilton, Z., & Simmons, J. (2001). The influence of actuarial risk assessment in clinical judgements and tribunal decisions about mentally disordered offenders in maximum security. *Law and Human Behaviour, 25*(4), 393–408.

Hotton, T. (2002). *Spousal violence after marital separation.* (Statistics Canada Cat. No. 85-002-XPE, Vol. 21, No. 7). Ottawa: Statistics Canada.

Jordan, H., & Howe, G. (1980). de Clérambault syndrome (erotomania): A review and case presentation. *Journal of the National Medical Association, 72*(10), 979–985.

Kamphuis, J., & Emmelkamp, P. (2001). Traumatic distress among support-seeking female victims of stalking. *American Journal of Psychiatry, 158,* 795–798.

Kamphuis, J., Emmelkamp, P., & Bartak, A. (2003). Individual differences in post-traumatic stress following post-intimate stalking. *British Journal of Clinical Psychology, 42,* 145–156.

Koss, M. P. (2000). Blame, shame, and community: Justice responses to violence against women. *American Psychologist, 11,* 1332–1343.

Lingg, R. (1993). Stopping stalkers: A critical examination of anti-stalking statutes. *St. John's Law Review, 76,* 347–377.

Logan, T. (2010). *Research on partner stalking: Putting the pieces together.* Lexington, KY: University of Kentucky, Department of Behavioral Science & Center on Drug and Alcohol Research.

Logan, T. (2012). *Intimate partner stalking: Comparing abusive partners who do and do not stalk.* NIJ, Office of Justice Programs. Retrieved from https://www.nij.gov /topics/crime/intimate-partner-violence/stalking/pages/stalkers-nonstalkers.aspx

Massachusetts Court System (2017). Official website of the Massachusetts Judicial Branch. Retrieved from http://www.mass.gov/courts/selfhelp/criminal-law /appeal-guilty-verdict.html

McEwan, T., Mullen, P., & Purcell, R. (2007). Identifying risk factors for stalking: A review of current research. *International Journal of Psychiatry and the Law, 30,* 1–9.

McIvor, R., & Petch, E. (2006). Stalking of mental health professionals: An underrecognized problem. *British Journal of Psychiatry, 188,* 403–404.

Meloy, J. (1998a). The clinical risk management of stalking: "Someone is watching over me. . . ." *American Journal of Psychotherapy, 51,* 174–184.

Meloy, J. (1998b). *The psychology of stalking.* San Diego, CA: Academic Press.

Meloy, J., Hoffmann, J., Guildimann, A., & James, D. (2011). The role of warning behaviors in threat assessment: An exploration and suggested typology. *Behavioral Sciences and the Law, 30*(3), 256–279. doi: 10.1002/bsl.999

Melton, H. (2000). Stalking: A review of the literature and direction for the future. *Criminal Justice Review, 25,* 246–262.

Miller, A. (2014). Threat assessment in action. *The Monitor of the American Psychological Association, 45*(2), 37.

Mitchell, B. (2007, May 29). Life sentence in Ross murder: Markham man found guilty of second degree murder of young woman. Retrieved from http://www.thestar .com/article/218866

Moriarty, L., & Freiberger, K. (2008). Cyberstalking: Utilizing newspaper accounts to establish victimization patterns. *Victims and Offenders, 3,* 131–141.

Mullen, P., Pathé, M., Purcell, R., & Stuart, G. (1999). Study of stalkers. *American Journal of Psychiatry, 156,* 1244–1249.

National Institute of Justice. (1996). *Domestic violence, stalking, and anti-stalking legislation: Annual report to Congress.* Washington, DC: U.S. Department of Justice.

Palarea, R., Zona, M., Lane, J., & Langhinrichsen-Rohlings, J. (1999). The dangerous nature of intimate relationship stalking: Threats, violence, and associated risk factors. *Behavioral Science and the Law, 17,* 269–283.

Pathé, M., & Mullen, P. (1997). The impact of stalkers on their victims. *British Journal of Psychiatry, 170,* 12–17.

Perez, C. (1993). Stalking: When does obsession become crime? *American Journal of Criminal Law, 20,* 263–280.

Philips, R. (2008). Celebrity stalkers. In D. Pinals (Ed.), *Stalking: A psychiatric perspective* (pp. 227–250). New York: Oxford University Press.

Prentky, R., Janus, E., Barbaree, H., Schwartz, B., & Kafka, M. (2006). Sexually violent predators in the courtroom: Science on trial. *Psychology, Public Policy, and Law, 12,* 357–393.

Purcell, R., Pathé, M., & Mullen, P. (2001). A study of women who stalk. *American Journal of Psychiatry, 158,* 2056–2060.

Purcell, R., Pathé, M., & Mullen, P. (2004). Stalking: Defining and prosecuting a new category of offending. *International Journal of Law and Psychiatry, 27,* 157–169.

Rathi, R. (2005). Zeta-Jones stalking case ends in plea. Retrieved from http://articles.latimes.com/keyword/dawnette-knight

Regehr, C., & Glancy, G. (2011). When social workers are stalked: Risks, strategies, and legal protections. *Clinical Social Work Journal, 39*(3), 232–242.

Regehr, C., & Kanani, K. (2010). *Essential law for social work practice in Canada* (2nd ed.). Toronto: Oxford University Press.

Roberts, A., & Dziegielewski, S. (2006). Changing stalking patterns and prosecutorial decisions: Bridging the present to the future. *Victims and Offenders, 1,* 47–60.

Rosenfeld, B. (2000). Assessment and treatment of obsessional harassment. *Aggression and Violent Behavior, 5*(6), 529–549.

Rosenfeld, B., & Harmon, R. (2002). Factors associated with violence in stalking and obsessional harassment cases. *Criminal Justice and Behavior, 29,* 671–691.

Schwartz-Watts, D., & Morgan, D. (1998). Violent vs. non-violent stalkers. *Journal of the American Academy of Psychiatry and the Law, 26,* 241–245.

Spitzberg, B., & Cupach, W. (2007). The state of the art of stalking: Taking stock of the emerging literature. *Aggression and Violent Behavior, 12,* 64–86.

Stalking cases appealed (n.d.). Retrieved from https://www.google.com/search?q=cases+of+stalking+convictions+appealed&rlz=1C1CHBF_enUS732US732&ei=wfLLWZPGBcT_abOOqpAG&start=20&sa=N&biw=1920&bih=949

Sreenivasan, H., Kirkish, P., Garrick, T., Wineberger, L., & Phenix, A. (2000). Actuarial risk assessment models: A review of critical issues related to violence and sex offender recidivism assessments. *Journal of the American Academy of Psychiatry and the Law, 28,* 438–448.

Statistics Canada. (2006). Violence against women in Canada: By the numbers. Retrieved from http://www42.statcan.ca/smr08/2006/smr08_012_2006-eng.htm

Storey, J., & Hart, S. (2011). How do police respond to stalking? An examination of the risk management strategies and tactics used in a specialized anti-stalking law enforcement unit. *Journal of Police and Criminal Psychology, 26*(2), 128–142.

Taylor, J. (2004, August 19). Alleged stalker found competent. Retrieved from http://articles.latimes.com/keyword/dawnette-knight

Telegraph. (2004, September 14). Woman claims Michael Douglas affair. Retrieved from http://www.telegraph.co.uk/news/1471717/Woman-claims-Michael-Douglas-affair.html

Tjaden, P. (2009). Stalking policies and research in the United States: A twenty-year perspective. *European Journal of Criminal Policy Research, 15*, 261–278.

Tjaden, P., & Thoennes, N. (1998). *Stalking in America: Findings from the National Violence Against Women Survey.* NCJ 169592.U.S. Washington, DC: U.S. Department of Justice, National Institute of Justice.

U.S. Department of Justice. (1997). *Domestic violence and stalking: The second annual report to Congress under the Violence Against Women Act.* Washington, DC: U.S. Department of Justice, Office of Justice Programs.

Wolfgang, M. (1961). Pioneers in criminology: Cesare Lombroso (1835–1909). *Journal of Criminal Law, Criminology and Police Science, 52*(4), 361–375.

Woodlock, D. (2017). The abuse of technology in domestic violence and stalking. *Violence against Women, 23*(5), 584–602.

Zona, M. A., Sharma, K. K., & Lane, J. C. (1993). A comparative study of erotomanic and obsessional subjects in a forensic sample. *Journal of Forensic Sciences, 38*(4), 894–903.

Zonana, H. (1999). *Dangerous sex offenders. A task force report of the American Psychiatric Association.* Washington, DC: American Psychiatric Association.

Zonana, H. (2000). Sex offender testimony: Junk science of unethical testimony. *Journal of the American Academy of Psychiatry and the Law, 28*, 386–388.

CHAPTER 11

Victims of Rape and Sexual Assault

OBJECTIVES

- To outline a theoretical framework of rape based on myths about sexual assault
- To outline measurement of the incidence of rape
- To describe rape reform efforts and rape-related legislation
- To describe military sexual trauma and campus sexual assault
- To describe programs of services for victims
- To outline a typology of sexual trauma
- To describe the dynamics of reporting a rape
- To describe a classification of rapists

KEY TERMS

Anger rapist

Blitz rape

Incest

Marital rape

Rape

Sexual assault

Sexual coercion

Sexual sadist

CASE

The threat of terrorism and biochemical warfare heralded the 21st century, impacting the nation's sense of safety and security. But a February 2006 rape and sadistic murder of a New York criminology student brought Americans back to the reality of rape, violence, its aftermath, and the inevitable victim blaming. Imette St. Guillen, a graduate student in criminal justice at John Jay College in New York City, was brutally sexually assaulted, stabbed, and bound. A sock had been stuffed into her mouth to suffocate her; her face was wrapped like a mummy in clear plastic packaging tape, suggesting her killer wanted to freeze the pained expression on her face. The killer chopped off her signature long, black hair before disposing of her body. About to turn 25, Imette was reportedly drinking and having a good time when she left a local club alone at 4:00 a.m., closing time. She never made it home. Her mutilated body was found in an isolated area miles away along a road in Brooklyn on February 25, 2006.

Within a short time investigators linked Darryl Littlejohn to St. Guillen's murder. Police investigated the potential links and similarities to three previous rapes and that of the rape and murder of Imette St. Guillen:

- Littlejohn had been known to impersonate law enforcement. He had a van.

- In the three previous attacks, the rapist had identified himself as an immigration officer before pulling the women into the van and throwing a blanket over their heads so they could not identify him. He then drove to an underground garage, where the women were raped and sexually assaulted.

- No DNA evidence was recovered from the three attacks. The victims told investigators that their attacker wiped them down after the rape with some sort of disinfectant swabs.

When police searched Littlejohn's home they recovered alcohol swabs, plastic ties, sections of his carpet, hair samples, and fibers. Police also located his 1992 blue-gray minivan. In another strange coincidence of possible linkage between the crimes, all of the assaults took place between 4:00 a.m. and 6:00 a.m. One of the previous rape victims was Japanese. Sources say a busboy at The Falls, the SoHo bar where St. Guillen was last seen alive, told them he heard Littlejohn ask the exotic-looking St. Guillen, "Are you Japanese?" just before he walked her outside.

The St. Guillen family filed several civil suits over the death of Imette naming The Falls bar, the federal probation department, the state parole board, and a company where Littlejohn took bounty-hunting classes. At the time of the murder, Littlejohn was on supervised release after serving a three-and-a-half-year federal prison sentence for a 2000 bank robbery. The Federal Chief of Probation for the Eastern District of New York was quoted in court papers admitting that his office had no contact with him since 2000 when a pre-sentence report was completed and that it was human error on the part of his department. The chief added that they were reforming the system to make this less likely to happen in the future (Fisher, 2017). In 2009, St. Guillen's family settled a confidential suit against The Falls bar for negligent hiring; Littlejohn's criminal record made him ineligible to work as a bouncer in New York City (Fisher, 2011). The family reported they would use some of the settlement money to support the Spirit of Imette Foundation (Shifrel, 2009). In March 2011, the St. Guillen family settled with the federal government for $130,000 for failing to keep tabs on Darryl Littlejohn, a violent ex-con who was supposed to be on supervised release. Tracking software for postrelease offenders was later named after St. Guillen (Fisher, 2011).

Introduction

Talk shows expressed shock and outrage at the brutality of the rape and murder of Imette St. Guillen, but many suggested that Imette was "asking for it" and "inviting" trouble because she stayed out late and had a lot to drink. Women were again reminded to "stay home" and "be safe." Noted Boston attorney Wendy Murphy's editorial in the *Boston Globe* (2006) argued that there is no doubt that if women stayed home serial killers or evil bouncers at nightclubs might not murder them. Nevertheless, she continued, shouldn't the message be that rapists and murderers, rather than the victim, should be afraid of public shame, humiliation, and punishment? This case highlights the inequity of sexual violence as a form of victimization and the challenges faced by victims and those working with victims.

All states include legislative statutes that define **rape** and **sexual assault**. It is important that a consistent definition be used in order to monitor the prevalence of sexual violence and to examine trends over time. In addition, a consistent definition helps in determining the magnitude of sexual violence and aids in comparing the problem across jurisdictions. Consistency allows researchers to measure risk and protective factors for victimization and perpetration in a uniform manner. This ultimately informs prevention and intervention efforts (Basile, Smith, Breiding, Black, & Mehendra, 2014). This chapter uses the Centers for Disease Control and Prevention (CDC) definition of sexual violence (Basile et al., 2014):

> Sexual violence is defined as a sexual act committed against someone without that person's freely given consent. Sexual violence is divided into the following types:
>
> - Completed or attempted forced penetration of a victim
> - Completed or attempted alcohol/drug-facilitated penetration of a victim
> - Completed or attempted forced acts in which a victim is made to penetrate a perpetrator or someone else

- Completed or attempted alcohol/drug-facilitated acts in which a victim is made to penetrate a perpetrator or someone else
- Non-physically forced penetration that occurs after a person is pressured verbally or through intimidation or misuse of authority to consent or acquiesce
- Unwanted sexual contact
- Noncontact unwanted sexual experiences

Sexual violence may include attempted and/or completed rape, sexual coercion and harassment, sexual contact with force or threat of force, and threat of rape (Fisher, Daigle, Cullen, & Turner, 2000). Rape, on the other hand, has a more specific definition. In December 2011, U.S. Federal Bureau of Investigation (FBI) Director Robert S. Mueller III told Congress that a new definition of rape had been approved by the FBI Advisory Board to define rape as "Penetration, no matter how slight, of the vagina or anus with any body part or object, or oral penetration by a sex organ of another person, without the consent of the victim" (Ryan, 2011, p. 1). This revised definition includes both males and females. Although legal definitions of rape and sexual assault vary greatly from state to state, in this chapter the terms are used interchangeably. The terms *rape* and *sexual assault* in this chapter refer to any unwanted contact of the sexual organs of one person, whether male or female, by another person, regardless of gender, with or without penetration and with or without resulting physical injury.

Scope of the Problem

Attempts to collect data on rape against women began in the 1980s. Estimates were derived from two primary sources, statistics from the Uniform Crime Reporting (UCR) Program and the nationwide crime victimization survey, the National Crime Survey (NCS). Despite these efforts, researchers and feminists believed that the true incidence of rape was underestimated. The criticism of the NCS was that it used too narrow a definition of rape and poorly designed interview questions. The criticism of the UCR Program was that many rapes were not reported to the police (Fisher, 2004). These criticisms prompted the development of new surveys and the redesign of existing ones. For instance, Koss, Gidycz, and Wisniewski (1987) developed the Sexual Experiences Survey to address methodological concerns about existing surveys. The survey was designed to use graphic language to describe specific behavioral acts and assessed a wide range of criminal elements of victimization (e.g., unwanted sexual contact, sexual coercion, and attempted and completed rape) (Fisher, 2004). Similarly, in 1992, the NCS was redesigned to address methodological shortcomings inherent in the NCS and was renamed the National Crime Victimization Survey (NCVS). The intent of the NCVS was to expand the definition of rape by adding screening questions to uncover additional incidents of rape and sexual assault to make it as "comparable as possible" to annual rape estimates from the National Violence Against Women Survey (NVAWS) (Bachman, 2000, p. 839). Nevertheless, critics continue to argue that their different methodologies are responsible for divergent rape estimates. Despite attempts to improve the NCVS, Bachman concluded that "the NVAWS has a greater likelihood of capturing incidents of intimate-perpetrated rape . . . compared to the NCVS" (p. 860). Her conclusion supports the critics who first argued that NCS, the precursor to NCVS, underestimated rape (Fisher, 2004).

Several problems exist in determining rape statistics. First, the manner in which rape is defined affects incidence and prevalence rates. *Prevalence* measures how many people have experienced sexual assault during their lifetimes. *Incidence* gives a snapshot of how many people have been sexually assaulted during a particular period of time, often one year. The varying definitions of sexual assault and rape result in differing rates of incidence and prevalence. For instance, determining the yearly incidence using the UCR depends on the victim and the police interpretation of what occurred. Victims must (1) perceive a rape has occurred, (2) decide it was an illegal act, and (3) decide whether or not to disclose it and (4) the police (or researcher) must decide whether the act meets the definition of an illegal act. For that act to come before a court of law, the prosecutor must decide if the evidence meets the charge. Only if the authority's classification concurs with that of the victim does the incident become recorded and thus counted in some of the measurement systems.

Second, underreporting makes it difficult to determine the number of sexual assaults. Guilt, fear of retribution, humiliation, lack of knowledge and trust in the legal and medical system, and impaired cognitive processing that occurs after intense trauma are some reasons persons may not report (Burgess, Fehder, & Hartman, 1995). In the original Burgess and Holmstrom study (1974), someone other than the victim was involved in reporting the sexual assault to police in more than half of the cases. According to the U.S. Department of Justice (2002), only 39% of rapes and sexual assault crimes were reported to law enforcement officials for the years 1992–2000. NVAWS found that only one in five adult women (19%) report their rapes to police (Tjaden & Thoennes, 2006). A study of nonincarcerated sex offenders found that 126 men admitted they had committed a total of 907 rapes involving 882 different women, with the average number of different victims per rapist being 7 (Abel et al., 1987).

Using the findings from the NVAWS, 17.6% of women and 3% of men have been raped at some time in their lives (Tjaden & Thoennes, 2006). Rape was defined in the study as an act that included attempted and/or completed vaginal, oral, and anal penetration. Thus, in the United States the prevalence of rape is equivalent to 1 of every 6 women and 1 of every 33 men. Because some victims were raped more than once, the NVAWS estimated that 17.7 million women and 2.8 million men have been forcibly raped at some time in their lives, with over 300,000 women and over 92,000 men forcibly raped in the year before the survey (Tjaden & Thoennes, 2006). According to the FBI (2010), 88,097 forcible rapes were reported to the police, at a rate of 56.6 crimes per 100,000 female residents in 2009.

In the United States in 2015, 0.98% of all persons age 12 or older (2.7 million persons) experienced at least one violent victimization, and 0.41% (1.1 million persons) experienced at least one serious violent victimization (rape or sexual assault, robbery, and aggravated assault). Less than half (47%) of violent victimizations and more than half (55%) of serious violent victimizations were reported to police. A greater percentage of robberies and aggravated assaults (62% each) were reported than simple assaults (42%) and rape or sexual assaults (32%). From 2014 to 2015, there were no statistically significant changes in the percentages of violent or serious violent victimizations reported to police (Truman & Morgan, 2016).

TABLE 11-1 offers statistics for rape and sexual assault in the United States.

Subpopulations of Victims

Although there is now a large body of research on sexual assault, additional data are needed to help document the extent to which certain subpopulations are impacted, the consequences and reporting (or nonreporting) of victimization incidents, and strategies for preventing and reducing the risk

TABLE 11-1 Rape and Sexual Assault Statistics

- An estimated 90,185 rapes (legacy* definition) were reported to law enforcement in 2015. This estimate was 6.3% higher than the 2014 estimate, 7.1% higher than the 2011 estimate, but 4.5% lower than the 2006 estimate.
- Annually, rape costs the U.S. more than any other crime ($127 billion), followed by assault ($93 billion), murder ($71 billion), and drunk driving ($61 billion).
- 8% of rapes occur while the victim is at work.
- Of those raped, 81% of women and 35% of men report significant short-term or long-term impacts such as posttraumatic stress disorder (PTSD).

* Legacy forcible rape is the carnal knowledge of a female forcibly and against her will. The new FBI expanded definition of forcible rape was operationalized in 2012.
Data from: FBI Uniform Crime Reports. 2010.

of sexual assault and effectively responding to victims. Two subpopulations that are currently a focus are victims of campus sexual assault and military sexual trauma.

CAMPUS SEXUAL ASSAULT

In the 1950s, Kanin and Kirkpatrick were one of the first teams to examine sexual aggression on college campuses and found that a significant proportion of college women (20% to 25%) reported being sexually coerced (Kanin, 1957; Kirkpatrick & Kanin, 1957). In the 1980s, Koss and colleagues published a series of landmark studies (1987) that provided concrete evidence of the problem of sexual assault on college campuses. Koss (1987) coined the term "date rape," and one of her studies found that 7.7% of male students volunteered anonymously that they had engaged in or attempted forced sex, but, more surprising, few considered it to be a crime. The male students had no shame, no regret, and faced no consequences. Koss identified three situational risk factors for college sexual abuse: a culture of high alcohol consumption, male peer pressure to prove one's sexual prowess, and men's own attitudes favoring impersonal sex (Kamenetz, 2014).

In the early 2000s, the National Institute of Justice sponsored the Campus Sexual Assault Study using a sample of 5,446 undergraduate women. The researchers found that almost 20% of undergraduate women had experienced attempted or completed sexual assault since entering college (Krebs, Lindquist, Warner, Fisher, & Martin, 2007).

Slowly, the media picked up on campus rape cases and highlighted them. In 2011, reporter Gwen Florio exposed multiple reports of sexual assault involving University of Montana football players that had gone unpunished by the school or local authorities. This led to a Justice Department investigation into 80 reported rapes in Missoula over a period of 3 years. The investigation resulted in settlements between the federal government, local law enforcement, and university officials (Gray, 2015, para, 1). By 2013, campus sexual assault was not a national story but the documentary on sexual assault in the military, *The Invisible War,* was being promoted by producer Kirby Dick (2013). When Dick heard of sexual assault occurring at colleges and universities, he was prompted to produce *The Hunting Ground* and to criticize fraternities and athletes and university officials from not keeping students safe (Dockterman, 2015, March 5, para.3).

In November 2014, a *Rolling Stone* story of a gang rape and the subsequent administrative mishandling of the incident was top news. But then criticism raised questionable journalistic ethics as investigators found significant problems at every stage of the reporting, editing, and fact-checking processes

(Hartmann, 2015). The story was retracted and several groups filed libel suits and importantly, critics argued the story hurt rape activism and advocacy (Gray, 2015, para. 3).

Again in 2015, the media covered criminal cases of Vanderbilt University former football athletes who were convicted of aggravated rape and aggravated sexual battery. Evidence included video and graphic photographs of the athletes carrying an unconscious woman and pictures of a sexual assault (Docterman, 2015, January 29).

Campus rape statistics have been fairly consistent since the 1950s. The National Crime Victimization Survey (NCVS) compares the rape and sexual assault victimization of female college students and nonstudents. Surveys of students and nonstudents for the period 1995–2013 have found the following (Sinozich & Langton, 2014):

- Among student victims, 20% of rape and sexual assault victimizations were reported to police, compared to 32% reported among nonstudent victims ages 18 to 24.

- The rate of rape and sexual assault reporting was 1.2 times higher for nonstudents (7.6 per 1,000) than for students (6.1 per 1,000).

- For both college students and nonstudents, the offender was known to the victim in about 80% of rape and sexual assault victimizations.

- Most (51%) student rape and sexual assault victimizations occurred while the victim was pursuing leisure activities away from home, compared to nonstudents who were engaged in other activities at home (50%) when the victimization occurred.

- The offender had a weapon in about 1 in 10 rape and sexual assault victimizations against both students and nonstudents.

- Rape and sexual assault victimizations of students (80%) were more likely than nonstudent victimizations (67%) to go unreported to police.

- About a quarter of student (26%) and nonstudent (23%) victims who did not report to the police believed the incident was a personal matter, and one in five (20% each) stated a fear of reprisal.

- Student victims (12%) were more likely than nonstudent victims (5%) to state that the incident was not important enough to report.

- Fewer than one in five female students (16%) and nonstudent (18%) victims of rape and sexual assault received assistance from a victim services agency.

In many ways, college students are a high-risk group for rape. Converging risk factors that set a scene for rape on college campuses include:

- *Age of the victims*. An abundance of young women who are open to the culture of socializing, "hooking up," and dating.

- *Victim access*. Numerous opportunities for easy access to potential victims; many of these opportunities are designed to promote socializing and hooking up.

- *Social culture*. Emphasis on informal, casual "dating" (e.g., hooking up, friends "with benefits"). More than 80% of the rapes that occur on college campuses are committed by someone with whom the victim is acquainted; approximately 50% are committed on dates.

- *Availability of alcohol and rape drugs*. Alcohol facilitates disinhibition, along with readily available "rape drugs" that produce anterograde amnesia, such as the benzodiazepine, Rohypnol, and the CNS depressant GHB (gamma-hydroxybutrate).

- *Coercion-supporting peer groups*. Peer groups may condone rape-supportive attitudes and attitudes characterized by hostile and negative masculinity.

- *Age of the offenders*. Typically young men aged 18 to 22 years who still possess the same psychosocial and neurocognitive judgement of the late teen years, with tendencies of risk taking, impulsivity, and inconsistent judgement and decision-making.

MILITARY SEXUAL TRAUMA

Over the past two decades, sexual assault in the military has received increasing attention. Reports of sexual assault and harassment among active duty personnel and cadets have catalyzed public law and research focused on the potential traumatic stress associated with these experiences (Hyun, Pavao, & Kimerling. 2009).

Military sexual trauma (MST) is the term used by the Veterans Administration (VA) to refer to experiences of sexual assault or repeated, threatening sexual harassment that a veteran experienced during his or her military service. This definition comes from federal law (Title 38 U.S. Code 1720D) and is "psychological trauma, which in the judgment of a VA mental health professional, resulted from a physical assault of a sexual nature, battery of a sexual nature, or sexual harassment that occurred while the veteran was serving on active duty or active duty for training." Sexual harassment is further defined as "repeated, unsolicited verbal or physical contact of a sexual nature that is threatening in character."

The military first pledged to crack down on sexual assault and harassment in 1992 in the wake of a scandal that surfaced at the Navy Fliers' 35th Annual Tailhook Association Convention in Las Vegas. At the convention, more than 100 U.S. Navy and United States Marine Corps aviation officers were alleged to have sexually assaulted 83 women and 7 men, or otherwise engaged in "improper and indecent" conduct at the Las Vegas Hilton. The scandal spurred a Congressional mandate in 1992 for the Department of Veterans Affairs to treat distress related to military sexual trauma (Healy, 1992). By 1995, 61% of VA medical centers had developed sexual trauma treatment teams.

However, in 1997 there was yet another scandal. At Maryland's Army Aberdeen Proving Grounds assault charges were brought against a dozen male officers for sexual assault of female trainees. When a hotline was established, 200 investigations were launched in response to more than 1,000 incoming phone calls requesting assistance (Spinner, 1997). In 2003, the U.S. Air Force Academy was accused of systemically ignoring an ongoing sexual assault problem on its campus. More than 50 cases of sexual assault were identified as having occurred at the U.S. Air Force Academy between January 1993 and December 2002 (Schemo, 2003).

The Department of Defense and the Veterans Administration have both developed surveys to obtain estimates of the numbers of service members (active, reserves, and retired) who have experienced sexual assault and/or harassment. The Department of Defense (DoD) has assessed service member experiences with sexual assault and harassment since 1996, when Public Law 104-201 first required a survey of the "gender relations climate" experienced by active-component forces. Congress mandates the Workplace and Gender Relations Survey of Active Duty Members (WGRA) every two years as an independent assessment of the rates of sexual assault, sexual harassment, and gender discrimination in the military (Stand-To, 2016).

Since 2002, "Workplace and Gender Relations Surveys," as they are known in 10 U.S.C. §481, have been conducted with active-component forces (see Research—DoD SAPR, 2016). The results of the 2012 survey suggested that more than 26,000 service members in the active reserves had experienced unwanted sexual contacts in the prior year, an estimate that received widespread public attention and concern. In press reports and congressional inquiries, questions were raised about the validity of the estimate, about what "unwanted sexual contact" included, and about whether the survey had been conducted properly.

Because of these questions, some members of Congress urged the Department of Defense to seek an independent assessment of the number of service members who experienced sexual assault or sexual harassment. The Sexual

Assault Prevention and Response Office (SAPRO) within the Office of the Secretary of Defense selected the RAND Corporation to provide a new and independent evaluation of sexual assault, sexual harassment, and gender discrimination across the military. As such, the Department of Defense asked the RAND research team to redesign the approach used in previous Department of Defense surveys, if changes would improve the accuracy and validity of the survey results for estimating the prevalence of sexual crimes and violations. In the summer of 2014, RAND fielded a new survey as part of the RAND Military Workplace Study (RMWS) (Morral, Gore, & Schell, 2015).

Specifically, the RMWS measures sexual assault, which captures three mutually exclusive categories: penetrative, nonpenetrative, and attempted penetrative crimes. It also measures *sexual harassment*, which consists of the following:

- *Sexually hostile work environment*. A workplace characterized by severe or pervasive unwelcome sexual advances, comments, or physical conduct that offends service members.

- *Sexual quid pro quo*. Incidents in which someone uses his or her power or influence within the military to attempt to coerce sexual behavior in exchange for a workplace benefit.

- *Gender discrimination*. Incidents in which service members are subject to mistreatment on the basis of their gender that affects their employment conditions.

The survey found that 1.5% of the active duty population had experienced at least one sexual assault in the past year, thus impacting between 18,200 and 22,400 service members. This represents approximately 1.0% of men (1 in 100) and 4.9% of women (5 in 100) in the service. Almost one-half of the women who experienced a sexual assault in the past year and about one-third of the men were classified as experiencing a penetrative sexual assault. These rates are higher than previously understood using earlier survey methods, and this difference is particularly large among men.

The RMWS study is the first survey of the military that included a large enough sample of men to provide details on their sexual assault experiences and provide important differences in experiences of men and women. Men who were sexually assaulted were more likely than women to have experienced multiple incidents in the past year, to have been assaulted by multiple offenders during a single incident, and to have been assaulted at work or during duty hours. Men also were more likely to describe an event as hazing or intended to abuse or humiliate them. Sexual assaults of men were less likely to involve alcohol than assaults of women, according to the study. Men who experienced a sexual assault were less likely to report it to authorities or tell anyone about the incident.

Risk of sexual assault was found to vary substantially by branch of service. Men and women in the Air Force experienced substantially lower rates of sexual assault than those in the Army, Navy, and Marine Corps. All RMWS reports are available online at http://www.rand.org/surveys/rmws.html.

Another resource for addressing the problem of military sexual assault is Military Investigation and Justice Experience Survey (MIJES). The results of the 2016 MIJES presented in this report represent the culmination of an extensive effort by the Office of People Analytics (OPA) to assist the department in assessing the investigative and legal processes/services experienced by military members who have made a report of sexual assault. The 2016 MIJES has proven to be a valuable tool for the department to evaluate its SAPR programs/resources, as well as assisting survivors through the military justice process. The findings reveal, among other issues, what is working for military members who bring forward a report of sexual assault, and what can be improved (Namrow et al., 2016).

The Veterans Administration surveys patients seen at their clinics. As reported in the *PTSD Research Quarterly* (2009), PTSD is the most common mental health condition observed among veterans who report MST. MST appears to be a significant source of traumatic stress among both men and women seeking VA disability for PTSD, where 4.2% of men and 71.0% of women report sexual assault during their military service. Using medical record data from all outpatients in 2003, researchers found strong associations between MST and PTSD, with stronger effects observed for women than for men. Among former reservists, researchers also found that sexual assault and harassment during military service were significantly associated with PTSD symptoms, as well as current and lifetime PTSD diagnosis (Hyun et al., 2009).

Prevalence estimates have remained fairly consistent since then, with clinical populations reported at 48,106 women and 43,693 men as of 2008. Despite the lower prevalence of MST among men, the populations are similar in size because VHA treats more men than women. The VHA was authorized to provide MST-related counseling in the early 1990s. In a 1994–1995 national study of female VHA outpatients even higher lifetime prevalence rates were found, where more than half (55%) of women reported sexual harassment and more than 20% reported sexual assault during their military service (Hyun et al., 2009).

The Canadian military has also sought to determine the severity of MST in its ranks. Military populations consist largely of young people who are a group at risk for sexual assault, with factors similar to students living on a college campus. Military members usually live on a base, in close quarters with one another, with men greatly outnumbering and frequently outranking women. After a sexual assault, victims fear reporting will negatively affect their career, experience feelings of betrayal, and fear continuous exposure to the perpetrator when he or she is a member of the same unit.

Watkins, Zamorski, and Richer (2017) analyzed 2013 data from the cross-sectional representative Canadian Forces Mental Health Survey of Canadian Regular Force personnel (*n* = 6,696). The definition used for the survey question on lifetime military-related sexual assault was forced or unwanted sexual activity or that occurred on deployment or in another military workplace, or was committed by any military personnel. All other sexual assault was defined as non-military-related sexual assault.

Results of the survey found self-reported sexual assault was more prevalent among women (non-military-related sexual assault 24.2%, military-related sexual assault 15.5%) than among men (5.9% and 0.8%, respectively). About a quarter of women who reported military-related sexual assault said they experienced a minimum of one event on deployment.

Canadian military women are at increased risk for sexual assault and military-related sexual assault relative to their male counterparts. Deployment may be a period of elevated risk for military-related sexual assault, and women who reported military-related sexual assault are more likely to have experienced mental disorders, especially posttraumatic stress disorder (Watkins et al., 2017).

Legislative Framework

Laws greatly shape public opinion and attitudes. Legislation in the form of law reform can be both instrumental and symbolic. Such was the case with rape-law reform, especially in conveying the concept of rape as an injurious, if not always physically damaging, act. Changes in rape laws helped to influence attitudes within both the criminal justice and general communities, although some would argue that jurors/citizens are still inclined to view rape in morality terms rather than criminal terms.

U.S. criminal rape laws were derived from British common law. Codification of the law against sexual violence began with the Statutes of Westminster in 1275 and 1285 and established rape as a serious crime with the possibility of a death penalty. Three elements needed to be proven: carnal knowledge of a woman by force and against her will. Two influential legal theorists were

17th-century jurist Lord Chief Justice Matthew Hale and the Edwardian-era scholar John Henry Wigmore (1863–1943). Hale's belief that rape is "an accusation easily made, and hard to be proved, and harder to be defended by the party accused, though ever so innocent" (Hale, 1847, p. 634) was reflected in both American jury instructions and standards of proof. Similarly, Wigmore's concern about sexually precocious minors and unchaste women who fantasize about rape gave rise to the corroboration doctrine and influenced such practices as the routine polygraph examination of victims (Wigmore & Chadbourn, 1970). Although neither man's assertions were supported by empirical data, they received widespread endorsement by legal bodies. As a result, U.S. law would reflect a concept of rape as a sexual rather than a violent offense and would impose a vast array of safeguards against false accusations by the turn of the 20th century (Largen, 1988).

The need for rape-law reform was clearly noted by women's rights movements, who were encouraging former victims to speak publicly about insensitive and indifferent treatment they had experienced in the criminal justice system. These disclosures fostered recognition for systematic change that women activists believed must begin with the law itself. To this end, movement activists organized to develop a rape-law reform agenda, solicit public support for reform, and present their case to state legislators. Although the political climate was favorable to these citizen-initiated efforts, it was a growing presence of women and sympathetic men within the legal and lawmaking professions that reduced most resistance to change. A review of rape-law reform by Largen (1988) suggested, among other things, that in most states social concepts of sexual assault were changing more rapidly than legal concepts. Again, this was evidence of the radical shift in the concept of unacceptable behavior.

The rape-law reforms implemented in the 1970s and 1980s in the United States were noted to be successful only to the extent that victims increasingly accessed the systems through reporting rape. Bachman and Paternoster (1993) analyzed the NCVS from 1973 to 1990 to examine the extent to which rape reporting changed during those years compared to the change in reporting for robbery and nonsexual assaults. The NCVS data demonstrated that rape victims who reported to police increased by 10% compared to a 4% increase for assault and a 12% decrease for robbery. Based on these findings, Bachman and Paternoster concluded, "rape victims were slightly more likely to report their victimizations after statutory reforms were in place" (1993, p. 566). Data from the NVAWS comparing rape-reporting practices before rape-law reforms (pre-1975) and after rape-law reforms (1980–1996) found a more significant change in reporting. Clay-Warner and Burt (2005) reported the likelihood of women reporting rape to police in the modern reform period (1990–1996) was 88% more likely to be reported than a rape occurring before 1975. A sexual assault that occurred in the middle reform period (1975–1989), however, was no more likely to be reported than one occurring before the enactment of reforms (Clay-Warner & Burt, 2005).

Similarly, a review of rape-law reform in Canada held that the 1983 reform addressed some of the key issues relating to sexual assault but that critical issues still remained. These issues were underreporting of sexual assault; low founding, charging, and conviction rates; the status of rape shield rules; and the defense of honest but mistaken belief of consent. Collective and social actions on the part of women's groups and education are seen as important policy tools to counter sexual assault (Tang, 1998).

Rape Shield Laws

During the 1970s in the United States, as the problem of rape came into focus, several groups and organizations joined a movement to reform rape laws with the intention of increasing the reporting of rape victimizations (Torres, 2008). One product of reform was the emergence of rape shield laws to "limit the introduction of sexual history evidence in rape trials" and "challenge the view that women with extensive sexual histories more frequently fabricate charges of rape than other women" (Flowe, Ebbesen, & Putcha-Bhagavatula, 2007, p. 159). Torres (2008) explained that the purposes of rape shield laws vary and suggested that rape shield laws encourage focus on the culpability of the accused rather than on the victim's sexual history. This is supported by the idea that no matter how promiscuous, a victim's sexual history should be irrelevant to the offender's culpability. In addition, Torres claimed that rape shield laws serve to encourage and facilitate victims coming forward to report rape (Torres, 2008).

Because of concerns surrounding false allegations of rape, laws governing rape remained stagnant and unfavorable to victims for many years before the 1970s. There was also significant skepticism toward claims of rape by victims that were met with "cautionary instructions to the jury warning of women's propensity to make false charges of rape" (Flowe et al., 2007, p. 160). In addition, evidence of promiscuity was frequently admitted at trial in an attempt to discredit a complainant and establish the likelihood of consent to sexual intercourse (Flowe et al., 2007). It is evident that false rape allegations may have a drastic impact on a person who is wrongly accused. However, the emotional and physical trauma that rape victims endure must also be considered in decisions made in the courtroom. Flowe and colleagues (2007) argued that "rape shield provisions attempt to balance protecting the complainant from potentially capricious invasions of privacy, and the defendant's rights to confront and cross-examine witnesses about potentially probative information" (p. 160). This is especially true for cases of "he said, she said" where physical evidence and witnesses are limited or absent.

Rape shield laws are intended to limit the exploration of complainants' sexual psychological history and protect them from "embarrassment and unnecessary publicity by dredging up irrelevant information on their background" (Meadows, 2004, p. 282). Meadows added that probing into a victim's prior sexual history would be humiliating and would discourage victims from reporting rape and pursuing charges (Meadows, 2004).

Anderson (2004) argued that despite the good intentions of rape-law reform, the functionality of rape shield laws was limited in providing protection to complainants. Furthermore, the useful application of these laws was exempted from many cases, especially those involving women who were previously intimate with the defendant, women who were deemed promiscuous, and prostitutes. Anderson (2004) attributed the inefficiency of rape shield laws to "their exceptions [which] routinely gut the protection they purport to offer" (p. 1). The Federal Rule of Evidence 412 states as follows (Anderson, 2004, p. 1):

> Evidence to prove a rape complainant's "other sexual behaviour" or "sexual predisposition" is inadmissible, except: (1) when it is offered "to prove that a person other than the accused was the source of semen, injury, or other physical evidence," (2) when it is offered to prove consent and it consists of "specific instances of sexual behaviour by the alleged victim with respect to the person accused," or (3) when the exclusion of the evidence "would violate the constitutional rights of the defendant."

Anderson (2004) further argued that the second exception defeats the purpose of rape shield laws because "62% of adult rapes are committed by prior intimates—spouses, ex-spouses, boyfriends, or ex-boyfriends" (p. 1). She also argued that the third exception has the same effect because "courts routinely misinterpret and exaggerate the scope of the defendant's constitutional right to inquire into the complainant's sexual history" (p. 1).

Rape shield laws are also known to be used and applied inconsistently across the United States. Although some states diminish the use of rape shield laws through exceptions defined in state legislatures, other states may permit exceptions based on requirements by the constitution, based on a judge's discretion, or based on the purpose for which the evidence is offered at trial. For example, evidence of sexual history of the accuser may be admitted for the purpose of attacking the credibility of the accuser in one state, whereas the same evidence might be used to prove the accuser had given consent in another state (Torres, 2008). TABLE 11-2 provides a more detailed classification of rape shield laws.

Although inconsistencies in the application of rape shield legislation and exceptions to these laws can favor defendants, incorrect application can have damaging implications to defendants. In 1998, a case involving the conviction of Oliver Jovanovic for an attack of a 20-year-old student created significant controversy and revealed possible injustices created by rape shield legislation. After having met a woman over the Internet and having explicit conversations with her involving sadomasochistic subject matter, the two met on several occasions where such acts took place. Jovanovic's lawyer attempted to undermine the woman's claims of physical injury by submitting evidence of her consent, which

TABLE 11-2 Application of Rape Shield Legislation: Manner and Degree to Which Women's Sexual History Is Admitted as Evidence

Types of Laws	Description
Legislated exception laws	25 states have enacted legislation that prohibits evidence of the victim's sexual predisposition or history unless: • There have been relevant instances of prior consensual sex between the accuser and the defendant. • Someone other than the defendant was the source of semen, other bodily fluids, or the cause of injury. • There has been a relevant pattern of prior sexual conduct of the complainant. • There is bias or bad motive that could cause fabrication of the accusation. • Evidence that shows that the accused believed the complainant gave consent. • There have been previous instances of false accusations on the part of the accuser.
Constitutional catch-all laws	11 states have enacted legislation that resembles the legislated exception laws with an added exception: • Evidence of previous sexual history of the complainant will be admitted if the judge determines that the inadmissibility of such evidence will violate the defendant's constitutional right.
Judicial discretion laws	Nine states grant the judge broad discretion to determine whether evidence of the complainant's sexual history should be admitted: • The judge will balance the evidence's relevancy and probative value against its prejudicial effect.
Evidentiary purpose laws	Four states determine admissibility of previous sexual history evidence based on the purpose of doing so in trial. For example: • In California and Delaware, sexual history cannot be offered to prove consent, but using it to attack the complainant's credibility is permissible. • In Nevada and Washington, the opposite occurs; evidence for attacking credibility is prohibited but using it to prove consent is allowed.

Data from: Anderson, M. J. 2004. Understanding Rape Shield Laws. The National Alliance to End Sexual Violence.

was believed to be apparent in emails exchanged between the two. The judge refused the emails as evidence, improperly citing the state's rape shield laws. Under a new trial ordered by the appellate court, the following was found: "Jovanovic was precluded not only from bringing out the degree to which the complainant seemed to be inviting sadomasochism but also from exploring whether she was a less reliable narrator of events than she appeared to be at trial" (Meadows, 2004, p. 286). The conviction was eventually overturned on appeal and a new trial ordered on the grounds that Jovanovic was not allowed to present an adequate defense, but not until he had spent 20 months in prison and suffered an assault from another inmate. (The woman was denounced as a habitual liar by some members of her own family.) The New York Supreme Court dismissed all charges after the accuser was no longer willing to testify.

Title IX

Title IX of the Education Amendments of 1972, signed into law by then-President Richard Nixon, prohibits discrimination on the basis of sex in all education programs or activities that receive federal financial assistance. The aim at that time was to ensure equal disbursement of women's athletic scholarships, as well as funding for women's collegiate sports programs. The Obama-era "Dear Colleague" letter, which was created by then-Vice President Joe Biden in 2011, is a comprehensive set of guidelines that essentially serve as a reminder to universities and Title IX administrators that schools need to follow the Title IX law especially when it comes to campus sexual assault. The letter to university administrators established sexual assault and harassment as critical Title IX issues. The letter said that schools should try to complete an investigation within 60 days and evaluate cases based on the weight or "preponderance of the evidence" standard, rather than the more stringent "clear and convincing evidence" standard some had used. Victims did not need to sign nondisclosure agreements and colleges were told they would be put on notice if they did not work immediately to prevent harassment of victims. Investigations were opened by the department's Office of Civil Rights, or OCR, into more than 300 schools for failing to respond to sexual violence after the letter came out (Cauterruci, 2017).

In 2014, President Obama established the White House Task Force to Protect Students from Sexual Assault with the goal to bring more transparency to the federal government's enforcement activities around this issue. All colleges, universities, and K–12 schools receiving federal funds must comply with Title IX. Schools that violate the law and refuse to address the problems identified by OCR can lose federal funding or be referred to the U.S. Department of Justice for further action (Cauterruci, 2017). On May 1, 2014, the OCR released a list of more than 70 higher education institutions that were under investigation for possible violations of federal law over how the university was handling sexual violence and harassment complaints (U.S. Dept. Education, 2014).

The Obama administration also recommended evidence-based prevention programs and requiring schools to conduct surveys about sexual violence on campus. The Republican platform of 2016 countered the Obama directives, stating that sexual assault claims should be "investigated by civil authorities and prosecuted in a courtroom, not a faculty lounge." Republicans argued that Obama had set out to "micromanage" universities' systems for addressing rape (Cauterruci, 2017).

Under the Trump administration, U.S. Secretary of Education, Betsy De Vos, in a September 2017 speech, criticized the Obama enforcement methods for failing to engage the public on controversial issues such as campus sexual assault. Rather, she noted, that the Department's Office for Civil Rights has issued letters from the desks of un-elected and un-accountable political appointees and sent out a "Dear Colleague" letter, which provided instructions on how schools must investigate and adjudicate accusations of sexual violence. The letter admitted it could not create any new legal obligations, because it was issued without the process of public comment that is required to make an agency's pronouncements legally binding. The non-binding status of the Obama-era letter meant that a new Administration could easily retract it with another letter, but DeVos pointedly did not do this emphasizing that ruling by letter was over. Rather, the agency would engage in precisely the notice-and-comment rulemaking process that the Obama Administration chose not to do. Although some have portrayed DeVos's speech as a rollback of Title IX, it clearly embraces a framework of compatibility: one in which Title IX seriously addresses sexual violence and also requires fairness to the accuser and the accused. According to some, DeVos appears to be proceeding exactly as an agency head should: give notice, take comments, and explain why a given policy is being adopted (Gersen, 2017).

Typologies of Rape and Sexual Assault

Incest

Incest is considered sexual activity between close relatives that is illegal in the jurisdiction where it takes place and is conventionally considered a taboo. Incestuous unions have an ancient history in that they were frowned upon and considered a violation of the natural and social order. In current times, sexual activity between adults and underage children is illegal and considered one of the most extreme forms of childhood abuse, often resulting in serious and long-term psychological trauma, especially in the case of parental incest.

Statistics on incest are difficult to gather and generalize. The Canadian Incidence Study on Child Abuse and Neglect (Trocmé et al., 2005) reported that in 22% of cases of child sexual abuse the perpetrator was the father or stepfather of the child; in an additional 40% of cases the perpetrator was another relative, totaling 62% of all child abuse cases. Similarly, the National Incidence Study in the United States revealed that 60% of cases of child sexual abuse are perpetrated by a biological parent or nonbiological parent (U.S. Department of Health and Human Services, 2010).

Statutory Rape

Statutory rape is defined as nonforcible sexual intercourse with a person who is younger than the statutory age of consent. The underlying premise is that young people under a certain age are incapable of fully understanding the nature and consequences of sexual activity and are thus vulnerable to manipulation and exploitation by adults. The actual age of consent across the United States ranges from 13 (in Delaware and Kentucky) to 18 years of age (in California and Arizona). Many of these statutes refer to the offense as unlawful sexual intercourse with a minor or child who is not one's spouse. Penalties can range from one year of imprisonment in Nebraska and two years in Texas and Tennessee up to the possibility of life imprisonment in several states. In 2000, the U.S. Department of Justice reported one statutory rape for every three forcible rapes of a juvenile (Troupe-Leasure & Snyder, 2005). Ninety-five percent of reported statutory rapes involved female victims, two-thirds of whom were aged 14 or 15. If the victim was a female, the offender was a male in 99% of cases. If the victim was a male, 94% of offenders were female (Troupe-Leasure & Snyder, 2005). In one highly publicized case, Mary Kay Letourneau, a 37-year-old Seattle schoolteacher, was imprisoned from 1997 to 2004 for child rape charges because of the sexual relationship she had with a 13-year-old student, Vili Fualaau. She gave birth to two of Fualaau's children while on probation. After her release from prison in 2004, Letourneau married Fualaau, and they are raising their two daughters.

Sexual activity between an adult and young person that appears to be "voluntary" is a troubling problem for law and society. Hines and Finkelhor (2007, p. 311) identified the following vulnerability factors and risks for young people involved in sex with adults:

- Youth experiencing family conflict who may seek out other adults to help them gain independence.

- Youth who are estranged from peers may seek out adult relationships.

- Youth with limited employment opportunities seek out adults to provide a route to motherhood or family formation.

- Youth who are sexually active may seek out adults for sexual opportunities not available among their peers.

- Youth who are gay or have sexual concerns may make them vulnerable to sexual offers from adults.

Adolescents involved in statutory relationships are more likely to have histories of abuse and have troubled or nonexistent relationships with their parents. Statutory relationships are associated with higher rates of teenage pregnancy, single parenthood, and poverty. Indeed, research suggests that in two-thirds of cases of teenage pregnancy the father is an adult male. In the case of younger teenagers who are pregnant, the father of the baby is on average 10 years older. Consequently, several teen advocacy and pregnancy prevention programs have called for increased utilization of existing statutory rape laws to protect young women and reduce teenage pregnancy (Harner, Burgess, & Asher, 2001).

Marital Rape

Marital rape is nonconsensual sex in which the perpetrator is the victim's spouse. On July 5, 1993, marital rape became a crime in all 50 states. In fact, marital rape was once widely condoned or ignored by law, and to this day it is widely tolerated and accepted as a husband's prerogative. This legal attitude was exemplified by Michael Hale, Chief Justice in England in the 17th century, who stated that a husband could not be guilty of the rape of his wife "for by their mutual matrimonial consent and contract the wife hath given up herself in this kind unto the husband which she cannot retract" (Russell, 1990, p. 17). In the late 1970s, advocates began efforts to change these laws, and currently the rape of a spouse is a crime in all 50 states and the District of Columbia. The Criminal Code of Canada formally recognized marital rape as a crime in 1983.

Acquaintance Rape

Acquaintance rape, also described as *date rape* or *hidden rape*, is a relatively common problem in American society, especially in the teenage and young adult years. Psychologist Mary Koss (1988) defined rape as being subjected to unwanted sexual intercourse, oral sex, anal sex, or other sexual contact through the use of force or threat of force. Unsuccessful attempts are also subsumed within the term rape. **Sexual coercion** is defined as unwanted sexual intercourse or any other sexual contact subsequent to the use of menacing verbal pressure or misuse of authority (Koss, 1988). Acquaintance rape remains a controversial topic, primarily due to the lack of agreement on the definition of consent. Publicized trials indicate that an increased awareness of sexual coercion and acquaintance rape has been accompanied by important legal decisions and changes in legal definitions of rape. Views on acquaintance rape also appear quite capable of creating opposing camps. Despite the violent nature of acquaintance rape, the belief that many victims are actually willing, consenting participants is held by both men and women alike. "Blaming the victim" seems to be an all too prevalent reaction to acquaintance rape (Curtis, 1997).

In a 2011 case, WikiLeaks founder Julian Assange was accused by two women of committing sexual offenses. His defense team countered the women were lying. One woman said she had consensual sex with Assange, but the condom broke and he used his body weight to hold her down, presumably to complete the act. She hosted a party for him the next evening. A few days later, Assange had sex with another woman—allegedly while she was asleep—also without wearing a condom. Both women reportedly acknowledged they freely chose to engage in sex acts with Assange, but that some of his conduct was nonconsensual. One woman reported that he engaged in unwanted, unprotected sex while she was asleep, an act considered criminal in Sweden. Assange denied the allegations, suggesting that the women were expressing the anger of jilted lovers. In his defense, Assange's attorneys sought to cast doubt on both the accusers and Swedish prosecutors. To this end, one of the witnesses called to the stand was a former Swedish judge who testified that Marianne Ny, the Swedish prosecutor, was an overzealous women's rights crusader with a bias against men (Faiola & Adam, 2011).

Sexual Homicide

The St. Guillen case reported earlier in this chapter illustrates not only a rape case but also a sexual homicide. So, what are the statistics in this area? Data on murder and murder victims and circumstances are obtained from the annual Supplemental Homicide Reporting program of the FBI (FBI, n.d.). Since the latter half of the 1980s, the percentage of all murders with known circumstances in which investigators have identified rape or other sex offenses as the principal circumstance underlying the murder has been declining, from about 2% of murders to less than 1%. The good news is that cases are declining. However, the decline is predicated on whether a homicide victim is examined for sexual assault. A study of sexual homicide determined many rapes were missed because medical examiners did not know the variations of sexual assault in a homicide (Ressler, Burgess, & Douglas, 1988). Between 1976 and 1994, there were an estimated 405,089 murders in the United States. Of these, the circumstances surrounding the murder were known in 317,925, or 78.5% of

TABLE 11-3 Comparing Murders Involving Sexual Assault and Not Involving Sexual Assault

- Known offenders in sexual assault murders were more likely to have been male.
- Sexual assault murders are more likely than all murders to involve a White offender (58% vs. 48%).
- Sexual assault murder offenders are on average about 5 years younger than all murderers.
- Sexual assault murder victims are more likely to be female and White.
- Sexual assault murder victims are both younger and older than the aggregate of all murder victims (25% under age 18 vs. 15% of all murder victims; 1 in 7 sexual assault murder victims are 60 or older vs. 1 in 14 murder victims).
- About 8 of 10 sexual assault murders are intraracial (i.e., the offender and victim are of the same race).
- Sexual assault murders are about twice as likely as all murders (39.2% vs. 20.9%) to involve victims and offenders who were strangers.

Data from: Ressler, R. K., Burgess, A. W., & Douglas, J. E. (1988). *Sexual homicide: Patterns and motives*. New York: Free Press.

the cases. Among the cases with known circumstances, an estimated 4,807, or 1.5%, were classified as involving rape or another sex offense. Sexual assault murder victims differ markedly from other murders, as indicated in TABLE 11-3.

Rape Myths

Among the challenges confronting women who are raped are the myths that surround the issue of rape and the culpability of the victim. Rape myths can be categorized into classic rape myths and contemporary rape myths. The theoretical framework on rape and sexual assault is predicated on a legal and cultural theory of rape that has as a basis classic rape myths. Great efforts are made to encourage women to report a rape immediately; however, societal expectations concerning the reporting of rape are in conflict. One expectation is that if a woman is raped she should be too upset and ashamed to report it, and therefore this crime goes largely unreported. The other is that if a woman is raped she should be so upset she would report it. Both expectations exist simultaneously; it is the latter one, however, that is written into law. This legal principle was researched and reported by Brownmiller (1975) to have been carried since the 13th century, when, according to Henry of Bratton (Bracton), who lived and wrote in the 13th century and is considered an authority for the ancient Saxon times, the procedure for a raped virgin went like this:

> She must go at once and when the deed is newly done, with the hue and cry, to the neighboring townships and show the injury done to her to men of good repute, the blood and her clothing stained with blood and her torn garments.
>
> (Brownmiller, 1975, p. 17)

The rule then continues that if the accused man protests his innocence, the raped virgin must then have her body examined by four law-abiding women sworn to tell the truth as to whether she was defiled or is still a virgin (Brownmiller, 1975). Thus, in modern language, this is called "making the fresh complaint."

Research on rape myths has been reported in the literature for about three decades, beginning with Burt (1980). Burt (1980) defined a rape myth as "prejudicial, stereotyped or false beliefs about rape, rape victims, and rapists" (p. 217). Lonsway and Fitzgerald (1994) argued for a conceptually grounded definition of the concept of rape myths as "attitudes and beliefs that are generally false yet are widely and persistently held, and that serve to deny and justify male sexual aggression against women" (p. 158). An underlying support for the cultural theory of rape myths is the example of the "just world" concept (e.g., Gilmartin-Zena, 1987). This concept purports that the world is a just place where bad things happen only to those who deserve them. Thus, people will search for evidence that victims provoked or deserved their misfortune (Lerner, 1980). The function of this myth is to explain why a victim "asked for it" by her dress or behavior. The prevailing rape myths include factors around (1) false accusations of rape, (2) only certain women are raped, (3) victim–offender relationship, (4) violence of the assault, (5) resistance of the victim, (6) emotional response of the victim, and (7) sexual history of the victim (Koss, 1987).

The contemporary or newer generation of rape myths derive from research since the 1980s, where studies revealed that most sexual assaults were not committed by strangers but by acquaintances or nonstrangers. Terms such as *date rape* and *acquaintance rape* began to take hold. Victims of date rape were typically viewed as less harmed than those raped by strangers, and date rapists were viewed as less serious offenders and less culpable than stranger rapists. Often, the context of the rape included shared culpability by the two parties because of too much alcohol and too little clear communication regarding consent (Lisak, 2011).

Rape myth acceptance is played out in the courtroom wherein the victim is treated like the offender. Technically, only the man is on trial. But as the drama of the courtroom unfolds it becomes clear in people's minds the victim is as much on trial as the defendant (Holmstrom & Burgess, 1978). Clearly, her character is being judged as much as his. Her statements are viewed with as much suspicion as his. She says he raped her. He says either in testimony or by pleading not guilty that he did not. The jury or judge must decide which of these contradictory statements to believe.

Tomlinson (1999) observed barriers of police reporting "stem directly from rape myths that are deeply embedded in our general culture" (p. 86). The following are common myths: women falsely accuse men of rape, rape is not harmful, risky behavior of women leads to rape, only certain women are raped, women enjoy it, rape is sexually motivated, most rape is committed by strangers, violence characterizes the assault, victims can resist, and sexually "loose" women cannot be raped (Ben-David & Schneider, 2005; Boeschen, Sales, & Koss, 1998; Burt, 1980; Koss, 1987).

Dynamics of Reporting Rape

Rape has been termed the *hidden crime* because it occurs at high rates yet frequently goes unreported to police and other authorities (Abbey, Zawacki, & McAuslan, 2000). The NVAWS (Tjaden & Thoennes, 2000) documented that 1 of 6 U.S. women and 1 of 33 U.S. men have experienced an attempted or completed rape as a child and/or adult, indicating how pervasive rape is in our society. However, data have consistently shown that rape and sexual assault victims, more so than victims of other crimes of comparable severity, keep their victimization hidden. According to a report by the Bureau of Justice Statistics (Rennison, 2002), only 31.6% of all rapes and sexual assaults were reported to law enforcement officials in 1998 compared to 62% of all robberies, 57.6% of all aggravated assaults, and 40.3% of all simple assaults. Data from the NCVS for the years 1992 through 1994 found that only 25% of rape and sexual assault victims reported the crime to the police (Bachman, 1998), and when surveying college women, Fisher, Daigle, Cullen, and Turner's (2003b) national-level study found that only 13.3% of rapes and 14.3% of sexual assaults were reported to the police.

Statistics for sexual violence are difficult to measure due to different definitions and methodology used in surveys. The national organization RAINN (Rape, Abuse, & Incest National Network) is the largest anti-sexual violence organization in the United States. RAINN provides current information to more than 1,000 sexual assault service providers and operates the DoD Safe Helpline for the Department of Defense. On its website, RAINN publishes statistics for each topic on sexual violence using the National Crime Victimization Survey (NCVS), which is an annual study conducted by the Justice Department (See RAINN website). RAINN reports there are on average 321,500 victims (age 12 or older) of rape and sexual assault each year in the United States (Department of Justice, 2015).

A number of factors increase the chances of a rape being reported. Bachman (1998) noted that reporting a rape is strongly related to the perceived seriousness of the offense, indicated by the presence of injuries; if another crime was committed during the rape (i.e., theft); or if the offender used threats and weapons. DuMont, Miller, and Myhr (2003) found that reporting was more likely to occur when the victim was injured. Women who sustained bruises, lacerations, abrasions, bumps, internal injuries, and/or fractures were approximately three and one-half times more likely to contact the police than those who were not clinically injured. The presence of weapons, threats or use of force, completion of rape, and monetary losses were other aspects that influenced the seriousness of the incidents. In a study of 897 women who reported experiencing victimization, Gartner and Macmillan (1995) found that harm, economic loss, and use of a weapon together explained approximately 15% of the variation in reporting to police. Women who were physically coerced (had their clothes torn and/or were slapped, kicked, hit, or choked) were approximately three times more likely to contact the police than those who were not. This finding is consistent with Bachman's (1998) examination of American NCVS data. Her analysis of 235 incidents of rape found that victims were more likely to report if the assailant had used physical force.

The motivation to take corrective action may be stronger because victims believe a serious crime occurred and they deserve justice (Bachman, 1998). Furthermore, the woman may believe the physical injury provides the "physical evidence" she needs for the police to take her complaint more seriously and eliminate any suspicions about false claims. Injuries may function to corroborate the victim's claims of forced sex. Police, prosecutors, and judges were more likely to believe an allegation of rape was false if a woman had not been injured. In Fisher, Daigle, Cullen, and Turner's (2003a; 2003b) study of college women, one-third to 40% of their sample did not report to the police because they believed they lacked proof the incident happened and thought the police would not believe it was serious enough.

Physical injury may also facilitate prosecution by having physical evidence to hold the perpetrator accountable for his criminal behavior. Findings from empirical examinations of police and prosecutorial decisions tend to support this supposition. A review of sexual assaults reported to the police in Canada between 1993 and 1997 found a significant relationship between the presence of mild, moderate, or severe injury and the laying of charges (McGregor, DuMont, & Myhr, 2002). Rape cases with physical evidence of rape are more likely to move forward in the criminal justice system, according to Horney and Spohn's (2001) study of rape case processing in Detroit. In another study, Bouffard (2000) found that the victim agreeing to the forensic exam increased the probability that a case would remain open, suggesting the role that physical evidence and injury play in prosecutors' rape case processing decisions (as cited by Sommers, Fisher, & Karjane, 2005).

It still is a major concern among rape advocates that women and men are not reporting. Clinicians and researchers acknowledge low reporting rates in women they are treating or studying. Additionally, rape crisis center staff document the numbers of women who do not report under the mechanism of a third-party report. That is, they report the rape to law enforcement but withhold the name and identifying information of the victim. TABLE 11-4 illustrates some of the barriers and facilitators of rape reporting.

Wolitzky and colleagues (2011) analyzed data from 3,001 women who participated in the National Women's Study–Replication and conveyed that less than 1 in 6 rapes, less than 1 in 5 forcible rapes, and just above 1 in 10 incapacitated rape/drug-alcohol facilitated rape (IR/DAFR) are reported to the police, suggesting that reporting of rape continues to be at historically low levels compared to 1992 (Kilpatrick et al, 1992). The findings

TABLE 11-4 Barriers and Facilitators to Reporting Rape

Factor	Characteristics of Reporting
Demographic	Women who are older, more educated, and earn higher incomes are more likely to report sexual assaults (Gartner & Macmillan, 1995; Pino & Meier, 1999). Findings regarding race and reporting conflict. Bachman (1998) found that African American women are more likely to file a sexual assault police report, whereas other studies found White women are more likely to do so.
Assault characteristics	*Alcohol*: Studies have indicated there is a belief that crimes against intoxicated students who have not reached the legal drinking age should not be reported to the police. *Relationship to the assailant*: Victims are less likely to report an assault to the police of a known offender versus a stranger (Gartner & Macmillan, 1995; Pino & Meier, 1999). *Seriousness of assault*: Victims are more likely to report when they perceive their assault to be a serious one. *Weapons*: Other factors include the presence of weapons, threats or use of force, completion of a rape, and monetary losses (Bachman, 1998; Felson, Messner, & Hoskin, 1999; Gartner & Macmillan, 1995; Pino & Meier, 1999; Williams, 1984).
Personal issues	Personal reasons for not reporting an assault include the following (Tjaden & Thoennes, 2006): • *Fear* of retaliation from the assailant (22.1%) • *Shame* and embarrassment regarding the assault (18.1%) • *Fear of blame*: Police would not believe me or would blame me (11.9%)

note a significant percentage of women who are raped do not acknowledge that their experience is a rape. Women continue to be concerned about negative responses from others after a rape, including fear that they would be blamed, that family members or others would find out about the rape if it was reported, and of getting pregnant and/or contracting an STD including HIV.

Nonreporting

Less than half of persons who are raped report the rape to the authorities. Reasons for this nonreporting are discussed below.

DENIAL

Before a rape is reported, the victim needs to be able to acknowledge that the act was a rape. In many cases, victims deny that they have been raped. In a study of college women, Fisher, Daigle, Cullen, and Turner (2003a) noted that although the act met the legal definition of rape, less than half (46.5%) personally defined the experience as rape. Another study using university women as participants conducted by Bondurant (2001) found that 64% of women did not acknowledge their rape experiences.

Women who perceived their rapes as more violent were more likely to acknowledge the rapes (Bondurant, 2001), which is consistent with the rape mythologies stating that rapes are violent acts. In a nationwide study of university women, Fisher and colleagues (2003a) found that incidents were considered rape three times more often when the offender used physical force than when the offender did not, and six times more when a weapon was used. When an injury was sustained, incidents were considered rape almost four times more than when an injury was not sustained (Fisher et al., 2003a). Layman, Gidydz, and Lynn (1996) reported that a significant proportion of the women who were acknowledged, as opposed to unacknowledged, rape victims were threatened with force, had their arms twisted or held down, and were hit or slapped during the rape.

Only one measure of the victim's behavior significantly increased the odds of the incident being considered a rape. The victim's use of forceful verbal resistance increased the odds of the incident being considered a rape almost three times more than when the victim did not vocalize (Fisher et al., 2003a).

Because injuries are commonly viewed as a social criterion of violent crime, they may assist a woman in defining her experience as a sexual assault. This is problematic insofar as the evidence suggests a substantial proportion of sexual assaults do not involve physical violence.

Data from the Office of Victim Services Bureau of Justice Statistics from 2005–2010 revealed the following statistics:

- In 2005–2010, more than half (58%) of female victims of sexual violence suffered some type of physical injury during the attack; the injuries included cuts, bruises, internal injuries, broken bones, gunshot wounds, or rape injuries. This percentage remained unchanged from 1994–1998 to 2005–2010.

- The percentage of females who received some type of treatment for their physical injuries after a sexual assault increased from 26% in 1994–1998 to 35% in 2005–2010.

- In 2005–2010, more than three-fourths of female victims (80%) who were treated for physical injuries received care in a hospital, doctor's office, or emergency room as compared to 65% in 1994–1998.

FEAR OF THE LEGAL SYSTEM

A common rationale for the underreporting of rape is the treatment that victims receive from societal institutions, especially the legal system. This realization is not a contemporary idea but one that initiated reforms in the 1970s and 1980s to shift the focus from the consent of the victim to the behavior of the offender (Bachman, 1998).

Campbell, Wasco, Ahrens, Sefl, and Barnes (2001) found that only 25% of participants' cases that were reported to the legal system were prosecuted. Of the 25% that were actually prosecuted, 10% of the reported rapes were tried but the rapist was not convicted at trial, 10% were tried and convicted, and 5% were resolved by a guilty plea from the assailant. A study examining legal outcomes of women seeking treatment for sexual assault in an urban emergency room found that of 888 women seeking treatment, only 132 (15%) had charges filed by the prosecutor (Wiley, Sugar, Fine, & Eckert, 2003). Most cases resulted in either a plea before trial (70%) or a guilty verdict by the jury (15%). Another 13% of cases were dismissed or acquitted (Wiley et al., 2003). This is consistent with previous research showing that the most typical disposition for cases accepted for prosecution is not trial but a plea agreement. In response to agreeing to plead guilty and saving the state the expense of a trial, the offender is allowed to admit to a lesser crime (Koss, Bachar, Hopkins, & Carlson, 2004).

Victims who do have their cases prosecuted may find the procedures are traumatizing. Defense attorneys will use rape myths to convince the jury the victim consented to the rape (Koss et al., 2004). Victims can be subjected to probing and embarrassing questioning by the police and prosecutors to verify that a crime has occurred, and the extent to which the victim used (or did not use) physical resistance may be a factor (Pino & Meier, 1999).

FEAR OF RETALIATION

Some victims do not report because they fear retaliation by their offender, especially when he is known or is a boyfriend or partner. In Bachman's (1998) analysis of NCVS, more than 1 in 10 victims said they did not report because they were afraid of reprisal by the offender. Among college-aged women, Fisher et al. (2003b) noted that 39.5% of victims cited the fear of reprisal by the assailant or others as factors influencing their decision not to report the crime.

GUILT AND BLAME

Prevailing stereotypes of rape depict self-blame and guilt as central issues for victims. Rape myth attitudes, which are commonly held beliefs that shift the blame for a sexual assault from the assailant to the victim, serve to minimize the prevalence and seriousness of rape and may play a major role in why women feel blame. Some of the most pervasive myths include the beliefs that women falsely accuse men of rape, rape is not harmful, women want or enjoy rape, or women cause or deserve rape by inappropriate or risky behavior (Frese, Moya, & Megias, 2004). These underlying assumptions about rape suggest that women are essentially responsible for male sexual behavior.

Wiehe and Richards (1995) found guilt and self-blame to be primary reasons a sample of 236 victims of acquaintance rape did not report their victimizations to the police. They reported that self-blame was a recurring theme in survivors' comments and was reinforced by family or friends who overtly or covertly blamed the victim for what occurred by questioning her behaviors ("Why did you invite him to your apartment?" "Why did you go to his house?" "Were you drinking at the time?"). These and similar questions, although appearing to be asking for information, can be seen as blaming the victim for what happened (as cited by Bachman, 1998).

Self-blame was especially prevalent when victims were under the influence of alcohol at the time of the incidences and when victims perceived their own actions led to their being sexually victimized (Fisher et al., 2003b). In addition, women who had alcohol-related assaults received more negative reactions from formal and informal sources than did women who did not have alcohol-related assaults. Specifically, women who experienced alcohol-related assaults received more blaming and stigmatizing responses than women whose assaults did not involve alcohol (Ullman & Filipias, 2001). Notably, in Fisher et al.'s (2003b) sample of college-aged women, alcohol and/or drugs were present in 7 of 10 incidents.

PERSONAL MATTERS

In Bachman's (1998) analysis of NCVS data, victims overwhelmingly said the incident was a "personal matter" and they dealt with it another way. These data are supported by the Bureau of Justice Statistics, from the years 1992 to 2000, in which the most often cited reason for rape, attempted rape, and sexual assault victims not reporting to the police was that it was a personal matter. In addition, 16% of rape victims from the NVAWS reported they were too ashamed or wanted to keep the incident private (Tjaden & Thoennes, 2000). Victims may elect to keep their experiences private for a wide variety of reasons. It could be a feeling of embarrassment at having been victimized, lacking confidence that reporting would lead to arrest, wishing to avoid the stigma associated with being a crime victim, or protecting their families or those close to the perpetrators (Fisher et al., 2003b). Alternatively, it could be fear of making the rape public. If the rape goes to trial, they are expected to testify about the details of sexual assault in an open court, and they may fear what their family, friends, and community members may think of them (Koss et al., 2004).

VICTIM–OFFENDER RELATIONSHIP

The closer the relationship between victim and offender, the more difficult the road to prosecution. Rapes committed by a stranger are still viewed as more serious and legitimate than rape by acquaintances, romantic partners, or husbands. Studies suggest acquaintance rape victims are less likely to label their assaults as rapes than woman assaulted by strangers (Fisher et al., 2003a). The Bureau of Justice Statistics data from 1992 to 2000 reported that the closer the relationship between the female victim and the offender, the greater the likelihood the police would not be told about the rape or sexual assault (Rennison, 2002). When the offender was a current or former husband or boyfriend, 77% of completed rapes and 75% of sexual assaults were not reported to the police. When the offender was a friend or acquaintance, 61% of completed rapes, 71% of attempted rapes, and 82% of sexual assaults were not reported. When the offender was a stranger, 54% of completed rapes, 44% of attempted rapes, and 34% of sexual assaults were not reported to the police (Rennison, 2002).

Nonstrangers commit approximately 74% of rapes or sexual assaults; thus, if victims are less likely to report such assaults, most offenses will not come to the attention of police (Fisher et al., 2003a). Other studies have replicated these results. Survey data from a community study by Ullman and Filipias (2001) found that more women sexually assaulted by strangers (78%) told formal support sources (including police, physicians, rape crisis counselors) than did women assaulted by known men (57.6%).

Rape treatment outcome research found that 51.6% of victims were raped by strangers (Vickerman & Margolin, 2009). This finding was similar in studies by Frazier (2003) and Resick, Jordan, Girelli, Hutter, and Marhoeder-Dvorak (1988) in which 45% and 54% of victims, respectively, were assaulted by a stranger. In one cross-sectional correlational study of 1,172 patients presenting to a local emergency department with a complaint of rape, the relationship between the victim and perpetrator was documented in 88.5% of cases ($n = 1,037$) (Avegno, Mills, & Mills, 2009). Of the total, 550 patients (53.0%) reported knowing their attacker, 437 (42.2%) did not know the perpetrator, and 50 (4.8%) were unsure. Results indicated that victims who were African American as opposed to White (62.6% vs. 43.5%, respectively, $P < 0.0001$) and young (age < 26 years) reported significantly higher rates of known perpetrators than older victims (58.1% vs. 49.2%, respectively, $P < 0.005$). Victims who reported knowing their attacker most often categorized the relationship as "acquaintance" (50.8%) or "friend" (30.8%) (Avegno et al., 2009). Contrary to other studies, categorizing the relationship as a "date" comprised only 9.6% of cases, as spouse or partner 4.0%, and as family member 4.9%.

For rapes reported to the police, the question becomes whether the victim–offender relationship actually influences legal outcomes. Some studies point to the fact that stranger rapes result in more positive legal outcomes. For example, Campbell et al. (2001) found that 80% of the prosecuted cases in their sample involved stranger rapes and 20% were nonstranger rapes. In contrast, Wiley et al.'s (2003) study of legal outcomes in women who presented to the emergency department with a complaint of sexual assault found significantly greater likelihood of a legal outcome if one's partner or spouse was the assailant (60%) compared to 31% in those cases not involving a partner or spouse. A stranger as the assailant did not affect legal outcome, and a friend or acquaintance as the assailant negatively influenced legal outcome (Wiley et al., 2003).

However, partner or spousal sexual assault is more likely to include physical violence and to result in physical injuries to the victim than sexual assault from an acquaintance (Stermac, DelBove, & AdSdison, 2001). An earlier study by Stermac, Dumont, and Dunn (1998) of 1,162 women seeking treatment also found intimate partner sexual assaults were more similar to stranger assaults, as both had greater physical violence and injuries than acquaintance assaults. It is possible that if a woman reports to the emergency department after sexual assault by an intimate partner, she may have experienced a more violent assault with more physical trauma than women assaulted by a stranger. The victim–offender relationship then becomes secondary to the presence of injuries, which validates the crime. It is also possible that assailants who are strangers may not be located, in contrast to a spouse/partner who is an assailant.

COPING BEHAVIOR AND CRIME FACTORS

The behavior of victims confronted by the threat of a rape attack, the attack itself, and the period immediately thereafter can be analyzed as coping. Burgess & Holmstrom studied the coping behavior of 92 women diagnosed as having rape trauma and identified three phases (Burgess & Holmstrom, 1974, 2006). In court, crime factors of relationship, reporting, use of force and/or weapon, and forensic findings play a critical role to the jury. TABLE 11-5 illustrates some of these factors when classified into the three phases of a rape.

Despite 30 years of public attention to the prevalence of rape and sexual assault in our society, the validity of reports is often questioned and rape victims continue to be blamed. Not reporting rape has negative consequences. It reduces the likelihood that an offender will be arrested or convicted by failing to initiate the criminal justice system. If rapists perceive the likelihood of apprehension from authorities is low, this undermines any deterrent value the legal system may have in preventing rape (Bachman, 1998). By not reporting, victims may not have access to victim-assistance services provided by the criminal justice system, such as support programs, or to medical treatment.

TABLE 11-5 Rape Beliefs and Phase of Rape

Phase of Rape	Crime Factors	Rape Attitudes and Beliefs
Before the rape	Stranger vs. nonstranger relationship Time between incident and report Use of force	She is acquainted with the offender. She meets him in a risky setting (e.g., bar). Her behavior is provocative (drinking, demeanor, clothing).
During the rape	Location of assault Weapon shown	She consents (then changes her mind). She doesn't resist or scream or call for help.
After the rape	Weapon used Resistance of victim	She doesn't immediately report or tell anyone for a while. She has no bruises or torn clothing. She doesn't go for a medical exam or the exam has no forensic findings. She stays with the offender or sees him again or resumes her usual lifestyle.

Typology of Sexual Trauma

The rape trauma syndrome was one of three typologies identified by Burgess and Holmstrom in 1974 and published in the *American Journal of Psychiatry*. The typologies were the result of personal interviews with 146 people who ranged in age from 3 to 73 years at the time of admission to the Boston City Hospital emergency department. The individuals all were admitted with the complaint of rape. Three types of sexual trauma were conceptualized from the sample of 146 and based on consent (or not) to have sex: rape trauma (no consent), pressured sex (coerced sex), and sex stress (initial consent but then denial of consent). Of the 146 individuals, 92 women ages 18 to 73 were classified as rape trauma victims and their responses to the assaultive experience formed the basis for the rape trauma syndrome.

Rape: Sex Without the Victim's Consent

Control is a key ingredient of a rape. In practical terms, the assailant has two goals: physical and sexual control of the victim. In listening to victims describe the assailants' styles of attack, it was clear that some rapists gained control in a direct physical action, such as a sudden surprise attack, whereas others used verbal ploys in an attack with the qualities of a confidence game. In both types the rapist gains sexual control of the victim by force and without her consent.

BLITZ RAPE

The **blitz rape** occurs "out of the blue" and without any prior interaction between assailant and victim. The person is leading a normal everyday life. A split second later that life is shattered and that individual is a victim. One 36-year-old victim told the rape advocate that the man appeared out of nowhere. She said she had no way to get away because it happened so fast, like a shock of lightning, that she didn't have time to think of an escape. From the victim's point of view there is no ready explanation for the man's presence. He suddenly appears, his presence is inappropriate, he is uninvited, and he forces himself into the situation. Often, he selects an anonymous victim and tries to remain anonymous himself. He may wear a mask or gloves or cover the victim's face as he attacks.

The "mark," to use the language of the criminal world, is the person destined to become a victim of some form of illegal exploitation. The classic example of the blitz-type rape is a woman walking down the street and who, from the assailant's viewpoint, is the "right mark at the right time." He is looking for someone to capture and attack, she happens on the scene, and she becomes the target. The surprise attack outdoors is a common blitz-type rape. However, it is not unusual for victims to be attacked while they are asleep in their own beds because the assailant has gained entry into the home. The following case illustrates such a rape in which the victim was in her own apartment sleeping.

Lauren, age 22, lived with two roommates in a second-floor apartment. Neither roommate was home when she went to bed around midnight. She awoke about 5:30 a.m. to a man on top of her and wearing a Halloween-type mask and a pair of gloves. Lauren tried to scream, and he put his hands over her mouth and nose and was choking her. He ripped off her nightclothes. She believed he would kill her. He told her to "Shut up" and proceeded to rape her. When he finished, he got up and walked out of the room. Lauren jumped up, locked the door, and looked for her cordless phone. She believed the assailant was in the apartment and that she had to escape. She cut the window screen with a pen, jumped out, and continued running to several doors, pounding on them for someone to help her. At about the third door a man responded and let her use his phone to call 911 and report the rape.

In blitz-type rapes, victims describe being jumped on, grabbed, pushed, or shoved when the assailant approached them from behind. Other victims describe being in the process of entering their cars or apartments or stopped at a traffic light when a man opened the unlocked passenger side door. Other victims describe being pulled into cars or grabbed outside and taken to an indoor area such as a hallway, building, or car. One woman had just stepped into her shower when the lights went out and the man grabbed her and took her into a bedroom.

CONFIDENCE RAPE

The confidence rape is a subtler setup than the blitz style and is an attack in which the assailant obtains sex under false pretenses by using deceit, betrayal, and often violence. The assailant and the victim interact before the assault. He may know the victim from some other time and place and thus already may have developed some kind of relationship with her. Or, he may establish a relationship as a prelude to attack. Often, there is quite a bit of conversation between victim and assailant. Like the confidence man, he encourages the victim to trust him and then betrays this trust as in the following example.

About 6:20 p.m. Sarah, age 23, was on the phone with a friend when a person, known to her as one of the workmen who had been in her apartment once, knocked on her door to tell her he needed to fix a leak for the apartment below hers. She unlocked her door, and he checked under her sink and in the bathroom. As he was leaving the apartment he suddenly locked the door handle. He then said he wanted to date Sarah; she was shocked and said no and asked him to leave several times. He then grabbed her wrists; she fought to get away, and he hit her on the sides of her face and proceeded to rape her.

Pressured Sex: Inability to Consent

In rape, the type of victimization discussed above, the victim, whether adult, adolescent, or child, clearly does not consent to the sexual activity. The sexual acts are against their will and they are forced by the assailant to do them. In pressured sex, the types of victimization discussed in this section, the victims aid or contribute in a secondary manner to the sexual activity. The victims' collaboration comes about because of their inability to consent or not consent due to their stage of personality or cognitive development.

It should be noted that we do not define ability to consent arbitrarily by age. In all these cases, the primary person involved, the assailant, stands in a relationship of power over the secondary person, the victim, because he is older, an authority figure, and so on.

The assailant gains access to this victim by three methods: (1) pressures the victim to take material goods, (2) pressures the victim to accept human contact, and (3) pressures the victim to believe the sexual activity is appropriate and enjoyable. In each of these three approaches, the assailant makes sure the victim gets something out of the sexual encounter; thus, at the time the encounter is not a totally negative experience for the victim.

Sex Stress Situation: Sex with Initial Consent

The third type of victimization is a sex stress situation rather than forced or pressured sex. They are not cases of the male's gaining access without the female's initial consent. Nor are they cases in which the victim, for personality or cognitive reasons, was incapable of making a decision of consent. Rather, in this type, the male and female initially agreed to have sexual relations but then something drastically "went wrong." Usually, what went wrong was the male exploited this agreement in several ways. In some cases, what went wrong was that authorities—police or parents—came upon or found out about the consenting couples and then these authorities themselves defined the situation as rape or caused the person to say it was rape as a way out of a dilemma of being caught.

Also, in some of these sex stress cases the person who referred to the problem as rape in reality wanted some service from the hospital and believed she could not directly ask for it. After all, given the prevailing attitudes, a young teenager cannot walk into a hospital and say that she and her boyfriend had sex the evening before, she is scared of getting pregnant, and she needs medication to prevent pregnancy. It should be emphasized that very few of these sex stress victims took the case to court; they did not become "spite cases"; that is, cases in which the female sought to "get the guy" on a rape charge simply out of spite.

Workplace Harassment

Confidence rapes also occur in the workplace or school setting where the victim needs to be present, harassment occurs, and authority (school or employer) fails to intervene. Consider the following case.

Michelle was in her senior year of high school when she began to work afternoons at a local fast food restaurant. She soon became upset with the work environment, in particular the sexual language and talk, references to women as "sluts," and unwanted physical contact. One employee in particular, Victor, frightened Michelle. He was over 6 feet tall and in his 30s. He would tell her she was sexy, pretty, and hot and that he wanted to have sex with her; he would also touch her despite her telling him to stop. Her coworkers or the supervisors took no action. Victor's behavior escalated to attempting to lift her skirt, rub her body, and kiss her. He threatened harm to her if she told anyone. Michelle tried to avoid Victor by procrastinating going to work and trying to work when Victor was not present. The sexual pressuring and harassment continued until Victor forced Michelle into a small, unlocked, unsupervised closet in the restaurant where he forced her to perform oral sex on him. The sexual assaults were reported to Victor's probation supervisor, the police, and Michelle's family.

Psychological Impact of Sexual Assault

The study of victim response revealed a differential response to sexual assault and rape: that symptoms persisted over a long period of time and that some symptoms did not abate despite therapeutic efforts. It was realized that more fundamental changes had occurred as a consequence of the sexual assault. These fundamental changes suggested a type of trauma learning that caused biological shifts. These assumptions have been bolstered by the rapidly developing areas of neuroscience and biology and have revealed substantive changes and alterations in basic central nervous system functioning.

One of the conclusions reached by Burgess and Holmstrom (1974, 2015) as a result of studying 92 adult rape victims was that victims suffer a significant degree of physical and emotional trauma during a rape. This trauma can be noted immediately after the assault and over a considerable time period afterward. Victims consistently described symptoms that included flashbacks, intrusive thoughts of the rape, fear, anxiety, nightmares, daymares, and the development of phobias. A cluster of symptoms was described as the rape trauma syndrome. The rape trauma syndrome has two phases: the immediate or acute phase, in which the victim's lifestyle is completely disrupted by the rape crisis, and the long-term process, in which the victim must reorganize this disrupted lifestyle. The syndrome includes physical, emotional, and behavioral stress reactions that result from the person being faced with a life-threatening event to one's life or integrity.

The Burgess and Holmstrom study had a clinical focus on victim response to rape and an institutional focus. The study made clear that rape does not end with the assailant's departure; rather, the profound suffering of the victim can be diminished or heightened by the response of those who staff the police stations, hospitals, and courthouses. Ironically, the institutions that society has designated to help victims may in fact cause further damage (Holmstrom & Burgess, 1978).

Rape trauma syndrome was accepted as a nursing diagnosis into the North American Nursing Diagnosis Association official nomenclature in 1979. Also included were two variations of rape trauma syndrome: silent response to rape and compounded reaction to rape. The silent response to rape was observed in persons who had never told anyone of a childhood rape experience but later (months or years) the assault was revealed. In the Burgess and Holmstrom study (1974), women talked freely of these early experiences in the context of the new assaultive experience. In the compounded rape trauma, the individual had a primary presenting medical or psychological disorder through which the rape trauma symptoms were filtered. Examples include elders with dementia, persons with a psychiatric disorder or physical disorder, and persons with an intellectual disability.

Posttraumatic Stress Disorder

Rape trauma syndrome preceded the term posttraumatic stress disorder by six years. When the American Psychological Association's work group on anxiety disorders was considering how to classify a number of traumatic events (e.g., combat stress, natural disasters, and rape trauma), it was decided to make an umbrella term under which the various life-threatening events could fall. The designated term, *posttraumatic stress disorder* (PTSD), came into the official nosology of the American Psychological Association in 1980, with the publication of the third edition of the *Diagnostic and Statistical Manual of Mental Disorders*.

In 2013, the American Psychiatric Association revised the PTSD diagnostic criteria in the fifth edition of its *Diagnostic and Statistical Manual of Mental Disorders* (APA, 2013). The diagnostic criteria include a history of exposure to a traumatic event that meets specific stipulations and symptoms from each of four symptom clusters:

- Intrusion: Involuntary, recurrent thoughts and memories of trauma.
- Avoidance: Efforts to avoid reminders of the trauma.
- Negative alterations in cognitions and mood: Persistent negative emotional state.
- Alterations in arousal and reactivity: Irritability.

The sixth criterion concerns duration of symptoms, the seventh assesses functioning, and the eighth criterion clarifies symptoms as not attributable to a substance or co-occurring medical condition.

When the traumatic event is a rape or sexual assault, the designation is usually rape-related PTSD, to distinguish it from other traumatic events, such as combat-related PTSD.

Classifying Rapists

To more fully appreciate rape victimization, it is helpful to understand the dynamics of the offender. What prompts men to rape? What are such offenders like? Do they progress from less serious to more aggressive offenses? What determines their choice of victims? What can a potential victim do, when faced with such an assailant, to deter him? Will the offender return? These are some of the questions commonly asked about rapists, and it is difficult to provide simple and unequivocal answers to them.

Early Research

Early research for classifying the underlying motivational intent for sexual assault identified three domains: power, anger, and sexuality (Groth, Burgess, & Holmstrom, 1977). This early classification was taken from the perspective of the rapist and clinical work with him.

Clinical work with offenders and victims in the 1970s through the 1990s revealed that rape was in fact serving primarily nonsexual needs: it was the sexual expression of power and anger. Rape was viewed as motivated more by retaliatory and compensatory motives than sexual ones; it was a pseudo-sexual act, complex and multidetermined but addressing issues of hostility (anger) and control (power) more than desire (sexuality).

The defining issue in rape is the lack of consent on the part of the victim. Sexual relations are achieved through physical force, threat, or intimidation. Rape is therefore first and foremost an aggressive act, and in any given instance of rape multiple psychological meanings may be expressed in regard to both the sexual and the aggressive components of the act.

The most basic observation one can make regarding rapists is that not all such offenders are alike. They do not do the very same thing in the very same way or for the very same reason. In some cases, similar acts occur for different reasons, and in other cases, different acts serve similar purposes. Clinical experience both with identified offenders and with victims of reported sexual assault note that in all cases of forcible rape, three basic components are always present: anger, power, and sexuality (Groth et al., 1977). The hierarchy and interrelationships among these three factors, together with the relative intensity with which each is experienced and the variety of ways in which each is expressed, may vary from one offense to another. Yet there is sufficient clustering so that distinguishable patterns of rape become evident: the anger rape, in which sexuality becomes a hostile act; the power rape, in which sexuality becomes an expression of conquest; and the sadistic rape, in which anger and control become eroticized. In every act of rape, then, both aggression and sexuality are involved. However, it is clear that sexuality becomes the means of expressing other, nonsexual needs and feelings that operate in the offender and motivate his assault. Rather than being primarily an expression of sexual desire, rape is, in fact, the use of sexuality to express issues of power and anger. It is a sexual act that is concerned much more with status, aggression, control, and dominance than with sexual pleasure or sexual satisfaction. It is sexual behavior in the service of nonsexual needs, and in this sense, rape is clearly a distortion of human sexuality.

Theory of Interpersonal Aggression

Rape and sexual assault are acts ensuing from interpersonal aggression that result in sexual victimization to person(s) who may or may not be known to the offender. These rapes and sexual assaults are not primarily motivated by material gain and are not sanctioned by a group. Rather, an underlying emotional conflict or psychological issue propels the offender to commit rape and sexual assault. Although the case may be legally defined as rape, the term *sexual assault* is used in this classification to encompass a wide range of forced and pressured sexual activities. (Douglas, Burgess, Burgess, & Ressler, 2006; Prentky & Burgess, 2000).

Exploitative Rape

In *exploitative rape*, sometimes called *power reassurance rape*, expressed aggression is generally low and does not exceed what was necessary to force victim compliance. Callous indifference to the victim is evident. Issues of power and control are underlying psychological conflict.

Sexualization essentially refers to a high degree of preoccupation with gratifying one's sexual needs. In this type of sexual assault, the offender quickly gains control over his victim. The evidence of such power and control is that the victim submits to sexual demands on the part of the offender. The offender places his victim in a situation through verbal threat, intimidation with a weapon, and/or physical force where she cannot refuse or resist him, and this provides the offender with a reassuring sense of power, security, strength, mastery, and control. In this fashion, he compensates for underlying feelings of inadequacy, vulnerability, and helplessness.

This type of rapist often shows little skill in negotiating interpersonal relationships and feels inadequate in both sexual and nonsexual areas of his life. Having few other avenues of personal expression, sexuality becomes the core of his self-image and self-esteem. Rape becomes the means by which he reassures himself of his sexual adequacy and identity, of his strength and potency. Usually, the goal of the assault is to effect sexual intercourse as evidence of conquest, and to accomplish this the victim may be kidnapped, tied up, or rendered helpless in some fashion.

Because it becomes a test of his competency, the rape experience for this offender is one of anxiety, excitement, and anticipated pleasure. The assault is premeditated and preceded by an obsessional fantasy in which, although his victim may initially resist him, once overpowered she will submit gratefully to his embrace because she will be so impressed with his sexual abilities. In reality, this offender may often be handicapped by impotency or premature ejaculation. If not, he still tends to find little sexual satisfaction in the rape. The assault is disappointing because it never lives up to his fantasy. The power rapist commits his offense in an effort to resolve disturbing doubts about his sexual adequacy and masculinity. He aims to place a woman in a helpless, controlled position where she cannot refuse him or reject him and thus shore up his failing sense of worth and adequacy.

Often, he must convince himself that his victim became attracted to him, really wanted sex but could not admit it, and clearly consented nonverbally to, and enjoyed, the sexual contact. Yet, at some level, he realizes that he has not found what he is looking for in the offense; he senses that something he cannot clearly define is lacking. He does not feel reassured by either his own performance or his victim's response to the assault; therefore, he must go out and find another victim—this time the "right one."

The offenses become repetitive and compulsive. The amount of force used in the assault may vary, and there may be an increase in aggression over time as the offender becomes more desperate to achieve that indefinable experience that continues to elude him. Usually, this offender does not have a conscious intent to hurt or degrade his victim; his aim is to have complete control over her so she will have no say in the matter and will be submissive and gratify his sexual demands. Aggression, then, may constitute a show of force or a reaction to resistance on the part of the victim. That is, when the victim resists the advances of her assailant, he retaliates by striking or hitting her. Aggression here usually becomes expressed less as an anger motive and more as a means of dominating, controlling, and being in charge of the situation. Rape becomes an assertion of the offender's virility or a reassurance of his competence—a reflection of the inadequacy he experiences in terms of his sense of identity and effectiveness.

Anger Rape

Sexual assault in this category is characterized by high expressive aggression (unprovoked physical and verbal aggression or physical force in excess of that necessary to gain victim compliance must be present). Rage is evident in this offender. He may have manifested behaviors listed for sadistic sexual assault, but these must appear to be punishing actions done in anger, not to increase sexual arousal. The primary motive for the offense is anger and not sexual gratification. When the offender knows the victim, the assault on that victim appears to be the result of the offender's easy access to that victim. These offenses are predominantly impulse driven (e.g., opportunity alone, possibly coupled with impaired judgment due to drugs/alcohol).

The degree of force used in this type of assault is excessive and gratuitous. The violence is an integrated component of the behavior even when the victim is compliant. Resistance from the victim is likely to increase the aggression, and serious injury or death may occur. The rage is not sexualized, suggesting the assault is not fantasy driven. The violence is a lifestyle characteristic that is directed toward males and females alike. The rape is but one feature in a history of unsocialized aggressive behavior noted across various social settings.

In some cases of sexual assault it is very apparent that sexuality becomes a means of expressing and discharging feelings of intense anger, rage, contempt, hatred, and frustration; the assault is characterized by excessive brutality. Far more physical force is used in the commission of the offense than is required simply to overpower and subdue the victim. Instead, the assault is one of explosive physical violence to all parts of the victim's body. This type of offender approaches his victim by striking and beating her; he tears her clothes, knocks her to the ground, uses abusive and profane language, rapes her, and frequently makes her perform or submit to additional degrading acts.

The **anger rapist** finds it difficult to explain his assault, when he cannot deny it, except to rationalize that he was drunk or on drugs. Often, the specific details are lost to his memory in that he becomes "blind with rage" during the assault. Satisfaction and relief result from the discharge of anger rather than from sexual gratification. Pleasure is derived from degrading and humiliating his victim.

His relationships to important women in his life are fraught with conflict, irritation, and irrational jealousy, and he is often physically assaultive toward them. His sexual offenses tend to be episodic and sporadic, triggered by conflicts in his relationships to these actual women in his life.

Sadistic Rape

In the sadistic rape, aggression itself is eroticized. The offender, referred to as a **sexual sadist**, derives satisfaction in the sexual abuse of his victim. Sexuality and aggression become intertwined into a single psychological experience: sadism. The assault itself appears ritualistic and usually involves bondage and torture. Sexual areas of the victim's body—her breasts, genitals, and buttocks—become the focus of injury. The rape experience for this type of offender is one of intense and mounting excitement. He finds pleasure in the victim's torment, anguish, distress, and suffering. His assault is deliberate, calculated, and premeditated. The victim is stalked, captured, abused, and, in extreme cases, murdered. The nature of the assault may or may not involve the offender's genitals: The victim may be raped with an instrument or foreign object, such as a spoon or bottle. In some cases, sexual penetration may take place after she is dead.

Sexual Predators in the Community

Although research on sex offenders has expanded our knowledge of the behavior and characteristics of rapists, their motivation, and their developmental antecedents, the studies have been conducted on incarcerated offenders. However, because many victims do not report their rape, the offenders remain undetected, not subject to prosecution, and therefore in the community. Psychologist David Lisak and colleagues began a series of interviews of undetected rapists primarily in college environments and found similarities to incarcerated offenders in that they shared the same motivational matrix of hostility, anger, dominance, hypermasculinity, impulsiveness, and antisocial attitudes. It was also noted that these men were likely to be serial offenders (Lisak & Miller, 2002).

Lisak characterized the modus operandi of undetected rapists as follows. First, they are adept at identifying possible victims and testing prospective victims' boundaries. Second, these offenders plan and premeditate their attacks using sophisticated strategies to groom the victim and isolate her for an assault. Third, they use only enough aggression to control and coerce the woman into submission. Fourth, they use psychological weapons of power, control, manipulation, and threats rather than weapons of knives or guns. Fifth, they use alcohol deliberately to render victims more vulnerable to attack or sometimes to make them unconscious (Lisak, 2011).

False Allegations of Rape and Sexual Assault

On August 23, 2011, a New York judge dropped all criminal sexual assault charges against former International Monetary Fund chief Dominique Strauss-Kahn. The decision ended a case that generated three months of sordid headlines about a hotel maid who accused Strauss-Kahn of attempting to rape her in his luxury Manhattan hotel suite (Ax & Trotta, 2011).

Prosecutors stated they were not convinced of his culpability beyond a reasonable doubt due to serious issues in the complainant's credibility and inconclusive physical evidence and therefore could not ask a jury to believe it. Prosecutors pointed to a "pattern of untruthfulness" about the 32-year-old woman's past that included a convincingly delivered story of being gang raped by soldiers in her native Guinea; she later admitted to fabricating the story, and prosecutors characterized her ability to recount a fictionalized sexual assault with complete conviction as "fatal" to her credibility. She had also denied an interest in making money from the case, despite a recorded conversation prosecutors said captured her discussing just that with her fiancé, a detainee in an immigration jail in Arizona, shortly after the encounter in the hotel (Ax & Trotta, 2011).

The case pitted supporters of Strauss-Kahn, who said he was the victim of an overzealous U.S. criminal justice system, against backers of the woman, Diallo, who complained it was an example of race, class, and gender where sexual assault victims are denied justice (Ax & Trotta, 2011).

Potential Consequences of a False Allegation

Imprisonment of men falsely accused of rape has been described since Biblical times. Potiphar, an Egyptian captain of Pharaoh's guard, employed Joseph to watch over his household. Potiphar's wife "cast her eyes upon Joseph . . . caught him by his garment, saying lie with me." Joseph resisted this temptation, but his rejection of her caused her to say that the Hebrew servant came to "mock her," that she lifted up her voice and cried, and that he fled, leaving his garment with her. Potiphar imprisoned Joseph for two years (Genesis, 39).

Although not resulting in imprisonment, a more contemporary, and nationally infamous, false allegation case occurred in the 1980s in Duchess County, New York. Tawana Brawley, a 15-year-old African American girl from the quiet little town of Wappingers Falls, New York (population 5,000), was missing for four days when she was found on November 28, 1987. She was observed in the backyard of a townhouse, previously occupied by her family, standing in a green garbage bag and literally hopping around the yard before lying down and pulling the bag over her head. Her hair had been cut short, she had feces smeared on her body, and "KKK" and "nigger" had been printed on her body with a sootlike substance. She refused to speak with police but, speaking through her aunt and mother, reported she had been abducted, taken to a wooded area, and repeatedly raped by four to six White men, one of whom had a police-style badge. Reverend Al Sharpton and others became involved, and it was alleged that the county police and prosecutor were involved in a cover-up to protect members of the local police force. Consequently, the national news media became involved, and then-Governor Cuomo asserted state jurisdiction over the investigation that resulted in the formation of a combined state and federal task force. After an intensive and lengthy criminal and state grand jury investigation lasting more than seven months, it was concluded that Brawley had falsified the story. Additionally, the grand jury found no evidence of a cover-up by law enforcement officials and recommended that their minutes be released to the public.

Another, but equally infamous, incident involved an African American female alleging that several White Duke University lacrosse players had assaulted her. Again, the national news media became involved because of inflammatory statements made by the local prosecutor. This matter collapsed from a preponderance of evidence supporting the defense, a lack of evidence supporting the allegation, and numerous conflicting statements given by the alleged victim. The state attorney general intervened and issued a blistering statement concerning the abilities and motivation of the local prosecutor.

Difficulty of Measuring Rates of False Allegations of Rape

For centuries there has been an assumption that many women allege being raped for purposes of revenge or other motives. In the 17th century, the suggestion of rape being an easily made accusation formed the basis of corroboration warnings issued by judges to the jury, cautioning of "women's propensity to make false charges of rape" (Flowe et al., 2007, p. 160). It is unclear whether this skepticism originated from a high frequency of false charges, because research findings on false rape allegations vary considerably from estimates of 1.5% to 90% (Lisak, Gardinier, Nicksa, & Cote, 2010). To obtain an accurate rate, the definition of a false allegation of rape must be clearly outlined. The International Chiefs of Police explained this definition as follows (Lisak et al., 2010, p. 1,319):

> The determination that a report of sexual assault is false can be made only if the evidence establishes that no crime was committed or attempted. This determination can be made only after a thorough investigation. This should not be confused with an investigation that fails to prove a sexual assault occurred. In that case, the investigation would be labeled unsubstantiated. The determination that a report is false must be supported by evidence that the assault did not happen.

Evidence that the assault did not happen may include physical evidence or credible witnesses who may contradict key aspects of the victim's version of the story. According to the International Chiefs of Police, uncooperative victims, insufficient evidence, inconsistencies in victim statements, lying on behalf of the victim, delayed reporting of a rape incident, or incidents that involved intoxication are all factors that, by themselves, do not make a rape allegation false (Lisak et al., 2010). As mentioned above, false allegations can also be confused or combined with the category of unfounded or unsubstantiated claims that are commonly defined as "lacking a sound base, groundless, unwarranted" (Lisak et al., 2010, p. 1,321). Lisak et al. (2010) claim that "both terms are used to code and administratively clear sexual assault cases that are often mislabelled as false allegations" (p. 1,321). The UCR, for example, reports 8% of rape allegations are unfounded. Lisak et al. (2010, p. 1,321) explain as follows:

> The UCR guidelines also make clear that the category of "unfounded" is broader than the category of false allegation, since "unfounded" includes cases that are determined to be "baseless." A case can be classified as "baseless" if, for example, a victim reports an incident that, while truthfully recounted, does not meet, in the eyes of investigators, the legal definition of a sexual assault. For example, if a victim reports to the police that she was raped while she was intoxicated, and truthfully states that she cannot

clearly recall whether there was penetration, investigators might classify such a case as "baseless/unfounded." This classification is clearly distinct from a case in which a victim deliberately fabricates an account of being raped, yet the "unfounded" category is very often equated with the category of "false allegation."

This is further evidence of how variations in the classifications and definitions of false rape allegations and differing methodologies of measuring false rape allegations add to a bank of unreliable data. In fact, Rumney (2006) concluded that the current research literature cannot be used to determine the rate of false rape allegations. Lisak et al. (2010) add that, "There is considerable evidence of widespread misclassification by police departments and enormous disparities among police agencies in how cases are classified" (p. 1,322).

Lisak et al. (2010) developed a list of studies that, according to them, use a clear definition of a false allegation, explain the source of data used, and attempt to evaluate data received from law enforcement agencies. TABLE 11-6 provides the studies with most consistent rates of false rape allegations per Lisak et al.

Lisak et al. outlined the importance of providing reliable and accurate data on false rape allegations that contradict widely held stereotypes that false rape allegations are common. Such a stereotype may result in increased

TABLE 11-6 Rates of False Allegations of Rape

Study	Sample Size	Rate of False Reports
Toronto (1970)	116	10.3% false
Philadelphia (1972–1975)	709	15% unfounded, 3% false
British Home Office Study (1985)	302	24% no crime, 8.3% false
British Home Office Study (1996)	483	25.5% no crime, 10.9% false
British Home Office Study (15-year period)	2,643	8.2% false, 2.5% recalculated false under more stringent criteria
Australian Study (3-year period)	812	2.1% false
Making a Difference Study by End Violence Against Women (18- to 24-month period)	2,059	6.8% false

Data from: Lisak, D., Gardinier, L., Nicksa, S. C., & Cote, A. M. 2010. False Allegations of Sexual Assault: An Analysis of Ten Years of Reported Cases. *Violence Against Women, 16*(12); 1324.

underreporting because victims may be under the impression their claims are less likely to be believed. The stereotype may also influence law enforcement agents to handle victims' allegations through hostile interrogation rather than fact finding (Lisak et al., 2010). Furthermore, incorrect assumptions about false rape allegations may inhibit appropriate policy developments surrounding rape reform and legislature (Rumney, 2006).

Reasons for False Allegations of Rape

Studies have revealed that some false allegations of rape may be motivated by malicious intent, medical conditions leading to a mistaken account of rape (such as Munchausen's syndrome), or complainants who thought they might have been sexually assaulted while they were highly intoxicated or asleep (Rumney, 2006). In Kanin's study (1957), 109 false allegations were revealed as a means for acquiring sympathy or attention, retaliation against a rejecting male, or serving as an alibi function to explain a consensual encounter or account for some other event (Kennedy & Witkowski, 2000). Other studies concluded that the most frequent motive for fabricated rape were instances that involved consensual sex that led to some sort of problem for the accuser, such as contracting a sexually transmitted disease or becoming pregnant (Gross, 2009, p. 68).

EMOTIONAL PROBLEMS IN NEED OF ATTENTION

Frequently, those who make false allegations have legitimate problems worthy of attention in their own right. However, if their complaints are accepted at face value, the underlying problem will go untreated and may surface at a later date. When rape complaints are determined to be false, investigators would be wise to seek the assistance of mental health professionals.

Investigators may suspect a false allegation when the victim repeatedly changes his or her accounts of the assault. This was one of the issues in the Duke lacrosse case. Care must be taken to distinguish a true changing of the story from a legitimate recollection of additional data. In both true and false claims, new information and more detail may be added in subsequent interviews. The false claimant wishes to "shore up" the allegation to make it more believable, whereas the genuine victim (as composure and equilibrium are regained) may remember more detail and descriptive data in the days after the assault.

Related to this same discussion is the distinction one must make between deliberate deceit and an honest mistake. The person making a false allegation may offer data that differ from the original report to further deceive and mislead the authorities. In the initial stages of an investigation, a legitimate rape victim, because of stress and psychic pain, may provide incorrect information related to an altered ability to accurately process information.

When a rape, or for that matter any crime, occurs, there must be three elements: perpetrator(s), act(s), and a setting or set of conditions. One can make a false allegation with reference to any or all of these elements.

Care for Victims of Sexual Violence

National Sexual Violence Resource Center

The National Sexual Violence Resource Center (NSVRC), founded by the Pennsylvania Coalition Against Rape and funded by the Centers for Disease Control and Prevention's Division of Violence Prevention, is the nucleus of a national movement to prevent sexual violence and to sustain a national momentum that influences practice, research, policy, and, ultimately, public attitudes and belief (CDC, 2017). The broad goals of the NSVRC are as follows:

- To strengthen the support system serving sexual assault survivors by providing competent leadership, resources, and information to develop capacity of national sexual assault organizations, state sexual assault coalitions, community-based programs, and allied professionals

- To provide accurate and comprehensive information and technical assistance in supporting effective intervention in the prevention of sexual violence

- To identify emerging policy issues and research needs to support the development of policy and practice leading to the prevention of sexual violence

- To develop the organizational structure and technological capacity supporting the development and implementation of NSVRC activities

The NSVRC is housed in Enola, Pennsylvania, and provides information and resources, technical assistance, and access to research through its toll-free number and email address. Organizational partners who collaborate with the NSVRC include the Violence Against Women Prevention Resource Center, the VAWnet/National Resources Center, the National Alliance of Sexual Assault Coalitions, and the National Coalition Against Sexual Assault.

Nationally, the sexual assault nurse examiner (SANE) and/or sexual assault response team model has grown exponentially. Although virtually all these programs were developed to facilitate standard comprehensive and expert care

TABLE 11-7 Evidentiary Care for Victims of Sexual Assault

Type of Care	Description
Initial medical evaluation	This is not a routine physical exam. Vital signs of the victim are taken; however, there is no treatment of injuries until the SANE documents injuries with pictures and collects evidence. The victim is advised of this procedure and must sign a consent form.
Evidentiary exam	The SANE is responsible for conducting the evidentiary exam and ensures the victim's dignity is protected and the victim is not retraumatized by the exam. Victims are a part of the decision process throughout the evidence collection phase. Most protocols suggest the exam be completed within 72 hours after the sexual assault. All evidentiary exams include the following: • Written consent from the victim, documentation of assault history • Forms of violence used and where • Medical information of the victim, including pregnancy status • Physical exam for trauma, genital, and nongenital • Collecting the victim's clothing and packaging according to state policy • Specimen collections, including skin, hair, and nails • Body fluid and orifice specimen collection • Blood draw and urine specimen for drug analysis DNA screen • Prophylactic treatment of sexually transmitted infections or culturing
Maintaining chain of evidence and evidence integrity	The SANE is responsible for ensuring complete documentation with signatures and the disposition of evidence. Additionally, the SANE is also responsible for identifying, collecting, and preserving evidence and for securing evidence in an area designated free of contaminants.
Crisis intervention and counseling	This includes a mental health assessment and referral for follow-up counseling. This is usually the primary role of the rape crisis center advocate. However, the SANE also provides crisis intervention and ensures follow-up counseling services are available.

Data from: Ledray, L. 1999. *Sexual assault nurse examiner (SANE) development & operations guide*. Washington, DC: Office for Victims of Crime, U.S. Department of Justice.

of sexual assault survivors, the literature clearly shows that policies and procedures do vary from program to program (TABLE 11-7).

In addition, SANE programs use specialized forensic equipment, such as a colposcope, which is a noninvasive, lighted, magnifying instrument for examining the perineum and anogenital area for the detection of small lacerations and bruises (Voelker, 1996). Other equipment may include a camera attached to the colposcope, and toluidine blue dye may be used for the detection of very small lacerations and abrasions. SANEs also document bruises and injuries using photography, usually digital cameras. SANEs are also trained in identifying and documenting patterned injuries, treatment of injuries, maintaining chain of evidence, and providing expert witness testimony (Ledray, 1999).

Conclusion

Rape and sexual assault are acts of aggression where sexual activity is used to degrade and humiliate the victim. Rape affects the lives of victims and their significant others with various physical and emotional consequences. Great strides have occurred over the past 30 years in terms of reform in the sexual assault law and protection of women. Many of these reforms come from the implementation of sexual assault response teams and of rape crisis centers developing services and programs for victims of rape.

Studying the motivation and characteristics of the sex offender has captured the television scene with interviews with offenders shown to illustrate their plan and how they carried out their crimes. Such information helps for prevention efforts and is used in educational programs. In addition, it is critical for the clinician to understand the factors that have injured the victim in order to assess and provide a treatment protocol. Law enforcement officers and agents benefit from understanding the dynamics that exist for both apprehension and investigative purposes.

Key Terms

Anger rapist: Displaces his anger, rage, and hatred onto a victim.

Blitz rape: Sudden, out of the blue, physical attack.

Incest: Sexual activity between close relatives that is illegal in the jurisdiction where it takes place.

Marital rape: Nonconsensual sex in which the perpetrator is the victim's spouse.

Rape: Use of sexuality to express issues of power and anger.

Sexual Assault: Any sexual act, attempt to obtain a sexual act, unwanted sexual comments or advances, or acts to traffic, or otherwise directed, against a person's sexuality using coercion.

Sexual coercion: Unwanted sexual intercourse or any other sexual contact subsequent to the use of menacing verbal pressure or misuse of authority.

Sexual sadist: An offender who finds pleasure and excitement in the suffering of his victim.

Discussion Questions

1. Discuss the barriers and facilitators of reporting a sexual assault to law enforcement.

2. Outline the history of rape reform in the United States and Canada, and evaluate rape reform in your jurisdiction.

3. What are the similarities and differences between rape trauma syndrome and posttraumatic stress disorder?

4. What are some dynamics and motivational factors noted in rapists?

5. How can a classification of rape be useful to the criminal justice system?

6. Compare campus sexual assault and military sexual trauma.

7. What might be some solutions to increase reporting of sexual assault in college student populations?

Resources

Federal Bureau of Investigation. Crime in the United States, 2016 https://ucr .fbi.gov/crime-in-the-u.s/2016

National Center for Victims of Crime https://victimsofcrime.org/

National Resource Center on Domestic Violence http://www.nrcdv.org/dvrn/

National Sexual Violence Resource Center http://www.nsvrc.org

References

Abbey, A., Zawacki, T., & McAuslan, P. (2000). Alcohol's effects on sexual perception. *Journal of Studies on Alcohol, 61*, 688–697.

Abel, G. G., Becker, J. V., Mittelman, M. S., Cunningham-Rathner, J., Rouleau, J. L., & Murphy, W. D. (1987). Self-reported sex crimes of nonincarcerated paraphilics. *Journal of Interpersonal Violence, 2*(1), 3–25.

American Psychiatric Association. (2013). *Diagnostic and Statistical Manual of Mental Disorders*. (5th ed.). Arlington, VA: American Psychiatric Publishing.

Anderson, M. J. (2004). Understanding rape shield laws. The National Alliance to End Sexual Violence. Retrieved from http://naesvorg.ipower.com/Resources/Articles /UnderstandingRapeShieldLaws.pdf

Avegno, J., Mills, T., & Mills, L. (2009). Sexual assault victims in the emergency department: Analysis by demographic and event characteristics. *Journal of Emergency Medicine, 37*(3), 328–334.

Ax, J., & Trotta, D. (2011, August 22). Strauss-Kahn criminal sexual assault charges dropped. Reuters. Retrieved from http://www.reuters.com/article/2011/08/23 /us-strausskahn-idUSTRE77J20620110823

Bachman, R. (1998). The factors related to rape reporting behavior and arrest: New evidence from the National Crime Survey. *Criminal Justice and Behavior, 25*, 8–29.

Bachman, R. (2000). A comparison of annual incidence rates and contextual characteristics of intimate-partner violence against women from the National Crime Victimization Survey (NCVS) and the National Violence Against Women Survey (NVAWS). *Violence Against Women, 6*(8), 839–867.

Bachman, R., & Paternoster, R. (1993). A contemporary look at the effects of rape law reform: How far have we really come? *Journal of Criminal Law and Criminology, 84*, 554–574.

Basile, K. C., Smith, S. G., Breiding, M. J., Black, M. C., & Mahendra, R. R. (2014). *Sexual violence surveillance: Uniform definitions and recommended data elements, version 2.0.* Atlanta, GA: National Center for Injury Prevention and Control, Centers for Disease Control and Prevention.

Ben-David, S., & Schneider, O. (2005). Rape perceptions, gender role attitudes, and victim-perpetrator acquaintance. *Sex Roles, 53*, 385–399.

Boeschen, L. E., Sales, B. D., & Koss, M. P. (1998). Rape trauma experts in the courtroom. *Psychology, Public Policy, and Law, 4*, 414–432.

Bondurant, B. (2001). University women's acknowledgment of rape: Individual, situational, and social factors. *Violence Against Women, 7*, 294–314.

Bouffard, J. A. (2000). Predicting sexual assault case closure categories from case characteristics. *Journal of Criminal Justice, 28*(6), 527–542.

Brownmiller, S. (1975). *Against our will: Men, women, and rape.* New York: Simon & Schuster.

Bureau of Justice Statistics. (2016). Criminal victimization, 2015. Summary. NCJ 250180. Retrieved from https://www.bjs.gov/content/pub/pdf/cv15_sum.pdf

Burgess, A. W., & Holmstrom, L. L. (2006). Coping behavior of rape victims. *The American Journal of Psychiatry*, Published online: April 01, 2006. Previous article Volume 133, Issue 4, April 1976, pp. 413–418.

Burgess, A. W., Fehder, W. P., & Hartman, C. R. (1995). Delayed reporting of the rape victim. *Journal of Psychosocial Nursing and Mental Health Services, 33*(9), 21–29.

Burgess, A. W., & Holmstrom, L. L. (1974). Rape trauma syndrome. *American Journal of Psychiatry, 131*, 981–986.

Burt, M. R. (1980). Cultural myths and supports for rape. *Journal of Personality and Social Psychology, 38*(2), 217–230.

Campbell, R., Wasco, S., Ahrens, C., Sefl, T., & Barnes, H. (2001). Preventing the "second rape": Rape survivors' experiences with community service providers. *Journal of Interpersonal Violence, 16*, 1239–1260.

Cauterruci, C. (2017, February 2). What will happen to Title IX under Trump? Slate. Retrieved from http://www.slate.com/articles/double_x/doublex/2017/02/trump_could_undo_obama_s_title_ix_protections_for_rape_victims_and_trans.html

Clay-Warner, J., & Burt, C. H. (2005). Rape reporting after reforms: Have times really changed? *Violence Against Women, 11*, 150–176.

Curtis, D. G. (1997). Perspectives on acquaintance rape. *The American Academy of Experts in Traumatic Stress, Inc.* Retrieved from http://www.aaets.org/article13.htm

Department of Justice, Office of Justice Programs, Bureau of Justice Statistics, National Crime Victimization Survey, 2010–2014 (2015).

Department of Justice, Office of Justice Programs, Bureau of Justice Statistics (2013). Over 60 Percent Decline in Sexual Violence Against Female from 1995 to 2010. Retrieved from http://www.bjs.gov/

Dick, K. (2013). The Invisible War. Retrieved from http://www.pbs.org/independentlens /films/invisible-war/

Docterman, E. (2015). The Vanderbilt rape case will change the way victims feel about the courts. *Time,* January 29, 2015. Retrieved http://time.com/3686617/the -vanderbilt-rape-case-will-change-the-way-victims-feel-about-the-courts/

Dockterman, E. (2015). The hunting ground reignites the debate over campus rape. *Time,* March 5, 2015. Retrieved http://time.com/3722834/the-hunting-ground -provocative-documentary-reignites-campus-rape-debate/

Douglas, J. E., Burgess, A. W., Burgess, A. G., & Ressler, R. K. (2006). *Crime classification manual.* San Francisco: Jossey-Bass.

DuMont, J., Miller, K. L., & Myhr, T. (2003). The role of "real rape" and "real victim" stereotypes in the police reporting practices of sexually assaulted women. *Violence Against Women, 9,* 466–487.

Faiola, A., & Adam, K. (2011). Assange sex assault allegations debated for 2nd day. Retrieved from http://www.canada.com/news/Assange+assault+allegations+debated /4244862/story.html#ixzz1V2Nm7unI

Federal Bureau of Investigation (FBI). (2011). Supplemental reports. Sex and murder statistics. Retrieved from https://ucr.fbi.gov/crime-in-the-u.s/2011/crime-in-the -u.s.-2011/offenses-known-to-law-enforcement/expanded/expanded-homicide-data

Federal Bureau of Investigation (FBI). (2008). *Crime in the United States, 2007.* Retrieved from http://www.fbi.gov/about-us/cjis/ucr/ucr

Federal Bureau of Investigation (FBI). (2010). *Crime in the United States, 2009.* Retrieved from https://archives.fbi.gov/archives/news/pressrel/press-releases/fbi -releases-2009-crime-statistics

Felson, R. B., Messner, S. F., & Hoskin, A. W. (1999). The victim–offender relationship and calling the police in assaults. *Criminology, 37,* 931–947.

Fisher, B. (2004). Measuring rape against women: The significance of survey questions. Retrieved from https://www.ncjrs.gov/pdffiles1/nij/199705.pdf

Fisher, B., Daigle, L., Cullen, F., & Turner, M. (2000). *The sexual victimization of college women.* Washington, DC: U.S. Department of Justice, National Institute of Justice, and Bureau of Justice Statistics.

Fisher, B. S., Daigle, L. E., Cullen, F. T., & Turner, M. G. (2003a). Acknowledging sexual victimization as rape: Results from a national-level study. *Justice Quarterly, 20,* 535–574.

Fisher, B. S., Daigle, L. E., Cullen, F. T., & Turner, M. (2003b). Reporting sexual victimization to the police and others: Results from a national-level study of college women. *Criminal Justice and Behavior, 31*(1), 6–38.

Fisher, J. (2011). Imette St. Guillen's family settles federal law suit. Greenwich Village and SOHO. Retrieved from https://www.dnainfo.com/new-york/20110325/greenwich-village-soho/family-of-college-student-murdered-soho-bar-settles-with-federal-government

Flowe, H. D., Ebbesen, E. B., & Putcha-Bhagavatula, A. (2007). Rape shield laws and sexual behavior evidence: Effects of consent level and women's sexual history on rape allegations. *Law and Human Behavior, 31*(2), 159–175.

Frazier, P. (2003). Perceived control and distress following sexual assault: A longitudinal test of a new model. *Journal of Personality and Social Psychology, 84*, 1257–1260.

Frese, B., Moya, M., & Megías, J. L. (2004). Social perception of rape: How rape myth acceptance modulates the influence of situational factors. *Journal of Interpersonal Violence, 19*(2), 143–161.

Gartner, R., & Macmillan, R. (1995). The effect of victim–offender relationship on reporting crimes of violence against women. *Canadian Journal of Criminology, 37*, 393–429.

Gersen, J. S. (September 8, 2017). Betsy DeVos, Title IX, and the "Both Sides" Approach to Sexual Assault. *The New Yorker*. Retrieved from https://www.newyorker.com/news/news-desk/betsy-devos-title-ix-and-the-both-sides-approach-to-sexual-assault

Gilmartin-Zena, P. (1987). Attitudes toward rape: Student characteristics as predictors. *Free Inquiry in Creative Sociology, 15*, 175–182.

Gray, E. (2015). Jon Krakauer defends new book on college rape. *Time,* April 23, 2015. Retrieved from http://time.com/3828787/jon-krakauer-defends-new-book-on-college-rape/

Gross, B. (2009). False rape allegations: An assault on justice (case study). *Forensic Examiner, 18*(1), 66–70.

Groth, A. N., Burgess, A. W., & Holmstrom, L. L. (1977). Rape: Power, anger, and sexuality. *American Journal of Psychiatry, 134*, 1239–1243.

Hale, M. (1847). *The history of the pleas of the crown* (Vol. 1). Philadelphia: R. H. Small.

Harner, H., Burgess, A. W., & Asher, J. (2001). Caring for pregnant teenagers: Medicolegal issues for nurses. *Journal of Obstetric, Gynecologic, & Neonatal Nursing, 30*(2), 139–147.

Hartmann, M. (2015). Everything we knew about the UVA rape case [Updated] *New York Magazine,* July 30. Retrieved http://nymag.com/daily/intelligencer/2014/12/everything-we-know-uva-rape-case.html

Healy, M. (1992). Pentagon blasts tailhook probe, two admirals resign. The Tech Online Edition. Volume 112 >> Issue 44.

Hines, D., & Finkelhor, D. (2007). Statutory sex crime relationships between juveniles and adults: A review of social scientific research. *Aggression and Violent Behavior, 12*, 300–314.

Holmstrom, L. L., & Burgess, A. W. (1978). *The victim of rape: Institutional reactions.* New York: Wiley.

Horney, J., & Spohn, C. (2001). The influence of blame and believability factors on processing of simple versus aggravated rape cases. *Criminology, 34*(2), 135–162.

Hyun, J. K., Pavao, J., & Kimerling, R. (2009). Military sexual trauma. *PTSD Research Quarterly, 20,* 1–4.

Kamenetz, A. (2014, November 30). The history of campus sexual assault. NPR. Retrieved from http://www.npr.org/sections/ed/2014/11/30/366348383/the-history -of-campus-sexual-assault

Kanin, E. J. (Sep. 1957). Male Aggression in Dating-Courtship Relations. *American Journal of Sociology, 63*(2), 197–204.

Kennedy, D. B., & Witkowski, M. J. (2000). False allegations of rape revisited: A replication of the Kanin study. *Journal of Security Administration, 23*(1), 41–46.

Kilpatrick, D. G., Edmunds, C. N., & Seymour, A. K. (1992). Rape in America: A report to the nation. Washington, DC: National Victim Center.

Kirkpatrick, C. & Kanin, E. J. (1957). Male sex aggression on a college campus. *American Sociological Review, 22*(1), 52–58.

Koss, M. (1987). The scope of rape. *Journal of Consulting and Clinical Psychology, 55,* 162–170.

Koss, M. P. (1988). Hidden rape: Sexual aggression and victimization in the national sample of students in higher education. In M. A. Pirog-Good & J. E. Stets (Eds.), *Violence in dating relationships: Emerging social issues* (pp. 145–168). New York: Praeger.

Koss, M. P., Bachar, K., Hopkins, C. Q., & Carlson, C. (2004). Expanding a community's justice response to sex crimes through advocacy, prosecutorial, and public health collaboration: Introducing the RESTORE program. *Journal of Interpersonal Violence, 19,* 1435–1463.

Koss, M. P., Gidycz, C. A., & Wisniewski, N. (1987). The scope of rape: Incidence and prevalence of sexual aggression and victimization in a national sample of higher education students. *Journal of Counseling and Clinical Psychology, 55*(2), 162–170.

Krebs, C. P., Lindquist, C. L., Tara, D., Warner, T. D., Fisher, B. S., & Martin, S. L. (2007). Campus Sexual Assault (CSA) study, final report. Washington, DC: National Institute of Justice.

Largen, M. A. (1988). Rape-law reform: An analysis. In A.W. Burgess (Ed.), *Rape and sexual assault II* (pp. 271–292). New York: Garland Press.

Layman, M. J., Gidydz, C. A., & Lynn, J. (1996). Unacknowledged vs. acknowledged rape victims: Situational factors and posttraumatic stress. *Journal of Abnormal Psychology, 105,* 124–131.

Ledray, L. (1999). *Sexual assault nurse examiner (SANE) development & operations guide.* Washington, DC: Office for Victims of Crime, U.S. Department of Justice.

Lerner, M. J. (1980). *The belief in a just world: A fundamental delusion.* New York: Plenum Press.

Lisak, D. (2011). *Sexual assault report, 14*(4), 49–50, 56–57. Kingston, NJ: Civic Research Institute, Inc.

Lisak, D., Gardinier, L., Nicksa, S. C., & Cote, A. M. (2010). False allegations of sexual assault: An analysis of ten years of reported cases. *Violence Against Women*, *16*(12), 1318–1334.

Lisak, D., & Miller, P. M. (2002). Repeat rape and multiple offending among undetected rapists. *Violence and Victims*, *17*, 73–84.

Lonsway, K. A., & Fitzgerald, L. F. (1994). Rape myths in review. *Psychology of Women Quarterly*, *18*, 133–164.

McGregor, M., Dumont, J., & Myhr, T. (2002). Sexual assault forensic medical examination: Is evidence related to successful prosecution? *Annals of Emergency Medicine*, *39*(6), 639–647.

Meadows, R. (2004). Rape shield laws: A need for an ethical and legal reexamination? *Criminal Justice Studies*, *17*(3), 281–290.

Morral A. R., Gore, K. L., & Schell, T. L. Sexual Assault and Sexual Harassment in the U.S. Military, Vol. 2. Estimates for Department of Defense Service Members from the 2014 RAND Military Workplace Study. Santa Monica, CA, RAND Corp, 2015.

Murphy, W. (2006, March 8). The murder of Imette St. Guillen. *Boston Globe*, p. 6.

Namrow, N. A., De Silva, S., Barry, A., Klahr, A., & Ely, K. (2016). 2016 Military Investigation and Justice Experience Survey (Mijes): Overview Report. Office of People Analytics. Retrieved from http://www.sapr.mil/public/docs/reports/FY16_Annual /Annex_2_2016_MIJES_Report.pdf

National Crime Victimization Survey. (2000). Washington, DC: Bureau of Justice Statistics.

Pino, N., & Meier, R. (1999). Gender differences in rape reporting. *Sex Roles*, *40*, 979–990.

Prentky, R. A., & Burgess, A. W. (2000). *Forensic management of the sex offender*. New York: Plenum.

National Sexual Violence Resource Center (NSVRC) (2017). Centers for Disease Control and Prevention, Department of Health & Human Services. Retrieved from https:// catalog.data.gov/dataset/national-sexual-violence-resource-center-nsvrc

RAINN website statistics. Retrieved from https://www.rainn.org/about-rainns-statistics

Rennison, C. M. (2002). *Rape and sexual assault: Reporting to police and medical attention, 1992–2000*. Washington, DC: U.S. Government Printing Office.

Resick, P. A., Jordan, C. G., Girelli, S. A., Hutter, C. K., & Marhoeder-Dvorak, S. (1988). A comparative outcome study of behavioral group therapy for sexual assault victims. *Behavior Therapy*, *19*, 385–401.

Ressler, R. K., Burgess, A. W., & Douglas, J. E. (1988). *Sexual homicide: Patterns and motives*. New York: Free Press.

Rumney, P. (2006). False allegations of rape. *Cambridge Law Journal*, *65*(1), 128–158.

Russell, D. E. H. (1990). *Rape in marriage: Expanded and revised edition with a new introduction*. Bloomington and Indianapolis: Indiana University Press.

Ryan, J. (2011). FBI to change definition of forcible rape. Retrieved from http:// abcnews.go.com/blogs/politics/2011/12/fbi-to-change-definition-of-forcible-rape/

Schemo, D. J. (2003). Air Force Ignored Sex Abuse at Academy, Inquiry Reports. *New York Times*. Retrieved from http://www.nytimes.com/2003/09/23/us/air-force-ignored-sex-abuse-at-academy-inquiry-reports.html

Shifrel, S. (2009). Imette suit is settled: Family to get cash from the bar where she was abducted. *Daily News*. Retrieved from http://www.nydailynews.com/news/crime/imette-suit-settled-family-cash-bar-abducted-article-1.377971

Sinozich, S., & Langton, L. (2014). Special report: Rape and sexual assault victimization among college-aged females, 1995–2013. Retrieved from https://www.bjs.gov/content/pub/pdf/rsavcaf9513.pdf

Spinner, J. (11/07/1997). In Wake of Sex Scandal, Caution Is the Rule at Aberdeen. *Washington Post*, p. B01.

Sommers, M. S., Fisher, B., & Karjane, H. (2005). Using colposcopy in the rape exam: Health care, forensic, and criminal justice issues. *Journal of Forensic Nursing, 1*, 28–36.

Stand-To (2016). Workplace and Gender Relations Survey. Retrieved from https://www.army.mil/standto/2016-07-27

Stermac, L., del Bove, G., & Addison, M. (2001). Violence, injury, and presentation patterns in spousal assault. *Violence Against Women, 7*(11), 1218–1230.

Stermac, L., Du Mont, J., & Dunn, S. (1998). Violence in known-assailant sexual assaults. *Journal of Interpersonal Violence, 13*, 398–412.

Tang, K. (1998). Rape law reform in Canada: The success and limits of legislation. *International Journal of Offender Therapy and Comparative Criminology, 42*(3), 258–270.

Tjaden, P., & Thoennes, N. (2000). *Full report of the prevalence, incidence, and consequences of violence against women: Findings from the National Violence Against Women Survey.* NCJ183781. Washington, DC: National Institute of Justice, Office of Justice Programs, U.S. Department of Justice.

Tjaden, P., & Thoennes, N. (2006). Special report on the extent, nature, and consequences of rape victimization: Findings from the National Violence Against Women Survey. Retrieved from http://www.ncjrs.gov/pdffiles1/nij/210346.pdf

Tomlinson, D. (1999). *Police-reporting Decisions of Sexual Assault Survivors: An Exploration of Influential Factors.* Alberta, Canada: Alberta Law Foundation.

Torres, J. (2008). Rape shield laws and game theory: The psychological effects on complainants who file false rape allegations. *Law & Psychology Review, 32*(1), 135–151.

Trocmé, N., Fallon, B., MacLaurin, B., Daciuk, J., Felstiner, C., Black, T., . . . , Barter, K. (2005). *Canadian incidence study of reported child abuse and neglect—2003: Major findings.* Ottawa: Canadian Child Welfare Research Portal.

Troupe-Leasure, K., & Snyder, H. (2005). Statutory rape known to law enforcement. Juvenile Justice Bulletin. Retrieved from http://www.ojp.usdoj.gov/

Truman, J. L., & Morgan, R. E. (2016). Criminal victimization, 2015. NCJ 250180. Bureau of Justice Statistics. Retrieved from https://www.bjs.gov/index.cfm?ty=pbdetail&iid=5804

Ullman, S., & Filipias, H. (2001). Correlates of formal and informal support seeking in sexual assault victims. *Journal of Interpersonal Violence, 16*(10), 1028–1047.

U.S. Department of Defense Sexual Assault Prevention and Response Office website. Research. Retrieved from http://www.sapr.mil/index.php/research

U.S. Department of Education. (2014). U.S. Department of Education releases list of higher education institutions with open Title IX sexual violence investigations. Retrieved July from https://www.ed.gov/news/press-releases/us-department-education-releases-list-higher-education-institutions-open-title-i

U.S. Department of Health and Human Services. (2010). Fourth national incidence study on child abuse and neglect. Retrieved from http://www.acf.hhs.gov/programs/opre/abuse_neglect/natl_incid/reports/natl_incid/natl_incid_title.html

U.S. Department of Justice. (2002). *Rape and sexual assault: Reporting to police and medical attention, 1992–2000*. Washington, DC: Government Printing Office.

Vickerman, K. A., & Margolin, G. (2009). Rape treatment outcome research: Empirical findings and state of the literature. *Clinical Psychology Review, 23*, 18–34.

Voelker, R. (1996). Experts hope team approach will improve the quality of rape exams. *Journal of the American Medical Association, 275*, 973–974.

Wiehe, V. R., & Richards, A. L. (1995). *Intimate betrayal: Understanding and responding to the trauma of acquaintance rape*. Thousand Oaks, CA: Sage.

Wigmore, J. H., & Chadbourn, J. H. (1970). *Evidence in trials at common law* (Vol. 3A). Boston: Little, Brown.

Wiley, J., Sugar, N., Fine, D., & Eckert, L. (2003). Legal outcomes of sexual assault. *American Journal of Obstetrics and Gynecology, 188*(6), 1638–1641.

Williams, J. E. (1984). Secondary victimization: Confronting public attitudes about rape. *Victimology, 9*, 66–81.

CHAPTER 12

Elder Abuse Victims

OBJECTIVES

- To identify the incidence and pervasive nature of abuse against the elderly
- To discuss types of abuse and categories of abusive situations involving the elderly
- To introduce screening tools to assess abuse in the elderly
- To present models of intervention in elder abuse
- To discuss typologies of sexual offenders against the elderly

KEY TERMS

Alzheimer's disease

Cognitively impaired

Dementia

Elder abuse

Fiduciary

Medically fragile

Power of attorney

Psychological abuse

CASE

Mickey Rooney, the legendary American actor, appeared in over 200 films and received a Juvenile Oscar in 1939, an honorary Oscar for Lifetime Achievement in 1983, an Emmy Award, and two Golden Globes ("Mickey Rooney," 2011). But in March 2011, he made the news for a very different reason. Ninety-year-old Mickey Rooney appeared before a Senate Special Committee in Washington, DC, stating he was a victim of elder abuse (FIGURE 12-1). Mr. Rooney testified that

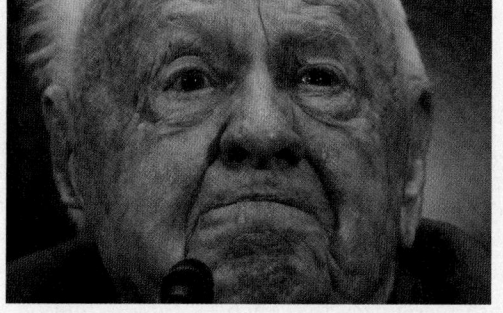

FIGURE 12-1 Mickey Rooney giving testimony on his abuse before a Senate Special Committee on Capitol Hill in Washington, DC.

© Jim Young/Thomson Reuters.

he had been victimized by Chris Alber, the son of his eighth wife ("Mickey Rooney speaks out," 2011). He stated that his stepson withheld food and medication, interfered with his finances, and subjected him to intimidation, bullying, and harassment (Freeman, 2011). Rooney told the Senate committee he suffered in silence for years: "I didn't want to tell anybody. I couldn't muster the courage and you have to have courage. . . . I needed help and I knew I needed it. Even when I tried to speak up, I was told to shut up and be quiet" (Cohen, 2011; "Mickey Rooney claims to be elder abuse victim," 2011). In his statements, Mr. Rooney made this impassioned plea: "I'm asking you to stop this elderly abuse. I mean to stop it. Now. Not tomorrow, not next month, but now." He urged the committee to pass legislation against elder abuse and send it

to be signed into law by President Barack Obama so the nation could say, "it's a crime and we will not allow it in the United States of America" (Cohen, 2011).

In September 2011, Rooney's court-appointed conservator filed suit against the Albers, alleging elder abuse and misappropriation of his likeness. The suit alleged that after Rooney let his stepson handle his personal and business affairs, Albers and his wife stole Rooney's money for their own use, kept him in the dark about his own finances, used threatening and abusive language, and refused him basic necessities, such as food and medicine. In October 2013, Rooney's conservator agreed to a $2.8 million stipulated judgment against the Albers.

Since Rooney's death from a heart attack in April 2014 at the age of 93, his family has been locked in a bitter legal struggle for the remains of the actor's estate, thought to be worth as little as $18,000. His funeral was even delayed by several weeks while the family rowed over his final resting place, before he was finally given a spot in the Hollywood Forever Cemetery.

By coming forward, Rooney did a service for millions of elderly in this country by helping to publicize financial elder abuse. As is often the case, celebrities can use star status to shed light on important issues. Rooney's courage will hopefully further the progress that is being made at the national level to fight the epidemic of elder abuse in this country (Gjertson, 2014).

Introduction

The U.S. Census Bureau provides the primary source of statistical information about the nation's people and counts the entire U.S. population every 10 years. The 2016 data estimates there are more than 323.1 million people in the United States (U.S. Census Bureau, 2016). The elderly population, in particular, is fast expanding as the "baby boomers" turn 65. About 13% of the current U.S. population is aged 65 or older, and this is expected to increase to 16.8% by 2020 (Morgan & Mason, 2014). Extending out to 2050, the population aged 65 and over is projected to be 83.7 million, almost double its estimated population of 43.1 million in 2012. The number of people in the oldest old age group, which refers to those aged 85 and over, is projected to grow from 5.9 million in 2012 to 8.9 million in 2030. In 2050, this group is projected to reach 18 million (U.S. Census Bureau, 2016).

Although there is no universally accepted definition of **elder abuse**, the National Center of Elder Abuse recognizes that each existing definition has its own merit and value. However, longstanding divergences in the definitions and data elements used to collect information on elder abuse make it difficult to measure elder abuse nationally; to compare the problem across states, counties, and cities; and to establish trends and patterns in the occurrence and experience of elder abuse (Centers for Disease Control and Prevention, 2016). Two examples of definitions include those offered by the World Health Organization (WHO) and the Centers for Disease Control and Prevention (CDC).

In 2002, the WHO published the *Toronto Declaration on the Global Prevention of Elder Abuse*, which included the following definition:

> Elder abuse is a single or repeated act, or lack of appropriate action, occurring within any relationship where there is an expectation of trust, which causes harm or distress to an older person. It can be of various forms: physical, psychological/emotional, sexual, financial, or simply reflect intentional or unintentional neglect.
>
> (pp. 3–4)

Further, the declaration states, "Elder abuse is the violation of human rights and a significant cause of injury, illness, lost productivity, isolation, and despair. Confronting and reducing elder abuse requires a multi-disciplinary approach" (WHO, 2002, pp. 3–4). This statement by the WHO underlines that elder abuse is a universal issue and is not limited to any one culture or country. Indeed, a special issue of *Educational Gerontology* in 2006 contained articles highlighting the problem of elder abuse in Israel (Rabi, 2006), Japan (Arai, 2006), Germany (König & Leembruggen-Kallberg, 2006), Brazil (Bezerra-Flanders, & Clark, 2006), and African Americans (Tauriac & Scruggs, 2006).

The CDC defines elder abuse as an intentional act or failure to act that causes or creates a risk of harm to an older adult. An older adult is someone age 60 or older. The abuse occurs at the hands of a caregiver or a person the elder trusts (CDC, 2017).

Scope of the Problem

While elder abuse is believed to have existed for centuries, it was first published in the medical literature in the 1970s (Burston, 1975). Not only has it been difficult to obtain consensus for a definition of elder abuse, but it is equally difficult to determine how large a problem it is. The first large-scale random survey on elder abuse was conducted by Pillemer and Finkelhor (1988) on 2,020 community-dwelling elderly persons living in the Boston area. The study produced an elder maltreatment rate of 32 elderly persons per 1,000 and identified spouses as the primary perpetrators. Twenty years later, a systematic review of elder abuse studies produced higher estimates of 6% of older adults reporting abuse in the last month and 5.6% of older couples reporting intimate partner violence (IPV) in the last year (Cooper, Selwood, & Livingston, 2008). The National Elder Mistreatment Study found similar rates to those just described, and, unfortunately, no evidence of improvement in the more than three decades since efforts began to monitor elder abuse (Acierno et al., 2010). The National Elder Mistreatment Study found that in a community sample of over 5,000 elders, the 1-year prevalence rate for emotional abuse was 4.6%, 1.6% for physical abuse, and 5.2% for current financial abuse by a family member. In total, 1 in 10 respondents reported some form of maltreatment in the past year.

WHO estimates of elder abuse across Canada, the Netherlands, the United States, Finland, and Great Britain range from 4% to 6%. Data from the United States are consistent with these estimates. The 2008 National Social Life, Health, and Aging Project was the first U.S. population-based, nationally representative study to ask older adults living in the community about their recent experiences regarding mistreatment by family members. Over 3,000 Americans between the ages of 57 and 85 participated in the survey. Results revealed that 9% of older adults reported verbal mistreatment, 3.5% reported financial mistreatment, and 0.2% reported physical mistreatment in the past year (Laumann, Leitsch, & Waite, 2008).

In this analysis and others, reports of financial mistreatment were significantly higher among older African Americans than among older White adults (Beach, Schulz, Castle, & Rosen, 2010). Older Latinos were less likely than others to report either financial or verbal mistreatment (Beach et al., 2010).

Using a broader definition of perpetrator that was not limited to family members, a recently released U.S. nationally representative sample of 5,777 older adults found that 5.1% of adults over the age of 60 reported emotional mistreatment, 5.2% reported financial abuse, 1.6% reported physical mistreatment, and 0.6% reported sexual mistreatment in the past year (Amstadter et al., 2010).

In Canada, similar to previous years, family members made up one-third of those accused in police-reported incidents of violent crime against seniors (aged 65 and over) in 2013, with just over 2,900 seniors (56.8 victims per 100,000 seniors) victimized by a family member that year. In total, nearly 8,900 (173.9 victims per 100,000 seniors) of persons aged 65 and over were the victims of a violent crime in Canada in 2013. The adult children of the senior victims of family violence were most likely to be the perpetrators. Statistics noted 4 in 10 elder victims of police-reported family violence were perpetrated by their grown child and in 28% of the cases, the spouse was the second most likely family member to be the perpetrator of family violence against the senior. More than half (55%) of violence committed against seniors by family members was an act of common assault. Weapons were used in one in six (15%) family violence incidents. Threats and/or physical force occurred in most incidents (85%). Physical injuries did not occur in a majority (61%) of senior victims of family violence and most minor injuries required little or no medical attention. Family violence involving homicide against seniors is rare with the overall rate of family-related homicides being 3.2 for every 1 million persons aged 65 and over (Statistics Canada, 2013).

Why is elder abuse a growing concern? The population of older adults in the Western world is growing rapidly with improved health care, nutrition, and living conditions, and elders are living longer. In Canada in 2016, there were over three-quarters of a million (770,780) people aged 85 and older living, with about 13.0% of the population aged 65 and older representing 2.2% of the Canadian population overall. The number of seniors aged 85 and older grew by 19.4% over the period from 2011 to 2016, nearly four times the rate for the overall Canadian population. Most interesting is the centenarian population (i.e., those aged 100 and older) grew even faster, with 8,230 elders or 41.3%, making it the fastest-growing age group between 2011 and 2016 (Statistics Canada, 2017). In the United States, older adults comprised 13% of the population in 1990 (11 years earlier than Canada), with 31 million Americans at least 65 years of age. By 2030, it is expected that 85 million people will be age 65 years or older, and 8 million will be older than age 85 years. Other countries already have much higher proportions of persons aged 65 years or older than do Canada and the United States. In Japan, Germany, and Italy roughly one person in five is aged 65 years or older.

Increasingly, older adults are living with family members and spouses. As people become more medically fragile or cognitively impaired, they place an increased burden on family members physically, emotionally, and financially. Increased family frustration combined with increased vulnerability of the elderly person can create a dangerous environment.

Elder Abuse Legislation

In the United States, the issue of elder abuse is addressed in both state and federal law. Combined hearings held by the Senate and House Committees on Aging in 1980 resulted in the proposed Prevention, Identification, and Treatment of Adult Abuse Act. This bill, which was never enacted, was modeled on child abuse legislation and called for, among other things, mandatory reporting (Dubble, 2006). The federal Older Americans Act was amended in 1987 to provide definitions of elder abuse and direct the use of federal funds for awareness and coordination activities (American Bar Association Commission on Law and Aging, 2005). Subsequently, the Elder Justice Act, first introduced in 2005, became law in March 2010, as part of the Patient Protection and Affordable Care Act (Elder Justice Coalition, 2011). Under this act, the Elder Justice Coordinating Council is charged with providing reports on activities, accomplishments, and challenges in this area and with making recommendations to congressional committees (Dong & Simon, 2011). The act further provides states with resources to prevent elder abuse, increase prosecution of those who mistreat the elderly, and provide victim assistance.

The Violence Against Women Act established federal domestic violence crime law that may be applied to cases of elder abuse. These federal crimes are limited to abuse that occurs in the federal territories or involve crossing state, federal, or tribal boundaries to commit or attempt to commit a crime of violence against an intimate partner (18 U.S.C. 2262), to stalk or harass (in person or by mail or computer) (18 U.S.C. 2261A), or to violate a qualifying protection order (18 U.S.C. 2262).

A special issue in nursing home care of vulnerable elderly people relates to the care of elderly sexual offenders previously convicted of crimes such as rape. The legislation was championed by Wes Bledsoe, an activist in the rights of elderly nursing home victims after reports that a 43-year-old man accused of killing four people had been ordered by a judge to live in a nursing home (Associated Press, 2008). Further study revealed that 30 registered sexual offenders lived in nursing home facilities in Oklahoma and that more than 500 older sexual offenders were due to be released from prison within the next 10 years in that state, many of whom may have required long-term care. A U.S. Government Accountability Office report further determined that more than half of the registered sexual offenders in nursing homes were younger than age 65 years, compared to only 10% of other residents who were younger than age 65 years (Adams & Calloway, 2009). As a result, Governor Brad Henry of Oklahoma signed the first U.S. legislation forbidding registered sexual offenders from being in standard nursing home facilities and requiring the establishment of a separate facility to address their needs (Associated Press, 2008). This represented another important step in the protection of vulnerable elderly individuals.

Laws enacted in all U.S. states establish systems for reporting and investigating abuse through adult protective services. In general, these laws require mandatory reporting of elder abuse, requiring certain groups of people (healthcare providers, bank tellers, police officers, etc.) to report suspected cases of abuse to the appropriate social service (U.S. Government Accountability Office, 2011). The statutes vary widely with respect to types of abuse, definitions of abuse, reporting requirements, investigation procedures, and remedies. For example, although virtually all state legislation covers physical abuse, neglect, and financial abuse, some states exclude psychological abuse, sexual abuse, and abandonment. Some states cover only older adults who live in the community, whereas others also cover abuse that occurs within institutions. Some states cover this abuse as a criminal offense, and others define it as a civil matter (American Bar Association Commission on Law and Aging, 2005).

Financial abuse of elderly individuals is not limited to abuse perpetrated by family members or caregivers but also includes investment fraud schemes that target vulnerable individuals, particularly the elderly. Yet, despite concern about the widespread nature of this type of abuse, few states have enacted legislation that specifically targets this issue. Florida enacted legislation in 2004 that identified civil remedies for fraud committed by a person in a position of trust against a vulnerable adult, defined as someone who lacks the capacity to consent. Nevada similarly enacted a statute in 2003 that stipulated a person who exploits an older or vulnerable adult is liable for two times the actual damages. Illinois, Oregon, and Tennessee, on the other hand, limit liability in these circumstances to cases where there has been a criminal charge or indictment (Catalano & Lazaro, 2008).

The Criminal Code of Canada does not specifically address elder abuse; thus, cases of elder abuse must be addressed through various other provisions. For example, financial abuse may be addressed through provisions related to theft, forgery, criminal breach of trust, or fraud; physical and sexual abuse under provisions such as criminal negligence causing bodily harm, assault, sexual assault, or failure to provide the necessities of life; and psychological abuse under provisions related to intimidation, uttering threats, or criminal harassment (Donovan & Regehr, 2010). Further, the Code does include a provision whereby the court must take into account for the purposes of sentencing whether the offense was motivated by age- or disability-based bias (Department of Justice Canada, 2007). Four Canadian provinces—Nova Scotia, New Brunswick, Prince Edward Island, and Newfoundland—have adult protection laws that cover elderly persons. These laws give specific health or social service departments responsibility to respond to abuse or neglect cases brought to their attention. However, in reviewing the use of these forms of legislation to protect older adults, the courts and policy analysts have expressed concerns that actions taken under the legislation are contrary to individual rights to liberty and self-determination. That is, cases have been reviewed where elderly people have been removed from the living situations determined to be neglectful or abusive and forcibly placed in institutional care (Gordon, 2001).

Therefore, the main controversy in the implementation of legislation to prevent elder abuse is the right of elderly individuals to self-determination and the understandable resistance to treating elderly individuals as essentially equivalent to children in need of protection.

At what point do people no longer have the right to determine how they will live, who they will live with, and how they will use their financial resources? When is a person incapacitated to the point that mandatory reporting of suspected abuse is warranted? As with other forms of court-mandated practice, these issues raise ethical, clinical, and civil liberties concerns for all those attempting to intervene in cases of abuse and neglect of elder people (Regehr & Antle, 1997).

Types of Elder Abuse

As with other forms of victimization that target a particular population, the various types of elder abuse are categorized based on the nature of the injury. TABLE 12-1 describes the types of elder abuse.

TABLE 12-1 Types of Elder Abuse

Type	Description	Examples
Physical	Any act of violence or the intentional inflicting of pain whether or not it results in physical injury	Hitting, misusing physical restraints or medication, forcible confinement
Neglect	Intentional or unintentional failure to care for or meet the needs of a dependent elderly person	Failing to provide adequate food, clothing, or shelter
Sexual	All forms of nonconsensual sexual activity	Rape, coerced nudity, and sexually explicit photography
Psychological	Attempts to dehumanize or intimidate older adults through verbal or nonverbal acts	Threats of violence or abandonment, lying, making insulting derogatory comments
Financial	Financial manipulation, exploitation, or dishonesty by a person in control	Homes sold without consent, checks cashed without authorization or via forged signatures, possessions stolen

Physical Abuse

Physical abuse includes any act of violence or the intentional inflicting of pain whether or not it results in physical injury. Obvious forms of physical abuse include beating, burning or scalding, pushing or shoving, hitting, or rough handling. However, it may also include tying an older person to furniture, misusing physical restraints, excessive restraint through drugs or alcohol, and confining the person to rooms or spaces. Older adults who are frail may also suffer abuse within the context of the healthcare system, such as overmedication or performing a medical procedure without consent.

Neglect

Neglect is the intentional or unintentional failure to care for or meet the needs of a dependent elderly person. Typically, this involves failing to provide adequate nutrition, clothing, and a safe, clean environment, resulting in dehydration, malnutrition, and poor hygiene. It can also involve the refusal to provide necessary medical care or leaving incapacitated elderly persons alone without proper care or supervision.

Sexual Abuse

Sexual abuse involves all forms of nonconsensual sexual activity. As with other populations, this may involve touching, rape, coerced nudity, and sexually explicit photography. Although this constitutes less than 1% of all elder abuse, it is nevertheless highly disturbing to imagine that the abuse can occur in the community as well as independent living facilities for seniors.

Ramsey-Klawsnik and colleagues (2007) identified five types of perpetrators of sexual abuse against elderly persons: (1) abuse by strangers or acquaintances, (2) abuse by care providers, (3) incestuous abuse, (4) marital or partner sexual abuse, and (5) sexual abuse perpetrated by another resident of a long-term care facility. In their research, the vast majority of victims were female and were highly dependent. Almost all offenders were male, 81% were care providers, and 78% were family members, generally husbands or adult sons. About one-fourth of the assaults occurred within an institution. Two types of cases to highlight involve care providers and stranger assaults. The following Albert Lea case involved young nursing aides as offenders while staff ignored the red flags.

In the Albert Lea nursing home in Minnesota, two teenage female nursing home aides, Ashton Larson and Brianna Broitzman, were sentenced for sexually and psychologically abusing residents suffering from Alzheimer's disease and other dementia disorders between January 1 and May 1, 2008

(Collin, 2010; Myfox.com, 2010). Police reports documented the perpetrators shut the residents' doors and pulled the privacy curtain that protected them from being observed and held the residents down, covered residents' mouths, pinched their breasts, applied pressure on their perineal area, and inserted their fingers into the residents' vaginas and/or rectums. Larson wept in court as families of her victims told a judge what her actions had done (Collin, 2010). During the time the abuse was noted to be occurring, the victimized residents had daily episodes of yelling and were rude, critical, verbally aggressive (swearing), and physically aggressive (hitting) (Myfox.com, 2010). However, after the perpetrators were suspended, it was reported that the residents' moods dramatically improved.

The second category of stranger rapes are difficult. Few people believe that the elderly are targets for sexual predators; however, the following three cases dispel that myth.

Case 1: Elders, regardless of age, are targets to rapists. Police in Houston, Texas, arrested a man who broke into a window at a senior independent living facility and raped an 88-year-old resident who was lying in her bed watching TV on June 11, 2017. Newspaper reports stated windows at the facility were not locked, there was no full-time security guard after hours, and no working security camera system in the complex at the time of the assault. Police noted that there had been an attempted burglary in late May at the same facility and no security upgrades had been made (ABC Eyewitness News, 2017).

The victim was beaten, smothered with a pillow, anally raped, and was repeatedly asked, "Do you like this?" The perpetrator was linked to the crime with fingerprints as evidence and was a suspect in several other sexual assaults that occurred at senior living facilities in the same area. The 21-year-old homeless suspect had an extensive criminal record (Flynn, 2017).

Case 2: Serial rapists also prey on seniors in living facilities. In Los Angeles, a 33-year-old was sentenced to 50 years to life in state prison for raping two senior citizens less than a year apart at the same living facility, including an 89-year-old woman, and assaulting two other elderly victims, a woman in her 80s in July 2015 and a 91-year-old man in October 2015. Rape charges involved a September 2015 attack on a 71-year-old woman who had just returned home and was dragged to her bedroom and sexually assaulted, and a May 2016 attack of an 80-year-old woman where a caretaker came to her aid and called 911 (NBC, 2017).

Case 3: A 2017 case received media attention for several reasons, including the victim's age, the multiple acts and injuries committed on her, and the crime and drug spree of the offender. Court documents reported that a 31-year-old-man entered a 65-year-old woman's bedroom through a window, ordered the woman onto the ground, tied her hands and feet with scarves from her dresser, blindfolded her, and threatened death while he sexually assaulted her. The rapist stole the woman's phone and her car. Police learned that the offender had a criminal history in three states, had been arrested at least 20 times for offenses ranging from burglary and drug possession to auto theft, obstructing a public officer, and hit and run. Along with local charges, the offender had been deported back to Mexico on several occasions. He also told investigators in March 2017 that he had a long history of using methamphetamine and was currently using on a daily basis (Fox News, 2017).

Psychological Abuse

Psychological abuse is when an individual attempts to dehumanize or intimidate older adults through verbal or nonverbal acts. This can involve threats of violence or abandonment, lying, making insulting derogatory comments, ignoring or excessively criticizing, and treating the elders like servants or children. Other forms of psychological abuse can involve dismissive and isolating behavior where the person is simply treated as though he or she does not exist.

The impact of psychological abuse is more difficult to identify and quantify than abuse that causes physical or financial harm. Each person is affected differently by psychological abuse, with some being highly vulnerable and others being mostly unaffected. In addition, there is a cultural overlay in which behavior in one cultural context that may be viewed as minimally harmful or benign can, in another cultural context, be experienced as highly harmful. Tam and Neysmith (2006) provided an interesting analysis on the cultural basis of psychological abuse. In their study of elderly Chinese Canadians, psychological abuse took the form of disrespect, which violates the basic Chinese cultural norms of values and behaviors. In their study, bossy, rude, or dismissive behavior of children or grandchildren and refusal to place the elderly person in a place of honor was considered to be highly damaging abuse that has no equivalent in Western culture.

Financial Abuse

Older adults can be vulnerable to financial manipulation or exploitation in such forms as fraud, theft, or forgery. At times, older adults' property or money is used in a dishonest manner or without consent. For example, homes can be sold without consent, checks can be cashed without authorization or via forged signatures, possessions can be stolen, or deception can be used to have the person sign **power of attorney** forms. Trusted individuals, such as healthcare providers, visitors to long-term care facilities, other residents, or relatives, may misappropriate funds while promising to act in the person's best interest.

Elderly persons are frequently targets of consumer fraud, telemarketing schemes, and identity theft because their isolation makes them vulnerable to deception (Nerenberg, 2006). A study of consumer fraud in a psychogeriatric population in Canada revealed that all victims were women with an average age of 85 years and all had designated power of attorney to another person who was unaware of the financial abuse (Cohen, 2006). These individuals are ideal victims for many reasons. Older women are of a generation that was not taught money management, and thus they frequently hand over financial issues to men. Older people frequently have significant financial resources and are motivated to donate to charitable causes, which in cases of fraud are not legitimate. Their isolation limits their ability to consult and determine the legitimacy of financial management companies or charitable organizations.

Stopping financial abuse and recovering property is extremely difficult. A possible means for protecting the financial resources of an elderly person is through awarding power of attorney to a trusted individual. A power of attorney is the authority granted by one person to another to act on behalf of the grantor in making personal (or financial) decisions for the grantor. A person may not act as a power of attorney for an individual if he or she is paid to provide health care, residential, social training, or support services to that individual, unless the person is the individual's spouse, partner, or relative. The authority given may be comprehensive or may be restricted to specific acts or types of decisions. The appointed attorney acts as a **fiduciary** and must act in concert with the wishes and best interests of the grantor. A person who is capable of giving a power of attorney may revoke it as long as he or she is still mentally capable (Hiltz & Szigeti, 2004; Regehr & Kanani, 2010). When the grantor has lost capacity, the power of attorney may be terminated if the appointed attorney resigns or by application to the court (Fowler, 2004).

In a family case of financial abuse, Anthony D. Marshall, the 89-year-old son of the Manhattan society doyenne Brooke Astor, surrendered in 2013 to begin a prison sentence for stealing millions of dollars from his mother during her final years of life, ending a seven-year legal battle. His life of wealth and accomplishment—receiving a Purple Heart in World War II, serving as a U.S. diplomat, and producing Broadway shows—took a major turn in 2006 when his son Philip alleged in court papers that his father had unduly enriched himself from Mrs. Astor's fortune.

Mr. Marshall and Francis X. Morrissey, Jr., an Astor family lawyer, were convicted in 2009 of stealing tens of millions of dollars from Mrs. Astor. Prosecutors said the two tricked Mrs. Astor, who by then was more than

100 years of age and had Alzheimer's disease, into altering her will to give tens of millions of dollars to Mr. Marshall. She died in 2007 at age 105.

Both men were to serve one to three years in prison but were allowed to remain free pending the outcome of their appeals. Those appeals were exhausted in 2013, when New York State's highest court declined to review the case (Buettner, 2013). Two months after starting his prison sentence, the State Parole Board approved Mr. Marshall's request for medical parole, ruling that he was so sick and frail as to be eligible for release under the state's so-called compassionate release law. He was released and died several months later at age 90 (McFadden, 2014).

Categories of Abusive Situations

Abuse of the elderly occurs both as a result of actions or inactions of family members, intimate partners, institutional caregivers, and, on rarer occasions, strangers to the victim.

Spousal Violence as Elder Abuse

As noted earlier, spouses make up a substantial percentage of elder abusers, and frequently there is a history of one member of the relationship exerting control over the other through intimidation and violence. In a stratified random sample of 2,000 community members older than age 65 years, Pillemer and Finkelhor (1988) discovered that 58% of perpetrators of sexual abuse were intimate partners. Although Statistics Canada (2013) data suggest that acts of family-related violence against both male and female seniors are most commonly perpetrated by victims' grown children, female seniors were more likely than male seniors to be victimized by a spouse.

Women of the elder generation preceded public awareness and outrage regarding intimate partner violence (IPV). By the time the issue of IPV was recognized in the late 1970s, these women had raised their children. The emerging shelters aimed at protecting women and their young children were not geared toward them. The empowerment messages of the feminist movement against IPV were not directed toward them. To many in the youth movement, these women were part of a generation of oppressors. Later, when elder abuse became an issue of concern in the late 1980s, the attention was focused on those who were abused outside of the marital relationship (Fisher & Regan, 2006).

Older women who are victims of intimate partner violence have many experiences that are similar to those of their younger counterparts. However, they additionally face challenges related to isolation, social roles, and income

(Desmarais & Reeves, 2007). Older women are less likely to have independent sources of income. They are less likely than younger women to have higher education. They were not encouraged to enter the workforce until after the end of World War II, and in fact were encouraged to relinquish jobs they may have had during the war to returning veterans. As a result, they frequently have no pensions beyond that offered through the federal government. Older women were raised in an era where divorce was a source of shame, whereas today, considering the high divorce rates, it has almost become a developmental stage in adulthood. These elder women became wives and mothers in the prefeminist era when gender roles were more strictly defined and marriage and family were the primary, and perhaps only, responsibilities of women. Many have never lived alone. Many have never learned independent skills at managing finances, negotiating contracts (such as leases), or interacting with lawyers. Although many women in abusive relationships experience tremendous obstacles to leaving and ensuring their own safety, older women often feel more trapped and have fewer resources and options on which to rely.

Abuse by Adult Children and Relatives

Motivations to care for an elderly relative are often multifaceted. Some individuals may view the cost of nursing home care to be a waste of the elderly person's assets, which would otherwise be inherited. At times, the elderly person may be able to contribute to the household through housework, cooking, or child care, although in time this may be limited by physical or mental infirmity. Other individuals provide care to their elderly relatives out of a sense of love, duty, or obligation (Fryling, Summers, & Hoffman, 2006). Similarly, elderly persons may elect to live with a relative because they have no alternative and choose not to live in an institution or because they truly desire to live their lives with their children and grandchildren. In situations where a relative (most often a child) cares for an elderly person, often a type of role reversal ensues; the parent becomes the dependent. The caregiver experiences more obligations and less time for other responsibilities or interests. Both the elderly person and his or her caregiver(s) experience less privacy. Regardless of the initial motivations for caring, if the arrangement becomes abusive and violent, the lack of autonomy experienced by the elderly person can make it very difficult to end the abuse.

Research has demonstrated two main types within the category of children as abusers. In the first type, adult child abusers, individuals are dependent on their victims for financial assistance, housing, and other supports. This is frequently because of personal problems, including mental illness, substance abuse, and dysfunctional personality characteristics. As a result, the adult child as caregiver has a decreased ability to tolerate stress and frustration and controls the elderly relative through violence and abuse (Gordon & Brill, 2001). Financial abuse in these cases may result from a need for money to support a drug habit, gambling, or a generally dysfunctional lifestyle. In such situations, there may also be a longstanding history of difficult relationships, perhaps involving the parent historically abusing the child. Alternately, the child may have witnessed violence between his or her parents and learned this is the method to deal with stress, anxiety, and frustration (Hightower, Smith, & Hightower, 2006). The adult child abuser has few resources on which to draw, and the abusive behavior is generally consistent with his or her other interactions with the world.

The following clinical case example illustrates this type of abuse. Iris was 80 years of age and continued to live in a relatively spacious apartment above the store in which she had worked for 42 years on a main street of a large city. She suffered from diabetes and quite advanced arthritis that limited her ability to walk down the stairs from her second-floor apartment. In her younger years, Iris supported both herself and her two sons on her income from her job as a sales clerk. Her husband, an abusive alcoholic, had suffered a brain injury in his early 30s, which Iris believed may have been caused by substance abuse or may have been a stroke. As a result, he was significantly disabled. Because of his highly abusive behavior toward her, Iris refused to take him home, and he remained institutionalized for the remainder of his life. Two years earlier, Iris's son, Paul, returned to live with his mother. Paul had a long history of substance abuse like his father and throughout his life worked in a series of jobs, including short-order cook, bartender, and waiter. He had a series of short-term relationships, and when he returned to his mother's home at the age of 50 years, he had just separated from his current common-law wife and lost his job. After moving in, Paul had his mother's phone number changed so she would not "be bothered by other people who just wanted to use her." He decided to get rid of some of her prized possessions because they "took up too much room in the apartment." Paul intercepted his mother's mail and cashed her checks so he could "buy groceries and her medications," but very scarce amounts of food actually came into the home, and he "forgot" to buy her medication. This left her in significant pain and further limited her mobility and her ability to care for her personal needs. When Iris would protest, Paul would yell at her, demean her, and berate her for "robbing" him of a father when he was growing up. Finally, Iris collapsed due to inadequate control of her diabetes, and Paul phoned an ambulance to take her to the hospital, where she disclosed her situation.

A second type of adult children as abusers can emerge as a result of caregiver stress caused by the demands of caring for an individual who may suffer from dementia or other illnesses that manifest themselves in a high need for physical care or disruptive behaviors. In these situations, the caregiver may strike out and assault the person for whom they are caring. A significant degree of caregiver stress has emerged from the results of government policies that focus on deinstitutionalization or the movement of care of elderly and infirm individuals from institutional care to the community. Part of this move has been ideological; that is, it is better for individuals to be in the community. However, part of this move has also been financial in that community-based care is far less expensive than institutional care. The lower cost is in large part due to limited resources flowing to community care and a reliance on family members to take over care responsibilities.

Caregiver burden is the negative impact on one's social, occupational, and personal well-being as a result of caring for an infirm person, usually a relative. The greatest area of research regarding caregiver burden is with caregivers of elderly individuals with dementia, a general term for memory loss and other cognitive abilities serious enough to interfere with daily life. **Alzheimer's disease** is the most common form of dementia, accounting for 60% to 80% of dementia cases. The burden experienced by caregivers of those with Alzheimer's disease or other forms of dementia results from functional deficits of the ill person, the degree to which the ill person depends on family members for personal care (such as hygiene), disorientation of the ill person, and difficult behaviors such as wandering and aggression (Sussman, 2006). As a result of this burden, family members often experience depression and a variety of physical health problems related to stress (Gonzalez-Salvador, Arango, Lyketsos, & Barba, 1999). In one study of family caregivers for individuals with Alzheimer's disease, 65% exhibited symptoms of depression (Papastavrou, Kalokerinou, Papacostas, Tsangari, & Sourtizi, 2007). Certainly only a small percentage of those caring for individuals with Alzheimer's disease or other forms of dementia abuse their family members, and thus stress cannot be equated with abuse. However, familial caregivers who strike out against those with dementia are more likely to suffer from low self-esteem and clinical depression (McDonald, Collins, & Dergal, 2006).

Institutionally Based Abuse

CBS News reported the tragic case of Mrs. Helen Love, who had been attacked by a staff member in the nursing home in which she resided (CBS News, 2000). On a visit to their mother, her sons Bruce and Gary discovered bruises on her neck, chin, and legs. When they questioned the injuries, they were informed her injuries were caused by her "medical illnesses." Upon examination in a local emergency room, at the insistence of her sons, it was discovered that Mrs. Love had a dislocated neck and a broken wrist in addition to the visible bruises.

In an interview with police, Mrs. Love revealed a nursing home attendant, Tim Saelee, had attacked her in retribution for soiling herself. She reported, "He got real ferocious and started beating me all around the bed. . . . He choked me and went and broke my neck . . . and broke my wrist." Mrs. Love believed she survived only by playing dead. Two days after she was interviewed on videotape, Helen Love died. Saelee pled guilty to assault and received one year in jail. Although this was his first conviction, it was not his first accusation of abuse. At previous times he was warned and fired for abusive behavior (CBS News, 2000).

Institutional abuse refers to older adults who are abused while they are residents of long-term care facilities. A relatively small percentage of older adults live in institutional environments (7% of older adults in Canada), and this may be one reason institutional abuse has been less a subject of examination than community-based abuse (McDonald, 2007). Nevertheless, by definition these are the most vulnerable elderly individuals because their need to live in institutions demonstrates their need for care and protection.

In a survey of 577 nurses and nurse's aides conducted in the United States, 36% of participants reported having seen at least one incident of physical abuse perpetrated by a staff member of an institution in the past year, most frequently the inappropriate use of restraints. Eighty-one percent reported seeing at least one incident of psychological abuse in the past year, most frequently yelling at the older person (Pillemer & Moore, 1989). Most surprising about this study was that 10% of staff members admitted to having committed physical abuse and 40% admitted to psychological abuse (mostly yelling). A report from the Committee on Government Reform of the U.S. House of Representatives (2001) indicated that over 30% of nursing homes in the United States had been cited for abuse.

The causes of institutional abuse are complex, but McDonald (2007) reported the results of several studies that point to the following factors:

- Lack of comprehensive policies governing care in institutions for the elderly and poor enforcement standards.

- The financial structure of institutions for the elderly reward low-cost measures that often result in poor care.

- Lack of qualified, well-trained staff in part due to poor wages and stressful working conditions.

- Vulnerability of the residents and/or resident aggression toward staff.
- Detrimental organizational culture and staff burnout.

Flowing from these causes, prevention of abuse and neglect of elderly persons in institutions is relatively straightforward. The National Center on Elder Abuse (2005) recommends coordination between law enforcement and adult protection workers, education and training of nursing home workers on managing behavior and conflict resolution, improved working conditions in long-term care institutions, strict enforcement of mandatory reporting, improved hiring practices and compliance with federal requirements regarding staffing, and the support and strengthening of residents' councils.

Investigations of allegations of institutionally based elder abuse are complex. Nursing homes do not promptly report allegations of sexual or physical abuse, which results in delays in the investigation. Often, evidence has been compromised and investigations delayed, which results in a reduced likelihood of a successful prosecution (Burgess, Prentky, & Dowdell, 2000). Reasons for untimely reporting of allegations are as follows: (1) residents may fear retribution if they report the abuse, (2) family members are troubled with having to find a new place because the nursing home may ask the resident to leave, (3) staff members do not report abuse promptly for fear of losing their jobs and recrimination from coworkers and management, and (4) nursing homes want to avoid negative publicity and sanctions from the state.

A problem that is more common than physical abuse by staff in long-term care facilities, emphasize Pillemar, Chen, and Van Haitsma (2012), is abuse of older residents by other residents. Studies have uncovered high rates of interpersonal violence and aggression toward older adults (Rosen, Lachs, Bharucha, et al., 2008). An intervention described by Blowers and colleagues (2008) includes the use of multidisciplinary teams to address the complex needs and problems of resident-on-resident elder abuse. These interdisciplinary interventions require an expanded role for nurses, physicians, social workers, and mental health staff in assessing and treating victims of elder abuse and in referring them for further care (Pillemar et al., 2012).

Societal Neglect

Although not traditionally viewed as a form of elder abuse, the neglectful practices of a society can also be highly abusive to vulnerable elderly individuals. A striking example occurred in August 2003 when a heat wave swept through southern Europe and temperatures rose to 40°C (104°F). The sweltering temperatures hit those most vulnerable—elderly individuals with health problems and limited mobility. By the end of the heat wave, scientists at Inserm (the National Institute for Health and Medical Research), using data supplied by funeral directors, deduced that 14,802 more deaths occurred in that three-week period than would have been expected in an average year. Almost all who died were elderly individuals who suffered from dehydration and hyperthermia. The heat wave hit when most of France was on annual vacation and large numbers of doctors, nurses, and hospital staff were away. Many bodies were not claimed for several weeks because relatives were on vacation. Others were never claimed, and on September 3, 2003, 57 unclaimed bodies were buried in Paris. In the end, the government of France was forced to admit that many of its 4.6 million people aged 75 years and older were ignored and left to fend for themselves or die (CNN, 2003; Crumley, 2003; "France heat wave," 2003).

Sexual Assault

Sexual assault against elderly persons is similar in many ways to sexual violence committed against people at all stages of life. However, the particular nature of the victim often belies general attitudes the public may hold for causes of sexual violence. Frequently, these views include victim-blaming attitudes, which people find more difficult to apply to elderly victims. Burgess, Commons, Safarik, Looper, and Ross (2007) presented a typology of motivations for sexual violence against the elderly based on the typologies for sexual offenders originally proposed by Prentky, Cohen, and Seghorn (1985). In their study, they classified 77 convicted sexual offenders of elderly victims.

TYPOLOGIES OF SEXUAL OFFENDERS AGAINST THE ELDERLY

Burgess and colleagues (2007) identified several types of sexual offenders against elders:

1. *Opportunistic rapists.* An opportunistic motive pertains to an impulsive rapist type who shows little planning or preparation. The offender usually has a history of unsocialized behavior, and the rape serves as an example of the degree to which the rapist lacks interpersonal awareness. These rapists show no concern for the welfare or comfort of their victims. The rape is for immediate sexual gratification rather than the enactment of a highly developed fantasy or sexualized ritual. The rape is in the service of dominance and power. In the study by Burgess and colleagues (2007), 13% of offenders fell into this category. Interestingly, offenders in this classification often claimed not to have penetrated the victim but rather committed acts of fondling, kissing, and molestation. In this way, these offenses are similar in nature to the sexual act committed by some child molesters.

2. *Pervasive anger rapists.* Pervasive anger is a second typology of elder rape in which the use of force is excessive and gratuitous, represented by 22% of offenders in the Burgess et al. study sample (2007). The violence for this group is an integrated component of the behavior even when the victim is compliant. Resistance from the victim is likely to increase the level of aggression where serious injury or death may occur. The rage is not sexualized, suggesting the assault is not fantasy driven. The violence is a lifestyle characteristic that is directed toward males and females alike. The rape is but one feature in a history of unsocialized aggressive behavior noted across various social settings.

3. *Sexual-type rapists.* In sexual-type motivations, there is a high degree of preoccupation with gratifying one's sexual needs. This was represented by 40% of the offenders in the Burgess et al. study (2007). Sexual preoccupation is typically evidenced by highly intrusive, recurrent sexual and rape fantasies; frequent use of pornography; reports of frequent uncontrollable sexual urges; use of a variety of alternative outlets for gratifying sexual needs (e.g., massage parlors, X-rated movies, sex clubs, strip bars); and engaging in other deviant sexual behaviors (paraphilias), such as voyeurism, exhibitionism, or fetishism. The sexual assaults of these offenders are often well planned, as evidenced by a clear, scripted sequence of events, possession of assault-related paraphernalia, and an apparent plan to procure the victim and elude apprehension after the assault. Sexual-type rapists include sexual sadistic rapists and sexual nonsadistic rapists:

- *Sexual sadistic rapists.* These rapists intend to inflict fear or pain on the victim and manifest a high level of aggression. The cardinal feature is the intertwining or fusing of the two feelings such that an increase in one leads to an increase in the other. There are two subgroups in the sexual sadistic rapist category:

  - *Overtly sadistic rapists.* These rapists appear to be angry, belligerent people who, except for their sadism and the greater planning of their sexual assaults, seem to be very similar to the pervasive anger rapists.

  - *Muted sadistic rapists.* For muted sadistic rapists the victim's fear or discomfort, or the fantasy of violence, contributes to the offender's sexual arousal (or does not inhibit such arousal), and the amount of physical force used in the sexual assault does not exceed what is necessary to gain victim compliance. Symbolic expressions of sadistic fantasy characterize these offenders, who may use various forms of bondage or restraint, noninjurious insertion of foreign objects, and other sexual aids. What is absent is the high level of expressive aggression that is clearly manifest in the overt sadism type. In general, muted sadistic offenders, except for their sadistic fantasies and their slightly higher lifestyle impulsivity, resemble the highly socially competent, nonsadistic rapists.

– *Sexual nonsadistic rapists.* For these rapists, the thoughts and fantasies that drive their sexual assault behavior lack the blended relationship between sex and aggression noted with the sadistic types. Indeed, these two rapist types show less aggression than any of the other rapist types. If the victim resists, sexual nonsadistic rapists may just leave rather than force the victim to comply. Their fantasies and behaviors generally reflect sexual arousal, distorted male beliefs about women and sexuality, feelings of social and sexual inadequacy, and lack of a contemporary masculine self-image. Compared to the other rapist types, these offenders have fewer problems with impulse control in behaviors outside of sexual aggression.

4. *Vindictive-type rapists*: These rapists have a basic belief of anger at women. Unlike pervasive anger rapists, women are the primary focus of vindictive rapists' anger. Their sexual assaults are physically injurious and intend to degrade, demean, and humiliate their victims. The misogynistic anger evident in these assaults range from verbal abuse to brutal murder. As noted, these offenders differ from pervasive anger rapists in that they show minimal anger toward men (e.g., instigating fights with or assaulting men). This group constituted 21% of the Burgess et al. sample (2007).

Assessment of Elder Abuse

Although healthcare practitioners are most likely to be in a position to identify abuse in an elderly person, everyone has an obligation to ensure that vulnerable individuals in our society are safe from harm. This moral obligation is reinforced by legislation enacted in several jurisdictions requiring people in a range of occupations to report suspected elder abuse.

People with dementia are particularly vulnerable to abuse because of impairments in memory, communication abilities, and judgment. Prevalence rates for abuse and neglect in people with dementia vary from study to study, ranging from 27.5% to 55% (Tronetti, 2014). Studies note that as dementia progresses, so does the risk of all types of abuse signaling a serious outcome for the victimized elder (Cooney et al., 2006). Research on elder abuse of people with dementia is inherently difficult. Abuse among this population is a hidden offense, perpetrated against vulnerable people with memory impairment, by those on whom they depend. Prevalence estimates are influenced, and possibly underestimated, by the fact that many people with dementia are unable, frightened, or embarrassed to report abuse (NCEA, 2016).

For those elderly who are in highly dependent situations, there may appear to be no safe way to report the abuse. Impairments, such as dementia, may be one factor that limits the ability of a victim to report and stop the abuse. In addition, like victims of sexual violence of any age, reporting the abuse is frequently experienced as humiliating, and victims fear their claims will not be believed (Ardovini, 2006). The rape or sexual assault of an elder is a felony. In some states, the sentence for the crime carries special sanctions because of the victim's advanced age.

Several factors shown in TABLE 12-2 are associated with increased risk of abuse and should be considered when abuse is suspected (U.S. Government Accountability Office, 2011).

In addition to general factors that may lead one to suspect abuse, a number of tools exist that assist with identification of abuse; some require training and others are simple to administer without training (Fulmer, Guadagno, Bitondo, & Connolly, 2004). One of the most user-friendly tools

TABLE 12-2 Factors Associated with Risk of Abuse

Factor	Description and Examples
Physical impairment	Elderly individuals with poorer health or limited mobility are at higher risk of abuse. Physically impaired individuals are less able to defend themselves.
Mental health problems	Clinical depression is associated with financial and psychological abuse. Victims of abuse are more likely to suffer from mental health problems. Alcohol abuse is associated with aggressive behavior in perpetrators of elder abuse.
Cognitive impairment	Cognitively impaired adults are at greater risk of abuse. Cognitively impaired individuals often cannot report abuse. Dementia in an elderly person may cause increased caregiver stress.
Lack of social support	Social contact can diffuse tension and allow others to monitor behavior. Social dependency on caregivers increases risk of abuse.

Data from: GAO. 2011. Elder Justice. Report of the Chairman, Special Committee on Aging, U.S. Senate. GAO-11-208.

TABLE 12-3 Elder Abuse Screening Survey

1. Are you afraid of anyone in your family?
2. Has anyone close to you tried to hurt or harm you recently?
3. Has anyone close to you called you names, put you down, or made you feel bad recently?
4. Does someone in your family make you stay in bed or tell you you're sick when you aren't?
5. Has anyone forced you to do things you did not want to do?
6. Has anyone taken things that belong to you without your permission?

Data from: Bomba, P. 2006. Use of a single page elder abuse assessment and management tool: A practical clinician's approach to identifying elder mistreatment. In J. Mellor & P. Bownell (Eds.), *Elder abuse and mistreatment: Policy, practice, and research* (pp. 103–122). Birmingham, NY: Haworth Press; and Fulmer, T., Guadagno, L., Bitondo, C., & Connolly, M. (2004). Progress in elder abuse screening and assessment instruments. *Journal of the American Geriatrics Society, 52*(2), 297–304.

is distilled into six short screening questions found in TABLE 12-3 (Bomba, 2006; Fulmer et al., 2004). The use of these questions not only identifies abuse but demonstrates an openness to discussing issues of abuse and the desire to offer assistance.

If elder abuse is suspected, there are three issues to consider (Bomba, 2006):

1. Is the person safe?
2. Will the person accept intervention?
3. Does the person have the capacity to refuse intervention?

Not all abuse situations constitute an emergency; thus, if the person is safe, it is possible to develop a longer-term relationship and move toward a plan to end the abuse if the person agrees to intervention. If the person does not agree to allow assistance, intervention can be forced only if the person does not have the capacity to consent to or refuse intervention. That is, people are allowed the self-determination to remain in abusive situations if they fully understand the nature and consequences of their decision. If they are not competent to consent or refuse, other options, such as adult protective services, can be called in to assist.

Rosen and colleagues (2016) reviewed legal records from adjudicated cases to describe acute precipitants for physical elder abuse. In collaboration with a large, urban district attorney's office, the researchers reviewed 87 successfully prosecuted physical elder abuse cases from 2003 to 2015 and identified 10 categories of acute precipitants that commonly triggered physical elder abuse: (1) the victim attempting to prevent the abuser from entering or demanding that he or she leave, (2) the victim threatening or attempting to leave/escape, (3) the threat or perception that the victim would involve the authorities, (4) conflict about a romantic relationship, (5) presence during/intervention in ongoing family violence, (6) issues in multigenerational child rearing, (7) conflict about the abuser's substance abuse, (8) confrontation about financial exploitation, (9) dispute over theft/destruction of property, and (10) disputes over minor household issues. The researchers recommend an improved understanding of these acute precipitants for escalation to physical violence and their contribution to elder abuse may assist in the development of prevention and management strategies (Rosen et al., 2016).

Interventions

Intervention strategies with regard to elder abuse fall into several categories, including prevention programs, adult protection programs, and domestic violence programs. Each intervention strategy is based on a particular view of the causes of elder abuse. For example, domestic violence programs target elder abuse as a form of family violence and focus on intimate partner or spousal violence, and adult protective services focus on vulnerability and often intervene when the abuser is an adult child or community caregiver.

Prevention Programs

One form of prevention attempts to address family stress caused by caregiving. In this approach, increased services are offered in the community, such as community nursing day treatment programs for elderly individuals with physical disabilities (e.g., those caused by stroke) or dementia. The notion is that increased services will result in reduced stress and burden, which, in turn, will reduce abuse caused by caregiver stress. A study of spousal caregivers of people with dementia, however, suggested that services alone do not provide a simple solution to caregiver stress. Using interviews and surveys, Sussman and Regehr (2009) found that in-home services, such as homemakers, nurses, occupational therapists, and case managers, did little to reduce the burden of spouses who care for their partners with dementia. In fact, the stress of dealing with multiple service delivery people in the home created additional stress for some. Rather, the only effective service in reducing caregiver stress in this study was the provision of adult day treatment programs (sometimes referred to as day care), which provided not only respite for the spousal caregivers but also opportunities for social interaction for their partners with dementia (Sussman & Regehr, 2009). Thus, investment in day treatment would seem to be an effective means for reducing elder abuse caused by stress.

Another form of prevention focuses more on education. The premise behind this approach is that, as with child abuse and spousal assault, increased knowledge by service providers, community members, and victims themselves will result in early detection, increased reporting, and therefore increased safety. In some jurisdictions, specific interventions have been established and have met with success. New York City's Domestic Violence Prevention Project (DVPP) began in 1983 as a joint program of the police and victim services. In this program, a police officer and a domestic violence counselor visit homes a few days after the police have responded to a domestic violence emergency call. The counselor meets with the victim to discuss the abuse and establish a safety plan. The police officer meets with the offender, if possible, and informs the offender the police are watching the household. Evidence suggests that this project has been successful in assisting the victim in contacting the police, but it has not resulted in lower levels of violence (Davis & Medina-Ariza, 2001). Although elder abuse cases were theoretically included in the DVPP model, in most situations in which the DVPP intervened the victims were younger spouses. Subsequently, an elder abuse prevention project was initiated where public education about elder abuse was distributed to 30 of 60 public housing projects in New York City. If cases were reported to police, the DVPP attended and provided service. These interventions saw a significant increase in reports of abuse both to the police and to researchers who asked about the incidence of abuse. Hopefully, the increased reporting indicated an increased awareness among elderly persons of their rights and an increased willingness to seek assistance.

Adult Protection Programs

Mandatory reporting laws and adult protective services are integrally linked. That is, as previously stated, most jurisdictions require professionals of varying types to report suspected elder abuse. This report, in turn, triggers an assessment and possible intervention by adult protective services. At this point an adult protective services worker generally investigates the report of abuse and determines the most appropriate course of intervention. When an elderly person is determined to be abused and he or she agrees to the intervention, safety plans and alternate living arrangements can be initiated. The problem arises when the person is unwilling to agree to the intervention. In such cases, a determination must be made whether the individual is competent to consent. For a person to have the capacity to consent, the person must be able to understand information that is provided to him or her and how that information applies to his or her specific situation. The Ontario Health Care Consent Act (1996), for example, states that a person is capable of consenting to treatment if "the person is able to understand the information that is relevant to making a decision about the treatment . . . and able to appreciate the reasonably fore-seeable consequences of a decision or lack of decision" (s. 4(1)). Capacity is not viewed as a blanket status; it is specific to a particular procedure and particular time frame. Thus, a person may be incapable of consenting to some treatments yet capable of consenting to others. For example, a person may be able to consent to such procedures as bloodwork but not to major procedures such as cardiac surgery. In addition, consent is fluid. A person may be capable of consenting to a particular procedure at one time but incapable of consenting to the same procedure at another time (Regehr & Kanani, 2010). As a result of the complexities around the issue of consent and the risk of undermining the civil rights and self-determination of elderly individuals, adult protective services as an approach to elder abuse remains highly controversial (Anderson & Mangels, 2006).

Domestic Violence Programs

Domestic violence programs as an approach to elder abuse are modeled on woman abuse intervention programs. They can include telephone hotlines, criminal charges against offenders that are made by police, protection orders, emergency shelters, and counseling services for both victims and offenders (McDonald, 2007). For example, changes in the criminal justice system in the United States include laws to enhance sentences in elder abuse cases, train-ing programs for police and judges, and special units within police depart-ments and prosecutors' offices to deal with cases of elder abuse (Anderson & Mangels, 2006). Problems with this approach also mirror those in domestic violence, including the inadequacy of restraining orders, the reluctance of police to criminalize domestic matters, and shortage of resources for inter-vention and shelter (McDonald, 2007).

A program established in New York City called Hebrew Home is an excellent example of a domestic violence model of service. This center uses a multidisciplinary team approach, which includes the district attorneys' offices, adult protective services, a medical center, and an advocacy organiza-tion. Services offered by the center include legal advocacy, short-term emer-gency housing, long-term care planning and possible admission, education and support for caregivers, public education and training, meals-on-wheels, and law enforcement training (Reingold, 2006). This integrated system pro-vides a spectrum of services that address immediate safety needs and long-term needs for ongoing care or intervention.

◼ Conclusion

The abuse and neglect of the elderly—either by a society that fails to adopt health, legal, and social service measures to meet the needs of older people; by staff members in institutions who have a fiduciary responsibility for vulnerable older people; or by relatives who are either stressed by or take advantage of vulnerability—is perhaps one of the saddest secrets of most societies. Seniors worked to develop societies into the form they take today, they nurtured and educated leaders, and they created economies. Yet, aging is a dreaded outcome of living, and the elderly are often relegated to insignificant roles and are viewed as a burden. Added to these prejudices are issues related to vulnerability and autonomy. Although many agree that the vulnerability of children justifies mandated protection services, societies are less clear when an older person loses the right to individual choice and the need for protection takes precedence. In recent years, many countries have moved to address these issues, but as yet there is no perfect solution.

◼ Key Terms

Alzheimer's disease: A slowly progressive disease of the brain characterized by impairment of memory and eventually by disturbances in reasoning, planning, language, and perception.

Cognitively impaired: A brain disorder in which thinking abilities are impaired.

Dementia: A condition in which memory loss has progressed to such a point that normal independent functioning is impossible and affected individuals can no longer successfully manage their finances or provide for their own basic needs.

Elder abuse: Any physical, sexual, verbal, psychological, or financial abuse perpetrated against an older adult.

Fiduciary: A business or person who may act for another with total trust, good faith, and honesty and who has the complete confidence and trust of that person.

Medically fragile: Individuals who have *medically* intensive needs that usually result in chronic health-related dependence.

Power of attorney: Authority granted by one person to another to empower the grantee to make financial and healthcare decisions on the grantor's behalf.

Psychological abuse: When an individual attempts to dehumanize or intimidate older adults through verbal or nonverbal acts.

Discussion Questions

1. What community, institutional, and legal policies or laws protect older persons from abuse?

2. What challenges are faced when attempting to address allegations of abuse in nursing homes?

3. If an educational program is to be focused on helping elderly people to find assistance if they are abused, what would be the most effective messages to convey?

4. What factors differentiate the assault and abuse of the elderly from similar assaults and abuse of people in other age groups?

5. How would you develop a prevention plan for elders living alone in the community?

Resources

Canadian Network for the Prevention of Elder Abuse http://www.cnpea.ca

National Center on Elder Abuse https://ncea.acl.gov/

National Committee for the Prevention of Elder Abuse http://www.preventel derabuse.org/elderabuse/

World Health Organization, Elder Abuse http://www.who.int/ageing/projects /elder_abuse/en/

References

Acierno, R., Hernandez, M., Amstadter, A., Resnick, H., Steve, K., Muzzy, W., & Kilpatrick, D. (2010). Prevalence and correlates of emotional, physical, sexual, and financial abuse and potential neglect in the United States: The National Elder Mistreatment Study. *American Journal of Public Health*, 100(2), 292–297.

Adams, J., & Calloway, M. (2009). Convicted sex offenders: New responsibilities for long-term care facilities. Virginia Department of Health Office of Licensure and Certification. Retrieved from www.vhca.org/IlluminAgeApps/whatsnewApp /files/69383C9C6.pdf

American Bar Association Commission on Law and Aging. (2005). *Information about laws related to elder abuse*. Newark, DE: National Center on Elder Abuse.

Amstadter, A., Cisler, J., McCauley, J., Hernandez, M., Muzzy, W., & Acierno, R. (2010). Do incident and perpetrator characteristics of elder mistreatment differ by gender of the victim? Results from the National Elder Mistreatment Study. *Journal of Elder Abuse & Neglect*, 23(1), 43–57.

Anderson, J., & Mangels, N. (2006). Helping victims: Social services, healthcare interventions in elder abuse. In R. Summers & A. Hoffman (Eds.), *Elder abuse: A public health perspective* (pp. 139–166). Washington, DC: American Public Health Association.

Arai, M. (2006). Elder abuse in Japan. *Educational Gerontology, 32*(1), 13–23.

Ardovini, J. (2006). Sexual violence against older women. In R. Summers & A. Hoffman (Eds.), *Elder abuse: A public health perspective* (pp. 131–138). Washington, DC: American Public Health Association.

Associated Press. (2008, June 18). Governor signs sexual predator bill. Retrieved from   http://www.tulsaworld.com/news/article.aspx?articleID=20080610_12_OKLAH04125

Beach, S., Schultz, R., Castle, N., & Rosen, J. (2010). Financial exploitation and psychological maltreatment among older adults: Differences between African Americans and non-African Americans in a population-based survey. *Gerontologist, 50*(6), 744–757.

Bezerra-Flanders, W., & Clark, J. (2006). Perspectives on elder abuse and neglect in Brazil. *Educational Gerontology, 32*(1), 63–72.

Blowers, A. N., Davis, B., Shenk, D., Kalaw, K., Smith, M., Jackson, K. A multidisciplinary approach to detecting and responding to elder mistreatment: creating a university-community partnership. *American Journal of Criminal Justice,* 2012;37:276–290.

Bomba, P. (2006). Use of a single-page elder abuse assessment and management tool: A practical clinician's approach to identifying elder mistreatment. In J. Mellor & P. Brownell (Eds.), *Elder abuse and mistreatment: Policy, practice, and research* (pp. 103–122). Birmingham, NY: Haworth Press.

Buettner, E. (2013, June 22). Appeals exhausted, Astor case ends as son is sent to jail. *New York Times.* Retrieved from http://www.nytimes.com/2013/06/22/nyregion/astors-son-his-appeals-exhausted-goes-to-prison.html

Burgess, A. W., Commons, M. L., Safarik, M. E., Looper, R. R., & Ross, S. N. (2007). Sex offenders of the elderly: Typology and predictors of severity of crime. *Aggression and Violent Behavior, 12,* 582–597.

Burgess, A.W. & Phillips, S. L. (2006). Sexual Abuse and Dementia in Older People. *Journal of the American Geriatrics Society, 54*(7), 1154–1155.

Burgess, A. W., Prentky, R., & Dowdell, E. (2000). Sexual predators in nursing homes. *Journal of Psychosocial Nursing, 38,* 9–17.

Catalano, L., & Lazaro, C. (2008). Financial abuse of the elderly: Protecting the vulnerable. *PIABA Law Journal,* 1–15.

CBS News. (2000, December 27). Tracking abuse in nursing homes. Retrieved from http://www.cbsnews.com/stories/2002/01/31/health/main327525.shtml

Centers for Disease Control and Prevention (CDC). (2016). National Center for Injury Prevention and Control fact sheet. Retrieved from https://www.cdc.gov/violenceprevention/pdf/em-factsheet-a.pdf

Centers for Disease Control and Prevention. (2017). CDC 24/7. Saving Lives, Protecting People. Retrieved from https://www.cdc.gov/violenceprevention/elderabuse/definitions.html

CNN. (2003, August 29). French heat toll tops 11,000. Retrieved from http://www.cnn.com/2003/WORLD/europe/08/29/france.heatdeaths/

Cohen, C. (2006). Consumer fraud and the elderly: A review of Canadian challenges and initiatives. In J. Mellor & P. Brownell (Eds.), *Elder abuse and mistreatment: Policy, practice, and research* (pp. 137–144). Birmingham, NY: Haworth Press.

Cohen, T. (2011). Mickey Rooney tells Senate panel that he was the victim of elder abuse. Retrieved from http://articles.cnn.com/2011-03-02/entertainment/rooney.elderly.abuse_1_elder-abuse-marie-therese-connolly-elder-population?_s=PM:-SHOWBIZ

Collin, L. (2010, December 22). 2nd Nursing home worker sentenced for abuse. Retrieved from http://minnesota.cbslocal.com/2010/12/22/2nd-nursing-home-worker-sentenced-for-abuse/

Committee on Government Reform of the U.S. House of Representatives. (2001). Abuse of residents is a major problem in U.S. nursing homes. Retrieved from http://oversight.house.gov/documents/20040830113750-34049.pdf

Cooper, C., Selwood, A., & Livingston, G. (2008). The prevalence of elder abuse and neglect: A systematic review. *Age and Ageing, 37*(2), 151–160.

Cooney, C., Howard, R., & Lawlor, B. (2006). Abuse of vulnerable people with dementia by their caregivers: Can we identify those most at risk? *International Journal of Geriatric Psychiatry, 21*(6), 564–571.

Crumley, B. (2003, August 24). Elder careless. Retrieved from http://www.time.com/time/magazine/article/0,9171,901030901-477899,00.html

Davis, R., & Medina-Ariza, J. (2001). *Results from an elder abuse prevention experiment in New York City.* National Institute of Justice: Research in Brief. Washington, DC: U.S. Department of Justice.

Department of Justice Canada. (2007). Abuse of older adults. Retrieved from http://www.justice.gc.ca/en/ps/fm/adultsfs.html

Desmarais, S., & Reeves, K. (2007). Gray, black, and blue: The state of research and intervention for intimate partner abuse among elders. *Behavioral Sciences and the Law, 25,* 377–391.

Dong, X., & Simon, M. (2011). Enhancing national policy and programs to address elder abuse. *Journal of the American Medical Association, 305*(23), 2460–2461.

Donovan, K., & Regehr, C. (2010). Elder abuse: Clinical, ethical, and legal issues in social work practice. *Clinical Social Work Journal, 38*(2), 174–182.

Dubble, C. (2006). A policy perspective on elder justice through APS and law enforcement collaboration. *Journal of Gerontological Social Work, 46*(3/4), 35–55.

Elder Justice Coalition. (2011). Elder Justice Act. Retrieved from http://elderjusticecoalition.com/legislation.htm

Fisher, B., & Regan, S. (2006). The extent and frequency of abuse in the lives of older women and their relationship with health outcomes. *Gerontologist, 46,* 200–209.

Fowler, L. (2004). *Powers of attorney.* Toronto: Law Society of Upper Canada.

FOX News. (2008, December 2). Six teens charged in nursing home abuse. Retrieved from http://www.foxnews.com/story/2008/12/02/6-teens-charged-in-nursing-home-abuse.html

FOX News. (2017, July 30). Portland man accused of sexually assaulting a 65-year-old woman had been deported. Retrieved from http://www.foxnews.com/us/2017/07/30/portland-man-accused-sexually-assaulting-65-year-old-had-been-deported-20-times.html

France heat wave death toll set at 14,802. (2003, September 25). Retrieved from http://www.usatoday.com/weather/news/2003-09-25-france-heat_x.htm

Freeman, D. (2011). Mickey Rooney: Elder abuse victim? Retrieved from http://www.cbsnews.com/8301–504763_162–20032211–10391704.html

Fryling, T., Summers, R., & Hoffman, A. (2006). Elder abuse: Definition and scope of the problem. In R. Summers & A. Hoffman (Eds.), *Elder abuse: A public health perspective* (pp. 5–18). Washington, DC: American Public Health Association.

Fulmer, T., Guadagno, L., Bitondo, C., & Connolly, M. (2004). Progress in elder abuse screening and assessment instruments. *Journal of the American Geriatrics Society, 52*(2), 297–304.

Gjertsen, E. (2014, April 10). The 'double life' of Mickey Rooney. CNBC. Retrieved from https://www.cnbc.com/2014/04/10/the-double-life-of-mickey-rooney.html

Gonzalez-Salvador, M., Arango, C., Lyketsos, C., & Barba, A. (1999). The stress and psychological morbidity of the Alzheimer patient caregiver. *International Journal of Geriatric Psychiatry, 14,* 701–710.

Gordon, R. (2001). Adult protection legislation in Canada: Models, issues, and problems. *International Journal of Law and Psychiatry, 24,* 117–134.

Gordon, R., & Brill, D. (2001). The abuse and neglect of the elderly. *International Journal of Law and Psychiatry, 24,* 183–197.

Health Care Consent Act. (1996). S.O. 1996, C.2.

Hightower, J., Smith, M., & Hightower, H. (2006). Hearing the voices of older abused women. In J. Mellor & P. Brownell (Eds.), *Elder abuse and mistreatment: Policy, practice, and research* (pp. 205–227). Birmingham, NY: Haworth Press.

Hiltz, D., & Szigeti, A. (2004). *A guide to consent and capacity law in Ontario.* Toronto: LexisNexis Canada.

König, J., & Leembruggen-Kallberg, E. (2006). Perspectives on elder abuse in Germany. *Educational Gerontology, 32*(1), 25–35.

Laumann, E., Leitsch, S., & Waite, L. (2008). Elder mistreatment in the United States: Prevalence estimates from a nationally representative study. *Journal of Gerontological Behavioral, Psychological Sciences, and Social Sciences, 63*(4), S248–S254.

McDonald, L. (2007). Elder abuse and neglect. In E. Birren (Ed.), *The encyclopedia of gerontology* (2nd ed., Vol. 1, pp. 1–10). New York: Academic Press.

McDonald, L., Collins, A., & Dergal, J. (2006). The abuse and neglect of older adults in Canada. In R. Alaggia & C. Vine (Eds.), *Cruel but not unusual: Violence in Canadian families: A sourcebook for educators and practitioners* (pp. 624–688). Waterloo, Ontario: Wilfrid Laurier University Press.

McFadden, R. (2014, December 1). Anthony D. Marshall, Astor son who was convicted in swindle, dies at 90. *New York Times*. Retrieved from https://www.nytimes.com/2014/12/02/nyregion/anthony-d-marshall-son-of-brooke-astor-convicted-in-swindle-dies-at-90.html?_r=0

Mickey Rooney. (2011). Biography. Retrieved from http://www.mickeyrooney.com/biography.html

Mickey Rooney claims to be elder abuse victim. (2011). Retrieved from http://www.thestar.com/entertainment/article/947875--mickey-rooney-claims-to-be-elder-abuse-victim

Mickey Rooney speaks out against elder abuse. (2011). Retrieved from http://www.theglobeandmail.com/news/arts/video/mickey-rooney-speaks-out-against-elder-abuse/article1927308/

Morgan, R., & Mason, B. (2014). Crimes against the elderly, 2003–2013: Special report. Washington, DC: U.S. Department of Justice.

Myfox.com. (2010, October 22). Sentencing in Alberta Lea nursing home abuse. Retrieved from http://www.myfoxtwincities.com/dpp/news/minnesota/sentencing-in-albert-lea-nursing-home-abuse-oct–22–2010

National Center on Elder Abuse (NCEA). (2005). *Nursing Home Abuse Risk Prevention Profile and Checklist.* U.S. Administration on Aging. Retrieved from www.ncea.aoa.gov/main_site/pdf/publication/NursingHomeRisk.pdf

NBC. (2017). Retrieved from http://www.nbclosangeles.com/news/local/Man-Sentenced-50-Years-for-Rape-Elderly-Women-North-Hollywood-442372573.html#ixzz4uHzdzCnE

NCEA. (2017). Research/data. Retrieved from https://ncea.acl.gov/whatwedo/research/statistics.html

Nerenberg, L. (2006). Communities respond to elder abuse. *Journal of Gerontological Social Work, 46*(3/4), 5–33.

Papastavrou, E., Kalokerinou, A., Papacostas, S., Tsangari, H., & Sourtizi, P. (2007). Caring for a relative with dementia: Family caregiver burden. *Journal of Advanced Nursing, 58*(5), 446–457.

Peasance, C. (2015). Abused by a wife who was desperate for fame, and kept on the road by her son who frittered his money away: New allegations surface about tragic actor Mickey Rooney's final years. *Daily Mail*. Retrieved from http://www.dailymail.co.uk/news/article-3283722/Abused-wife-desperate-fame-kept-road-son-frittered-money-away-New-allegations-surface-tragic-actor-Mickey-Rooney-s-final-years.html#ixzz4oQ5ck1sB

Pillemer, K., & Finkelhor, D. (1988). The prevalence of elder abuse: A random sample survey. *Gerontologist, 28*, 51–57.

Pillemer, K., & Moore, D. (1989). Abuse of patients in nursing homes: Findings from a staff survey. *Gerontologist, 29*(3), 321–327.

Pillemer, K., Chen, E. K., Van Haitsma, K. S., et al. Resident-to-resident aggression in nursing homes: results from a qualitative event reconstruction study. Gerontologist, 2012;52:24–33.

Prentky, R. A., Cohen, M. L., & Seghorn, T. K. (1985). Development of a rational taxonomy for the classification of sexual offenders: Rapists. *Bulletin of the American Academy of Psychiatry and the Law, 13*, 39–70.

Rabi, K. (2006). Israeli perspectives on elder abuse. *Educational Gerontology, 32*(1), 49–62.

Ramsey-Klawsnik, H., Teaster, P., Mendiondo, M., Abner, E., Cecil, K., & Tooms, M. (2007). Sexual abuse of vulnerable adults in care facilities: Clinical findings and a research initiative. *Journal of the American Psychiatric Nurses Association, 12*(6), 332–339.

Regehr, C., & Antle, B. (1997). Coercive influences: Informed consent in court mandated social work practice. *Social Work, 42*(3), 300–306.

Regehr, C., & Kanani, K. (2010). *Essential law for social work practice in Canada.* Toronto: Oxford University Press.

Reingold, D. (2006). An elder abuse shelter program: Build it and they will come, a long-term care based program to address elder abuse in the community. In J. Mellor & P. Brownell (Eds.), *Elder abuse and mistreatment: Policy, practice, and research* (pp. 123–135). Birmingham, NY: Haworth Press.

Rosen, T., Lien, C., Stern, M. E., Bloemen, E. M., Mysliwiec, R., McCarthy, & Flomenbaum. N. E. (2017). Emergency Medical Services Perspectives on Identifying and Reporting Victims of Elder Abuse, Neglect, and Self-Neglect. *The Journal of Emergency Medicine.* Published online: July 13, 2017.

Rosen, T., Lachs, M. S., Bharucha, A. J., et al. Resident-to-resident aggression in long-term care facilities: insights from focus groups of nursing home residents and staff. *Journal of the American Geriatrics Society,* 2008;56:1398–1408.

Shaw, M. (June 20, 2017). ABC Alleged rape at senior living center prompts review of security. Eyewiness News, Houston, Texas, Retrieved from http://abc13.com/news/alleged-rape-at-senior-living-center-prompts-review/2120104/

Statistics Canada. (2002). *Family violence in Canada: A statistical profile.* Ottawa: Author.

Statistics Canada. (2007). *Family violence in Canada: A statistical profile.* Ottawa: Author.

Statistics Canada. (2013). *Family violence in Canada: A statistical profile.* Ottawa: Author.

Sussman, T. (2006). Negotiating community care as a stress: The experience of spousal caregivers. Paper presented at the Fourth Annual National Gerontological Social Work Conference, February 16–18, 2006. Chicago, Illinois.

Sussman, T., & Regehr, C. (2009). The influence of community-based services on the burden of spouses caring for their partners with dementia. *Social Work in Health Care, 34*(1), 29–39.

Tam, S., & Neysmith, S. (2006). Disrespect and isolation: Elder abuse in Chinese communities. *Canadian Journal on Aging, 25*(2), 141–151.

Tauriac, J., & Scruggs, N. (2006). Elder abuse among African Americans. *Educational Gerontology, 32*(1), 37–48.

Tronetti, P. (2014). Evaluating abuse in the patient with dementia. *Clinics in Geriatric Medicine 30*(4), 825–38.

U.S. Census Bureau, Population Division (2016). Retrieved from https://www.census .gov/data/tables/2016/demo/popest/nation-total.html

U.S. Government Accountability Office. (2011). *Elder justice. Report of the Chairman, Special Committee on Aging, U.S. Senate.* GAO-11-208. Washington, DC: Author.

World Health Organization (WHO). (2002). Toronto declaration on the global prevention of elder abuse. Retrieved from http://www.who.int/ageing/projects /elder_abuse/alc_toronto_declaration_en.pdf

© Peyker/Shutterstock.

CHAPTER 13

Homicide: Victims, Their Families, and the Community

Ann Wolbert Burgess and Paul Thomas Clements

OBJECTIVES

- To identify types of homicide by victim and motive
- To outline homicide statistics and trends
- To explain the theories of violent crime and homicide
- To identify victimization concepts related to homicide
- To outline homicide typologies, including homicide-suicide
- To describe the grief, bereavement, and trauma response of homicide covictims

KEY TERMS

Classic mass murder

Covictim

Homicide

Murder

Recidivism

Serial murder

Spree murder

Traumatic bereavement

Traumatic grief

Uniform Crime Reporting (UCR)

CASE

Until his double life came to light with his arrest in February 2011, Canadian Air Force officer Russell Williams had a brilliant future. He had been entrusted with flying various prime ministers, as well as Queen Elizabeth II, and was the commander of Canada's largest air force base. Colonel David Russell Williams, the former Canadian commander unmasked as a thief and killer, videotaped his extended, brutal assaults on the two women he murdered (FIGURE 13-1). His first murder victim was Corporal Marie-France Comeau, an air force flight attendant from Colonel Williams's base. Prosecutors said that after hours of repeatedly being raped and beaten in the head with a large flashlight she was suffocated by duct tape covering her mouth and nose. After Corporal Comeau's body was discovered, Colonel Williams sent her father a letter of condolence in his capacity as base commander. Jessica Lloyd, the second murder victim, had been spotted by the colonel as he drove on a road near a cottage he owned. Williams had targeted the corporal after meeting her while she worked on a military flight.

Williams pleaded guilty to the murders, two other sexual assaults, and 82 break-ins. The disturbing accounts of the crimes were drawn from Colonel Williams's own meticulous records and videotapes of his 2-year rampage, which began with home break-ins to steal girls' and women's underwear for his sexual arousal and then culminated in the murders. Williams took pictures of himself wearing the underwear in the women's bedrooms. He then stored the photographs on a computer hard drive. Williams burgled at least 47 homes, starting in 2007. Many of the targeted homes

FIGURE 13-1 Colonel Russell Williams.
© Master Corporal Miranda Langguth/Department of National Defence/Thomson Reuters.

were on the same street as Williams's cottage in Tweed, Ontario. Other targeted homes were in the vicinity of Williams's main home in Orleans, outside Ottawa (BBC, 2010). Williams was given a life sentence with no chance of parole for 25 years for the two murders and sexual assaults (Austen, 2010).

The Canadian Forces stripped Williams of his rank and medals and later dismissed him in disgrace (dishonorable discharge). In addition, Williams's uniform was burned and his medals were cut into pieces. His commission scroll (a document confirming his status as a serving officer) was also shredded.

Four years after he was sentenced, Williams reached an out-of-court financial settlement with some of his many victims. The civil lawsuits included one by "Jane Doe," Williams's first sexual assault victim, and a second by the mother and brother of Jessica Lloyd, who was kidnapped from her Belleville, Ontario home and murdered inside the former air force commander's cottage. The lawsuits also accused his long-time spouse, Mary Elizabeth Harriman, of participating in a "fraudulent" and "clearly suspicious" property transfer aimed at shielding their assets. These actions were dismissed against Mary Elizabeth Harriman on a without-costs basis (Friscolanti, 2014).

A third lawsuit filed by Laurie Massicotte, who was ambushed in her living room and assaulted at knifepoint just weeks before Williams committed his first murder, was settled in 2016. Massicotte's claim included accusations that the Ontario Provincial Police had failed to warn the neighborhood about a potential predator. Her lawsuit also claimed that Williams's wife knew of her husband's activities but chose not to report him to the police. Massicotte settled with the police department, which did not handle her investigation very well. One officer even suggested she made the whole thing up, despite the fact there was a similar attack on the same street 10 days before (Warmington, 2016).

Introduction

Homicide can be operationally defined as the intentional and sometimes unintentional or accidental killing of another person. It is a tragic phenomenon that has aroused great public and professional concern for decades. By virtue of its lethality, there is no doubt that murder is the ne plus ultra of crimes (Delisi, Kosloscki, Sween, et al., 2010, p. 1). **Murder** is the unlawful taking of human life. It is a behavioral act that terminates life in the context of power, personal gain, brutality, and sometimes sexuality. Murder is a subcategory of homicide, which also includes lawful taking of human life, such as manslaughter, and deaths resulting from criminal and noncriminal negligence, such as unpremeditated vehicular deaths (Riedel & Hunnicutt, 2012). By definition, a murder is a homicide (the killing of one human being by another) that is committed intentionally or with malice aforethought. Although a distinction is made in the literature among homicide, murder, and killing, for the purpose of this text the terms are used interchangeably.

Scope of the Problem

When it was established, the Federal Bureau of Investigation's **Uniform Crime Reporting (UCR)** Program was the first system to classify homicide in the United

States. The U.S. homicide rate steadily decreased throughout the decade of the 1990s. In 1991, the homicide rate was 9.8 per 100,000 inhabitants. By 2000 it had fallen to 5.5 per 100,000 inhabitants (Fox, 2001). However, it began to increase in 2001. In 2001, the nation's homicide rate was 5.6 per 100,000, and it remained at 5.6 in 2005 (Federal Bureau of Investigation [FBI], 2006). Between 2004 and 2005 the number of homicides increased by 2.4% (FBI, 2006). However, some states saw much higher increases than others: Alabama (+46.0%), Rhode Island (+31.2%), Delaware (+30.0%), Wyoming (+26.6%), Wisconsin (+25.2%), Utah (+19.3%), West Virginia (+17.4%), Virginia (+16.9%), Pennsylvania (+16.0%), Ohio (+15.5%), Missouri (+12.8%), South Carolina (+8.7%), and New Jersey (+6.05). In 2006, the homicide rate was an estimated 5.7 murders per 100,000 inhabitants. An estimated 17,034 persons were murdered nationwide in 2006, an increase of 1.8% from the 2005 estimate (FBI, 2007). More recent data reflects that 13,594 persons were murdered in 2014 and 15,192 in 2015, representing an 11.8% increase across those 2 years (FBI, 2017). FIGURE 13-2 presents homicide numbers by the type of weapon used; almost half (47.32%) of murders were caused by handguns and 14.14% by unknown firearms. Knives and cutting instruments comprised 13.38% of murder weapons; other weapons, 13.6%; hands, fists, and so on, 5.87%; shotguns, 3.07%; and rifles, 2.55% (FBI, 2011).

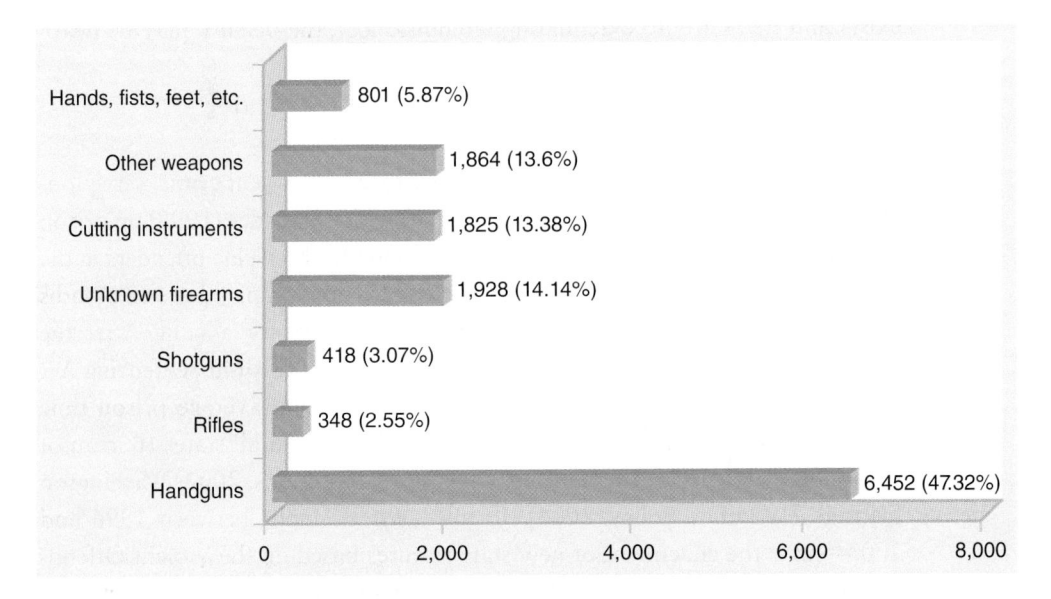

FIGURE 13-2 Number of murders by type of weapon used.

Data from: FBI Uniform Crime Report – Crime in the United States. 1977, 1981, 1987, 1989, 2003, 2007. Washington, DC: Department of Justice.

The murder rate in Canada is considerably lower than that in the United States. The number of murders in Canada rose 12% in 2004, after hitting a 36-year low in 2003. This, however, was due to increases in the population, as the rate of 1.9 homicides for every 100,000 population was 5% lower than it was 10 years earlier. In 2006, the number of homicides decreased, with a total of 606 murders reported across the country. Numbers have remained relatively stable since then, at 1.8 homicides per 100,000. In 2015, police reported 604 homicide victims, 83 more than the previous year and the highest number of homicides reported since 2011 (Statistics Canada, 2015).

The highest homicide rates are traditionally reported in the Northern Territories and western Canada, whereas the lowest rates were reported in Atlantic Canada. Nunavut, a region in Canada with a very sparse population, has a staggering murder rate of 18.64 per 100,000, whereas the Yukon and the Northwest Territories have rates of 5.94 and 4.60 per 100,000, respectively. Provincially, Manitoba reported the highest rate in 2009 (4.66 per 100,000), followed by Saskatchewan (3.49 per 100,000). Among the nine largest cities, Winnipeg has the highest homicide rate, followed by Edmonton and Vancouver. The cities of Quebec and Ottawa reported the lowest rates (Statistics Canada, 2011).

Legislative Framework

All legal codes classify murder as a major crime. Where the element of intent exists and there are no extenuating circumstances, the penalty may be death or life imprisonment.

Penalties for Homicide

Homicide offenders, in comparison to other forms of violent crime, serve longer prison terms. One study by the Bureau of Justice Statistics (1998) on prison sentencing in 1994 showed the average sentencing for homicide offenders in the United States was 266.4 months (slightly over 22 years) compared to 123 months for rape, 88.8 months for robbery, and 47.8 months for assault. After the enactment of the Violent Offenders Incarceration and Truth-in Sentencing Act of 1994, the average length of sentencing given to and average prison time served by homicide offenders further increased in almost all states (Bureau of Justice Statistics, 1995; Illinois Department of Corrections, 2002; Washington Institute for Public Policy, 2004). In Iowa, for example, between 1996 and 2003—after the enactment of new state statutes based on the Violent Offenders Incarceration and Truth-in Sentencing Act—the average length of stay for second-degree homicide offenders increased from 190 months to 510 months

(168%); for attempted homicide from 85 months to 255 months (200%); and homicide by vehicle Class B from 85 months to 255 months (200%) (Iowa Legislative Services Agency, 2003). Between 1986 and 2003, the average length of stay in prison by homicide offenders in the state of Washington increased by about 116% (Washington Institute for Public Policy, 2004). These trends of growth in sentencing and time served by homicide offenders in recent years have significantly impacted not just state correctional budgets and populations but also issues related to their reentry and reintegration to society. Currently, for example, 31 states have capital punishment as a penalty for murder under certain circumstances (which is down from 36, due to state-by-state legislative determination based on violation of state constitutions or as cruel and unusual punishment). In general, these circumstances include first-degree murder, aggravated murder, murder involving sexual assault or kidnapping, or murder involving drug trafficking. The Bureau of Justice Statistics (2017) reported that at year-end 2014, 34 states held 2,943 inmates on death row (41 fewer than year-end 2013), and at year-end 2015, 33 states held 2,881 under the sentence of death. In 2014, seven states executed 25 inmates, and in 2015, six states executed 28 inmates (61 fewer than in 2014).

Recidivism

One of the significant challenges for prison reentry is the high rate of recidivism and reincarceration. In 2004, one study noted that of the more than 650,000 released prisoners from federal and state prisons every year, about 67% (435,500) were rearrested and 50% (325,000) were reincarcerated within 3 years (National Governors Association Center for Best Practices [NGA], 2004). One of the major studies done on recidivism by the Bureau of Justice Statistics (2002) tracked 272,111 prisoners for 3 years after their release from prisons in 15 states in 1994. The rate of recidivism among homicide offenders was about 40.7%. Of 19,268 homicide offenders released, 3,051 committed homicides again within 3 years. The study also found the released homicide offenders accounted for about 7.7% of other crimes committed between 1994 and 1997. The homicide offenders committed 10% of other crimes within a year after their release. More recently, a study by the recidivism rate found that inmates released from state prisons had a 5-year recidivism rate of 76.6% and those from federal prisons, 44.7%.

Consequently, these statistics raise several questions: Is homicide typology a good predictor of assessing the risk of repeat offending by homicide offenders? Is there a configuration of offender characteristics that can predict whether a particular homicide offender will reoffend? In other words, is there a homicide typology that can make reasonably valid predictions about the nature of reoffending by homicide offenders? Homicide offenders are released to communities in large numbers. Research is ongoing about how these offenders fare after release. Clearly, it is imperative to examine recidivism patterns among released homicide offenders to assess to what extent predictors for recidivism are similar to those for other violent offenders, and to study whether the degree of recidivism differs by type of homicide (Liem, Zahn, & Tichavsky, 2014).

Civil Litigation

Civil litigation is one option open to families affected by homicide. Two areas of law can be used: denial of equal protection and failure to act. In denial of equal protection, liability can occur when an agency or organization fails to respond to a crisis. Cases involving 911 calls for victims of spousal abuse have attempted to force police departments to arrest the perpetrators of family violence. In some cases, local agencies have been held responsible in civil suits for failing to act. These situations can include lack of proper training, lack of proper supervision, or lack of protection on the part of law enforcement.

Classification of Homicides

The UCR, prepared by the FBI in conjunction with the U.S. Department of Justice, presents statistics for crimes committed in the United States within a given year. According to the UCR, percentages for all categories of murder except the unknown motives category have decreased. The number of murders classified in the unknown category, however, has risen dramatically. In 2003, of 14,054 murders, 31% were categorized in the unknown category (FBI, 2005). However, in 2011, of the 12,664 murders, 38% were categorized as unknown circumstance (FBI, 2011). This trend is particularly noteworthy in that it suggests both the heterogeneity of motives that give rise to murder and the clear inadequacy of a system that partitions murder essentially into three categories: felony, noncriminal, and miscellaneous. The miscellaneous and unknown motives categories represent wastebasket classifications. A classification system that fails to capture 40% to 50% of the cases (other and unknown) clearly is suboptimal in its ability to explain the universe of behavior. The FBI Academy's Behavioral Science Unit at Quantico, Virginia, began contributing to the literature on the classification of homicide with the Hazelwood and Douglas (1980) publication on typing lust murderers, followed by the classifying of homicides by number of victims, type, and style (Douglas, Burgess, Burgess, & Ressler, 2013).

Single Homicide

A single homicide, as illustrated by the Cosby murder described next, is defined as one victim and one homicidal event. Mikhail Markhasev murdered Ennis Cosby, age 27 and only son of entertainer Bill Cosby, on January 16, 1997, in Los Angeles, California. Cosby had pulled his Mercedes to the side of Interstate 45 to change a flat tire when he was confronted by Markhasev. According to prosecutors, Markhasev demanded money from Cosby and then shot him in the head and fled the scene. Markhasev was convicted after a jury trial and sentenced to life in prison without the possibility of parole. The main evidence used to convict him was that his DNA was found in a cap wrapped around the murder weapon and the testimony of a man to whom he had sent incriminating letters and told of the location of the murder weapon. Markhasev confessed his guilt in 2001 in a letter to the court stating he wished to discontinue his appeals, also stating in the letter that he "wanted to do the right thing. . . . More than anything, [he] wanted to apologize to the victim's family" (Robinson, 2004, p. 1). Markhasev is serving his sentence in a California prison. Ennis Cosby's family and the larger community felt the tragedy of his death due to his father's high-profile reputation as a television star and entertainer.

Double Homicide

A double homicide is defined as two victims who are killed at one time in one location. The January 27, 2001 murder of Dartmouth College Professors Half and Suzanne Zantop by teenage classmates James Parker and Robert Tulloch is an example of a double homicide. The two teenagers posed as students taking a survey as the lure to gain entrance into a home where the motive was robbery. Investigators who traced the knives to Parker, who bought them online, solved this case. They also were identified by fingerprints and boot prints. The pair were located hitchhiking west in Massachusetts and taken into custody (Weber, 2002). Parker testified against Tulloch and pled to second-degree murder. He is eligible for parole in 2026 at age 41. Tulloch is serving a life sentence without parole.

Another example of a double homicide, the bodies of 27-year-old Rachel Entwistle and 9-month-old Lillian were found on January 22, 2006, in the master bedroom of the family's rented Massachusetts home, where the Entwistles had been living for only 10 days. Autopsy results showed that Rachel died of a gunshot wound to the head and the baby died of a gunshot wound to the stomach. Police located the husband and father, British-born Neil Entwistle, at his parents' home in England, where he had fled after claiming to have discovered the bodies. Entwistle told the police he was so distraught upon seeing the corpses of his wife and daughter that he decided to kill himself. However, because he was unable to bring himself to end his life, he decided to fly home to England to see his parents. The defense theory was that Rachel was depressed, killed her baby, and then shot herself in a murder-suicide act (Leonard, 2008).

Entwistle's DNA was found on the handle of the .22 handgun owned by his father-in-law, which he told authorities he had never touched. Additionally, DNA matching that of his wife Rachel was found on the gun's muzzle. A search of Entwistle's computer also revealed that days before the murders Entwistle viewed a website that described "how to kill people" and searched for escort services. Entwistle had been unemployed since September 2005 and was essentially penniless at the time of the killings. Authorities suspected a financial motivation for the killings (Leonard, 2008).

After deliberating for nine hours over two days, on June 25, 2008, the jury found Entwistle guilty to the charge of first-degree murder. He was also found guilty of the illegal possession of a firearm and ammunition. He was sentenced to life in prison without the possibility of parole on June 26, 2008, the mandatory sentence for someone convicted of first-degree murder in the state of Massachusetts. Entwistle's appeal for a new trial was heard in court in April 2012 (Ellement, 2012).

Triple Homicide

A triple homicide is defined as three victims killed at one time in one location. The triple homicide of young college students illustrates the targeting of victims and a hate crime. On August 5, 2007, four young adults in Newark, New Jersey, were shot in the head at close range in a school parking lot, killing all but one (Schweber & Santos, 2007). One victim was shot in the schoolyard where the four were sitting, and three victims were taken to a secluded area and shot. The shootings happened just a few weeks before these four young college students were to start their fall semester at Delaware State University in Dover, Delaware. The victims were friends from Newark who had gone to the schoolyard to hang out and listen to music; some of the victims' belongings had been stolen. Newark homicide detectives apprehended four males between the ages of 15 and 28 in the Newark area, and two males were apprehended on August 19, 2007, in Oxen Hill, Maryland, and the Woodbridge section of northern Virginia. The detectives had received a tip that the perpetrators were heading to Mexico and then to El Salvador, the birthplace of the violent gang MS-13. The suspects were believed to be members of a Central American gang, which has a strong presence in Washington, DC; Prince George's County, Maryland; and Newark, New Jersey. The motives for the shootings have been heavily debated between robbery and a gay hate crime. The victims were believed to have planned to participate in a Black Gay Parade the following day. An adult suspect, Jose Carranza, 28, and a 15-year-old juvenile were apprehended in August 2007 (Scroope, 2007).

Mass Murder

Any single-event, single-location homicide involving four or more victims is classified as *mass murder*. The two subcategories of mass murder are (1) classic mass murder and (2) family mass murder. **Classic mass murder** involves one person operating in one location at one period of time, which could be minutes or hours or even days. The prototype of a classic mass murder is a mentally disordered individual whose problems have increased to the point that he acts out against groups of people who are unrelated to him or his problems, unleashing his hostility through shootings and stabbings. One classic mass murderer was Charles Whitman, who in 1966 armed himself with boxes of ammunition, weapons, ropes, a radio, and food; barricaded himself in a tower at the University of Texas at Austin; and opened fire for 90 minutes. He had committed a double homicide the evening before when he shot and killed his mother and wife. He left a suicide note in which he described himself as appearing as an average intelligent person. He then wrote of his recurring disturbing thoughts that seemed to be taking over his concentration and required significant mental energy to control (Douglas & Olshaker, 1999).

The second type of mass murder is family mass murder. If four or more family members are killed and the perpetrator takes his or her own life, it is classified as a mass murder-suicide. Without the suicide and with four or more victims, the murder is classified as family mass murder. An example is John List, an insurance salesman who killed his mother, wife, and their three children in 1972. Along with the bodies, List left a note to his pastor wherein he wrote that there was too much evil in the world and that he had ended the lives of his family to save their souls. List had difficulty holding a job and was taking money from his mother's account to pay the mortgage. List disappeared after the crime, and his car was found at an airport parking lot. He was located 17 years later in Virginia following a television program describing the murders and posting an age-progressed picture of how he might look in 1989. A neighbor recognized him from the horn-rimmed glasses he was wearing in the picture. He died at age 82 from complications of pneumonia (Stout, 2008).

Spree Murder

A **spree murder** is defined as a single event with two or more locations and no emotional cooling-off period between murders. The single event in a spree murder can be of short or long duration. On September 6, 1949, spree murderer

Howard Unruh of Camden, New Jersey, took a loaded German Lugar pistol and extra ammunition and randomly fired the handgun while walking through his neighborhood, killing 13 people and wounding 3 in about 20 minutes. Although Unruh's killing took a short length of time, it was not classified as a mass murder because he moved to different locations (Douglas et al., 2013). Unruh was diagnosed with paranoid schizophrenia and never stood trial. He was confined for 60 years to the high-security prison for the criminally insane in New Jersey and died at age 88 (Goldstein, 2009).

Andrew Phillip Cunanan was an American spree killer who murdered five people, including fashion designer Gianni Versace, in a cross-country journey during a three-month period in 1997, ending with Cunanan's suicide at the age of 27.

Serial Murder

Serial murder was initially defined as three or more separate events in three or more separate locations with an emotional cooling-off period between homicides. At a 2005 FBI conference on serial murder (Morton & Hilts, 2005), discussion focused on the number of events needed for classification as serial murder. There was considerable support for reducing the number to two or more events to qualify as serial in nature. The serial murder is hypothesized to be premeditated, involving offense-related fantasy and detailed planning. When the time is right and the serial murderer has cooled off from the last homicide, he selects the next victim and proceeds with his plan. The cooling-off period can last for days, weeks, or months and is the key feature that distinguishes the serial killer from other multiple killers. Ted Bundy is an example of a serial murderer. Bundy killed 30 or more times over a period of many years in at least five different states.

Other differences are hypothesized to distinguish mass, spree, and serial murderers. In addition to the number of events and locations and the presence or absence of a cooling-off period, the classic mass murderer and spree murderer are not concerned with who their victims are; they will kill anyone they come into contact with. In contrast, serial murderers usually select a type of victim. Serial murderers think they will never be caught, and sometimes they are not. Serial murderers carefully monitor their behavior to avoid detection, whereas spree murderers, who often have been identified and are being closely pursued by law enforcement, are usually unable to control the course of events. Serial killers, by contrast, plan and choose their victims and locations, and sometimes stop the act of murder if the situation does not meet their requirements. With a sexually motivated murderer, the offense may be classified as any of the aforementioned types.

FIGURE 13-3 Robert Pickton was charged with the first-degree murders of 27 women.

© Getty Images News/Getty Images/Staff.

Canadian serial killers include the child killer, Clifford Olson, who murdered a total of 11 children. He pleaded guilty at his trial in 1982, was sentenced to life in prison, and died of cancer in 2011 at age 71 (Canadian Press Files, 2011). Paul Bernardo and his wife Karla Homolka killed three teenage girls, including Homolka's sister. Bernardo was sentenced to life for the three murders and Homolka pled guilty to manslaughter, was sentenced to 12 years in prison, and was released on parole in July 2005 (Serial Killer Profiles, 2009). Pig farmer Robert Pickton (**FIGURE 13-3**) was charged with the first-degree murders of 27 women. Pickton is alleged to have killed and dismembered the bodies of his victims on his farm in Port Coquitlam, British Columbia. He was convicted of second-degree murder in the deaths of six women in 2007 and sentenced to life imprisonment. The remaining 21 first-degree murder charges were stayed by Crown prosecutors, noting that there could be no further sentence imposed (Cameron, 2011).

Homicide-Suicide

The incident of a homicide followed by suicide is generally defined as a two-stage sequential act in which a person kills one or more individuals and then commits suicide shortly thereafter. Homicide-suicide incidents can have long-term traumatic effects on those closely associated with the incident and frequently have a profound psychological impact on communities. In the following case, the impact extended to the wrestling community. On June 25, 2007, professional wrestler Chris Benoit; his wife, Nancy; and their 7-year-old son, Daniel, were found dead in their Fayetteville, Georgia, home at around 2:30 p.m. Police entered Benoit's home on a "welfare check" after several missed shows (including the "Vengeance" pay-per-view event) and found the three bodies. The Fayette County, Georgia, Sheriff's Department closed their investigation on February 12, 2008, having reached the conclusion that Benoit, over a three-day period, murdered his wife and son and then committed suicide (ABC News, 2007).

Homicide-suicide cases have been difficult to study for several reasons: (1) until recently there has been no centralized database for analysis; (2) because there is no medicolegal distinction of homicide-suicide, cases typically do not result in a criminal charge or trial to provide in-depth analysis of the perpetrator; (3) researchers have had to rely on newspaper accounts of cases, and thus cannot report on prevalence or incidence; (4) the research community arrives separately at suicide from a clinical orientation or homicide from a forensic orientation rather than engaging the combination of lethal behaviors; and (5) with the death of the perpetrator, classifying a case based on assumed psychopathology or motive is particularly prone to speculation. As a result, there is a missing theoretical foundation to understand motivation in specific subcategories of homicide-suicide that, in turn, can direct prevention strategies.

For example, the psychoanalytical literature has a long history of proposing a link between homicidal and suicidal tendencies, characterized by Freud's notion of the death instinct. This notion was further elaborated on by Menninger (1938), who posited that suicide involved the wish to kill, to be killed, and to die. However, there is minimal evidence to support or refute this link.

Some studies have proposed typologies for categorizing these incidents based on the victim–perpetrator relationships and generally include the following, by order of commonality: intimate partner–related homicide-suicide, familicide (killing of all family members in a household) or filicide (killing of children), and extrafamilial homicide-suicide (killing of nonfamily members). Some incidents are also of mixed type, where there are familial and extrafamilial victims involved. Other studies have evaluated homicide-suicide incidents within selected populations (e.g., among the elderly), in individual states, and across multiple cities and other countries. Few population-based studies on homicide-suicide incidents from multiple states are available in the literature.

The Centers for Disease Control and Prevention (CDC) established a national surveillance system, the National Violent Death Reporting System, that collects data from selected states on all homicides, suicides, injuries of unknown intent, and firearm accidents (TABLE 13-1). Information is gathered from death certificates with death investigation reports filed by law enforcement

TABLE 13-1 Surveillance Data for Violent Deaths (CDC)

Sources and Causes	Data
Sources of data	Death certificates
	Coroner/medical examiner reports
	Toxicology results
	Law enforcement reports
	Hospital records/documentation
	Other reports related to each death
Causes of violent death in 2014	Homicide: Number of deaths: 15,872 (5.0 deaths per 100,000 population)
	Firearm homicide: Number of deaths: 11,008 (3.0 deaths per 100,000 population)
	Suicide: Number of deaths: 42,826 (13.4 deaths per 100,000 population); 10th most common cause of death
	Gang-related homicide: 15,500 homicides per 100,000 population

Data from: Centers for Disease Control. (CDC). 2007. The effectiveness of universal school-based programs for the prevention of violent and aggressive behavior: A report on recommendations of the Task Force on Community Preventive Services. MMWR 2007; 56 (No. RR-7). Center for Disease Control. (CDC). 2002. Atlanta, Georgia.

and coroner or medical examiner offices. Although the Violence Policy Center (2006) reported that U.S. statistics on homicide followed by suicide represents an estimated 5% to 6% of homicides and 2% of suicides, this dual behavior remains a very serious form of interpersonal violence that occurs in families, the workplace, schools, and community settings. Homicide-suicide accounts for 1,000 to 1,500 deaths annually, or 20 to 30 violent deaths weekly (Violence Policy Center, 2006). It can result in dyadic death or multiple victims, as in the 32 deaths at Virginia Tech in 2007.

The study of homicide-suicides has resulted in mixed advances. On the positive side, both workplace homicide and school shootings as phenomena have inspired successful public health intervention and threat assessment. Recent tragedies around the country have focused attention on workplace violence in the United States. The Census of Fatal Occupational Injuries (CFOI) conducted by the Bureau of Labor Statistics (2013) provides an annual count of fatal work injuries in the United States, including homicides. From 2006 to 2010, an average of 551 workers per year were killed as a result of work-related homicides. In 2010 (the last year for which final data are available), the CFOI reported a total of 518 workplace homicides, or 11% of all fatal work injuries that occurred that year. A total of 77 of those were multiple-fatality homicide incidents in which two or more workers were killed, including 69 homicides and 8 assailant suicides, all of whom were in work status at the time of the incident. Shootings accounted for 78% of all workplace homicides in 2010 (405 fatal injuries). More than four-fifths (83%) of these workplace homicides from shootings occurred in the private sector, whereas only 17% of such shootings occurred in government workplaces. However, minimal progress has been made in preventing family annihilation crimes.

Violent Death Data

Gang-related violent death is an increasing type of crime. Awareness of gang-related homicides has increased, subsequently resulting in an ever-increasing interface between gang members and the healthcare system. For example, recent focus has been on the highly organized gang known as MS-13 (Mara Salvatrucha), which has between 6,000 and 10,000 members in 46 states, according to FBI statistics (Vincent, 2017). The FBI has designated MS-13 as the most dangerous gang in America. Given that gangs are no longer an urban phenomenon, particularly since they are steadily relocating to suburban and rural areas, it is of importance to have an awareness of the significant number of homicides related to retaliation and revenge (which are two cardinal tenets of gang memberships).

Homicide Victimization Theories

Criminologists develop theories that try to explain why some people murder others. In contrast, victimologists describe theories from the injured parties' perspective. From this perspective, the question becomes why the victim was killed (Doerner & Lab, 2008).

One of the earliest theories was *social interactionalism*, the idea of victim precipitation of the crime. Drawing on von Hentig's insight that in many violent crimes "the victim shapes and molds the criminal" and "assumes the role of a determinant" (von Hentig, 1948, p. 384), Wolfgang (1958) introduced the concept of *victim precipitation* into the study of homicide. Wolfgang reviewed Philadelphia police records between 1948 and 1952 and determined that in 26% of the 150 cases reviewed the victims were the first ones to display a weapon, throw a punch, or use other physical action to escalate the violence to a lethal outcome.

Victim risk, by virtue of the person's lifestyle or routine activities, is another way to explain homicide events. This theory suggests that individuals may be put at risk by their everyday behavior. Hindelang, Gottfredson, and Garofalo (1978) wrote on the lifestyle of persons influencing their risk for victimization. This view is based on the assumption that some types of interactions between people are nonrandom and their results may, in fact, be predictable.

Social learning theories have also been advanced to explain homicide. Modeling theory suggests that people learn by imitating the behavior of others (Bandura, 1973). Differential association theory suggests that learning comes from interpersonal contacts and that individuals will act from input they have from authority figures in their life (Sutherland, 1947). Differential identification argues that personal contact is not necessary for the transmission of behavior but that viewers can model what they see on a media screen.

For nearly 100 years the effects of exposure to violent media (e.g., comic books, movies, television, and video games) have come under scrutiny by the scientific, political, and public communities (Anderson & Bushman, 2002). As early as 1910, comic strips published in newspapers were believed (by some) to be a menace to society, to weaken the use of good manners, to teach lawlessness, to cheapen life, and to increase the chance of mental illness (Starker, 1989). By the 1950s, there was concern that violence in comic books might increase aggression in children (Wertham, 1954). This concern led to the development of a Comics Code Authority, a self-censoring agency for comic book content developed and enforced by the producers of comic books (Savage, 1990). In the 1970s, the U.S. Surgeon General warned of the potential negative effects of violent television (U.S. Surgeon General's Scientific Advisory Committee, 1972). In 2000, a hearing was held on the effects of violent video games on children and adolescents by the U.S. Senate Commerce, Science, and Transportation Committee (U.S. Senate Commerce, Science, and Transportation Committee, 2003). Research has demonstrated that exposure to violent media appears to increase aggressive behavior, thoughts, and feelings in young people. However, in spite of these findings, Anderson and Bushman (2002) noted the impact of media violence continues to be underreported by news services. Bersin (2010) noted that with greater access to firearms and explosives, the scope and efficiency of violent behavior has had serious consequences. In fact, more families have televisions than telephones. Over half of all children have a television set, laptop computer, and smartphone in their bedrooms. This gives a greater opportunity for children to view programs and, more important, to access the Internet and social media without parental supervision. Studies reveal that children watch approximately 28 hours of television a week, more time than they spend in school. The typical American child will view more than 200,000 acts of violence, including more than 16,000 murders before age 18. Television programs display 812 violent acts per hour; children's programming, particularly cartoons, displays up to 20 violent acts hourly. Although no direct correlation has been established, it is suggested that such ongoing and extensive exposure can have an impact on how violence is perceived. For example, the American Psychological Association (APA, 2015) reported, based on four meta-analyses that reviewed more than 150 research reports published before 2009, that violent video game play is linked to increased aggression in players, but insufficient evidence exists about whether the link extends to criminal violence or delinquency. The APA (2015) stated that "The research demonstrates a consistent relation between violent video game use and increases in aggressive behavior, aggressive cognitions, and aggressive affect, and decreases in prosocial behavior, empathy, and sensitivity to aggression." Clearly, ongoing research is required.

Demographic Correlates and Homicide Offending

The demographic variables most consistently examined in homicide research are race, ethnic origin, gender, social class, age, and victim–offender relationship. The FBI's *Supplementary Homicide Reports 1980–2004* reported that Blacks represented 48.38% of homicide offenders in 1980 (FBI, 2005). This high representation of Blacks among homicide offenders has remained consistent. In 2004, Blacks, who constitute about 13% of the U.S. population, represented 49.42% of the homicide offenders (FBI, 2005). Between 1980 and 2004, Blacks committed 50.50% of all total homicides reported to law enforcement, compared to 46.29% by Whites, 1.24% by Asians, and less than 1% by Native Americans (FBI, 2005).

Homicide offending also shows consistent patterns of variation in terms of gender, age, victim–offender relationship, and weapons used in the commission of homicide. Homicide is primarily a male crime. According to the FBI's Supplementary Homicide Reports, 1980–2004, in 1980, males represented 86.10% of all homicide offenders (FBI, 2005). According to Homicide Trends in the United States, 1980–2008 (Bureau of Justice Statistics, 2011), males represented 77% of homicide victims and nearly 90% of offenders. Specifically, the victimization rate for males (11.6 per 100,000) was three times higher than the rate for females (3.4 per 100,000). In terms of age, most homicide offenders are relatively young but are not juveniles. In 2008, children younger than age 18 accounted for only 8.42% of homicides. Adults between 18 and 34 were responsible for 44.44%, and those between 25 and 59 accounted for 42.09% (Bureau of Justice Statistics, 2011). In highly populated cities, acquaintance homicide is consistently the most frequent type of homicide, with stranger homicide a close second, followed by family-related homicides. The Bureau of Justice Statistics (2011) reported that during the years of 2009 and 2010, with regard to acquaintance homicides, 23% involved being killed by a male acquaintance and 6% by a female acquaintance. Further, 40% of homicides were stranger homicides and 42% were family-related homicides. Firearms are the most often used weapon in homicides. This has remained consistent since the 1980s. In 2013, firearms were used in 62.77% of homicide cases. In 2014, firearms were used in 63.62% of cases (CDC, 2017c).

Supplemental homicide report data are collected and compiled by the FBI as part of the UCR Program and provide incident-level details on the location, age, sex, and race of the victims and offenders; the victim–offender relationship; weapons used; and the circumstances of the homicide. A large amount of literature in recent years has empirically substantiated these variations in homicides in terms of race, gender, age, victim–offender relationship, and the use of weapons. Race combined with social class has a strong correlation to homicide. Disadvantaged minority group members were overrepresented as both perpetrators and victims of homicide. In examining Black–White differentials in adult homicide mortality, it was found that Blacks living in the inner city had a higher risk of homicide compared to Whites living in the inner city despite controlling for age and gender. Much of the racial gap seems to be highly correlated with socioeconomic status, especially low marriage rates, low educational attainment, and high unemployment rates. Disadvantaged communities with large amounts of social disorganization, economic and social distress, drug use, and street gang membership have a large number of homicides (FBI, 2005, 2007, 2011).

Homicide Offender Typologies

In addition to their efforts to understand the nature of homicide offender characteristics and the sociodemographic contexts of homicide offending, criminologists and criminal justice researchers have also developed a number of homicide typologies or classificatory schemas to profile and explain the personality and the inner motivations of homicide offenders.

Organized and Disorganized Offenders: Typology of Crime Scene Dynamics

One of the oldest and widely known typologies is between organized and disorganized homicides, originally described by FBI agents Robert Hazelwood and John Douglas (1980). Megargee (1966) properly described it as a syndrome rather than as a typology and delineated two categories—the organized nonsocial category and the disorganized asocial category—that were not intended to embrace all cases of sexual homicides. These categories were derived from the understanding of crime scene behavior. A brief history of the development of the typology and the dichotomy of organized/disorganized follows (Ressler, Burgess, & Douglas, 1992) (TABLE 13-2).

During the 1970s, special agents at the Behavioral Science Unit at the FBI Academy were becoming quite experienced in assessing violent criminality patterns. Police photography departments from around the United States were routinely sending crime scene and investigative reports of unusual murder cases where no suspect had been identified. These crime scenes included grisly murders, mutilations, and bodies thrown into ravines. FBI agents had to communicate back to the police departments, and that required developing a

TABLE 13-2 Profile Characteristics of Organized and Disorganized Offenders

	Organized	Disorganized
Offender characteristic	Average to above-average intelligence Socially competent	Below-average intelligence Socially inadequate
Crime characteristics	Skilled work preferred	Unskilled work
	Sexually competent	Sexually incompetent
	High birth order status	Low birth order status
	Father's work stable	Father's work unstable
	Inconsistent childhood discipline	Harsh discipline as child
	Controlled mood during crime	Anxious mood during crime
	Use of alcohol with crime	Minimal use of alcohol
	Precipitating situational stress	Minimal situational stress
	Lives with partner	Living alone
	Mobility with car in good condition	Lives/works near crime scene
	Follows crime in news media	Minimal interest in news media
	May change jobs or leave town	Significant behavior change (drug/alcohol abuse,
	Planned offense	religiosity, etc.)
	Victim a targeted stranger	Spontaneous offense
	Personalizes victim	Victim/location known
	Controlled conversation	Depersonalizes victim
	Crime scene reflects overall control	Minimal conversation
	Demands submissive victim	Crime scene random and sloppy
	Restraints used	Sudden violence to victim
	Aggressive acts before death	Minimal use of restraints
	Body hidden	Sexual acts after death
	Weapon/evidence absent	Body left in view
	Transports victim or body	Weapon/evidence often present
		Leaves body at death scene

language the detectives could understand. To characterize the types of offenders, a terminology was needed that was not psychiatric in nature, as the typical police officer had no training in psychology. The agents needed to speak to the police in terms they could understand to assist them in their searches for killers, rapists, and other violent criminals. One of the important findings of the Ressler et al. (1992) serial murderer study was the dichotomy of organized and disorganized offenders.

The organized versus disorganized crime scene distinction became the great divide, a fundamental way of separating two very different types of crime scenes and types of personalities who commit multiple murder (Canter, Alison, Alison, & Wentink, 2004). The term *organized* was selected to imply a nonpsychotic person who was organized in his criminal behavior patterns and more often than not fit the criteria for a sexual criminal psychopath. The term *disorganized* applied to a person who had mental problems more likely than not as the basis of his criminality, either as being a borderline psychotic, having a full-blown mental illness, or being a substance abuser (Douglas et al., 2013).

Some crime scenes and some murderers displayed organized as well as disorganized characteristics, and those were called "mixed." For instance, Ed Kemper was a highly organized killer, but his mutilation of bodies after death was more typical of a disorganized one. Ed Kemper at age 14 was incarcerated until age 22 for killing his grandparents after being sent to live with them on their farm after his parents divorced. Upon his release, he murdered seven coeds from the university where his mother worked. He also killed his mother and her friend. He knew she was planning a trip with an elderly friend and, after killing his mother, telephoned the woman to come over to the house. He then strangled her, supposedly to prolong his confrontation with the police (Douglas et al., 2013).

ORGANIZED OFFENDER

The key attribute of the organized offender is his planning of the crime. Logic is displayed at the crime scene. Organized crimes are planned; they are not spontaneous or spur of the moment. The planning derives from the offender's fantasies, which develop (in strength) over time.

John Joubert, an 18-year-old airman in the U.S. Air Force, killed three young males ranging in age from 11 to 14 years. His assaults dated back to age 15 and eventually led to the murder of three young boys. He had assaulted others with a knife, building up to the murder. Bite marks on two of his victims were matched against his teeth marks, providing evidence. John Joubert told of having crimes in mind for years before the opportunity for a slashing murder presented itself and he crossed the line into action. Monte Rissell, too, had violent fantasies for years before a likely victim showed up in the parking lot after the night when, in his mind, his former girlfriend had spurned him.

Most victims of organized offenders are targeted strangers. The offender stakes out or patrols an area, hunting for someone who fits a certain type of victim he has in mind. Age, appearance, occupation, hairstyle, and lifestyle may be elements of choice. David Berkowitz, also known as "Son of Sam," looked for women who were alone or sitting with men in parked cars. Berkowitz was an early serial killer with at least six known victims. His shootings were of opportunity, with some shot while sitting in a car and others while sitting on a porch. He was looking for vulnerable women (Douglas et al., 2013). His crimes were similar to the Washington, DC, beltway sniper shootings by Lee Boyd Malvo and John Allen Mohammed in 2002.

The organized offender often uses a ruse or con to gain control over his victim. The offender often has good verbal skills and a high degree of intelligence, enough to lure a victim into a vulnerable area. Control is of the essence for an organized offender. An organized offender might offer a prostitute a 50-dollar bill, give a hitchhiker a ride, assist a disabled motorist, and tell a child he is taking him to his mother. Because the crime has been planned, the offender has devoted time to figuring out how to obtain a victim and may have perfected the ruse. John Gacy, who was known as the "Killer Clown," murdered 33 young males in the Chicago area in 1970s. He buried 29 of the young men under the floorboards of his homes in Des Plaines, and the remainder were dumped in a nearby river. John Gacy promised money to young men in a homosexual transient district in Chicago if they would come home and perform sex acts with him (Ressler et al., 1992).

During the criminal act, the organized offender adapts his behavior to the exigencies of the situation. After Ed Kemper shot two young women on a college campus, he had the presence of mind to drive past security officers at the gate with two dying women in his car, without alarming the officers. Although admittedly in a state of anxiety, Kemper was not on a hysterical shooting spree. He was able to adapt his behavior to the danger of getting by the checkpoint. Adaptability and mobility are signs of an organized offender. Moreover, organized killers learn as they go on from crime to crime; they get better at what they do, and this shows their degree of organization.

Further evidence of planning that sometimes becomes available to police investigators lies in the organized offender's use of restraints—handcuffs, ropes, and the like. Many murderers take "rape kits" along when they hunt for victims so they do not have any difficulty restraining those whom they wish to assault.

Taking one's own car or a victim's car is part of a conscious attempt to obliterate evidence. Similarly, the organized offender brings his own weapon to the crime and takes it away once he is finished. He knows fingerprints on the weapon or ballistic evidence may connect him to the murder and so he removes it from the crime scene. He may wipe away fingerprints from the entire scene, wash away blood, and do many other things to prevent identification either of the victim or himself. The longer a victim remains unidentified, of course, the greater likelihood the crime will not be traced back to the offender. Usually, the police will find the victim of an organized offender to be nude; without clothing, the victim is less easily identified. It may seem a large step from wiping fingerprints off a knife to decapitating a body and burying the head in a different place from the torso, but all these actions serve to prevent identification of the victim and of the killer.

The organized offender often takes personal items belonging to his victims as trophies or to deny the police the possibility of identifying the victim. Wallets, jewelry, class rings, articles of clothing, photographs—all these, once belonging to victims, have been found in the dwellings of organized killers after their arrests. Usually, these are not items of intrinsic value, such as expensive jewelry, but rather items used to recall the victim. These trophies are taken for the incorporation of the offender's postcrime fantasies and as acknowledgment of his accomplishments. Many take photographs of their crimes to keep alive the excitement of the crime. Although Monte Rissell stole money from the purses of his victims, he also took jewelry from them and kept them in his apartment. He further extended his fantasy involvement with the victims by driving their cars for hours after he had killed them (Ressler et al., 1992).

These crimes are sexual in nature even if there is no completed sexual act with the victim. The truly organized offender generally completes a sexual act with a living victim, taking full advantage of the situation to rape and torture before murdering the victim. The organized offender seeks to increase his erotic interest through keeping the victim alive and performing perverted and destructive acts on the victims near death several times before the murder so he can enjoy their suffering while he rapes them. During rapes, the organized offender demands that the victim display submissive behavior and act fearful and/or passive. If a victim fights back, the organized offender's aggressive behavior usually becomes heightened, sometimes so much that a man who had originally planned on only raping a victim escalates in violence into murder when the victim resists.

The organized offender takes steps to hide the bodies of his victims, or otherwise attempts to conceal their identity, and then keeps track of the investigation. He does so to elongate the time period in which his fantasy seems to be in control of events. In one particularly egregious case of postcrime fantasy, the killer was a hospital ambulance driver. He would kidnap his victims from the parking lot of a restaurant and transport them elsewhere for rape and murder. Unlike many organized offenders, he would leave their bodies in locations that were only partially concealed and then would call the police to report finding a body. As the police rushed to the location of the body, the offender rushed back to the hospital so when the call from the police came to the hospital for an ambulance to be dispatched, he would be in a position to answer that call. He derived special satisfaction from driving the ambulance to the dumpsite, retrieving the body that he himself had killed, and transporting it back to the hospital (Douglas et al., 2013).

Organized offenders generally had a father who had steady employment and who inconsistently disciplined, often leaving the offender with a feeling that he was entitled to everything. The organized offender as a child "acts out" in school, with aggressive and sometimes senseless acts. They externalize their hurt, anger, and fear. Organized offenders feel superior to nearly everyone. Gacy, Bundy, and Kemper all belittled the police who were too stupid, they said, to catch them and the psychiatrists who were too inept to understand them. They overcompensate, often believing themselves to be the smartest and most successful even when they are only moderately so and not particularly distinguished except for the monstrousness of their crimes. After the crime, they often follow the progress (or nonprogress) of the investigation in the news media.

Organized offenders also perform well sexually. Often, they have multiple sex partners. As good con artists with excellent verbal skills, they are often able to convince women (and men, in some cases) to have sex with them. They may be superficially attractive and be good amateur psychologists. Their lives are characterized by having many partners, none of whom stick with them very long. An ex-girlfriend of Bundy said he was an unexciting sex partner. Most if not all organized offenders have tremendous anger toward women, often expressed in the belief that a certain woman is not "woman" enough to "turn him on." The ranks of organized offenders contain many rapists who beat up women, they report, because the women did not stimulate them to orgasm. Organized offenders are angry at their girlfriends, at themselves, at their families, and at society in general. They believe they have been mistreated during their entire lives and that everything is stacked against them. These men strike back in their murders not only at individual victims but at society as a whole.

DISORGANIZED OFFENDER

Whereas the organized offender displays planning and logic in every aspect of his crime, the disorganized offender's actions are devoid of normal logic. Until he is caught and can tell his version of the crimes, chances are no one can follow the twisted reasoning he uses to pick his victims or to commit his crimes. Many times the disorganized offender is too mentally ill to drive a vehicle and control his victims, so he will have walked to the scene or taken public transportation. If the disorganized offender owns a car, it will often appear unkempt and in poor condition; so, too, will his dwelling.

The disorganized offender may pick up a steak knife in the victim's home, plunge it into her chest, and leave it sticking there. Use of such a "weapon of opportunity" (anything within reach or nearby to the criminal encounter) is not uncommon (PoliceOne, 2008). Such a disorganized mind does not care about fingerprints or other evidence. If police find a body rather readily, that is a clue the crime was done by a disorganized offender.

A disorganized crime scene displays the confusion of the killer's mind and his spontaneous and symbolic qualities that are commensurate with his delusions. If the victim is found, as is often the case, he or she will likely have horrendous wounds. This may include signs of overkill which, particularly in disorganized interpersonal violence, often involves interpersonal violence and often presents in patterns of injuries that are usually directed to the throat, chest, and abdomen of the victims (Fox & Levin, 1996, Gerberth, 1998). Sometimes the depersonalization of the victim by the attacker manifests itself in an attempt to obliterate the victim's face or in mutilation after death. Often, the death scene and the crime scene are the same for the disorganized offender; he does not possess the mental clarity of mind to move the body or conceal it.

The disorganized offender does not take symbolic trophies; rather in his confused mental state he takes an obscure item such as a body part, a lock of hair, or an article of clothing as a souvenir whose value cannot be discerned.

These crimes all have a sexual component whether or not there is a completed sexual act with the victim. The disorganized offender often does not complete the sex act or, if he does, completes it only with a dead or entirely inanimate victim. The disorganized killer kills quickly, with a blitz style of attack.

Organized and disorganized killers have very different personalities. The ways in which the personalities develop, and the behavioral consequences of these developmental patterns, are often important to unraveling a crime. The disorganized offender grows up in a household where the father's work is often unstable, where childhood discipline is harsh, and where the family is subject to serious strain brought on by alcohol, mental illness, and the like.

The disorganized offender grows up to internalize hurt, anger, and fear. Although normal people also internalize these emotions to some degree—which is necessary to live together in our society—the disorganized offender goes way beyond the norm in his internalization. He is unable to let off steam and lacks the verbal and physical skills for expressing these emotions in the proper arenas. He cannot be easily counseled because he cannot tell the therapist very much about the emotional turmoil inside him.

Part of the reason for the unexpressed anger within disorganized offenders is that they are not necessarily handsome people. They do not appear attractive, as measured by others, and they have a very poor self-image. They may have physical ailments or disabilities that make them different, and they are not comfortable being different. Rather than accepting their disabilities, they believe themselves to be inadequate, and they act in an inadequate manner, thus reinforcing their hurt, anger, and isolation. Disorganized offenders tend to withdraw from society almost completely, to become loners. Whereas many organized killers tend to be reasonably attractive, outgoing, and gregarious, disorganized killers are incapable of relating to other people at all. Therefore, disorganized offenders most likely do not live with a member of the opposite sex, probably not even with a roommate. If they live with anyone else, chances are it will be with a parent and probably a single parent. No one else will be able to tolerate their strange ways, so disorganized offenders are alone, possibly recluses. Such offenders actively reject the society that has rejected them.

Commensurate with these disorganized offenders' poor self-image is that they are underachievers. In general, they are less intelligent than are organized offenders, but most are not seriously deficient. However, they never live up to their potential either in school or in the workplace. If they work at all, it will be at a menial job, and they are habitually disruptive because of their inability to get along with other people. They also accept that they underachieve. When police questioned one killer, he said he was an unemployed actor. That was wishful thinking. Actually, he was an unemployed stagehand—certainly by his own admission, an underachiever in the theatrical profession.

Other Typologies Based on Crime Scene Dynamics

Under the leadership of Unit Chief John Douglas, FBI agents Robert Ressler and others associated with the FBI's National Center for the Analysis of Violent Crime, which is part of the FBI's Behavioral Science Unit, expanded the twofold typology into a fourfold typology of homicide motivations. These typologies are also primarily based on crime scene indicators. The four types are (1) criminal enterprise homicides (contract murders, gang-motivated murders, insurance/inheritance–related killings, and felony murders); (2) personal cause homicides (domestic violence–related murders, political and religious murders, or mercy killings); (3) sexual homicide (rape and murder, child rape, and child serial killings); and (4) group cause homicides (cult-related homicides and homicides related to extremism and terrorism) (Douglas et al., 2013).

Later, Holmes and Holmes (1998, 2001) classified homicide offenders, particularly serial killers, in terms of four categories: visionary killer, mission killer, hedonistic killer, and power or control killer. Visionary killers kill in the name of God, a devil, or an angel. They believe they are commanded from some supernatural powers to kill. Mission killers are driven by earthly missions to establish a just regime or a group. They are driven by their own constructed rationality of removing the ills of society. Hedonistic killers, on the other hand, kill for thrills, lust, and pleasure. Killing for them is the expression of their pleasure principle. Power killers kill to symbolize their power over and control of the victims. Killing for them is a way of regaining the control of their fractured minds and personalities.

A considerable number of homicide studies have been generated in recent years on the basis of a model developed by C. Gabrielle Salfati of the Center for Investigating Psychology of the University of Liverpool, England. Salfati (2011) and Salfati and Grey (2002) classified homicides into two categories on the basis of 36 crime scene indicators: expressive homicide and instrumental homicide. Expressive homicides are anger induced and linked to rape, arson, or physical attack. Extreme violence, multiple wounds, and the use of multiple weapons, suffocation, and dismemberment of the bodies of the victims characterize expressive crime scenes. Instrumental homicides are linked to violence, theft, robbery, and burglary, where the offenders are motivated by some ulterior aims for money or sex. In instrumental crime scenes, bodies are not hidden and the offenders leave traces of weapons, blood, clothes, semen, and shame and guilt.

Fox and Levin (1996, 2005, 2006) have studied the issue of homicide typology for several decades. They divided homicide into three main categories: serial murders, mass murders, and spree killing. On the basis of these three categories they developed a fivefold motivational typology: power-based homicides, revenge-based homicides, loyalty-based homicides, profit-based homicides, and terror-based homicides.

These typologies, used as tools in much empirical analysis, have considerably improved our knowledge of the nature of homicide offending and homicide offenders (TABLE 13-3). What is missing in most of these typologies, however, is an analysis of how and whether they can predict homicide recidivism. The core concern in most of these typologies is to be able to comprehend the inner mind

TABLE 13-3 Typologies of Homicides

Source	Nature	Homicide Categories	Core Focus
Hazelwood & Douglas (1980)	Twofold typology	Disorganized homicides Organized homicides	Crime scene analysis for determining a suspect
Douglas, Burgess, Burgess, & Ressler (2013)	Fourfold typology	Criminal enterprise Personal cause homicides Sexual homicides Group cause homicides	Material gain Narcissistic gain Sexual intent Ideology of group
Holmes & Holmes (1998, 2001)	Fourfold typology	Visionary killers Mission killers Hedonistic killers Power killers	Motivations of the killer
Salfati (2001)	Twofold typology	Expressive homicides Instrumental homicides	Homicide motivations
Fox & Levin (2005)	Fivefold typology	Power Revenge Loyalty Profit Terror	Homicide intent by ideology of murderer
Roberts, Zgoba, & Shahidullah (2007)	Fourfold typology based on underclass homicides	Altercation/argument–precipitated homicides Felony homicides Intimate partner violence Accident homicides	Perception of loss; dispute Involving sex, love, and emotion Driver under the influence of alcohol or drugs

of the homicide offenders—the complex trajectories of motivations for homicide. The search for homicide motivation is a genuine intellectual challenge in criminology and criminal justice. But the extent to which motivational understanding can help us develop an understanding of the social trajectory where the offenders live and commit the crime and the degree to which the complex nature of homicide motivations are amenable to empirical analysis are open to questions (Canter & Wentink, 2004; Goodwin, 1998, 2002).

Most typologies based on motivational understanding are drawn from the Freudian theory of psychodynamics; that is, they are based on assumptions that most homicide offenders are driven by the unconscious and their psychopathic personalities are the byproducts of childhood trauma and victimization. It seems that in order to use homicide typologies as predictors of recidivism and to develop evidence-based reentry policies, we need a typology that is based on a more structural understanding of the social ecology within which the offenders live and where offenders will return after they are released (Sampson & Wilson, 1995). Roberts, Zgoba, and Shahidullah (2007) suggest that a typology is needed that can provide a more empirically grounded analysis of offender characteristics and their complex relations with homicide offending and recidivism. Their empirical analysis of 336 homicide offenders drawn from New Jersey aims to contribute to this end through the development of a new typology and an analysis of its application and relevance to homicide reentry and recidivism (Roberts et al., 2007).

Underclass Homicide Typology

Criminal profiling and typifying criminal personalities is one of the enduring scientific passions in criminology and criminal justice, a passion that goes back to the Italian criminologist Cesare Lombroso's *Criminal Man*, originally published in 1876. Lombroso's theory of anthropological criminology essentially stated that criminality was inherited and that someone "born criminal" could be identified by physical defects. These defects were identified as a large jaw, a forward projecting jaw, a low sloping forehead, high cheekbones, a flattened or upturned nose, handle-shaped ears, a large chin, a very prominent hawklike nose or fleshy lips, hard shifty eyes, scanty beard or baldness, insensitivity to pain, and long arms. Very few criminologists today lend scientific credence to Lombroso's physiognomic approach to the understanding of criminality, but the search for a typology of criminal offenders, particularly homicide offenders, has remained as a genuine curiosity (Lombroso-Ferrero, 1972).

Homicide research is disproportionately dominated by intellectual passion and scientific curiosity to understand the mind of the serial and brutal killers—the high class of the murderers—who make headlines, create terror, and generate a collective sense of national traumas (Fox & Levin, 2005). Many even believe that the classification of serial killers is a misleading venture (Hickey, 2002). Hundreds of thousands of homicide offenders do not make headlines and do not raise any collective sense of terror and tragedy. They commit the crime, serve the time, and get back to the community only to return to prison after committing new crimes. The understanding of the nature and peculiarities of this "underclass" of homicide offenders is far more significant from the point of view of increased stress and strains on criminal justice. They commit violence and kill people for few dollars and over few stretches of arguments. They come from a fragile social ecology, fragmented families, and failed communities. They come from communities where some even glorify and justify a culture of violence (Sampson, Raudenbush, & Earls 1997; Sampson & Wilson, 1995).

Toward a New Homicide Typology

We have come a long way since Marvin Wolfgang's doctoral dissertation and book was completed at the University of Pennsylvania in the 1950s. Those criminologists, such as the authors, who study offender typologies based on the victim–offender relationship owe a great debt to Wolfgang's classic study. Dr. Wolfgang provided the first sociological and statistical analysis of 588 homicide victims and 621 homicide offenders in the city of Philadelphia between 1948 and 1952 (Wolfgang, 1958). The Roberts et al. (2007) typology of homicide offenders and recidivism builds on the early classification of homicide by Wolfgang. Wolfgang conceptualized the term *victim-precipitated homicide* because most homicide offenders in his study were acquaintances or close relatives of the victims.

The Roberts, Zgoba, and Shahidullah (2007) typology emphasized that although there is no excuse or rational reason for almost all homicides, the interaction and distorted perceptions of many homicide offenders do result in lethal outcomes. Despite the unique characteristics, circumstances, and criminal history of each of the 336 homicide offenders, as a result of longitudinal analysis, four patterns and types of homicide were documented: stranger to stranger/felony homicide, domestic violence, accidental (usually drunk driving related), and altercation/argument precipitated.

Despite a great deal of information on various types of offenders, limited longitudinal data are available on the offending patterns, typologies, and recidivism of different types of homicide perpetrators. Also, knowledge of the underclass and lower socioeconomic class type of homicide offender included in the Roberts et al. (2007) study is limited compared to notorious middle-class serial killers. Roberts et al. (2007) examined a random sample of 336 homicide offenders who were released between the years 1990 and 2000 from the New Jersey Department of Corrections and then followed for a minimum of five years. The offenders were tracked to determine whether incarcerated homicide offenders who had no criminal histories before their homicide conviction recidivated less and to identify specific variables correlated with recidivism. Based on the data, the researchers conceptualized a new fourfold typology of homicide offenders: (1) offenders who committed a homicide that was precipitated by a general altercation or argument, (2) offenders who committed a homicide during the commission of a felony, (3) offenders who committed a domestic violence–related homicide, and (4) offenders who were charged with a degree of homicide after an accident. Statistical analysis was completed to determine which variables correlated with the different types of recidivism and which of the four types of homicide offenders recidivated. In conclusion, none of the 336 homicide offenders committed another murder. However, they did find that those at highest risk of recidivism for new violent or drug crimes were the felony homicide group (slightly over one-third), followed by the altercation-precipitated homicide offenders (27%), which was in sharp contrast to the domestic violence homicide offenders, with less than 10% recidivism due to a new violent or drug offense, and the accidental homicides, with 17% recidivism due to a new violent or drug offense. This exploratory study demonstrates that a homicide typology can be a good indicator of homicide offender recidivism if it is structurally grounded to examine the complex articulation of relations between offender characteristics and their post incarceration behavior (Roberts et al., 2007).

During the past decades, particularly after the formation of the Homicide Research Working Group in 1991, a considerable amount of literature has emerged on issues of understanding the social and demographic characteristics of homicide offenders and their behavioral peculiarities, motivational contexts, crime scene behavior, and typology. See TABLE 13-4.

TABLE 13-4 A Fourfold Typology of Homicides

Homicide Type	Nature and Characteristics	Case-Based Data and Homicide Circumstances
Altercation- or argument-precipitated homicides	Magnified perception of money or property loss; argument over money or property; dispute over relatively small amount of money or possessions; verbal dispute escalates into fight and fight into stabbing and shooting. In this category, homicides are driven by what Salfati (2001) called instrumental expressions.	Argument and fight over $4.00. Victim died from beating. Defendant hit victim in the head with a 2×4 because they were fighting over a bike. Shot victim over argument about dog. Victim was shot after argument over money. Beat victim with a bat and dumped his body in the woods over argument about drugs.
Felony homicides	Perpetrators kill their victims during the commission of a felony crime. Homicides are committed as a means to commit other crimes. Most felony offenders have records of past criminal histories.	Robbery, burglary, grand theft, kidnapping, and other felony crimes induce homicides.

(continues)

TABLE 13-4 A Fourfold Typology of Homicides (*Continued*)

Homicide Type	Nature and Characteristics	Case-Based Data and Homicide Circumstances
Domestic violence or intimate partner violence–induced homicides	Perpetrators are family members, current or ex-spouses, cohabitating intimate partners, or girlfriends or boyfriends. This category of homicides is mostly precipitated not because of intentions to commit a felony crime or achieve any instrumental goals but because of complexities and fragilities in relations involving sex, love, and emotion.	Shot victim. He believed she was unfaithful. Shot wife after she left him. Defendant used car to run over and kill husband who had beaten her badly in the car. Shot and killed victim after years of emotional abuse. Defendant stabbed boyfriend in chest with kitchen knife after argument.
Accident homicides	Perpetrators cause death of victims usually by automobiles.	Driving under the influence of alcohol or drugs. Driving after binge drinking.

Data from Canter, 2004; Fox & Levin, 2005; Hickey, 2002; Holmes & Holmes, 2002; Petherick, 2005; Ressler et al., 1992; Salfati, 2001.

Covictims of Homicide

The term **covictim** is used synonymously with *survivor* and emphasizes the depth of the trauma of a homicide. In the aftermath of the murder it is the covictim who deals with the medical examiner, the criminal or juvenile justice system, and the media. The term *covictim* may be expanded to any group or community that is touched by the murder: a classroom, a dormitory, a school, an office, or a neighborhood. Most of the individuals who make up these communities are wounded emotionally, spiritually, and psychologically by a murder, some more deeply than others. Common problems that confront covictims are outlined in TABLE 13-5.

Covictim Response to Family Member Homicide

Darlene R., age 53, began working at Food King in 1975 and married Bill Bowen, owner of the store, in 1978. She started as an office manager and eventually became a vice president working in all parts of the store, including public relations and customer relations. Darlene and Bill raised three children. In the fall of 1996, Darlene was recuperating from neck surgery. In part to celebrate their wedding anniversary and also to visit their daughter Terry, who was enlisted in the military at Kessler Air Force Base, the Bowens decided to travel to Gulfport over the weekend of October 25, 1996. The couple checked into a local inn on Thursday, October 24, 1996. Their daughter joined them for dinner and then left to return to her quarters to study. Darlene and Bill went

TABLE 13-5 Issues Confronting Covictims

Issue	Examples
Financial considerations	Covictims are faced with unplanned expenses related to funeral, burial, medical treatment, mental health care for family members, and other costs. These unexpected issues contribute to the continuing distress experienced.
Criminal or juvenile justice system	Covictims of homicide will be asked to participate in and understand the complex issues of a cumbersome legal system. They must sit through proceedings without comment or outburst lest they be barred from the courtroom. They may be exposed to graphic crime scene photography, descriptions of victim torture and suffering, and horrific depictions of the last moments of death.
Employment	A covictim's mental and cognitive ability to function, be motivated, and to perform on the job are diminished. They experience emotional mood swings and can be impatient with trivia. Some covictims now suddenly find themselves being required to be the primary provider for the family. Some covictims use work as a way to manage their grief.
Marriages	Marital partners may have difficulty relating, and they may even separate after a death due to homicide. Partners tend to grieve differently. They may blame each other for the loss, may each wish to turn away from the memories that the other partner evokes, and sometimes are unable to help each other because they cannot help themselves.
Children	Parents may ignore or fail to communicate with their children when they are preoccupied with their own issues. The children, in turn, fear adding to their parents' pain and simply withdraw. Children who witness the murder can experience significant emotional trauma, including posttraumatic stress disorder, and need a referral for intervention.
Religious faith	Questions for, anger at, and challenges to religious beliefs and faith can occur. Oversimplistic placations and responses to questions about "God's will" by clergy and church members sometimes create more problems for covictims who are questioning the "why" of the murder. Covictims may experience feelings of guilt for being angry at God. They may perceive the homicide as punishment from God.
Media	Homicide covictims are subjected to the intrusion of an insensitive media. Covictims may learn of the death from news broadcasts. Reporters may override the covictim's need for privacy and reminders of the violence associated with the homicide. News of the event may be repeated on local or national newscasts, resulting in constant reminders of the death. There is often shame and embarrassment as neighbors, peers, coworkers, and the community-at-large learn of the homicide (even if the victim was not involved in high-risk behavior related to the homicide).
Dealing with professionals	Covictims report that professionals (police, court personnel, hospital personnel, funeral directors, clergy, school personnel, psychologists, and psychiatrists) often demonstrate by their comments and actions that they do not fully understand the impact of death by homicide on the remaining family members.
Substance use and abuse	Covictims may seek to self-medicate the traumatic memories with alcohol and/or drugs after the homicide, particularly for depression, anxiety, and sleep disturbances. Misperception that medication will eliminate all connection to the homicide (i.e., "make it go away"). Careful attention to this potential problem is required.

Data from: 1999 *National Victim Assistance Academy*, Chapter 11: Homicide. Authors: Carroll Ann Ellis and Janice Lord, Editors: Grace Coleman, Mario Gaboury, Morna Murray, and Anne Seymour.

sightseeing, ending up visiting a food store and then a casino. They returned later that evening to the inn. After several loud knocks to the door, the door burst open, a man dragged Bill out of the room, and gunshots were heard. A gun was placed to Darlene's head with the threat of death if she didn't stop screaming. She turned around and was hit over the top of her head. More shots were fired and the gunmen left. Darlene screamed for help, called on the room telephone, and eventually the police arrived. Bill was pronounced dead at the scene.

Darlene, a witness to the murder of her husband and a victim of a head and neck assault, suffered traumatic bereavement and symptoms of chronic posttraumatic stress. Immediately after the murder, Darlene's daughter and sister arrived to help. She was taken to the military base and provided room in the officer's quarters. Armed guards were placed outside her room to make her feel safe. Darlene stayed in a state of shock for months. She described how she lost time and had no memory of those months. Her friends became so concerned about her they made arrangements for her to see a doctor. However, she had problems remembering appointments and would just stay at home. She developed severe headaches and neck pain from the assault to her head. She sought help with pain management and medication. She had injections into her neck. Nothing relieved the headaches and the pain. Darlene had continual flashbacks to the murder and recurring nightmares. She needed sleeping medication but then would be exhausted all day. She believed she was losing her mind. She refused to see her friends or be with people she knew. She felt paranoid. She did not want to talk with anyone. She was irritable and cried constantly. She missed her husband. She could not take care of the business and had to sell it. This made her feel like a failure, saying not only had she lost her husband but also the store. She did not feel she could manage without him. She would not answer the telephone because she did not want to talk to people.

Two years after the murder, Darlene believed she was making some progress but had a setback after her deposition for a civil suit. All the traumatic memories came back. She withdrew by sleeping. She believed she lost several years. When reminded of something she said, she said her mind was a blank. She used to be very social, managing public relations for the store. After the murder she could hardly get through a dinner with friends. She hyperventilated in social settings. She became suspicious of people, a new behavior. She could not stay in a hotel. She was chronically fatigued and had little interest in current events. She watched reruns of television shows from the 1970s and 1980s. On the radio she listened to oldies but goodies music. She would read but stopped if there was any violence. She went to a movie with her sister, became ill while watching a scene where someone was shot, vomited, and had to leave the movie. Then she felt guilty. She had mood dysregulation and many crying spells. Her weight fluctuated.

Darlene's experience is not uncommon, as the murder of a family member leaves more than just bodies behind. Murder leaves survivors to struggle and cope with sudden and violent loss of life. The impact of violence on families is a complex issue (Buka, Stichnick, Birdthistle, & Earls, 2001). Parents, spouses, siblings, and children are forever marred by the horrific event. From media coverage and those speaking out against the horrors of murder, the focus is usually on adults, often the parents or spouses of the deceased. In addition, however, children are profoundly affected by the experience of loss yet may think about the victim, feel about the murder, and express their grief in ways that are significantly different from adults.

Death and Notification

Based on case study interviews with families of murder victims (Clements & Burgess, 2002), one of the most distressing issues is the significant number of agencies that swing into action when a homicide is reported. There is a flurry of media coverage and a police investigation ensues at the crime scene. Emotions run high with fear and disbelief, with the focus usually on the deceased and the assailant. Families search desperately for answers and, if a body has not yet been found, live in hope for a happy ending that over time seems more and more remote.

Law enforcement usually has the responsibility of ringing the doorbell and announcing to the family that one of their members has been murdered. News of a homicide is inherently sudden and traumatic in nature and raises many questions. What happened? Who is the murderer? Why did it happen? Death notification requires families to face a horrifying reality and then immediately move to complete a number of activities, including identifying the victim, making funeral arrangements, and notifying friends and family, while at the same time juggle investigative demands with daily life activities, such as caring for children.

The medical examiner's office plays a critical role in the aftermath of a homicide. The medical examiner's office is the final voice of the victim in that he or she makes a final determination of the cause and manner of death from the information gleaned from the forensic autopsy. In the search for answers, however, family members can become obsessed with the details of the death. Some family members insist on seeing pictures of the deceased or crime scene; others want details regarding the physical state of the body from autopsy and other reports. Most want to know if the victim suffered before the actual time of death. One study of parents who lost a child to violent death reported an unending quest for information, for instance, seeking to find out how much water was in the lungs in the case of a drowning murder (Janzen, Cadell, & Westhues, 2004). All these questions seem to be part of the search to find answers and create meaning out of the unthinkable.

Funeral Activities and the Immediate Aftermath

One of the duties that occupies the family's time in the first week after a homicide is attending to the funeral details and arrangements. Such decisions as to whether or not to have an open casket must be made. This may depend on the physical appearance of the body and can be a difficult decision for the family. In the case of a child murder, families often express an interest in being a part of the process of preparing and bathing the body. While planning the funeral, families must also take into account how newspaper reporting has handled the situation in terms of what peoples' fantasies might be of the injuries to the deceased. Murder is newsworthy and as a crime it becomes an act against the community. There is no confidentiality. Murder victims are named and family members are thrown into the public's view. Privacy for grief and stabilization of the family system is lost.

Post-Funeral Life

After the crisis of the death notification and funeral activities, friends and relatives typically must return to the daily routines from which they came before the death. The house, which may have been burgeoning with love, support, and numerous shoulders to cry on, may now seem like an empty shell, filled with haunting reminders and echoes of the person who is now dead. Returning to work, school, or church can be quite ominous. The immediate time period after the death notification and funeral is one of shock and disbelief for the family and the children. Families are numb and confused and generally have a number of physical concerns. Insomnia, sleep pattern disturbance, headaches, and gastrointestinal upsets are common.

Because the return to work or school may occur within a time frame of less than a week after the murder, the reentry into this subcommunity has been described as pivotal in dealing with trauma. It can be distressing in this phase. Family members may feel misunderstood by employers, coworkers, teachers, and peers. There may be little validation of the homicide of the family member. People may not know what to say. Children may be unable to concentrate and have difficulty completing certain school tasks. They can become defiant, verbally aggressive, and, in some cases, physically violent. They may skip class, refuse to do their work, and succeed in being sent home.

Intersections Between Grief and Trauma

The horror of murder and the events that lead to it cannot be overstated with respect to the grieving process of those left behind. Kristen French was kidnapped, tortured, sexually assaulted, and murdered by Paul Bernardo and his wife, Karla Homolka, in what became known as the Ken and Barbie murders due to the good looks of the two serial murderers. Donna French, mother of Kristen, became a well-known figure after the deaths, championing the cause for those who are covictims of murder. Donna French stated at a 2010 conference, "The details of Kristen's captivity wiped me out. I had no idea such evil existed. Each detail [of the trial] seemed to physically assault me. Day after day, I would listen to graphic details and try to avoid looking at explicit pictures." Eight years after the murders she still indicated, "Not a day goes by I'm not filled with thoughts of Kristen. The emptiness is all encompassing," French said (Edwards, 2010, pp. 1–2).

Family members are hit with a sudden death and are aware of the violence and horror experienced by their loved one, but they are also faced with the context in which it occurs, be it during a sexual assault or argument; as an act of arson; or as the result of torture, drunk driving, or a "romantic triangle" (Gross, 2007). Grief and mourning are part of the bereavement process. Grief is a subjective experience and behavior noted after a significant loss, whereas mourning refers to the process of the attenuation of grief as an adaptation to loss (Horowitz, Krupnick, Kaltreider, Leong, & Marmar, 1981). Family members feel sad, depressed, guilty, preoccupied, lonely, and angry and struggle to adjust to their environment, including home, school, and peers. Unlike other losses, however, when family members are faced with murder, their grief is intertwined with trauma. Trauma-related responses include avoiding reminders of the deceased; feeling purposeless and futile about the future; sensing numbness or detachment resulting from the loss; feeling shocked, stunned, or dazed by the loss; denying the reality of the death; feeling that life is empty and unfulfilling without the deceased; and feeling a fragmented sense of trust, security, and control and anger over the death (Regehr & Sussman, 2004), as well as intense and often paralyzing fear and thinking near-consuming thoughts of revenge (Gross, 2007).

Such experiences have led to a new conceptual framework called traumatic grief (Regehr & Sussman, 2004) or traumatic bereavement (Henry-Jenkins, 1996; Pearlman et al., 2014). Several factors differentiate traumatic grief and bereavement from "normal" grief. These factors include the *closeness of the relationship* with the deceased (Gleser, Green, & Winget, 1981), the *violence* associated with the death (Kaltman & Bonanno, 2003; Thompson, Norris, & Ruback, 1998), the sense of *injustice* (Armour, 2002; Rock, 1998), and the *explicit circumstances* surrounding the death (i.e., did the victim suffer) (Regehr & Sussman, 2004). In addition to the cause of death, factors related to perceptions of justice include the age of the deceased, whether the death was expected, and the co-occurrence of other losses or stressors (Gross, 2007). Of note, it has been posited that traumatic grief is a disorder distinct from bereavement-related depression and anxiety; specifically, that the magnitude of traumatic grief can easily develop into a diagnosable depressive disorder or posttraumatic stress disorder, both of which typically manifest in three symptom clusters: traumatic grief, bereavement-related depression, and bereavement-related anxiety (Boelen, van den Bout, & de Keijser, 2004). Subsequently, research results and anecdotal reports suggest that different treatment methods may be required for the various syndromes that develop in people who fail to recover from bereavement (e.g., medication for symptoms of depression and anxiety management). In any case, it has been determined that trauma and grief related to the homicide must be treated simultaneously, versus individually, because they are inherently intertwined.

Guilt and Blame

Murder undermines one's faith in the world as an ordered and secure place, and covictims are faced with *shattered assumptions* about other individuals, members of the community, and society at large. They no longer believe that the world is benevolent, meaningful, and predictable; they can no longer assume that people are invulnerable or that each person is worthy of having a fulfilling life (Janoff-Bulman, 2002). Studies show that untimely natural deaths shake one's confidence in this sense of security. Blaming someone for a tragedy is a less disturbing alternative than facing the fact that life is uncertain. It allows people control by putting the responsibility onto another person. Not being able to explain a situation makes people feel helpless. People look for a target to project their feelings. A main target, of course, is the assailant; however, some people blame themselves. Another target is the criminal justice system. Families want justice and the assailant prosecuted. Families can become angry with the police for being unsuccessful in finding the assailant. And not infrequently the victim may be blamed. This concept holds that no victim is entirely innocent but rather participates to some degree in the crime. Family members may have thoughts of how they could have prevented the death. This phenomenon is known as *survivor's guilt*, and is not uncommon, and it can be extremely disturbing.

Stigma

Homicides are often sensationalized in the media, and thus a violent death can damage the social network of the victim's family. In some cases, people deliberately avoid the victim's family, and consequently are not supportive. Such cases may involve drugs in which the victim "squealed" to federal agents. Thus, the victim is not seen as worthy of grieving, and the family members receive no support. Family members may feel "different" and embarrassed, especially if the death revolved around a crime such as drug trafficking and this was on the news. In other situations, people unwittingly avoid the family. Such cases usually involve horrific situations that overwhelm the social network to the point people do not know what to say to the family.

Fears and Phobias

As with crime victims, fears and phobic reactions are common and develop according to the specific circumstances surrounding the events of the crime. Families become very aware of the potential for a crime occurring and cope by adding protective measures. Adults will obtain permits to carry guns or will put burglar alarms in their homes.

Supporting the Covictim

Several points are helpful to review in providing support to homicide covictims. It is critical to learn the details of the case before speaking to the covictim or family for determining their wishes for talking to the media, assistance with funeral details, and needs for contact and information as the investigation progresses. Staff members need to understand the stages of bereavement and grief as they meet with covictims, have available the names of support groups, and provide court services that are available to family members and witnesses. Exploring application to the Victim of Crime Act fund may alleviate some of the financial stress of the burial and other unanticipated expenses. The Crime Victims Fund was established by the Victims of Crime Act of 1984 (VOCA) and serves as a major funding source for victim services throughout the country (U.S. Department of Justice, 1999). Each year millions of dollars are deposited into this fund. Victims and covictims can receive compensation for the following crime-related expenses: medical costs, mental health counseling, funeral and burial costs, lost wages or loss of support, and crime scene clean-up.

Clinicians need to alert the prosecutor of the covictims' concern for safety and inform covictims of their rights to file civil suits, if applicable. Staff need to be prepared to provide long-term victim assistance in cases involving the death penalty, as well as to provide information on their rights and services available in the post-sentencing phases of their cases, including victim protection, notification of offender status and location, restitution, victim input, and parole release hearings (Tennessee Victim Assistance Academy Participant Manual, 2008).

In death penalty cases, covictims have the right to witness the execution. Depending on the state, covictims may also have a face-to-face meeting with the criminal. For those covictims who have restructured their lives after a homicide, they can be asked whether they wish to participate in victim impact panels, where they can provide firsthand knowledge of victim trauma and the injustices victims endure (Ellis & Lord, 1999).

Grief work is the psychological process that moves the person from being preoccupied with thoughts of the lost person, through painful recollections of the loss experience, to the final step of settling the loss as an integrative experience (Parkes, 1972). Successful mourning allows for the slow withdrawal of the attachment to the deceased and the increased availability of psychic energy to forge new or stronger relationships. In addition, however, those experiencing traumatic grief may need interventions that focus on managing the trauma-related symptoms such as the fears, nightmares, and physiological arousal (Regehr & Sussman, 2004).

Conclusion

In summary, this chapter has examined homicide and how victimology concepts of victim–offender relationship and victim risk information provide important directions for understanding the criminal and his victim. Based on research and crime trends the important conclusions are as follows. First, the United States has a high crime and homicide rate when compared to other industrialized nations. Second, homicide is an interactional crime whereby victim risk and offender risk result in a lethal outcome affecting not only the victim but also the victim's family members and the community. Third, a large number of characteristics of victims, offenders, and situations can increase the risk of a violent outcome. Homicides can be decreased or prevented as people are educated and resources are available to persons before they become victims.

Key Terms

Classic mass murder: One murderer operating in one location at one period of time, which could be minutes or hours or even days.

Covictim: Immediate family, significant others, work associates, and close personal friends who had dealings with the deceased.

Homicide: The intentional and sometimes unintentional or accidental killing of another person.

Murder: A subcategory of homicide, which also includes lawful taking of human life.

Recidivism: The commission of new crimes by the offender.

Serial murder: Two or more separate events in three or more separate locations with an emotional cooling-off period between homicides.

Spree murder: A single event with two or more locations and no emotional cooling-off period between murders.

Traumatic grief, traumatic bereavement: Grief associated with traumatic loss, such as murder.

Uniform Crime Reporting (UCR): The earliest homicide reporting system.

■ Discussion Questions

1. Compare and contrast the type of homicide by motive in the single, double, and triple homicide cases cited in this chapter and the dynamics of homicide-suicide.

2. What homicide theory best describes your perception of victimization by homicide?

3. Which of the various homicide typologies best explains the hotel murder of Bill (last case in the chapter)?

4. What treatment intervention would you recommend for Bill's wife, Darlene?

5. Debate whether (or not) recidivism differs by type of homicide.

6. Discuss the type of homicide, victim risk, crime scene, and motive in the following case:

   A 41-year-old separated woman was found dead in her home, clad in a short nightgown covering to the waist. There was no sign of forced entry. The assault began at the entry (kitchen) door, with the assailant stabbing and slashing at the victim, pursuing her from the kitchen area back to the victim's daughter's bedroom and back to the hallway where she died. The victim put up a fight and suffered numerous defensive wounds along with indications that she did grab the blade of the knife at some point with both hands. Her hands were severely cut. The throat slashing was postmortem. There was no evidence of sexual assault. Victimology noted the victim maintained a low social profile, was employed as a telephone sales representative, and lived in a single-family house on a rural farm with her teenage daughter.

Resources

Compassionate Friends www.compassionatefriends.org

Mothers Against Drunk Driving https://www.madd.org

National Center for Victims of Crime https://victimsofcrime.org/

National Organization for Victim Assistance (NOVA) http://www.trynova.org

Parents of Murdered Children (POMC) www.pomc.com

References

ABC News. (2007). Chris Benoit's murder, suicide: Was brain damage to blame? *Nightline*. Retrieved from http://abcnews.go.com/Nightline/chris-benoits-dad-son -suffered-severe-brain-damage/story?id=11471875

American Psychological Association. (2015, August 13). APA review confirms link between playing violent video games and aggression. Retrieved from http://www .apa.org/news/press/releases/2015/08/violent-video-games.aspx

Anderson, C. A., & Bushman, B. J. (2002). Human aggression. *Annual Review of Psychology, 53*, 27–51.

Armour, M. (2002). Experiences of co-victims of homicide. *Trauma, Abuse, and Violence, 3*, 109–124.

Austen, I. (2010, October 19). Canadian commander videotaped murders. Retrieved from http://www.nytimes.com/2010/10/20/world/americas/20canada.html

Bandura, A. (1973). *Aggression: A social learning analysis.* Englewood Cliffs: NJ: Prentice Hall.

Bersin, E. V. (2010). The impact of media violence on children and adolescents: Opportunities for clinical interventions. *American Academy of Child and Adolescent Psychiatry*. Retrieved from https://www.aacap.org/aacap/Medical_Students_and_Residents /Mentorship_Matters/DevelopMentor/The_Impact_of_Media_Violence_on _Children_and_Adolescents_Opportunities_for_Clinical_Interventions.aspx

Boelen, P.A., van den Bout, J., & de Keijser, J. (2003). Traumatic grief as a disorder distinct from bereavement-related depression and anxiety: A replication study with bereaved mental health care patients. *The American Journal of Psychiatry, 160*, 1339–1341.

British Broadcasting Corporation (BBC). (2010). Full horror of Canada's pilot murders revealed. Retrieved from http://www.bbc.co.uk/news/world-us-canada-11577048

Buka, S. L., Stichnick, T. L., Birdthistle, I., & Earls, F. J. (2001). Youth exposure to violence: Prevalence, risks, and consequences. *American Journal of Orthopsychiatry, 71*(3), 298–310.

Bureau of Justice Statistics. (1995). *Violent offenders in state prison: Sentences and time served*. Washington, DC: Department of Justice, Office of Justice Programs.

Bureau of Justice Statistics. (1998). *Justice in the United States and in England and Wales*. Washington, DC: Department of Justice, Office of Justice Programs.

Bureau of Justice Statistics. (2002). *Recidivism of prisoners released in 1994* (Special Report by P. A. Langan & D. J. Levin). Washington, DC: Department of Justice, Office of Justice Programs.

Bureau of Justice Statistics. (2011). Homicide trends in the United States, 1980–2008. Retrieved from https://www.bjs.gov/content/pub/pdf/htus8008.pdf

Bureau of Justice Statistics. (2017). Capital punishment, 2014–2015: Statistical brief. Washington, DC: Department of Justice, Office of Justice Programs.

Bureau of Labor Statistics. (2010). Workplace shootings fact sheet. Retrieved from http://www.bls.gov/iif/oshwc/cfoi/osar0014.htm

Bureau of Labor Statistics. (2013). Injuries, illnesses, and fatalities: Workplace homicides from shootings. Retrieved from https://www.bls.gov/iif/oshwc/cfoi/osar0016.htm

Burgess, A. W., Regehr, C., & Roberts, A. R. (2013). *Victimology: Theories and applications* (2nd ed.). Sudbury, MA: Jones & Bartlett Learning.

Cameron, S. (2011). *On the farm: Robert William Pickton and the tragic story of Vancouver's missing women*. New York: Random House Digital.

Canadian Press Files. (2011). Serial killer Kenneth Olsen dies. Retrieved from http://www.cbc.ca/news/canada/story/2011/09/30/clifford-olson-death.html

Canter, D. (2004). Offender profiling and investigative psychology. *Journal of Investigative Psychology and Offenders Profiling, 1*, 1–15.

Canter, D. V., Alison, L. J., Alison, E., & Wentink, N. (2004). The organized/disorganized typology of serial murder: Myth or model? *Psychology, Public Policy, and Law, 10*(3), 293–320.

Canter, D. V., & Wentink, N. (2004). An empirical test of Holmes and Holmes' serial murder typology. *Criminal Justice and Behavior, 3*(4), 488–515.

Centers for Disease Control and Prevention. (2017a). *All injuries*. Atlanta, GA. Retrieved from https://www.cdc.gov/nchs/fastats/injury.htm

Centers for Disease Control and Prevention. (2017b). *Assault and homicide*. Atlanta, GA. Retrieved https://www.cdc.gov/nchs/fastats/homicide.htm

Centers for Disease Control and Prevention. (2017c). *National Violent Death Reporting System: Web coding manual*. Atlanta, GA: Author. Retrieved from https://www.cdc.gov/violenceprevention/nvdrs/index.html

Clements, P. T., & Burgess, A. W. (2002). Children's responses to family member homicide. *Family and Community Health, 25*(1), 1–11.

Delisi, M., Kosloski, A., Sween, M., Hachmeister, E., Moore, M., & Drury, A. (2010). Murder by numbers: Monetary costs imposed by a sample of homicide offenders. *Journal of Forensic Psychiatry and Psychology, 31*(4), 501–513.

Doerner, W. G., & Lab, S. P. (2008). *Victimology*. Cincinnati, OH: Anderson Publishing.

Douglas, J., Burgess, A.W., Burgess, A., & Ressler, R. (2013). *Crime classification manual* (3rd ed.). San Francisco: Jossey-Bass.

Douglas, J., & Olshaker, M. (1999). *The anatomy of motive.* New York: Scribner.

Edwards, J. (2010). A victim speaks. Canada: Simcoe.com. Retrieved from http://www .simcoe.com/news/article/835045--a-victim-s-story

Ellement, J. R. (2012, April 6). Neil Entwistle's attorney argues before SJC that searches in murder case were illegal. *Boston Globe*, Metro D, p. 1. Retrieved from http:// www.boston.com/Boston/metrodesk/2012/04/neil-entwistle-attorney-argues -before-sjc-that-searches-murder-case-were-illegal/2cQ8nIqjf94ZmmbysDToAO /index.html

Ellis, C. A., & Lord, J. (1999). Homicide. In G. Coleman, M. Gaboury, M. Murray, and A. Seymour (Eds.), *National victim assistance academy text.* Retrieved from http:// www.crimevictimservices.org/page/victimtypes/81

Federal Bureau of Investigation (FBI). (2005). *Supplementary homicide reports 1980–2004.* Washington, DC: Department of Justice.

Federal Bureau of Investigation (FBI). (2006). *Uniform crime report—Crime in the United States.* Washington, DC: Department of Justice.

Federal Bureau of Investigation (FBI). (2007). *Uniform crime report—Crime in the United States.* Washington, DC: Department of Justice.

Federal Bureau of Investigation (FBI). (2011). *Uniform crime report—Crime in the United States.* Washington, DC: Department of Justice.

Federal Bureau of Investigation (FBI). (2017). *Uniform crime report—Crime in the United States.* Washington, DC: Department of Justice.

Fox, J. A. (2001). Uniform Crime Reports [United States]: Supplementary homicide reports, 1976–1999. ICPSR 3180.

Fox, J. A., & Levin, J. (1996). *Overkill: Mass murder and serial killing exposed.* New York: Bantam Books.

Fox, J. A., & Levin, J. (2005). *Extreme killing: Understanding serial murder.* Thousand Oaks, CA: Sage.

Fox, J. A., & Levin, J. (2006). *Will to kill: Explaining senseless murder.* Boston: Allyn Bacon.

Friscolanti, M. (2014, August 25). Ex-Colonel Russell Williams settles out of court with some vicitms. *MacLean's.* Retrieved from http://www.macleans.ca/news/canada /ex-colonel-russell-williams-settles-out-of-court-with-numerous-victims/

Gerbeth, V. J. (1998). Domestic violence homicides. *Law and Order,* 46(112), 51–54.

Goodwin, M. (1998). Reliability, validity, and utility of extant serial murder classifications. *The Criminologist,* 22, 194–210.

Goodwin, M. (2002). Reliability, validity, and utility of criminal profiling typologies. *Journal of Police and Criminal Psychology,* 17, 1–18.

Gleser, G., Green, B., & Winget, C. (1981). *Prolonged psychosocial effects of disaster: A study of Buffalo Creek.* New York: Academic Press.

Goldstein, R. (2009, October 20). Howard Unruh dies at 88; Killed 13 people in Camden in 1949. *New York Times*, NY Region. Retrieved from http://www.nytimes.com/2009/10/20/nyregion/20unruh.html?_r=1&pagewanted=all

Gross, B. (2007). Life sentence: Co-victims of homicide. *Annals of the American Psychotherapy Association*. Retrieved from http://www.annalsofpsychotherapy.com/articles/fall07.php?topic=article10.

Hazelwood, R., & Douglas, J. (1980). The lust murderer. *FBI Law Enforcement Bulletin*, 49(3), 18–22.

Henry-Jenkins, W. C. (1996). *Just us: Overcoming and understanding homicidal loss and grief*. Omaha, NE: Centering Corporation.

Hickey, E. (2002). *Serial murderers and their victims* (3rd ed.). Belmont, CA: Wadsworth.

Hindelang, M. J., Gottfredson, M. R., & Garofalo, J. (1978). *Victims of personal crime: An empirical foundation for a theory of personal victimization*. Cambridge, MA: Ballinger.

Holmes, R. M., & Holmes, S. T. (1998). *Serial murder* (2nd ed.). Thousand Oaks, CA: Sage.

Holmes, R. M., & Holmes, S. T. (2001). *Mass murder in the United States*. Upper Saddle River, NJ: Prentice Hall.

Holmes, R. M., & Holmes, S. T. (2002). *Profiling violent crime: An investigative tool* (3rd ed.). Thousand Oaks, CA: Sage.

Horowitz, M. J., Krupnick, J., Kaltreider, N., Leong, A., & Marmar, C. (1981). Initial psychological response to parental death. *Archives of General Psychiatry*, *137*, 316–323.

Illinois Department of Corrections. (2002). *Statistical presentation, 2001: Part II: Length of stay*. Springfield, IL: State of Illinois.

Iowa Legislative Services Agency. (2003). *Review of Iowa's 85.0% sentencing laws*. Des Moines, IA: State Capital.

Janoff-Bulman, R. (2002). *Shattered assumptions: Towards a new psychology of trauma*. New York: Free Press.

Janzen, L. M, Cadell, S., & Westhues, A. (2004). Dealing with the sudden death of a child: Advice to professionals from parents. *Omega: Journal of Death and Dying*, *48*(2), 175–190.

Kaltman, S., & Bonanno, G. (2003). Trauma and bereavement: Examining the impact of sudden and violent deaths. *Anxiety Disorders*, *17*, 131–147.

Leonard, T. (2008, June 6). Neil Entwistle lived a double life, U.S. court told. *The Daily Telegraph* (London). Retrieved from http://www.telegraph.co.uk/news/worldnews/northamerica/usa/2085878/Neil-Entwistle-lived-a-double-life,-US-court-told.html

Liem, M., Zahn, M. A., & Tichavsky, L. (2014). Criminal recidivism among homicide offenders. *Journal of Interpersonal Violence*, *29*(14), 2630–2651.

Lombroso-Ferrero, G. (1972, c1911). *Lombroso's criminal man*. Montclaire, NJ: Patterson Smith.

Megargee, E. I. (1966). Estimation of CPI scores from MMPI protocols. *Journal of Clinical Psychology*, 22(4), 456–458.

Menninger, K. (1938). *Man against himself*. New York: Harcourt Brace.

Morton, R. J., & Hilts, M. A. (2005). Serial murder. Retrieved from http://www.fbi.gov/stats-services/publications/serial-murder

National Governors Association Center for Best Practices [NGA], 2004. Retrieved from https://www.nga.org/cms/center

Parkes, C. M. (1972). *Bereavement: Studies of grief in adult life*. New York: International Universities Press.

Pearlman, L. A., Wortman, C. B., Feuer, C. A., Farber, C. H., & Rando, T. A. (2014). *Treating traumatic bereavement: A practitioner's guide*. New York: Guilford Press.

Petherick, W. (2005). *The science of criminal profiling*. New York: Barnes and Noble.

PoliceOne. (2008, February 15). Weapons of opportunity. Retrieved from https://www.policeone.com/Officer-Safety/tips/1661806-Weapons-of-opportunity/

Regehr, C., & Sussman, T. (2004). Intersections between grief and trauma: Towards an empirically based model for treating traumatic grief. *Journal of Brief Treatment and Crisis Intervention*, 4(3), 289–309.

Ressler, R., Burgess, A., & Douglas, J. E. (1992). *Sexual homicide*. New York: Free Press.

Riedel, M., & Hunnicutt, G. (2012). Chapter Homicide victimization. In Criminology. Retrieved from http://www.oxfordbibliographies.com/view/document/obo-9780195396607/obo-9780195396607-0131.xml

Roberts, A. R, Zgoba, K., & Shahidullah, S. M. (2007). Recidivism among found types of homicide offenders: An exploratory analysis of 336 homicide offenders in New Jersey. *Aggression and Violent Behavior*, 12(5), 493–507.

Robinson, B. (2004, February 9). Convicted killer of Ennis Cosby confesses. ABC News. Retrieved from http://abcnews.go.com/US/story?id=94100&page=1

Rock, P. (1998). *After homicide: Practical and political responses to bereavement*. Oxford, UK: Oxford University Press.

Salfati, C. G. (2001). A European perspective on the study of homicide. *Homicide Studies*, 5(4), 286–291.

Salfati, C. G. (2011, November). Behavioral and victim consistency patterns by serial sexual homicide offenders. Paper presented at the First Annual International Multidisciplinary Collaborative Conference on Violence Research & Evidence-Based Practice: Sexual Homicide, Binghamton, NY, University of Binghamton.

Salfati, C. G., & Grey, J. (2002, November). Profiling U.S. homicide. Paper presented at the Annual Meeting of the American Society of Criminology, Chicago, IL.

Sampson, R. J., Raudenbush, S. W., & Earls, F. (1997). Neighborhoods and violent crime: A multilevel study of collective efficacy. *Science*, 277, 918–924.

Sampson, R. J., & Wilson, W. J. (1995). Towards a theory of race, crime, and urban inequality. In J. Hagan & R. D. Peterson (Eds.), *Crime and inequality* (pp. 37–52). Stanford, CA: Stanford University Press.

Savage, W. W. (1990). *Comic books and America, 1945–1954*. Norman, OK: University of Oklahoma Press.

Schweber, N., & Santos, F. (2007, August 6). Shooting of 4 college friends baffles Newark. *New York Times*. Retrieved from http://www.nytimes.com/2007/08/06/nyregion/06newark.html?_r=1

Scroope, H. (2007, August 10). Suspect pleads not guilty in New Jersey students' execution-style deaths. Retrieved from http://www.foxnews.com/story/0,2933,292717,00.html

Serial Killer Profiles. (2009). Famous serial killers. Retrieved from http://www.serialkillers.ca/paul-bernardo-and-karla-homolka/

Starker, S. (1989). *Evil influences: Crusades against the mass media*. New Brunswick, NJ: Transaction Publishers.

Statistics Canada. (2011). Homicide offences, number, and rate, by province and territory. Retrieved from http://www40.statcan.gc.ca/l01/cst01/Legal12b-eng.htm

Statistics Canada (2015). Homicide in Canada, 2015. Retrieved from https://www.statcan.gc.ca/pub/85-002-x/2016001/article/14668-eng.htm

Stout, D. (2008, March 25). John E. List, 82, Killer of 5 family members, dies. *New York Times*. Retrieved from http://www.nytimes.com/2008/03/25/nyregion/25list1.html

Sutherland, E. H. (1947). *Principles of criminology*. Philadelphia: J.B. Lippincott.

Tennessee Victim Assistance Academy Participant Manual. (2008). Retrieved from http://www.utc.edu/Academic/CriminalJustice/documents/Chapter15-Homicide_000.doc

Thompson, M., Norris, F., & Rubach, R. (1998). Comparative distress levels of inner-city family members of homicide victims. *Journal of Traumatic Stress*, 11(2), 223–242.

U.S. Department of Justice, Office of Justice Programs. (1999). Office for the Victims of Crime fact sheet: Victims of Crime Act Victims Fund. Retrieved from https://www.ncjrs.gov/ovc_archives/factsheets/cvfvca.htm

U.S. Senate Commerce, Science, and Transportation Committee. (2003). Hearing on the impact of interactive violence on children on April 14, 2000. Washington, DC: Government Printing Office.

U.S. Surgeon General's Scientific Advisory Committee on Television and Social Behavior. (1972). *Television and growing up: The impact of televised violence*. DHEW Publication No. HSM 72–9086. Washington, DC: U.S. Government Printing Office.

Vincent, I. (2017, June 10). This is the most dangerous gang in the nation. *New York Post*. Retrieved from http://nypost.com/2017/06/10/this-is-the-most-dangerous-gang-in-the-nation/

Vincent, I. (2017). I was an MS-13 gang member –and got out alive. New York Post, Metro, June 10, 2017. Retrieved from http://nypost.com/2017/06/10/i-was-an-ms-13-gang-member-and-got-out-alive/

Violence Policy Center. (2006). American roulette: Murder-suicide in the United States. Retrieved from http://www.vpc.org/studies/amroul2006.pdf

Von Hentig, H. (1948). *The criminal and his victim*. New Haven, CT: Yale University Press.

Warmington, J. (2016, October 11). Russell Williams settles suit with sexual assault victim. *Toronto Sun*. Retrieved from http://www.torontosun.com/2016/10/11/russell-williams-settles-suit-with-sex-assault-victim

Washington Institute for Public Policy. (2004). *Sentencing for adult felons in Washington. Part 1. Historical Trends*. Olympia, WA. Retrieved from http://www.scribd.com/doc/11202120/Sentences-for-Adult-Felons-in-Washington-Options-to-Address-Prison-Overcrowding-Part-II-Recidivism-Analyses

Weber, H. R., & Associated Press. (2002, June 28). "False leads in Dartmouth murder case took investigators elsewhere." *Boston Globe*. Retrieved from http://www.boston.com/news/daily/28/tulloch_leads.htm

Wertham, F. (1954). *Seduction of the innocent*. New York: Holt, Rinehart & Winston.

Wolfgang, M. E. (1958). *Patterns of homicide*. Philadelphia: University of Pennsylvania Press.

CHAPTER 14

Hate Crimes

Sarah B. Gregorian

OBJECTIVES

- To discuss the nature and sources of hate crimes
- To discuss legal controversies related to hate crimes
- To identify types of hate crimes
- To identify typologies of hate crime offenders
- To identify the impact of hate crimes on victims

KEY TERMS

Anti-Semitism

Genocide

Hate crime

Hate speech

Islamophobia

Suicide bomber

White supremacist

Xenophobia

CASE

On January 24, 2011, two young men from Shenandoah, Pennsylvania, Derrick Donchak, age 20, and Brandon Piekarsky, age 19, (see FIGURE 14-1) were sentenced to 9 years in prison for the beating death of 25-year-old Luis Ramirez, an undocumented Mexican immigrant (CNN, 2011) in 2008. During the trial, witnesses provided evidence the accused had repeatedly warned Ramirez to leave their neighborhood (which was 97% White) because they did not like immigrants. It was stated they made racial slurs before and during the attack in which they threw Mr. Ramirez to the ground and repeatedly kicked him in the head. Three Pennsylvania police officers, Chief

Matthew Nestor, Officer William Moyer, and Officer Jason Hayes, were acquitted of charges of conspiracy to obstruct a federal investigation. It was alleged they attempted to cover up the 2008 murder. In summarizing the entire case, U.S. Department of Justice prosecutor Myesha K. Braden stated, "Because of Mr. Ramirez's race, he was somehow worthy of being beaten like a dog. Mr. Ramirez's race is the reason that he died. . . . Every Hispanic member of the community was victimized. What happened to Luis Ramirez was no different than what happened in the 1940s, 1950s, and 1960s" (Bortner, 2010).

The two defendants, Brandon Piekarsky and Derrick Donchak, were convicted in federal court for the traumatic beating and subsequent death of Luis Ramirez. The Defendants were charged with criminal violation of the Fair Housing Act, 42 U.S.C. §3631. This charge penalizes actions taken against an individual on account of his race, color, or national origin, and with the specific intent to intimidate the victim from exercising his right to housing free of discrimination. On appeal, the defendants argued that the District Court erred in instructions to the jury that the government did not need to prove that issues of race and occupancy were the Defendants' only motivations in beating Ramirez.

FIGURE 14-1 Derrick Donchak and Brandon Piekarsky.
© Nick Meyer/Republican-Herald/AP Photos.

Other issues raised by the Defendants on appeal included whether double jeopardy barred their federal trial and whether the evidence was sufficient to support a conviction under §3631. The Court wrote in their opinion that they considered the Defendants other arguments but found them to be without merit. The Appeals Court affirmed the final conviction, judgment, and sentence of the District Court, in all respects. Opinion filed June 18, 2012 (United States Court of Appeals for Third Circuit, 2012).

Introduction

A **hate crime** is criminal conduct motivated in whole or in part by a preformed negative opinion or attitude toward a group based on race, ethnicity, religion, gender, sexual orientation, or disability. The perpetrator views the victim as lacking in full human worth based on those characteristics (California Department of Justice, 2000). Victims of hate crimes include members of racial, ethnic, and religious minority groups and people with disabilities. **Hate speech** is defined as words used as weapons to ambush, terrorize, wound, humiliate, and degrade (Lawrence, Matsuda, Delgado, & Crenshaw, 1993). These messages threaten the individual's freedom and dignity in addition to his or her psychological and emotional state. These messages also continue the oppression and subordination of groups whose history has included discrimination. Lawrence and colleagues (1993) argued that by protecting hate speech society supports those who hate in further subjugating oppressed groups. Conversely, others have suggested that hate legislation and suppression of free speech can equally be used against oppressed and minority groups, restricting their ability to express views that contradict majority opinion (Cowan, Resendez, Marshall, & Quist, 2002). As American jurisprudence leans heavily on free speech as opposed to speech regulation, many challenges exist in attempting to address hate speech. Therefore, "hateful and offensive online speech enjoys the same robust First Amendment protections as any other form of speech" (Henry, 2009, p. 236).

A prime example of the conflict between the right to freedom of expression and the right to be protected from hate is the case of the Jones family in St. Paul, Minnesota. In the spring of 1990, an African American family, the Joneses, moved into a predominantly White neighborhood where within a few months they were subject to slashed tires, racial slurs, and finally a burning cross on the front lawn. A young man known to be a skinhead was convicted on trespassing and vandalism (Cowan et al., 2002). A St. Paul city ordinance allowed for legal prosecution of hate crimes, and thus the offender was charged. However, on appeal in 1992, the St. Paul ordinance was overturned by the Supreme Court of the United States on the basis that the ordinance violated the U.S. Constitution, specifically the right to free speech under the First Amendment. This Supreme Court ruling jeopardized all city and state laws throughout the United States regarding hate crimes. Hate crime debates therefore focus on what is the most fundamental right: the right to be protected from hatred or the right to free expression of one's views.

Scope of the Problem

Estimates of the incidence of hate crimes are variable and are fraught with controversy. In the United States, hate crime data come from two main sources: the Federal Bureau of Investigation (FBI) Uniform Crime Reporting (UCR) Program and the Bureau of Justice Statistics. As a result of Congress passing the Hate Crime Statistics Act of 1992, the FBI has been reporting hate crime numbers conveyed by law enforcement agencies since 1994. According to the FBI's 2015 Hate Crime Statistics, 14,997 law enforcement agencies were participating in the Hate Crime Statistics Program. Of these

Analysis of the 5,462 single-bias incidents reported by law enforcement during 2014 revealed the following biases:

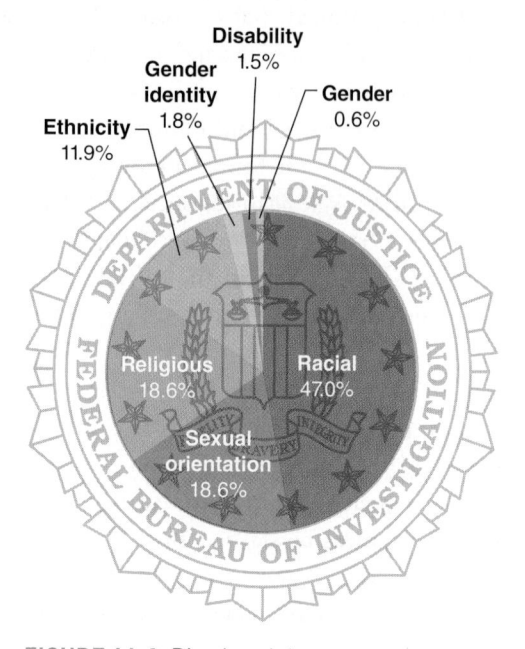

Disability 1.5%

Gender identity 1.8%

Ethnicity 11.9%

Gender 0.6%

Religious 18.6%

Racial 47.0%

Sexual orientation 18.6%

FIGURE 14-2 Bias breakdown.

Data from Federal Bureau of Investigation. Hate crime statistics 2014.

agencies, 1,742 reported 5,818 hate crime incidents involving 6,885 offenses (see **FIGURE 14-2**).

Analysis of the 5,818 single-bias incidents reported in 2015 revealed that:

- 56.9% were motivated by a race/ethnicity/ancestry bias (3,310 incidents).

- 21.4% were prompted by religious bias (1,244 incidents).

- 18.1% resulted from sexual-orientation bias (1,053 incidents).

- 2.0% were motivated by gender-identity bias (114 incidents).

- 1.3% were prompted by disability bias (74 incidents).

- 0.4% were motivated by a gender bias (23 incidents).

Some critics have suggested that these numbers are extremely low for the entire population of the United States and propose that such low numbers confirm that hate crimes are not as serious a problem as the media and society believe (Jacobs & Henry, 1996; Morgan, 2002). Consequently, these critics suggest that hate crime laws should be abandoned. Others suggest that these numbers reflect significant underreporting of hate-related offenses to police. They argue that low numbers represent fear on the part of victims who choose not to self-identify through police reports and bias on the part of law enforcement who are reluctant to classify crimes as motivated by hate. Perhaps confirming that suspicion, the Bureau of Justice Statistics reports considerably higher numbers than those of the FBI. Using interview data and extrapolating to the population base, they estimated an annual average of 191,000 incidents in the United States between 2000 and 2003, affecting 210,000 victims (Shively & Mulford, 2007).

In 2006, the 12 major police forces in Canada reported a total of 892 hate-motivated crimes (Dauvergne, Scrim, & Brennan, 2006). Overall, 61% of the hate crimes were motivated by race or ethnicity, 27% were motivated by religion, and 10% were motivated by sexual orientation. Half of all racially motivated hate crimes were directed toward Black people, and two-thirds of religiously motivated crimes were directed toward Jewish people. Half of all hate crimes involved property, 23% involved assault, and almost 15% involved threats or harassment. One hate crime resulted in murder, and one involved sexual assault. Hate crimes were more likely to involve young people; victims were most likely to be between the ages of 12 and 24, and the perpetrators of hate crimes were most likely to be between the ages of 12 and 17. In most cases (77%), the perpetrator was a stranger to the victim. The offender was identified in approximately one-half of the incidents. Men constituted 90% of the known offenders. Only 10% of the offenders had previously been involved with criminal activity (Dauvergne et al., 2006).

Canada has a diverse and multicultural population and it is expected to increase over the coming decades. As Canada's demographics change, the potential may arise for hate-motivated crimes against individuals or groups (Chongatera, 2013). For example, Canadian police reported 1,362 criminal incidents in 2015 that were motivated by hate. These figures marked an increase of 5% or 67 more incidents than were reported in 2014. The increase in the total number of incidents reflected an increase in police-reported hate crimes motivated by hatred of a religion (+40 incidents) or of a race or ethnicity (+30 incidents) (Statistics Canada, 2017).

A newer venue for hate crimes is the Internet. In March 1995, former Klansman Don Black created the first neo-Nazi website, which featured links, essays, and graphics promoting White supremacy, Nazism, and guerrilla warfare and attesting to Jewish conspiracies and Black inferiority. By March 1998,

163 active sites in North America publicized racial hatred. Of these, 29 were based on Klan beliefs, 27 were founded by skinheads, and 25 were focused on anti-Semitism (Southern Poverty Law Center, 1998). The Southern Poverty Law Center publishes a list of Hate Groups in the United States. Their statistics note 917 such groups between 1999–2016 (SPLC, 2017).

With the explosion of information on the Internet since that time, current estimates of websites that promote hate are not available. The popularity of the Internet for extremists is due in part to the low cost, the ease of global distribution, and the anonymity with which someone can access and contribute to the discourse without ever self-identifying or attending a meeting (Levin, 2002a). These sites can provide tools for extremists; for example, a prominent animal liberation site offers do-it-yourself instructions for creating basic incendiaries from easily acquired materials. They also provide lists of possible victims, for example, a radical antiabortion site lists the names of physicians who perform abortions, complete with their driver's license information, home addresses, and images. Names of those who have been murdered feature slash marks. Hate on the Internet is especially hard to regulate due to the unlimited number of access points, the lack of legal precedence and mechanisms for defining Internet-based activity, and the tremendous flexibility and technology growth of the medium (Levin, 2002a).

Hate Crime Legislation

Although violence on the basis of hate has a long history, its legislative history is very short. As stated earlier, in the United States this was in large part due to the difficulties in prohibiting hate speech and subsequent actions due to the emphasis on freedom of speech in the U.S. Constitution (Morgan, 2002). The first attempts to address hate crimes in the United States occurred from the 1920s to the 1940s when legislators sought to enact statutes to deter the incitement of hatred and the lynching of African Americans. However, although there were a few successes in creating state legislation to address this terrifying issue, most early efforts failed to find a means to prohibit hate-based crime. In the 1950s, seven U.S. states and several large cities adopted group libel statutes that addressed hate speech, and in 1952, the Supreme Court upheld the constitutionality of these statutes (Dixon & Ray, 2007).

During the 1980s and 1990s, most U.S. states, beginning with California in 1978, moved to criminalize actions against persons or property motivated by hate. In 1981, the Anti-Defamation League drafted model legislation that served as a template for similar legislation in other states (McPhail, 2000). By 2013,

Congress and 45 states and the District of Columbia had enacted hate crime penalty–enhancement laws, many based on a model law the Anti-Defamation League wrote in 1981. Most of these states also delineated particular groups as being specific targets of hate crimes. The 2015 *Hate Crime Statistics* report has added seven additional religious anti-bias categories (anti-Buddhist, anti-Eastern Orthodox, anti-Hindu, anti-Jehovah's Witness, anti-Mormon, anti-other Christian, and anti-Sikh), as well as an anti-Arab bias motivation (FBI, 2016).

Highlights from hate crime victimization from 2004–2015 reported by the Bureau of Justice Statistics include the following (Langton, 2017):

- Each year from 2004–2015, U.S. residents experienced an average of 250,000 hate crime victimizations.
- In the same reporting period, there was no statistically significant change in the annual rate of violent hate crime victimization (about 0.7 per 1,000 persons age 12 or older).
- The overwhelming majority (99%) of victims reported offenders' use of hate language as evidence of a hate crime.
- Between 2011–2015, racial bias was the most common motivation for hate crime (48%).
- Over half (54%) of hate crime victimizations were not reported to police during 2011–2015.

The media have played a major role in publicizing hate crimes. The first time the term *hate crime* appeared in the media is believed to be on December 20, 1986, when an incident was reported that stoked racial tensions in New York City and captured national headlines. Three Black men were attacked by a group of White teenagers yelling racial slurs in Howard Beach. The men were driving from Brooklyn to Queens, when their car broke down near Howard Beach. They walked several miles to Howard Beach to ask to use a phone to call for assistance. After being told there was no phone available, the men left the store and they were confronted by a gang of teens. One of the men, Michael Griffith, 23, was chased into traffic on the Belt Parkway and died after being hit by a car. A second man, Cedric Sandiford, was severely beaten, while the third man, Timothy Grimes, outran the assailants and escaped without serious injury (History.com staff, 2009).

State-based legislation has been enhanced by federal legislation, including the Hate Crimes Prevention Act of 2000, the 1990 Hate Crime Statistics Act, and the 1994 Hate Crime Sentencing Act (Jenness, 1999). In the Hate Crime Sentencing Act, enhanced penalties are allowed if a victim or property was selected by the offender because of the actual or perceived race, color, religion, national origin, ethnicity, gender, disability, or sexual orientation.

Despite the aim of these statutes to both symbolically and practically deal with the special harms created by crimes motivated by hate, it is suggested that prosecutions are rare, and when they are attempted they often fail due to practical and legal difficulties (Franklin, 2002). To begin with, initial decisions about whether to charge someone with a hate crime are made by frontline police officers, who are influenced not only by their own beliefs but also by the belief systems within their communities and organizations. Variations between policing divisions in laying charges related to hate crimes are quite striking, particularly when the offenses are committed by youth (Franklin, 2002). When a decision to lay a charge related to hate is made, the next challenge is to prove the motivation behind the crime, and the final decision on the guilt of an offender rests with a judge and/or jury, who bring their own biases to the table.

In Canada, hate crimes are addressed under three sections of the national Criminal Code. Section 318, Advocating Genocide, is defined as supporting or arguing for the killing of members of an identifiable group. Advocating **genocide** is an indictable offense and can result in a prison term of up to five years. Section 319, Public Incitement of Hatred, occurs when a person (1) communicates statements (2) in a public place (3) that incite hatred against an identifiable group (4) in such a way that there will likely be a breach of the people. Conviction can result in a sentence of up to two years. Finally, under Section 320, physical hate propaganda material kept on any property for distribution can be seized (Criminal Code of Canada, 2004). Although originally the "identifiable groups" in these provisions were defined by color, race, religion, and ethnic origin, Bill 59-11, which was passed in 2004, extended the definition to include sexual orientation.

The most famous case related to hate crime legislation in Canada is that of Ernst Zündel, who was jailed several times in Canada for publishing literature that claimed the Holocaust was a hoax and incited hatred against Jews. Zündel immigrated to Canada in 1958 from West Germany. In the 1970s, he established a publishing company, which by the early 1980s had become a major worldwide distributor of Nazi memorabilia, books, and pamphlets denying the Holocaust and books denouncing Zionism. His mailing list in the United States alone included 29,000 addresses, and in 1978 to 1979, the West German government seized over 200 shipments of material bound for distribution there. Zündel was criminally tried and convicted in 1985 and 1988 for hate crimes, but this was overturned on appeal to the Supreme Court of Canada in 1992, on the grounds the conviction violated the right to free speech under the Canadian Charter of

Rights and Freedoms. Having been denied citizenship in Canada, his permanent residency status in Canada expired, and he went to the United States, where he was arrested and then deported back to Canada in 2003 for overstaying a visa. Upon his return to Canada, a national security certificate was issued and deportation to Germany was sought. After two years of court battles and appeals during which Zündel was held in solitary confinement, he was extradited to Germany in 2005, where he faced 14 charges of inciting racial hatred. Finally, in February 2007, he was convicted in a German court and sentenced to five years in prison, the maximum allowed for such an offense under German law (CBC News, 2007). Ernst Zündel was freed from a German prison after serving five years, saying upon his release, "I'm back out after seven years, three weeks, three prisons, and three countries," adding, "It's kind of a sad situation; there's a lot to say. I'll certainly be careful not to offend anyone and their draconian laws" (Frey, 2010).

Zündel wanted to move to the United States from Germany and would normally have been able to obtain a visa, because his wife of 16 years is a U.S. citizen. However, he was classified as inadmissible by the U.S. Department of Homeland Security Administrative Appeals Office because he had been convicted of foreign crimes for which the sentence was five years or more (Volokh, 2017). This case is perhaps the most telling example of the difficulty that various Western legal systems have in dealing with activities that incite racial and other forms of hatred.

In 2004, the Council of Europe, the United States, Canada, South Africa, and Japan entered into the Cybercrime Convention. As of December 2016, 52 countries had ratified the convention, and 4 others had signed the convention but not ratified it. The Cybercrime Convention mandates countries to have unified legislation for international crime prevention to address cross-jurisdictional issues related to cybercrime. The convention is supplemented by a Protocol on Xenophobia and Racism, encompassing xenophobia and racism committed on the Internet. This protocol prohibits:

> any written material, any image, or other representation of ideas or theories, which advocates, promotes, or incites hatred, discrimination or violence, against any individual or group of individuals, based on race, color, descent, or national or ethnic origin, as well as religion if used as pretext for any of these factors.
>
> (Council of Europe, 2006, Ch. 1, A.1)

It also prohibits Internet sites that deny or minimize crimes against humanity, including the Holocaust. The United States, while signing the Cybercrime

Convention, did not sign the protocol on racism due to concerns that it conflicted with the First Amendment. Thus, any hate-related website originating in the United States is safe from recrimination under the treaty (Henry, 2009).

Typology of Hate Crimes

Hate crimes are motivated by extremist views related to the characteristics of a particular individual or group. This chapter highlights hate crimes motivated by discrimination based on race, religion, gender, sexual orientation, and disability. In addition, although all hate crimes may have an underlying political motivation, some are committed specifically for the purposes of effecting political responses.

Race

Although hate crimes based on race can be directed at many different racial groups, both historically in North America and to the present day the majority of racially motivated hate crimes are directed toward individuals who are Black. As Levin (2002b) pointed out, "The text of the Declaration of Independence leaves the impression that the notion of harmful status-based deprivations did not exist at America's founding: 'We hold these truths to be self-evident, that all men are created equal.' Yet status-based violence and deprivations are old as the nation itself" (p. 228). Slavery, and the concomitant violence committed against slaves, would easily fit under current definitions of hate crimes. Nevertheless, courts were clear that slaves were not to be afforded basic rights of safety. In an 1829 North Carolina case in which a slave master shot an escaping female slave, the judge declared the power of the master and the submission of slaves were absolute regardless of the resultant harm (*State v. Mann*, 1829). Decisions of this sort were upheld by the Supreme Court, which in 1857 found that Blacks, due to their inferior nature, were incapable of being citizens of the United States and thus were not subject to the rights of citizenship (*Scott v. Sandford*, 1857). Seven years later, the Civil Rights Act of 1866 extended citizenship and other rights to Blacks, and in 1871, legislation was enacted banning the activities of the Ku Klux Klan.

Despite protective legislation, the 1870s saw a rise in hate crimes against Blacks in America, with lynching one of the major forms of violence where victims were mutilated, burned, or hung in public arenas. By 1915, the Ku Klux Klan reemerged, and by the mid-1920s it had 4.5 million members. Klan members held influential roles in state and national assemblies (Levin, 2002b). Legislation in the late 1920s placed restrictions on membership in these groups, so they largely went underground, reemerging in the 1960s. Thus, hate crimes committed against Blacks in North America have a long tradition, initially sanctioned by law and only very recently condemned by law.

James Byrd, Jr. was a 49-year-old African American man living on disability income in a subsidized apartment in Jasper, Texas. In June 1998, he accepted a ride from three young White men, Shawn Allen Berry, Lawrence Russell Brewer, and John William King. Instead of driving him home, however, they beat him and chained him by his ankles to the back of a pickup truck. At the trial a pathologist testified that Mr. Byrd was alive through much of the dragging, and it appeared that he attempted to keep his head off the ground. However, about one-half of the way through the three-mile drag he hit a culvert and was decapitated. His body was then dumped in a cemetery. It was determined that two of the defendants, King and Brewer, were members of a White supremacist group. King's body was covered in tattoos that depicted, among other things, a Black man hanging from a tree, Nazi symbols, and the words "Aryan Pride." All three defendants were found guilty of capital murder, two were sentenced to death, and the third, Berry, was sentenced to life in prison (CNN, 1999; Reuters, 1999). Lawrence Russell Brewer was executed in Texas on September 21, 2011. King lost an appeal in 2016. He can still appeal to the Fifth Circuit Court in New Orleans, but a judge in Jasper County could set an execution date if the court denies the appeal. In 2004, several years after Byrd's murder, two White teenagers were charged with desecrating his grave (Barnes, 2004).

The horrific death of James Byrd, Jr., is not an isolated incident and merely serves as an example of many tragic crimes committed against people. Racially based crimes often occur in waves, whereby a single incident emotionally incites a community and causes a ripple effect of retaliation and further offending. Police in the United Kingdom, in awareness of this tendency, work to identify critical incidents and critical periods of time and then attempt to engage with the community to ward off further attacks (Dixon & Ray, 2007). Offending against a socially excluded group becomes justified by community prejudice, and victims become dehumanized.

In the 1940s, scholars advanced a theory that hate crimes are associated with economic conditions; that is, aggression toward a particular group stems from frustration associated with economic downturns even when the group has no real responsibility for the economic decline. Early studies in the 1940s identified the correlation between lynching of Blacks in the American South and economic conditions as measured by cotton prices and economic growth between 1882 and 1930. More recent research has challenged these analyses and has suggested that the roots of racially motivated hate crimes are far more complicated than economic conditions alone would explain (Espiritu, 2004; Green, Glaser, & Rich, 1998).

Another analysis of racially motivated hate crimes relates to the conception that they are caused by xenophobia (Perry, 2002). Groups such as the American-Arab Anti-Discrimination Committee and the National Asian Pacific American Legal Consortium have raised concerns about increased violence against members of their communities. These groups believe that the increase in hate crimes has emanated from fears resulting from the 9/11 attack on America.

The USA PATRIOT Act was signed into law by President George W. Bush on October 26, 2001. With its 10-letter abbreviation (USA PATRIOT) expanded, the full title was "Uniting and Strengthening America by Providing Appropriate Tools Required to Intercept and Obstruct Terrorism Act of 2001." The law was intended to help government agencies detect and prevent possible acts of terrorism or sponsorship of terrorist groups.

The USA PATRIOT Act expanded law enforcement to allow for the conduct of searches, phone and Internet surveillance, and access to personal medical, financial, student, and mental health records. It also required foreign-born immigrants from certain countries to register under the National Security Entry/Exit Registration System with U.S. Immigration and Customs Enforcement (Akiyama, 2008).

The USA Freedom Act (Pub.L. 114–23) that was signed into law on June 2, 2015, by President Obama restored in modified form several provisions of the USA PATRIOT Act, which had expired the day before. The USA Freedom Act ends the National Security Agency's (NSA) bulk collection of Americans' telephone records, limits other ways the government collects large amounts of records, and adds new transparency measures to the way the government collects information.

Concerns are that such government policies will also be reflected in public attitudes of Islamophobia, and ultimately in the commission of hate crimes. Islamophobia is defined as an exaggerated fear, hatred, and hostility toward Islam and Muslims that is perpetuated by negative stereotypes resulting in bias, discrimination, and the marginalization and exclusion of Muslims from social, political, and civic life (Ali et al., 2011).

Islamophobia existed before the terrorist attacks of September 11, 2001, but it has increased in frequency and notoriety since then. The Runnymede Trust in the United Kingdom, for example, identified eight components of Islamophobia in a 1997 report, and then produced a follow-up report in 2004 after 9/11 and the initial years of the Afghanistan and Iraq wars.

The second report found the aftermath of the terrorist attacks had made life more difficult for British Muslims (Beutel, 2011). In the United States, the FBI reported that the number of attacks on mosques and other hate crimes against Muslims in 2015 was higher than at any other time except following the 9/11 attack when 481 incidents were reported. In 2015, there were 257 anti-Muslim incidents, up from 154 in 2014—over a two-thirds (67%) increase (FBI, 2015).

Globally, many Muslims report not feeling respected by those in the West. Significant numbers of people in several Western countries share this sentiment as well, saying that the West does not respect Muslim societies. Specifically, 52% of Americans and 48% of Canadians say the West does not respect Muslim societies. Smaller percentages of Italian, French, German, and British respondents agree (Gallup News, 2016).

This sentiment has encouraged psychologists to research this vulnerable population and to document the impact anti-Muslim bias is having on Muslim Americans. The aim is to develop interventions to help ensure Muslim Americans receive the mental health treatment they need with the ultimate goal to reduce societal prejudice of all kinds (Clay, 2017).

Religion

On the night of April 5, 2004, the library of United Talmud Torah, a Jewish elementary school in Montreal, Canada, erupted into flames after a kerosene bomb crashed through the window. Although no one was injured in the nighttime attack, it caused $500,000 in damage and destroyed 10,000 books. A note discovered on the scene indicated the attack was in retaliation for Israel's assassination of Hamas leader Sheikh Ahmed Yassin. The note indicated Jews should be punished for Israeli actions and promised to strike again if Israeli policy did not change. It read, "Here is the consequence of your crimes and your occupation. Here is the riposte of your assassinations. Here is where terrorist Ariel Sharon has led you" (Center for Policing Terrorism, 2007, p. 2). The following year, 19-year-old Sleiman Elmerhebi was sentenced to 40 months in jail for the crime (CBC News, 2005; Peritz, 2005). This attack against a Jewish institution in Montreal was not an isolated occurrence. In 2006, a firebombing occurred at a Jewish boys' school, and in 2007, the Jewish Community Centre was firebombed. A report from B'nai Brith's League for Human Rights identified Montreal as a hotbed of anti-Jewish activity in 2006, identifying 215 separate occurrences, including desecration of synagogues, destruction of property, and assaults. Property crime, particularly vandalism, is the most common type of religiously motivated hate crime and includes burning of religious institutions and painting of swastikas on buildings.

In both Canada and the United States, much of religiously motivated hate crime is directed against people who are Jewish. As indicated earlier, Jewish people are the most common victims of all hate crimes in Canada. According to the FBI (2009), 70.1% of all religiously motivated hate crimes in the United States in 2009 were anti-Semitic in nature, down from 86% in 1996. In 2015, 52.1% were victims of crimes motivated by their offenders' anti-Jewish bias and 21.9% were victims of anti-Islamic (Muslim) bias (FBI, 2015).

A 2005 report by the U.S. Department of State noted, "The increasing frequency and severity of anti-Semitic incidents since the start of the 21st century, particularly in Europe, has compelled the international community to focus on anti-Semitism with renewed vigor" (p. 1). According to this report, the European Union Monitoring Center for Racism and Xenophobia identified France, Germany, the United Kingdom, Belgium, and the Netherlands as the countries with the most significant increases in anti-Semitic incidents. As a result, governments in France, Germany, and Belgium are providing enhanced protection to members of the Jewish community and Jewish properties.

It has been suggested that this type of hate crime is frequently based on normative beliefs about acceptable violence toward a particular group. Amjad and Wood (2009) conducted two studies examining whether normative beliefs about aggression predicted whether youth in Pakistan would join an extremist anti-Semitic organization. In this study, university students completed a questionnaire eliciting their beliefs and then were approached by a confederate and asked to join a specific organization. Beliefs about normative aggression toward Jews were strongly associated with willingness to join the organization.

Despite the preponderance of religious bias hate crimes being anti-Semitic, other groups are also targeted. During 2001, after the attack on the World Trade Center, the FBI (2015) reported a 17-fold increase in anti-Muslim hate crimes, and in 2004, 13% of religiously motivated hate crimes were against Islamic individuals; however, by 2009, this was reduced to 8.4%. Other discriminatory activities directed toward Muslims post-9/11 included "airport screenings, search and surveillance powers without sufficient review, guilt by association, investigations and deportations, and special alien registration" (Abu-Raz & Suarez, 2009, p. 50). FBI data indicate that hate crimes against Muslims rose between 2014 and 2015 (FBI, 2015). Jewish Americans continue to be the most targeted for hate crimes.

Disability

The pervasive stigma that people apply to both mental and physical illness is expressed in many forms of discriminatory behaviors against those with disabilities, including placing disabled persons at increased risk of physical and sexual abuse (American Psychological Association, 1998). Research confirms that people with disabilities experience heightened risk of sexual, physical, and emotional abuse (McMahon, West, Lewis, Armstrong, & Conway, 2004). Where disability and gender discrimination intersect, the incidence of violence is alarming. For example, the risk of physical and sexual assault is 4 to 10 times higher for adults with developmental disabilities than for other adults (Sobsey, 1994). Sobsey found that 84% of disabled people who were victims of sexual violence were female, and 93% of offenders were male. Further, studies repeatedly demonstrate high rates of victimization among people suffering from mental illness (Clement, Brohan, Sayce, Pool, & Thornicroft, 2011). Nevertheless, tremendous barriers exist to reporting these crimes and to prosecuting them, including myths in the criminal justice system that women with intellectual disabilities who are victims of sexual violence will not be credible witnesses due to their intellectual or speech limitations and that women with disabilities are promiscuous (Keilty & Connelly, 2001).

The fact that people with disabilities experience discrimination was acknowledged by the U.S. federal government in the Americans with Disabilities Act of 1990. This act proclaimed "that disabled persons have been subjected to a history of purposeful unequal treatment" (42 USC 12101, SEC. 2(7)). It is perhaps the seemingly incomprehensible act of attacking someone who is rendered vulnerable by disability that disability was not added to the Hate Crime Statistics Act until 1994. One of the issues in defining crimes against those with a disability as hate crimes is the individualized nature of these crimes. In hate crimes against those with disabilities, there are no crosses burning on lawns and no swastikas painted on walls; rather, individual vulnerability is exploited.

Waxman (1991) chronicled the history of treatment of those with disabilities and indicated that the abuse and murder of children with disabilities were commonplace in traditional societies. This was a result of several factors: utilitarianism (the greatest good for the greatest number of people); value systems that emphasized strength, beauty, and intelligence; and shame related to beliefs that disability was punishment for sin or disobedience of God. In more recent times, forced institutionalization may have somewhat different, yet somewhat similar, motivations (Waxman, 1991). These biases against those with disabilities result in loss of control, loss of worth, social isolation, and ultimately increased vulnerability. Further, individuals with disabilities are more likely to live in poverty, are less likely to be employed on a full-time basis, are more likely to be reliant on public transit, and are more likely to be reliant on others for personal care (McMahon et al., 2004). On a social level, disabled persons are less likely than others in society to have learned social skills to protect themselves against crime.

According to the U.S. Census Bureau (2012), 14% of the American population is considered to have a disability, such as a hearing, vision, cognitive, ambulatory, self-care, or independent-living limitation that restricts their full participation at school, at work, at home or in the community. Because older adults are far more likely to have disabilities than younger people, this number is likely to increase as the U.S. population ages.

Consider the following findings from the Bureau of Statistics based on data from the Bureau of Justice Statistics' (BJS) National Crime Victimization Survey (NCVS) between 2009–2015 (Harrell, 2017):

- People with disabilities are 2.5 times more likely to be victims of violent crimes.

- Persons with cognitive disabilities had the highest rates of total violent crime (57.9 per 1,000).

- The rate of serious violent crime (rape or sexual assault, robbery, and aggravated assault) for persons with disabilities (12.7 per 1,000) was more than three times the rate for persons without disabilities (4.0 per 1,000).

- Violent crime (rape or sexual assault, robbery, and aggravated assault) for persons with disabilities (12.7 per 1,000) was more than three times the rate for persons without disabilities (4.0 per 1,000).

- Particulars of the crimes were also different. Crimes against people with disabilities were more likely to occur during daylight hours. The violence was also more likely to be committed by someone the victim knew (40%).

Gender

Twenty-five-year-old Marc Lépine (born Gamil Gharbi) walked into the École Polytechnique de Montréal on December 6, 1989, carrying a Ruger Mini-14 semiautomatic rifle. He entered a second-floor classroom, separated the men from the women, and then ordered the approximately 50 men to leave. Claiming he was fighting feminism, he shot the nine women who remained, killing six and injuring the rest. He is reported to have screamed, "I hate women." After this, Lépine moved to other areas of the building, killing a total of 14 women and 4 men and injuring 10 additional women. The incident ended when Lépine turned the gun on himself. In a letter found in his jacket, Lépine indicated the attack was politically motivated. That is, he wished to kill feminists for ruining his life. The letter contained the names of 19 other women he wished to kill. The Montreal Massacre became a galvanizing moment in which mourning turned into outrage about all violence against women (CBC Digital Archives, 1989). The date is remembered by a walk and vigil in cities across Canada.

The pervasive nature of violence against women in our society has led many to advocate for this violence to be considered a hate crime. Portraying violence against women as hate based underscores the public and societal nature of the crime and moves the focus away from the individual victim, thereby reducing the possibility of victim blaming. During a congressional hearing on the Hate Crime Statistics Act, the president of the National Organization for Women presented feminist research and theory to argue that women were a group targeted for violence due to hate. Nevertheless, gender was not included in the language of the bill (McPhail & DiNitto, 2005). More recently, gender-based violence has been added to federal legislation, to the legislation of 20 states, and to the model hate crime statute prepared by the Anti-Defamation League. However, gender has rarely been used in hate crime prosecutions, and as of 2005, McPhail and DiNitto reported only two successful prosecutions of gender-related hate bias crimes. Their study of prosecutors' attitudes supports the notions that those in the justice system find it difficult to fit violence against women into the hate crime model. Thus, although legislation supports gender as a basis for hate crime, there is no evidence that practice will change in the near future.

Sexual Orientation

On a cold October night in 1998 in Laramie, Wyoming, Matthew Shepard, a 21-year-old gay college student, was robbed, savagely beaten, tied to a fence in a remote rural area, and left to die. Eighteen hours later, he was found alive but unconscious. He died of head injuries five days later in a Colorado hospital. The high-profile murder galvanized gay rights activists but also fueled anti-gay opponents. Tensions were so high that Matthew Shepard's father wore a bulletproof vest under his suit when he spoke at his son's funeral (ABC News, 2004). The public response to the attack was instantaneous. Thousands of people staged candlelight vigils, prominent figures issued statements condemning the attack, and Matthew Shepard became a symbol of anti-gay hate crimes (Hoffman, 2011).

Local residents Aaron McKinney and Russell Henderson were both convicted of kidnapping and murder and sentenced to two consecutive life terms in prison. However, because Wyoming did not have a statute addressing hate crimes, a bill was introduced into the Wyoming legislature that defined attacks motivated by hate. The bill was voted down in the Wyoming House of Representatives. On May 3, 2007, the Matthew Shepard Act (HR 1592) passed the U.S. House of Representatives, and on September 27, 2007, it passed the Senate. However, the hate crimes provision was not included in the final version of the bill. The act that sought to extend federal hate crime legislation to include individuals who are victims of hate as a result of gender, sexual orientation, or disability fell victim to House opponents of hate crimes (Human Rights Campaign, 2008).

In the United States, the number of adults identifying as lesbian, gay, bisexual, or transgender (LGBT) increased to 4.1% in 2016 compared to 3.5% in 2012. The data were drawn from a random sample of more than 1.6 million U.S. adults as part of Gallup Daily tracking. The figures represent the largest sample of LGBT Americans and imply that more than an estimated 10 million adults now identify as LGBT in the U.S. today, approximately 1.75 million more compared with 2012 (Gates, 2017).

It is difficult to get an accurate count of the LGBT population due to stigma and methodological problems. However, the following statistics are the best estimates from surveys around the world (Catalyst, 2017).

Canada: 1.7% of Canadians between the ages of 18–59 are gay or lesbian, and an additional 1.3% are bisexual. In Japan, 5.9% of the population is LGBT; in the United Kingdom, 1.7% are LGB; in Australia, 1% of all couples are same-sex couples. Numbers of transgendered persons have been equally difficult to estimate. However, findings from the first national sample of 6,450 transgender and gender non-conforming study participants who took the time and energy to answer questions about their lives have been published. The data present major findings about transgender and gender non-conforming people in the U.S. and provide critical data points as follows.

Discrimination in the combination of anti-transgender bias and structural racism was especially notable. People of color in general fare worse than White participants across the board, with Black transgender respondents faring worse than all others in many areas examined. The respondents lived in extreme poverty with persons nearly four times more likely to have a household income of less than $10,000/year compared to the general population. The mental health issues were serious with 41% of respondents reported attempting suicide compared to 1.6% of the general population, and especially for those who lost a job due to bias (55%), were harassed/bullied in school (51%), had low household income, or were the victim of physical assault (61%) or sexual assault (64%) (Grant et al., 2011).

Political

Politically motivated hate crimes are often based on conspiratory beliefs of the offender or deep-seated religious beliefs. As indicated earlier with regard to hate crimes facilitated by the Internet, the identification and killing of physicians who perform abortions is an example of a politically motivated hate crime. Pro-life movement members, frustrated by legislation to limit abortion restrictions, resort to extremist methods. Born in 1923, Henry Morgentaler studied gynecology upon his release from Auschwitz and went to Canada where, in 1969, he gave up his family practice and began to perform illegal abortions in Montreal. By the time Morgentaler opened his Toronto clinic in 1983, abortion was the most controversial issue in Canada. In the decade that followed, attempts were made on the life of Morgentaler and other physicians; the clinic was bombed, shot at, and desecrated on numerous occasions; and women who entered the clinic were harassed and assaulted. Although abortion was legalized in the United States in 1973 by the Supreme Court ruling in *Roe v. Wade*, statutory restrictions to abortions in Canada were not overturned until 1988, in the Supreme Court case of *Morgentaler v. Her Majesty the Queen*. Despite the Supreme Court ruling, or perhaps fueled by it, attacks on Morgentaler and his clinics continued well into the 1990s. To this day, he lives behind bulletproof glass.

Conspiracy beliefs are another motivation for political bias hate crimes. Timothy McVeigh's bombing of the government building in Oklahoma City, which killed 168 people and injured 850 more, is the deadliest case of domestic terrorism in the United States. McVeigh was a former member of the U.S. Army who specialized in explosives and demolition. Upon his release he lived a transient life, acting as a vendor in gun shows and visiting Waco, Texas, at the time of the Waco siege. McVeigh claimed the bombing was in response to the government crimes at Waco and instructed his lawyers to use a necessity defense and to argue that his bombing of the federal building was justifiable. Nevertheless, McVeigh was sentenced to death by lethal injection.

Typology of Offender Motivation

McDevitt, Levin, and Bennett (2002) developed a typology of hate crime offenders based on an examination of 169 cases of the Boston Police Department. The four types—thrill seeking, defensive, retaliatory, and mission—are widely accepted and taught in law enforcement training and have been corroborated

TABLE 14-1 Typology of Offenders of Hate Crime Motivation

Type	Description
Thrill seeking	Desire for excitement Youths acting in groups
Defensive	Seen as necessary from offender's prejudiced point of view Committed near victim's home, school, or business
Retaliatory	In response to real or believed incident committed by someone in the targeted group Seen as avenging the death of someone
Mission	Attempt to rid the world of perceived evil Usually a member of an organized group

Data from: McDevitt, J., Levin, J., & Bennett, S. 2002. Hate crime offenders: An expanded typology. *Journal of Social Issues, 58*(2), 303–317.

in other research (Franklin, 2000). A summary of these typologies can be found in TABLE 14-1.

Thrill-seeking offenders are motivated by a desire for excitement and constituted 66% of the cases in McDevitt and colleagues' study. This category consists mainly of youths who act in groups. When perpetrating these crimes, youths have frequently been out drinking together and when caught they frequently explain to police they were bored and looking for some fun. Groups of youths engaged in thrill-seeking hate crimes generally leave their own neighborhoods and seek a target such as a gay bar, synagogue, or minority neighborhood where they inflict violence against persons or property and in doing so make slurs or leave graffiti that is indicative of hate. These offenders have no previous relationship with the victim. Their weapons tend to be hands, feet, and rocks or other easily accessible items because the premeditation and consideration of consequences are limited. Their behavior is often not consistent with the typical behaviors of these youths. Further, their general attitudes are often not of deep-seated hate; rather, they may have been swept up in the moment. Because the commitment to the bias of these groups is frequently limited, there is a strong possibility of deterrence from further criminal activities of this type simply by police intervention. Parents are frequently stunned this has occurred when they are notified by police, and they act as a further force for deterrence.

Defensive offenders constituted 25% of the hate crimes examined. These attacks are committed, from the offenders' prejudiced point of view, because they are necessary to protect their neighborhood from others who are considered to be outsiders. These offenders report to police that members of a minority group had moved into a previously all-White neighborhood, school, or workplace and introduced the risk that more of their group would follow, resulting in lower property values, heightened crime, more drugs, and so on. Because such defensive crimes are based on firmly held beliefs that the minority group represents a danger, offenders in this category tend to have limited worldviews, have not been exposed to people in the "other category," and due to their fears and prejudices are unlikely to allow themselves to have sufficient exposure to those in the feared group to develop relationships and quell fears. As a result of their belief systems, deterrence through individual criminal charges or therapeutic interventions is unlikely. Externally imposed strategies, such as the forced integration of schools in the South, coupled with security for those in the minority group, eventually lead to change. These crimes tend to be perpetrated by groups of young people and occur near the home, school, or business of the offenders. There are often previous acts of intimidation by the offenders in which threatening messages are spray painted on homes, racist comments are made directly to individuals, physical intimidation is used, or actual physical assaults are perpetrated.

Retaliatory hate crimes occur after a real or believed incident was committed by someone within the group that is now targeted. For example, after the attack and shooting death of a 16-year-old Black adolescent, Yusuf Hawkins, in a White working-class neighborhood of Brooklyn in August 1989, violence erupted throughout New York City. Hawkins and three friends were confronted by a crowd of 10 to 30 White youths, some of whom had baseball bats and one had a handgun. The youths mistakenly believed Hawkins was dating a local girl. Although the original attack on Hawkins could be viewed as falling into the defensive category of hate crimes, what followed was a number of retaliatory attacks resulting in the month with the largest number of hate crimes in New York City's history (McDevitt et al., 2002; Pinderhughes, 1993). Thus, retaliatory hate crime offenders act on the belief that they are avenging the death or violation of someone who is like them. The attack frequently follows merely the rumor that a crime was committed against someone in the offender's own group and rarely is any effort put into verifying the rumor. The actual target of the attack needs only to be someone in the targeted group and is not the actual perpetrator of the original crime. The attack is likely to be on the turf of the victim and can involve lethal weapons as a result of premeditation.

Mission is the final category of hate crime offender motivations. In this category, offenders are totally committed to bigotry, and this becomes the focus of their life. In mission hate crimes, the perpetrator seeks to rid the world of perceived evil. A mission offender is usually a member of an organized group, such as the Ku Klux Klan, although the offender may operate alone. Commitment to the belief system is complete, and the methods of attack are premeditated and often lethal. This type of offender will not be deterred by reason or legal intervention. In McDevitt and colleagues' study (2002), deterrence occurred in less than 1% of cases. The ultimate example of the mission-motivated hate crime is the suicide bomber.

Suicide Bombers as Perpetrators of Hate Crimes

Suicide bombing, as a form of terrorism, is the targeted use of self-destructing human beings against civilian populations to effect political change. It serves as a weapon of psychological warfare intended to affect a large population. The primary targets are not those killed in the attack but those who witness it (Atran, 2003). This type of activity can best be viewed as theater for the media (Hutchinson, 2007). What separates suicide bombings from other forms of hate crimes is that they are rarely conducted independently by one individual, but rather the individual is executing an attack that has been planned by an organization. Suicide bombings are, however, consistent with other hate crimes in that they are random attacks based on hatred toward a particular group of people. The outcomes of such terror are often highly successful, and governments frequently capitulate to the demands of the terror group in fear of further widespread death and destruction.

Classical literature describes suicides where there is clearly declared hostile and aggressive intent toward an enemy. These include suicide out of revenge in Greek writings and suicide by devotion by Roman soldiers. Although the history of suicide attacks is long, in modern times the first noted examples were the Japanese kamikazes, who used aircraft as flying bombs to destroy Allied ships during World War II. It has been suggested that in the Battle of Okinawa, all requests for volunteers met with unanimous acceptance, although no shame was to be associated with refusal (Atran, 2003). However, in a study of the diaries of the pilots, Ohnuki-Tierney (2004) disputed this contention and concluded that most of these pilots did not die for the emperor, and they did not fully embrace the military ideology. They did not volunteer but were coerced through social forces in a totalitarian regime.

Modern suicide bombing started in the Middle East during the 1980 Iran–Iraq War. This was punctuated in December 1981, when the Iraqi embassy in Beirut was destroyed, leaving 27 dead and 100 wounded (Hutchinson, 2007). Then, in April 1993, the first of 20 suicide attacks between 1993 and 1997 occurred in Israel. These 20 attacks killed 175 people and injured 928. The second, more lethal wave began in 2000, and by 2005, suicide bombers had killed 657 people in Israel and injured 3,682 others (Brym & Araj, 2006). Finally, on September 11, 2001, suicide attackers crashed commercial aircrafts into the World Trade Center in New York City and the Pentagon in Arlington, Virginia. A third plane failed to meet its target and crashed in Somerset County, Pennsylvania. In all, 2,986 people were recorded dead after the attacks on that single morning.

Earlier theories regarding the nature of suicide bombers have been disputed by research. One such theory is that suicide bombers are unstable individuals, plagued with psychopathology and harboring a death wish. However, interviews with prospective suicide bombers and reconstructions of biographies indicate there is no greater incidence of psychopathology in this group than in the general population and that the incidence may indeed be lower (Brym & Araj, 2006). A second explanation focuses on deprivation and the motivation for suicide bombing as being to act out against those in positions of power who withhold resources. However, studies of Arab suicide bombers indicate they have higher levels of education and are from higher socioeconomic classes than others in their society (Brym & Araj, 2006). Scholars have begun to consider suicide bombing in terms of strategically rational political action—a means of coercing a foreign state. Within this framework, specific motivations are revenge against a state for their actions against the group to which the suicide bomber belongs, the desire to achieve a strategic gain (e.g., the withdrawal of Israel from occupied territories), or the desire to achieve a religious goal (such as the defense or spread of Islam). Studies of Palestinian suicide bombers, for example, suggest they are motivated by the effectiveness of the attacks as a means to revenge national and personal humiliation and hatred of Israel and America (Grimland, Apter, & Kerkhof, 2006).

For the individual suicide bomber, the process begins with indoctrination, where leaders of the organization embrace the bomber and reinforce his or her preexisting beliefs and motivations. The second stage is to obtain commitment to the group and its goals. Group dynamics then serve to solidify motives and create social pressure to act. Finally, the suicide bomber is asked to make a personal pledge committing to the act. This pledge is frequently videotaped, making it extremely difficult to change one's mind (Hutchinson, 2007).

After interpreting sensationalized narratives of suicide bombers, the terrorism studies literature has evolved from viewing suicide bombers as pathological or fanatical to identifying that bombers often believe their acts are rational because the acts follow an identifiable strategic logic. Lyness (2014) argues in her study of female suicide bombers that they can go undetected, such as disguising fake pregnancies, and that presents a uniquely risky and ungovernable subject.

Impact of Hate Crimes on Victims

The impact of hate crimes on victims will depend in some measure on the motivation behind the crime. In the last decades, motivations have shifted significantly with the largest increase, according to the victims, based on ethnicity bias. Over 50% (51%) of cases reported in 2012 cited ethnicity (e.g., ancestral, cultural, social, or national affiliation), up from 30% in 2011 and 22% in 2004. Also, the percentage of hate crimes where the perceived cause was religious bias nearly tripled—from 10% in 2004 to 28% in 2012, and gender bias more than doubled, from 12% to 26% (Wilson, 2014).

Violent attacks against one's person, loved ones, or property have well-known psychological effects. When the cause of the crime is hate, however, some research suggests these effects can be more severe. Hate crime victims have reported trying to be less visible and relocating to attempt to reduce the possibility of further attacks on their emotional or physical selves. Victims of hate-based assaults report higher symptoms of intrusive thoughts and higher levels of anxiety and anger than victims whose assaults were not hate based (Sullaway, 2004). One reason is that when hate-based crimes involve physical assault, the severity of the assaults is significantly higher than that of other assaults, and people are more likely to require hospitalization. From a psychological perspective, the lack of control a victim of a hate-based crime experiences is another possible factor. Unlike other victims who may believe they can reduce the risk of further assaults by changing their behavior (e.g., not going to dangerous areas), victims of hate-based crimes cannot change many of the factors that make them identifiable targets. For example, people obviously cannot change the color of their skin, and the only option may be to move to another area.

In an early study, Barnes and Ephross (1994) explored the nature of hate attacks and victims' responses to them in a sample of 59 victims that included Black, White, and Asian individuals. More than half of the victims reported experiencing a series of attacks rather than a single attack.

About one-third of the victims moved from the neighborhood, purchased a gun, decreased social participation, prepared to fire a gun, bought home security devices, or increased safety precautions for children in the family. Of the 59 victims, 24% received physical injuries as a result of the most recent attack. Minor injuries were sustained by 10%, and 9% received medical treatment for injuries inflicted in the attack. The severe injuries inflicted on 5% of the victims required hospitalization. In 41% of the most recent attacks, victims incurred property damage.

Participants identified several emotional reactions to the most recent attack on them. Irwin, a Jewish victim who had a swastika spray-painted on his mailbox, experienced a feeling of anger, which nearly 68% of the participants reported. About 51% of the participants indicated fear that they or their families would be physically injured. One-third of the victims felt very saddened by the incident.

About one-third of the participants made plans to avoid potential future victimization. A Cambodian refugee was assaulted by a Black man in a suburban park. Shortly after the attack, she moved to another county because of fear that the man would find and attack her again. Her responses represent the avoidance behavioral coping that some victims adopted.

In contrast to avoidance, some victims made preparations for retaliation. One Black man stated, "I am scared that I might catch one of these people. . . . The scariest thing is I got guns and can use them."

Herek, Gillis, and Cogan (1999) hypothesized that lesbian, gay, and bisexual people might be particularly vulnerable to hate crimes for two main reasons: (1) sexual prejudice is still acceptable in many segments of society, and thus the crime may reinforce internalized negative views, and (2) the development of sexual identity often occurs in opposition to family and community, thereby reducing resources and support. Their research about the victimization experiences of 2,259 Sacramento-area lesbians, gays, and bisexuals confirmed that gay and lesbian victims of hate crimes manifested significantly more symptoms of depression, anger, anxiety, and posttraumatic stress than those who were victims of violent crimes not associated with hate. Hate crime victims also displayed significantly more crime-related fears than victims of violent crimes that were not motivated by bias and those who were not crime victims. Comparable differences were not found among bisexuals, perhaps indicating differing identity and support issues among bisexuals than among gays and lesbians.

Hate crimes affect not only individuals but also communities. The fact that a member of a group has been targeted simply because of his or her skin color, religion, or sexual orientation sends shockwaves throughout the group. All members become acutely aware of the risks they face, and their sense of safety and security is severely undermined. The response of police and the justice system can serve to allay fears or intensify the sense of vulnerability depending on whether the crime is taken seriously and whether offenders are apprehended, charged, and convicted. In the absence of this, a fear develops that it is open season on violence. The increased fear in the gay and lesbian community that was documented by researchers is an excellent example of this point (Noelle, 2002). Indeed, there does appear to be escalations in violence toward a group after a highly publicized hate crime. For example, there was a twofold increase in hate crimes after the mob attack of a young Black man in New York in 1986 (Craig, 1999). Further, a group's historical experiences of oppression, denial of rights, and violence are resurrected in the aftermath of hate-based crimes, and fears of a return to earlier days emerge.

◼ Conclusion

Hate against one group by members of another group is a pervasive aspect of human history. Hate crimes and hate speech are direct attempts to degrade, oppress, and control members of certain groups. Victims tend to be innocent members of the targeted group and generally have no previous relationship with the offenders. Unpredictability and the fact that the behavior is unprovoked serve to keep not only the victims but all members of that group in a state of anxiety or even fear. Despite the highly destructive qualities of hate crimes, Western societies have found it tremendously difficult to define and control them in a legal context. What constitutes statements of hate and what constitutes valid opinion continues to be a point of debate that does not appear will be settled anytime soon.

A cautionary note is offered from one study that analyzed data from the Crime Survey for England and Wales on racially motivated crime. The study suggests that not all victims report being affected by hate crime, not all victims are affected the same way, and some victims of racially motivated crime report less of an emotional impact than some victims of equivalent but otherwise motivated crimes. Thus, researchers Iganski and Lagou (2015) recommend that just as there is variation in victim impacts, there will be variation in offender culpability and advise discretion and flexibility in sentencing to ensure justice for offenders.

Key Terms

Anti-Semitism: Hostility toward or prejudice against Jews or Judaism.

Genocide: Systematic murder of an entire political, cultural, or religious group.

Hate crime: Criminal conduct motivated in whole or in part by a preformed negative opinion or attitude toward a group based on race, ethnicity, religion, gender, sexual orientation, or disability.

Hate speech: Words used as weapons to ambush, terrorize, wound, humiliate, and degrade members of an identified group.

Islamophobia: Hostility toward or prejudice against Muslims.

Suicide bomber: The targeted use of self-destructing human beings against civilians.

White supremacist: A person who believes White people are racially superior to others and should therefore dominate society.

Xenophobia: Fear and hatred of strangers or foreigners or of anything that is strange or foreign.

Discussion Questions

1. Some would suggest there is a fine line between hate speech and freedom of speech. Discuss.
2. How do hate crimes affect a community, and how do such acts differ from other forms of crime?
3. Discuss possible intervention strategies for hate crime offenders based on offender typologies.
4. Create a treatment plan for victims of hate crimes.
5. What is the intersection between suicide bombing and hate crimes?
6. What is Islamophobia? Provide examples.

Resources

Bureau of Justice Assistance, *A Policymaker's Guide to Hate Crimes* www.ncjrs.gov/pdffiles1/bja/162304.pdf

FBI, Hate Crimes. https://ucr.fbi.gov/hate-crime

Reading Hate, Hate Crime Research and Scholarship in Canada http://www
.criminologyandjustice.uoit.ca/hatecrime/index.html

Southern Poverty Law Center http://splcenter.org

■ References

ABC News. (2004, November 26). New details emerge in Matthew Shepard murder.
Retrieved from http://abcnews.go.com/2020/story?id=277685&page=1

Abu-Raz, W., & Suarez, Z. (2009). Muslim men and women's perception of discrimination, hate crimes, and PTSD symptoms post 9/11. *Traumatology, 15*(3), 48–63.

Akiyama, C. (2008). When you look like the enemy. *Journal of Brief Treatment and
Crisis Intervention, 8*(2), 209–213.

Ali, W., Clifton, E., Duss, M., Fang, L., Keyes, S., & Shakir, F. (2011, August 26).
Fear, Inc.: The roots of the Islamophobia network in America. Washington, DC:
Center for American Progress. Retrieved from http://www.americanprogress.org
/issues/2011/08/pdf/islamophobia.pdf

American Psychological Association (APA). (1998). Hate crimes today. Retrieved from
http://www.apa.org/releases/hate.html

Americans with Disabilities Act. (1990). Including changes made by the ADA Amendments Act of 2008 (P.L. 110-325). Retrieved from http://www.ada.gov/pubs
/adastatute08.htm

Amjad, N., & Wood, A. (2009). Identifying and changing the normative beliefs about
aggression, which lead young Muslim adults to join extremist anti-Semitic groups
in Pakistan. *Aggressive Behavior, 35*, 514–519.

Atran, S. (2003). Genesis of suicide terrorism. *Science, 299*, 1534–1539.

Barnes, A., & Ephross, P. H. (1994). The impact of hate violence on victims. *Social
Work, 39*, 247–251.

Barnes, S. (2004, May 12). Teenagers charged in grave desecration. *New York Times*.
Retrieved from http://www.nytimes.com/2004/05/12/us/national-briefing-southwest
-texas-teenagers-charged-in-grave-desecration.html?n=Top%2FReference
%2FTimes%20Topics%2FSubjects%2FC%2FCemeteries

Beutel, A. J. (2011). Data on Post-9/11 terrorism in the United States. Washington, DC:
Muslim Public Affairs Council. Retrieved from http://www.mpac.org/assets/docs
/publications/MPAC-Post-911-Terrorism-Data.pdf

Bortner, P. (2010, October 20). Donchak, Piekarsky in Pike County Correctional Facility.
Retrieved   from   http://newsitem.com/news/donchak-piekarsky-in-pike-county
-correctional-facility–1.1051243#axzz1RKn0b1o4

Brym, R., & Araj, B. (2006). Suicide bombing as strategy and interaction: The case of
the second intifada. *Social Forces, 84*(4), 1969–1986.

California Department of Justice. (2000). Hate crime in California 2000. Retrieved
from http://ag.ca.gov/cjsc/publications/hatecrimes/hc2000/preface.pdf

Catalyst. (2017). Knowledge Center, LGTB Workplace Issues. Retrieved from http://www.catalyst.org/knowledge/lesbian-gay-bisexual-transgender-workplace-issues

CBC Digital Archives. (1989, December 6). The Montreal massacre. Retrieved from http://archives.radio-canada.ca/IDD–1-70-398/disasters_tragedies/montreal_massacre/

CBC News. (2005, January 18). Man given two years for firebombing Montreal Jewish school. Retrieved from http://www.cbc.ca/canada/story/2005/01/18/firebombsentence-jewishschool0118.html

CBC News. (2007, February 15). Ernst Zundel sentenced to five years for Holocaust denial. Retrieved from http://www.cbc.ca/world/story/2007/02/15/zundel-germany.html

Center for Policing Terrorism. (2007). Analysis: Firebombing of Jewish elementary school in Montreal in 2004. Retrieved from http://www.cpt-mi.org/pdf/jewishschool1.pdf

Chongatera, G. (2013). "Hate-crime victimization and fear of hate crime among racially visible people in Canada: The role of income as a mediating factor." *Journal of Immigrant & Refugee Studies*. Vol. 11. p. 44–64.

Clay, R. C. (2017). Islamophobia. Monitor on Psychology, 48(4), p. 34. Retrieved from http://www.apa.org/monitor/2017/04/islamophobia.aspx

Clement, S., Brohan, E., Sayce, L., Pool, J., & Thornicroft, G. (2011). Disability hate crime and targeted violence and hostility: A mental health and discrimination perspective. *Journal of Mental Health*, 20(3), 219–225.

CNN. (1999, February 22). Closing arguments today in Texas dragging-death trial. Retrieved from http://www.cnn.com/US/9902/22/dragging.death.03/

CNN. (2011, February 23). Men convicted of hate crime sentenced to nine years in prison. Retrieved from http://articles.cnn.com/2011-02-23/justice/pennsylvania.hate.crime_1_derrick-donchak-brandon-piekarsky-federal-court?_s=PM:CRIME

Council of Europe. (2006). Additional Protocol to the Convention on cybercrime, concerning the criminalisation of acts of a racist and xenophobic nature committed through computer systems. Retrieved from http://www.coe.int/t/dghl/cooperation/economiccrime/cybercrime/Default_en.asp

Cowan, G., Resendez, M., Marshall, E., & Quist, R. (2002). Hate speech and constitutional protection: Priming values of equality and freedom. *Journal of Social Issues*, 58(2), 247–263.

Craig, K. (1999). Retaliation, fear, or rage: An investigation of African American and White reactions to racist hate crimes. *Journal of Interpersonal Violence*, 14(2), 138–151.

Criminal Code of Canada. (2004). R.S., c. C-46, s. 318–319.

Dauvergne, M., Scrim, K., & Brennan, S. (2006). *Hate crime in Canada*. Canadian Centre for Justice Statistics Profile Series. Ottawa: Statistics Canada.

Dixon, L., & Ray, L. (2007). Current issues and developments in race hate crime. *Journal of Community and Criminal Justice*, 54(2), 109–124.

Espiritu, A. (2004). Racial diversity and hate crime incidents. *Social Science Journal*, *41*, 197–208.

Federal Bureau of Investigation (FBI). (2009). Hate crime statistics, 2009. Retrieved from http://www2.fbi.gov/ucr/hc2009/incidents.html

Federal Bureau of Investigation (FBI). (2015). Hate crime statistics, 2015. Retrieved from https://ucr.fbi.gov/hate-crime/2015

Federal Bureau of Investigation (FBI). (2016). Latest hate crime statistics released. Retrieved from https://www.fbi.gov/news/stories/2015-hate-crime-statistics-released

Franklin, K. (2000). Antigay behaviours among young adults: Prevalence, patterns, and motivations in a noncriminal population. *Journal of Interpersonal Violence*, *15*(4), 339–362.

Franklin, K. (2002). Good intentions. *American Behavioral Scientist*, *46*(1), 154–172.

Frey, G. (2010, August 1). Holocaust denier Ernst Zundel released from prison. *The Star*. Retrieved from https://www.thestar.com/news/world/2010/03/01/holocaust _denier_ernst_zundel_released_from_prison.html

Gates, G. (2017). In U.S., more adults identify in as LGBT, Gallup News Social Issues. Retrieved from http://news.gallup.com/poll/201731/lgbt-identification-rises.aspx?g _source=lgbt&g_medium=search&g_campaign=tiles

Gallup News. (2016). Islamophobia: Understanding anti-Muslim sentiment in the West. Retrieved from http://www.gallup.com/poll/157082/islamophobia-understanding -anti-muslim-sentiment-west.aspx

Grant, J. M., Mottet, L. A., Tanis, J., Harrison, J., Herman, J. L., & Keisling, M. Injustice at Every Turn: A Report of the National Transgender Discrimination Survey. Washington: National Center for Transgender Equality and National Gay and Lesbian Task Force, 2011.

Green, D., Glaser, J., & Rich, A. (1998). From lynching to gay bashing: The elusive connection between economic conditions and hate crime. *Journal of Personality and Social Psychology*, *75*(1), 82–92.

Grimland, M., Apter, A., & Kerkhof, A. (2006). The phenomenon of suicide bombing. *Crisis*, *27*(3), 107–118.

Harrell, E. (2017). Crimes against persons with disabilities, 2009–2015 statistical tables.

Henry, J. (2009). Beyond free speech: Novel approaches to hate on the Internet in the United States. *Information and Communications Technology Law*, *18*(2), 235–251.

Herek, G., Gillis, R., & Cogan, J. (1999). Psychological sequelae of hate-crime victimization among lesbian, gay, and bisexual adults. *Journal of Consulting and Clinical Psychology*, *67*(6), 945–951.

History.com staff. (2009). Man chased to his death in Howard Beach hate crime. Retrieved from http://www.history.com/this-day-in-history/man-chased-to-his -death-in-howard-beach-hate-crime

Hoffman, S. (2011). "Last night, I prayed to Matthew": Matthew Shepard, homosexuality, and popular martyrdom in contemporary America. *Religion and American Culture: A Journal of Interpretation*, *21*(1), 121–164.

Human Rights Campaign. (2008). The local law enforcement hate crimes prevention act/Matthew Shepard act. Retrieved from http://www.hrc.org/5660.htm

Hutchinson, W. (2007). The systemic roots of suicide bombing. *Systems Research and Behavioral Science, 24,* 191–200.

Iganski, P., &, Lagou, S. (2015). Hate crimes hurt some more than others: implications for the just sentencing of offenders. *Journal of Interpersonal Violence.* Jun;30(10):1696–1718.

Jacobs, J., & Henry, J. (1996). The social construction of a hate crime epidemic. *Journal of Criminal Law, 86*(2), 366–391.

Jenness, V. (1999). Managing differences and making legislation: Social movements and the racialization, sexualization, and gendering of federal hate crimes law in the U.S. 1985–1998. *Social Problems, 46*(4), 548–571.

Johnson, S., & Byers, B. (2003). Attitudes toward hate crime laws. *Journal of Criminal Justice, 31,* 227–235.

Keilty, J., & Connelly, G. (2001). Making a statement: An exploratory study of barriers facing women with an intellectual disability when making a statement about sexual assault to police. *Disability and Society, 16*(2), 273–291.

Langton, L. (2017). Hate Crime Victimization, 2004–2015. Bureau of Justice Statistics, Office of Justice Programs. Retrieved from https://www.bjs.gov/index.cfm?ty=pbdetail&iid=5967

Lawrence, C., Matsuda, M., Delgado, R., & Crenshaw, K. (1993). Introduction. In M. Matsuda, C. Lawrence, R. Delgado, & K. Crenshaw (Eds.), *Words that wound: Critical race theory, assaultive speech, and the First Amendment* (pp. 1–15). Boulder, CO: Westview Press.

Levin, B. (2002a). Cyberhate. *American Behavioral Scientist, 45*(6), 958–988.

Levin, B. (2002b). From slavery to hate crime laws: The emergence of race and status-based protection in American criminal law. *Journal of Social Issues, 58*(2), 227–245.

Lyness, C. (2014). Governing the suicide bomber: reading terrorism studies as governmentality. *Critical Studies in Terrorism, 7*(1).

McDevitt, J., Levin, J., & Bennett, S. (2002). Hate crime offenders: An expanded typology. *Journal of Social Issues, 58*(2), 303–317.

McMahon, B., West, S., Lewis, A., Armstrong, A., & Conway, J. (2004). Hate crimes and disability in America. *Rehabilitation Counselling Bulletin, 47*(2), 66–75.

McPhail, B. (2000). Hating hate: Policy implications of hate crime legislation. *Social Science Review, 74*(4), 635–653.

McPhail, B., & DiNitto, D. (2005). Prosecutorial perspectives on gender-bias hate crimes. *Violence Against Women, 11*(9), 1162–1185.

Morgan, J. (2002). U.S. hate crime legislation: A legal model to avoid in Australia. *Journal of Sociology, 38*(1), 25–48.

Noelle, M. (2002). The ripple effect of the Matthew Shepard murder. *American Behavioral Scientist, 46*(1), 27–50.

Ohnuki-Tierney, E. (2004). Betrayal by idealism and aesthetics. *Anthropology Today*, 20(2), 15–21.

Peritz, I. (2005, January 19). Library bomber jailed two years. Retrieved from http://www.theglobeandmail.com/servlet/story/RTGAM.20050119.wbomber19/BNStory/National/

Perry, B. (2002). Defending the color line: Racially and ethnically motivated hate crime. *American Behavioral Scientist*, 46(1), 72–92.

Pinderhughes, H. (1993). The anatomy of racially motivated violence in New York City: A case study of youth in southern Brooklyn. *Social Problems*, 40(4), 478–492.

Reuters. (1999, November 19). Third defendant is convicted in dragging death in Texas. *New York Times*. Retrieved from http://www.nytimes.com/1999/11/19/us/third-defendant-is-convicted-in-dragging-death-in-texas.html

Scott v. Sandford. (1857). 19 How. 393.

Shively, M., & Mulford, C. (2007). Hate crime in America: The debate continues. *National Institute of Justice Journal*, 257, 1–13.

Sobsey, D. (1994). *Violence and abuse in the lives of people with disabilities: The end of silent acceptance?* Baltimore, MD: Brookes.

Southern Poverty Law Center. (1998). Intelligence project. Monitoring hate and extremist activity. Retrieved from http://www.splcenter.org/intel/intpro.jsp

Southern Poverty Law Center. (2017). Hate map. Retrieved from https://www.splcenter.org/hate-map

State v. Mann. (1829). 13 NC (2 Dev) 263.

Sullaway, M. (2004). Psychological perspectives on hate crime laws. *Psychology, Public Policy, and Law*, 10, 250–292.

U.S. Census Bureau. (2012). Newsroom Archive. Dept. of Commerce. Retrieved from https://www.census.gov/newsroom/releases/archives/miscellaneous/cb12-134.html

U.S. Court of Appeals for the Third Circuit. *United States of America v. Brandon Piekarsky and Derrick Donchak*. No. 11-1567. Retrieved from www2.ca3.uscourts.gov/opinarch/111567p.pdf

U.S. Department of State. (2005). Report on global anti-Semitism. Retrieved from http://www.state.gov/g/drl/rls/40258.htm

Volokh, E. (2017, April 24). Holocaust denier Ernst Zundel barred from moving to the U.S., though his wife is an American citizen. *Washington Post*. Retrieved from https://www.washingtonpost.com/news/volokh-conspiracy/wp/2017/04/24/holocaust-denier-ernst-zundel-barred-from-moving-to-the-u-s-though-his-wife-is-an-american-citizen/?utm_term=.69fc376a8807

Waxman, B. (1991). Hatred: The unacknowledged dimension against disabled people. *Sexuality and Disability*, 9(3), 185–199.

Willis, D. (2004). Hate crimes against gay males: An overview. *Issues in Mental Health Nursing*, 25, 115–132.

Wilson, M.M. (2014). Hate crime victimization, 2004–2012 Statistical Tables. Bureau of Justice Statistics. Retrieved from https://www.bjs.gov/content/pub/pdf/hcv0412st.pdf

© Peyker/Shutterstock.

CHAPTER 15

Victims of Social Media

Elizabeth B. Dowdell

OBJECTIVES

- To define the types of violence trending on social media
- To identify the characteristics of social media violence
- To indicate appropriate resources for assisting victims of social media violence

KEY TERMS

Internet risk behaviors

Self-exploitation

Sexting

Sextortion

Social media

CASE

Eighteen-year-old Michelle Carter urged her high school boyfriend, Conrad Roy, to kill himself in the summer of 2014, through a series of texts and phone calls. A Massachusetts jury found her responsible for his death and guilty of involuntary manslaughter in June 2017.

Carter and Roy met in 2012. Although they lived an hour apart, they communicated frequently, almost exclusively via text and phone calls. The case hinged on the power of words—Michelle Carter's words—and whether they could be deadly. At the heart of the case was the question of whether Carter's texts and messages

pushed Roy to take his life or if he would have done so anyway.

Some of the most compelling evidence in the case were texts in which Carter explicitly told Roy to follow through with his suicide plan, using a gas-powered water pump to fill the cabin of his pickup truck with carbon monoxide.

When issuing the verdict, Judge Lawrence Moniz said Carter had a legal obligation to call for help when she realized Roy was in danger, but instead "admitted in subsequent texts that she did nothing." The verdict in this landmark case, which drew national attention, is likely to reverberate across the country and potentially reshape criminal law relating to virtual communications (McGovern, 2017).

On August 3, 2017, Michelle Carter was sentenced to 2.5 years in prison for involuntary manslaughter, with 15 months to be served and the rest suspended followed by 5 years of probation. She is currently free while her case is being appealed.

Matt West/The Boston Herald via AP, Pool.

Introduction

A whole new class of victimization has evolved as a result of communication technologies. While the Internet has provided many new and exciting advances, it also has resulted in victimization. The relationship between social media and the Internet is complex. Individual Internet behavior involves a myriad of factors that contribute either safety or risk-taking behaviors that can begin in adolescence. Studies suggest that individuals, especially children and adolescents, who participate in one **Internet risk behavior** are more likely to participate in additional Internet risk behaviors. The danger is that the combined risk behaviors increase the individual's potential for mental health issues and negative psychological outcomes associated with engagement in patterns of risky off- or online behavior. This chapter reviews the structure of the Internet and identifies some of the victims of social media.

As of March 2017, the Internet had approximately 3.7 billion users, or 49.6% of the world's 7 billion population (Internet World Statistics, 2017). Two key advances have marked its evolution in recent years: the social web and mobile technology. These two innovations have changed the way people use the Internet. The social web has given people new ways to communicate. For example, since its creation in 2004, Facebook has grown into a worldwide network of over 1.7 billion subscribers. Mobile technology has greatly increased the reach of the Internet, growing the number of Internet users everywhere (Internet World Stats, 2017).

The use of electronic media is an important part of life for many people, and children and adolescents especially. Studies report that in the United States, media exposure among school-aged children and adolescents is nearly eight hours a day, even when taking multitasking into account (Rideout, Foehr, & Roberts, 2010). From 2004 to 2009, total media exposure in a typical day among U.S.

adolescents increased by more than two hours (Rideout et al., 2010), even though the recommendation from the American Academy of Pediatrics (2001) for total media use was only one to two hours of quality programming per day.

Today's children are growing up immersed in digital media, which has both positive and negative effects on healthy development. They are growing up in a media-saturated environment that includes broadcast and streamed television, interactive video games, and social media. These immersive media allow youths to experience the role of both media creator and consumer (Moreno, 2016).

To help parents develop a personalized media approach for their child, the American Academy of Pediatrics (AAP) introduced an interactive Family Media Plan (www.HealthyChildren.org/MediaUsePlan) that allows families to prioritize daily activities. Health, academic, and social goals are met first, and then media use is considered. Using the plan, critical health practices are followed daily, including attaining 1 hour of exercise and 8 to 12 hours of sleep (depending on age). To ensure that sleep is restful, the AAP says that children should not sleep with media devices in their rooms and should avoid any screen time for at least an hour before bed. The plan also suggests designating screen-free locations at home, such as the bedroom, as well as media-free times, such as family dinnertime or while driving. Families are guided to prioritize these health practices, to consider other responsibilities such as homework, sports, and time with friends, and then to determine how much time is "left over" that may be considered for media use (Moreno, 2016).

Despite organizations' efforts to promote limits on social media use for children, an alarming number of young people show what appear to be signs and symptoms of excessive social media use. Young people seem especially vulnerable to social media overload, with case studies highlighting students whose academic performance suffers as they spend extensive time online. Some also suffer health consequences from loss of sleep, as they stay up late to chat online, to check for social network status updates, or to reach the next game levels (Wallace, 2014).

Researchers in a variety of countries have documented adverse health effects of excessive online activity. For example, a study of 15-year-olds ($n = 5,402$) from Finland, France, and Denmark analyzed data on participants' sleep and symptoms of feeling low, irritability/bad temper, nervousness, headache, stomachache, backache, and feeling dizzy. The results suggested that sleep duration may be a potential underlying mechanism behind the association between computer use and health symptoms (Nuutinen et al., 2014).

Asian countries reported on youth symptoms at the 2007 International Symposium on the Counseling and Treatment of Youth Internet Addiction in Seoul. At that time, South Korea considered online gaming to be one of its most serious public health issues, with the South Korean government estimating that approximately 210,000 South Korean children (2.1% of those aged 6 to 19 years) were afflicted and required treatment. As of June 2007, South Korea had trained 1,043 counselors in the treatment of Internet addiction and enlisted over 190 hospitals and treatment centers and introduced preventive measures into schools. It was estimated that the average South Korean high school student spent about 23 hours each week gaming, and that 1.2 million were at risk for addiction and required basic counseling. In particular, therapists were worried about the increasing number of individuals dropping out from school or work to spend time on computers. The Chinese government noted similar concerns, reporting that 13.7% of Chinese adolescent Internet users, about 10 million teenagers, met the diagnostic criteria for Internet addiction. As a result, in 2007, China began restricting computer game use; current laws now discourage more than three hours of daily game use (Block, 2008).

Social Media Structure

Today, online access can be achieved from any location, with 24/7 electronic contact to anyone with a cell phone, email account, or Internet access. National studies have found that the majority of today's youth are using the Internet as a venue for social interaction, sharing of ideas, artistic creations, photography, school work, and online journaling or blogging (Duggan & Brenner, 2013; Lenhart, 2015a).

Computer technology can be classified into two types: hardware and software. *Hardware* has become an essential part of everyday life with handheld data devices such as smartphones, laptops, and tablets, each improving every year with faster service, more memory, and increased storage. Studies report that 94% of teenagers who have access to the Internet on mobile devices use them daily to communicate online with peers as well as to access social networking sites, blogs, and online resources (Lenhart, 2015a; Patchin & Hinduja, 2010).

Software technology includes social media programs that have been written specifically for the Internet, such as Facebook, Twitter, Snapchat, Tumblr, Instagram, and online blogs. These social media sites allow users to join or create networks based on similar interests or behaviors. Facebook, for example, allows users to generate a profile containing self-description, demographic information, personal likes, hobbies, and affiliations. Users can also interact through viewing profiles, writing posts, sharing pictures, sending private messages, and online chatting (Duggan & Brenner, 2013; Lenhart, 2015a). See TABLE 15-1 for an overview of some of the most popular social media sites.

TABLE 15-1 Social Media Websites

Social Media	Number of users as of April 2017	Services
Baidu Tieba	300,000,000	Largest Chinese social media site. Features communities organized around interest groups. Anonymous posting is not allowed. Users can post at most 10 pictures and one video from certain broadcast websites. Users cannot edit published posts.
Facebook	1,968,000,000	Online social networking site that allows users to create personal profiles, share photos and videos, and communicate with other users.
Gab	200,000+	Users called "Gabbers" read and write short messages of up to 300 characters called "gabs." The site also offers multimedia functionality.
Google+	300,000,000	Users can post photos and status updates to the stream or interest-based communities. Also allows users to group people by different types of relationships.
Instagram	600,000,000	Photo-sharing application and service that allows users to share pictures and videos.
LinkedIn	500,000,000	Primarily a professional networking website. Used for job searches and recruitment and to stay in touch with past colleagues and potential clients.
QQ	868,000,000	Instant messaging software service that supports online social games, music, shopping, microblogging, movies, and group and voice chat.
QZone	595,000,000	Social networking website that allows users to write blogs, keep diaries, send photos, listen to music, and watch videos.
Pinterest	150,000,000	Users can upload, save, sort, and manage images—known as pins—and other media content (e.g., videos) through collections known as pinboards.
Reddit	234,000,000	Users submit content such as text posts or direct links. Users can then vote submissions up or down, which determines their position on the page. Submissions with the most up-votes appear on the front page or the top of a category. Content entries are organized by areas of interest called *subreddits*.
Snapchat	300,000,000	An image messaging and multimedia mobile application on which pictures and messages are only available for a short time before they become inaccessible.

(continues)

TABLE 15-1 Social Media Websites (*Continued*)

Social Media	Number of users as of April 2017	Services
Tumblr	550,000,000	Microblogging and social networking website that allows users to post multimedia and other content to a short-form blog.
Twitter	319,000,000	An Internet service that allows users to post "tweets" for their followers to see updates in real-time.
Viber	260,000,000	A free, cross-platform instant messaging and voice over IP (VoIP) application. Users can exchange images, video, and audio media messages by sending files to each other.
WeChat	889,000,000	A Chinese social media mobile application software that features instant messaging, e-commerce, and payment services.
Weibo	313,000,000	A Chinese microblogging website. Akin to a hybrid of Facebook and Twitter.
WhatsApp	1,200,000,000	An instant messaging service for smartphones. Can be used to make voice calls and one-to-one video calls.
Wikia	300+ (2016)	A wiki hosting service.
YouTube	1,000,000,000	An American video-sharing website.

User numbers from Statista. Retrieved 14 July 2017.

Twitter is an online social networking service that enables users to send and read short 140-character messages called "tweets" in real time. Registered users can read and post tweets, but unregistered users can only read them.

Not surprisingly, children, adolescents, and young adults can and do share a wide range of information about themselves on social media sites because the sites themselves are designed to encourage the sharing of information and the expansion of networks. According to a Pew Research Center report, 92% of teenagers in the United States aged 13 to 17 years went online daily, and 24% reported being almost constantly on the Internet (Lenhart, 2015a). The current high school generation has grown up in a technology-based society where equipment has gotten more powerful in memory, easier to use, and much more portable in size.

With the fast expansion of social media, misuse can be a legal issue. Thus, social media platforms usually have terms of service. Consider Twitter's terms of service as an example:

- *Violent threats (direct or indirect)*: Threats or promotion of violence including threatening or promoting terrorism is not allowed.

- *Harassment:* Inciting or engaging in targeted abuse or harassment of others is not allowed. Questions considered when evaluating abusive behavior include the following:

  - Is the reported account to harass or send abusive messages to others?

  - Is the behavior one-sided or includes threats?

  - Is the account prompting others to harass another account?

  - Is the account sending harassing messages to multiple accounts?

- *Hateful conduct*: Violence that attacks or threatens other people on the basis of race, ethnicity, national origin, sexual orientation, gender identity, religious affiliation, age, disability, or illness is not allowed.

Types of Social Media Victimization

Youth risk behaviors have been studied and well documented in the health arena with regards to smoking, substance use, and sexual experimentation. Now, with the Internet being a part of daily life, risk-taking behaviors are moving online. Adolescence and young adulthood are periods when people are at risk for Internet victimization. This generation has grown up with changing technology, has experienced having their technology use monitored by adults, and are now in charge of their own online independence.

Technology and the devices associated with online access present a number of hazards, such as the potential for electronic aggression, self-exploitation, cyberbullying, online harassment, access to pornography, online predators, sexual solicitation, identity theft, and cyberstalking. Bullying is one increasingly common experience for youth. In a nationwide high school study, 20.1% of high school students reported having been bullied on school property during the prior 12 months, with more girls (22.0%)

than boys (18.2%) reporting the experience (Eaton et al., 2012). The most frequent forms of in-school and online bullying involved name-calling or insults, and the online incidents most typically took place through instant messaging.

Internet risk behaviors that have been found to cluster together include posting of personal information (name of school, email address, photos), sexualized pictures or videos, corresponding online with an unknown person (meeting the person offline), online-initiated harassment (playing jokes), online-initiated sex sites, and overriding Internet filters or blocks (Dowdell, Burgess, & Cavanaugh, 2009; Duggan & Brenner 2013; Hepburn, Azrael, Molnar, & Miller, 2012; Lenhart, 2015a; Tokunaga, 2010).

Self-Exploitation

Sexting involves the sending or forwarding via cell phone of sexually explicit photographs or videos of the sender or someone known to the sender (Lorang, McNiel, & Binder, 2016). Many adolescents use cell phones and indicate that text messaging is their preferred means of communication. Because transferring and viewing sexually explicit material of a minor subject is considered to be child pornography in many jurisdictions, there can be serious legal consequences. Sexting involves taking nude photos of oneself (auto-pornography or self-exploitation) and can also include individuals in the acts of undressing each other, touching each other, or having sex. While sexting and other self-exploitative behaviors are becoming increasingly common, Ahern and Mechling (2013) argue there is a lack of recognition of the consequences and increased risks of sexting (e.g., shame and guilt, earlier sexual behavior, bullying, incarceration, substance abuse, depression, suicide) for youth as a vulnerable population.

Rice and colleagues (2012) reported that sexting is associated with sexual activity, sexual risk behaviors, and knowing others who have sent a sext. It is not surprising that a link has been reported between sexting and offline sexual behaviors, as well as between electronic aggression and sending a sext or receiving a sexting message. Studies indicate that troubling academic behaviors with teachers, failing grades, suspensions, and being expelled from school are higher among students who sext and receive sexting messages than students who do not. Researchers have also found that teens who send and receive sexting messages and view sexually explicit material online are more likely to create, send, and view sexualized material. Basically, students who view sexualized material online copycat what they see to create what they like (Dowdell, 2015).

Sexting Case: Protecting One's Electronic Reputation

In 2010, in Olympia, Washington, Margarite, an eighth-grade girl, posed naked before her bathroom mirror, held up her cell phone, snapped a picture, and sent the full-length frontal photo to her new boyfriend, Isaiah. They broke up soon after. A few weeks later, Isaiah forwarded the photo to an eighth-grade girl, once a friend of Margarite's, who posted a text message on the photo saying, "Ho Alert! If you think this girl is a whore, then text this to all your friends." In turn, hundreds of students were estimated to have received the sexted photo with its tagged message, and Margarite was bombarded by texts from worried friends and propositions from boys she scarcely knew. The next morning the school was buzzing. "When I opened my phone I was scared," recalled a student, "I knew who the girl in the picture was. It's hard to unsee something like that" (Hoffman, 2011a).

The incident was reported to police. Isaiah admitted they agreed to exchange pictures. He sent a picture without a shirt on. After the photo went viral, Margarite transferred schools in an effort to put the experience behind her, but within weeks she was recognized and more students began to taunt her, calling her a whore and slut. She became depressed and begged to stay home from school (Hoffman, 2011a).

The county prosecutor initially charged three students—Isaiah, the former girlfriend, and a 13-year-old girl who was also instrumental in propagating the photo—with felony charges of dealing in depictions of a minor engaged in sexually explicit conduct.

A month later, the prosecutor amended charges from a child pornography felony to a gross misdemeanor of telephone harassment. Isaiah and the two girls would be eligible for a community service program that would keep them out of court, and the case could be dismissed. The three teens would have to create public service material about the hazards of sexting, attend a session with Margarite to talk about what happened, and otherwise have no contact with her.

One year later, Margarite transferred back to her old school, after talking with her former friend to be sure the incident was settled between them.

This sexting case illustrates how a nude photo caused harassment, betrayal, social ostracism, legal intervention, social justice, and family and community intervention. Several commentaries published on the case are instructive (Hoffman, 2011b):

- *College professor*: Teenagers have constant access to technology and are growing up in a culture that celebrates body flaunting. Sexting is easy, unremarkable, and even compelling. One reason teenagers sext is to look cool and sexy to someone they find attractive.

- *Prosecutor*: Naked pictures of a partner on a cell phone is an advertisement of being sexually active and can give the person status. Sexting is not illegal. But when that sexually explicit image includes someone who is under 18, child pornography laws may apply.

- *Isaiah (boyfriend):* He didn't know sexting was against the law.

- *College professor*: The contemporary teenager's world, in many developed countries, is steeped in highly sexualized messages. Extreme pornography is easily available on the Internet. Hit songs and music videos promote stripping and sexting. You can't expect teenagers not to do something they see happening all around them.

- *Attorney*: "We have to protect kids from themselves sometimes. We're on the cusp of teaching them how to manage their electronic reputations."

- *Margarite's father*: "I could say it was everyone else's fault, but I had a piece of it, too. I learned a big lesson about my lack of involvement in her use of the phone and texting. I trusted her too much. The photo most certainly still exists on cell phones, and perhaps on social networking sites, readily retrievable. She will have to live with this for the rest of her life."

- *School support*: School authorities held forums about sexting for the school's teachers, parents, and student delegations from the town's four middle schools.

- *Margarite's advice*: "If they are about to send a picture and they have a feeling, like, they're not sure they should, then don't do it at all. I mean, what are you thinking? It's freaking stupid!"

Sexting Ring Case

Sexting cases can have variations on the theme, as in the following case that involved multiple students who tried to sell explicit photos.

In January 2016, five high school students were arrested and another 20 were referred to a community-based review board in Newtown, Connecticut, for their involvement in a "sexting" ring that circulated sexually explicit images and videos of other students. The probe began in 2015, when school administrators learned that several boys and girls were sexting—sharing nude photos and videos of themselves and their classmates—through smartphone apps such as Snapchat, FaceTime, iMessage, and Kik. Some of the students who received copies of the images tried to profit by selling the pictures and videos for $10 to $20 apiece. The students whose images were shared were also held accountable for their actions in taking the pictures and forwarding them even though they never intended the images to go beyond the person to whom they were sent. Charges for those arrested included misdemeanor counts of obscenity, transmitting or possession of child pornography by a minor, as well as felony counts of possession of child pornography and obscenities as to minors (Ferrigno, 2016).

In another high school sexting case in Colorado, reported by Ferringno (2016), students used a photo vault app that hides nude photos by storing them in an app that appears to be a calculator or media player. Within the app, when a certain button is held long enough a prompt for a password appears. Once that password is entered, any messages that have been sent from photo vault to photo vault start showing up. The app is similar to Snapchat in that the photo can be deleted from the device.

Electronic Aggression

Electronic aggression, or cyberbullying, is any behavior performed through electronic or digital media by individuals or groups that repeatedly communicates hostile or aggressive messages intended to inflict harm or discomfort on others. Electronic aggression can occur in many forms such as bullying through social networking sites, email, harmful texting, or instant messaging (IM). It can occur in a chat room, on a website, or through digital messages or images sent to a cell phone (Huang & Chou, 2010; Patchin & Hinduja, 2010).

Studies on gender differences have found that girls are more likely than boys to report having been the victim of electronic aggression by being sexually harassed online and to be the recipients of threatening text and email messages at least once (Rivers & Noret, 2010). Girls also are more likely than boys to engage in behaviors that raise their risk level for victimization, including posting pictures online, chatting with strangers online, disclosing school information or instant messenger screen names, and flirting online (Sengupta & Chaudhuri, 2011).

Studies comparing students who have used the Internet to intentionally harass others with those students who have not harassed have uncovered concerning differences. Researchers have found that students who intentionally harass are more likely to have trouble in school, report being a below-average student, have been bullied, drink alcohol, smoke cigarettes, and use other substances (Dowdell, 2015). Additionally, when examined in the context of other Internet risk behaviors, such as receiving aggressive or threatening online messages, viewing sexually explicit material, browsing online sex sites, as well as receiving sexting messages, and using a webcam, an image emerges of an electronically aggressive adolescent with negative experiences both in his or her online and offline life (Dowdell, 2015).

Dangerous Cases Using Social Media

The use of social media can also have lethal consequences. In a study of Internet stalking and homicide, criminologist Dr. Jane Mockton Smith and colleagues at the University of Gloucestershire in England completed a six-month study of 358 cases, which occurred in Britain between 2012 and 2014 and found a strong correlation between stalking and homicide. In fact, criminologists found stalking behavior present in 94% of cases they studied, and the researchers found that 85% of the murders occurred in victims' homes. In one case, the offender set up a bogus profile on Facebook and stalked his ex-partner before constantly bombarding her with texts and calls. Police later found the victim's body in her apartment, where he had left Oasis's "Stop the Clocks" playing on repeat (Grierson, 2017).

Legal Issues

Sexting Laws

With regard to sexting, the trend has been that minors involved in sexting without other exacerbating circumstances should be charged with a less serious offense; however, consensus is lacking on exactly how they should be adjudicated (Lorang et al., 2016). As of July 2015, 20 states have enacted sexting laws: Arizona, Arkansas, Connecticut, Florida, Georgia, Hawaii, Illinois, Louisiana, Nebraska, Nevada, New Jersey, New York, North Dakota, Pennsylvania, Rhode Island, South Dakota, Texas, Utah, Vermont, and West Virginia. Eleven of these states classify the offense as a misdemeanor and prescribe out-of-court "diversion" remedies or informal sanctions such as counseling. Four of the 20 states, however, also allow for felony charges (Lorang et al., 2016).

Modern sexting laws often provide leniency to adolescents as long as the sexting is consensual and is considered a misdemeanor mistake in exploring sexuality. Lorang and colleagues (2016) cite two cases showing the treatment of such cases. In a Pennsylvania case, the minor (and an unknown number of other people) received a text message with recordings of the consensual sexual acts of two other minors, aged 16 and 17, and further disseminated the recording. The trial court dismissed the charges related to sexual abuse of children because the child pornography statutes when applied to teenage sexting failed to "provide a teenager of ordinary intelligence fair notice of what is prohibited." The appeals court dismissed the charges because of the vagueness of the penal codes as applied to the defendant. The court reasoned that a teenager would have understood that child pornography was illegal and that the law was there to protect children. The judge continued to write that the same teenagers, unless prosecuted, would be clueless that their conduct falls within the parameters of the Sexual Abuse of Children statute. Not only is sexting prevalent in their world, but it is doubtful they would connect sexting with the sexual exploitation of children (Pa. Cnty Ct., 2012).

In an Ohio case, however, in which a 13-year-old female juvenile defendant sent nude self-images to a juvenile male, the court of appeals held that the court did not err in overruling the defendant's motion to dismiss. They stated that, as applied to juveniles, the statute was not unconstitutionally vague. The defendant filed a motion to dismiss, which was denied. The defendant then entered a no-contest plea. She was sentenced to 30 days in detention, but the sentence was suspended. She was ordered to complete 16 hours of community service, to attend an educational program on sexting, and to write an essay. She was also banned from using a cell phone for six months (Ohio Ct. App., 2012).

Internet Luring

Internet luring is called *child luring* when a minor is involved. The Royal Canadian Mounted Police (RCMP) defines child luring as follows: "Adults aged 18 or more who attempt, through the Internet, to contact minors for the purpose of inciting them to have sexual contact." These actions are considered criminal under the Criminal Code of Canada, Section 172. The RCMP recommends that in the event of cyberbullying the user should save all messages; block the sender via the website or app's security features; never respond to the messages; talk to a trusted adult; and contact the local police service in order to file a complaint. The RCMP cite the case of 15-year-old Rehtaeh Parsons, who hanged herself in her bathroom after four boys raped her and spread a photograph of the assault, causing classmates and friends to taunt and cyberbully her. The attack left Rehtaeh an outcast at her high school, where her rapists were also students. Her mother later described how friends, students, and strangers taunted her. Boys texted her all the time, saying, "Will you have sex with me?" Girls texted her, saying, "You're such a slut." According to her mother, "She was never left alone. She had to leave the community. Her friends turned against her. People harassed her . . . It just never stopped" (Warren, 2013).

Sextortion

Sexual extortion, or sextortion, is another form of Internet crime. The Canadian Centre for Child Protection defines sextortion as "adults using technology to exploit children for a sexual purpose." Consider the example of 15-year-old Amanda Todd, who had exposed her breasts on a webcam while interacting with a group online. A man in the virtual audience turned out to be an Internet predator known as a "capper." Cappers troll the Internet looking for young people who have posted some type of sexual image in order to extort them. The predator then threatens to post the screenshot of the behavior with the victim's parents, teachers, employers, and others if the victim does not provide the capper with more sexually explicit materials. The capper who targeted Todd then contacted her via Facebook and demanded three more photos of her breasts in order to make him disappear. The predator warned that it would not matter if Todd changed schools, made new friends, or got a new boyfriend; he would find her to continue the harassment. The predator turned out to be a 35-year-old man from the Netherlands. He was charged with extortion, Internet luring, criminal harassment, and the possession and distribution of child pornography in relation to Todd's case (Victims of Violence, 2016; Yuen, 2017).

Mental Health Implications

Internet Addiction

Internet addiction goes by a few different names, including Internet addiction disorder (IAD), compulsive Internet use (CIU), problematic Internet use (PIU), or iDisorder. It may include playing online video games in excess, compulsive online shopping, or constant checking of social media sites. Use becomes disordered when computer use interferes with a person's daily life and their relationships (Gregory, 2017).

In the clinical history of addiction disorders, more than 20 years ago, psychiatrist Ivan Goldberg, in 1995, satirically theorized IAD as a disorder, and listed seven symptoms on psycom.net, a psychiatry bulletin board (Gregory, 2017). Hundreds of people who heard of the diagnostic test logged on, clicked through, and diagnosed themselves as being Internet addicts. Goldberg's test was a parody on the *Diagnostic and Statistical Manual* (DSM), and in 1997, he commented that having an Internet addiction support group was as logical as having a support group for coughers (Srinivasan, 2014).

Srinivasan (2014) studied the problem of IAD for over five years and noted that since Goldberg's prank about 100 scientific journals in psychology, sociology, neuroscience, anthropology, healthy policy, and computer science have published on the Internet addiction question in some form. And after two decades of ridicule, research, advocacy, and pushbacks, Srinivasan arrived at two basic questions: What should it be called? Does the "it" exist?

What should it be called? Should it be called addictive, maladaptive, pathological, or excessive use; Internet addiction disorder; or problematic Internet use? Does it belong in the DSM under gaming disorders? And does the condition involve certain types of software, such as video games or social media, or certain types hardware, such as mobile phones or laptops (Srinivasan, 2014)?

Other clinicians and researchers have joined the nomenclature pursuit. Wallace (2014) suggests problematic Internet use, dysfunctional Internet use, Internet dependency, pathological Internet use, and compulsive Internet use as ways to describe these behaviors. Cheng and Li (2014) define Internet addiction (IA) as an impulse control problem characterized by an inability to inhibit Internet use. Because of the inability to control the behavior, there is an adverse impact on major life domains (e.g., interpersonal relations, physical health) (Cheng & Li, 2014).

Does Internet addiction (IA) really exist? Trying to find how many people have any type of health condition is a challenge. Behavior is hard to measure, and there's no diagnostic standard. Researchers have used many different tests across the world. Sampling bias also complicates any measure. How much of a population actually has access to the web, and how often? Prevalence statistics for IA vary between less than 1% to more than 8% in the United States. Norway reports 2%; Poland 5.8%; England at 18.3%; Italy at 5.4%; and China and Korea between 2% to 35% among adolescents (Srinivasan, 2014).

Cheng and Li (2014) designed a study to address the issue of IA prevalence through a meta-analysis, using amalgamated data to give more conclusive evidence for a global estimate. The Middle East had the highest prevalence (10.9%) and the lowest was in Northern and Western Europe with 2.6%. IA prevalence was higher for nations with greater traffic time consumption, pollution, and dissatisfaction with life in general. (Cheng & Li, 2014).

Studies have also examined pathological gaming. Gaming behaviors have been studied as to whether some youth are "addicted" to video games. Using a national sample, Gentile and his team (2009) gathered information from a randomly selected sample of 1,178 American youths ages 8 to 18 about their video-gaming habits and parental involvement in gaming to determine the percentage of youth who meet clinical-style criteria for pathological gaming. The researchers found 8% of video-game players showed pathological patterns of play, and they had poorer grades in school. These results confirm that pathological gaming can be measured reliably (Gentile, 2009).

Signs and Symptoms of Internet Addiction

Internet addiction is described as a compulsive-impulsive spectrum disorder that involves at least three subtypes: excessive gaming, sexual preoccupations, and email/text messaging (Block, 2008). About 86% of IA cases have some other DSM diagnosis such as depression or ADHD and the issue of comorbidity further complicates diagnosis as well as treatment (Block, 2008). IA is characterized by changes in mood, preoccupation with the Internet and digital media, the inability to control the amount of time spent online, the need for more time or a new game to achieve a desired mood, withdrawal-like symptoms when not engaged online, a level of family conflict associated with time spent online, and a diminishing social life as well as poor performance in school or work (Cash, Rae, Steel, & Winkler, 2012). IA has four components (Block, 2008; Cash, Rae, Steel, & Winkler, 2012):

1. *Excessive use* that is often associated with a loss of sense of time or a neglect of basic drives.

2. *Withdrawal*, including feelings of anger, tension, and/or depression, occurs when the computer is inaccessible.

3. *Tolerance*, including the need for better computer equipment, more software, or more hours of use.

4. *Negative repercussions*, including arguments, lying, poor achievement, social isolation, and fatigue.

Young (1998) designed the following questions for assessing social media use:

1. Do you feel preoccupied with the Internet (think about previous online activity or anticipate next online session)?

2. Do you feel the need to use the Internet with increasing amounts of time to achieve satisfaction?

3. Have you repeatedly made unsuccessful efforts to control, cut back, or stop Internet use?

4. Do you feel restless, moody, depressed, or irritable when attempting to cut down or stop Internet use?

5. Do you stay online longer than originally intended?

6. Have you jeopardized or risked the loss of a significant relationship, job, educational, or career opportunity because of the Internet?

7. Have you lied to family members, therapists, or others to conceal the extent of involvement with the Internet?

8. Do you use the Internet as a way of escaping from problems or of relieving a dysphoric mood (e.g., feelings of helplessness, guilt, anxiety, depression)?

Addiction is present if the person answers positive to five (or more) of the questions as occurring during a six-month period. In the following case, an extreme reaction to withdrawing from gaming illustrates the severity of symptoms.

Case of Withdrawal Psychosis

Paik, Oh, and Kim (2014) reported a case of a patient with withdrawal psychosis. The symptoms included disorganized behaviors, agitation, irritability, and a persecutory delusion. The symptoms developed one day after the 25-year-old man stopped playing an Internet game that he had been playing every day all day for two years. He had no abnormal brain imaging findings from laboratory tests on admission, and upon antipsychotic medication (quetiapine up to 800 mg) his psychotic symptoms resolved after four days of treatment. This case report suggests that a brief psychosis can develop during withdrawal after excessive use of technology, suggesting that the pathology beneath the IAD is not an impulse control issue but more likely a form of addiction.

Interventions

Prevention

As previously noted, many parents have questions about how to manage or control their children's screen time. The American Academy of Pediatrics (AAP) convened a working group to develop policy guidelines for parents. They recommend that pediatricians consider a child's "media diet" as a part of wellness exams, considering not just the quantity of media but also the quality. The AAP recommends that parents and caregivers develop a family media plan that takes into account the health, education, and entertainment needs of each child as well as the whole family (Moreno, 2016). According to the AAP (2016):

- Parents should be mindful of their child's media consumption, and should co-view media and co-play games with their children.

- Protect children under age 6 from all virtual violence, because they cannot always distinguish fantasy from reality.

- Policy-makers should consider legislation to prohibit easy access to violent content for minors and should create a robust and useful "parent-centric" media rating system.

- Pediatricians should advocate for and help create child-positive media, collaborating with the entertainment industry on shows and games that don't include violence as a central theme.

- The entertainment industry should create content that doesn't glamorize guns or violence, doesn't use violence as a punch line and eliminates gratuitous portrayals of violence and hateful, misogynistic or homophobic language unless also portraying the impacts of these words and actions.

- In video games, humans or living targets should never be shot for points.

- The news media should acknowledge the proven scientific connection between virtual violence and real-world aggression and stop portraying the link as controversial.

Interventions with regard to sexting should address initial acts of nonconsensual distribution of explicit images as well as the potential for continuing harassment from others, and interventions for students and adults who are upset by the sexts. Interventions should be organized around a collaborative effort between professionals, school administrators, and family members to mitigate the potential harms, stigma, and psychological distresses associated with cases of sexting with cyberbullying that are shown to affect the normal functioning of a young victim. Symptoms of sexting and cyberbullying overlap (National Center for Missing & Exploited Children, 2012a, 2012b):

- Child avoids the computer, cell phone, and other technological devices or appears stressed when receiving an email, instant message, or text.

- Child withdraws from family and friends or acts reluctant to attend school and social events.

- Child avoids conversations about computer use.

- Child exhibits signs of low self-esteem including depression and/or fear.

- Child has declining grades.

- Child has poor eating or sleeping habits.

Identifying Victims of Electronic Aggression

Prevention of electronic aggression, in any form, as well as risk-taking behaviors and addiction to the Internet is a priority goal. A first step is having conversations with adolescents and young adults about sexting, bullying, and online relationships. Second, they should be asked directly about social media use. The NCMEC (2017b), as part of its Netsmartz Workshop on Sexting, offers questions to use as discussion starters:

- Has anyone ever sent you a sext?
- Have you known anyone who sent or received a sext?
- Has anyone ever asked or pressured you to sext?
- What should someone do if they receive a sext?
- What could happen to you if someone forwarded you a naked picture?
- What are some ways a private photo sent to one person could be seen by others?

If an individual has already sexted or has seen a sext, further assessment is needed to determine the extent of the sexting or exposure to sexting.

Questions to ask about cyberbullying include (NCMEC, 2017a):

- Have you ever been upset with someone online? How did you deal with it?
- Has someone ever sent you a mean message online? How did it make you feel?
- If you knew someone was being cyberbullied, what would you do?
- Do you know where to report cyberbullying on the websites and apps you use? Who would you talk to at school?

Due to the increasing threat of cyberbullying, it is recommended that social media platforms adopt, implement, and evaluate policies and programs on an ongoing basis, and publish anti-bullying policies on their websites.

▓ Conclusion

In summary, the Internet has provided many new and exciting advances while changing the way individuals communicate with each other. Online access is easier with open WiFi, hand-held data devices, touch screens, and voice activation commands, which suggests the continued expansion of what the Internet can offer the world. While the Internet has delivered an evolving world of new social media sites, applications, and means of connecting, a new class of victimization, victims, and offenders have emerged. Technology and the devices associated with online access also comes with a number of hazards such as the potential for electronic aggression, self-exploitation, cyber bullying, sexting, addiction, online harassment, online predators, sexual solicitation, identity theft, and cyber stalking. The relationship between social media and the Internet is complex. Individual Internet behavior involves a myriad of factors that contribute to the occurrence of safety or risk-taking behaviors that can begin in adolescence and continue across the lifespan into late adulthood.

The cases highlighted in this chapter demonstrate that Internet victims can experience significant negative outcomes from sexting, bullying, harassment, and risk taking. Interventions should be organized around a collaborative effort between providers, professionals, and family members. Professionals who interact with clients across the lifespan have a unique role in providing risk screening, identification, education, and referrals of victims of social media for treatment. Understanding that high-risk Internet behaviors cluster and screening for high-risk individuals will lead to evidence-based best practices through identification, assessment, intervention, and evaluation. Each person can be easily screened during each interaction by asking questions specific about time spent online, description of life created online, feelings about being online compared to offline, aggression (electronic aggression and traditional bullying), sexting (inappropriate photos), online relationships, and any offline meetings.

Professionals can ask direct questions and listen, actively remembering to document every response while reviewing the history in addition to following up on all risk behavior questions that get a response of "yes." Support systems are essential to continued screening and interventions for individuals who are victimized using social media outlets. Social supports, which should also include access to any professional supports, may be peers, family members, extended family members, school/work associates or resources, parish or religious support systems, as well as law enforcement or legal response. Identifying online risk potential as well as individuals who have been victimized can be a challenge as many do not share their experiences, believing that it can be better to stay quiet and to forget. Professionals can utilize these suggested resources for screening, educating and referring, as well as content that can be shared with adolescents, parents, family members, and others.

Key Terms

Internet risk behaviors: Sharing of personal information (e.g., name of school, email address, picture of self); corresponding online with an unknown person or later meeting the person offline; engaging in online-initiated harassment (e.g., malicious or offensive jokes); visiting online-initiated sex sites; and overriding Internet filters or blocks.

Self-exploitation: The creation and distribution of explicit or inappropriate pictures of oneself or peers.

Sexting: Involves the sending or forwarding via cell phone sexually explicit photographs or videos of the sender or someone known to the sender.

Sextortion: Sexual exploitation that occurs primarily online and in which non-physical forms of coercion are utilized, such as blackmail, to acquire sexual content (photos/videos) of an individual, obtain money from that individual, or engage in sex with them.

Social media: Forms of electronic communication, such as websites for social networking and microblogging, through which users create online communities to share information, ideas, personal messages, and other content (such as videos).

Discussion Questions

1. Discuss the advantages and disadvantages of social media across the lifespan.
2. What are the implications of Internet risk behaviors within educational systems?
3. What are the implications of Internet risk behaviors within health systems?
4. What are the implications of Internet risk behaviors within legal systems?
5. What is another way to look at Internet addiction?

Resources

Cyberbullying Research Center https://cyberbullying.org

National Center for Missing & Exploited Children http://www.missingkids
.org/home

NetSmartz Workshop websites (NCMEC):
http://www.netsmartz.org/Educators
http://www.netsmartz.org/LawEnforcement
http://www.netsmartz.org/Sexting

References

Ahern, N. R., & Mechling, B. (2013). Sexting: Serious problems for youth. *Journal of Psychosocial Nursing and Mental Health Services*, 51(7), 22–30.

American Academy of Pediatrics, Committee on Public Education. (2001). Retrieved from http://pediatrics.aappublications.org/content/pediatrics/107/2/423.full.pdf

American Academy of Pediatrics (AAP). (2016, July 18). Virtual violence impacts children on multiple levels. Retrieved from https://www.aap.org/en-us/about-the-aap/aap-press-room/pages/Virtual-Violence-Impacts-Children-on-Multiple-Levels.aspx

Anderson, M., & Perrin, A. (2017, May 17). Tech adoption climbs among older adults. Pew Research Center, Internet and Technology. Retrieved from http://www.pewinternet.org/2017/05/17/tech-adoption-climbs-among-older-adults/

Block, J. J. (2008). Issues for DSM-V: Internet addition. *The American Journal of Psychiatry*, 165(3), 306–307.

Cash, H., Rae, C. D., Stell, A. H., & Winkler, A. (2012). Internet addiction: A brief summary of research and practice. *Current Psychiatry Reviews*, 8(4), 292–298.

Chakraborty, K., Basu, D., & Vijaya Kumar, K. G. (2010). Internet addiction: Consensus, controversies, and the way ahead. *East Asian Archives of Psychiatry*, 20(3), 123–132.

Cheng, C., & Li, A. Y. (2014). Internet addiction prevalence and quality of (real) life: A meta-analysis of 31 nations across seven world regions. *Cyberpsychology, Behavior, & Social Networking*, 17(12), 755–760.

Dowdell, E. B. (2015). Self-exploitation and electronic aggression: High-risk Internet behaviors in adolescents. Final Report of Award No. 2010-MC-CX-0002. Washington, DC: Office of Juvenile Justice and Delinquency Prevention, Office of Justice Programs, U.S. Department of Justice.

Dowdell, E. B., Burgess, A. W., & Cavanaugh, D. J. (2009). Clustering of Internet risk behaviors in a middle school student population. *Journal of School Health*, 79, 547–553.

Duggan, M., & Brenner, J. (2013). The demographics of social media users, 2012 (Vol. 14). Pew Research Center's Internet & American Life Project. Retrieved from http://www.pewinternet.org/2013/02/14/the-demographics-of-social-media-users-2012/

Eaton, D. K., Kann, L., Kinchen, S., Shanklin, S., Flint, K.H., Hawkins, J., . . . Wechsler, H. (2012). Youth Risk Behavior Surveillance—United States, 2011. *MMWR Surveillance Summaries*, *61*(5), 1–165. Retrieved from https://www.cdc.gov/mmWr/preview/mmwrhtml/ss6104a1.htm

Elder, S. (2014, August 15). A Korean couple let a baby die while they played a video game. *Newsweek*. Retrieved from http://www.newsweek.com/2014/08/15/korean-couple-let-baby-die-while-they-played-video-game-261483.html

Englander, E. K. (2014). Contemporary bullying and cyberbullying: Knowing what to look for. Paper presented at the 61st Annual Meeting of the American Academy of Child and Adolescent Psychiatry (AACAP), San Diego.

Ferrigno, L. (2016, January 27). Newtown High School students charged in "sexting" ring. *CNN News*. Retrieved from http://www.cnn.com/2016/01/27/us/connecticut-high-school-sexting-ring/index.html

Gentile, D. (2009). Pathological video-game use among youth ages 8 to 18: A national study. *Psychological Science*, *20*, 594.

Gregory, C. (2017). Internet addiction disorder: Sign, symptoms, and treatment. Psycom.net Retrieved from https://www.psycom.net/iadcriteria.html

Grierson, J. (2017, April 24). Stalking behaviour identified in 94% of murders, study shows. *The Guardian*. Retrieved https://www.theguardian.com/uk-news/2017/apr/24/stalking-behaviour-murders-study-shows

Hepburn, L., Azrael, D., Molnar, B., & Miller, M. (2012). Bullying and suicidal behaviors among urban high school youth. *Journal of Adolescent Health*, *51*(1), 93–95.

Hoffman, J. (2011a, March 27). A girl's nude photo, and altered lives. *New York Times*. Retrieved from http://www.nytimes.com/2011/03/27/us/27sexting.html

Hoffman, J. (2011b, April 10). When a 'sext' goes viral. ChinaDaily. Retrieved from http://www.chinadaily.com.cn/cndy/2011-04/10/content_12298807.htm

Huang, Y. Y., & Chou, C. (2010). An analysis of multiple factors of cyberbullying among junior high school students in Taiwan. *Computers in Human Behavior*, *26*, 1581–1590.

Internet World Stats. (2017, March). World internet usage and population statistics. Retrieved from www.internetworldstats.com/stats.htm

Korenis, P., & Villick, S. B. (2014). Forensic implications: Adolescent sexting and cyberbullying. *Psychiatric Quarterly*, *85*, 97–101.

Lenhart, A. (2015a). Teens, social media, and technology overview, 2015. Pew Research Center. Retrieved from http://www.pewinternet.org/files/2015/04/PI_TeensandTech_Update2015_0409151.pdf

Lenhart, A. (2015b). Teens, technology, and friendships. Pew Research Center. Retrieved from http://www.pewinternet.org/2015/08/06/teens-technology-and-friendships/

Lenhart, A., Madden, M., Macgill, A. R., & Smith, A. (2007). Teens and social media: The use of social media gains a greater foothold in teen life as they embrace the conversational nature of interactive online media. Pew Research Center. Retrieved from   http://www.pewinternet.org/files/old-media/Files/Reports/2007/PIP_Teens _Social_Media_Final.pdf.pdf

Lorang, M. R., McNiel, D. E., & Binder, R. L. (2016). Minors and sexting: Legal implications. *Journal of the American Academy of Psychiatry and the Law*, 44(1), 73–81.

McGovern, B. (2017, June 16). Michelle Carter found guilty in landmark texting suicide case. *Boston Herald*. Retrieved from http://www.bostonherald.com/news /local_coverage/2017/06/michelle_carter_found_guilty_in_landmark_texting _suicide_case

Merriam-Webster Dictionary. (2017). Social media (definition). Retrieved from https:// www.merriam-webster.com/dictionary/social%20media

Mitchell, K. J., Finkelhor, D., Jones, L. M., & Wolak, J. (2012). Prevalence and characteristics of youth sexting: A national study. *Pediatrics*, 129(1), 13–20.

Mitchell, K. J., Finkelhor, D., & Wolak, J. (2001). Risk factors for and impact of online sexual solicitation of youth. *Journal of the American Medical Association, 285*(23), 3011–3014.

Mitchell, K. J, Wolak, J., & Finkelhor, D. J. (2008). Are blogs putting youth at risk for online sexual solicitation or harassment? Child Abuse Neglect, 32, 277–294.

Moreno, M. (2016). Media use for 5- to 18-year-olds should reflect personalization, balance. *American Academy of Pediatrics*. Retrieved from http://www.aappublications .org/news/aapnewsmag/2016/10/21/MediaSchool102116.full.pdf

Murray, R. (2012, October 12). Teen who posted video about cyberbullying commits suicide. *New York Daily News*. Retrieved from http://www.nydailynews.com /news/world/cyberbullied-teen-commits-suicide-article-1.1181875

Naragon, K. (2015). Subject: Email, we just can't get enough. *ADOBE NEWS*. Retrieved from https://blogs.adobe.com/conversations/2015/08/email.html

National Center for Missing and Exploited Children (NCMEC). (2012a). Netsmartz workshop: Cyberbullying. Retrieved from https://www.netsmartz.org/Cyberbullying

National Center for Missing and Exploited Children (NCMEC). (2012b). Netsmartz workshop: Sexting. Retrieved from http://www.netsmartz.org/Sexting

National Center for Missing & Exploited Children (NCMEC). (2017). Sextortion (defined). Retrieved from http://www.missingkids.com/Sextortion

Nuutinen, L., Roos, E. B., Ray, C., Tynjala, A., Rasmussen, M., . . . Leger, D. (2014). Computer use, sleep duration, and health symptoms: a cross-sectional study of 15-year olds in three countries. *International Journal of Public Health*. Retrieved from https:// www.researchgate.net/publication/262564288_Computer_use_sleep_duration_and _health_symptoms_a_cross-sectional_study_of_15-year_olds_in_three_countries

Ohio Ct. App., 2012. In re JP, 2012-Ohio-1451, 2012 Ohio App. LEXIS 1298 (Ohio Ct. App., 2012).

Pa. Cnty Ct. 2012. In re CS, 2012 Pa. Dist. & Cnty. Dec. LEXIS 403 (Pa. Cnty Ct. 2012).

Paik, A., Oh, D., & Kim, D. (2014). A case of withdrawal psychosis from Internet addiction disorder. *Psychiatry Investigation*, 11(2):207–209.

Patchin, J. W., & Hinduja, S. (2010). Cyberbullying and self-esteem. *Journal of School Health*, *80*(12), 614–621.

Pawloski, G. (2010, February 17). Prosecutor drops felony child porn charges in sexting case. *The Olympian*. McClatchy DC Bureau. Retrieved from http://www .mcclatchydc.com/news/crime/article24573847.html

Rice, E., Rhoades, H., Winetrobe, H., Sanchez, M., Montoya, J., Plant, A., & Kordic, T. (2012). Sexually explicit cell phone messaging associated with sexual risk among adolescents. *Pediatrics*, 130(4):667–673.

Rice, E., Winetrobe, H., Holloway, I. W., Montoya, J., Plant, A., & Kordic, T. (2014). Cell phone Internet access, online sexual solicitation, partner seeking, and sexual risk behavior among adolescents. *Archives of Sexual Behavior*, *44*(3), 1–9.

Rideout, V., Foehr, U., & Roberts, D. (2010). Generation M2: Media in the lives of 8- to 18-year-olds. Menlo Park, CA: Kaiser Family Foundation.

Rivers, I., & Noret, N. (2010). 'I h8 u': Findings from a five-year study of text and email bullying. *British Education Research Journal*, *36*(4), 643–671.

Robertson, A. (2017, April 24). Most killers stalk victims on social media before murdering them say criminologists. DailyMail.com. Retrieved from http://www.dailymail .co.uk/news/article-4439130/Most-killers-stalk-victims-social-media-murder .html#ixzz4ocoHm1zg

Sengupta, A., & Chaudhuri, A. (2011). Are social networking sites a source of online harassment for teens? Evidence from survey data. *Children and Youth Services Review*, *33*, 284–290.

Srinivasan, V. (2014, May 15). Internet addiction: Real or virtual reality? *Scientific American*. Retrieved from https://blogs.scientificamerican.com/mind-guest-blog/ internet-addiction-real-or-virtual-reality/

Tokunaga, R. S. (2010). Following you home from school: A critical review and synthesis of research on cyberbullying victimization. *Computers in Human Behavior*, *26*, 277–287.

Valkenburg, P. M., & Peter, J. (2011). Online communication among adolescents: An integrated model of its attraction, opportunities, and risks. *Journal of Adolescent Health*, *48*(2), 121–127.

Victims of Violence. (2016). Crimes on the Internet. *Canadian Centre for Child Protection*. Retrieved from http://www.victimsofviolence.on.ca/research-library /crime-on-the-internet/#source

Wallace, P. (2014). Internet addiction disorder and youth. EMBO Reports: Science & Society. Retrieved from http://onlinelibrary.wiley.com/doi/10.1002/embr.201338222/full

Warren, L. (2013, April 9). "Gang-rape victim," 17, kills herself "after her attackers took picture of the assault and sent it to classmates who branded her a slut." DailyMail

.com. Retrieved from http://www.dailymail.co.uk/news/article-2306494/Rehtaeh-Parsons-Gang-rape-victim-17-kills-attackers-took-picture-assault-sent-classmates-branded-slut.html#ixzz4ohTNuUXA

Ybarra, M. L., Diener-West, M., & Leaf, P. J. (2007). Examining the overlap in Internet harassment and school bullying: Implications for school intervention. *Journal of Adolescent Health*, 41, S42–S50.

Young, K. S. (1998). Internet addiction: The emergence of a new clinical disorder. CyberPsychology and Behavior, Vol. 1 No. 3., pages 237–244.

Yuen, J. (2016, September 25). Sextortion of children on the rise. *Toronto Sun*. Retrieved from http://www.torontosun.com/2016/09/25/sextortion-of-children-on-the-rise

CHAPTER 16

Victims of Cybercrime

Kevin R. Powers and Elizabeth S. Dillon

OBJECTIVES

- To identify types of computer- and Internet-based crimes
- To identify the incidence and costs of cybercrime
- To discuss legal approaches to cybercrime
- To discuss the impact of cybercrime on victims
- To identify strategies for preventing cybercrime

KEY TERMS

Botnets

Child sexual victimization on the Internet

Computer hacking

Copyright piracy

Cyberbullying

Cybercrime

Cyberstalking

Cyberterrorism

Distributed denial of service (DDoS)

Identity theft

Internet fraud

Mail fraud

Malware

Phishing

Ransomware

Spam

Spear phishing

Telemarketing fraud

Telephone hacking

Terrorism

CASE

According to Greenberg (2017):

> The WannaCry ransomware attack has quickly become the worst digital disaster to strike the [I]nternet in years, crippling transportation and hospitals globally. But it increasingly appears that this is not the work of hacker masterminds. Instead, cybersecurity investigators see in the recent meltdown a sloppy cyber-criminal scheme, one that reveals ama-teur mistakes at practically every turn.

Palmer (2017) reports that security pro-fessionals are still trying to determine how WannaCry was able to infect so many machines. Although official confirmation has not identified those responsible for the original WannaCry attack, private cybersecurity firms and investi-gating government agencies have been focused on North Korea as the culprit. The Bitcoin wal-lets associated with WannaCry contained only 338 payments amounting to $140,000. Although that could be considered a small amount, the ransomware infected hundreds of thousands of computers. More serious is the potential for WannaCry to inspire other malware cre-ators to copycat WannaCry's wormlike features (Palmer, 2017).

By exploiting vulnerabilities in how com-puters using Microsoft Windows communicate with other devices (McGoogan et al., 2017), the WannaCry ransomware software encrypted victims' computers, demanding payment in bit-coin exchange for "unlocking" the encrypted files (Woollaston, 2017). Targeted computers were "infected" when victims unknowingly clicked certain links or downloaded certain files (McCoogan et al., 2017). Targets included individual victims as well as hospitals, banks, telecommunications companies, and ware-houses (Sherr, 2017) (**FIGURE 16-1**). Although the WannaCry attack was largely halted within a few days, approximately 200,000 machines in 150 countries were ultimately affected (McGoogan et al., 2017).

FIGURE 16-1 The United Kingdom's National Health Service was among the victims of the WannaCry ransomware attack.
© Ben Stansall/ AFP/ Getty Images.

Introduction

Broadly speaking, **cybercrime** is any illegal activity conducted through a com-puter or handheld device. These crimes usually occur through global Internet networks. The Internet is the largest single component of cyberspace. Spanning the globe, it has over 3 billion users worldwide (Internet World Stats, 2017).

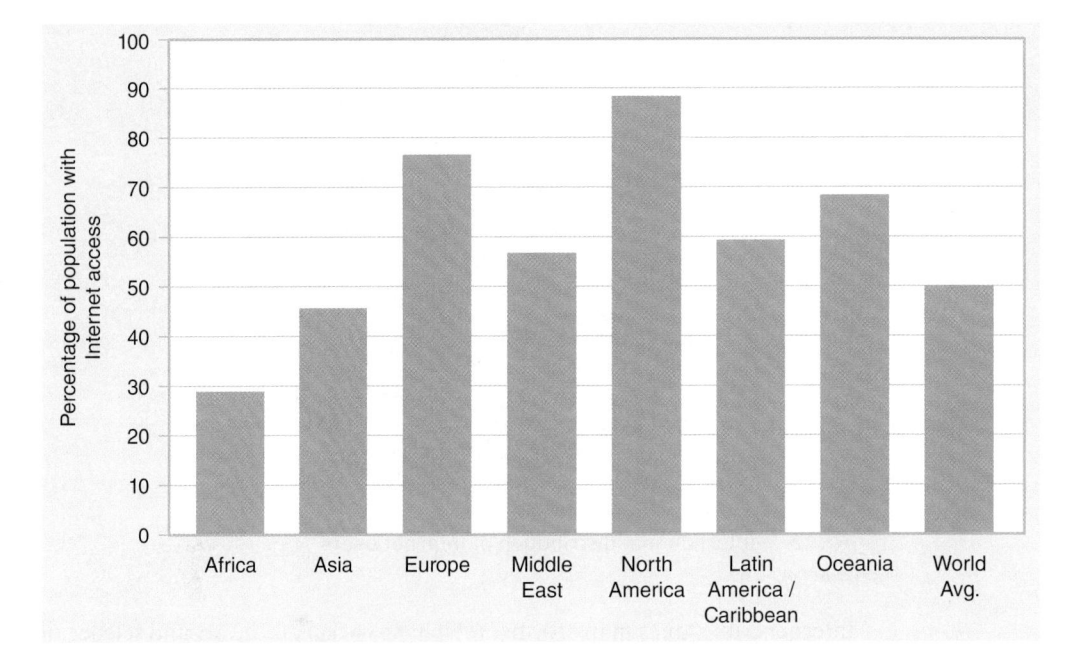

FIGURE 16-2 Global Internet penetration.
Data from Internet World Stats, 2017.

North America has the highest percent of the population with Internet access of any continent, with 88.1% of the population having access (see **FIGURE 16-2**), due to the high percentages of the population having Internet access among *all* of the countries comprising North America, with Greenland at 90.2%, Canada at 79.2%, Bermuda at 78.6%, and the United States at 78.2%. However, when the number of individuals with Internet access in a population is considered, rather than the percent of the population with Internet access, Asia represents 50.1% of world Internet users, while North America represents just 8.6% (see **FIGURE 16-3**) (Internet World Stats, 2017).

In addition to traditional access of the Internet via desktop and laptop computers, Internet use through mobile devices has risen dramatically. In 2015, Americans sent and received more than 2.11 trillion texts, videos, and photo messages, or more than 4 million texts per minute. In the same year, Americans used 9.5 trillion megabytes of mobile data, a 137.6% increase over 2014 (Cellular Telecommunications and Internet Association, 2016). This surge is reflective of the 2.8 trillion minutes Americans spent using their mobile phones and the 5.2 billion mobile users as of 2015 (Cellular Telecommunications and Internet Association, 2015, 2016).

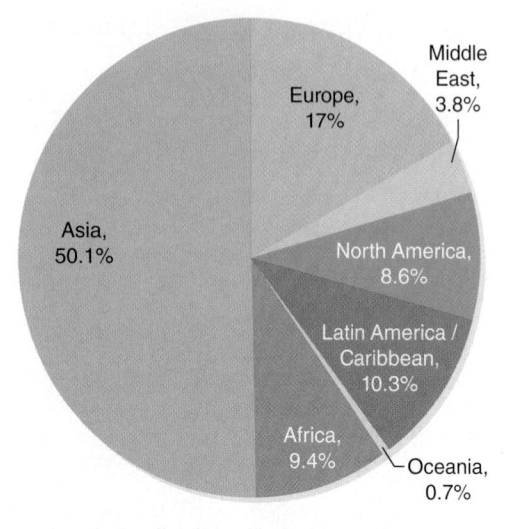

FIGURE 16-3 International distribution of Internet users.

Data from Internet World Stats, 2017.

Internet crime takes many forms. **Telephone hacking** is the art and science of cracking into a telephone network. Originally, telephone hacking was primarily used for making free long-distance phone calls, but now involves seeking private information on individuals. **Computer hacking** refers to unauthorized access to a computer or network, which may be motivated to publicize beliefs, to protest against a certain cause, or for personal gain. Hacking may be simply annoying or may turn to **cyberterrorism**, where essential services, such as medical systems or banking systems, can be disrupted (Chung, Chen, Chang, & Chou, 2004). **Internet fraud** is deception conducted through the Internet for the purpose of financial gain. **Copyright piracy**, although not necessarily viewed as a serious crime by the general public, is receiving a great deal of attention by law enforcement officials. Growing concerns are child pornography and **child sexual victimization on the Internet**, as well as the victimization among young people in the form of **cyberbullying**. **Ransomware**, as noted in the opening case, refers to malicious software that holds computer files hostage though encryption until the victim pays an agreed-upon ransom. **Identity theft** occurs when a criminal fraudulently assumes the victim's identity in order to secure financial gains. **Spam** refers to the sending of unwanted and often irrelevant emails and other communications to a large amount of individuals. **Phishing** occurs when a criminal fraudulently pretends to be a reputable company and sends emails or other communications for financial gain. **Spear phishing** is a targeted form a phishing, where criminals use known information about victims to obtain confidential information or for financial gain. **Botnets** are networks of computers that criminals control to perform coordinated cyberattacks. A **distributed denial of service (DDoS)** is a type of cyberattack in which multiple devices at varied locations all become infected, usually with **malware**. The group of infected devices then acts as a single system that hits a target simultaneously, resulting in a denial of service (DoS).

The type of disruption and damage caused by such an attack is illustrated by the massive DDoS attack against domain host Dyn in October 2016 (DeCesare, 2016). Dyn is a DNS provider, meaning it helps direct domain names back to certain IP addresses for many major companies. Dyn estimated that the attack, which was highly sophisticated, involved tens of millions of IP addresses and was powered by a botnet of hacked DVRs and webcams known as Mirai. The Mirai botnet looks for certain Internet of Things (IoT) devices, such as those that are using default usernames and passwords in smart home devices, and turns them into bots for use in cyberattacks similar to the one perpetrated against Dyn (Forrest, 2016). IoT refers to the connection of various devices to the Internet. For example, smartphones, cars, home and kitchen appliances, and even heart monitors can all be connected through the IoT, and as the IoT becomes more connected over the next few years the list will continue to grow (Meola, 2016). During the Dyn attack, online behemoths such as Twitter, Amazon, Reddit, Netflix, and others were without service multiple times during the day of the attack (Forrest, 2016). According to DeCesare (2016), "This attack was big, disrupting consumer services like Spotify and Netflix, all the way to enterprise-grade providers like Heroku and Zendesk . . . it's likely that this attack will have impacted more people, in more ways, than any other in memory" (DeCesare, 2016). Other major websites, including Okta, CNN, and Pinterest, were disrupted as well, which "provided a grim reminder of the vulnerability of a key element of the Internet's infrastructure" (Jackson Higgins, 2016).

In addition, the Internet can be used as a mechanism to lure people (especially children) into other forms of victimization. On July 27, 2017, law enforcement authorities apprehended two suspects in a sex trafficking operation spanning three states and affecting 13 victims, some as young as 15 years old. Investigators determined that the suspects used the Internet and cellular phone applications to lure the victims into their sex trafficking ring. In response to the arrests, Mike Boudreaux, the Sherriff of Tulare County, California, warned parents, "Be vigilant. Pay attention to what your children are doing online. Ask those very difficult questions. Who are you speaking with? Who are you talking to? Be a proactive parent" (Garcia, 2017). Similarly, in May 2017, a Los Angeles man was arrested for using his online multiplayer gaming avatar to lure approximately 67 child victims in different countries into sending him sexually explicit videos of themselves (Shaw, 2017). In April 2017, an ex-school board president in Adams County, Colorado, admitted to posting an explicit ad on the website Craigslist.com seeking "Daddy Daughter Role Play," in order to solicit a child to engage in inappropriate sexual activity (Garcia, 2009; Low, 2017).

Scope of the Problem

Cybercrime statistics are not collected in the same uniform manner as other crimes, in part because they fall into the jurisdiction of many different agencies. Although the scope of cybercrime is difficult to measure, a number of indicators point to the widespread nature of the problem:

- An estimated 15.4 million Americans, representing about 1 in every 16 adults, were victims of identity theft in 2016. The total financial cost of this identity theft in the United States was $16 billion (Sullivan, 2017).

- In 2016, almost 90,000 complaints were filed by Canadians to the Canadian Anti-Fraud Centre reporting that they had been victim to more than 30 different types of mass marketing fraud (Competition Bureau, 2017).

- In a 2016 study, 47% of American Internet users reported having experienced online harassment or abuse, including physical threats, cyberstalking, offensive name-calling, impersonation, hacking, and denial of access to an online platform (Lenhart et al., 2016).

- In a study of 5,700 U.S. schoolchildren, researchers found that 33.8% reported being bullied online (Patchin, 2016).

- The FBI's National Infrastructure Protection Center identified the vulnerability of the United States to cyberterrorism, noting that the government is 100% dependent on information systems and computer systems to run the nation (Goodman, Kirk, & Kirk, 2007).

- In 2016, NATO warded off an average of 500 cyberattacks per month that warranted a response (Browne, 2017).

- A 2015 survey of 58 U.S. organizations that had experienced cyberattacks in that year found that 97% had been subject to a malware attack and 100% had experienced attacks relating to viruses, worms, and Trojan horses. The survey reported that these companies saw, on average, 160 discernible cyberattacks per week (Ponemon Institute, 2015).

- The number of new ransomware families increased by 752% in 2016, which helped cybercriminals to steal about $1 billion from businesses (TrendLabs, 2017).

- The National Center for Missing and Exploited Children estimated that, in 2015, more than 26 million sexual abuse images and videos were reviewed by their analysts (U.S. Department of Justice, 2016a).

- 3,672 individuals were arrested in the United States in 2006 for possession of child pornography (Wollak, Finkelhor, & Mitchell, 2011).

- In April 2015, President Barack Obama issued an Executive Order declaring cybercrime to be a national emergency (Obama, 2015).

The Legal Context

The vast expansion of cybercrime and its consequences in human suffering and financial losses have resulted in a variety of attempts to fight it, including legal, organizational, and technological approaches. Many countries have instituted legislative approaches; however, the transnational nature of these crimes requires international cooperation and coordination (Kierkegaard, 2006). For example, in 1997, the G8 developed an action plan that required members to criminalize cybercrime and to protect the integrity and confidentiality of data systems (Chung et al., 2004). In 2001, the Council of Europe, the United States, Canada, South Africa, and Japan passed the Convention on Cybercrime, also known as the Budapest Convention, which mandates countries to have unified legislation for international crime prevention. The Budapest Convention was entered into force in 2004, and 55 countries have signed and ratified the agreement as of 2017. This agreement attempts to deal with the problem that Internet crime often originates in a jurisdiction that may be halfway around the world from the jurisdiction in which the victim lives. In this case, law enforcement then is hampered by cross-jurisdictional issues, including differing laws, definitions, and standards for Internet use, as well as crime descriptions, evidence collection procedures, and offender detention practices. The Convention is supplemented by a Protocol on Xenophobia and Racism committed on the Internet (Council of Europe, 2017).

National approaches to Internet crime prevention, detection, and prosecution are complicated by the vast array of types of Internet crime. As a result, legislation that addresses Internet crime is not unified in any way. In the United States, the range of legislation that addresses cybercrime is very broad, including the Cyber Security Enhancement Act of 2002, which modified the Homeland Security Act; amendments to the USA PATRIOT Act related to computer crime and electronic evidence; amendments to the federal Criminal Code that address, among other things, fraud-related activity pertaining to computers, wire and electronic communications interceptions, and recording of dialing, routing, addressing, and signaling information; the Cybersecurity Enhancement Act of 2013, which provides for voluntary public-private partnerships to improve cybersecurity research, development, awareness, and preparedness; the Cybersecurity Act of 2015, which requires that the director of National Intelligence and the departments of Homeland Security, Defense, and Justice develop procedures to detect and share cyber threat information with private entities and the public and work with private entities to help remove the risk; and new sentencing guidelines related to cybercrime. These legislative amendments demonstrate the developing and changing world of cybercrime and the challenges in addressing it. To ensure future success in combating Internet crime, the U.S. Cyber Security Research and Development Act (2002) authorized an expenditure of $903 million for research in this area.

Additionally, President Barack Obama issued several Executive Orders in response to the increasing threat of cybercrime. These Executive Orders addressed federal responses to cyberincidents, the responsibility of companies and organizations to share information related to cybersecurity risks, collaboration between the private sector and critical infrastructure with the federal government in response to cyberincidents, and the establishment of the Commission on Enhancing National Cybersecurity in the Department of Commerce.

Specific legislation also exists for particular types of cybercrime. For example, in the fall of 1998, the U.S. Congress passed the Identity Theft and Assumption Deterrence Act. This legislation created a new offense of identity theft, which prohibits knowingly transferring or using, without lawful authority, a means of identification of another person with the intent to commit, or to aid or abet, any unlawful activity that constitutes a violation of federal law, or that constitutes a felony under any applicable state or local law (18 U.S.C. §1028(a)(7)). This offense, in most circumstances, carries a maximum term of 15 years of imprisonment, a fine, and criminal forfeiture of any personal property used or intended to be used to commit the offense. Schemes to commit identity theft or fraud may also involve violations of other statutes, such as identification fraud (18 U.S.C. §1028), credit card fraud (18 U.S.C. §1029), computer fraud (18 U.S.C. §1030), mail fraud (18 U.S.C. §1341), wire fraud (18 U.S.C. §1343), or financial institution fraud (18 U.S.C. §1344). Each of these federal offenses are felonies that carry substantial penalties—in some cases, as high as 30 years of imprisonment, fines, and criminal forfeiture.

In January 2010, Canada revised the Criminal Code to more effectively target identity theft. Three new offenses carry a maximum five-year sentence: obtaining and possessing identity information, trafficking identity information, and unlawfully possessing or trafficking government-issued identity information.

Despite these laws, however, the ability of law enforcement agencies to address Internet crime is often hampered by the fundamental right for privacy. The Federal Bureau of Investigation (FBI), for example, has reported that its investigations are strictly limited by the Fourth Amendment of the U.S. Constitution, which guarantees the right of the people to be secure in their persons, houses, papers, and effects against unreasonable searches and seizure. Following legal action by the FBI against Apple for refusing to provide a program to bypass iPhone security without wiping the data from the phone of the man responsible for the San Bernardino shooting in 2015, law enforcement organizations have been pushing to require companies to provide "backdoor" methods to access the private data on the phones, computers, and other devices of individuals (Selyukh, 2016). Although the European Convention on Cybercrime calls for member states to ensure a proper balance between the interests of law enforcement and respect for fundamental human rights, the influence of the cyberspace in the organization of terrorism and other crimes has sparked conversation in increasing law enforcement's ability to better ensure public safety (Armstrong & Forde, 2003).

Child pornography is a good example of efforts to deal with serious Internet crime. Child pornography is a category of expression that is not protected by the First Amendment of the Constitution, and until 2002 it was covered by the 1996 Child Pornography Prevention Act. In 2003, President Bush signed the PROTECT Act, which redefined child pornography to include not only images of real children engaging in sexually explicit conduct but also computer-generated depictions that were indistinguishable from real children. The Canadian government enacted an amendment to the Criminal Code in 2002 that addressed child pornography on the Internet and using the Internet to lure children (Schell, Martin, Hung, & Rueda, 2007). In response, a report released in 2005 indicated that charges related to child pornography against those living in Canada had increased eight times between 1998 and 2003, suggesting that the new laws may have had some effect. In December 2011, the Canadian government introduced legislation that made the failure to report suspected cases of child pornography possession a crime. Failure to alert authorities about someone who possesses videos, photographs, or online material can result in a maximum fine of up to $100,000 for corporations, a maximum six-month jail term, and a fine of up to $10,000 (Department of Justice Canada, 2011).

As crime spreads across the Internet, law enforcement has begun to catch up with those using the web for illicit purposes. In December 2014, the U.S. Department of Justice's Criminal Division created the Cybersecurity Unit within the Computer Crime and Intellectual Property Section, with its objective to:

> [S]erve as a central hub for expert advice and legal guidance regarding how the criminal electronic surveillance and computer fraud and abuse statutes impact cybersecurity. Among the unit's goals is to ensure that law enforcement authorities are used effectively to bring perpetrators to justice while also protecting the privacy of every day Americans. In pursuing that goal, the unit is helping to shape cyber security legislation to protect our nation's computer networks and individual victims from cyber attacks. The unit also engages in extensive outreach to the private sector to promote lawful cybersecurity practices.
>
> (U.S. Department of Justice, 2017)

The National White Collar Crime Center (NW3C), based in Richmond, Virginia, offers operational support to law enforcement and functions as an information clearinghouse for cybercrime. The complexity of these cybercrimes, and the fact that they cross many traditional boundaries, means that, for any given cybercrime, several law enforcement agencies are responsible for each type of crime in the United States alone (see **TABLE 16-1**). These agencies work together to generate more funding to help law enforcement keep up with the ever-changing computer world. All cybercrime in the United States can be reported to the Internet Crime Complaint Center (http://www.ic3.gov /default.aspx).

TABLE 16-1 Agencies Responsible for Internet Crime in the United States

Type of Crime	Responsible U.S. Agency
Hacking	FBI (local office) U.S. Secret Service
Password trafficking	FBI (local office) U.S. Secret Service
Child pornography and child exploitation	FBI (local office) U.S. Customs and Immigration Enforcement

TABLE 16-1 Agencies Responsible for Internet Crime in the United States (*Continued*)

Type of Crime	Responsible U.S. Agency
Internet fraud and spam	FBI (local office)
	U.S. Secret Service (Financial Crimes Division)
	Federal Trade Commission
	Securities and Exchange Commission
Internet harassment	FBI (local office)
Internet bomb threats or trafficking in firearms	FBI (local office)
	Bureau of Alcohol, Tobacco, and Firearms
Copyright piracy	FBI (local office)
	U.S. Customs and Immigration Enforcement
Ransomware	FBI (local office)
Theft of trade secrets/economic espionage	FBI (local office)

Data from the U.S. Department of Justice (2017) and Federal Bureau of Investigation.

Types of Internet Crime

Internet crime comes in many different forms. Some of these forms are directed at particular individuals or groups, whereas others are not specifically targeted, but rather seek general disruption.

Hacking

Hacking (sometimes called *network intrusion*) refers to gaining unauthorized access to a computer or network. Hackers are individuals or groups who use the Internet to attack computer systems on a global scale. *Phone hacking* refers to intercepting phone calls or voice-mail messages of a user without his or her knowledge. Software for hacking is readily available and easily downloadable at little or no cost. Hackers share and barter their tools and information and mentor those who share their values. For instance, a simple Internet search using the term "phone hacking" reveals how-to videos and free software for casual hackers. Motivation for hacking can come from a number of factors, including the thrill and excitement of illegal activity, the challenge of outsmarting corporations and professional computer security experts, recognition of their activities through media attention, and the power of being able to affect many people and bring down powerful organizations (Armstrong & Forde, 2003).

Hackers may also be motivated by profit, vengeance, or political aims. Hackers use various types of encryption methods to hide their activities. They retain anonymity by using pseudo-names, remailers, and anonymous servers.

The Ponemon Institute, in cooperation with IBM Security, conducted a cost of data breach research study in 2017 with 63 U.S. companies in 16 industry sectors that experienced loss or theft of protected personal data. Fifty-two percent of the respondents indicated that the data breach involved a malicious or criminal attack, and 47% indicated that malicious or criminal attack was the root cause of the breach, rather than system glitches or negligent employees. The average total cost of the data breaches for the study's 63 companies was $7.35 million, an increase of 4.7% from 2016. Of those breaches, those due to malicious or criminal attack were the costliest, at $244 per capita in contrast to $209 per capita for system-glitch-caused breaches and $200 per capita for human error. It took companies a mean time of 235 days to detect breaches caused by malicious or criminal attack and a mean time of 68 days to contain them, compared to 181 days to detect and 38 days to contain a breach due to system glitch or 168 days to detect and 44 days to contain a breach due to human error (Ponemon Institute, 2017).

Beyond financial losses, however, hacking can lead to the damaging of data files and programs, disruption of work in progress, and undermining of public and consumer confidence.

Although the first computer viruses that appeared in the 1980s were unsophisticated codes written by hackers primarily in search of glory, new viruses are highly sophisticated and lucrative for the designers. In 2003, the first of these viruses, called SoBig.A, allowed the designer to monitor commands and control the host computer after a computer was infected (Bradbury, 2007). Since that time, the ability to control computers through network servers has intensified, and now hackers are able to use a host to send spam messages throughout the world, control online gambling and commerce sites, and hold access to personal data files for ransom. Groups of coders are creating networks that sell software intended for criminal use of another computer and even offer software support for the criminal who is using it.

A report by the U.S. Department of Justice identifies the challenges faced by prosecutors and investigators in identifying computer hackers (Morris, 2005). First, hackers may hide or "spoof" their IP address or bounce their messages through intermediary computers. Second, victims often do not discover the hacker's activities until it is too late and all traces of the hacker's identity are gone. In addition, some Internet service providers (ISPs) do not keep records that would allow hackers' identities to be disclosed with a subpoena. Some hackers alter ISP records, thereby obscuring their identity. Finally, some leads may go through foreign countries where hacking is not considered to be a crime. For example, earlier in the history of cybercrime in the United Kingdom, several arguments were put forth, both in support of and against the criminalization of hacking. Under British law, there was no general right to privacy, and thus the interference with privacy involved in hacking was more analogous to trespass and did not constitute criminal activity (Tan & Newman, 1991). The new European-wide agreements have shifted this legislative framework.

Despite problems with apprehension, ample evidence indicates that in some countries the courts are taking a very serious approach to hacking when offenders are apprehended. One example is Simon Vallor, a 22-year-old Welshman who was sentenced in a London, England, court proceeding to two years in prison after pleading guilty to creating three computer viruses. The judge noted that virus writers are not merely "computer buffs" or "nerds," but rather criminals whose activities cause destruction, disruption, and financial loss (Barton, Nissanka, & Waterhouse, 2003). Further, in July 2017, Russian hacker Alexander Tverdokhlebov was sentenced by a U.S. federal court to more than nine years in prison and three years of supervised release following his prison term after pleading guilty to engaging in illegal business ventures on the "dark net," including laundering stolen money and operating several "botnets" that he used to steal more than 40,000 credit card numbers and other financial information (Dunn, 2017). However, other countries, such as the Netherlands, have taken a very lenient approach, sentencing the author of the Anna Kournikova worm to just 150 hours of community service in 2001.

Cyberterrorism

The most dangerous form of hacking is cyberterrorism. Terrorists are individuals or groups of people who attempt to induce fear through threats and random acts of violence that inflict mass casualty or considerable economic loss for the purposes of calling attention to a political viewpoint. Cyberterrorism is the convergence of terrorism and the cyberspace (Stohl, 2006). It is the use of computers and networks to intimidate or coerce governments, organizations, or individuals for a particular political motivation. Whereas in the past terrorism relied upon deadly explosive materials to launch devastating attacks, cyberterrorism creates unprecedented opportunities for committing acts of terror through ubiquitous multimedia communication tools (Chu, Deng, & Chao, 2011). Cyberterrorism can lead to deaths through explosions, plane crashes, water contamination, or the disruption of medical or emergency response systems.

Since the 9/11 attack on the World Trade Center, the Western world has been aware of the threat of terrorism like never before. Ron Dick, former director of the FBI's National Infrastructure Protection Center, highlighted the modern vulnerability to cyberterrorism and noted that the United States is 100% dependent on information systems and computer systems to run the nation (Goodman et al., 2007). Critical infrastructures that depend on the Internet include transportation, banking and finance, energy distribution, emergency preparedness and response, public health, water, and others. In 2011, the Pentagon concluded that cybersabotage originating from another country could be considered an act of war. Should such an attack result in the death, destruction, or high-level disruption that a military attack may cause, use of force could be involved in the retaliation (Gorman & Barnes, 2011).

In cyberterrorism, extremist groups merely exploit modern tools to attain the same goals they have in the past. Chu and colleagues (2011) described the use of a smartphone using a popular web application and publicly accessible Wi-Fi to perform an act of terrorism. They determined that the digital forensics of mobile phones lags considerably behind computer forensics and that, as this becomes a growing mode for terrorist activities, forensic analysis approaches must be developed. Since 2011, digital forensics of mobile phones have vastly improved; however, the constant advancements being made in both smartphone and computer technology make it difficult to remain up-to-date with security and forensics.

Cyberspace is attractive to terrorist groups for a number of reasons. First, the anonymity of cyberspace allows people to gather information, create communication networks, and collaborate without detection. Innovative social media allows for nimble and vigorous revolutionary movements that can serve to attack existing social and political structures (Deibert & Rohozinski, 2010). Those engaging in this activity are difficult to track down to a particular location or identity because of easily accessible encryption software and their ability to move information in multiple formats and reroute it through multiple locations. Further, the Internet is increasingly accessible to people in all parts of the world, essentially flattening the traditional hierarchy of information access. Information and propaganda can be spread to large numbers of people with relative ease.

As an example of cyberterrorism, it is reported that Al-Qaeda used the Internet to coordinate operations, solicit donations via Internet transfers, and recruit volunteers through invitation-only chat rooms in preparation for the 9/11 attack (Goodman et al., 2007). The Internet, therefore, provides a means for distributing horrifying messages to vast populations, instilling fear and help-lessness. One stunning example of this was the beheading of *Wall Street Journal* reporter Daniel Pearl in February 2002, which was broadcast via videos posted on Islamic websites (Stohl, 2006). This was then picked up by the mainstream press, and the propaganda messages and subsequent fear spread further. The Internet continues to be used as a means to spread radical political ideas, recruit violent extremists, and scheme terror plots. Efforts by the United States and its partners to work with social media companies to curtail and counter terrorist activity on the Internet has proven effective, showing a 75% decline in Islamic State (ISIS) content on the Internet from 2015 to 2016 and a 45% decline in ISIS-related Twitter traffic from 2014 to 2016 (U.S. Department of State, 2016). Despite this progress, terrorist groups continue to direct attacks around the world. The efforts of the United States and other countries to combat **terrorism** and terrorist activities was best summarized in a report to Congress by the U.S. Department of State following the 9/11 attacks, which stated:

> Terrorism cast its lethal shadow across the globe—yet the world's resolve to defeat it has never been greater. . . . This chilling report details the very clear and present danger that terrorism poses to the world and the efforts that the United States and our partners in the international community are making to defeat it. The cold, hard facts presented here compel the world's continued vigilance and concerted action.
>
> (2001, para. 2)

Cyberbullying

Traditionally, bullying occurred most frequently on or around school property. However, the current generation of children has been raised on electronic media. This relatively new medium for communication and information sharing has changed individuals' social interactions, learning strategies, and choice of entertainment. Young people use email, webcams, text messaging, Instagram, Twitter, Facebook, and other social media sites to communicate with one another. The well-worn joke of the teenager's excessive use of the family telephone no longer applies. The dramatic change in the activities of youth related to the Internet is evidenced by the fact that the Internet is now a preferred pastime over watching television for young people (Mishna, McLuckie, & Saini, 2009). According to a 2015 study by from the Pew Research Center, 92% of teens go online daily, with 24% of those teens going online "almost constantly," and 56% saying they go online several times a day (Lenhart, 2015). This virtual world and easy access to communication has opened up a whole new area in terms of young people's ability to victimize one another. This is not to say that young people are meaner than they used to be or that the Internet has created bullies; rather, a study by Raskauskas and Stoltz (2007) revealed that almost all the youth who admitted to being cyberbullies also admitted to other more traditional forms of bullying. This suggests that, through the Internet, those who are prone to be bullies merely have more effective and efficient means of hurting other children.

Literature and incidence data on Internet-based bullying confirm its prevalence among school-aged children. The National Center for Education Statistics estimated that approximately one in every five students ages 12 through 18 were bullied from 2014 to 2015 (U.S. Department of Education, 2016). However, according to a 2016 study of a nationally representative group of 5,700 middle and high school students by the Cyberbullying Research Center, 33.8% of students reported being cyberbullied in their lifetime, and 16.9% of students reported being cyberbullied within the 30 days prior to the study (Patchin & Hinduja, 2016). The forms of harassment in the previous 30 days included mean or hurtful comments online (22.5%) and rumors online (20.1%), among nine other methods. Of the students who were cyberbullied, 25.7% reported experiencing one or more of these types of harassment two or more times in the past 30 days. In the same study, 11.5% of the students admitted to cyberbullying other students in their lifetime and 6% admitted to cyberbullying others in the 30 days prior to the study. The most commonly reported harassment methods by these cyberbullies in the last 30 days included posting mean or hurtful comments about someone online (7.1%), spreading rumors about someone through text messages or emails (5.4%), and posting a mean or hurtful picture of someone online (4.2%), among other forms of harassment. Also in the 30 days prior to the study, 8.1% of the student cyberbullies admitted to inflicting one or more of these forms of harassment on another student two or more times (Patchin & Hinduja, 2016). Based on data from the 2014 Canadian General Social Survey, about 17% of the Canadian population aged 15 to 29 who accessed the Internet at some point between 2009 and 2014 (a group representing approximately 1.1 million people) reported that they experienced cyberbullying or cyberstalking. Of this group, 36% reported that they had experienced cyberbullying but not cyberstalking, 33% reported experiencing just cyberstalking, and 31% reported experiencing both (Hango, 2016). Unfortunately, survey data from the National Center for Education Evaluation and Regional Assistance in 2010 shows that 64% of bullying incidents went unreported to teachers or other adults (Petrosino, Guckenburg, DeVoe, & Hanson, 2010).

Typical Internet bullying includes rumors being spread about someone through the use of emails or website postings; embarrassing or compromising pictures of a young person, sometimes taken in places like locker rooms; or modified pictures in which the young person's face is attached to a pornographic picture. When these messages are unleashed on the Internet, they are impossible to stop, as was a situation in which a movie taken of a teenage boy was distributed worldwide. The most famous cyberbullying case began on November 4, 2002, when a 15-year-old teenager in Trois-Rivières, Quebec, filmed himself acting out scenes from the movie *Star Wars* using a golf ball retriever as a lightsaber. The film was discovered by classmates and was loaded onto Kazaa, a global file sharing network. Subsequently, adapted versions were created with added music and special effects, and the original video was merged with other movies. The clumsy young man became world famous under the name "Star Wars Kid," and by 2006 his video had been viewed 900 million times. Television spoofs of the video appeared on major network shows such as *American Dad!* and *Arrested Development*. As a result of this worldwide attention, students in the young man's school leaped on tables whenever he entered the room yelling "Star Wars Kid, Star Wars Kid." They harassed him verbally and poked him to get a reaction. As a result of this unbearable attention, the teenager became depressed and dropped out of school. Three years later, the teenager and his family reached an out-of-court settlement with the families of three former schoolmates who initiated the bullying (Ha, 2006).

In 2016, 15-year-old Phoebe Prince was the victim of a three-month cyberbullying campaign by classmates, including through harassing messages on Facebook and via text messages. As the apparent result of this incessant harassment, Prince committed suicide by hanging, shaking the community of her 17,000-resident Western Massachusetts town (James, 2010). Ultimately, the three teenage perpetrators of the cyberbullying were prosecuted on various charges of harassment (Webley, 2011).

Cyberbullying can also include threatening emails, text messages, and other messages sent anonymously. In other instances, insulting or damning messages are sent to others under the guise of being sent by the bullying victim. In such cases, the young person suddenly discovers that he or she is ostracized by others and is unaware of what the cause may be. Bullying is extremely challenging to deal with in any situation; however, as with other cybercrimes, the inability to identify an offender can make addressing cyberbullying, a seriously damaging problem, next to impossible. This problem is exacerbated by the fear that victims have in coming forward to report cyberbullying, particularly given the threat of potential ongoing retaliation for "tattling" (Giacobbe, 2010).

The outcomes of cyberbullying parallel those of traditional bullying. Beran and Li (2005) administered a survey asking students about their reactions to cyberbullying. The majority of students reported feelings of sadness, anxiety, and fear, and stated that it affected their ability to concentrate on their schoolwork and to attain good marks. Additionally, data from the 2014 Canadian General Social Survey found that 60.4% of individuals who reported being only cyberbullied and not cyberstalked had a low level of trust in the people in their neighborhood, and 37.9% of those individuals had low levels of trust in their peers at school or work. For individuals who experienced both cyberbullying and cyberstalking, these statistics were measured at 47.5% and 39.0%, respectively (Hango, 2016). Research in this area displays the devastating effect cyberbullying can have on victims, altering their mental health, relationships with others, and ability to perform in work and school.

Child Sexual Exploitation on the Internet

Sexual exploitation of children on the Internet takes many forms. Definitive data as to the extent of Internet child pornography are unavailable. However, it has been estimated that there are approximately 14 million pornographic websites, with some posting more than 1 million child abuse images. In addition, somewhere between 23,000 and 40,000 websites advertise chat rooms that defend adult–child sexual relations (Sinclair & Sugar, 2005). One indication of the extent of online child pornography is through police arrests and seizures. For instance, the Child Exploitation and Online Protection Centre seized a database of 877,000 unique images during police investigations in the United Kingdom alone (Quayle & Jones, 2011). Analysis of another website by the FBI found that it hosted about 1.3 million images of children subjected to violent sexual abuse (U.S. Department of Justice, 2016b). As of 1999, the FBI had opened 1,500 new cases of child pornography in America, and many experts contended that it was the fastest-growing criminal frontier in cyberspace. Supporting that claim, the National Juvenile Online Victimization Study revealed that arrests in the United States for possession of child pornography rose from 1,713 in 2000 to 3,672 in 2006 (Wolak et al., 2011). Since 2003, when U.S. Immigration and Customs Enforcement and Homeland Security launched Operation Predator, which aimed to dismantle groups and individuals involved with the spread of child pornography, more than 35,000 criminal investigations and 13,000 arrests of child predators have been made (U.S. Department of Justice, 2016b).

The child pornography industry yields billions in profits. An FBI investigation into one child pornography website operated by Landslide Productions revealed that this one site grossed $1.4 million in 1 month and had 35,000 individual subscribers (Taylor & Quayle, 2003). The images posted on the Internet of child sexual abuse are used by offenders for sexual gratification, to support beliefs about the acceptability of adult–child relations, to lower inhibitions of victims, and to entrap and control victims.

Although in the past obtaining child pornography was difficult because it required a degree of exposure through visiting a specialized store that distributed the material or providing an address where material could be delivered, the Internet has made child pornography not only accessible, but has also made its acquisition private. Thus, fears of exposure and humiliation no longer serve as barriers to those individuals seeking child pornography. Many of the people who are eventually apprehended and charged have huge collections of images—up to 40,000 pictures (Taylor & Quayle, 2003). Increasingly, it appears that individuals are obtaining child pornography through peer-to-peer networks, such as Tor, that bypass central networks and allow users to surf the web with total anonymity (Wolak et al., 2011). This makes it more difficult to discover perpetrators and track the incidence of this activity.

Worryingly, purchasers of child pornography do not appear to limit themselves to fantasy alone, and one report suggested that 80% of these individuals are active child molesters (Seto, Cantor, & Blanchard, 2006; Schell et al., 2007). Similarly, in a study of 21 samples of Internet offenders with known offending histories, on average one in eight had an official criminal record for contact sexual offending, and of those offenders who self-reported their offending histories 55% admitted to a history of contact sexual offending (U.S. Department of Justice, 2016a). Child pornography is viewed as both addictive and progressive. Individuals who view the images become desensitized and seek out more and more violent and shocking material (Schell et al., 2007).

The range of people involved in child pornography crosses boundaries of class, income, and profession. The National Online Juvenile Victimization Survey found that among a sample of 605 people arrested for child pornography, perpetrators were overwhelmingly single (61%) White (80%) males (99%), in all age and income groups. However, 31% were married or living common-law and lived with children younger than age 18 (Wolak et al., 2011). Alexy, Burgess, and Baker (2005a) examined a convenience sample of 225 cases published in the news media to identify the types of people who engage in Internet child pornography. More than one-fifth of the offenders lived outside the United States. The largest occupational category of Internet offenders was professional (64%) and included persons in the fields of education, computers, medicine, and law. Other occupational categories included laborer (11.2%), unemployed (8.8%), military (5.6%), student (7.2%), and clergy (3.2%). These findings contradict the stereotypes about those who purchase and use child pornography and demonstrate the manner in which this offense infiltrates society. Parents who warn their children of the dangers associated with strangers rarely instruct them that child molesters may also be people they have come to know either in person or online.

The cases identified by Alexy and colleagues (2005a) were classified using law enforcement terminology to describe Internet offenders as traders, travelers, or combination traders/travelers. *Traders* are Internet offenders who trade and/or collect child pornography online. They may be involved with any or a combination of the following: production, possession, and distribution of child pornography online. More than half of the cases in this sample involved traders (59.1%). Descriptions of the Internet traders noted that they could be charged with child pornography, be interested in a wide variety of sexual acts with children, produce Internet child pornography, distribute child pornography, amass a very large collection of child pornography, operate as partners, and/or operate for profit. *Travelers* seek to meet a child in person after communicating through email or in a chat room. Characteristics of travelers include offenders with a wide range of sexual interests involving children, including sadistic and homicidal acts. *Combination traders/travelers* are individuals who participate in trading child pornography as well as traveling across state and/or national boundaries to engage in sexual interactions with a child. Slightly more than 19% of the analyzed cases involved offenders who engaged in a combination of trader and traveler activities.

As noted in the category of travelers, the Internet is also used to contact children. One example of this is the use of Internet advertising for access to child prostitutes in other countries, allowing child sexual tourism to flourish in countries where poverty contributes to an active sex trade industry and there is poor policing enforcement to limit sexual relations with minors (Sinclair & Sugar, 2005). In Honduras and Costa Rica, for example, pedophilic tourism increased 60% in 1999 as a result of a website that offered children for prostitution.

Another example is child luring through the Internet (Taylor & Quayle, 2003). In 2000, Finklehor, Mitchell, and Wolak estimated that approximately one in five youths receive sexual approaches from people they encounter online each year. Some of these approaches are from others in their own peer group, but some are from adults seeking illegal contact with teens. In a follow-up study conducted in 2007, it was determined that most Internet-initiated sex crimes involve an adult male who meets and seduces an underage adolescent into sex. Of these cases, only 5% of the perpetrator pretended to be younger than their actual age (Wolack, Finkelhor, Mitchell, & Ybarra, 2008). Wolack and colleagues (2008) suggested that these type of Internet sexual offenses fall into the legal category of statutory rape; that is, the youth agrees to meet and have sex with the perpetrator, but that the victim is under the legal age of consent. They estimated that crimes involving Internet luring account for approximately 7% of all statutory rapes in the United States. In these situations, an offender enters chat rooms that are frequented by children and poses as someone younger or of the other gender. Relationships are then established with vulnerable children by the offender becoming a confidant who understands and empathizes with the child's fears and struggles. Eventually, trust is established and the offender suggests a meeting where they can cement their friendship. The child or youth may agree to the meeting, believing that he or she is about to see someone approximately his or her own age with similar hopes, fears, and dreams. In extreme cases, the outcome is kidnapping, assault, or murder. Therefore, preventive education of young people appears to be vital. Mishna and colleagues (2009) conducted a review for The Campbell Collaboration to summarize the best available knowledge on school-based intervention programs to help protect children from cyberabuse. They concluded that participation in psychoeducational programs focusing on Internet safety do increase the safety knowledge of children. However, very discouragingly, such interventions do not change risky online behavior.

A key component of Internet sexual abuse investigations is identifying victims and tracking offenders. Images can be reproduced indefinitely with no loss of quality, and they can originate from anywhere in the world and be sent anywhere in a fraction of a second. In 2016, the Internet Watch Foundation found that 60% of child sexual abuse content originated in Europe (including Russia and Turkey) and 37% originated in the United States. The report identified that 92% of all child abuse URLs were hosted in five countries: the Netherlands, the United States, Canada, France, and Russia (Internet Watch Foundation, 2017). The international nature of the problem has presented tremendous challenges for law enforcement professionals in their aims to apprehend offenders and rescue children.

As a result of frustration caused by technological limitations, in January 2003, the Toronto Police Service contacted Microsoft Corporation to ask for assistance in dealing with online sexual exploitation of children. Their message was simple: "the bad guys are winning." A collaborative effort between the Toronto Police Service, the Royal Canadian Mounted Police, and Microsoft emerged, which included a $2.5 million investment by Microsoft Canada that resulted in a software package entitled the Child Exploitation Tracking System (CETS), which allows global police agencies to share information to track online child predators (Microsoft, 2005). In December 2004, after consultations were held with police specialists in North America, the United Kingdom, and Interpol, the product was ready for international deployment (National Child Exploitation Coordination Centre, 2008; Sher, 2007). Groups that came together for the development of this tracking system later formed the Innocent Images International Task Force, which would become the Violent Crimes Against Children International Task Force, and now includes law enforcement officers from 40 countries.

In 2013, after a request from the British prime minister, Microsoft and Google implemented measures to end web-based child pornography by removing child pornographic content from their search engine indices, filtering search results, and returning warnings to the user when specific search terms are used. For example, if an individual were to search for sexually explicit content involving children on Microsoft's search engine, Bing, the return is an ad to the user with a warning that says, "Child porn, exploitative, or abusive content is illegal. Get help now." Google searches for child pornography yield a similar warning. Following these measures, query volume for sexually explicit content involving children fell by 67% on Google from 2013 to 2014. Query volume on Bing also saw similarly significant drops to Google following the announcement of their plan to combat this content (Steel, 2015).

Additionally, undercover investigations are also commonly used to catch child sexual predators on the Internet. These investigations are conducted in a variety of ways, including having investigators pose as minors, having investigators pose as mothers who want to teach their children about sex, or having investigators pose as child pornography traders or sellers. However, research conducted by Mitchell, Wolak, and Finkelhor (2005) revealed that most investigators who used this method posed as female adolescents younger than the age of 12 years. All 124 offenders who were apprehended were male, most were White (91%), and most were employed full time (91%). A substantial proportion of these offenders (37.7%) had annual incomes greater than $50,000. When charges were laid, 91% pleaded guilty. As with other types of undercover work, the investigator falsifies his or her true identity and develops a sense of trust and acceptance by the targeted person(s). These officers are specially trained and work with national and international networks aimed at child exploitation. In a study of 51 people convicted of offenses involving enticing children over the Internet, 90% were apprehended as a result of an Internet sex sting (Briggs, Simon, & Simonsen, 2011).

More recently, in 2016, the FBI, with a warrant, quietly took over the "world's largest" child pornography site, Playpen, and placed malware on all of the computers that were logged on to the site for two weeks. This malware exposed the users' IP addresses, despite being hidden behind Tor's anonymity. In February 2015, the Playpen site had 215,000 registered members (Nakashima, 2016). Ongoing investigation from this FBI sting, as of May 2017, has resulted in the arrest of 350 suspects in the United States and 548 arrests internationally, as well as the persecution of 25 child pornography producers. The creator of Playpen has also since been arrested and sentenced to 30 years in prison (Schladebeck, 2017). Nevertheless, concerns have been raised about the ability to successfully prosecute cases involving undercover operations and deception. Courts have been concerned about entrapment, specifically whether undercover officers manufacture crimes or simply give offenders an opportunity to commit them (Arkin & Lichtblau, 2014; Mitchell et al., 2005).

Cyberstalking

Gary Dellapenta was a 50-year-old security guard who met 28-year-old Randi Barber at church. When she rejected his romantic approaches, Dellapenta became obsessed with Barber and placed advertisements of her on the Internet under the names of "playfulkitty4U" and "kinkygal30." Impersonating his victim, he posted her address and phone number along with a message that she fantasized about being raped on Internet bulletin boards and in chat rooms. He answered email inquiries about the ads and invited the potential attackers to come to her home and even offered suggestions about how to get past her security locks. As a result, six different men appeared at the victim's door and indicated that they wanted to rape her. Dellapenta had online accounts with four out-of-state companies, which required considerable policing resources to track down and acquire search warrants necessary to collect evidence. As the first person prosecuted under a California law on cyberstalking, Dellapenta pleaded guilty in April 1999 to one count of stalking and three counts of solicitation of sexual assault. In the end, he received a six-year sentence (Simpson, 2000).

Janet Reno, while serving as the Attorney General of the United States, delivered the first **cyberstalking** report to then Vice President Al Gore in September 1999. In the report she stated, "As we travel the information super-highway into the next millennium, we must do all we can to ensure the safety of computer users. We must also ensure that our federal and local laws can effectively deal with the threats present in the new electronic age" (U.S. Department of Justice, 1999). The Attorney General's report included the following recommendations: (1) states should review their laws to determine whether they address cyberstalking, and if not, they should promptly expand laws to address cyberstalking; (2) federal laws should be amended to prohibit the transmission of any communication in interstate or foreign commerce with intent to threaten or harass another person where such communication places that person in reasonable fear of death or bodily injury; (3) law enforcement agencies should acquire training on the extent of cyberstalking and appropriate investigative techniques; and (4) the Internet industry should create an industry-supported website containing information about cyberstalking and what to do if a person is confronted with the problem.

The 1999 Reno report suggested that 475,000 people may be victims of cyberstalking each year in the United States, and, quoting police figures, she estimated that 20% of all stalking cases involved cyberstalking. Reno's estimate was not far off. The 2006 Supplementary Crime Victimization Survey revealed that 1 in 4 victims of stalking identified some form of cyberharassment, and 1 in 13 reported being victims of electronic monitoring, including GPS monitoring, listening devices, or bugs (Baum et al., 2009). A 2011 study by the National Centre for Cyberstalking Research at Bedfordshire University in England found that cyberstalking had become more common than physical stalking, with 324 of the 353 study participants stating that they had experienced some form of harassment through electronic communication. The prevalence of cyberstalking continues to increase, as shown through the Data & Society Research Institute's 2016 report on Online Harassment, Digital Abuse, and Cyberstalking in America, which found that 8% of American Internet users say they have been cyberstalked to the point of feeling unsafe or afraid (Lenhart et al., 2016). The same study also found that women are twice as likely to be cyberstalked than men. More specifically, 20% of women younger than age 30 reported being cyberstalked, contributing a significant portion to the statistic that 14% of total Internet users younger than age 30 reported being cyberstalked. Additionally, Lenhart and colleagues (2016) found that repeated online contact that made the individual feel afraid or unsafe was four times as likely among lesbian, gay, and bisexual Americans than among heterosexual Americans.

Despite the dramatic example of Gary Dellapenta earlier in this section, the most common methods of cyberstalking involve harassing or threatening emails, text messages, calls, and voicemails, as well as inappropriate e-greeting cards and digitally altered pornographic photos that lead to harassment of the victim (Glancy, Newman, Potash, & Tennison, 2007). More sophisticated means of cyberstalking may involve the use of spyware to track the victim's activities and communications. Physical stalking and cyberstalking have similarly destructive effects on their victims. Victims commonly experience fear, depression, stress, anxiety, lowered self-esteem, and loss of trust in others. Posttraumatic stress disorder (PTSD) is also prevalent among victims of cyberstalking, at rates comparable to other traumatic events, such as sexual assault and combat. These reactions to cyberstalking result in adverse effects on the victim's social relationships and occupational activities (Short, Guppy, Hart, & Barnes, 2015). One way in which the impact of cyberstalking distinguishes itself from that of physical stalking, however, is its uncontrollable, anonymous form, which leads to a fear of the unknown in the victim (Glancy et al., 2007). Indeed, the 2006 National Crime Victimization Survey revealed that the worst fears of stalking victims in general are not knowing what will happen next (46.1%) and believing that the behavior will not stop (29.1%) (Baum et al., 2009). A study on the impact of cyberstalking found that in 21.7% of cyberstalking cases the harasser was a total stranger (Short et al., 2015). Cyberstalking makes it easier to harass the victim at work and at home without any inconvenience to the stalker. Nevertheless, individuals can take steps to prevent and manage cyberstalking (see TABLE 16-2).

TABLE 16-2 Preventing and Managing Cyberstalking

Preventing cyberstalking	• Keep your primary email address private.
	• Do not assume that any transaction on the Internet is confidential.
	• Choose online names with care; avoid seductive nicknames.
	• Create strong passwords that you change frequently and never share them with others.
	• Do not fill out online profiles or use privacy settings on all your online accounts to limit your online sharing.
	• Watch what you say online. Avoid sharing where you plan to be and when.
	• Avoid chat rooms.
	• Use firewalls and antivirus protection.
	• Log out of computer and mobile programs when you step away from these devices and monitor physical access to these devices.
Managing cyberstalking	• Notify the Internet provider from which the harassing email originates.
	• Save all harassing communications.
	• In a neutral manner, inform the harasser that the communication is unwanted.
	• Do not have further contact with the harasser.
	• Contact the police.
	• If you suspect the use of spyware software on your computer, only use public computers or telephones to get help.

Data from: Glancy, G., Newman, A., Potash, M., & Tennison, J. 2007. Cyberstalking. In D. Pinals (Ed.), *Stalking: Psychiatric perspectives and practical approaches*. pp. 212-226. New York: Oxford University Press; and Pathé, M. 2002. Surviving stalking. New York: Cambridge University Press.

Internet Fraud

On November 25, 2002, the U.S. government charged Philip Cummings with wire fraud and conspiracy in connection with his participation in a massive identity theft scheme that spanned nearly 3 years and involved more than 30,000 victims. Cummings worked at Teledata Communications, Inc. (TCI), a company in Long Island, New York, that provided the computerized means for banks and other entities to obtain consumer credit information from the three commercial credit history bureaus: Equifax, Experian, and TransUnion. TCI provided software and other computerized devices to its client companies enabling them, through the use of confidential computer passwords and subscriber codes, to access and download credit reports of consumers for legitimate business purposes. Cummings worked at TCI from about mid-1999 through about March 2000 as a help desk employee and was responsible for helping TCI's clients. As such, he had access to these companies' confidential passwords and codes. With these codes, Cummings had the ability to access and download credit reports himself.

Starting in early 2000, Cummings agreed to provide credit reports to a coconspirator (CW) in return for money. He also taught CW how to access the credit bureaus and download the reports. Ford Motor Credit Company was one entity whose confidential TCI password and subscriber code were misappropriated for 10 months to download approximately 15,000 credit reports. Ford discovered the scheme after reviewing bills for those credit histories and receiving numerous complaints from consumers who had been the subject of identity theft and fraud. After searching its databases of passwords and subscriber codes of its various corporate customers, Experian discovered that the number of victims of compromised credit reports exceeded 30,000. Consumers whose credit reports had been stolen in this scheme reported many forms of identity fraud. Bank accounts holding tens of thousands of dollars in savings were depleted; credit cards were used to the tune of thousands of dollars without authorization; address changes were made to accounts at various financial institutions; checks, debit cards, ATM cards, and credit cards were sent to unauthorized locations; and identities of victims had been assumed by others. This resulted in more than $2.7 million in confirmed financial losses (U.S. Department of Justice, 2002).

Fraud is defined as the purposeful, unlawful act to deceive, manipulate, or provide false statements to damage others, often in a material sense. Schemes to defraud involve intentionally depriving victims of something of value, generally money or property (Neese, Ferrell, & Ferrell, 2003). As a whole, fraud is estimated to cost U.S. corporations in excess of $600 billion annually, or about 6% of the average company's total annual revenue. In 2016, 6.15% of consumers were victims of identity fraud, an increase of more than 2 million people from 2015. Additionally, as consumers continue to make more frequent purchases online, so, too, do more fraudsters move to the Internet to find their victims, which is reflected in the 40% increase in card-not-present fraud from 2015 to 2016 (Javelin Strategy & Research, 2017).

Fraud is by no means a new concept, with the first recorded laws relating to fraud dating back to the 4th century BCE in Greece (Burns, Whitworth, & Thompson, 2004). In the United States, the first **mail fraud** statute was enacted in 1872, in an effort to protect the integrity of the U.S. Postal Service. In more recent years, it has been expanded to include other forms of delivery, including courier services (Neese et al., 2003). Wire fraud legislation followed, which, over time, included wire, radio, or television writings, signals, pictures, or sounds. **Telemarketing fraud** is the third type of legislation in this area. According to Department of Justice Canada:

> Telemarketing fraud has become one of the most pervasive forms of white-collar crime in Canada and the United States, with annual losses in both countries in the billions of dollars. In recent years, authorities have observed concentrations of offenders in metropolitan areas including Atlanta, Houston, Las Vegas, Los Angeles-Orange County, Miami-Fort Lauderdale, Montreal, Tampa-St. Petersburg, Toronto, and Vancouver.
>
> (2015, para. 2)

As a result of this type of cross-border crime, a special Canada–U.S. working group was set up to address the issue (Department of Justice Canada, 2015).

As with other forms of cybercrime, the Internet merely provides a new mechanism for engaging in deception and theft. Internet fraud refers to any scheme involving the Internet, such as chat rooms, email, message boards, or websites that are used to conduct fraudulent transactions or solicit individuals for fraudulent purposes. TABLE 16-3 provides some of the more common attempts to scam the public as reported by the FBI's Internet Fraud Complaint Center.

What is surprising with respect to Internet fraud is how vulnerable even seemingly savvy consumers may be. Grazzioli (2004) conducted a study with 80 MBA students, exposing them to both fraudulent and legitimate marketing websites. Only 15% of the students correctly identified fraudulent sites. The authors concluded that the lack of widespread consumer awareness and training on Internet commerce is a significant obstacle to limiting Internet fraud. The 2017 Identity Fraud Study by Javelin Strategy & Research provides a silver lining on this issue, however, when comparing offline and online fraud.

TABLE 16-3 Types of Internet Fraud

Auction fraud	• Misrepresentation of product for sale. • Nondelivery of a product sold on an auction site. • Frequently originating in Romania. • May also result in courier fraud where an apparently legitimate courier emails the buyer for upfront payment of transportation costs.
Credit card fraud	• Unauthorized use of credit card. • Card information often stolen from unsecured websites.
Debt elimination	• Advertises legal ways to eliminate mortgage or debts. • Pay fee of $1,500 to $2,000. • Signs power of attorney for scammer to manage funds.
Employment/business opportunity schemes	• Offer the opportunity to "work at home." • Often involves reselling or shipping merchandise. • Asks to provide personal information to be "hired." • Asks to make an investment in the enterprise.
Lottery fraud	• Notification that person has won a lottery. • Request for fee to obtain.
Nigerian Letter or "419"	• Named for violation 419 in the Nigerian criminal code. • Email representing self as government official or royalty. • Need to get money out of the country. • Person is asked to send banking information for money transfer.
Phishing, spear phishing, spoofing	• Email sent from an apparent legitimate business. • Recipient instructed to sign in via a provided link. • Asked to provide password that is then used fraudulently.

Data from the FBI Internet Crime Complaint Center.

The study found that "offline consumers," meaning those individuals with little online presence and distrust of both online and mobile banking, take, on average, over 40 days to detect fraud and suffer higher fraud amounts than "e-commerce shoppers." E-commerce shoppers are defined in the study as individuals with an online presence particularly when it comes to making online purchases. Individuals in the e-commerce group have a high prevalence of fraud, but 78% of these fraud victims detected the fraud within 1 week of it beginning (Javelin Strategy & Research, 2017).

Internet fraud is not limited to individual victims, however. In a survey of senior executives from companies around the world, 75% reported to having been victim to a fraud incident within the past year, with 69% suffering financial loss as a result. Eighty percent of these executives believed that their organizations had become more vulnerable to fraud in the past year, and 51% admitted that their companies were highly or moderately vulnerable to information theft risk, including cyberincidents. When the target of Internet fraud is a corporation or organization, upwards of 81% of the perpetrators are insiders or employees of the organization. The position of the offender within the company has a significant impact on cybercrime. The study showed that, of fraud incidents caused by an insider, only 36% of the insiders came from senior or middle management, but the losses in these instances were significantly higher due to increased access to secure and confidential data and the perpetrator's increased ability to hide his or her activities (Economist Intelligence Unit, 2016).

Laws related to Internet fraud in the United States are adaptations of mail fraud acts. Although fraud is an age-old problem, the Internet makes the identities of the people in communication difficult to verify; increases the deceiver's reach; makes deception less costly and time consuming; and makes legal prosecution more difficult. It has been suggested that law enforcement agencies are under-resourced and undertrained to deal with Internet fraud. The skills of personnel with years of street experience are not useful in this context, and agencies must therefore rely upon young techies to deal with the issue (Burns et al., 2004). To adequately address these challenges, enforcement agencies are training staff, developing new competencies, and developing new procedures of operation. In 2013, the Police Executive Research Forum conducted a study of 213 law enforcement agencies to examine the role of the local police in the battle against cybercrime. Of these agencies, 42% reported having a computer crime or cybercrime unit. When asked about the biggest challenges to investigating cybercrime, 54% of agencies responded with lack of staffing, 31% said lack of funding, and 29% said a lack of in-house experience. Many of these local agencies also indicated that they refer cybercrime cases elsewhere, with 66% referring cases to the FBI and 51% referring to the U.S. Secret Service, among other agencies and task forces (Police Executive Research Forum, 2014).

New initiatives by the U.S. Department of Justice are addressing these concerns. Specifically, the Fraud Section of the Department of Justice works to combat economic crime, often in collaboration with the United States Attorneys offices and foreign law enforcement agencies. The Fraud Section is often the national leader in large, complex financial fraud investigations and prosecution. It is staffed with more than 150 prosecutors, over 20 federal support staff, and more than 130 contract support staff. These employees are divided among five units, including the Strategy, Policy, and Training (SPT) Unit; the Administration and Management Unit; and three litigating units—the Foreign Corrupt Practices Act (FCPA) Unit, the Health Care Fraud (HCF) Unit, and the Securities and Financial Fraud (SFF) Unit (U.S. Department of Justice, 2016c).

Identity Theft

Identity theft occurs when someone uses another person's personal information, such as that person's name, Social Security number, or credit card number, to commit fraud. The 2014 Victims of Identity Theft Supplement to the National Crime Victimization Survey estimated that approximately 17.6 million people, or 7% of American age 16 years or older, were victims of one or more incidents of identity theft in 2014. These crimes included existing bank accounts (8.1 million victims) and credit card accounts (8.6 million victims) as the most common types of misused information. Households more likely to experience identity theft had incomes of $75,000 or higher (Harrell, 2015). Rebovich, Layne, Jiandani, and Hage (2000) reported that the National White Collar Crime Center's project that measured public attitudes regarding identity theft crimes found that one in three households had been victimized by white collar crime in 1999. Although 60% of the respondents thought that those most victimized were older than age 60 years, the study indicated that 18- to 34-year-olds with some college education were high-risk targets. The reporting of identity theft was low, with less than 1 in 10 reporting. The 2014 Victims of Identity Theft Supplement found that only 2.6 million (approximately 14%) of identity theft victims in 2014 were age 65 or older (Harrell, 2015).

Stolen identities can be used in a large number of fraudulent ways, as indicated in TABLE 16-4. The 2014 Victims of Identity Theft Supplement provided further information beyond the most common type of identity theft: the unauthorized or attempted misuse of existing bank or credit accounts. Other types of identity theft included fraudulent use of credit cards; attempted or successful misuse of an existing telephone, online, or insurance account; use of information to open a new account, such as a credit card or loan; and use of personal information to get medical care, employment, or other benefits. In 2014, the most common way identity theft crimes were discovered was when the victim was contacted by a financial institution about suspicious activity (45%) or when the victim noticed fraudulent charges on an account (18%). Nine out of 10 of these identity theft victims did not know anything about the

TABLE 16-4 Uses of Stolen Identities

Credit card fraud	• Opening new credit card accounts
	• Cloning and using existing credit cards to run up charges
Phone or utilities fraud	• Opening new accounts
	• Renting property or other items in the victim's name
Banking fraud	• Creating counterfeit checks
	• Opening a new account
	• Cloning ATM card and emptying the account
	• Taking out a loan in the victim's name
Government document fraud	• Getting a driver's licence or official identification
	• Using the victim's Social Security number to obtain benefits
	• Filing a fraudulent tax return
Other	• Obtaining employment with the victim's Social Security number
	• Obtaining medical care with the victim's health insurance information
	• Giving false information at the time of arrest (if the offender does not appear in court, a warrant is issued under the victim's name)

offender's identity, and most victims did not know how this offender obtained their personal information (Harrell, 2015). As another example of how stolen identities can be used, the police in Montreal reported that in 2006, a man was shocked to discover that he had a criminal record, his driver's license had been revoked, and that his car was about to be impounded. It evolved that two years earlier a criminal had been arrested for impaired driving and when questioned by the police, instead of identifying himself correctly, he provided the name, address, date of birth, and Social Security number of the victim. On further questioning, he was even able to provide the names of the victim's parents.

Information that allows others to falsely assume an identity is acquired in a wide variety of ways: dumpster diving (rummaging through trash); skimming (storing credit card information when the victim makes a purchase and his or her card is swiped); phishing and spear phishing (sending spam messages from financial institutions that ask for personal data); changing the victim's address (redirecting mail to the offender); and simply stealing the victim's wallet. Identity theft impacts victims in pervasive and unexpected ways.

In one notorious case of identity theft, the criminal, a convicted felon, not only incurred more than $100,000 of credit card debt; obtained a federal home loan; and bought homes, motorcycles, and handguns in the victim's name, but he called his victim to taunt him, saying that he could continue to pose as the victim for as long as he wanted—because identity theft was not a federal crime at that time—before filing for bankruptcy, also in the victim's name. The victim and his wife spent more than 4 years and more than $15,000 of their own money to restore their credit and reputation, and the criminal served a brief sentence for making a false statement to procure a firearm but made no restitution to his victim for any of the harm he had caused. This case, and others like it, prompted Congress in 1998, to create a new federal offense of identity theft.

Who is the victim is a major question in identity theft crime: Is it the individual whose identity is stolen, or is it the business, company, or agency upon whom the fraud is perpetrated? Watkins (2000) argued that most police departments consider the business or company to be the victim and the individual who had his or her identity stolen to be a witness. The Privacy Rights Clearinghouse (2000) argued that victims often got little or no help from authorities because the crimes were not investigated. A report by the Privacy Rights Clearinghouse (2000) on 66 identity theft complaints found that the burden of cleaning up the mess fell to victims to repair both their credit rating and their emotional well-being (National Victim Assistance Academy, 2000). The Financial Crimes Division of the U.S. Secret Service (Leas & Burke, 2000), the Los Angeles Police Department (n.d.b), and Tworkowski and Madge (1999) concluded that victims needed months or years to restore their credit and reputation. More recently, information provided in the 2014 Victims of Identity Theft Supplement (Harrell, 2015) revealed that about 7% of U.S. residents age 16 or older (an estimated 17.6 million Americans) were victims of identity theft in 2014. An overwhelming 86% of victims experienced the misuse of an existing credit card or bank account, while 4% of victims had their personal information used for fraudulent activity.

In addition to financial and identity harm, victims of financial crimes can suffer psychological and physical effects and can require assistance and intervention (Alexander & Seymour, 1998; National Victim Assistance Academy, 2000). In the 2014 Victims of Identity Theft Supplement, for instance, 29% of victims who spent 6 months or more resolving the issue reported that the experience was severely distressing (Harrell, 2015). However, identity theft victims do not necessarily have the same rights as violent crime victims, and they do not have an organized constituency group. Victims of financial crime often blame themselves, feel embarrassed and betrayed, describe a violation of their personal integrity and sense of trust, and are reluctant to discuss their victimization with others. They can feel isolated and find the criminal justice process unsympathetic, intimidating, and stressful. Identity theft cases can become very complex because multiple jurisdictions may be involved. Victims may experience numerous instances of unauthorized and fraudulent use of their identity. To become an effective, strong advocate for one's own case, it is vital to impose a form of organization on an identity theft case from the first day. TABLE 16-5 provides suggestions on how to respond to identify theft.

Law enforcement responses to identity fraud have been hampered by both technological and legislative barriers. The Montreal case of a man who acquired a criminal record as a result of having his identity stolen added to the impetus to create a new method of tracking identity theft in Canada using the nationwide Canadian Police Information Centre (CPIC), which includes the names and descriptions of not only criminals but also victims who have had their identification stolen. In attempting to protect consumers, the California legislature enacted a statute in 2002 that requires all agencies, businesses, or individuals that conduct a business in which personal data is collected to notify their customers of any security breaches. Federal legislators have passed the Identity Theft and Assumption Deterrence Act (1998), the Identity Theft Penalty Enhancement Act (2004), and the Identity Theft Enforcement and Restitution Act (2008). In 2000, the Office for Victims of Crime designed a new curriculum module on financial crime for the National Victim Assistance Academy. In one of the units on identity theft, the crime is defined as occurring when one individual misappropriates another person's identification information and uses it to take over existing credit card or bank accounts, apply for a mortgage or car

TABLE 16-5 Responding to Identity Theft

Documentation and evidence are key to legally reclaiming one's identity.
• Because all documents can be evidence, they should be kept in a safe place for future use.
• Keep a record of all conversations related to your case, including names and contact information of persons with whom you have spoken.
• Request written confirmation of all discussions—email follow-up of discussions as a tool for creating a paper trail.
• Write summaries of your case every month or so in order to keep dates and progress clear so you can describe what has transpired.

Data from: Privacy Rights Clearinghouse. 2009a. Fact sheet 17: Reducing the risk of identity theft. Retrieved from http://www.privacyrights.org/fs/fs17-it.htm; and Privacy Rights Clearinghouse. 2009b. Fact sheet 17(a): Identity theft victims guide. Retrieved from http://www.privacyrights.org/fs/fs17a.htm.

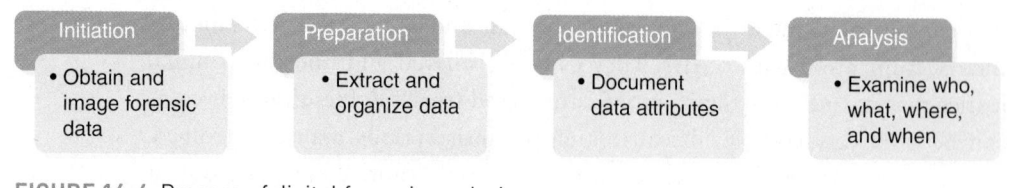

FIGURE 16-4 Process of digital forensic analysis.
Courtesy of Ann Burgess.

loan, make large purchases, and/or apply for insurance. Further, in 2000, the FBI, in cooperation with the National White Collar Crime Center, established the Internet Crime Complaints Center, which focuses on public education and responding to complaints of Internet fraud and identity theft. The investigation process can be found in **FIGURE 16-4**.

Internet Copyright Piracy

In 2004, in response to increasing concerns regarding intellectual property crime (IPC), the U.S. Department of Justice launched the Task Force on Intellectual Property, later to become the Intellectual Property (IP) Task Force in 2010. This task force is charged with addressing crime related to copyrights, trademarks, trade secrets, and patents, with a particular emphasis on public health and safety, theft of trade secrets and economic espionage, and large-scale commercial counterfeiting and piracy. Perhaps of greatest interest to most people is the issue of copyright, which includes the protection of music, movies, books, and artwork. Copyright law grants the exclusive right to authors and developers for distributing, recording, displaying, and performing their work. While copyright laws have been in effect since 1909, the Internet provides new opportunities and challenges for distribution of materials. This is of particular concern to legislators given the vast contribution that the sale and distribution of copyrighted materials adds to the national economy. A report of the Task Force on Intellectual Property indicated that "Copyright industries in the United States sold and exported an estimated $89.26 billion in 2002 to foreign nations. Copyright industries exceeded other major industries including the chemical, food and live animal, motor vehicle, and aircraft sectors" (U.S. Department of Justice, 2004, p. 7). Thus, itemized in the report are numerous cases of individuals who have been prosecuted for counterfeit DVDs, stolen satellite signals, and illegal movie distribution. In 2016, U.S. Customs and Border Protection and U.S. Immigration and Customs Enforcement–Homeland Security Investigations seized 31,560 goods in violation of intellectual property rights, up 9% from the previous year, resulting in 451 arrests, 304 indictments, and 272 convictions. If the seized goods had been genuine, the total estimated manufacturer's suggested retail price would have been over $1.3 billion (U.S. Department of Homeland Security, 2016).

Perhaps the most famous case of Internet copyright infringement is the case of the online music downloading service, Napster. Napster allowed individuals to exchange songs by trading computer files in MP3 format. Beginning with a suit launched by Metallica and Dr. Dre, the music industry sought to shut down Napster in 2000 on the basis that it violated copyright law. In a counterargument, Napster claimed that the Record Industry Association of America (RIAA) was trying to suppress technology to maintain its dominance in the $39 billion global music business. In 2001, Napster settled with Metallica and Dr. Dre and moved to transition from free file sharing to digital music sales (CNN, 2001).

Conclusion

Computer crime is a relatively new and growing area where individuals and organizations can become victimized. Computer-based crimes span a wide range of activities, including child pornography, cyberstalking and cyberbullying, computer and telephone hacking, cyberterrorism, copyright theft, and fraud and identity theft. Offenders in this category are perhaps the most diverse of any crime category, spanning all nationalities, all ages, and all socioeconomic groups. However, with the possible exception of hacking for the purposes of vandalism, the Internet has not created new categories of crime; rather it has created new opportunities for criminals to use technology for their own personal ends. Nevertheless, it has created many new challenges for legislators, prosecutors, and law enforcement agencies who work in systems that have been unprepared to deal with this new wave of victimizing activity. In this area of crime, perhaps more than any others, individuals and organizations must actively work to protect themselves on a daily basis through cautious sharing of information and general suspicion regarding the identity and motives of those they cannot see or hear in person.

Key Terms

Botnets: Networks of computers that criminals control to perform coordinated cyberattacks.

Child sexual victimization on the Internet: Use of the Internet to distribute or view child pornography or to contact children for the purposes of sexual abuse or exploitation.

Computer hacking: The unauthorized use of an information system or network by circumventing or bypassing the security mechanisms; illegally accessing other people's computer systems for destroying, disrupting, or carrying out illegal activities on the network or computer systems.

Copyright piracy: Unauthorized use or sale of copyrighted material.

Cyberbullying: Bullying though means of email, instant messages, text messages, blogs, cell phones, pagers, and websites with the goal of tormenting, threatening, harassing, humiliating, or embarrassing a person.

Cybercrime: Crime committed using the Internet; includes attacks that cause electronic commerce sites to lose money, identity theft, sale of contraband, stalking, or disrupting operations with malevolent programs.

Cyberstalking: The use of the Internet to stalk another person.

Cyberterrorism: Any premeditated, politically motivated attack against electronic information or systems to cause physical, real-world harm or severe disruption.

Distributed denial of service (DDoS): A type of cyberattack in which multiple devices at varied locations all become infected, usually with malware. The group of infected devices then acts as a single system that hits a target simultaneously, resulting in a denial of service (DoS).

Identity theft: Use of a person's identifying information, including name, Social Security number, or credit card number, without permission, to commit fraud or other crimes.

Internet fraud: Deception conducted through the Internet for the purpose of financial gain.

Mail fraud: The willful use of the national mail service to defraud or obtain money or property by means of false pretenses, representations, or promises.

Malware: A software program designed to damage or cause unwanted actions on a computer system, including viruses, worms, and Trojan horses.

Phishing: An attempt to obtain financial or other confidential information from a user, typically by sending an email that mimics a legitimate organization, but contains malware (e.g., a keylogger) that operates in the background to collect sensitive information.

Ransomware: A type of malware that restricts access to computer systems until the target pays a ransom to the malware operators to remove the restriction.

Spam: The sending of unwanted and often irrelevant emails and other communications to a large number of individuals.

Spear phishing: A highly personalized form of phishing where an email appears to be from a friend or financial institution and contains an attachment or link to a site that downloads malware (usually spyware or a keylogger) that operates in the background to collect sensitive information.

Telemarketing fraud: Fraudulent selling conducted over the phone. It most often targets the poor and elderly.

Telephone hacking: The illegal access to a telephone network for free phone calls or to obtain personal information.

Terrorism: Use of violence and intimidation, especially against civilians, in the pursuit of political aims.

Discussion Questions

1. Despite new international agreements, what international challenges continue to exist in combating cybercrime?

2. If you were working with a telecommunications company to develop safeguards for Internet bullying, what elements of the issue would you consider?

3. Describe aspects of an education campaign for college-aged adults to protect themselves from cyberstalking.

4. You have been asked to develop a program to help victims of identity theft. What would you include in your program?

Resources

FBI, Internet Fraud Complaint Center (IC3) http://www.ic3.gov/default.aspx

Royal Canadian Mounted Police, Online Child Exploitation http://www.rcmp -grc.gc.ca/ncecc-cncee/index-accueil-eng.htm

Royal Canadian Mounted Police, Scams and Fraud http://www.rcmp-grc .gc.ca/scams-fraudes/index-eng.htm

StopBullying.gov http://www.stopbullying.gov

U.S. Department of Justice, Office for Victims of Crime https://www.ovcttac .gov

References

Alexander, E., & Seymour, A. (1998). *Roles, rights, and responsibilities: A handbook for fraud victims participating in the federal criminal justice system.* Washington, DC: Police Executive Forum.

Alexy, E. M., Burgess, A. W., & Baker, T. (2005a). Internet offenders: Traders, travelers, and combination trader-travelers. *Journal of Interpersonal Violence, 20*(7), 804–812.

Arkin, W. M., & Lichtblau, E. (2014, November 16). More federal agencies are using undercover operations. *New York Times.* Retrieved from https://www.nytimes.com/2014/11/16/us/more-federal-agencies-are-using-undercover-operations.html

Armstrong, H., & Forde, P. (2003). Internet anonymity practices in computer crime. *Information Management & Computer Security, 11*(5), 209–215.

Barton, P., Nissanka, V., & Waterhouse, F. (2003). Cyber-crime—criminal offense or civil wrong? *Computer and Security Report, 19*(5), 401–405.

Baum, K., Catalano, S., Rand, M., & Rose, K. (2009, January). Stalking victimization in the United States. Bureau of Justice Statistics Special Report. NCJ 224527. U.S. Department of Justice, Office of Justice Programs.

Beran, T., & Li, Q. (2005). Cyber-harassment: A study of a new method for an old behavior. *Journal of Educational Computing Research, 32*(3), 265–277.

Bradbury, D. (2007, December 6). Technique is new, crime is not. *National Post,* SR4.

Briggs, P., Simon, W., & Simonsen, S. (2011). An exploratory study of Internet-initiated sexual offenses and the chat room sex offender: Has the Internet enabled a new typology of sex offender? *Sexual Abuse: A Journal of Research and Treatment, 23*(1), 72–91.

Browne, R. (2017, January 19). NATO: We ward off 500 cyberattacks each month. CNN Politics. Retrieved from http://www.cnn.com/2017/01/19/politics/nato-500-cyberattacks-monthly/index.html

Burns, R., Whitworth, K., & Thompson, C. (2004). Assessing law enforcement preparedness to address Internet fraud. *Journal of Criminal Justice, 32,* 477–493.

Canadian Anti-Fraud Centre. (2010). Annual statistical report on mass media fraud and identity theft activities. Retrieved from http://www.antifraudcentre-centreantifraude.ca/english/statistics_statistics.html

Cellular Telecommunications and Internet Association. (2015). 5.2 billion mobile phone users worldwide. Retrieved from https://ctia.org/industry-data/facts-and-infographics-details/fact-and-infographics/5-2-billion-mobile-phone-users-worldwide

Cellular Telecommunications and Internet Association. (2016). Americans' data usage more than doubled in 2015. Retrieved from https://ctia.org/industry-data/press-releases-details/press-releases/americans-data-usage-more-than-doubled-in-2015

Chu, H., Deng, D., & Chao, H. (2011). Potential cyberterrorism via a multimedia smartphone based on a web 2.0 application via ubiquitous Wi-Fi access points and corresponding digital forensics. *Multimedia Systems, 17,* 341–349.

Chung, W., Chen, J., Chang, W., & Chou, S. (2004). Fighting cyber-crime: A review and the Taiwan experience. *Decision Support Systems*, *41*, 669–682.

CNN. (2001, July 12). Napster settles suit. CNN Money. Retrieved from http://money .cnn.com/2001/07/12/news/napster/

Competition Bureau. (2017). Fraud facts 2017—Recognize, reject, report fraud. Retrieved from http://www.competitionbureau.gc.ca/eic/site/cb-bc.nsf/eng/04201.html

Council of Europe. (2017). Budapest Convention and related standards. Retrieved from http://www.coe.int/en/web/cybercrime/the-budapest-convention

DeCesare, M. (2016, October 22). How massive DDoS attacks are undermining the Internet. TechCrunch. Retrieved from https://techcrunch.com/2016/10/22 /how-massive-ddos-attacks-are-undermining-the-internet/

Deibert, R., & Rohozinski, R. (2010). Risking security: Policies and paradoxes in cyberspace security. *International Political Sociology*, *4*, 15–32.

Department of Justice Canada. (2011). Legislation protecting children from online sexual exploitation comes into force. Retrieved from https://protectchildren.ca /app/en/media_release_national_mandatory_reporting_leg

Department of Justice Canada. (2015). Report of the Canada–United States working group on telemarketing fraud. Retrieved from http://www.justice.gc.ca/eng /dept-min/pub/tf/sum-som.html

Dunn, J. (2017, July 10). Russian cybercriminal caught with $272,000 in $100 bills, $5 million in bitcoin. *North Bay Business Journal*. Retrieved from http://www .northbaybusinessjournal.com/home/7185526-181/russian-hacker-had-272000 -in?artslide=0

Economist Intelligence Unit. (2016). Global fraud report: Vulnerabilities on the rise. Kroll. Retrieved from http://anticorruzione.eu/wp-content/uploads/2015/09 /Kroll_Global_Fraud_Report_2015low-copia.pdf

Federal Bureau of Investigation. (2001). Protecting yourself against identity theft. Retrieved from http://www.fbi.gov/con-tact/fo/norfolk/19999/ident.htm

Federal Bureau of Investigation (2011). Internet crime schemes. Internet Fraud Complaint Center. Retrieved from http://www.ic3.gov/crimeschemes.aspx#item-1

Finkelhor, D., Mitchell, K., & Wolak, J. (2000). *Online victimization: A report on the nation's youth*. Alexandria, VA: National Center for Missing and Exploited Children.

Forrest, C. (2016, October 24). Dyn DDoS attack: 5 takeaways on what we know and why it matters. TechRepublic. Retrieved from http://www.techrepublic.com /article/dyn-ddos-attack-5-takeaways-on-what-we-know-and-why-it-matters/

Garcia, S. (2017, July 28). Missing girl helps investigators bring down entire human trafficking ring. ABC. Retrieved from http://abc7chicago.com/news/human -trafficking-sex-ring-busted;-13-victims-rescued/2257267/

Giacobbe, A. (2010, June). Who failed Phoebe Prince? *Boston Magazine*. Retrieved http://www.bostonmagazine.com/2010/05/phoebe-prince/

Glancy, G., Newman, A., Potash, M., & Tennison, J. (2007). Cyberstalking. In D. Pinals (Ed.), *Stalking: Psychiatric perspectives and practical approaches* (pp. 212–226). New York: Oxford University Press.

Goodman, S., Kirk, J., & Kirk, M. (2007). Cyberspace as a medium for terrorists. *Technology Forecasting and Social Change, 74*, 193–210.

Gorman, S., & Barnes, J. (2011, May 31). Cyber combat: Act of war. *Wall Street Journal.* Retrieved from http://online.wsj.com/article/SB10001424052702304563104 576355623135782718.html

Grazzioli, S. (2004). Where did they go wrong? An analysis of the failure of knowledgeable Internet consumers to detect deception over the Internet. *Group Decision and Negotiation, 13*, 149–172.

Greenberg, A. (2017, May 15). The WannaCry ransomware hackers made some real amateur mistakes. *Wired.* Retrieved from https://www.wired.com/2017/05 /wannacry-ransomware-hackers-made-real-amateur-mistakes/

Ha, T. (2006, April 7). "Star Wars Kid" cuts a deal with tormenters. *Globe and Mail.* Retrieved from http://www.theglobeandmail.com/servlet/story/RTGAM.20060407 .wxstarwars07/BNStory/National/home

Hango, D. (2016). Cyberbullying and cyberstalking among Internet users aged 15 to 29 in Canada. Statistics Canada. Retrieved from http://www.statcan.gc.ca/pub /75-006-x/2016001/article/14693-eng.htm

Harrell, E. (2015). Victims of identity theft, 2014. Bureau of Justice Statistics. Retrieved from https://www.bjs.gov/content/pub/pdf/vit14.pdf

Hunton, P. (2011). The stages of cybercrime investigations: Bridging the gap between technology examination and law enforcement investigation. *Computer Law and Security Review, 27*, 61–67.

Internet Watch Foundation. (2017). IWF annual report, 2016. Retrieved from https:// annualreport.iwf.org.uk/

Internet World Stats. (2017). Usage and population statistics. Retrieved from http:// www.internetworldstats.com/

Jackson Higgins, K. (2016). DDoS Attack on DNS Provider Disrupts Okta, Twitter, Pinterest, Reddit, CNN, Others. *Dark Reading.* Retrieved from http://www .darkreading.com/attacks-breaches/ddos-attack-on-dns-provider-disrupts -okta-twitter-pinterest-reddit-cnn-others/d/d-id/1327252

James, S. (2010). Immigrant teen taunted by cyberbullies hangs herself. ABC News. Retrieved from http://abcnews.go.com/Healthcyber-bullying-factor-suicide -massachusetts-teen-irish-immigrant/story?id=9660938

Javelin Strategy & Research. (2017). Identity fraud hits record high with 15.4 million U.S. victims in 2016, up 16 percent according to new Javelin Strategy & Research study. Retrieved from https://www.javelinstrategy.com/press-release/identity -fraud-hits-record-high-154-million-us-victims-2016-16-percent-according-new

Kierkegaard, S. (2006). EU framework decision on cyber attacks. *Computer Law and Security Report, 22*, 381–391.

Leas, M., & Burke, T. (2000). Identity theft: A fast-growing crime. *FBI Law Enforcement Bulletin*, 69(8), 8–13.

Lenhart, A. (2015). Teens, social media, and technology overview 2015. Pew Research Center. Retrieved from http://www.pewinternet.org/2015/04/09/teens-social-media-technology-2015/

Lenhart, A., Ybarra, M., Zickuhr K., & Price-Feeney, M. (2016). Online harassment, digital abuse, and cyberstalking in America. *Data & Society Research Institute, Center for Innovative Public Health Research*. Retrieved from https://www.datasociety.net/pubs/oh/Online_Harassment_2016.pdf

Los Angeles Police Department. (n.d.b). Identity theft. Retrieved from http://www.lapdonline.org/search_results/content_basic_view/1364

Low, R. (2017, April 27). Ex-school board president confesses on tape to Internet luring of 12-year old. *FOX News*. Retrieved from http://kdvr.com/2017/04/27/school-board-members-confession-on-tape-internet-luring-of-12-year-old/

McGoogan, C. (2017, May 18). What is WannaCry and how does ransomware work? *The Telegraph*. Retrieved http://www.telegraph.co.uk/technology/0/ransomware-does-work/

Meola, A. (2016). What is the Internet of Things (IoT)? *Business Insider*. Retrieved from http://www.businessinsider.com/what-is-the-internet-of-things-definition-2016-8

Merritt, M. (n.d.). Straight talk about cyberstalking. Norton by Symantec. Retrieved from https://us.norton.com/cyberstalking/article

Microsoft. (2005, April 7). Microsoft collaborates with global police to develop child exploitation tracking system for law enforcement agencies. Retrieved from https://news.microsoft.com/2005/04/07/microsoft-collaborates-with-global-police-to-develop-child-exploitation-tracking-system-for-law-enforcement-agencies/#pGwMrTOFwGZY8eTq.97

Mishna, F., McLuckie, A., & Saini, M. (2009). Real-world dangers in an online reality: A qualitative study examining online relationships and cyber abuse. *Social Work Research*, 33(2), 107–118.

Mitchell, K., Wolak, J., & Finkelhor, D. (2005). Police posing as juveniles online to catch sex offenders: Is it working? *Sexual Abuse: A Journal of Research and Treatment*, 17(3), 241–267.

Morris, D. (2005). Tracking a computer hacker. Retrieved from http://www.usdoj.gov/criminal/cybercrime/usamay2001_2.htm

Nakashima, E. (2016, January 21). This is how the government is catching people who use child porn sites. *The Washington Post*. Retrieved from https://www.washingtonpost.com/world/national-security/how-the-government-is-using-malware-to-ensnare-child-porn-users/2016/01/21/fb8ab5f8-bec0-11e5-83d4-42e3bceea902_story.html?utm_term=.591081f12113

National Centre for Cyberstalking Research. (2011). Cyberstalking in the United Kingdom: An analysis of the ECHO pilot survey. University of Bedfordshire. Retrieved from https://www.beds.ac.uk/__data/assets/pdf_file/0003/83109/ECHO_Pilot_Final.pdf

National Child Exploitation Coordination Centre. (2008). Child exploitation tracking system. Retrieved from http://www.rcmp-grc.gc.ca/ncecc-cncee/cets-eng.htm

National Victim Assistance Academy. (2000). *Financial crime.* Washington, DC: Office of Victims of Crime.

Neese, W., Ferrell, L., & Ferrell, O. (2003). An analysis of federal mail and wire fraud cases related to marketing. *Journal of Business Research, 58,* 910–918.

Obama, B. (2015). Blocking the property of certain persons engaging in significant malicious cyber-enabled activities. Federal Register. Retrieved from https://www .treasury.gov/resource-center/sanctions/Programs/Documents/cyber_eo.pdf

Palmer, D. (2017). WannaCry ransomware attack at LG Electronics takes systems offline. ZDNet. Retrieved from http://www.zdnet.com/article/wannacry -ransomware-attack-at-lg-electronics-takes-systems-offline/

Patchin, J. W., & Hinduja, S. (2016). *2016 cyberbullying data.* Cyberbullying Research Center. Retrieved from https://cyberbullying.org/2016-cyberbullying-data

Pathé, M. (2002). *Surviving stalking.* New York: Cambridge University Press.

Petrosino, A., Guckenburg, S., DeVoe, J., & Hanson, T. (2010). What characteristics of bullying, bullying victims, and schools are associated with increased reporting of bullying to school officials? National Center for Education Evaluation and Regional Assistance. Retrieved from https://ies.ed.gov/ncee/edlabs/regions /northeast/pdf/REL_2010092_sum.pdf

Police Executive Research Forum. (2014). *Critical issues in policing series: The role of local law enforcement agencies in preventing and investigating cybercrime.* Washington, DC: Author. Retrieved July 27 2017, from http://www.policeforum.org /assets/docs/Critical_Issues_Series_2/the%20role%20of%20local%20law%20 enforcement%20agencies%20in%20preventing%20and%20investigating%20 cybercrime%202014.pdf

Ponemon Institute. (2015). 2015 cost of cyber crime study: United States. Retrieved from http://img.delivery.net/cm50content/hp/hosted-files/2015_US_CCC_FINAL_4.pdf

Ponemon Institute. (2017). 2017 cost of data breach study: United States. Retrieved from https://www-01.ibm.com/common/ssi/cgi-bin/ssialias?htmlfid =SEL03130USEN&

Privacy Rights Clearinghouse. (2000). Identity theft: How it happens, its impact on victims, and legislative solutions. Retrieved from http://www.privacyrights.org/ar /id_theft.htm

Privacy Rights Clearinghouse. (2009a). Fact sheet 17: Reducing the risk of identity theft. Retrieved from http://www.privacyrights.org/fs/fs17-it.htm

Privacy Rights Clearinghouse. (2009b). Fact sheet 17(a): Identity theft victims guide. Retrieved from http://www.privacyrights.org/fs/fs17a.htm http://www.publicsafety .gc.ca/media/nr/2010/nr20101101-eng.aspx

Qualye, E., & Jones, T. (2011). Sexualized images of children on the Internet. *Sexual Abuse: A Journal of Research and Treatment, 23*(1), 7–21.

Raskauskas, J., & Stoltz, A. (2007). Involvement in traditional and electronic bullying among adolescents. *Developmental Psychology, 43*(3), 564–575.

Rebovich, D. J., Layne, J., Jiandani, J., & Hage, S. (2000). *The national public surveys on white collar crime*. Morgantown, WV: National White Collar Crime Center.

Schell, B., Martin, M., Hung, P., & Rueda, L. (2007). Cyber child pornography: A review paper of the social and legal issues and remedies—and a proposed technological solution. *Aggression and Violent Behavior, 12*, 45–63.

Schladebeck, J. (2017, May 6). Creator of 'world's largest' child porn site sentenced. *New York Daily News*. Retrieved from http://www.nydailynews.com/news/crime /creator-world-largest-child-porn-site-sentenced-article-1.3142151

Selyukh, A. (2016, December 3). A year after San Bernardino and Apple-FBI. Where are we on encryption? NPR. Retrieved from http://www.npr.org/sections/alltech considered/2016/12/03/504130977/a-year-after-san-bernardino-and-apple-fbi -where-are-we-on-encryption

Seto, M., Cantor, J., & Blanchard, R. (2006). Child pornography offenses are a valid diagnostic indicator of pedophilia. *Journal of Abnormal Psychology, 115*, 610–615.

Shaw, B. (2017, July 17). Dad says predator was luring kids in popular online children's game. 2017. KHOU. Retrieved from http://www.khou.com/tech/dad-says -predator-was-luring-kids-in-popular-online-childrens-game/457400979

Sher, J. (2007). *One child at a time: The global fight to rescue children from online predators*. Toronto: Random House.

Sherr, I. (2017, May 19). WannaCry ransomware: Everything you need to know. CNET. Retrieved from https://www.cnet.com/news/wannacry-wannacrypt-uiwix -ransomware-everything-you-need-to-know/

Short, A., Guppy, A., Hart, J. A., & Barnes, J. (2015). The impact of cyberstalking. *Studies in Media and Communication, 3*(2), 23–37. Retrieved from http://redfame .com/journal/index.php/smc/article/viewFile/970/913

Simpson, D. (2000, June 12). Feds find dangerous cyberstalking hard to prevent. CNN. Retrieved from http://archives.cnn.com/2000/TECH/computing/06/12/cyberstalkers .idg/index.html

Sinclair, R., & Sugar, D. (2005). Internet-based sexual exploitation of children and youth environmental scan. Retrieved from http://www.rcmp-grc.gc.ca/ncecc-cncee /factsheets-fichesdocu/enviroscan-analyseenviro-eng.htm

Steel, C. M. S. (2015). Web-based child pornography: The global impact of deterrence efforts and its consumption on mobile platforms. *Child Abuse and Neglect, 44*, 150–158.

Stohl, M. (2006). Cyber terrorism: A clear and present danger, the sum of all fears, breaking point, or patriot games? *Crime, Law, and Social Change, 46*, 223–238.

Sullivan, B. (2017, February 6). Identity theft hit an all-time high in 2016. *USA Today*. Retrieved from https://www.usatoday.com/story/money/personalfinance /2017/02/06/identity-theft-hit-all-time-high-2016/97398548/

Tan, L-M., and Newman, M. (1991). Computer misuse and the law. *International Journal of Information Management, 11*, 282–291.

Taylor, M., & Quayle, E. (2003). *Child pornography: An Internet crime*. New York: Routledge.

Titus, R. M., Heinzelmann, F., & Boyle, J. M. (1995). Victimization of persons by fraud. *Crime and Delinquency, 41*(1), 51–72.

TrendLabs. (2017). Trendlabs 2016 Security Roundup: A Record Year for Enterprise Threats. Retrieved from https://documents.trendmicro.com/assets/rpt/rpt -2016-annual-security-roundup-a-record-year-for-enterprise-threats.pdf

Tworkowski, N., & Madge, B. E. (1999). Identity crisis survival: Learning the scams of identity theft. *The White Paper, 13*(4), 18–21, 40, 48–49.

U.S. Department of Education. (2016). *Student Reports of Bullying: Results from the 2015 School Crime Supplement to the National Crime Victimization Survey.* NCES 2017-015. Retrieved from https://nces.ed.gov/pubs2017/2017015.pdf

U.S. Department of Homeland Security. (2016). Intellectual property rights seizure statistics: Fiscal year 2016. Retrieved from https://www.cbp.gov/sites/default/files /assets/documents/2017-Jan/FY%2016%20IPR%20Stats%20FINAL%201.25.pdf

U.S. Department of Justice. (1999, September). Attorney general Janet Reno delivers cyberstalking report to the vice president. Retrieved from http://www.usdoj.gov /opa/pr/1999/September/421ag.htm

U.S. Department of Justice. (2002). U.S. announces what is believed the largest identity theft case in American history; losses are in the millions. Retrieved from http:// www.usdoj.gov/criminal/cybercrime/cummingsIndict.htm

U.S. Department of Justice. (2004). Report of the Department of Justice's Task Force on Intellectual Property. Retrieved from https://www.justice.gov/sites/default/files/olp /docs/ip_task_force_report.pdf

U.S. Department of Justice. (2005). Computer virus broker arrested for selling armies of infected computers to hackers and spammers. Retrieved from http://www.justice .gov/criminal/cybercrime/anchetaArrest.htm

U.S. Department of Justice. (2016a). *Protecting Children Online: Using Research-Based Algorithms to Prioritize Law Enforcement Internet Investigations, Technical Report.* Retrieved from https://www.ncjrs.gov/pdffiles1/ojjdp/grants/250154.pdf

U.S. Department of Justice. (2016b). *The National Strategy for Child Exploitation Prevention and Interdiction.* Retrieved from https://www.justice.gov/psc/file/842411 /download

U.S. Department of Justice. (2016c). *Fraud Section year in review 2016.* Retrieved from https://www.justice.gov/criminal-fraud/page/file/929741/download

U.S. Department of Justice. (2017). Reporting computer, Internet related, or intellectual property crime. *Computer Crime and Intellectual Property Section.* Retrieved from https://www.justice.gov/criminal-ccips/reporting-computer-internet-related-or -intellectual-property-crime

U.S. Department of Justice, FBI. (2017). Cybercrime. Retrieved from https://www.fbi .gov/investigate/cyber

U.S. Department of State. (2001). Patterns of global terrorism. Retrieved from http:// www.state.gov/s/ct/rls/pgtrpt/

U.S. Department of State. (2016). *Country Reports on Terrorism 2016.* Retrieved from https://www.state.gov/j/ct/rls/crt/2016/272228.htm

Watkins, M. (2000). Identity theft a nightmare, not impostor in Internet age. *Police*, *24*(7), 26–29.

Webley, K. (2011, May 5). Teens who admitted bullying Phoebe Prince sentenced. *Time*. Retrieved from http://newsfeed.time.com/2011/05/05/teens-who-admitted-to-bullying-phoebe-prince-sentenced/

Wolak, J., Finkelhor, D., Mitchell, K., and Ybarra, M. (2008). Online "predators" and their victims: Myths, realities, and implications for prevention and treatment. *American Psychologist*, *63*(2), 111–128.

Wolak, J., Finkelhor, D., Mitchell, K. (2011). Child pornography possessors: Trends in offender and case characteristics. *Sexual Abuse: A Journal of Research and Treatment*, *23*(1), 22–42.

Woolaston, V. (2017, May 22). WannaCry ransomware: What it is and how to protect yourself. *Wired*. Retrieved from http://www.telegraph.co.uk/technology/0/ransomware-does-work/

© Peyker/Shutterstock.

CHAPTER 17

Other Forms of Victimization

OBJECTIVES

- To discuss property-related crime and its victims
- To discuss victims of workplace violence
- To discuss the effects of victims of natural disasters
- To discuss the effects of terrorism
- To expose the harms caused by major forms of white-collar and corporate crime
- To identify issues related to the accused as victims, including wrongful convictions and racial profiling

KEY TERMS

Burglary	Racial profiling
Corporate victimization	Robbery
Home invasion	Terrorism
Larceny	Theft

CASE

Home Invasion and Carjacking

On Monday, July 18, 2011, a federal jury in Greenbelt, Maryland, convicted Jason Thomas Scott for a series of violent home invasions, carjackings, and firearms offenses, as well for the molestation of a teenage girl. The three-week trial portrayed Jason Scott as a professional, methodical, dangerous criminal as he escalated his activities from committing burglaries and demanding PIN numbers for his victims' bank accounts to armed home invasions. Scott admitted to 28 burglaries and 9 armed home invasions and to sexually assaulting and photographing the teenage girl (Castaneda, 2011). These convictions were added to his recent homicide convictions. On January 26, 2009, he had entered the home of Karen Lofton, a 45-year-old nurse, and fatally shot both her and her 16-year-old daughter, Karissa. Three months later, the bodies of Delores Dewitt, a 42-year-old nurse, and her 20-year-old daughter, Ebony, were found in a burning car less than a mile away from the Lofton's home after what was believed to be a carjacking. Police believed Scott might also have committed murders in Washington, DC, Texas, and Florida that remained unsolved (Thomas & Francis, 2010). Scott, who had a degree in computer science from the University of Maryland and worked for a courier company, researched police forensic tactics and may have used his employer's database to research potential victims (Castaneda, 2011; Thomas & Francis, 2010). Scott faces a mandatory minimum sentence of 97 years in prison for the federal offenses.

Wrongful Conviction

Dr. Charles Smith, a renowned forensic pathologist in Toronto, conducted over 1,000 autopsies of children over a 24-year period, many of which involved suspicious deaths. A number of these cases involved "shaken baby syndrome," a condition often leading to death where an infant incurs brain injury due to intentional shaking. However, over the course of the 1990s, he was subject to an increasing amount of criticism by the judicial system regarding his methods, competence, and, in particular, his testimony at trial. In 2005, the chief coroner for Ontario instituted a review into 45 cases of homicide about which Smith had expressed professional opinions that the death was either homicide or criminally suspicious. The coroner's review determined that Smith made questionable conclusions of foul play in 20 cases, 13 of which resulted in criminal convictions. Subsequently, a commission was established in which Justice Stephen Goudge was charged with examining 20 cases identified in the earlier chief coroner's review (Glancy & Regehr, 2012). In one of these cases, William Mullins-Johnson was convicted of murder in the 1994 death of his niece. After 10 years in jail, Mullins-Johnson was released on bail pending review of his conviction. In 2007, he was acquitted of the murder.

The opening pages of the Goudge inquiry report emphasized the high costs of misleading expert testimony. The attorney for Mullins-Johnson asked Smith to apologize to his client, who was in the audience at the inquiry. The emotionally charged exchange follows (Goudge, 2008, p. 5):

Dr. Charles Smith: Could you stand, sir? [brief pause] Sir, I don't expect that you would forgive me, but I do want to make it—I'm sorry. I do want to make it very clear to you that I am profoundly sorry for the role that I played in the ultimate decision that affected you. I am sorry.

Mr. William Mullins-Johnson: For my healing, I'll forgive you but I'll never forget what you did to me. You put me in an environment where I could have been killed any day for something that never happened. You destroyed my family, my brother's relationship with me and my niece that's still left and my nephew that's still living. They hate me because of what you did to me. I'll never forget that, but for my own healing I must forgive you.

On February 1, 2011, Smith was stripped of his license during a hearing by the College of Physicians and Surgeons of Ontario examining "disgraceful conduct."

Introduction

People can become victims of a wide variety of crimes. At times, these crimes are specific to particular populations, such as children, the elderly, women, or individuals and groups of a specific race or religion. At other times, the crimes are more general in who is targeted, such as in the case of Internet and white-collar crime. This chapter focuses on the following forms of victimization: (1) victims of property-related crime, (2) victims of terrorism, (3) victims of violence in the workplace, (4) corporate and white-collar victimizations, and (5) victims of the justice system.

Victims of Property-Related Crime

Although the estimated number of violent crimes in 2016 increased 4.1% when compared with 2015 data, the FBI's annual Report on Crime in the United States documented a 1.3% decrease in property crimes. These figures marked the 14th consecutive year that estimates of property crimes had declined. Property crimes are reported to the United States FBI's Uniform Crime Reporting (UCR) Program and include the offenses of burglary, larceny-theft, motor vehicle theft, and arson. The intent of these offenses is the theft of money or property, but there is usually no threat or force used against the victims. Arson is included in the property crime category because it involves the destruction of property; however, only limited data are available for arson (FBI URC Property Crime, 2016).

Crimes related to property can involve the loss of property alone or they can also include sexual violence, other forms of physical assault, or murder. Further, the level of threat to the victim differs in these crimes. For example, theft involves minimal personal threat, whereas a home invasion or carjacking can involve a lethal threat.

Police-reported crime in Canada in 2015, as provided by the Crime Severity Index (CSI), reflected that the crime rate had increased for the first time since 2003. The change was caused by increases in fraud, breaking and entering, robbery, and homicide. Canadian police-reported crime rates in 2015 for all types of property crimes increased: fraud (+15%), possession of stolen property (+13%), theft over $5,000 (excluding motor vehicles) (+8%), identity fraud (+9%), motor vehicle theft (+6%), and breaking and entering (+4%) (Statistics Canada, 2016).

The volume of police-reported crime in Canada also increased in 2015, rising 3% from the previous year to 5,198 incidents per 100,000 population. This was about the same rate as reported in 2013 (5,195 per 100,000 population) and 29% lower than a decade earlier in 2005. Excluding traffic offenses, there were almost 1.9 million police-reported Criminal Code incidents in 2015, approximately 70,000 more incidents than in 2014 (Statistics Canada 2016).

Robbery

Robbery is both a property crime and a violent crime depending on the severity and threat to the victim. The Federal Bureau of Investigation's Uniform Crime Reporting (UCR) Program defines **robbery** as the "taking or attempting to take anything of value from the care, custody, or control of a person or persons by force, or threat of force or violence and/or by putting the victim in fear" (FBI UCR Property Crime, 2016). **Larceny** (or **theft**) concerns the taking of a person's property without the permission of the property owner or possessor of that property but does not involve threat, intimidation, or violence to the individual in possession of the property. The charge applied in any particular case depends on the value of the merchandise stolen or the amount of money stolen (Basics of a Burglary Case, 2011). Legislation in various jurisdictions differentiates between petty larceny and grand larceny based on a particular value (e.g., over $1,000). *Grand larceny* is a felony offense. *Personal larceny* involves the theft or attempted theft of property or cash directly from the victim by stealth but without force or threat of force, such as in the case of pickpocketing.

Robbery is different from theft in that it involves the use of force, the threat of force, the use of violence, or the threat of violence to intimidate the victim or put the victim in fear for his or her safety. If there is a struggle between the victim and the offender during a theft, it will more likely be classified as a crime of robbery (National Center for Victims of Crime, 2011). Robbery may be further classified according to the degree of force used or threatened; thus, a jurisdiction might consider armed robbery a more serious crime than robbery without a weapon.

According to the FBI, an estimated 327,374 robberies occurred nationwide, accounting for an estimated $390 million in losses (average dollar value of stolen property per reported robbery was $1,190). Firearms were used in 40.8% of the robberies (FBI UCR, 2016). The most common place to be robbed is on the street (41% of all robberies). However, 16.8% of people were robbed in their own homes, and 23.7% were robbed in a workplace such as a commercial building, gas station, or convenience store. Although banks are the least likely place for a robbery to occur (1.8% of all robberies), they result in the highest average loss per offense ($3,884). Among the robberies for which the UCR Program received weapons information in 2015, strong-arm tactics were used in 43%, firearms in 40.3%, and knives or cutting instruments in 7.9%. Other dangerous weapons were used in 8.8% of robberies in 2015 (FBI URC Property Crime, 2016).

People fear robbery because it not only entails loss of property but also involves the threat or actual use of violence. The upfront confrontation with a threatening offender strips victims of their sense of control, leaving them feeling both helpless to protect themselves and self-blaming for not resisting. When a weapon is involved, the loss of control is even more acutely experienced, often resulting in both short-term crisis reactions and long-term distress (Bard & Sangrey, 1986). Frighteningly, this crime often occurs in the victim's home, place of work, or on the street in his or her local neighborhood. This undermines the person's general sense of safety and can often lead to restricting activities to avoid further risk, inability to work, and excessive fear at home. Studies of bank tellers, shop owners, and others who experience armed robbery at work demonstrate trauma profiles very similar to that of other violent crimes. This has led the banking industry to invest in crisis counseling services to assist those affected by robbery.

Most property lost in robberies is never recovered. When stolen property is recovered by a police department, it is kept in the police property room until it is known whether it will be needed as evidence at trial. If the defendant pleads guilty, the property is not needed as evidence, and efforts are made to release the property to its legal owner. The police agency first is required to photograph the item and identify it on a printed form prepared by the prosecuting attorney's office. The victim is required as the true owner of the possessions to sign a statement indicating ownership of the items recovered. In those instances in which the property is needed as evidence at trial, it cannot be released until completion of the trial and appeal process, which may take years (Hancock County, 2011).

Burglary

Under U.S. law, **burglary** is the uninvited and illegal entry into a person's property, cargo container, or any vehicle or vessel. In Canada, the equivalent term, *break and enter*, refers to the entrance into a building for the purpose of committing an indictable offense or the unlawful entrance into a home, house, or abode. In both countries, the entry may involve force, such as breaking a lock or window, or may involve entry through an unlocked door.

Between 2014 and 2015 there was a decrease in the overall property crime rate, which includes household burglary, theft, and motor vehicle theft. The rate of theft declined from 90.8 victimizations per 1,000 households in 2014 to 84.4 per 1,000 in 2015 (Bureau of Justice Statistics, Criminal Victimization, 2016).

The four types of burglary described by the U.S. Bureau of Justice Statistics (2016) are as follows:

- *Completed burglary.* A form of burglary in which a person who has no legal right to be present in the structure successfully gains entry to a residence, by use of force, or without force.

- *Forcible entry.* A form of completed burglary in which force is used to gain entry to a residence. Some examples include breaking a window or slashing a screen.

- *Unlawful entry without force.* A form of completed burglary committed by someone having no legal right to be on the premises, even though no force is used.

- *Attempted forcible entry.* A form of burglary in which force is used in an attempt to gain entry.

According to the FBI (2016), a home burglary occurs every 13 seconds, with the front door being the most common entry point. Other entry points to a home burglary are reported as follows (ReoLink, 2016):

- Front door: 34%
- First-floor window: 23%

- Back door: 22%
- Garage: 9%
- Unlocked entrance: 4%
- Second floor: 2%

Although definitions and penalties for burglary differ across the various U.S. states, the severity of the crime is influenced by certain common factors:

- Type of property (residential or commercial property, cargo container, or type of vehicle or vessel)
- Whether there are people in the property at the time
- Possession of a weapon while committing the burglary
- If the burglar is under the influence or in possession of illegal drugs
- Intent to commit a crime and the severity of that crime

Burglary is frequently a secondary crime or by-product of the intention to commit another crime, typically a more serious crime such as arson, murder, kidnapping, identity theft, sexual assault, destruction of property, or violation of civil rights (Basics of a Burglary Case, 2011).

Although victims of burglary usually do not encounter the burglar, they nevertheless express considerable fear and often report a feeling of personal violation. Further, the fear of home burglaries makes people anxious about leaving their homes unattended even to go away for a weekend or to go to work. Additionally, people can lose significant amounts of property during burglaries. It is estimated that victims of burglary offenses suffered an estimated $3.6 billion in property losses in 2015, with an average dollar loss per burglary offense of $2,316 (FBI URC 2015 Burglary).

Home Invasion

Home invasion is a situation in which one or more perpetrators force entry into a home where inhabitants are present for the purposes of robbery, rape, or other criminal activity. Also known as *push-in robberies*, home invasions frequently involve highly violent activities. For example, Maxwell Bogel, aged 38 years, was a drug gang enforcer who was on the U.S. Marshals' Most Wanted list for many months. In 1998, he was sentenced in absentia to 68 years for kidnapping, rape, and robbery. His criminal activity involved forcing his way into the homes of people who owed the gang money, often keeping family members captive for more than a day. He would then repeatedly rape and sodomize the girls in the families until the money was paid (Cardwell, 2001).

Reports from Florida describe home invasions of elderly people, the perpetrators severely beating the inhabitants and then ransacking their homes (Hurley, 1995). Home invasion robberies can be distinguished from other types of robberies because in most commonplace robberies, the perpetrator avoids contact with the home owner. Such burglars tend to enter the house covertly through a back entrance. Their entire operation is based on stealth. In contrast, confrontation is often the key element of home invasion robberies (Hurley, 1995). These robbers carry weapons of control such as firearms, handcuffs, masks, and tape. Victims are forced to open safes and reveal their valuables. Although several theories attempt to explain the rise in home invasions, the answers are often tied to the drug trade for one category of offender, and in other cases the advanced technology that prevents robbery of institutions, such as banks, may have pushed armed robbers to an easier target. Not only is security much lower in residential properties, but alarms are generally off when the property is occupied.

Legislators and law enforcement personnel have attempted to manage this relatively new threat. In Florida, a law was passed in 1993 that makes home invasion robbery a first-degree felony even when no weapon is used. This law provides for stiff penalties (Hurley, 1995). In January 2008, after a burglary where a woman and her two daughters were murdered, the state senate in Connecticut similarly passed a law moving home invasion robbery to a first-degree offense. Sentences were made stiffer, and the requirement that the offender knew the home was occupied was dropped. The bill further requires global positioning monitoring of an additional 300 parolees. One senator was reported as saying, "The people in my district have had it. If you don't feel safe in your own home what else do you have?" ("Senate OKs new home invasion law," 2008).

Home invasion differs from burglary in that its perpetrators have a violent intent apart from the unlawful entry itself, specific or general, much the same way as aggravated robbery—personally taking from someone by force—is differentiated from mere larceny (theft alone). In the Petit family home invasion murders in July 2007, in Cheshire, Connecticut, two paroled men, Steven Hayes and Joshua Komisarjevsky, broke into the house and tied up the mother and two teenaged daughters. The mother was forced to withdraw money from her bank account and then when she returned to the home she was raped and strangled. The two men then poured gasoline all over the house and lit it on fire. Both girls died of smoke inhalation; it was later determined that the 13-year-old had also been raped. Komisarjevsky and Hayes were captured as they tried to escape the burning house in the family's car. The two men were convicted at separate trials and both sentenced to death. However, when the Connecticut State Supreme Court abolished the death penalty in May 2016, they were resentenced to life in prison without release (Altimari, 2016).

Carjacking

On January 28, 1993, Ellis McHenry approached a man at a gas station in Cleveland, Ohio, asked if he needed drugs, and then asked to rent his car. When the patron refused, McHenry revealed a gun with which he struck the victim and then stole his car. Over the subsequent week, McHenry committed two additional carjackings. One involved two women and the 2-year-old daughter of one of the victims. In the end, he robbed them at gunpoint and ordered them from the car, which he stole. The final carjacking involved a woman who was transporting two emotionally disturbed students, whom he held at gunpoint. McHenry was found guilty of three counts of carjacking, three counts of using a firearm in the commission of a crime of violence, and one count of receiving a firearm from an illegal alien (Blatt, 1998).

In 1992, a federal statute came into effect in the United States that criminalized carjacking. In 1994, the statute was amended, and carjacking was defined as follows in 18 U.S.C. §2119 (italics added):

> Whoever, *with intent to cause death or serious bodily harm* takes a motor vehicle that has been transported, shipped, or received in interstate or foreign commerce from the person or presence of another by force and violence or by intimidation, or attempts to do so, shall (1) be fined under this title or imprisoned not more than 15 years or both, (2) if serious bodily injury results, be fined under this title or imprisoned not more than 25 years, or both, and (3) if death results, be fined under this title or imprisoned for any number of years up to life, or both *or sentenced to death*.

In the United States, the number of carjackings has increased dramatically in recent years—a 40% increase per year between 1987 and 1992—and in 2003, it was estimated to average 49,000 per year (Jacobs, Topalli, & Wright, 2003). Concern about this crime has led to an extension of provisions related to home invasion to carjacking in some jurisdictions. For example, in 1998, Louisiana passed a "Shoot the Carjacker" law, which extended the defense of habitation law. This law makes justifiable a homicide committed by a person who is lawfully inside a motor vehicle against someone who is unlawfully attempting to enter the vehicle if the person believes that deadly force is necessary to prevent the entry or to compel the intruder to leave (Green, 1999).

While studies on robberies in general report how offenders manipulate fear in the victim, research has neglected studying victims and offenders of carjacking. This research gap is curious given that carjacking requires offenders to neutralize victims who can use their vehicles to escape or as a weapon or a shield. In an attempt to add to the carjacking literature, Jacobs (2013) conducted qualitative interviews with 24 active carjackers to study coercive decision making in predatory social exchange. His research examined fear as a link to compliance and how offenders manipulate the "severity" dimension of threat to influence compliance.

Carjacking is a concern in the United States, but it is an even more serious concern for Foreign Service officers working abroad. Carjackers in foreign countries range from well-connected terrorists to petty criminals. Carjackers always want the vehicle, and, on some occasions, they want the people in the car as well. In such cases, the crime of carjacking can include kidnapping and murder (ADST, n.d.). The carjacking, kidnapping, and murder of former Italian prime minister Aldo Moro is one example. On March 16, 1978, Moro's car was attacked by a dozen armed Red Brigade terrorists. His five guards were killed and Moro was abducted and taken to a secret location where he was held for two months while the terrorists tried to negotiate with the Italian government. On May 9, 1978, his body was found wrapped in a blanket and riddled by bullets, in the back of a car in the center of historic Rome (This day in history, 1978).

Victims of Workplace Violence

During the past decade, newspapers rarely have missed an opportunity to report the latest murder, robbery, physical or sexual assault, or stalking incident occurring in the workplace. Factories, offices, criminal courts, public schools, and hospitals are no longer the safe places they once were for employees. Other victimization in institutions can occur by peers, customers, and authority persons, as well as by strangers. The most high profile of these was a series of incidents between 1986 and 2006 in which current or former workers in the U.S. Postal Service committed mass murders in their places of work. Indeed, the term "going postal" has become a slang term for extreme and uncontrollable rage in the workplace. Examples of Postal Service–related shootings include the 1986 murder of 14 employees in Oklahoma by Patrick Sherrill, who then shot himself to death; two separate shootings on May 6, 1993, in Michigan and California that resulted in five dead and three wounded; and the mass murder of six Postal Service employees in California in 2006.

According to the Bureau of Labor Statistics, 409 workers in private industry and government were victims of workplace homicide in 2014. Of those victims who died from workplace violence, 83% were male, 49% were White, and 32% were working in a retail establishment. Violence can occur in any workplace and among any type of worker, but the risk for fatal violence is greater for workers in sales, protective services, and transportation, while the risk for nonfatal violence resulting in days away from work is greatest for healthcare and social assistance workers (National Institute for Occupational Safety and Health, 2014).

Violence in the workplace is a serious safety, health, and victim issue. As a victim issue, the victim's peer workers, employers, and families will need assistance in recovering from the dynamics of the incident. The most extreme forms of workplace violence—homicide or suicide—are the cause of fatal occupational injuries in the United States. As reported in 2015 by the U.S. Bureau of Labor Statistics, there were a total of 4,836 fatal work injuries, a slight increase from the 4,821 fatal injuries reported in 2014. For the first time the Census of Fatal Occupational Injuries (CFOI) published an annual and only release with no revisions for 2015 CFOI data. Key findings reported in the 2015 Census of Fatal Occupational Injuries are as follows:

- In 2015, the overall rate of fatal work injury for workers was 3.38 per 100,000 full-time workers, lower than the 2014 rate of 3.43.

- In 2015, Latino or Hispanic workers suffered 903 fatal injuries—the most fatalities since 937 in 2007.

- Older workers, 65 years and over, suffered 650 fatal injuries, the second-largest number for older workers since the first national census in 1992, but fatalities decreased from the 2014 number of 684.

- In 2015, roadway incident fatalities increased 9% from 2014 totals, accounting for over 25% of the fatal occupational injuries.

- While workplace suicides decreased 18% in 2015; workplace homicides increased 2% from 2014 totals.

- Tractor-trailer truck drivers suffered 745 fatal injuries, the highest of any occupation.

- In 2015, there were 937 fatal work injuries in the private construction industry and represented the highest total of fatalities since 975 cases in 2008.

- In 2015, fatal injuries in the private oil and gas extraction industries decreased 38% from 2014 figures.

- In 2015, 17% percent of victims were under contract and working for another business or government entity rather than for their direct employer at the time of the incident.

Workplace suicide is a serious concern for companies and organizations. The increase in this type of violence matches the rise in the overall number of suicides in the United States. In 2013, the Centers for Disease Control and Prevention (CDC) noted 41,149 suicides in the United States, compared with 29,199 in 1999—an increase of about 41%. Between 1999 and 2013, every year the number of suicides increased except for 2003. The CDC reported the suicide rate was 10.48 (per 100,000) in 1999, dropped very slightly to 10.44 in 2000, and then increased to 12.55 by 2013. In 2013, suicide was the 10th leading cause of all deaths in the United States and occurred more than twice as frequently as homicide. However, homicides were more likely to occur at the workplace than suicides. Although workplace homicides have decreased over time, they still occurred about 43% more frequently than workplace suicides in 2013 (Bureau of Labor Statistics, 2016).

American companies have identified workplace violence as one of the most serious threats they must manage. Beyond the human costs, workplace violence results in tangible costs such as those resulting from damage, sick time, and health and life insurance costs. It also adversely affects a company's ability to attract and maintain high-quality employees, undermines employee morale, and decreases productivity (Hunt & Hughey, 2010).

Environmental conditions associated with workplace violence and fatalities have been identified and control strategies implemented in a number of work settings. For instance, handling money while in contact with the public increases the risk of being victimized at work during a robbery. Workplace strategies to reduce the risk of robbery include installing locked drop safes, limiting the cash on site through the use of credit and debit cards, and creating physical barriers between the worker and the public. Other strategies involve use of closed-circuit cameras, alarm doors, and improved lighting (Loomis, Marshall, Wolf, Runyan, & Butts, 2002).

Individuals in health and social services are also at high risk of violence, in this case from patients or consumers of services. In one study, 82% of emergency department nurses had been assaulted in the previous year (Gacki-Smith et al., 2009). In a Canadian study, almost 70% of paramedics reported being assaulted and 56% reported being in situations where they believed their lives were at risk (Regehr & Bober, 2005). Environmental strategies in such settings involve reducing overcrowding and wait times that increase patient frustration, ensuring that healthcare workers operate in teams, and developing violence management skills in workers.

Despite the fact that victimization by the public is the more likely risk, media and other attention has focused on violence committed by employees of the organization, most specifically homicides. In these cases, typically a distressed employee perceives that he or she has been unfairly treated in the workplace and as a result threatens a coworker or supervisor. Such situations are more difficult to predict and guard against than robbery or patient violence in large part due to the rare nature of these events (they account for only about 7% of all workplace homicides). Nevertheless, Park Dietz, a psychiatrist specializing in threat assessment, suggested that all threats must be reported to those who are responsible for managing them. The company may have in-house specialists to assess the risk of each individual threat, may seek the assistance of external consulting firms that specialize in risk assessment, or may seek the assistance of FBI threat assessment specialists. Dietz (2009) suggested that threat assessment should be part of a comprehensive program of risk management that includes the following:

- Policies regarding violence, threats, misconduct, weapons, intimate partner violence, and bomb threats
- A system for reporting, investigating, assessing, and managing all threats, misconduct, and inappropriate behavior
- Access controls
- A security plan and procedures
- Preemployment screening procedures
- A drug-free workplace program
- An employee assistance program
- Critical incident response procedures
- Training of all employees in their roles in each of the above

Victims of Natural Disasters

Natural disasters such as major earthquakes, floods, and hurricanes occur periodically and have the capacity to disrupt daily life and cause devastation. Such disasters can cause loss of life as well as property losses. For example, Hurricane Katrina and Superstorm Sandy resulted in hundreds of deaths and billions of dollars in property losses. These disasters have the capacity to affect the psychological health not only of survivors, but family members living in other states or countries from the survivors.

It is important to acknowledge that each disaster is unique even though research on disasters shows there are common effects across disaster types.

Several factors may determine a given disaster's effects on survivors. For example, continuing aftershocks following an earthquake, life threat, loss of employment or income, and cultural beliefs are some of the factors that can affect both the physical and mental health of disaster survivors (PTSD, 2016).

Disasters involving large numbers of people are all too common events. In March 2011, a tidal wave hit the coast of Japan, destroying towns and killings thousands. Dramatic video footage demonstrates the overwhelming power of nature and human vulnerability (see for instance http://www.dailymail.co.uk /news/article-1366000/Japan-tsunami-video-shows-tidal-wave-destroying -path.html). Closer to home, Hurricane Katrina hit Louisiana on August 29, 2005. The collapse of two levees resulted in 80% of the city of New Orleans being submerged in up to six feet of water (CBC News, 2005).

In the fall of 2017, four hurricanes made a U.S. landfall. Hurricane Harvey on August 25 made landfall as a Category 4 hurricane with winds of 130 mph near Rockport, Texas, lingered around southern Texas for days, and dropped 40 to 61 inches of rainfall in southeast Texas and southwest Louisiana. Hurricane Irma hit Florida in early September, causing significant damage across the state. Hurricanes Harvey and Irma were Category 4 hurricanes and struck the United States in the span of just two weeks. Then hurricane Maria took a dramatic toll on property and power lines in Puerto Rico at the end of September with Irma-level winds and Harvey-level flooding, crippling communications, decimating buildings, and damaging a dam that placed downstream residents at risk of catastrophe. The devastation was described as apocalyptic (CNN, 2017). Hurricane Nate then hit Mississippi and Louisiana in early October, causing major property damage. While people try to recover from their property loss, the psychological effect can linger for years for the victims and their families.

Victims of Terrorism

While disasters resulting in devastation and loss take a huge toll on the people involved (Norris et al., 2002), the effects of disasters caused by human actions are more disturbing (North & Pfefferbaum, 2002; Weisaeth & Tonnessen, 2003). In 2001, the U.S. Department of State (2001, para. 2) provided a report to Congress on terrorism and terrorist activities:

> [T]errorism cast its lethal shadow across the globe—yet the world's resolve to defeat it has never been greater. . . . This chilling report details the very clear and present danger that terrorism poses to the world and the efforts that the United States and our partners in the international community are making to defeat it. The cold, hard

facts presented here compel the world's continued vigilance and concerted action.

The RAND Corporation, after the Oklahoma City bombing, developed a worldwide database on terrorist incidents occurring between 1968 and 2004. The database identified a total of 19,828 events and 86,568 casualties, of which 25,408 were fatal. Most terror-related events involved bombs and guns (Bogen & Jones, 2006).

In the face of disaster, the immediate response of people is often adaptive. Media coverage of the 100th anniversary of the Titanic highlighted stories of bravery and chivalry. Following the directive of Captain Edward Smith—"Women and children first!"—72% of women survived the disaster while only 19% of men arrived safely on shore (Boesveld, 2012). Similarly, in interviews of survivors of the 9/11 terrorist attack on the World Trade Center, the vast majority did not report becoming immobilized or incapacitated by their feelings or the circumstances. Rather, people described their actions as adaptive, looking for exits, joining coworkers and strangers in finding a way out of the damaged office floor, and moving in a deliberate and cooperative manner (Perry & Lindell, 2003; Regehr & Bober, 2005).

In the aftermath, however, victims of terrorist violence have a wide variety of responses. A nationally representative study of 512 Israelis who had been directly exposed to a terrorist attack and 191 who had family members exposed demonstrated that 76.7% had at least one symptom of traumatic stress and 9.4% met the criteria for posttraumatic stress disorder (PTSD) (Bleich, Gelkopf, & Solomon, 2003). Seven weeks after 9/11, the New York City Health Department and the Centers for Disease Control and Prevention conducted a door-to-door survey of those living in the neighborhood of the World Trade Center, which revealed that 40% of people reported having symptoms of PTSD (Galea et al., 2002). A national survey conducted three to five days after the attack revealed that 44% of the respondents reported one or more substantial symptoms (Schlenger et al., 2002). A similar survey conducted months later revealed that 17% of the U.S. population had trauma symptoms related to 9/11 at two months after the attack, and 5.8% had symptoms at six months after the attack (Ai, Evans-Campbell, Santangelo, & Cascio, 2006).

The widespread impact of terrorism reflected in these studies echoes the impact of hate crimes; that is, these crimes affect not only individuals, but also communities. The fact that a member of a group has been targeted simply because of his or her skin color, religion, or sexual orientation sends shock waves throughout the group. Community members become acutely aware of the risks they face, and their sense of safety and security is severely undermined.

At an individual level, those directly affected by the event understandably have higher levels of response. In a study conducted by Stellman and colleagues (2008) with over 11,000 World Trade Center employees 10 to 61 months after the 9/11 attack, over 60% of workers met diagnostic criteria for substantial stress reaction, over 10% of workers met criteria for probable PTSD, and other diagnostic categories for less than 10% included probable depression and probable panic disorder. The PTSD diagnosis for workers in this study was higher than the U.S. population and matched that seen in returning Afghanistan war veterans. PTSD was associated with loss of friends and family members; disruption of work, family, and social life; and higher rates of behavioral symptoms in their children (Stellman et al., 2008). A study of 777 people who were affected by 9/11 because they lived or worked near the site, witnessed the attack, knew a victim, or knew a recovery worker who revealed specific symptoms including somatic responses, such as stomach pain, back pain, headaches, chest pain, dizziness, or heart rate increases; depressive symptoms; and anxiety symptoms, including concentration difficulties and arousal (Colarossi, Heyman, & Phillips, 2005).

The U.S. State Department (2017) released its annual 2016 report, *Country Reports on Terrorism 2016*, which provides trends and events in international terrorism from January 1 to December 31, 2016. The report includes policy-related assessments; individual country figures; information on foreign government counterterrorism cooperation; and information on terrorist safe areas, state sponsors of terrorism, foreign terrorist organizations, and the challenge of nuclear, chemical, radiological, and biological terrorists (see report on www.state.gov/j/ct).

The 2016 National Consortium for the Study of Terrorism and Responses to Terrorism at the University of Maryland reported in its Statistic Annex that the number of terrorist attacks had decreased by 9% and the number of deaths due to terrorist attacks had decreased by 13% from 2015. This decrease was due to fewer attacks and deaths in Afghanistan, Syria, Yemen, Nigeria, and Pakistan. In 2016, terrorist attacks occurred in 104 countries. Over half (55%) of the attacks occurred in five countries (Iraq, Afghanistan, India, Pakistan, and the Philippines) and 75% of fatal terrorist attacks took place in five countries (Iraq, Afghanistan, Syria, Nigeria, and Pakistan).

In 2016, the top terrorist threat continues to come from ISIS-inspired terrorist cells, networks, and individuals around the world. In 2016 and part of 2017, ISIS lost a large amount of territory it had controlled due to the coordinated military operations of the 72-member Global Coalition to Defeat ISIS. Al-Qaeda continues to be a resilient threat and Iran remains the leading state sponsor of terrorism. Hezbollah, one of the terrorist groups supported by Iran, continues to threaten U.S. allies despite financial sanctions against its sponsors and law enforcement efforts.

Corporate Victimization

Corporate victimization has received far less attention from criminologists, victimologists, and law enforcement alike than many other forms of victimization. Croall (2001) identified that positivist victimologists have traditionally focused on conventional definitions of crime and when measuring crimes against organizations have limited their scope to such crimes as robbery or burglary. Similarly, she contended that while radical victimologists have been interested in the structural forces that underpin crime and victimization, they have nevertheless focused on street crime and interpersonal violence. Croall (2001, 2007) has suggested that this lack of attention in part may stem from the sense that victims are invisible, for instance in the case of environmental crimes, crimes against the government, or crimes against corporations. It may also stem from notions that victims of corporate crimes may be undeserving; that is, investors can be blamed for engaging in risky investments solely for the purpose of becoming wealthier. The absence of corporate crime in most crime analyses is particularly interesting given the long-standing awareness of these issues and the devastating consequences this type of crime holds for large numbers of people.

Heralded as the pioneer in the area of corporate crime is Edwin Sutherland, who in a presidential address to a joint meeting of the American Economic Society and the American Sociological Society in 1939, first raised the issue that he then wrote about 10 years later in his groundbreaking book *White Collar Crime* (Sutherland, 1949). Sutherland (1949) defined white-collar crime as "crime committed by a person of respectability and high social status in the course of their occupation" (p. 9). Braithwaite (1984) later modified this definition and suggested that corporate crime is "the conduct of a corporation, or employees acting on behalf of the corporation, which is proscribed and punishable by law" (p. 6).

More recently, white-collar crime has been front and center in public awareness as a result of a series of high-profile cases reported in the media and popular novels and movies based on real cases. In 2009, Bernie Madoff was sentenced to a jail term of 150 years by a New York federal court judge for swindling investors out of $65 billion (Moyer, 2009). The Hollywood film *Erin Brockovich* (2000) focused on the battle led by Brockovich, then a legal clerk, against Pacific Gas and Electric for allegedly poisoning the drinking water of a small town in Hinkley, California, resulting in a $333 million settlement.

Twenty years later in 2011, Brockovich returned to Hinkley due to concerns that the problem of contamination had returned (Schwartz, 2011). February 2012 marked the 40th anniversary of a flood in Buffalo Creek, West Virginia, caused by the bursting of a dam designed to hold back coal wastewater, four days after it was declared safe by a federal mine inspector. The resulting rush of 130 million gallons of sludge water killed 125 people, injured 1,100, and left 4,000 homeless (*Herald-Dispatch*, 2012).

Organizations are also the victims of corporate crime. In August 2017, a federal jury found Martin Shkreli guilty on multiple criminal securities fraud charges. Shkreli, who has been nicknamed "Pharma bro" and called "the most hated man in America," was found guilty of three of the eight charges brought against him, including convictions on securities fraud and conspiracy to commit both securities fraud and wire fraud. Prosecutors produced evidence that showed Shkreli had duped multiple investors into investing millions of dollars into hedge funds he ran, MSMB Capital and MSMB Healthcare. He did so by falsely claiming to have a superb record of running those types of funds and that his investment strategy was low risk. Not surprisingly, Shkreli spun the guilty verdicts as a victory, since he avoided some of the harsher criminal convictions (Mindock, 2017).

The Association of Certified Fraud Examiners (ACFE) released the 2016 Report to the Nations on Occupational Fraud and Abuse (RTTN) report, which included data compiled from 2,410 cases of fraud investigated between January 2014 and October 2015. It reported that organizations around the world lost an estimated 5% of their annual revenues to occupational fraud. As a percentage of 2014 estimated gross world product, this translates to a potential loss of more than $3.7 trillion.

Additional findings from the survey include the following:

- For all cases in the survey, the median financial loss was $150,000. Almost one-quarter (23.2%) of fraud cases had losses of $1 million or more.

- The most common form of occupational fraud was asset misappropriation. More than 80% of the cases had a median loss of $125,000.

- There was a median loss of $100,000 in billing schemes and a median loss of $158,000 in check tampering schemes. The greatest fraud risk was in other categories of asset misappropriation. Common red flags or behavioral warning signs noted by fraudsters were as follows:

  - Spending more than their finances could afford

  - Experiencing financial difficulties

– Developing too close an association with vendors or customers

– Having excessive control issues within work, family, and social relationships

– Exhibiting a "wheeler-dealer" attitude involving unscrupulous behavior

– Experiencing recent family problems

- A very small number (5.3%) of occupational fraud perpetrators had a prior conviction of a fraud-related offense. Only 8.3% had ever been fired by an employer for fraud-related conduct.

- Receiving tips was the most common fraud detection method (39.1% of reported cases). Tips that came into organizations with a reporting hotline (47.3%) were more likely to detect fraud through tips than organizations without hotlines (28.2%).

Thus, corporate crime can take many forms, ranging from defrauding people out of money to negligent practices causing injury and death. See **TABLE 17-1** for an overview of corporate crimes and their victims.

TABLE 17-1 Victims of Corporate Crimes

Victim	Examples
Government	Tax evasion by corporations Fraudulent billing for services (such as by consultants or construction firms)
Organizations	Embezzlement Employee theft
Investors and savers	Cheating of investors through bogus trades, insider trading, kickbacks, and falsified records (FBI, 2008)
Consumers	Deceptive advertising Deceptive mortgage and lending practices Internet, telecommunications, and mail fraud
Employees	Refusal to pay fair wages and benefits (e.g., to foreign workers) Neglect of health and safety regulations
The public	Environmental contamination including illegal emissions from industry, farming, and transport; littering; waste dumping; the pollution of land, water, and rivers; and noise pollution

Data from: Croall, H. 2011. Victims of white colar and corporate crime. Retrieved from http://www.uk.sagepub.com/stout/croall_white_collar%20-%20vics_crim_soc.pdf.

Legislative and law enforcement attempts to deal with corporate crime have varied according to the nature of the activity and are primarily divided into three categories: environmental, consumer protection, and corporate securities and commodities fraud. In 2001, the FBI established the Corporate Fraud Initiative, which focused on three categories of corporate fraud: falsification of financial information; self-dealing by corporate traders; and obstruction of justice, specifically to conceal criminal conduct. Investigations continue to focus on market manipulation, high-yield investment fraud, hedge-fund fraud, foreign exchange fraud, and broker embezzlement. The establishment of the FBI unit was followed one year later by the Sarbanes-Oxley Bill, which incorporated both corporate governance and criminal law and established provisions for increasing maximum sentences for corporate crimes (Moohr, 2007) and allowed for fines of up to $5 million for perpetrators who falsified company records. These changes reflected changing public attitudes toward the perpetrators of such crime (Price & Norris, 2009) but also arose from a need for government to appear to be addressing the economic crisis in which the United States and other nations found themselves (Simpson, 2002).

The Environmental Protection Agency (EPA) was established in 1970, and is the lead agency for developing and enforcing environmental regulations passed through the U.S. Congress (Gibbs & Simpson, 2009). Topics of legislation covered by the EPA include air pollution, water contamination, waste disposal, pesticides use, and toxic substances (EPA, 2012). One of the mechanisms for addressing environmental concerns is through the Comprehensive Environmental Response, Compensation, and Liability Act, which (1) taxes chemical and petroleum industries and (2) provides authority to respond to actual or threatened releases of toxic agents that may threaten public health or the environment (EPA, 2012). The EPA can also make recommendations to the Department of Justice that criminal charges be filed. In addition, as noted earlier, compensation for damages can be acquired through civil action as occurred in the case of Pacific Gas and Electric described previously.

The Federal Trade Commission Bureau of Consumer Protection is responsible for conducting investigations and initiating action in the case of consumer fraud. It coordinates with criminal investigation agencies, litigates civil actions, and enforces consumer protection laws (Federal Trade Commission, 2012).

Victims of the Justice System

Although much research has focused on individuals who were victimized primarily by those engaged in crime, victimization can also occur at a systemic level.

Victims of Wrongful Convictions

Sometimes the accused also becomes a victim by way of wrongful conviction. Wrongful convictions are of grave concern to society and to the administration of justice. As stated by U.S. Senator Patrick Leahy:

> These mistakes in our system of justice carry a high personal and social price. They undermine the public's confidence in our judicial system, they produce unbearable anguish for innocent people and their families and for the victims of these crimes, and they compromise public safety because for every wrongly convicted person, there is a real criminal who may still be roaming the streets.
>
> (2003, para. 3)

Concern about not only the incarceration but also the possible execution of innocent people led to the passing of the Justice for All Act in 2004. This act provides for the development of effective systems within states that have the death penalty for monitoring prosecutions and funding for obtaining DNA evidence. In addition, advocacy comes from the legal community and other parts of society to ensure that those who are wrongfully convicted are freed, the most famous initiative being the Innocence Project. According to its website, "The Innocence Project is a national litigation and public policy organization dedicated to exonerating wrongfully convicted people through DNA testing and reforming the criminal justice system to prevent future injustice" (Innocence Project, 2008, para. 1). At the time of this writing, the Innocence Project has helped to exonerate 307 people who were wrongly convicted.

The National Registry of Exonerations is a joint project of the University of California–Irvine Newkirk Center for Science and Society, the University of Michigan Law School, and the Michigan State University College of Law. It provides detailed information about every known exoneration in the United States since 1989—cases in which a person was wrongly convicted of a crime and later cleared of all the charges based on new evidence of innocence. The registry recorded 166 exonerations in 2016. The previous record—160 exonerations—was set the year before, in 2015. In total, the National Registry of Exonerations has recorded 1,994 known exonerations in the United States since 1989 (as of February 26, 2017). Since 2011, the annual number of exonerations has more than doubled. Currently, the average is more than three exonerations a week (National Registry of Exonerations, 2016).

Several causes for wrongful convictions have been identified by the Innocence Project (TABLE 17-2). In about 75% of convictions that are overturned, the issue has been eyewitness misidentification. At times these misidentifications are a result of variables outside the control of the criminal justice system, such as poor lighting, great distances, and stress experienced by the witness. They also may be the result of factors within the criminal justice system, such as the use of lineups or photo arrays that bias the witness in a particular direction. Perhaps the most striking case of injustice caused by eyewitness testimony was early in the 19th century when seven men were executed for a robbery committed by five men (Sporer, Koehnken, & Malpass, 1996). A large body of psychology literature focuses on the fallibility of eyewitness testimony, which, in general, concludes that such testimony is frequently highly unreliable and very amenable to manipulation (Malpass, 2006). As the Innocence Project and others weighed into the discussion of problems with eyewitness testimony with dramatic examples of wrongful convictions, the U.S. Department of Justice initiated a Technical Working Group for Eyewitness Evidence (n.d.b) that produced a report aimed at creating changes in the way that this testimony is acquired.

The first clinic reported to work on non-DNA exonerations was the Michigan Innocence Clinic. The following causes reported by the University of Michigan law clinic and noted on their website are found on Table 17-2.

TABLE 17-2 Causes of Wrongful Convictions

Eyewitness misidentification Eyewitness misidentification is a major cause of wrongful convictions nationwide. The human mind is not like a tape recorder; we neither record events exactly as we see them, nor recall them like a tape that has been rewound. Witness memory is like any other evidence at a crime scene; it must be preserved carefully and retrieved methodically, or it can be contaminated.

Junk science It has been found that in some cases, forensic testing methods have been applied with little or no scientific validation and with inadequate methodology and assessments of their significance or reliability. As a result, forensic analysts can testify in cases without providing evidence-based findings. And in some cases, forensic analysts have engaged in misconduct.

False confessions In some cases, innocent defendants may make incriminating statements, give outright confessions, or plead guilty. Regardless of the age, capacity, or state of the persons who confess, what they often have in common is a decision—made at some point during the interrogation process—that confessing will benefit them rather than continuing to maintain their innocence.

Government misconduct In some cases, government officials take steps to ensure that a defendant is convicted despite weak evidence or even clear proof of innocence.

Snitches Statements from people with incentives to testify—particularly incentives that are not disclosed to the jury—are strong evidence in convicting an innocent person. People have been wrongfully convicted in cases in which snitches are paid to testify or receive favors in return for their testimony.

Bad legal representation The failure of overworked lawyers to investigate, call witnesses, or prepare for trial has led to the conviction of innocent people.

Data from Michigan Innocence Project 2017 and the Innocence Project, 2008. Retrieved from http://www.innocenceproject.org/. and https://www.law.umich.edu/clinical/innocenceclinic/Pages/wrongfulconvictions.aspx

Another cause of wrongful conviction relates to scientific evidence. Despite what the public has been led to believe with television shows such as *CSI: Crime Scene Investigation*, the science on which criminal investigation and prosecution relies is highly inexact. All tests, including blood tests and DNA tests, have a margin of error and often rely on professional judgment in the interpretation of results. This is evident in the case of Dr. Charles Smith, discussed previously. Among his areas of expertise was shaken baby syndrome, a form of head trauma that often leads to death, in which an infant is vigorously shaken. The shaking can lead to hemorrhages in the retinas of the eyes, skull fractures, swelling of the brain, subdural hematomas (blood collections pressing on the surface of the brain), rib and long bone (bones in the arms and legs) fractures, and bruises around the head, neck, or chest. On the basis of Dr. Smith's testimony in 20 cases where he proclaimed that shaken baby syndrome had occurred, 13 individuals, primarily parents, were criminally convicted of murder for allegedly shaking a small infant to such an extent that brain damage and death resulted (CBC News, 2008). In 2010, the Province of Ontario announced a fund to pay compensation to 19 people who were directly impacted by the flawed testimony of Dr. Smith (Boyle, 2010).

Approximately 25% of cases of wrongful conviction involve false confessions of guilt. False confessions can occur as a result of many factors, including duress or coercion, intoxication, diminished capacity, and mental disorder. For example, juveniles in particular may be convinced that if they confess they can go home (Innocence Project, 2008). People of all ages may become exhausted under the scrutiny of interrogation and may believe they will have the opportunity to prove innocence at a later time. Of greatest concern, however, are individuals with mental impairments, who are disproportionately represented among those who give false confessions. An example is Eddie Joe Lloyd, a man with schizophrenia who was convicted in 1984 of the rape and murder of a 16-year-old girl. Mr. Lloyd wrote to the police on numerous occasions with suggestions on how to solve crimes. On this occasion the police interrogated Mr. Lloyd, and in doing so provided him with information about the crime. Mr. Lloyd confessed to the crime with the belief that he would assist the police in smoking out the real killer. After spending 17 years in prison for the crime, Mr. Lloyd was exonerated by DNA evidence (Innocence Project, 2008).

Clearly, more and more attention is being paid to ensuring that wrongful convictions do not occur. Nevertheless, many wrongfully accused individuals are currently incarcerated, and even with improved measures there is no fail-safe way to ensure that innocent persons are not found guilty of crimes they have not committed. Diligence is required to avoid creating new victims through wrongful convictions.

Victims of Racial Profiling and Disproportionate Penalties

Racial profiling, according to the Ontario Human Rights Commission (2003), is any action undertaken for reasons of safety, security, or public protection that relies on stereotypes about race, color, ethnicity, ancestry, religion, or place of origin (or a combination of these) rather than on reasonable suspicion to single out an individual for greater scrutiny or different treatment. A large body of evidence supports the view that there are biases in the criminal justice system against members of minority groups. To begin with, the use of race as a criterion for discretionary traffic and field stops is well documented and has long been a hotly debated topic (Birzer & Birzer, 2006; Parker, MacDonald, Alpert, Smith, & Piquero, 2004; Wilson, Dunham, & Alpert, 2004). Such a practice is related to the Fourth Amendment right of the police to exercise discretion, and this discretion, when applied to racial profiling, leads to increased danger of convicting an innocent minority (Georgakopoulos, 2004).

Thirty-two states have a death penalty sentence. Today, 3,035 inmates are on death row, and 1,392 people have been executed since 1976. The race breakdown of the defendants executed is approximately 56% White, 35% Black, 8% Hispanic, and 2% other race. The race of the victim was disproportionately White (76%), Black (15%), Hispanic (6), and other (3%) (Statistic Brain, 2016). And in 2006, the imposition of the death penalty was disproportionately applied to members of different races. For example, of persons under sentence and awaiting death in 2006, 1,802 were White, 1,352 were Black, 28 were Native American, 35 were Asian, and 11 were of unknown race (U.S. Department of Justice, n.d.a). This is significant considering that in a 2005 census 80.2% of the population was White, 12.8% was Black, 1% was Native American, and 4.3% was Asian (U.S. Census Bureau, 2006).

In Canada, the terms *Indigenous peoples* or *Aboriginal peoples* are the collective names for the original peoples of North America and their descendants. The Canadian Constitution recognizes three groups of Aboriginal peoples: Indians (more commonly referred to as First Nations), Inuit, and Métis. These are three distinct peoples with unique histories, languages, cultural practices and spiritual beliefs. Aboriginal people comprised 4.3% of the total Canadian population, with more than 1.4 million people in Canada identifying themselves as an Aboriginal, according to the 2011 National Household Survey (NHS). Aboriginal peoples are the fastest growing population in Canada, increasing by 20% between 2006 and 2011, compared to 5% for non-Aboriginal people. Aboriginals are also the youngest population in

Canada, with almost half (46%) being under the age of 25. This population is also becoming increasingly urban, with more than half (56%) living in urban areas (National Household Survey, 2011).

The situation facing Indigenous peoples of Canada in conflict with the law remains troubling. Between 2005 and 2015, the Indigenous inmate population grew by 50% compared to an overall offender growth rate of 10%. First Nations, Inuit, and Métis inmates now represent just over 25% of the in-custody population despite comprising just 4.3% of the Canadian population. Indigenous women, the fastest growing subpopulation in federal custody, now comprise 37% of all women serving more than a two-year sentence (National Household Survey, 2011). Aboriginal inmates are also more likely to be classified as maximum security, spend more time in segregation, and serve more of their sentence behind bars compared to non-Aboriginal inmates (Aboriginal Peoples Guide, 2011).

Facts and figures of this kind have led to the conclusion that discrimination against Aboriginal peoples pervades the operations of the Canadian justice system and that Aboriginal peoples are significantly disadvantaged as a result (Dylan, Regehr, & Alaggia, 2008). Some contend that the increased risk of apprehension and conviction is due to preexisting views of criminality, which can lead to unintentional racial profiling and prejudicial sentencing (Georgakopoulos, 2004). This is problematic because one of the issues in dealing with discriminatory practices is that the legal apparatus for antidiscrimination law is based on intentional discrimination. Others suggest that practices leading to increased apprehensions and convictions are clearly intentional and based on racist beliefs (Parker et al., 2004; Wilson et al., 2004).

These issues of overrepresentation of minority group members at all levels of the justice system have profound effects not only for those who are accused and convicted but also for the victims of crime. Victims from racialized communities, knowing that members of their community are unfairly treated under the law, may feel both personal pressure and community pressure to not report crimes committed against them or testify in court. The Ontario Human Rights Commission (2003) reported that racial profiling seriously erodes public confidence in public institutions. As a result, people are mistrustful of the criminal justice system, law enforcement, customs and border control, and the education system. According to a 2007 report by the Ontario Human Rights Commission, people of Aboriginal ancestry reported significant alienation from the criminal justice system. Many communities expressed a lack of faith and sense of uselessness of registering complaints with police, human rights commissions, or other complaint bodies because they believed they would not be taken seriously or, worse yet, would be treated like suspects. The Commission was also told that negative treatment received from various service providers discouraged many racialized individuals from taking advantage of services that are taken for granted by mainstream communities. This conclusion was reinforced by research conducted by Dylan and colleagues (2008) in which Aboriginal women reported reluctance to report crimes of violence committed against them as a result of previous experiences of being discounted, disbelieved, and accused of precipitating the violence.

On July 8, 2017, the Ontario Human Rights Commission (OHRC) and the Ontario Federation of Indigenous Friendship Centres (OFIFC) signed an agreement with the ultimate goal of ending anti-Indigenous discrimination in Ontario. This agreement sets the stage for future collaboration with urban Indigenous communities that is based on trust, dignity, respect, and a shared commitment to reconciliation and substantive equality.

Conclusion

A great deal of effort has been directed toward research in the area of victimology, legal policy analysis, and reform to improve protections for people to avoid victimization. Efforts are also needed to assist in obtaining justice for individuals and groups who have been victimized and in developing social service interventions to assist those suffering from victimization. For example, many forms of white-collar and corporate victimization reflect wider patterns of social and economic inequality and indicate a need for victim-centered initiatives to include these forms of crime. Added to these efforts are new innovations to further ensure safety and reduce harm caused by victimization. Nevertheless, victimization has a history as old as humankind, and the mechanisms to address the problem will continue to need refinement and creative new thinking.

Key Terms

Burglary: Unlawful entry of a residence, industry, or business, with or without force, with the intent to commit a larceny.

Corporate victimization: Classic white-collar crime involves personal gain at the expense of employers, the government, or clients (which can also be described as occupational crime).

Home invasion: Burglary of a dwelling while the residents are at home.

Larceny: Unlawful taking (or attempted taking) of property other than a motor vehicle from the possession of another by stealth with intent to permanently deprive the owner of the property.

Racial profiling: Any action undertaken for reasons of safety, security, or public protection that relies on stereotypes about race, color, ethnicity, ancestry, religion, or place of origin (or a combination of these) rather than on reasonable suspicion to single out an individual for greater scrutiny or different treatment.

Robbery: Unlawful taking or attempted taking of property that is in the immediate possession of another by force or threat of force.

Terrorism: Systematic use of terror, especially as a means of coercion.

Theft: Taking of a person's property without the permission of the property owner or possessor of that property.

Discussion Questions

1. Discuss why home invasions are increasing.

2. Describe a case of someone who has been victimized by a corporate crime.

3. What problems are associated with documenting and measuring victimization from white-collar and corporate crime?

4. How might society deal with the fact that a person has been imprisoned for a crime that it is later determined the person did not commit?

5. How does racial profiling harm victims of crime?

Resources

Environmental Protection Agency http://www.epa.gov

Innocence Project http://www.innocenceproject.org

National Crime Prevention Council www.ncpc.org

National Institute for Occupational Safety and Health http://www.cdc.gov /niosh/

Office for Victims of Crime https://ojp.usdoj.gov/ovc

References

Ai, A., Evans-Campbell, T., Santangelo, L., & Cascio, T. (2006). The traumatic impact of the September 11, 2001, terrorist attacks, and the potential protection of optimism. *Journal of Interpersonal Violence, 21*(5), 689–700.

Altimari, D. (2016, August 19). Cheshire killers Komisarjevsky, Hayes moved to Pennsylvania. *Hartford Courant*. Retrieved from http://www.courant.com/news/connecticut/hc-cheshire-killer-moved-to-pennsylvania-20160819-story.html

Association of Certified Fraud Examiners (ACFE). (2016). Report to the Nations on Occupational Fraud and Abuse. Retrieved from https://bkdforensics.com/2016/03/30/acfe-releases-2016-report-occupational-fraud-abuse/

Association for Diplomatic Studies and Training (ADST). (n.d.) Carjacking and the Foreign Service. Retrieved from http://adst.org/2015/07/dangerous-roads-carjacking-and-the-foreign-service/#.WdqONVtSyUk

Bard, M., & Sangrey, D. (1986). *The crime victim's book*. (2nd ed.). Secaucus, NJ: Citadel Press.

Basics of a Burglary Case. (2011). Retrieved from http://www.lawfirms.com/resources/criminal-defense/the-basics-a-burglary-case.htm

Birzer, M., & Birzer, G. (2006). Race matters: A critical look at racial profiling, it's a matter for the courts. *Journal of Criminal Justice, 34*(6), 643–651.

Blatt, D. (1998). The federal carjacking statute under commercial clause scrutiny after Lopez: *United States v. McHenry. University of Cincinnati Law Review, 66*, 747–774.

Bleich, A., Gelkopf, M., & Solomon, Z. (2003). Exposure to terrorism, stress-related mental health symptoms, and coping behaviors among a nationally representative sample in Israel. *Journal of the American Medical Association, 290*(5), 612–620.

Boesveld, T. (2012, April 14). Was chivalry's finest hour its last? *National Post*, p. A1.

Bogen, K., & Jones, E. (2006). Risks of mortality and morbidity from worldwide terrorism: 1968–2004. *Risk Analysis, 26*(1), 45–59.

Boyle, T. (2010, August 10). Province to compensate victims of Dr. Charles Smith. *Toronto Star*, p. A1.

Braithwaite, J. (1984). *Corporate crime in the pharmaceutical industry*. London: Routledge and Kegan Paul.

Bureau of Justice Statistics. (2015). Burglary. Retrieved from https://www.bjs.gov/index.cfm?ty=tp&tid=321

Bureau of Justice Statistics. (2016). Suicide in the workplace. Retrieved from https://www.bls.gov/opub/mlr/2016/article/suicide-in-the-workplace.htm

Cardwell, D. (2001, March 2). Fugitive gang enforcer arrested in push-in robberies in the Bronx. *New York Times*. Retrieved from http://www.nytimes.com/2001/03/02/nyregion/fugitive-gang-enforcer-arrested-in-push-in-robberies-in-bronx.html

Castaneda, R. (2011). Man convicted in federal carjacking, home invasion case. *Washington Post*. Retrieved from http://www.washingtonpost.com/blogs/crime-scene /post/man-convicted-in-federal-carjacking-home-invasion-case/2011/07/18/gIQAg OxNMI_blog.html

CBC News. (2005, September 4). Hurricane Katrina timeline. Retrieved from http://www .cbc.ca/news/background/katrina/katrina_timeline.html

CBC News. (2008, October 1). Dr. Charles Smith: The man behind the public inquiry. Retrieved from http://www.cbc.ca/news/background/crime/smith-charles.html

Colarossi, L., Heyman, J., & Phillips, M. (2005). Social workers' experiences of the World Trade Center disaster: Stressors and their relationship to symptom types. *Community Mental Health Journal, 41*(2), 185–198.

CNN. (2017, September 26). Apocalyptic devastation in Puerto Rico. Retrieved from http://www.cnn.com/2017/09/25/us/hurricane-maria-puerto-rico/index.html

Croall, H. (2001). The victims of white collar crime. In S. Lindgren (Ed.), *White collar crime research. Old views and future potentials* (pp. 35–54). Sweden: National Council for Crime Prevention.

Croall, H. (2007). White collar crime, consumers, and victimization. In G. Geis & H. Pontell (Eds.), *International handbook of white collar crime* (pp. 127–146). New York: Springer.

Dietz, P. (2009). Threat assessment: Workplace. *Wiley Encyclopedia of Forensic Science*. Published online. Retrieved from http://onlinelibrary.wiley.com/book /10.1002/9780470061589

Dylan, A., Regehr, C., & Alaggia, R. (2008). And justice for all? Aboriginal victims of sexual violence. *Violence Against Women, 14*(6), 678–696.

Environmental Protection Agency (EPA). (2012). Regulatory topics. Retrieved from http://www.epa.gov/lawsregs/topics/#air

Federal Bureau of Investigation (FBI). (2008). Financial crimes report to the public: Fiscal year 2008. Retrieved from http://www.fbi.gov/stats-services/publications/fcs _report2008/financial-crimes-report-to-the-public#corporate

Federal Bureau of Investigation (FBI). (2016). FBI 2016 Crime in the United States, property crime. Retrieved from https://ucr.fbi.gov/crime-in-the-u.s/2015/crime-in -the-u.s.-2015/offenses-known-to-law-enforcement/property-crime

Federal Bureau of Investigation (FBI). (2016). FBI 2016 Crime in the United States, burglary. Retrieved from https://ucr.fbi.gov/crime-in-the-u.s/2015/crime-in-the-u.s.- 2015/offenses-known-to-law-enforcement/burglary

Federal Trade Commission (FTC). (2012). About the Bureau of Consumer Protection. Retrieved from http://www.ftc.gov/bcp/about.shtm

Gacki-Smith, J., Juarez, A., Boyett, L., Homeyer, C., Robinson, L., & MacLean, S. (2009). Violence against nurses working in U.S. emergency departments. *Journal of Nursing Administration, 39*(7/8), 340–349.

Galea, S., Resnick, H., Ahern, J., Gold, J., Bucuvalas, M., Kilpatrick, D., . . . Vlahov, D. (2002). Posttraumatic stress disorder in Manhattan, New York City, after the

September 11th terrorist attacks. *Journal of Urban Health: Bulletin of the New York Academy of Medicine, 79*(3), 340–353.

Georgakopoulos, N. (2004). Self-fulfilling impressions of criminality: Unintentional racial profiling. *International Review of Law and Economics, 24,* 169–190.

Gibbs, C., & Simpson, S. (2011). Measuring corporate environmental crime rates: Progress and problems. *Crime, Law and Social Change, 51*(1), 87–107.

Glancy, G., & Regehr, C. (2012). From schadenfreude to contemplation: Lessons for forensic experts. *Journal of the American Academy of Psychiatry and the Law, 40*(1), 81–88.

Goudge, S. (2008). *Inquiry into pediatric forensic pathology in Ontario report.* Toronto: Ministry of the Attorney General.

Green, S. (1999). Castles and carjackers: Proportionality and the use of deadly force in defense of dwellings and vehicles. *University of Illinois Law Review, 1,* 1–42.

Hancock County. (2011). Information for victims of property crime. Hancock County, Indiana. Retrieved from http://www.hancockcoingov.org/property-crimes.html

Herald-Dispatch. (2012, February 26). Gallery: The Buffalo Creek flood. Retrieved from http://www.herald-dispatch.com/specialsections/100years/x1107815709/Gallery -The-Buffalo-Creek-Flood

Hunt, M., & Hughey, A. (2010). Workplace violence: Impact and prevention. *KCA Journal, 29*(1), 39–43.

Hurley, J. (1995). Violent crime hits home: Home invasion robbery. FBI Law Enforcement Bulletin. Retrieved from http://findarticles.com/p/articles/mi_m2194 /is_n6_v64/ai_17312586

Innocence Project. (2008). The Innocence Project. Retrieved from http://www .innocenceproject.org/

Jacobs, B. (2013) The manipulation of fear in carjacking. *Journal of Contemporary Ethnography, 42*(5), 523–544.

Jacobs, B., Topalli, V., & Wright, R. (2003). Carjacking, streetlife, and offender motivation. *British Journal of Criminology, 43,* 673–688.

Leahy, P. (2003). Leahy urges Senate to vote on DNA bill. Retrieved from http://leahy .senate.gov/press/200410/100704B.html

Loomis, D., Marshall, S., Wolf, S., Runyan, C., & Butts, J. (2002). Effectiveness of safety measures recommended for prevention of workplace homicide. *Journal of the American Medical Association, 287*(8), 1011–1017.

Malpass, R. (2006). A policy evaluation of simultaneous and sequential lineups. *Psychology, Public Policy and Law, 12*(4), 394–418.

Mindock, C. (2017, August 4). Martin Shkreli—once dubbed "most hated man in America"—convicted of securities fraud. *Independent.* Retrieved from http://www .independent.co.uk/news/world/americas/martin-shkreli-guilty-most-hated-man -america-pharma-bro-convicted-securities-wire-fraud-conspiracy-a7877836.html

Moohr, G. (2007). On the prospects of deterring corporate crime. *Journal of Business and Technology Law, 2*(1), 25–41.

Moyer, L. (2009, June 29). It could have been worse. *Forbes*. Retrieved from http://www .forbes.com/2009/06/24/bernie-madoff-prison-sentence-business-beltway-madoff .html

National Center for Victims of Crime. (2011). Robbery. Retrieved from http://www .ncvc.org/ncvc/main.aspx?dbName=DocumentViewer&DocumentID=32367

National Household Survey. (2011). Statistics Canada. Catalogue no. 99-011 -X2011035.

National Registry of Exonerations 2016. University of California, Irving. Retrieved form https://www.law.umich.edu/special/exoneration/documents/exonerations_in _2016.pdf

Norris, F. H., Friedman, M. J., Watson, P. J., Byrnie, C. M., Diaz, E., & Kaniasty, K. (2002). 60,000 disaster victims speak, part 1: An empirical review of the empirical literature, 1981–2001. *Psychiatry: Interpersonal and Biological Process*, 65(3), 207–239.

North, C. S., & Pfefferbaum, B. (2002). Research on the mental health effects of terrorism. *Journal of the American Medical Association*, 288(5), 633–636.

Ontario Human Rights Commission. (2003). Paying the price: The human cost of racial profiling. Retrieved from http://ohrc.yy.net/en/resources/news/NewsRelease .2006-05-17.8048765200

Parker, K., MacDonald, J., Alpert, F., Smith, M., & Piquero, A. (2004). A contextual study of racial profiling. *American Behavioral Scientist*, 47(7), 943–962.

Perry, R. W., & Lindell, M. K. (2003). Understanding citizen response to disasters with implications for terrorism. *Journal of Contingencies and Crisis Management*, 11(2), 49–60.

Price, M., & Norris, D. (2009). White collar crime: Corporate and securities and commodities fraud. *Journal of the American Academy of Psychiatry and the Law*, 37, 538–544.

PTSD. (2016). National Center for PTSD. Traumatic effects of certain types of disasters. Retrieved from https://www.ptsd.va.gov/professional/trauma/disaster-terrorism /traumatic-effects-disasters.asp

Regehr, C., & Bober, T. (2005). *In the line of fire: Trauma in the emergency services*. New York: Oxford University Press.

ReoLink. (2016). Home burglary and crime statistics. Retrieved from https://reolink .com/home-burglary-crime-statistics/

Schlenger, W., Caddell, J., Ebert, L., Jordan, K., Rourke, K., & Wilson, D. (2002). Psychological reactions to terrorist attacks: Findings from a national survey of American's reactions to September 11, 2001, terrorist attacks. *New England Journal of Medicine*, 345, 1507–1512.

Schwartz, N. (2011, March 9). Erin Brockovich returns to Hinkley testing chromium-polluted water. *Huffington Post*. Retrieved from http://www.huffingtonpost.com /2011/03/09/erin-brockovich-returns-to-hinkley_n_833423.html

Senate OKs new home invasion law. (2008). Retrieved from http://www.newstimes.com /latestnews/ci_8048791

Simpson, S. (2002). *Corporate crime, law, and social control.* Cambridge: Cambridge University Press.

Sporer, S., Koehnken, G., & Malpass, R. (1996). Introduction: 200 years of identification. In S. Sporer, R. Malpass, & G. Koehnken (Eds.), *Psychological issues in eyewitness identification* (pp. 1–6). Hillsdale, NJ: Erlbaum.

Statistic brain (2016). NAACP LDF Death Row, U.S.A., Gallup Poll, Bureau of Justice Statistics. Retrieved from http://www.statisticbrain.com/death-penalty-statistics/

Statistics Canada. (2011). Aboriginal Peoples Reference Guide. National Household Survey, 2011. Retrieved from http://www12.statcan.gc.ca/nhs-enm/2011/ref/guides /99-011-x/99-011-x2011006-eng.cfm

Statistics Canada. (2016). Police-reported crime statistics in Canada, 2015. Retrieved from http://www.statcan.gc.ca/pub/85-002-x/2016001/article/14642-eng.htm

Stellman, J., Smith, R., Katz, C., Sharma, V., Charney, D., Herbert, R., . . . , Southwick, S. (2008). Enduring mental health morbidity and social function impairment in World Trade Center rescue, recovery, and cleanup workers: The psychological dimension of an environmental health disaster. *Environmental Health Perspectives, 116*(9), 1248–1253.

Sutherland, E. (1949). *White-collar crime.* New York: The Dryden Press.

This day in history (May 09) Aldo Moro found dead. Retrieved from http://www .history.com/this-day-in-history/aldo-moro-found-dead

Thomas, P., & Francis, E. (2010, July 28). Maryland serial-killer suspect Jason Thomas Scott "evil," victim's mom says. Retrieved from http://abcnews.go.com/GMA/jason -thomas-scott-suspected-maryland-serial-killer-evil/story?id=11266673

U.S. Census Bureau. (2006). National population estimates. Retrieved from http://www .census.gov/popest/national/

U.S. Department of Justice. (n.d.a). Capital punishment statistics. Retrieved from http:// www.ojp.usdoj.gov/bjs/cp.htm

U.S. Department of Justice. (n.d.b). Technical working group for eyewitness evidence. Retrieved from http://www.ncjrs.gov/nij/eyewitness/tech_working_group.html

U.S. Department of Justice. (2010). Crime in the United States: Robbery. Retrieved from http://www.fbi.gov/about-us

U.S. Department of Labor. (2016). Workplace violence. Retrieved from https://www .osha.gov/SLTC/workplaceviolence/

U.S. State Department. (2001). Patterns of global terrorism. Retrieved from www.state .gov/s/ct/rls/pgtrpt

U.S. State Department. (2017). Country reports on terrorism, 2017. Retrieved from www.state.gov/j/ct.

Weisaeth, L., & Tonnessen, A. (2003). Responses of individuals and groups to consequences of technological disasters and radiation exposure. In R. Ursano (Ed.), *Terrorism and disaster: Individual and community interventions* (pp. 209–235). New York: Cambridge University Press.

Wilson, G., Dunham, R., & Alpert, G. (2004). Prejudice in police profiling. *American Behavioral Scientist, 47*(7), 896–909.

CHAPTER 18

Forensic Victimology and Investigative Profiling

OBJECTIVES

- To present cases where forensic victimology can be applied
- To highlight the utility of forensic victimology for investigative purposes
- To emphasize the critical role of collecting evidence from victims for prosecution
- To demonstrate how behavioral profiling can narrow a list of possible suspects
- To demonstrate how crime scene analysis plays a critical role in criminal investigations and legal proceedings

KEY TERMS

Cold case

Combined DNA Index System (CODIS)

Forensic victimology

Sexual assault nurse examiner (SANE)

Sixth Amendment

CASE

Three-year-old Riley Fox was abducted from her family's home in Wilmington, Illinois, where she had been sleeping in the living room. Her 6-year-old brother discovered that she was missing at 7:45 a.m. the morning of June 7, 2004. He awoke the father, Kevin Fox, who called the police and organized a community search. That afternoon, two female volunteers found Riley's body face down in a creek in the Forsythe Woods, around 2.5 miles from her home. The parents later learned that Riley had been bound, gagged with duct tape, sexually assaulted, and then drowned. The case went cold for five months.

In November, detectives called the parents to come to the station and immediately separated them. The father, Kevin, was taken into a very small room and interrogated for the next 14 hours while they told the mother they felt Kevin had killed Riley. Kevin denied the accusation, took a lie detector test, and was told he had failed it. Kevin believed that agreeing with the statements of the detectives was his only way out of that room. He signed a confession and then was charged with first-degree murder with a death penalty attached.

Attorney Kathleen Zellner met with Kevin Fox, believed he was innocent, and took on the case while Kevin was still in jail. She convinced the Will County prosecutor to send the samples to a lab in Virginia for retesting, as the Illinois state lab's equipment was not sophisticated enough to pick up on what little DNA existed. Y-STR testing checks the Y-chromosome, which is nearly identical in males of the same lineage and can be tested in small amounts. The partial profile may not be enough to completely identify a suspect, but it is enough to eliminate a suspect with 100% certainty. In Kevin Fox's case, it was what he needed to be eliminated as a suspect and he was released from jail.

Kathleen Zellner filed a civil suit, and a federal jury awarded Kevin and Melissa Fox, $15.5 million for false arrest and malicious prosecution in December 2007, the largest award ever given in Illinois for a civil rights case alleging wrongful arrest. An appeals court agreed with the jury's findings, but reduced the award, which had previously been reduced to $12.2 million, to $8 million (Schemadeke, 2010).

The 7th Circuit Court of Appeals criticized the investigators on the case, implying that their decision to quickly rule out the girl's death as the work of a sexual predator was "absurd." The court also found that detectives lacked probable cause to arrest Fox, given the "exceedingly weak evidence" they had assembled.

About four years later, law enforcement received a tip about a possible suspect, Scott Eby, who was in prison for sexually assaulting a relative. He had, in fact, been interviewed by police that very night and had even asked the police about the little girl. The investigators had failed to take a closer look at a pair of muddy shoes found near Riley's body with Eby's name written on the shoe (Schmadeke, 2011).

Eby was interviewed in prison by FBI agents. They also obtained a DNA sample and were able to get a statement from him. Eby confessed to killing Riley after first breaking into another home on the same block as the Foxes' and said he cut through the back screen door of the home and then pushed the door in. He abducted Riley, duct taped her mouth to silence her, put her in the trunk of his car, drove to the State Park about three miles away, and sexually assaulted her in the public bathroom. Eby said the bandana he had over his face had come down and Riley looked at him and said, "I want my Daddy." Thinking she could now identify him, Eby took her to the creek and drowned her.

Introduction

The Riley Fox case illustrates failures in evidence collection (overlooking the pair of shoes at the crime scene), the initial forensic testing (not sending samples to the proper lab), and bias in targeting the father and pressuring for a false confession. The tip by an ex-girlfriend then led the FBI to take over the case and obtain a correct confession and match the evidence to the offender.

This chapter focuses on the importance of understanding victimology from a forensic perspective in two important ways. First, the critical role of collecting evidence from the victim as essential in the prosecution of a case and second, the essential role played by victimology in the behavioral profiling of an offender to narrow a list of possible suspects.

Forensic Victimology

A crime is an interactional event between a victim and an offender. It starts with a victim but does not end with the departure of the assailant. When the crime is reported, a number of individuals and systems are mobilized, including emergency responders, law enforcement, hospitals, and courts. Each individual system is designated to respond to victims of a crime; a response that has significant impacts on the victim, on the victim's ability to provide an account of the criminal event, and on the legal proceedings that may follow.

911 Calls

A 911 call is often the first point of entry for a victim into the legal system. In such cases, the 911 call may be used as evidence in court. All conversation and utterances, outside of the 911 call, are typically documented. The 911 call is often maintained as evidence and may be played in court as the prosecutor's opening address to the jury.

In the Fox case, the call to the police department was answered by a communications dispatcher. He determined the nature of the emergency and routed it to a police officer, who, in turn, organized a volunteer missing child search team.

Statutes are in place that determine whether a 911 call can be introduced into court proceedings. In 2006, the U.S. Supreme Court ruled that certain 911 calls could be used as evidence in court proceedings where the victim refuses to testify. The **Sixth Amendment** to the U.S. Constitution grants the accused the right to confront their accuser. Before this ruling, 911 calls would not be admitted into evidence when the caller refused, or could not be located, to testify because the accused could not cross-examine his or her accuser.

The U.S. Supreme Court heard two domestic violence cases in 2006. In one case, *Davis v. Washington*, a woman called 911 to report her ex-boyfriend had beaten her with his fists and fled when she picked up the phone to make the emergency call. In the other, *Hammon v. Indiana*, a wife signed a statement after police questioning stating she had been punched, pushed, and shoved by her ex-husband. The victims did not testify in court in either case; however, based on the earlier accounts the victims gave both defendants were convicted.

The Washington case was upheld, based on the victim's nontestimonial account that was in an attempt to locate the accused during an active emergency. The judges in the Indiana case ruled the wife's police statement was testimonial because there was no longer an emergency. The statement would be inadmissible unless the wife testified in court.

The 911 ruling is an important ruling as it applies to other types of crimes where the victim is unable or refuses to appear in court. Based on this ruling, 911 call dispatchers can play a critical role for evidentiary purposes. A typical 911 call will provide the type of the incident and details such as persons involved, the caller's location, the presence or not of a suspect and his or her description, the presence of weapons, any recorded background noises (voices, screams, shouts, threats, breaking glass or furniture), and any information on the medical condition of any victims. The 911 call can be used as evidence providing the recording equipment is able to receive and record accurate calls from multiple sources and can provide secure storage and easy retrieval (Versadial, 2014).

Most 911 dispatch centers are equipped with sophisticated technology and software that can provide real-time assistance to call-takers. This may be helpful in mapping locations of the caller as well as available emergency resources, displaying high-resolution aerial images of specific locations, or bringing up relevant information from databases. In addition to the voice call, some elements of this visual data may be used and recorded for purposes of evidence as well.

Beyond the role of the 911 call as evidence, dispatchers are the first line of response to calls for assistance and help. Call-takers must be diligent in establishing the existence of an emergency and making sure relevant facts are uncovered so law enforcement and emergency services personnel can be adequately informed and prepared to carry out a prompt and effective response.

First on the Scene: Police, Paramedics, and Fire Personnel

The first responder may be a police officer, ambulance staff, or hospital worker. The initial responsibilities of the responding officer and other emergency personnel typically include ensuring the safety and well-being of the victims and other individuals present by eliminating existing threats and providing for or requesting medical assistance (if necessary).

The next critical stage of first response is the preservation of evidence, which is not the exclusive domain of police officers but it is often these individuals who take the lead in this task. The manner in which evidence is preserved and handled can make or break a case. As such, police may direct emergency personnel to avoid certain entry routes that may disturb evidence as long as it does not impede the prompt delivery of medical attention. A restricted perimeter using rope or some sort of barrier may be established and nonessential personnel will be escorted away from the scene.

Once the scene is secured, photographs, written records, sketches, or audiotaped documentations of the scene may be produced by other officers who arrive at the crime scene. If possible, testimonies may be taken from victims, but this may be difficult or impossible if the victim is in critical condition, is in shock, or is unable to provide an accurate account for any reason. Witnesses serve as an equally important resource for information and details about the incident. They may provide the identity of suspects and victims, confirm that a crime did indeed take place, reveal key events or details, or corroborate other testimonial evidence.

Forensic teams may be called in to collect physical evidence such as impressions (fingerprints, footprints, bite marks, etc.), biological samples (semen, blood, saliva, hair, etc.), trace evidence (gunshot residue, fibers, etc.), and accessories to the crime (weapons, tools, etc.) (Byrd, 2016).

Depending on the severity of the injuries and trauma experienced, victims may or may not be present at the crime scene for extended periods of time. Nevertheless, the victim leaves behind vital threads of evidence of the victimization event that are later woven together by investigators. In many cases, the hospital serves as a key site where the majority of evidence from victims, both testimonial and physical, is collected. The next section details the dual roles of hospital personnel as both healer and detective.

Hospital Personnel as Healers and Detectives

Hospital staff, when dealing with a crime victim, have two basic duties. Their therapeutic duty is to provide medical care, as they do with all patients, and their investigative duty is to collect legal evidence. When victims seek professional help after an assault, they are most likely to be directed to the medical system, specifically the hospital emergency department (ED). The survivor's body is its own crime scene, and due to the invasive nature of evidence collection, such as that performed in a rape case, medical personnel, rather than crime scene technicians, are the appropriate professionals to accomplish this task.

MECHANISM OF INJURY

The examiner notes the injury or tissue damage and classifies it as a contusion, laceration, abrasion, or fracture. *Contusions* are a region of injured tissue or skin in which blood capillaries have been ruptured (i.e., a bruise). A *laceration* involves a tearing in the layers of skin. An *abrasion* is the scraping/removal of the superficial layers of the skin while fractures involve broken bones.

Injuries to the body are carefully documented and can provide an account of the victim experience. The nature and location of injuries can assist in verifying the victim's account of the crime. Each injury is evidence of application of force during the assault and must be preserved as a piece of evidence. Preservation of this evidence occurs in three methods: a text description; diagrammatic illustration; and, if indicated, photography. The healthcare provider examining the victim/patient must document the location, size, shape, and color of each injury. To effectively communicate an injury site to the reader of the medical record, the hours on the face of a clock are used as a locator to ensure that there will be no confusion or misinterpretation of the injury location. Even if photographs are taken, it is still appropriate to use the clock methodology for courtroom testimony.

It is essential that all crime victims who present to healthcare facilities be thoroughly evaluated. Treating injuries alone is not sufficient in these cases. Staff who examine these patients must be educated and clinically prepared to collect evidence and document findings while maintaining the chain of custody. They should be able to coordinate crisis intervention and support for patients, and in cases of sexual assault provide sexually transmitted infection (STI) evaluation and care, pregnancy assessment, and discuss treatment options. They must be aware of and follow jurisdictional reporting policies, and be able to provide court testimony if necessary.

FORENSIC PRACTITIONERS

Forensic practitioners care for and treat individuals, families, communities, and populations in systems where intentional and unintentional injuries occur. These include but are not limited to patients who have been:

- Victims, suspects, or perpetrators of interpersonal violence (e.g., child abuse, elder abuse, intimate partner abuse and assault, sexual abuse/assault, gang violence)

- Victims, suspects, or perpetrators of manmade catastrophes (e.g., motor vehicle collisions, acts of terrorism)

- Victims of natural causes of trauma and population evacuation (e.g., seismic or weather-related disasters)

The forensic healthcare needs of victims include those of some of society's most vulnerable, marginalized and often disadvantaged populations, both living and deceased (e.g., children, individuals with congenital and developmental disabilities, transgendered individuals, residents of nursing homes, patients with mental illness, and individuals who are substance users, homeless, or incarcerated). Special consideration and care is required in these cases.

One well-known domain in forensic practice is that of responding to the trauma of assault and abuse, and intervening to mitigate the impact of violence on individuals, families, communities, and society. Patients report victimization in a variety of healthcare settings, including emergency departments and clinics. Forensic practitioners, often sexual assault nurses, are experts in history-taking, assessment, treatment of trauma response and injury, documentation (written and photographic) and collection of evidence and its management, emotional and social support required during a post-trauma evaluation and examination, and the documentation of injury and testimony required to bring such cases through the legal system (Ledray & Burgess, 2018). These specially trained personnel are not only vital to the health and well-being of victims, but can play a significant role in legal proceedings where they may provide expert testimony.

One special forensic group includes **sexual assault nurse examiners (SANE)**. SANE programs were created in the 1970s by the nursing profession, in collaboration with rape crisis centers/victim advocacy organizations, and rapidly proliferated across the nation during the 1990s (Ledray & Burgess, 2018). These programs were designed to circumvent problems with traditional hospital emergency department care by having specially trained nurses, rather than doctors, provide first-response care to sexual assault victims/survivors. SANE programs are staffed by registered nurses or nurse practitioners who have completed a minimum of 40 hours of classroom training and 40 to 96 hours of clinical training (Ledray & Burgess, 2018). Most SANE programs are hospital based, but some are located in community settings. Nearly all programs serve adolescents and adults, and approximately half serve pediatric victims. SANE programs strive "to minimize the physical and psychological trauma to the victim and maximize the probability of collection and preserving physical evidence for potential use in the legal system" (Ledray & Burgess, 2018).

DNA TESTING

Another step in the investigative process may include the collection of genetic material from the victim while under the care of hospital staff. Once samples are collected, they are sent to labs for analysis. The **Combined DNA Index System**, or **CODIS**, is a national DNA databank that allows for the exchange and comparison of DNA profiles electronically. Today, all 50 states, the FBI, and the U.S. Army can participate in the system. CODIS has two major indices that assist law enforcement in solving crimes. The first is the *forensic index*, which contains DNA profiles recovered from crime scenes such as the results obtained from the processing of sexual assault kits. The second major index is the *offender index* that includes the DNA profiles of known offenders, whose DNA samples were taken pursuant to various federal and state collection laws pertaining to a criminal offense. CODIS is also a component of the FBI's National Missing Person DNA Database program, wherein biological samples can be entered into the database to identify missing persons or unidentified human remains (Douglas et al., 2013).

Investigative Profiling

Every meaningful analysis of violent crime begins with victimology (i.e., a study of the victim). The scientific study of the victim has been especially useful to criminal profilers in analyzing crime scenes for the purpose of identifying unknown offender traits and profile characteristics. In turn, profile characteristics provide police with data on which to classify a crime and identify suspects in unsolved cases. The work of investigative analysts at the FBI Academy in Quantico, Virginia, led to an expansion of traditional crime categories. The result of this work was the publication of a book, *The Crime Classification Manual* (Douglas, Burgess, Burgess, & Ressler, 2013). To classify a crime using *The Crime Classification Manual*, questions about the defining characteristics of the crime need to be answered. These characteristics include information about the victim, the crime scene, and the nature of the victim–offender exchange.

Interest in criminal behavior profiling has increased in popularity since the 1980s. Television shows such as *Criminal Minds* and *Mindhunter* and the well-known film *Silence of the Lambs* have helped in increasing its popularity. Individuals who practice this specialized analysis have years of law enforcement experience and training to prepare them to examine criminal behavior. Nonetheless, debates persist, especially in academia, about the background, skills, and training needed to practice behavioral analysis in this arena.

Forensic victimology, a subspecialty of victimology, is the study of the victim with the application of legal and scientific or techniques used in connection with the detection of crime. This subspecialty came into the professional literature with studies of the battered child syndrome (Kempe, Silverman, Steele, & Droegemueller, 1962), rape victims (Burgess & Holmstrom, 1974), and battered women (Walker, 1979). According to Turvey (2014), forensic victimologists should be objective, dispassionate examiners and investigate as scientists, report as educators, and understand the gravity of their eventual courtroom testimony.

Forensic victimology is the collection and assessment of all significant information as it relates to the victim and his or her lifestyle, including the victim's personality, employment, education, friends, habits, hobbies, and marital status. Relationships, dating history, sexuality, reputation, criminal record, history of alcohol or drug use, physical condition, and neighborhood of residence are all pieces of the mosaic that comprises victimology. The bottom line is: Who was the victim, and what was going on in his or her life at the time of the event? For example, was the victim having any problems? Had the victim recently expressed any fears? Did the victim express any concerns about his or her security? Was the victim in a relationship?

Criminal profiling and typifying criminal personalities is one of the enduring scientific passions in criminology and criminal justice; a passion that dates back to the studies of Italian criminologist Cesare Lombroso's *Criminal Man*, originally published in 1876. Lombroso's theory of anthropological criminology essentially stated that criminality was inherited and that someone "born criminal" could be identified by physical defects, such as a forward-projecting jaw or low, sloping forehead. Very few criminologists today lend scientific credence to Lombroso's physiognomic approach to the understanding of criminality, but the search for a typology of criminal offenders, particularly homicide offenders, has remained as a genuine curiosity (Lombroso-Ferrero, 1972).

A history of offender profiling and how it has advanced into a more comprehensive analysis, including additional services to assist law enforcement agencies, can provide insight (Schrer & Jarvis, 2014). Investigative profiling is best viewed as a strategy that enables law enforcement to narrow the field of options and generate educated guesses about the perpetrator. It has been described as a collection of leads (Rossi, 1982), as an informed attempt to provide detailed information about a certain type of criminal (Geberth, 1981), and as a biological sketch of behavioral patterns, trends, and tendencies (Vorpagel, 1982). Geberth (1981) noted the investigative profile is particularly useful when the criminal has demonstrated some clearly identifiable form of psychopathology. In such a case, the crime scene is presumed to reflect the murderer's behavior and personality in much the same way as furnishings reveal a homeowner's character.

Investigative or criminal profiling is, in fact, a form of retroclassification, or classification that works backward. Typically, a known entity is classified into a discrete category based on presenting characteristics that translate into criteria for assignment to that category. In the case of homicide investigation, investigators have neither the entity (i.e., the offender) nor the victim. It is thus necessary to rely on the only source of information that typically is available: the crime scene. This information is used to profile, or classify, an individual. An important part of profiling is using the concepts of victimology and crime scene investigation. The assessment areas are described in the next section, followed by an analysis of a **cold case**.

Crime Scene Analysis

The five areas of modern crime scene analysis include: victimology, crime scene indicators, forensic findings, investigative considerations, and outcome for the offender and legal issues involved in court proceedings (Douglas et al., 2013).

Victimology

Victimology is critical to a crime investigation as a first step in determining motive. Victimology is the complete history of the victim and is a crucial part of the anatomy of a crime. The critical question is to evaluate why a particular person was targeted for a violent crime; ideally, the answer will lead to the offender's motive.

Victims are assessed as to their risk level in terms of lifestyle and situation. Lifestyle risk level is a function of the victim's age, physical size, race, marital status, living situation, location of residence, and occupation. Situational risk assesses the victim's location and activities at the time of the crime and interacts with lifestyle risk. For example, the situational risk of a person remains the same inside a residence unless the doors are unlocked. Traveling to a social site, workplace, or residence may increase a person's situational risk level. Situational risk level varies from day to day depending on a person's routine. An example of an individual with a high-lifestyle risk who increased his situational risk is a teenager who ran away from a youth residential shelter. The victim was found on a little-traveled rural road, dead of massive thermal burns, in the ashes of a cardboard barrel, the metal rings of which were in the debris. Paint thinner was used as the ignitable liquid, and the victim was identified through dental records. Victimology noted the victim to be a troubled youth, streetwise, and involved in drugs.

The very young and the elderly may be high-risk victims under certain situations. Children walking home from school or alone at home may be targeted or stalked. Elderly living alone may be targeted because of their situation and fragility. On New Year's Eve, several teenaged offenders entered the home of an elderly widow and beat her with fists about the head and face. There were no signs of forced entry. The victim was bound and found the next day in her backyard covered with a piece of sheet metal and boards. Her skull was struck many more times than necessary to kill her while jewelry and money were taken from the home. Victimology noted the widow lived alone in the residential area of a small town and it was rumored that she had money in the house.

Crime Scene Indicators

In cases involving medically unexplained, sudden, or violent deaths, the crime scene assessment is divided into four distinct scenes. The *initial contact scene* is where the victim first had contact with the offender. The *assault scene* is where the assault, physical or sexual, occurred. The *death scene* is where the death of the victim took place. The *body location scene* is where the body was discovered. These four scenes can be the same physical location, multiple locations within a single building, physically separated locations, or any combination of these. For each crime scene location, an assessment is made of the risk level of the victim and the offender. The initial contact scene risk is a function of location, time of day, number of people at the location, and the routine of the victim as to the location. The risk level of location for the offender is a function of the offender's risk at being at the crime scene.

Forensic Findings

Forensic findings are the analysis of physical evidence pertaining to a crime, evidence that is used toward legal proof that a crime occurred. This evidence is often called a *silent witness*, offering objective facts specific to the commission of a crime. The primary sources of physical evidence are the victim, the suspect, and the crime scene. Secondary sources include the home or work environment of a suspect; however, search warrants are necessary for the collection of such evidence (Douglas et al., 2013).

Investigative Considerations

Investigative considerations are discussed after the investigator has classified the offense (and thus the motive). The investigative considerations and search warrant suggestions can be used to give direction and assistance to the investigation.

Outcome

The *outcome* for the offender is the result of a trial or plea bargain. Legal proceedings can result in a conviction and the offender may be sentenced to imprisonment. The suspect may also be found not guilty due to a number of circumstances or if found guilty may have his or her sentence reduced due to insufficient or faulty evidence.

Several resources are available that can aid assessment and help build an accurate victimology. Investigators have a trove of previous cases at hand and can identify common themes among different crimes. The crime can also be classified according to the *Crime Classification Manual*, which provides a diagnostic system to classify different types of offenses (Douglas et al., 2013).

Case Example

Scherer and Jarvis (2014) provide an adjudicated case (with identification of names and locations changed) to illustrate how the range of FBI criminal investigative analysis services can most benefit during an investigation. The authors point out that this example only shows how criminal investigative analysis services were provided in one particular case. It does not illustrate the required protocol for services to be rendered in every case because this varies, nor does it endorse a required methodology.

In the late 1980s, a male offender was convicted of committing two homicides and was suspected in three others. The first victim was hitchhiking at the time of the crime and, victimology would classify her as high risk. Her body was found on the side of the road. A few months later, the second victim, also hitchhiking at the time of the crime, was found also on the side of a road. The investigating agency, noting the similarities between the two cases, sought assistance from FBI special agents trained in criminal investigative analysis. Two FBI special agents provided a general crime analysis, which consisted of identification of shared characteristics of the crimes, evaluation of case linkages, assessment of victimology, and analysis of crime signature aspects. That analysis produced an unknown offender profile for suspect identification for the type of person who would have committed these two homicides.

A threat assessment was conducted and suggested that the offender would kill again and that the community should be warned of this individual through a media release. The analysts provided media strategies. As the police pursued their investigation, a third victim was discovered. However, due to decomposition of the body, there was not sufficient evidence to assist in the investigation. Then, a month after finding the third body, a fourth victim disappeared and never was recovered. Because of the developments in the case, officers continued providing information to the FBI special agents to receive further investigative suggestions. A decoy operation using a female officer was set in place. Although dangerous for that female officer, the necessary information was gathered for identification of the suspect, as well as evidence that could help convict the offender of the first two murders.

At that time, research was also gathered for a search warrant to gain access to the suspect's car to search for possible fibers from inside of the vehicle. At the same time, a fifth victim had disappeared, but was disposed of in water (rather than on the side of the road). Investigators suspected that the offender watched the media accounts of the case and changed his methods of operation (MO). Thus, the criminal investigative analysts modified their investigative suggestions.

Subsequent profiling efforts were successful. Once the suspect was taken into custody, the investigators requested additional behavioral assistance with interview and interrogation techniques. This involved an indirect personality assessment (IPA) of the suspect. At trial, the IPA could be used in formulating a prosecutorial strategy. Trial strategies also are used during jury selection and opening and closing remarks. Additionally, expert testimony may be requested to educate the jury as to terms such as crime scene indicators, MO, signature, staging, or sexual homicide.

Case Featuring an Atypical Serial Killer

The following cases evolved in various states over a 10-year period. They are presented to illustrate the importance of victimology and DNA testing and the skills and failures of crime scene analysis.

Case 1

In January 2010, a Dodge Durango driving very slowly beside a bike path was noted in Arlington, Virginia. A police officer thought that the driver was acting suspiciously so he ran the plates. The Durango was again seen the next night raising the officer's suspicions that the driver had no particular destination or purpose but was just watching people (Jaffe, 2012).

This case helped solve two cold cases. Case 1 began in Virginia as an attempted abduction. A young nurse working the night shift in the District of Columbia was walking to her boyfriend's residence on a deserted street when she was approached from behind by a man with a gun. As she began walking faster the gunman ordered her to keep walking and to be quiet. When she asked where he was taking her, he pointed to the Dodge Durango.

She told him she was not getting in the car, that she was a nurse who had just left work. She offered her purse and tossed it into a pile of snow, distracting the man. She then bolted toward her boyfriend's place, screaming as she got to his door. He and his roommates came out when they heard her. The man and his car were gone (Jaffe, 2012).

Case 2

The second case occurred two weeks later. Two women returning from a night out in Washington, DC and an early morning meal at IHOP were accosted at the door to their apartment by a gunman ordering they give him their wallets and open the door. The three of them entered the apartment. They said no one else was home although a roommate was asleep upstairs. The gunman bound both their hands with the cord of a vacuum cleaner and left the room. They managed to get loose, but he returned with a kitchen knife and made them get back on their knees. He retied one victim's hands with the vacuum-cleaner cord and the other victim with the cord of an iron. He then ordered them into the bedroom, but one refused.

The gunman was small and seemed confused and unprepared to the victims. He tried to tape the mouth of one of the women with blue painter's tape. It fell off. He asked if they had duct tape. He seemed inept, but he had the knife and gun.

When he left the bedroom to search for tape, one victim threw herself against the door and slammed it shut. The man had patted them down but hadn't found one cell phone. The victim was able to dial 911.

Responding to the slamming door, the man returned, grabbed the cell phone, and smashed it against the wall. He pulled the smaller victim, by the arm and out into the street, the iron dangling below her tied hands.

The second victim banged the vacuum cleaner around until her roommate woke up, came downstairs and called 911. They managed to convey the details of the victim's abduction. It was 4:25 a.m.

Meanwhile, the gunman had dragged the victim to his car and ordered her to lie down on the back seat. He drove to an isolated area and raped her. He then wrapped packing tape around her face and head, pushed her down between the back and front seats and drove off. The victim could see they were on a highway, but she couldn't make out the signs. After a long drive, they pulled off the highway, drove aimlessly for a while, and turned onto rough terrain.

It was nearing dawn when the Durango came to a stop. The victim sat up and asked for water. The gunman scooped up some snow, pulled the tape from her mouth, and wet her lips. She could see she was in a wooded area. She could also make out cars on a road behind them. He got into the back seat and forced her to perform another sex act. She could see the gun on the front passenger seat. He removed the scarf she was wearing, then rewrapped it tightly around her neck. She struggled. He pulled harder. The scarf dug into her neck, and she felt her eyes bulge. She lost consciousness.

When she regained consciousness, she was face down in the snow. She was freezing, soaked in snow and slush. Her legs were weak. Using her arms and elbows, she dragged herself toward the road until she could kneel and then stand. She reached the road and tried to scream.

A passing motorist and his wife saw her, stopped and walked to her. Blood was coming from her head, and she was shivering and turning blue. The wife wrapped her in her coat, took her into the car, and turned on the heat. The victim told the couple she had been raped and beaten. The couple called 911, and drove her to the nearest hospital.

At the hospital, she was examined by a SANE. Her entire face was swollen, tiny red spots from burst blood vessels covered her face and neck, and her eyes were bloodshot and spotted—all consistent with strangulation. Dried blood surrounded her mouth, ears, and nose. Her hands and legs below her knees were cut and raw.

She was interviewed by the police and identified the car as a silver SUV. One of the policemen remembered seeing a silver SUV and contacted the Virginia DMV. Two hours later they had a tag and a driver's license photo. They called the victim who had escaped from the offender, to come to the station and she quickly identified her assailant as Jorge Avila Torrez.

The nurse from Case 1 was also called and was showed the photo ID pack. She also identified Torrez from the pack of photos (Jaffe, 2012).

Case Analysis

VICTIMOLOGY

The first three victims were single women in their 20s walking alone on a deserted street in the early hours of the morning. Normally, they would be considered low risk but being on a deserted street in early morning hours raised their risk level. The three victims were victims of opportunity and strangers to the offender. The offender was surveying the area, driving slowly. He parked his car and proceeded on foot to follow them to avoid their seeing his car.

CRIME SCENE INDICATORS

When victim 1 refused to get into his car, she interacted with him, tricked him by throwing her purse in the snow unexpectedly, and secured her escape by screaming as she ran to safety. The offender, afraid of identification and capture, left quickly in his car.

The crime scene for victims 2 and 3 was initially the street. He then forced both victims into the apartment of one of the victims, where he immediately took their purses (having learned from the first victim) and proceeded to tie both up with items of opportunity in the home—a vacuum cleaner cord with the vacuum cleaner still attached and with an iron cord with the iron still attached. He searched both victims but failed to find a cell phone. After the gunman realized they had called 911, he took the smaller victim to his car and started driving to find a suitable location not visible from the road for the assault. The third crime scene for the sexual assault was in his car. The fourth crime scene was where he attempted to murder his victim, strangling her until she passed out, and left thinking she was dead in the woods under power lines, indicating he was familiar with the area.

INVESTIGATIVE CONSIDERATIONS

The police immediately identified the car by the license plate that had been called in on a light-colored SUV. They created a composite offender picture from the three victim descriptions, went to each crime scene, and looked for tire prints in the snow and any other items.

FORENSIC FINDINGS

The Dodge Durango was seen by the three victims and matched the one reported earlier by police for suspicious behavior. The car tag was found, the car and owner identified, and a driver license photo obtained. This photo was identified by the first victim, and the police located his car. Looking through the windows of the car they saw the iron and other items reported by the victims. They then began following the suspect, a Marine named Jorge Torrez. Police obtained a search warrant for car and arrested the suspect. The car was searched for blood, semen, and jewelry and other items that might have been taken from the victims.

OUTCOME

Torrez was found guilty of all counts. In the interim, the police received information about other possible crimes that he may have committed. They decided to put an informant in the cell with the offender in case he decided to brag about his accomplishments. This act produced a confession of the rape murder of Petty Officer Amanda Jean Snell. Torrez's DNA was submitted to CODIS and it produced a hit with another murder in Zion, Illinois, five years earlier.

Case 3

Petty Officer Amanda Jean Snell was assigned to the office of the Chief of Naval Operations at the Pentagon in the fall of 2008 and moved into Joint Base Myer-Henderson Hall in Arlington, which housed Marines, sailors, and a few Air Force personnel. Snell had friends from civilian life, but had not made many new friends in Keith Hall barracks. She volunteered as a youth minister at a local church and described herself on the social networking website MySpace as feeling isolated.

Snell was scheduled to work on Monday, July 13, 2009, but when she did not report for duty, a room check was scheduled. They found the door was unlocked, the bed was made, and the room neat. Amanda Snell was found dead wedged into her clothes locker with a pillowcase over her head. An investigator took photographs of her room, searched for clues, bagged her bed linens, and interviewed everyone in the barracks. The autopsy showed no bruising, signs of struggle, or indication of sexual activity. A medical examiner's report ruled the cause of death to be "undetermined." (Jaffe, 2012).

Snell's family told investigators that she suffered from migraines and that one remedy to ease the pounding was to curl up in a dark place and cover her head. The lack of witnesses and evidence of a crime, her neat room, and a medical history to explain her location in a closet led authorities to think she might have died of natural causes.

The paperwork was reviewed by a veteran NCIS agent stationed with the criminal division. At the time, there were two camps within NCIS: Some believed that Amanda Snell had died of natural causes; others suspected foul play. Snell's laptop was missing, as was her iPod. The latter group did not accept the "undetermined" cause of death and began to pursue the case as a homicide. Jorge Avila Torrez lived seven doors from Amanda Snell. In the interview with Torrez, he denied having any type of contact with her. He then offered to help the agents with their investigation (Jaffe, 2012). They accepted and he inserted himself into the investigation, as most offenders try to do.

Case Analysis

VICTIMOLOGY

Amanda Snell was low risk because of her conservative life style, working at the Pentagon, traveling by government vehicle and having limited access to outside personnel. She was also low risk because she did not party with other residents, kept to herself, and did volunteer work with a local church. She was, however, open to risk from within the protective shell of the military.

CRIME SCENE INDICATORS

This was a single crime scene. The offender did not cause any noise or attention to his encounter with Officer Snell and was comfortable enough at the site to sexually assault, kill, and stuff her in her locker with a pillow over her head. He also remade the bed while removing the top sheet. The coroner could not determine if Snell was dead before being put into the locker or whether she died in the locker from suffocation.

FORENSIC FINDINGS

After the investigation was reopened, Torrez's semen was found on the bottom sheet, and it matched with the semen from the assault of victim in Case 2. Torrez's fingerprints were found in Snell's room showing he had been there, which he had denied in the earlier investigation.

INVESTIGATIVE CONSIDERATIONS

Torrez had already admitted to the snitch in a recorded conversation that he had killed Snell. The investigation was directed to obtain evidence to confirm his admission and convict him in court.

OUTCOME

Torrez was found guilty. Torrez's DNA put him at the following crime.

Case 4

Two second-grade girls who spent Sunday of Mother's Day in 2005 riding bikes around Zion, Illinois, a working-class town on the edge of Lake Michigan, were found dead of multiple stab wounds in a densely forested park early Monday morning. The bodies of the girls, Laura Hobbs, age 8, and Krystal

Tobias, age 9, and were found off a bicycle path in a wooded area on the north end of the city park. The father, Jerry Hobbs, and his father found the bodies by following a deer trail into the woods.

Laura Hobbs was murdered, sexually assaulted, stabbed 20 times, with stab wounds to both eyes, and her throat was cut. Krystal Tobias's throat was also cut and she was stabbed four times postmortem, but not sexually assaulted. Both victims showed signs of beating and slapping. Blood at the site indicated they were murdered there. One of the girls' bikes was recovered not far from the bodies. The second bike was found further from the bodies. No weapons were found. There were no other items at the body site.

Case Analysis

VICTIMOLOGY

May 8, 2005, Mother's Day. Laura Hobbs went to church and flew a kite before meeting Krystal Tobias, her close friend, for a bike ride. Both girls were medium risk as they were isolated in a wooded area but on a bike path.

CRIME SCENE INDICATORS

Krystal Tobias, according to the offender's confession, was killed first. He had engaged the girls in a game of hide and seek. After killing Krystal, he was able to capture Laura Hobbs and sexually assault her before walking her to where Krystal's body was located. He then killed Laura and inflicted postmortem wounds. There was one crime scene: the death scene and body recovery scene were at the same location. The bodies were located in a wooded area not visible from the bike path. Both victims were fully clothed and laying on their backs. One of Tobias's legs was straight and the other leg was bent giving a look of being spread. Hobbs's hips and legs were turned to one side. Their shoes were located near their bodies and their caps were close by.

INVESTIGATIVE CONSIDERATIONS

Jerry Hobbs, the father, was arrested and held in jail for five years. He had a criminal history and had just been paroled from prison. The prosecutor believed that because he found the bodies he was the main suspect.

The extreme violence, cutting of the throat, and stabbing of the eyes suggested that the offender was not a family member but was known to the victims. A great amount of anger and rage precipitated the crimes.

FORENSIC FINDINGS

By 2007, scientists had determined that the semen recovered from Laura's body did not match her father's DNA. However, prosecutors said the presence of another man's semen was not enough to clear him of the slayings, and that any sex crime committed against the girl could have happened before the killings.

In 2010, the DNA was shown to match Torrez after his arrest in Virginia, and prosecutors released Jerry Hobbs.

OUTCOME

Torrez is awaiting trial. Krystal Tobias's half-brother, Alberto, said Torrez was his friend growing up in Zion, and they kept in touch until he was arrested in February in Virginia.

Conclusion

This newest area of forensic victimology is important for the need to collect evidence for prosecutions and defense perspectives and for the need to narrow suspects in a crime by behavioral profiling from crime scene evidence. As noted in the case examples, crime scenes can be misread but when carefully analyzed can significantly strengthen both criminal investigations and legal procedures. The key factors for analysis include victimology, crime scene indicators, investigative considerations, forensic findings, and outcome.

Key Terms

Cold case: A criminal investigation that has not been solved for (generally) at least one year and, as a result, has been closed from further regular investigations.

Combined DNA Index System (CODIS): A national DNA database that compares DNA profiles electronically.

Forensic victimology: The scientific study of the victim to inform investigative and forensic issues for legal purposes.

Sexual assault nurse examiner (SANE): Nurses with special training in forensics.

Sixth Amendment: Amendment to the U.S. Constitution that grants the accused the right to confront their accuser.

Resources

Bureau of Justice Statistics: https://www.bjs.gov/

Center for Disease Control and Prevention of Violence Prevention: https://www.cdc.gov/violenceprevention/overview/index.html

CODIS: https://www.fbi.gov/services/laboratory/biometric-analysis/codis/codis
-and-ndis-fact-sheet

Cold Case Watch www.savagewatch.com

Office for Victims of Crime: https://www.ovc.gov/

Discussion Questions

1. How did Jorge Torrez manage to kill two little girls in one setting?

2. When can a 911 call be used in court proceedings?

3. When can CODIS be used?

4. Where does one find SANEs?

5. What are the five areas of crime scene analysis?

6. When does an investigation turn into a cold case?

References

Burgess, A. W., & Holmstrom, L. L. (1974). Rape trauma syndrome. *American Journal of Psychiatry*, *131*(11), 981–986.

Byrd, M. (2016). Duty description for the crime scene investigator. Crime Scene Investigator Network. Retrieved from http://www.crime-scene-investigator.net/dutydescription.html

Douglas, J. E., Burgess, A. W., Burgess, A. G., & Ressler, R. (2013). *Crime classification manual* (3rd ed.). New York: Wiley.

Geberth, V. J. (1981). Psychological profiling. *Law and Order*, *56*, 46–49.

Jaffe, H. (2012). Predator in the Ranks: Inside a Real-Life NCIS Murder Case. Washingtonian. Retrieved from https://www.washingtonian.com/2012/09/11/predator-in-the-ranks-inside-a-real-life-ncis-murder-case/

Kempe, C. H., Silverman, F. N., Steele, B., & Droegemueller, D. (1962). The battered-child syndrome. *Journal of the American Medical Association, 181*(1), 17–24.

Ledray, L. E., & Burgess, A. W. (2018). *Medical response to adult sexual assault*. Florrisant, MO: STM Learning.

Lombroso-Ferrero, G. (1972, c. 1911). *Lombroso's criminal man*. Montclair, NJ: Patterson Smith.

Rossi, D. (1982). Crime scene behavioral analysis: Another tool for the law enforcement investigator. *Police Chief*, *57*, 152–155.

Scherer, J. A., & Jarvis, J. P. (2014). Criminal investigative analysis: Practitioner perspectives (Part 1 of 4). *FBI Law Enforcement Bulletin*. Washington, DC.

Schmadeke, S. (2010 April 7). Court upholds finding that police framed Kevin Fox in the rape-murder of daughter Riley Fox, 3. *Chicago Tribune*. Retrieved from http://articles.chicagotribune.com/2010-04-07/news/ct-met-0408-riley-fox-verdict -appeal-20100407_1_riley-fox-foxes-attorney-kathleen-zellner

Schmadeke, S. (2011, February 26). I'm the 'lowest kind of slime,' killer of 3-year-old confessed. *Chicago Tribune*. Retrieved from http://articles.chicagotribune .com/2011-02-26/news/ct-met-eby-investigation-20110226_1_sharon-eby-riley -fox-scott-wayne-eby

Turvey, B. E. (2014). Forensic Victimology, 2nd ed. San Diego, Elsevier.

Versadial. (2014). Court admissibility of 911 calls and its importance to your PSAP. Retrieved from https://www.versadial.com/court-admissibility-of-911-calls-and -its-importance-to-your-psap/

Vorpagel, R. E. (1982). Painting psychological profiles: Charlatanism, charisma, or a new science? *Police Chief*, 49, 156–159.

Walker, L. A. (1979). *Battered woman syndrome*. New York: Springer.

Glossary

A

Adjudication: Includes all formal and informal steps within the criminal process. (5)

Alien: Term used in the Mann Act to denote foreign-born persons. (7)

Alzheimer's disease: A progressive disease of the brain characterized by impairment of memory and eventually by disturbances in reasoning, planning, language, and perception. (12)

Anger rapist: Rapist who displaces his anger, rage, and hatred onto a victim. (11)

Anti-Semitism: Hostility toward or prejudice against Jews or Judaism. (14)

B

Battered woman syndrome: The effects of intimate partner violence on victims. This syndrome (BWS) is a subcategory of post-traumatic stress disorder and results from long-term gender abuse. (9)

Battered woman syndrome defense: An extension of self-defense laws that appreciates battered women's perceptions of risk and the possibility of escape. (9)

Blitz rape: A rape that occurs suddenly, out of the blue. (11)

Botnets: Networks of computers that criminals control to perform coordinated cyberattacks. (16)

Bullying: A form of habitual aggressive behavior that is hurtful and deliberate. (8)

Burglary: Unlawful entry of a residence, industry, or business, with or without force, with the intent to commit a larceny. (17)

C

Celebrity stalking: Harassment of a well-known figure who generally does not know the stalker. (10)

Child maltreatment: Encompasses four types of maltreatment: physical abuse, sexual abuse, emotional abuse, and neglect. Children often are subject to more than one type of abuse. Abusers can be parents or other family members; caretakers, such as teachers or babysitters; acquaintances (including other children); and (in rare instances) strangers. (6)

Child pornography: Obscene photographing, filming, or depiction of children for commercial purposes or for arousal of self, subject child, or viewing audience. (7)

Child prostitution: Inducing or encouraging a child to engage in sex for financial or other gain. (7)

Child sexual exploitation on the Internet: Use of the Internet to distribute or view child pornography. Use of the Internet to contact children for the purposes of sexual abuse or exploitation. (16)

Child trafficking: Abduction and sale of children. (7)

Civil justice system: A network of courts and legal processes that enforce, restore, or protect private and personal rights. (5)

Classical criminology: A view that people have free will and that appropriate and timely punishment will deter crime. (3)

Classic mass murder: A murderer operating in one location at one period of time, which could be minutes or hours or even days. (13)

Cleared by exceptional means: Occurs when the police are unable to place formal charges against an alleged offender, for example, because the offender is dead, a victim refuses to cooperate, or extradition is denied. (2)

Cognitively impaired: A brain disorder in which thinking abilities are impaired. (12)

Cold case: A criminal investigation that has not been solved for (generally) at least one year and, as a result, has been closed from further regular investigations. (1, 18)

Combined DNA Index System (CODIS): A national DNA database that allows DNA profiles to be compared electronically. (18)

Complex child trauma: Describes both children's exposure to multiple traumatic events, often of an invasive, interpersonal nature, and the wide-ranging, long-term impact of this exposure. These events are severe and pervasive, such as abuse or profound neglect. (6)

Complex posttraumatic stress disorder: Reactions experienced by survivors of prolonged abuse, which include symptoms of posttraumatic stress disorder and personality changes. (9)

Computer hacking: Unauthorized use of an information system or network by circumventing or bypassing the security mechanisms. Illegally accessing other people's computer systems for destroying, disrupting, or carrying out illegal activities on the network or computer system. (16)

Conditional threat: Warns that a violent act will happen unless certain demands or terms are met. (8)

Copyright piracy: Unauthorized use or sale of copyrighted material. (16)

Corporal punishment: Punishment intended to cause pain. (8)

Corporate victimization: Classic white-collar crime that involves personal gain at the expense of employers, the government, or clients (which can also be described as occupational crime). (17)

Costs of victimization: Financial repercussions due to victimization that include health and medical costs, direct financial costs, intangible costs, and criminal justice costs. (1)

Covictim: Immediate family, significant others, work associates, and close personal friends who had dealings with the deceased. (13)

Credible threat: A legal term that indicates a clear threat that, to an outside observer, is a cause for concern for the safety of the victim. (10)

Crime victim: A person who has been directly and proximately harmed—physically, emotionally, or financially—as a result of the commission of an offense. (1)

Crime victims' rights: Eight rights included in Section 3771 of Title 18 of the U.S. Code, Crimes and Criminal Procedure. (1)

Criminal charges: A formal accusation of having committed a criminal offense. (5)

Criminal law: Branch of law concerned with actions that are harmful to society in which prosecution is pursued by the state, not the individual. (5)

Criminology: The study of the etiology of crime and the characteristics of the criminal. (1)

Critical criminology: Subdiscipline of criminology that combines an analysis of the state with the lived experience of victims. This model includes radical, Marxist, and feminist approaches. (3)

Cyberbullying: Bullying though means of email, instant messages, text messages, blogs, cell phones, pagers, and websites with the goal of tormenting, threatening, harassing, humiliating, or embarrassing a person. (16)

Cybercrime: Crime committed using the Internet. This is a broad term that includes attacks that cause electronic commerce sites to lose money, stealing a person's identity, selling contraband, stalking victims, or disrupting operations with malevolent programs. (16)

Cyberstalking: Use of the Internet to stalk another person. (10, 16)

Cyberterrorism: Any premeditated, politically motivated attack against electronic information or systems. The unauthorized use of computers and information technology to cause physical, real-world harm or severe disruption. (16)

D

Dark figure of crime: Phrase used to refer to the amount of unreported or undiscovered crime. (2)

de Clérambault's syndrome: A syndrome of delusional love first described by de Clérambault in 1942. (10)

Defendant: A person or institution against whom an action is brought in a court of law; the person being sued or accused. (5)

Dementia: A condition in which memory loss has progressed to such a point that normal independent functioning is impossible and affected individuals can no longer successfully manage their finances or provide for their own basic needs. (12)

Developmental disability: A cognitive, emotional, or physical impairment, especially one related to abnormal sensory or motor development, which appears in infancy or childhood and involves a failure or delay in progressing through the normal developmental stages of childhood. (6)

Developmental traumatology: The systemic investigation of the psychiatric and psychobiological impact of overwhelming and chronic interpersonal violence on the developing child. This relatively new area of study synthesizes knowledge from an array of scientific fields, including developmental psychopathology, developmental neuroscience, and stress and trauma research. (6)

Direct threat: Identifies a specific act against a specific target. (8)

Disclosure: A child telling that someone has abused or hurt him or her. This can be very difficult, and how the professional/investigator responds can be critical for all facets of subsequent intrapsychic and interpersonal recovery. (6)

Distributed denial of service (DDoS): A type of cyberattack in which multiple devices at varied locations all become infected, usually with malware. The group of infected devices then acts as a single system that hits a target simultaneously, resulting in a denial of service (DoS). (16)

Domestic violence: Incidents of interspousal physical or emotional abuse perpetrated by one of the spouses upon the other spouse. (9)

Double (or secondary) victimization: Retraumatization of the victim or experience of other adverse consequences as a result of the justice process. (1)

E

Elder abuse: Any physical, sexual, verbal, psychological, or financial abuse perpetrated against an older adult. (12)

English common law: The traditional, unwritten law of England that forms the basis of modern statutes. (5)

Erotomania: A syndrome of delusional loving. (10)

Eye movement desensitization and reprocessing (EMDR): A psychotherapy treatment designed to alleviate the distress associated with traumatic memories. (6)

F

Fetal abduction: Criminal removal of the fetus from the uterus of the pregnant mother. (7)

Fetal homicide: An act that causes the death of a fetus. Also called *feticide*. (6)

Fetal rights: The rights of any unborn human fetus, which is generally a developing human from roughly eight weeks after conception until birth. (6)

Fiduciary: A business or person who may act for another with total trust, good faith, and honesty and who has the complete confidence and trust of that person. (12)

Forensic victimology: The scientific study of the victim to understand forensic issues for legal purposes. (18)

G

Genocide: Systematic murder of an entire political, cultural, or religious group. (14)

Grand jury: A jury convened to inquire into accusations of crime and to evaluate the grounds for indictments. (5)

Grooming: Use of nonviolent techniques by one person to gain sexual access to and control over a child victim. (7)

H

Hate crime: Criminal conduct motivated in whole or in part by a preformed negative opinion or attitude toward a group based on race, ethnicity, religion, gender, sexual orientation, or disability. (14)

Hate speech: Words used as weapons to ambush, terrorize, wound, humiliate, and degrade members of an identified group. (14)

Hierarchy rule: Rule that requires counting only the highest offense and ignoring all others; it applies only to the crime reporting process and does not affect the number of charges for which the defendant may be prosecuted in the courts. (2)

Home invasion: Burglary of a dwelling while the residents are at home. (17)

Homicide: The intentional or sometimes unintentional or accidental killing of another person. (13)

I

Identity theft: Use of a person's identifying information, including name, Social Security number, or credit card number, without permission, to commit fraud or other crimes. (16)

Incest: Sexual activity between close relatives that is illegal in the jurisdiction where it takes place. Sexual intercourse with a descendent by blood or adoption. (6, 11)

Incidence: Number of crimes that take place during a particular period of time. (2)

Indirect threat: A threat that is vague, unclear, or ambiguous. (8)

Infant abduction: Kidnapping after an infant is born and is less than 6 months old, usually from a hospital, clinic, home, or other location. (7)

Internet fraud: Deception conducted through the Internet for the purpose of financial gain. (16)

Internet risk behaviors: Online risky behaviors that have been found to cluster together: sharing of personal information (e.g., name of school, email address, picture of self); corresponding online with an unknown person or later meeting the person offline; engaging in online-initiated harassment (e.g., malicious or offensive jokes); visiting online-initiated sex sites; and overriding Internet filters or blocks. (15)

Intimate partner violence (IPV): Any behavior within an intimate relationship that causes physical, psychological, or sexual harm to those in the relationship. (9)

Islamophobia: Hostility toward or prejudice against Muslims. (14)

J

Just world theory: Tendency of people to attribute blame to victims of crime to retain a sense that the world is safe. (3)

Juvenile justice system: That part of the justice system having jurisdiction over cases involving persons age 17 and younger. (5)

K

Keylogging: A technology that records consecutive keystrokes on a keyboard to capture username and password information. (16)

L

Larceny: Unlawful taking (or attempted taking) of property other than a motor vehicle from the possession of another by stealth with intent to permanently deprive the owner of the property. (17)

Laws: Define the criminal justice system within each jurisdiction and delegate the authority and responsibility for criminal justice to various jurisdictions, officials, and institutions. (5)

Learned helplessness: A cognitive state in which a victim no longer believes that any action can change an aversive situation. (9)

Lifestyle routine activities theory: Theory that personal characteristics and lifestyle activities increase or decrease an individual's risk of victimization. (3)

M

Mail fraud: The willful use of the national mail service to defraud or obtain money or property by means of false pretenses, representations, or promises. (16)

Malware: A software program designed to damage or cause unwanted actions on a computer system; includes viruses, worms, and Trojan horses. (16)

Marital rape: Nonconsensual sex in which the perpetrator is the victim's spouse. (11)

Medically fragile: Individuals who have medically intensive needs that usually result in chronic health–related dependence. (12)

Missing children: Children whose whereabouts are unknown to their parent, guardian, or legal custodian. (7)

Murder: A subcategory of homicide, which also includes lawful taking of human life. (13)

N

National Crime Victimization Survey (NCVS): A series of surveys, previously called the National Crime Survey, which collect data on personal and household victimization since 1973. (1, 2)

National Incident-Based Reporting System (NIBRS): A more detailed version of the Uniform Crime Reporting (UCR) Program. (2)

National Organization for Victim Assistance (NOVA): Established in 1975 as a national umbrella organization, this organization is dedicated to expanding current victim services, developing new programs, and supporting passage of victims' rights legislation. (4)

O

Obsessional harassment: Harassment causing fear that originates from the obsession of one individual with another individual who is uninterested in the relationship. (10)

P

Password trafficking: The act of sharing, selling, or buying stolen passwords. Stolen passwords can be used to access the victim's personal records and bank account. (16)

Peace bond: An order from a criminal court that restrains one person from bothering or threatening another. (10)

Personality: Pattern of collective character, behavioral, temperamental, emotional, and mental traits of an individual. (8)

Phishing: An attempt to obtain financial or other confidential information from a user, typically by sending an email that mimics a legitimate organization but contains malware (e.g., keylogger) that operates in the background to collect sensitive information. (16)

Physical bullying: Pushing, hitting, tripping, spitting at, and physical beating. (8)

Positivistic: Knowledge derived through the use of the scientific method. (3)

Posttraumatic stress disorder (PTSD): An anxiety disorder that develops in some individuals who have had major traumatic experiences. It is characterized by intrusive thoughts and images and heightened arousal. (9)

Power of attorney: Authority granted by one person to another to empower the grantee to make financial and healthcare decisions on the grantor's behalf. (12)

Pretrial: A conference held before the trial begins to bring the parties together to outline discovery proceedings and to define the issues. (5)

Prevalence: How many people experience a particular crime during their lifetime. (2)

Primary victimization: Victimization of the targeted or personalized victim. (4)

Protection order: A civil court order that is issued under family violence legislation. It provides various emergency and long-term orders to protect victims of family violence. (9, 10)

Psychiatric gating: When a sexually violent person is certified under provincial mental health legislation and sent to a hospital. (10)

Psychological abuse: When an individual attempts to dehumanize or intimidate older adults through verbal or nonverbal acts. (12)

R

Racial profiling: Any action undertaken for reasons of safety, security, or public protection that relies on stereotypes about race, color, ethnicity, ancestry, religion, or place of origin (or a combination of these) rather than on reasonable suspicion to single out an individual for greater scrutiny or different treatment. (17)

Ransomware: A type of malware that restricts access to computer systems until the target pays a ransom to the malware operators to remove the restriction. (16)

Rape: A legal term that involves unwanted and unlawful sexual activity by threat or actual coercion or force against either gender. (11)

Recidivism: The commission of additional crimes by an offender. (13)

Repeat victimization: Repeated criminal offences committed against a victim who has experienced prior victimization. (1)

Restraining order: An order issued after the aggrieved party appears before a judge that tells one person to stop harassing or harming another person. (10)

Robbery: Unlawful taking or attempted taking of property that is in the immediate possession of another by force or threat of force. (17)

S

Sexual assault nurse examiner (SANE): Forensic nurses who have received special training to conduct sexual assault evidentiary exams for rape victims. (18)

School dynamics: Patterns of behavior, thinking, beliefs, customs, traditions, roles, and values that exist in a school's culture. (8)

Secondary victimization: Victimization affecting impersonal victims, such as commercial establishments, churches, schools, and public transportation. (4)

Self-exploitation: The creation and distribution of explicit or inappropriate pictures of oneself or peers. (15)

Serial murder: Two or more separate events in three or more separate locations with an emotional cooling-off period between homicides. (13)

Sexting: Involves the sending or forwarding via cell phone sexually explicit photographs or videos of the sender or someone known to the sender. (15)

Sextortion: A relatively new form of sexual exploitation that occurs primarily online and in which nonphysical forms of coercion are utilized, such as blackmail, to acquire sexual photos/videos, money, or sex from the targeted individual. (15)

Sexually violent predator: Any person who has been convicted of or charged with a crime of sexual violence and who suffers from a mental abnormality or personality disorder that makes the person likely to engage in predatory acts of sexual violence if not confined in a secure facility. (10)

Sexual assault: A form of coercive or forced sexual violence, including unwanted harassment or comments, or acts to traffic, or otherwise directed, against a person's sexuality. (11)

Sexual coercion: Unwanted sexual intercourse or other sexual contact subsequent to the use of menacing verbal pressure or misuse of authority. (11)

Sexual sadist: An offender who finds pleasure and excitement in the suffering of his victim. (11)

Sixth Amendment: Amendment to the U.S. Constitution that grants the accused the right to confront his or her accuser. (18)

Social bullying: Rumors and behaviors aimed at deliberate social exclusion. (8)

Social media: Forms of electronic communication such as websites for social networking and microblogging through which users create online communities to share information, ideas, personal messages, and other content (such as videos). (15)

Spam: Refers to the sending of unwanted and often irrelevant emails and other communications to a large number of individuals. (16)

Spear phishing: A highly personalized form of phishing where an email appears to be from a friend or financial institution, with an attachment or link to a site that downloads malware, usually spyware or a keylogger that operates in the background to collect sensitive information. (16)

Spiritualistic theories: Theories that attribute victimization to the acts of gods, demons, cosmic forces, and other supernatural forces. (3)

Spree murder: A single event with two or more locations and no emotional cooling-off period between murders. (13)

Stalking: Any form of harassment that causes the person being harassed to have a reasonable fear for his or her safety. (10)

Statutory rape: Sexual intercourse between a person under the age of consent and an adult age 18 years or older. (6)

Stockholm syndrome: Dramatic and unexpected realignment of affections to the positive bond between hostage and captor and to the feelings of distrust and hostility on the part of the victim toward authority. (3)

Suicide bomber: The targeted use of self-destructing human beings against civilians. (14)

T

Telemarketing fraud: Fraudulent selling conducted over the phone. It most often targets the poor and elderly. (16)

Telephone hacking: Illegal access to a telephone network to enable free phone calls or to obtain personal information. (16)

Terrorism: Systematic use of terror especially as a means of coercion. (16, 17)

Tertiary victimization: Victimization that is diffuse and extends to the community at large. (4)

Theft: Taking of a person's property without the permission of the property owner or possessor of that property. (17)

Third-party liability: Responsibility held by a person or organization that did not commit the offense but may have contributed to or facilitated the offense. (5)

Threat: Expression of intent to do harm or to act out violently against someone or something. (8)

Thrownaways: Children who have been told to leave the household, are refused reentry into their home after running away, are not sought by parents or others when they run away, or are abandoned or deserted. (7)

Trauma-focused cognitive-behavioral therapy (TF-CBT): A psychotherapy approach for children and adolescents who are experiencing significant emotional and behavioral difficulties related to traumatic life events. (6)

Traumatic grief and bereavement: Grief associated with traumatic loss, such as murder. (13)

U

Uniform Crime Report (UCR): The earliest reporting system of homicide. Provides some of the most commonly cited crime statistics in the United States; it is concerned with index crimes that include attempted or completed murder and nonnegligent manslaughter, forcible rape, robbery, aggravated assault, burglary, larceny-theft, and motor vehicle theft. (2, 13)

V

Veiled threat: A threat that strongly implies but does not explicitly threaten violence. (8)

Verbal bullying: Taunts, threats, name calling, and derogatory comments. (8)

Victim impact statement: A statement given by the victim(s) that details how the crime has affected him or her. (5)

Victim Information and Notification Everyday (VINE) program: A program that enables victims of intimate partner violence to access court information. (4)

Victimology: The study of the victim from a bio-social-structural way of viewing crime and the law and the criminal and the victim. (1, 18)

Victims of Crime Act (VOCA): Federal law that established the Crime Victim's Fund, which is supported by fines collected from persons who have been convicted of criminal offenses. (4)

W

Whaling: A spear-phishing technique that targets high-net-worth individuals, family offices, and corporate executives. (16)

White supremacist: A person who believes White people are racially superior to others and should therefore dominate society. (14)

Wife battering: Assault against a woman by her husband. (9)

X

Xenophobia: Fear and hatred of strangers or foreigners or of anything that is strange or foreign. (14)

Y

Youth gang: A self-formed association of peers who have in common some sense of identity, some degree of permanence and organization, and an elevated level of involvement in delinquent or criminal activity. (8)

Name Index

This index contains proper names. For subject references, please see the separately presented Subject Index.

Subject Index

© Peyker/Shutterstock.

Tables, figures and boxes are indicated by an italic *t*, and *f*, respectively. Please see the separately presented Name Index for references to proper names.